P9-CBJ-037

CHILDREN AND THEIR ART, *Third Edition*

WITHDRAWN

THIRD EDITION

CHILDREN AND THEIR ART

Methods for the Elementary School

CHARLES D. GAITSKELL

AL HURWITZ

Coordinator of Arts
Newton Public Schools
Newton, Massachusetts

96443

HARCOURT BRACE JOVANOVICH, INC.

New York   Chicago   San Francisco   Atlanta

© 1958, 1970, 1975 by Harcourt Brace Jovanovich, Inc.

All rights reserved. No part of this publication may be reproduced or transmitted in any form or by any means, electronic or mechanical, including photocopy, recording, or any information storage and retrieval system, without permission in writing from the publisher.

ISBN: 0-15-507298-6

Library of Congress Catalog Card Number: 74-12519

Printed in the United States of America

CHILDREN AND THEIR ART, *Third Edition*

Gaitskell and Hurwitz

N350
. G32
1975

PREFACE

The third edition of *Children and Their Art,* like previous ones, deals with both the theoretical basis of art education and the practical methods for teaching art. A broad creative program is presented as a logical extension of art, its history in the schools, and its unique function in the lives of children. The problems that arise in the day-to-day process of teaching are given close attention, as are the preparation of an art room, the handling of displays, the correlation of art with the general school curriculum, and the evaluation of the children's progress.

This edition includes examples of children's art from many countries. It has been the good fortune of both writers to represent Canada and the United States at the World Council of the International Society for Education in Art (INSEA–UNESCO). Our long and affectionate association with this organization has made us acutely aware of the potential that art has as a socially unifying force in the lives of children.

In the third edition, increased interest in four areas of art education has demanded greater attention: the move toward behavioral goals or performance competency, the tendency toward greater integration of art into other areas of learning, the use of art in teaching retarded and handicapped children, and the more general problem of curriculum planning. A philosophy of group art, in keeping with current interest in the art world, is also discussed at some length.

The book has been revised in several other aspects as well: bibliographical material has been expanded, activities have been added at the conclusion of many chapters, and the case-histories section has been amended. The activities suggested for classroom use in all the chapters have been carefully tested, and new ones have been added.

Many of the illustrations come from two highly regarded school systems: the Dade County Schools in Florida and the Newton Schools in Massachusetts. In Dade County, the students of Pat Renick, Helen Donnell, Jacqueline Hinchey, and Sarah Maddox produced art of particular excellence; in Newton, the students of Maida Abrams, Lori Schill, Barbara Alan, Jean Kornbleuh, Ava Bond, Mary Baker, Ann Wiseman, Carolyn Shapiro, Beth Richman, Ann Forbes, Neil Jacobs, and Ken Roberts were equally creative. Special thanks are due to Jo Kowalchuck, Yvonne Anderson, Jim Robison, Jimmy Morris, and Allen Kaprow for their reviews of specific areas. We also wish to express our appreciation to Judith Burton for the painting used on the cover.

We are most grateful to the following INSEA members, who lent us the work of the children of their countries: Gunther Wagner, West Germany and Austria; Makni Ameur, Tunisia; Elizabetta Eichhorn, Italy; Dr. Loutfi Zaki, Egypt; Isaka Goan, Israel; Mitsui Nagamachi, Japan; Dr. Larry Kantnor, an American art teacher in Nepal; and Gillian Haynes, Great Britain.

Edmund Feldman of the University of Georgia and James Ackerman of the Fogg Museum at Harvard kindly permitted the use of transcripts of their classroom teaching. We are also grateful to William D. Francis of the University of Texas and Jon J. Moscartolo of Massachusetts State College at Framingham for their thoughtful and perceptive suggestions in relation to the entire text. Associates who were particularly helpful in the preparation of the section on art appreciation are Judy Morse and Pauline Josephs. Betty LaTona and Mark and Helen Hurwitz provided valuable secretarial assistance in preparing the manuscript.

C. D. Gaitskell
A. Hurwitz

CONTENTS

PART TWO   **TEACHING ART**

14
ART ACTIVITIES
FOR GIFTED CHILDREN 381

15
RELATING ART
TO THE GENERAL CURRICULUM 407

16
DISPLAYING CHILDREN'S ART 437

17
DEVELOPING CHILDREN'S
APPRECIATION OF ART 453

PART ONE

PREPARING TO TEACH ART

Contemporary values in the fine arts are often reflected in the pictorial approaches taught in the elementary school system. The exciting use of color and brushwork in this painting resembles the modern artist's interest in the manipulation of paint and in the use of color for design purposes.

CHARACTERISTICS
OF CONTEMPORARY ART EDUCATION

If art could do nothing better than reproduce the things of nature, either directly or by analogy, or to delight the senses, there would be little justification for the honorable place reserved to it in every known society. Art's reputation must be due to the fact that it helps people to understand the world and themselves, and presents to their eyes what they have understood and believe to be true.*

Many factors have influenced the nature of art education in our schools, but three demand particular attention. The first of these is the nature and tradition of art; the second, the philosophy of education in a democratic society with its concern for the freedom of the individual; and the third, the development of theories of teaching based on the discoveries of psychology. Art education today, therefore, is the result of an evolutionary process, and whatever degree of efficiency we now enjoy in our school program has not been achieved suddenly. By means of philosophical deliberation, systematic experimentation, and, sometimes, it must be admitted, trial and error, we have arrived at methods of teaching art that appear to be acceptable from the standpoint of both contemporary aesthetics and current trends in education. The major portion of this chapter is intended to show how the characteristics and objectives of a good contemporary art program have arisen out of the three influences mentioned above. The chapter closes with discussions of changes in art education, the role of creativity in the art classroom, and a summary of objectives in art education.

*From Rudolf Arnheim, *Art and Visual Perception*, p. 374. Copyright © 1954 the University of California Press, and used with their permission.

THE BELIEFS ON WHICH ART EDUCATION IS BASED

Good contemporary programs of art education seem to be founded on a set of widely shared beliefs. Each belief has both critics and advocates, and all beliefs are subject to modification. For the present, however, the ones discussed below form a theoretical framework within which art teachers work. There is certainly no dearth of information regarding either the convictions or the objectives of art educators. They are stated in position papers, keynote addresses, committee reports, and the writings of professionals who have devoted their lives to the subject. (See the Recommended Reading in the Appendix.) The principal beliefs in the current consensus would appear to be as follows:

Creative Ability in All Children

One of the most obvious characteristics of present-day art education is the belief of teachers in the creative ability of all children. Not so many decades ago the ability to create was usually thought to be an attribute of only a few learners, primarily those having artistic talent. Today creativeness apparently is no longer considered a special ability reserved for a gifted minority, nor is it assigned to a limited number of human activities. W. H. Kilpatrick[1] voiced this point of view when he said that creativeness is a characteristic of all learning, although it differs in degree from one situation to another. It is present in any of the novel situations that people continually face in life. Everyone can, and indeed must, create to live a normal life. C. E. Spearman,[2] a distinguished British psychologist, endorsed this view. John Dewey[3] and George W. Hartmann[4] went so far as to assert that the rediscovery of a solution to any problem, when achieved without the knowledge that the solution had already been found, might be considered a creative act and might be placed, from the standpoint of learning, in the same category as an original discovery. Such interpretations of the creative aspect of learning have encouraged the widely held belief that learners of almost any age in an art class have the ability to produce something that for them is new, superior, or unique when compared with previous performances.

Of all the characteristics discussed, the belief in the creative ability

---

[1] *A Reconstructed Theory of the Educative Process* (New York: Teachers College, 1935).

[2] *Creative Mind* (New York: Appleton-Century-Crofts, 1931).

[3] "All thinking is original in a projection of considerations which have not been previously apprehended." A child, says John Dewey, who realizes for the first time that 5¢ and 5¢ make 10¢ is a discoverer. See his *Experience and Education* (New York: Macmillan, 1938), p. 187.

[4] *Educational Psychology* (New York: American Book, 1941). It is interesting to note that Harold Rugg considers Hartmann (together with Raymond Wheeler) an author who interprets Gestalt psychology in a manner that is "by far the best for American conditions." See Harold Rugg, *Foundations for American Education* (New York: World Book, 1947), p. 149.

Figure 1.1 *Stimulating learning situations can be as valuable to the student as the final product of art work. (Photo by Educational Development Center.)*

of all children seems to have had the greatest impact on general education. Psychologists and art educators have produced a wide range of research on how to develop creative ability in children. It is generally felt that attention should be given not only to their findings but also to the attempt to apply some of their conclusions to the elementary art program. In general it may be stated that although the creative act involves a process leading to a product, current thinking about elementary art places as high a premium on the values of the learning *situation* as on its products. The creative personality in relation to the art program is discussed at some greater length on pages 40–43.

Probably no other phase of the present-day art program has caused more controversy than the beliefs of teachers concerning the acquisition of skills and the importance of these skills in expressive acts. It will be shown later in the chapter that earlier art programs set forth a number of exercises that were graded according to the difficulty of the skills required for their successful completion. It cannot be denied that those who were subjected to this program developed skills. These skills, however, were of the "watertight compartment" variety. That is to say, although pupils

Integrated Acquisition of Skills

might learn to draw a chalk box, shade in pencil, or lay down a watercolor wash acceptably, they were given little or no opportunity to use these skills in acts involving creative thinking.

Dewey pointed out in this connection that narrow modes of skill in any field cannot be of much service to the learner. To be of practical use, skills must be gained in such a manner as to allow the learner to achieve a deepening knowledge of and an increased insight into the subject under consideration. As skills are being acquired, he said, they must be readily put to use in new situations that are under the personal control of the learner.[5] Contemporary practice in art education, then, is influenced by the concept that the acquisition of skills should be related to the needs of the learner.

Skills may also be interpreted as including ways of handling materials and carrying out various processes (as in ability for printmaking, facility with tools, or self-direction in preparation for activity). These skills are valued for the role they play in the carrying through of ideas to satisfactory conclusions and must be approached as means to ends rather than as ultimate learning experiences.

Freedom of Thought and Feeling

Another characteristic of the contemporary art program, deriving from political and aesthetic sources, is the strong belief of teachers that learners must enjoy freedom of thought and feeling when they are engaged in artistic pursuits. Without such freedom, it is claimed, no one can produce art.

In those earlier art programs that were built on the acquisition of formal skills, little attention was paid to the individual thought of the learner. Rules and regulations were laid down for both production and appreciation of art forms. Pictures were produced according to standard rules of composition, and a masterpiece was considered good because it was conceived according to a formula. The pupil was deprived of the opportunity to respond to a subject on a personal level by a step-by-step method of teaching.

Children should be encouraged at a very early age to operate independently after having decided on a particular task. When they can follow a route from self-motivation through completion of a project, we may assume that a state of freedom has been attained through personal discipline. The kind of pseudo-expressive freedom that is associated with excesses of the progressive atmosphere of the 1930's too often led to chaos in the name of art education. The methods applied served to provide temporary therapy rather than meaningful activity and nourished a kind of formless, untrammeled laxity for which there is neither time nor money in the currently overburdened curriculum.

[5]John Dewey, *Democracy and Education* (New York: Free Press, 1966).

Artistic expression does not emerge from a void. As mentioned previously, any artistic effort worthy of the name expresses the thoughts and feelings, which of course reflect the experiences, of its author. Such is the fundamental nature of art, and any attempt by painters and other artists to express what they have not experienced results in shoddy and insincere performances that cannot rightly be called art.

Experience and Expression

As will be pointed out later in the chapter, one of the chief reasons for the failure of much of the school art of the past was that the children's experiences were not utilized for expressive purposes. The subject matter employed in drawing and painting was derived more from the experiences of adults than from those of children. In contrast, art teachers today try to build their programs around the true basis of artistic expression. An activity that does not engage the children's experiences in life as a motivating force for expression is rarely seen in the contemporary art program. This practice in no way limits the range of expression because children have an unlimited variety of experiences that lend themselves to expressive acts. Any situation that moves the children emotionally and stimulates them intellectually, it is believed, will provide a basis for expression.

In the art program of today, experience refers not only to the subject matter of expression but also to the tools and materials employed in an expressive act. Formerly, children were often presented with specific materials and tools and told in minute detail how to produce an object designed by someone else. The pupils had had little if any previous experience before they began work on the project selected by the teacher. As a result the children's insight into the properties of the materials being employed and the potentialities of the tools being used remained insufficiently developed. Whatever learning they gained was too narrow to apply to any activity but the one in progress. Today it is believed that the child should experiment freely with tools and materials, if within context.

"Experience," in the sense used here, goes beyond situations that involve the child purely on an objective level; it refers also to the "inner" world of emotional conflicts, dreams, reverie, speculation, and fantasy. A good teacher creates situations that call on the child's imagination, vision, and memory, any of which may function in an experiential sense. The teacher should use this type of experience to draw the child away from visual clichés and into creative behavior that is exciting and productive. We may assume, then, that the child's inner world is as much an artistic resource as are the materials of art.

It must be admitted that art programs of years past did little to develop taste beyond a sporadic pseudo-literary study of "famous" works of "great" artists. The result of these banal and tepid forays into appreciation was a severely limited conception of art on the part of the child, for in confining discussions to poor reproductions of painting, teachers gave the impression that industrial and commercial or architectural design was not

Development of Taste

worthy of mention. Thus students were denied the opportunity to gain even the slightest insight into artistic works (in the non–fine arts area) that they would encounter for the rest of their lives.

Beginning in the 1920's critics began to express serious concern about the general level of aesthetic taste. Roger Fry stated that in aesthetic matters we were "satisfied . . . with a grossness, a sheer barbarity and squalor which would have shocked the thirteenth century profoundly."[6] As early as 1934 Dewey asked, "Why is the architecture of our cities so unworthy of a fine civilization? It is not from lack of materials nor lack of technical capacity . . . yet it is not merely slums but the apartments of the well-to-do that are aesthetically repellent."[7]

Statements like these offered a challenge to education, for such condemnations referred indirectly to the mass of the people who were the product of public schools. The inference could be made, and indeed was made, that the program of art education was not effective in developing in people the ability to discriminate good design from bad. As a result art educators have only comparatively recently begun to give serious consideration to methods of developing a critical sense in children.

It has never been more apparent that aesthetic conditioning of one sort or another is constantly at work on our populace. The impact of mass media, the changing face of the city, the birth of new towns, and the despoliation of natural resources must somehow be brought to the attention of children—and in the most dramatic terms. How effective art teachers may be in their attempts to create a visual sensitivity is still a matter of speculation. Our world abounds in vulgarities of every sort—on television, in magazines, in our littered streets, and in our polluted waterways. Despite the emerging role of the designer and planner in our society, the defilers of our environment overwhelm, in volume, the objects that would humanize and enhance our lives. "Our unmastered crafts," asserts Teague, "have produced a squalid disorder as a too common setting of modern life."[8] In Gill's opinion, "Step by step things have been sacrificed to entries into account books."[9]

[6]*Vision and Design* (New York: Meridian, 1956), p. 23. This is the currently available edition of Fry's book, published originally in 1920. Throughout the text wherever possible the most recent editions of all books cited are given.

[7]John Dewey, *Art as Experience* (New York: Putnam, 1958), p. 344. See also G. Holme, *Industrial Design and the Future* (London: Studio, 1934).

[8]Walter Dorwin Teague, *Design This Day* (New York: Harcourt Brace Jovanovich, 1940), p. 115.

[9]Eric Gill, *Art and a Changing Civilization* (London: John Lane, The Bodley Head, 1934), p. 98. The trends in the design of the Studebaker automobile in the 1950's are worthy of note in this connection. In 1953 Raymond Loewy, a designer of repute, redesigned this vehicle. In a display that year of outstanding automobile designs, the Museum of Modern Art in New York included Studebaker but no other American automobile. But after 1953 the Studebaker—"one of the few really beautiful cars to come out of the United States . . . was loaded with irrelevant decoration, and finally replaced by something square, aggressive, and pretentious; something 'within the design trends of the industry,' as the handout said."—"Cars," *Design,* No. 92 (August 1956), p. 14. Studebaker, of course, felt compelled to make the change to sell its wares.

Perhaps it is still too soon to judge the effects of the new art program; perhaps people's desire for display and ostentation, together with the pressure of advertising, which often appeals to snobbishness and a desire to be up-to-date rather than to a respect for craftsmanship and honest quality, will hold back the efforts of the art educator.

Since in art education today emphasis is placed on the development of the individual as a person as well as a producer and consumer of art forms, the individual's behavior in relation to associates takes on considerable significance. Contemporary art education has been affected by the idea that the school "must be a place where pupils go, not merely to learn, but to carry on a way of life."[10] Hence the art program of today is not considered adequate unless it tends to bring about growth in the child's social skills and awareness, and one may find in the art class certain group activities designed to bring about this end. By the use of field trips and projects, and in some cases through cooperation with the social studies program, the art teacher is able to direct the child's attention to the arts as they exist beyond the museum, beyond even personal creative efforts.

Art and Citizenship

Citizenship can operate on two levels. One can be seen in terms of the interpersonal relations mentioned above and the other can be understood in terms of social or political behavior. First we learn to respect and live with our neighbors and then we attempt to improve the quality of everyone's life by taking the appropriate kind of political and artistic action to affect the broad social and environmental issues confronting the community. This is admittedly asking a lot of art education, but, if we are genuinely concerned about ultimate life goals, we must extend our view beyond the individual to society at large. A trip to a new housing project may be as important and as enlightening as a trip to a museum; a visit from a landscape designer as significant and engaging as one from a potter.

Encouraging a sensitivity to one's environment in children is a difficult task for many teachers to accept because of its apparent removal from what they conceive as the creative process. Social awareness through art asks that the students who have contact with an art program become so concerned with issues relating to the world in which they move that, as adults, they seek ways in which they may exercise control. Once they are committed to some program of action that they feel betters the community, they take on the role of worthy or enlightened citizens.

In particular, children must be made aware of the role that art can play in refining the quality of living. Such topics as pollution, conservation, and urban planning may now be seen as aspects of design. The ordering of visual elements may be extended from a painting to a poster, from a building to a housing development, even to a city itself. All such

[10] Boyd H. Bode, *Democracy as a Way of Life* (New York: Macmillan, 1937), p. 77.

Figure 1.2 *Art may begin anywhere. In this case a first grader makes his mark on the school's parking lot. (Photo by Jim Robison.)*

examples have in common a conception of human beings as designers, artists who manipulate elements of space and form for ends that range from the creation of an image to the development of an environment that shapes the attitudes and patterns of living of a segment of society. In such cases art becomes a social force rather than a vehicle for individual personal expression. It is hoped that the form and order found in art may help to bring about a similar regard for form and order in the lives of those who study it.

Development of Visual Perception

The body of theory that urges teachers to relate art activity to the perceptual process is drawn from such diverse sources as Rudolf Arnheim (a Gestalt psychologist), Bartlett Hayes (a curator, critic, and teacher), and the Bauhaus movement (an art movement which began in the 1920's). Whereas the basic design courses at most art schools and colleges use perception as the focus for the teaching of design, the elementary art teacher in a sense prepares the children for perceptual maturity by engaging them in problems that are found in visual learning situations as well as in picture-making. Art teachers must find time to do more than allow their students to draw, paint, print, and sculpt objects that embody experience and feeling; they now realize the importance of activities focusing specifically on visual relationships: figure to ground, tension to balance, reconciliation of opposing forces, and so on. Activities based on such problems can link intensity of vision to depth of feeling; they can help children not only to create their world but to view it with greater clarity. According to Bartlett Hayes,

> The case for Visual Perception rests on the premise that the informed and sensitive use of the eye is necessary for a broad understanding of the modern world. The complexity of our present environment is taken for granted; but how much does the ordinary person notice the details, know why they are shaped as they are, or see them as a meaningful whole? Abstract information is difficult to keep in order if the memory is not aided by the eye, and certain facts of nature are almost impossible to understand in terms of words—how easily could you understand or describe a crystallographic structure without microphotographs to help? As a visual apparatus, the camera can indeed help, but how important a role does it play in the present curriculum?[11]

A close reading of Chapter 3, "Design as a Basis for Art Activity," should demonstrate how perceptual theory relates to more familiar art activity.

Related to perceptual awareness is an area of appreciation that not only includes information about our cultural heritage (art history) but also places a value on the response to art (art criticism). Critical perception goes beyond simple perceptual training in that it ultimately deals with values. It offers children a visual vocabulary for looking in addition to requiring them to consider this vocabulary in affective terms—that is, in *qualities* of art such as intensity (Rouault and Van Gogh), compassion (Kollwitz and Rembrandt), and social content (Daumier and Ben Shahn).

The Value of Art Criticism

   Because appreciation of this sort is perhaps the newest area of art education there is relatively little research that can tell us how the operation of critical perception relates to growth levels of children. Philosophy, however, usually precedes empirical investigation, and until the researchers have caught up, the new art teachers will proceed on personal conviction, testing and refining their methods in the laboratory of the classroom. Chapter 17, "Developing Children's Appreciation of Art," points out that there is more information in this area for the upper grades than for the lower ones, but a number of approaches for the primary grades can be recommended.

DEVELOPMENTS IN ART EDUCATION

Teachers should not be surprised if they are often asked by their students to define art. It is well, therefore, to consider here briefly just what art is, before discussing how the theories of art have influenced art education.

---

[11] In Howard Conant, ed., *New York University Art Education Seminar* (Washington, D.C.: U.S. Office of Education, 1966), p. 120.

Educators and laymen are growing weary of generalizations and desire answers that are comprehensible and clearly stated. It may be presumptuous to attempt a definition of art in light of the extensive literature that exists on the subject, but for the purposes of elementary instruction one can come close to a meaningful definition of art based on speculation as well as observable behavior. The definition proposed in the discussion below has apparently been accepted by many children of the writer's acquaintance; presumably some adults will find it to be of use as well.

To obtain a basic understanding of art we may begin by projecting ourselves back into history, before the advent of personal adornment, even before the age of cave paintings. If we can push ourselves far back enough into the dim recesses of time, it may be possible for us to recognize the importance of one early achievement, the invention of containers. The seemingly simple realization that a hollow space would allow one to store water or grain must have been one of the wonders of primitive technology. How long people were satisfied with this breakthrough we do not know, but at some point someone must have noticed that if greater attention were given to such considerations as the *shape* of the container as well as the consistency of the wall's thickness, the containers would somehow be more "satisfactory." In perfecting the form in order to improve the function our anonymous fabricator was working on the level of enlightened craftsmanship.

At a later stage the person making the container, or "pot," felt an impulse to make adjustments on the *surface* of the vessel. This phase is highly significant simply because what happens on the "skin" of the pot has nothing at all to do with its *function*—that is, with how much it can carry or how much punishment it can take. It can only make the handling of the object a more *pleasurable* experience. There was yet another difference in this stage: whereas technical considerations (the relation of size to thickness to function) somewhat circumscribed the potmaker's realm of choice, the decorative stage released unlimited options in technique and design. Once the object was formed, shapes could be inscribed or painted in patterns that might include swirls, loops, straight lines, or combinations of any or all of these.

The next stage, which followed decoration, placed primitive people directly in the camp of their more sophisticated descendants, for they soon discovered that decoration could have *meaning,* that signs could stand for ideas. They found that symbols not only could clarify their fears, dreams, and fantasies, but that they could communicate their state of mind to others. Cave paintings reflected this function, for in these the animals depicted were more than recognizable shapes taken from the experience of the group—they represented a magical ritual whereby hunters could record their concern for survival. Decorations had now moved into the more profound sphere of the image as metaphor, and not every member of the tribe was capable of making such a transference. Those who could, we now call *artists*.

We have spoken of function and of communication, of symbol and of transference, and of the pleasure and excitement of observing and examining graphic and sculptural configurations. In essence, we have been speaking of art—both of the child and of the adult.

Perhaps the most obvious characteristic of art is that it is the result of forming, or making. Anyone who attempts to form or make anything is an artist in embryo. As one writer puts it, "We are no longer sure of *what* a work of art is in an objective way. . . . As we become unsure of standards, the finished work of art diminishes in importance while the artist becomes increasingly more interesting and important. Art becomes what an artist *does,* not what he makes."[12]

If art is to be produced, however, artists must have mastery of tools, materials, and processes. They usually achieve such mastery only through a rigorous self-discipline that keeps them striving for excellence of production. All artists worthy of the name engage in this search for excellence, never ceasing in a struggle to surpass in quality their former output.

As a result of this struggle for mastery, an artist may produce an organization, or assembly, of materials to which others respond favorably. This assembly is usually given such names as "composition," or "design." "The musical composition is arresting," we say, or, "The design of the bridge is excellent." Clive Bell called an arresting artistic assembly a "significant form." "In each [work of art]," he said, "lines and colors combined in a peculiar way, certain forms and relations of forms, stir our aesthetic emotions . . . these aesthetically moving forms I call 'significant form' and 'significant form' is the one quality common to all works of art."[13] Although Bell's statement is an important one, he failed to make entirely clear the meaning of "significant." To do so one must recognize the fact that art possesses qualities beyond that of fine form, or design. Bell did *not,* however, equate "significance" with beauty. Art can be controversial, stimulating, abrasive and at times shocking. The important consideration is that it *engage* us through its uniqueness.

Common to all art is the individuality of expression. All great art bears the imprint of the personality of its creator. "Even the art that allows the least play to individual variations," says Dewey, "like, say, the religious painting and sculpture of the twelfth century, is not mechanical and hence bears the stamp of personality."[14]

The personal nature of art is related to two factors—the source of the subject matter and the manner in which the design is developed. All great art represents a personal reaction of its creator to personal experi-

[12]Allen S. Weller, "Art, Artist, Teacher and Critic," *Art Education,* Vol. 18, No. 1 (January 1965), pp. 5-6.
[13]*Art* (New York: Stokes, 1914), p. 8.
[14]*Art as Experience,* p. 251. See also Paul Zucker, *Styles in Painting* (New York: Viking, 1950); Sheldon Cheney, *A Primer of Modern Art,* 14th ed. (New York: Tudor, 1966); and Herbert Read, *History of Modern Art* (New York: Horizon, 1953); all illustrate the intensely personal nature of contemporary art.

Figure 1.3 *All great art bears the imprint of the artist's personality, even when the work of art fits within an ancient tradition, as in this painting by Georges Rouault, which carries forward into this century the traditions of the stained glass windows of the twelfth and thirteenth centuries. Rouault's painting may be taken as an example of Expressionism. (Georges Rouault, The Old King, 1916–38. Oil on canvas app. 30¼ × 21¼ in. Collection, Museum of Art, Carnegie Institute [Patrons Art Fund]. ©1974 by SPADEM PARIS.)*

ences. The genius of El Greco, Picasso, Goya, Cézanne, Matisse, and a host of other great artists is reflected in the thought and emotion generated by contact with their environment. The greatest artists are those who have discovered a personal mode of expression that suits the reaction to experience they wish to convey. Thus, we can glance at a work of art and say immediately, "That is a piece of sculpture by Henry Moore," "That is a painting by Chardin," or "That is an etching by Rembrandt." In the individuality of the work rests its timeless and universal appeal.

We see, therefore, that art results from an act of self-expression involving emotions and intellect. Thus we may say that *art is a form of expression giving order to a human being's reaction to the environment.*[15] It is this concept of art—a traditional one—that governs to a great extent the art program in our schools today.

[15]See Dewey, *Art as Experience,* for further elaboration of this idea.

14

It has been said that science states facts and that art expresses meanings. Perhaps one way to understand what is valued in art education is to contrast the artistic with the scientific method. Scientific inquiry aims at verification and rejects emotional involvement; whereas the artist draws inspiration from the senses, the scientist refuses to be misled by them. Irving Kaufman notes that art "offers an infinite but subjective number of truths and generally stresses the individual character of the process, the product and the imaginative nature of the motivating experience."[16] The empirical nature of science demands repetition for verification; the artist avoids repetition at all costs. The scientist places a premium on logical processes; the artist, however, may consciously seek out the illogical in the search for a fresh statement.

Art and Science

Although artists are not anti-intellectual, their initial impetus toward their work is derived from experiences that are unique, often spontaneous, subjective, and at times even irrational. On the other hand there are verifiable aspects to art that could conceivably appeal to the scientist that exists in every artist. The structure and makeup of materials, the dynamics of space and color interaction, may all be studied without even engaging in studio activity. (One must, however, also admit that the speculative nature of the higher realms of physics and mathematics does correspond in many ways to the intuitive nature of art.) Learning, in both art and science, begins in the realm of sensory experience.

The history of art contains many periods in which views on the nature of art have changed, leading to changes in modes of expression. In some periods artists have emphasized subject matter of local interest at the expense of design. In others, design was given greater attention than subject matter because of new concepts, such as those of the Cubists. From time to time scientific discoveries, such as the laws of optics, have dominated both form (design) and content (subject matter). When one is sacrificed for the other—as, for example, design was neglected in the work of Landseer and other nineteenth-century painters, or as subject matter has been slighted in the output of some nonobjective painters—the quality of art inevitably suffers.

Some Periodic Changes in Artistic Theories

Of course these developments in art are often valuable because they reveal new potentialities for expression. Although they may upset the standard of production for a little while, they tend ultimately to enrich the mainstream of art. Each mode sinks into this stream, leaving some influence or disappearing entirely, according to its merits.

At least five aesthetic developments, which overlap to some extent, are worthy of our consideration, since each has influenced, or continues to influence, art education in varying degrees. The first of these is the

[16]*Art and Education in Contemporary Culture,* p. 337.

dominance of "beauty" as an ideal of artistic expression; the second is the movement called "Postimpressionism"; the third, "Expressionism"; and the fourth, the emergence of "nonrepresentational" art. The fifth development is more difficult to define because it involves not only a breakup of form but a desire to create new forms by combining the traditionally distinct modes of the painter, the sculptor, the craftsman, and even the engineer.

The Concept of "Beauty."   The view that art must be identified with concepts of beauty is of limited extent in the history of world art. As Read points out, it probably arose in Greece as the offspring of a humanistic philosophy of life, was inherited by Rome, and was revived by the Renaissance.[17]

The chief aim of Greek art was the portrayal of an ideal of humanity, one that gave great emphasis to physical beauty. But this, continues Read, is only one of several artistic ideals. The Byzantine ideal is the representation of the divine rather than the human; the primitive ideal is the control of awesome forces through powerful images; the Oriental ideal is the expression of abstract, metaphysical concepts. It would be difficult to bring beauty into service of all the artistic expressions of these several ideals.

Despite the fact that many artists have relied on beauty as a basis for expression, it is merely one of many possible approaches. Goya, for

[17]Herbert Read, *The Meaning of Art,* 3rd ed. (New York: Pitman, 1951).

Figure 1.4   *Artists within the Western tradition also have sought material for their work elsewhere than in concepts of ideal beauty. In this oil painting Jack Levine expresses a strong sense of anguish in response to the stresses of our time. (Kennedy Galleries, Inc.)*

Figure 1.5 *The ideal of beauty in art does not hold universally. This drawing by a six-year-old of a monster conveys a sense of dread similar to that of the sculpture in Figure 1.6.*

Figure 1.6 *This New Guinea sculpture was used as a fence post to protect a planted area. Neither this work nor the drawing in Figure 1.5 reflect a concern with the ideal of beauty. (The Museum of Primitive Art; Photo, Charles Uht.)*

example, found inspiration in the horrors of war as well as in the beauty of a woman's body; Daumier found themes for expression in political revolution; Toulouse-Lautrec, in the degradation of the body and soul. Art, in fact, embraces all of life and not only that small segment of it that may be considered ideally beautiful.

Beauty to the uninitiated is most often identified with execution as well as with subject matter. Thus in salon painting nobility and virtue are associated with technical virtuosity; high-blown sentiment with "realistic" rendering.

So powerful is the Greek-Roman-Renaissance influence on Western civilization that even to this day the concept of ideal beauty as a primary concern of art still exerts a major influence on professional art and hence on art education in our schools. Nevertheless, to impose such a limiting concept on children, as some teachers have done, is to deny them the opportunity of exploring the rich variety of themes that artistic expression traditionally includes.

Impressionism.   In the closing years of the nineteenth century one finds the origins of a second major influence on art education. Starting with a consideration of color, certain writers and painters attempted to interpret design in terms of physical laws and by means of intellectual analyses of surface composition.[18] Georges Seurat and Paul Signac attempted to find a logic in the use of color that their predecessors, the Impressionists, had employed with great charm but wholly intuitively. Scientists such as Chevreul, Helmholtz, and Ostwald provided an intellectual and theoretical summation of much that had been discovered intuitively by many artists in the past.

Impressionist painting had certain distinguishing characteristics in addition to a charming use of color. The traditional hierarchical organization of subject matter was abandoned in favor of a relatively modern preoccupation with light and color; flat tones and clear edges were avoided in favor of small strokes of color and indefinite contours, both of which tended to convey a sense of diffuse and often sparkling light. Artists moved their studios out of doors, and painters such as Monet found themselves doing multiple studies of a particular subject as they focused on the light of early morning, high noon, and twilight in relation to a cathedral, bridge, or haystack. One might say the Impressionists were primarily interested in the effect of light on objects in contrast to the Postimpressionists, who were interested in a variety of other artistic problems.

The Postimpressionists.   The more immediate forebears of twentieth-century art were a group of painters known as the Postimpressionists because of their close relationship to the earlier movement. The most significant of these artists were Vincent Van Gogh, Paul Cézanne, Paul Gauguin, and Georges Seurat. These four men, all highly individualistic, contributed their own distinctive perception of art to those who were to follow. The vivid, emotionally charged works of Van Gogh left their mark on the Expressionists; the broad, flat tones of Gauguin were to find their echoes in the work of Henri Matisse; and the construction of form in terms of planes undertaken by Paul Cézanne opened the door to Cubism, perhaps the most revolutionary of twentieth-century styles. Cézanne refused to limit his vision to the forms given by the tradition of painting and thus examined the structure beneath the outward aspects of objects. He invited viewers to study his pictorial subjects from multiple points of view and made the space between objects as meaningful as the objects themselves. Cézanne rejected the hazy softness of Impressionism and applied his paint

---

[18]The reader is referred to Jay Hambidge, *Elements of Dynamic Symmetry* (New York: Wittenborn, 1959), in which the ultimate in intellectual analysis of pictorial composition is to be found. Here the author resolves a number of masterpieces into mathematical formulas. How wrong one may go by following a formula may be seen in Faber Birren's *Monument to Color* (New York: McFarlane, 1938). One can only describe the illustrations in color as shockingly bad. The book, however, contains considerable technical and historical information about color theory.

Figure 1.7 *In the background of this Postimpressionist masterpiece, Les Poseuses by Georges Seurat, we see a portion of his even more famous La Grande Jatte. Notice the carefully arranged dots of pigments, characteristic of the method of painting known as "pointillism" developed by Seurat and his followers. (Collection Heinz Berggruen.)*

in clearly articulated flat strokes of color, which appeared to literally build his paintings as one small passage led to larger areas. This method of organizing the structure of a painting unified the entire work into a "fused, crystallized unit, within which the shapes and colors work together."[19]

Fauvism and Expressionism. Fauvism and Expressionism can be considered together, especially since they are closely related to one another and, in the early years of this century, were linked together under the rubric "Expressionismus." Expressionism, although difficult to define because it took numerous forms, was clearly the outgrowth of certain features in Postimpressionism, most notably those found in Van Gogh's work, but also to some degree those found in Gauguin's as well. Some people have claimed that the main feature of this movement is the expression of the artist's feelings rather than ideas. Others have stated that the movement relies chiefly on design used very abstractly to achieve an order and a rhythm that have greater significance than can be found in art that relies on nature as a basis for expression. Still others assert that Expressionism is mainly decorative.[20]

---

[19] Burton Wasserman. *Modern Painting* (Worcester, Mass.: Davis, 1970), p. 36.

[20] Concerning the nature of Expressionism, see: Clive Bell, *Since Cézanne* (New York: Harcourt Brace Jovanovich, 1922); Sheldon Cheney, *The Story of Modern Art* (New York: Viking, 1941), and *Expressionism in Art* (New York: Liveright, 1941); and Herbert Read, *Art Now,* 2nd ed. (New York: Pitman, 1960). A lively and entertaining account of Expressionism in America may be found in parts of Rudi Blesh, *Modern Art U.S.A.* (New York: Knopf, 1956).

A

B

C

D

E

G

F

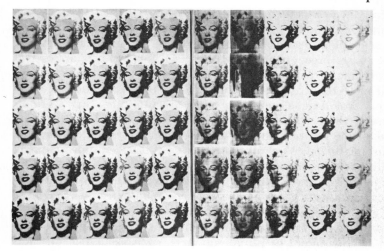

Figure 1.8 *The history of modern art reflects a varied approach to the problems of design and expressiveness.* **A** *is an example of Postimpressionism. Boy in a Red Waistcoat, 1893–95, Paul Cézanne. Oil on canvas, 35¼″ × 28¼″. Collection Mr. and Mrs. Paul Mellon.* **B** *is an example of Fauvism. Red Room (Harmony in Red), 1908–09, Henri Matisse. Oil on canvas, app. 71″ × 97″. Hermitage, Leningrad. For an example of Expressionism see Figure 1.3 and for Cubism see Figure 1.9.* **C** *is an example of Dadaism. To Be Looked At (from the Other Side of the Glass) with One Eye, Close To, for Almost an Hour, 1918, Marcel Duchamp. Framed doubleglass panel with oil paint, collage, lens, 20⅛″ × 16⅛″. Collection, Museum of Modern Art, N.Y., Katherine S. Drier Bequest. For an examplè of pure abstraction see Figure 1.10.* **D,** *Surrealism. The Eye of Silence, 1943–44, Max Ernst. Oil on canvas, 42½″ × 55½″. Collection, Washington University, St. Louis. © 1974 by SPADEM PARIS.* **E,** *Abstract Expressionism. Painting 1952, 1955–56, Franz Kline. Oil on canvas, app. 77″ × 100″. Present location unknown.* **F,** *Pop Art. Marilyn Monroe Diptych, 1962, Andy Warhol. Silk screen on canvas, 82″ × 114″. Leo Castelli Gallery. Collection Mr. and Mrs. Burton Tremaine, Meriden, Conn.* **G,** *Op Art Supernovae, 1959–61. Victor Vasarely. Oil, 59¾″ × 95½″. Tate Gallery, London.*

21

Perhaps at this point we should make a distinction between the Expressionists and the Fauves. Matisse, Rouault, and Derain may be taken as representative painters of the latter movement. Matisse, in particular, was the leader of a group of painters in France who extended the new use of color created by Gauguin and Van Gogh, carrying it to the point where the group earned the critically derisive term of "Fauves" or "Wild Beasts." The art-going public at the turn of the century, which had just begun to accept the radical innovations of the Postimpressionists, could not cope with the Fauves' strident use of pure color, their free-flowing arabesques, purley decorative line, and total disregard of local color (the specific color of a natural object). The Fauves were trying to paint according to Derain's clarion call of 1906, when he wrote: "We must, at all costs, break out of the fold in which the realists have imprisoned us."[21] The Fauves were creating their own reality and conceived of painting as a vehicle for expression that was totally autonomous, wholly independent of the viewer's perception of the world.

Expressionism, generally speaking, may be said to place emphasis on emotions, sensations, or ideas rather than on the appearance of objects. Expressionist artists present their reactions in a form that is almost invariably a pronounced distortion of the camera view of the environment. These qualities had their origins outside of France. Expressionism, in its narrower sense, was a development of early twentieth-century German art in response to the aesthetic furor taking place in France at the time. One can think of the Expressionist artists of Germany, Scandinavia, and Austria as merging the color and design theories of the Postimpressionists of France with attitudes toward subject matter that were uniquely Germanic in origin.[22] This merger gave German Expressionism its distinguishing characteristics: a heightened use of color, an extreme simplification of form and distortion of representational conventions for emotive reasons, a preoccupation with hallucinatory religious experience, and the investment of conventional or public subjects, such as landscapes and human figures, with private visionary or mythic meanings. Considerably influenced by the Fauves, the German Expressionists in turn affected French painters such as Rouault, especially in terms of the ideological substructure of art. Eventually, the artistic manners and attitudes of the German Expressionists were to have a wide influence and to assume the more generalized characteristics described previously. As time went on, Expressionism took the form of extreme abstraction. The liberating effects on painting that attended Expressionism can well be imagined.[23] Later we shall see that it had similar effects on art education, and that these effects are still being felt.

[21]Quoted in Werner Haftmann, *Painting in the Twentieth Century* (New York: Praeger, 1965), p. 36.

[22]The works of Edvard Munch, Arnold Böcklin, and the members of the Jugendstil, such as Gustav Klimt, had great influence on the formative years of German Expressionism.

[23]The reader is referred to Appendix II, "Recommended Reading for Teaching Art: Art Appreciation," for titles dealing with Expressionistic artists.

Figure 1.9 *The Cubists, reflecting the new consciousness of the relativity of time and space, offered the viewer a more flexible visual experience by presenting, simultaneously, different views of still-life objects. (Juan Gris. Breakfast (1914). Pasted paper, crayon, and oil on canvas, 31⅞″ × 23½″. Collection, The Museum of Modern Art, New York. Acquired through the Lillie P. Bliss Bequest. © ADAGP 1975.)*

Cubism. It was in 1907, when *Les Demoiselles d'Avignon* was painted, that Pablo Picasso took Cézanne's ideas one step further toward what is now known as Cubism. *Les Demoiselles* combined the simultaneous perspective of Cézanne with the simple, monumental shapes and sharply faceted surfaces of African and primitive Iberian art. As Picasso developed his ideas together with Georges Braque, the forms of Cubism became more complex. By 1911, Cubist compositions grew in complexity as planes overlapped, penetrated each other, and moved into areas of total abstraction. Space and form were now handled with a minimum of color in contrast to the rich hues of the Fauves and Expressionists. Their spontaneity and painterly qualities, born of their own emotionalism, were superseded by a more intellectual concern for order. As Haftmann describes it,

> Cubism embraces all the aspects of the object simultaneously and is more complete than the optical view. From the information and signs conveyed on the rhythmically moving surface, the imagination can reassemble the object in its entirety. . . . Cubism corresponds to that new modern conception of reality which it has been the aim of the whole pictorial effort of the 20th Century to express in visual terms.[24]

Surrealism. The precursors of Surrealism were artists such as Paul Klee, Giorgio di Chirico, and Marc Chagall, all of whom dealt with fantasy, dreams, and other states of mind. We may add to these influences the Dada movement whose anti-art theatrics and demonstrations challenged

---

[24] Werner Haftmann, *Painting in the Twentieth Century*, p. 80.

23

the most basic assumptions regarding art. André Breton, a poet, first used the term "surrealist" in his own publication, thus reflecting the close connection between an art movement and a literary one, a common situation in the history of art. The artists who were ultimately to be identified with the movement—Max Ernst, Hans Arp, Salvador Dali, Joan Miró, Yves Tanguy—all shared Breton's interest in Sigmund Freud's ideas regarding dreams, psychoanalysis, and the relation of the conscious and subconscious self. The Surrealists were intrigued by the possibilities of subconscious experience as the subject matter for art and strove to divorce themselves from rational and logical approaches. In searching for a definition of Surrealism that would apply equally to literature and art, Breton wrote "Surrealism: the dictation of thought free from any control of reason, independent of any esthetic or moral preoccupation . . . rests upon a belief in the superior reality of certain forms of association hitherto neglected, in the omnipotence of the dream, in the disinterested play of thought."[25]

Nonrepresentational Art.   One of the most revolutionary developments in the art of the early twentieth-century was the shift toward what was at first called "nonobjective" art. Wassily Kandinsky, a Russian who lived in Germany and France, is considered the father of nonobjective painting.[26] The concepts subsumed under this term are now usually referred

[25] Herbert Read, *A Concise History of Modern Painting* (New York: Praeger, 1959), p. 132.

[26] Kandinsky wrote an exposition of his art for the Guggenheim Foundation (New York: 1946) titled *On the Spiritual in Art*. See also his *Concerning the Spiritual in Art and Painting in Particular* (New York: Wittenborn, 1964). Piet Mondrian is another well-known nonrepresentational artist: see his *Plastic Art and Pure Plastic Art* (New York: Wittenborn, 1945).

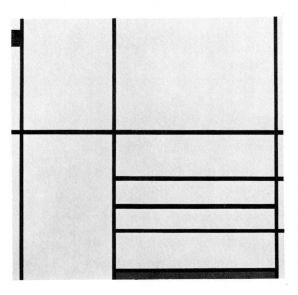

Figure 1.10 *In the early part of this century certain artists turned completely away from the representational functions of art and became solely concerned with the creation of pure relations among the design elements. One of the major figures in this movement was Piet Mondrian, whose Composition in White, Black and Red is a prime example of what has come to be called pure abstraction. (1936, Oil on canvas, 40¼″ × 41″. Collection, the Museum of Modern Art, New York. Gift of the Advisory Committee.)*

to as nonrepresentational and cover a much wider range of styles than originally. Nonrepresentational art now includes the works of such diverse artists as Kandinsky, Piet Mondrian, Hans Arp, Constantin Brancusi, Jackson Pollack, Mark Rothko, Louise Nevelson, and the artists associated with the Op, Minimal, and Hard-Edge schools of art, such as Victor Vasarely, Don Judd, Kenneth Noland, and Frank Stella. Before the arrival of nonrepresentational art, the subject matter of painting and sculpture derived almost universally from the natural world, although the degree of correspondence ranged widely from photographic likeness to highly abstract statement. The nonrepresentational painter, however, asserts that expression is based on the manipulation of the elements of design—line, mass and space, light and shade, texture, and color[27]—without reference to the visible world. Subject matter is in a sense eliminated. Although nonrepresentational painting has perhaps declined in popularity recently, art education has profited greatly from the nonrepresentational artists' experiments with media, techniques, and pictorial composition.

Fragmentation and Reconstruction.　When Picasso included fragments of newspaper clippings in his cubistic paintings, he was attacking much the same problem as the Futurist artist Boccioni when he integrated, at an earlier time, a real window frame into a piece of sculpture. Both were struggling with a traditional concern of the artist—that of stating the nature of reality in terms of one's own time. The "fixed" point of view, which began with the Renaissance painters' discovery of perspective, was seriously questioned by Cézanne and the Cubists and was followed by further movements that were not only to redefine traditional ideas of space and subject matter but to question the role of the very surface of the canvas itself. The collage approach, which combined diverse and un-related "found" textures, eventually led to the addition, some thirty years later, of real objects, as for example, Rauschenberg's stuffed birds and pillows. Artists such as Louise Nevelson and George Segal have either employed the real object as an adjunct to painting and sculpture or used it to create a new kind of symbol derived from both arts. The idea of creating situations werein "found" objects are set into fresh perspective by the creation of radically different frames of reference seems to be a part of the current thinking of the artist, who is freed from the limitations imposed by fixed media classifications. Thus, sculpture is not merely painted, it *moves,* and paintings wired for sound may speak to us literally as well as symbolically, thereby steadily weaning the viewer away from an attitude of passivity and contemplation toward greater degrees of participation.

　　How is the art teacher to respond to contemporary ideas that may seem shocking, frivolous, or even vulgar? The aesthetics of anti-art, high

---

[27]See Chapter 3 for a discussion of these elements.

Figure 1.11 *A fifth grader's felt-pen drawing, showing a design that relates a variety of shapes to linear divisions.*

camp, and pornographic art are admittedly difficult and perhaps cannot be introduced in the elementary classroom, yet there was a time when a problem in collage was considered very advanced. Time will tell which of the art movements currently in vogue are merely fads and which have significance for learning in art. It is pointless to be avant-garde when the children have no idea of the meaning behind the activities assigned them, yet there is much of contemporary art from which they can derive profit and enjoyment. Scrap sculpture is closely allied to the mysterious monochromatic assemblages of Louise Nevelson, and working with raw film, box cameras, and photograms allows children to relate designs to the technology of their time. We ask our students to create collages out of paper—why not create forms out of three-dimensional "found" objects? The art of our time, if presented through judicious use of slides and reproductions, field trips, and visiting artists, may provide a greater depth of understanding and excitement for both student and teacher. Students curious about color could learn much from the Hard-Edge or Op Art painters, and teachers preparing for the annual PTA poster project could stimulate the children by showing them the calligraphy and silkscreen prints of Corita Kent. The burden of presenting activities relating to not only the art of today but that of the past as well falls on the art consultant, but it is the responsibility of the classroom teacher to express to the art consultant an interest in such ideas. Conversely, the art consultant should recognize that the recent history of art has extended our perceptions so that the general public can now accept a ballet setting that uses surrealist images, for example, or illustrations and paintings that do not conform to the rules of photographic realism. The art teacher can and should look to the history of art as a rich source of ideas. There is a time for children to focus their attention on the external world and there is a time to honor our own dreams and inner desires; there should be opportunities to experiment with form, and there should be situations wherein the modes of one medium can borrow from another. The history of art provides ample evidence to support all such activities.

FREEDOM AND ART

Since art is of a highly personal nature, creating people must control the activities that engage them. To be in control of their work artists must enjoy a high degree of freedom in the choice of both subject matter and manner of expression.

At certain periods in history political and aesthetic restrictions have been placed on artists. Sometimes these restrictions have resulted not from the normal discipline of artistic production but rather from the repressive actions of dictatorships—such as the Nazi regime in Germany. The Nazi repression was, of course, promulgated for political reasons, as are the similar restrictions on Soviet artists today. In other periods, various groups of artists, salons, and academies have attempted to restrict artistic activities, often for the purpose of maintaining a *status quo* in which their members strongly believed. In England, France, and elsewhere, individuals or groups of influential artists have from time to time attempted to set forth canons for art and greatly discouraged deviations from them. Sometimes one person of remarkable ability and persuasive power has been able to influence artistic thought until it became derivative rather than creative. Under all such conditions, the art of the times has suffered.

Cheney has offered a number of examples demonstrating the disastrous effects that unnecessary restriction has on artists' output.[28] He mentions the Chinese, who, with their passion for regulating design, did not escape the cramping effects that attend the codification of rules related to composition. Cheney also cites the codification of the rules of architecture by Vitruvius. Originally written in the first century A.D., these rules were rediscovered and enthusiastically adopted by the architects of the Renaissance. The ascendancy of Vitruvius' "orders" has touched the environment of us all. Cheney maintains that until the second decade of this century submission to the classic mode of architectural design seriously impeded the development of a creative building art based on human need.

[28]Sheldon Cheney, *A New World History of Art* (New York: Holt, Rinehart and Winston, 1956).

A clear-cut example of dictatorial practice, one that almost completely stifled aesthetic expression, may be found in educational systems of the past. The lessons that educators have learned, therefore, from a study of artistic practice, and that today they apply to art education in our schools, are concerned with two freedoms. They believe that art cannot flourish, either in professional circles or in school, unless the creators are free, first, to employ those aspects of experience that truly arouse their emotions and stimulate their intellect, and second, to develop a form of expression that they find appropriate to the theme they wish to express. Today it is believed that the success of an art education program depends largely on adherence to these traditional freedoms. Furthermore, the quality of any art program may be judged by the degree to which the teacher advocates and encourages these freedoms.

The freedom necessary for the success of an aesthetic act cannot be separated from the freedom of thought and action that is the prerogative of the individual living in a democracy. A fact that perhaps has generally been overlooked is that art educators have been among the pioneers in developing a pedagogy compatible with democratic practices. What assisted them as much as anything else was their understanding that such a form of pedagogy suited the requirements of artistic expression. They recognized that art could not be taught successfully unless it was presented in an atmosphere designed to develop individual and, in a sense, nonconformist expression.

It should be noted that freedom in the art program does not mean unlimited license. Teachers, in attempting to move children beyond a plateau of development must constantly make certain decisions regarding their instructions. In so doing, however, they are always guided by the need for options—choices to be made by the individual child during the course of the art activity. It is this recognition of the value of personal decision-making that separates the art class from most others.

THE INFLUENCE OF GENERAL EDUCATIONAL THOUGHT

Modern education, like modern art, is not entirely a product of the last three or four decades. Many of the basic ideas to be found both in aesthetics and in teaching today may be traced to ideas held by philosophers and teachers who lived long ago, as well as to the psychologists of recent years. Contemporary art education, then, is a field that is fed by the history of art and general education. The development of current practice in art education is also supported by the investigations of psychologists into the learning process as a whole. Ultimately, our social goals determine the direction art education takes.

What a modern ring some of the ancient writings have! In the *Republic* of Plato (427–347 B.C.), for example, we find the germ of the concept called the "search for excellence" discussed earlier in this chapter. Montaigne (1533–92) and Francis Bacon (1561–1626) emphasized the need to base teaching on firsthand experience rather than on "logic chopping." Comenius (1592–1670) developed this idea in his *Didactica magna* and later made it practical in his *Orbis pictus.* In the latter, it is also interesting to note, he affirmed that children should not memorize what they do not understand. Rousseau (1712–88) believed that teaching should be related to childhood interests and that education should be concerned with the everyday life of the child. He emphasized these ideas in his *Émile:*

> What must we think of the barbarous education, which sacrifices the present to the uncertain future, which loads a child with chains of every sort, and begins by making him miserable, in order to prepare him, long in advance, for some pretended happiness which it is probable he will never enjoy?

Let children be children, Rousseau advocated, and let them learn through self-initiated activities. On the matter of competition—a question we are still debating in education—Rousseau declared that self-competition is preferable to rivalry between children and their fellows. It must be admitted that Rousseau was a theorist and a dreamer and that some of his ideas about teaching were quite impractical. It remained for future teachers to make pedagogical order out of Rousseau's theories. Three teachers—Johann Pestalozzi (1746–1827), Johann Herbart (1776–1841), and Friedrich Froebel (1782–1852)—contributed to this process.

Unlike most of his predecessors, the gentle Swiss, Pestalozzi, gave particular emphasis to the idea that education is more than the process of recording sense impressions on a passive mind. Learners must be active participants and must reorganize the experiences that they encounter. It was Pestalozzi also who thought the development of good citizens to be the chief aim of teaching.[29]

As a pioneer and experimenter, Pestalozzi made many mistakes, and he lacked the ability to systematize his thoughts into a teaching methodology. The task of developing a systematic pedagogy was left to Herbart, a learned German. Herbart gained inspiration to perform this task from Pestalozzi's school.[30] Although Herbart's methodology seems cold and formal to teachers today, his teachings nevertheless recognize in the learning process the natural capacities, interests, and activities of children.

Froebel, also a German and something of a mystic, established his

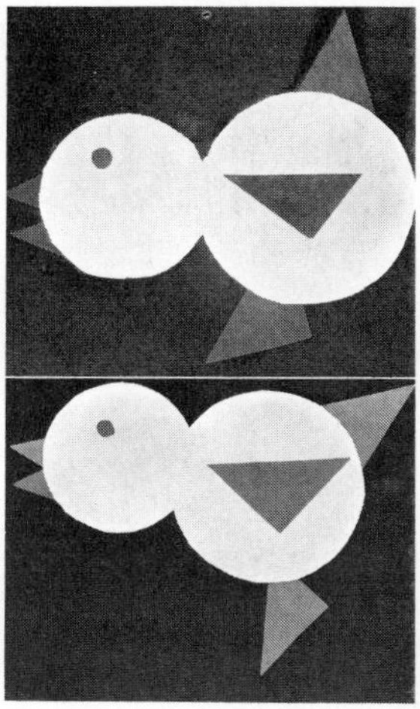

Influential Philosophical Theories

Figure 1.12 *Examples of the use of Froebel's "basic shapes." "Art" lessons that teach children to copy these forms are harmful to educational development.*

---

[29]See Pestalozzi's novel, *Leonard and Gertrude* (1781) and his book on education, *How Gertrude Teaches Her Children* (1801).

[30]Herbart wrote *ABC of Sense Perception* to explain Pestalozzi's views.

first kindergarten in 1837 after visiting Pestalozzi's school.[31] His teaching methods were founded on the naturalism preached by Rousseau and practiced by Pestalozzi. His mystical ideas prompted him to make use in the kindergarten of objects having a basic geometrical shape—cube, circle, prism, and so on—on the theory that a child would gain an awareness of unity, and indeed deity, by being in contact with some of these "perfect" forms. Froebel has exerted a profound influence on art education in kindergartens, but his influence is not always acceptable to modern art teachers, for reasons that will be explained later. His strong belief, however, that children should be taught from the concrete to the abstract and that a school should be a miniature society, is still considered sound.

In this respect at least, Froebel predated Jean Piaget's theories of children's concept development, for both men saw sensory experience as providing the natural basis for distinguishing between material and social realities. (In other words, if "working together" is one of the teacher's goals, role-playing or painting a class mural will be of greater educational significance to a first grader than will a discussion of the subject.)

Influential Psychological Theories

Although the educational theories and practices just described have had their effects on art teaching, an even stronger influence is to be found in the developments of psychological thought. Because a complete and detailed study of the effects of psychology on methodology is manifestly impossible here, we shall consider only a few of the most important influences on teaching methods in art. These influences include, first, what are known as "faculty" and "Herbartian" psychology, both of which are associated with the so-called introspective school of psychological thought; second, the "functional" school of psychology, from which developed E. L. Thorndike's S-R theory of learning and much of John Dewey's philosophy; and third, the "Gestalt" school of psychology.

The "faculty" psychologists believed that the mind was composed of a series of separate compartments, each of which housed a "faculty" such as memory, will, or reason. In order to train one's mind, a person must perform a series of intellectual exercises. "Those whose 'faculties' had not been trained by suitable exercises or who were deemed lacking in 'faculties' as the masses were sometimes thought to be had to be content with lowly social positions."[32] Because the faculty psychologists taught that the mental powers developed through exercise could be applied to all areas of human endeavor, including artistic effort, influence on early art education was great.

Herbart thought that the mind acted as a unit, maintaining that it has the power of what he called "apperception"—the capacity to assimi-

---

[31] His most important book is *Education and Man,* published in 1826.
[32] James Mulhern, *A History of Education* (New York: Ronald, 1946), p. 389.

late new ideas through ideas already acquired. Herbart developed teaching methods that he believed assisted the mind in making use of the power of apperception. His methods "elevated the importance of the teacher and made the pupil a listener, whose mind was to be molded according to a preconceived plan of studies and by formal steps of method."[33] By the middle of the nineteenth century, the Herbartian steps of teaching had become common practice—indeed, slogans—in almost every North American normal school. The methods used in drawing lessons were determined by these steps.[34]

In America, interest later developed in a psychological concept related to Darwinian biology. According to this concept, mind was thought to be the chief factor in adaptation to environment. Hence it was said to consist of functions rather than of the static structures suggested by earlier psychologies; this concept led to the so-called functional school of psychology.

John Dewey (1859–1952) is considered to be one of the founders of the functional school of psychology and was in his early years closely associated with it. As a philosopher, of course, Dewey later ranged far in his ideas, but they were unmistakably colored by functionalism. He was greatly concerned with the relationship of learners to their environment and to the society in which they live.[35] He regarded education as the "continuing re-creation of experience." According to Dewey, experience and education are not synonymous: education involves the direction and control of experience, and a meaningful experience implies some measure of control for future experiences. Knowledge is not static, Dewey said, nor is it gained in a static environment to be used in a static society. Learning must lead to more learning—the process is never-ending. Dewey's ideas readily lend themselves to the teaching of art. Indeed, he was a philosopher of aesthetics as well as of education and produced an admirable book on the subject, *Art as Experience,* which will be referred to again in this book.

John Dewey's ideas were supplemented by the work of G. Stanley Hall in the Child Study Movement during the early part of this century. Both Dewey and Hall saw *scholiocentric* (school-centered) situations giving way to the *pedocentric* (child-centered) curriculum. Hall thought that the selection of all learning activity should proceed from the study of child development and that a teacher's primary obligation is to study the child rather than the subject. As early as 1901 Hall stated, "The guardians of the young should strive first of all to keep out of nature's

---

[33]*Ibid.*

[34]The Herbartian steps of teaching are as follows: preparation, presentation, association, generalization, and application. See Herbart's *Text Book of Psychology,* published in 1816, and his *Outlines of Educational Doctrine,* published in 1835.

[35]Of the vast amount of writing Dewey produced on this theme, perhaps his *Democracy and Education* might be selected for reading by the student.

way and to prevent harm, and should merit the proud title of defenders of the happiness and rights of children."[36] Statements such as this one provided the groundwork for the laissez-faire methods of art instruction of the Progressive era. One of the tasks of today's art educator is to find ways of resolving the dilemma posed by respect for the rights and freedom of the child on the one hand, and, on the other, the possibly conflicting desire of the teacher to play a more positive role in structuring the learning environment.

A psychologist associated with the functional school of thought was E. L. Thorndike (1874–1949). Thorndike joined the staff of Teachers College, Columbia University, in 1901 and remained there until his retirement in 1940. Among his achievements were the development of a systematic animal psychology, the production of the first standardized tests in education, and the investigation of many learning problems.[37]

Thorndike based his educational theories on what is called a stimulus-response, or "S–R" theory. According to this theory, learning consists in the establishment of a series of connections, or pathways, in the brain, resulting from a specific stimulus that causes an equally specific response.[38] Between each nerve ending is a gap, or synapse, which tends to resist the impulse of the stimulus but which can be bridged by repeated stimuli. This physiological condition led Thorndike to believe that learning should be a matter of repetitive drill. The most efficient teaching would result from breaking a school subject into minute parts. Drill based on these minute details would then allow the learner to develop "a wonderfully elaborate and intricate system of connections."[39] When Thorndike's system was applied to art, it exhibited certain deficiencies. Although learning can undoubtedly occur as a result of a methodology based on such a system, the S–R theory failed, as we shall see, to promote the kind of creative thinking that art demands.

The system of psychology called "Gestalt" has had a strong influence on contemporary art education. In *The Growth of the Mind*[40] Kurt Koffka (1886–1941) produced evidence to show that, in learning, an organism acts as a total entity and does not exercise only certain parts. During the First World War, Wolfgang Köhler, a German psychologist, performed experiments with primates that supported the Gestaltist theories. In his experiments primates showed "insight" in solving problems.[41] On the basis of

[36]G. Stanley Hall, *The Forum,* Vol. 32 (1901–02), pp. 24–25.

[37]In 1913 and 1914 he published his three-volume *Educational Psychology,* comprising the following: Vol. I, *The Original Nature of Man;* Vol. II, *The Psychology of Learning;* Vol. III, *Work, Fatigue, and Individual Differences.*

[38]See Thorndike's description of this phenomenon in *The Psychology of Wants, Interests, and Attitudes* (New York: Appleton-Century-Crofts, 1935).

[39]E. L. Thorndike, *Educational Psychology: Briefer Course* (New York: Teachers College, 1914), p. 173.

[40]Totowa, N.J.: Littlefield, Adams, 1959.

[41]*The Mentality of Apes* (New York: Harcourt Brace Jovanovich, 1927).

such evidence, the Gestaltists maintained that wholes are primary; parts derive their properties and their behavior from them. The learner, in other words, acquires knowledge not by building bit-by-bit a system of nervous connections, but by achieving "insight," that is, *understanding the relationships among the various aspects of the learning situation.*

Rudolf Arnheim, in his book *Art and Visual Perception,*[42] has provided art teachers with the clearest and most completely stated view of Gestalt psychology. His book includes material ranging from an analysis of Picasso's *Guernica* to a discussion of the development of children's perception. How deeply Gestalt theories have affected art education today will be seen in the subsequent portions of this book.

CHANGES IN ART EDUCATION

Having studied some important influences on art education as we find it today, we may now examine the changes that have occurred in this area. Although art activities have apparently engaged people's attention for perhaps 30,000 years, art as a part of general education is relatively new. Many other fields of study had become traditional before the 1850's when art, in a restricted form, was placed on most programs of studies. Even at that time leaders in public education were usually reluctant to recognize its importance or support it as a serious part of the school program. Just a little over sixty years ago, educational thinkers such as Herbert Spencer held that art should be considered only as a leisure-time activity.[43] Spencer, like the functionalists, was greatly influenced by Darwin's *Origin of Species,* so that, to him, the fundamentals of a good education depended largely on activities contributing to human survival in a world of fierce biological competition. Art, therefore, was a luxury that might be indulged in only after all other "necessary" human activities had received their full share of attention. The Spencerian attitude toward art was long current in schools; educators who agree with Spencer may still be found today.

The Linear Drawing Program

Around the 1850's a type of work that in some respects might be considered the beginnings of school art appeared in several European and American institutions of learning. This work was usually called "linear drawing," and although it did not include expressive work, it involved some of the media associated with art. At first, linear drawing consisted for the most part of mapmaking, but as time went on, the content of the program was broadened. By the 1880's it included map-drawing and "the

---

[42] 4th ed. (Berkeley: University of California Press, 1964).
[43] *Education—Intellectual, Moral and Physical* (Totowa, N.J.: Littlefield, Adams, 1963).

delineation of common objects on paper, slates, and blackboard," by which advanced pupils might master the intricacies of linear perspective. This meager advance in thirty years may seem pitiful to us today, particularly in view of the tremendous strides being made at that time by such artists as Manet, Degas, Toulouse-Lautrec, and, above all, Cézanne.[44] Nevertheless, even this limited advance had the effect of breaching what had appeared to be an impregnable and almost universal wall of academic resistance to anything resembling art in the general education program.

The precise nature of the linear drawing program may be studied in several series of exercise books published beginning in the 1870's. These series usually consisted of eight books—one for each grade. They remained in vogue until the early 1900's, when "drawing" became "art," and a new point of view emerged. The early drawing books outlined a curious mixture of mechanical drawing and freehand copying and were planned according to an adult standard of draftsmanship. Influenced by the "faculty" type of psychology, they were built on the idea that it is necessary to master the elements of one small skill before progressing to an exercise involving another skill.

In North America, the *Smith Drawing Books* were one of the first series to be adopted for general use in the schools. Their author, Walter Smith, was at one time headmaster of the Leeds School of Art and Science, a training school in England for art teachers. He later became State Director of Art Education in Massachusetts. In 1872 he published a volume called *Art Education, Scholastic and Industrial*.[45] Smith seems to have been a man of considerable learning, for in this volume his remarks on the design of industrial objects are quite fitting.

In format, the many series of drawing books were very much alike. Most of them provided on the cover a statement of their educational objectives. Usually the purpose of the series was "the laying of a good foundation for more advanced art training." The following statements as to the particular aims of the books are typical:

1. To train the eye in the accurate perception of form, size, and proportion, and to exactness in the measurement of distances and angles.
2. To train the hand to freedom and rapidity of execution.
3. To train the memory to accurate recollection of the forms and arrangements of objects.
4. To cultivate and refine the taste by the study, delineation, and recollection of beautiful forms.

[44]Professional developments in drawing as illustrated in etchings of this period are strikingly displayed in Edward T. Chase, *The Etchings of the French Impressionists and Their Contemporaries* (New York: Crown, 1946).

[45]Boston: James R. Osgood.

In the teachers' colleges of this period the drawing books were often used as guides to methodology. The teachers-in-training were subjected to the same type of formal discipline in drawing as was advocated in the drawing books. A study of the drawing examinations they had to pass gives further insight into the emphasis placed on technical skill in drawing rather than on expression. The following are sample questions in an examination given at a teachers' college in 1878:

1. Give instructions in full as you would give them to a class for drawing a water pitcher. Be especially particular about the *lip* and *handle*. Show your construction lines.
2. Sketch a doorway with a door half open.
3. Draw a Roman cross showing its thickness; first, with the eye *below* it and to the left; second, with the eye *above* it and to the right.[46]

As time went on, a number of art schools became interested in the drawing program in the public schools and established courses for prospective teachers. In this way the influence of the drawing books tended to diminish. Unfortunately, the early program in the art schools often was as rigid as that set forth in the books. State departments of education apparently made it clear that no nonsense was to be tolerated in art classes. As one official in an education department put it:

> The subjects [in the art course] will be of a practical character. Take drawing, for example; it is not the purpose of the government to encourage amateurs whose sole object is to draw something agreeable, merely for the sake of representation, but rather to provide instruction which will assist in explaining the technicalities of that which is represented.

A representative "elementary" course for teachers-in-training might consist, therefore, of the following studies: "freehand outlines; model drawing; perspective; practical geometry." An advanced course might contain a continuation of the elementary-course subjects, with the addition of "historical ornament and painting of objects in oils." By the turn of the century, nature study was occasionally added to the list, and a study of famous paintings might appear in some art education programs.

That the program of linear drawing was anything but creative and expressive is obvious. Nevertheless, it deeply influenced art education. To this day one may find in some classrooms certain so-called art activities that are based on the program of linear drawing. Where they are not used merely to keep children quiet, coloring exercises, for example, are still offered in various schools in the belief that the hand and eye should be

[46]Teachers today might be expected to answer such questions, but they would, of course, not be judged solely on their ability to resolve correctly mechanical problems of this kind.

trained dissociated from thought. Step-by-step exercises in which the teacher does the planning and organizing of an art activity, and by which the children are taught to follow directions passively, are another manifestation of the fact that linear drawing and the Herbartian methodology persist in our educational systems. The educational inefficiency of exercises of this type has been proved over and over again, yet these practices continue.

The Influence of the S–R Theory of Learning

The influence of the S–R theory of learning was equally unfortunate. It led to an overemphasis on the intellectual content of art programs, rigidity, and the acceptance of a debased interpretation of Postimpressionism. Children were encouraged to make color wheels and value scales. They made prearranged designs to illustrate the standardized color arrangements known as monochromatic, complementary, split-complementary, and the like. Exercises in the use of classic proportion and line were found in many schools.

Certain activities in the linear drawing program were retained. Linear perspective was given even greater prominence because it provided a collection of neat intellectual tricks for teachers and pupils. The chalk box, drawn in two-point perspective, was laboriously delineated by many a weary pupil, as were lines of telephone poles and railway tracks. A number of principles that the pupils were expected to commit to memory were established for most activities.

Even the youngest children did not escape. Froebel's basic shapes were employed to teach drawing to them (see Figure 1.12). Teachers designed "people" and "birds" out of circles, "houses" out of triangles, and a host of objects out of oblongs. The children were expected to copy these. In so doing they were denied the opportunity to express any reaction to what they observed firsthand in their environment.

The Influence of Franz Cizek: Creative Expression

Until the advent of Expressionism, art education had remained remarkably aloof from the artistic tradition, and even then artistic thinking affected education only slowly. Expressionism first had its effect on art education largely through the work of one outstanding teacher, Franz Cizek.[47] Cizek, an Austrian, went to Vienna in 1865 to study art. At the close of his formal period of study, he turned to art education. In 1904, after achieving success in several teaching posts, he accepted the position of chief of the Department of Experimentation and Research at the Vienna School of Applied Arts. His now-famous art classes for children were developed in this department.

[47]See W. Viola, *Child Art and Franz Cizek* (New York: Reynal & Hitchcock, 1936). See also Thomas Munro, *Art Education: Toward Science in Aesthetics* (Indianapolis: Bobbs-Merrill, 1956).

Figure 1.13 *A picture produced in Cizek's school in Vienna. Cizek proved that children are capable of expressing themselves in a personal, creative, and acceptable manner.*

Cizek eliminated from these classes such activities as the making of color charts and the photographic drawing of natural objects. Rather, he encouraged children to present in visual form their personal reactions to happenings in their lives. In the output produced under his guidance, much of which has been preserved to this day, one finds that the young artists depicted themselves at play, attending happy gatherings, and in general doing the things that naturally engage the attention and interest of the young. Cizek always maintained that it was not his aim to develop artists. Instead, he held as his one goal the development of the creative power that he found in all children and that he felt could blossom "in accordance with natural laws."[48]

Much of the work produced in Cizek's classrooms reveals the charm of expression of which children, under sympathetic teachers, are capable. There are indications, however, that Cizek and his staff discouraged the young from venturing much beyond the concept of beauty as a theme for artistic expression. Some of the output seems oversweet and discloses pretty mannerisms, such as a profusion of stars in the sky areas of com-

[48]R. R. Tomlinson, *Picture Making by Children* (London: Studio, 1934), p. 27.

positions or a stylized expression of childish innocence in the faces. These mannerisms lead one to deduce that some of the classes may have been overly supervised, and that the artistic development of the children was brought about as much by some of Cizek's teachers as by "natural laws." Nevertheless, Cizek is an important figure in art education, and his work deserves the widespread admiration it has received. The contemporary belief that children, under certain conditions, are capable of expressing themselves in a personal, creative, and acceptable manner derives largely from his demonstrations in Vienna.

During the years in which Cizek held his classes, he had many visitors from abroad. Word spread, particularly to England and America, of the "new system of art teaching."[49] Those who understood its basic principles used the new system to bring about desirable modifications of their art programs. In education as elsewhere, however, new movements invariably attract some followers who do not completely understand them. Expressionism as related to art education was no exception. The term "self-expression" in the 1920's was closely allied with the Expressionist painters in Europe, and many teachers felt that children should be encouraged to work in the highly subjective manner of such artists as Van Gogh, Nolde, and Schmidt-Rotluff. German Expressionism and French Cubism are examples of the many ideas imported from abroad that were to feed into the mainstream of art education and to characterize art instruction during the era of Progressive education.

Another influence, felt in the late 1930's, was that of the Bauhaus, a German school committed to integrating the technology of its day into the work of the artist. As a result of this influence, plastics, photography, and visual investigation involving sensory awareness found their way into the secondary-school art program, and the elementary schools seemed also to be caught up in a headlong rush for novelty of materials. Bauhaus influences on current elementary-school practice, however, are far from negative. The interest in the technology of art—notably in the communications media—the concern for the elements of design, and a generally adventuresome attitude toward new materials are all consistent with the Bauhaus attitude. One could also point to the growing interest in the multisensory approach to art as well as the tendency to incorporate aesthetic concerns into environmental and industrial design, especially on the secondary level.

Many ideas that have merit on one level suffer in translation when

---

[49]Tomlinson made Cizek's methods well known in England; see his *Picture Making by Children*. His *Crafts for Children* (New York: Studio, 1955) is also an excellent book in which children's three-dimensional art activities are discussed in relation to Expressionism. Wilhelm Viola and Thomas Munro were among the many influential writers who brought word of Cizek to the United States. Developments along Cizek's lines in Canada were largely the result of the work of Arthur Lismer; see John McLeish, *September Gale, A Study of Arthur Lismer* (Toronto: Dent, 1955), especially Chapter 8.

applied to another. The theories of Progressive education, of the Bauhaus school, and of Expressionism and Cubism were all initiated by persons of great sophistication and professional commitment. One task of education is to narrow the gap between what is known and practiced by artists and university-based theorists and what is taught in art classrooms. If art teachers are not always successful in adapting to the changing nature of their discipline, neither have their colleagues in other disciplines been completely successful in this respect. The "new" math, the "process" approach to social studies, and the nonverbal student-centered ideas that are being introduced into the language arts programs are just a few signs of the struggle being carried on in other areas of the curriculum. All these attempts derive from a new partnership between educator and subject-matter specialist, professional artist, mathematician, historian, or linguist.

Although several observers of Cizek's methods found merit in the idea of "creative expression," they were unable to develop an adequate pedagogy to make his ideas practicable. Such teachers were convinced that the child could grow naturally, untrammeled by adult interference. Freedom to grow "according to natural laws" meant for them that the children should have license to do pretty much as they liked without the intervention of a teacher.

When certain educational administrators witnessed the artistic results of the program of "freedom without restriction" they were evidently disturbed. Instead of the orderly, neat, and disciplined delineation of railway tracks and chalk boxes and the bright circles of color charts, here were meaningless daubs of paint produced in noise and confusion. If this was art, they wanted no part of it. Said one official in an educational report: "There is no pretense at teaching the subject. . . . It is a method to keep children busy. The results obtained are deplorable." Much of this criticism was justified. When children are left to their own devices and lack stimulus and guidance from a teacher, the results are indeed often "deplorable."[50] Although art, as was observed earlier, cannot be produced without certain democratic freedoms, progress in expression cannot take place unless an acceptable pedagogy underlies classroom procedures.

In one sense the history of art education is the history of great teachers. Dewey, Hall, Cizek, and Dow were not only theorists and innovators, but also influences on great numbers of personal followers who in turn disseminated their teachers' ideas. Any list of such teachers would include Viktor Lowenfeld, who has left his mark on art education while fulfilling such roles as research psychologist, writer, lecturer, and chairman of the Department of Art Education at Pennsylvania State University.

---

[50] We still have the laissez-faire teachers with us and, paradoxically, there are none more dictatorial than they. Even if the children require instruction, they insist on witholding it from them and maintain that they will learn without urging or guidance. See Monica Haley, "Contradictions in Art Educational Theory and Practice," *Art Education*, Vol. 9, No. 5 (June 1956).

Theories change, however, and in the process yesterday's innovator becomes today's subject of serious questioning. A new generation of teachers is now questioning Lowenfeld's visual-haptic theories,[51] and some feel that he created an indefensible separation between process and product, thus placing undue emphasis on the *instrumental* function of art. Most, however, would agree that Lowenfeld's contribution was invaluable in showing how a knowledge of psychology could be of use to art teachers in directing attention to children's growth potential through art. It is doubtful that anyone who has read Lowenfeld and Brittain's *Creative and Mental Growth*[52] will ever use a coloring book or a numbered painting set, nor ever believe that the subject is more important than the child.

Another figure who, with Dewey and Lowenfeld, established a foundation for the art education of the 1950's was Sir Herbert Read. Before his interest in art education Read had established himself as a poet, essayist, and art critic. He thus brought an unusually broad and diverse background to the task of writing his impressive *Education Through Art*.[53] In this book he attempted to join philosophy (Plato) and psychology (Jung) to create his own theory of art education. Erudite and eclectic, Read's work still stands as one of the richest sources of information and ideas, particularly in his discussion of theories of developmental stages in drawing and his presentation of personality types.

CREATIVITY IN THE CLASS

The urge to investigate creativity may be viewed as the result of a shift in interest from art educators to psychologists. The progressive educational movement laid the groundwork for this investigation by relating the free and expressive aspects of art creativity to a theory of personality development. When the movement expired in the late 1950's, members of the American Psychological Association, acting on the suggestion of their president, J. P. Guilford,[54] assumed leadership in applying more rigorous techniques to such problems as the analysis of creative behavior and the identification of characteristic behavior of professionals in both the arts and the sciences. Within a decade what had formerly existed on the level of a philosophical mystique had been replaced by a science. The entire research paraphernalia of the psychologist—tests, measurements, computers, and so on—were brought to bear on that delicate, mercurial

[51]Lowenfeld distinguished between two types of students. *Visual* children are close observers of their environment and, working from a primarily perceptual basis, offer much information concerning what they *see. Haptic* children place themselves at the center of the action and, working from a sensory base, report what they *feel* about their subject. See Chapter 6, pp. 178–83, for a fuller discussion of these theories.

[52]4th ed. (New York: Macmillan, 1964).

[53]New York: Pantheon, 1958.

[54]"The Nature of Creative Thinking," *The American Psychologist* (September 1950).

process whereby people of all ages and in all areas of learning arrived at fresh solutions to problems.

Psychologists, of course, are not newcomers to the examination of artistic processes and products. In 1898 G. V. Dearborn conducted an investigation of the imaginative responses of college students, and in 1900 Kilpatrick's inkblot tests demonstrated that children in the first three grades were more imaginative than those in the upper elementary grades. James Sully, the English psychologist, published his *Studies of Childhood* in 1892 (revised in 1903),[55] and four years earlier Bernard Perez, working in France, had written *Art and Poetry of the Child.*[56] The psychologists' concern with the projective values of visual symbols is hardly new; what the 1950's brought, however, was a fresh look at the creative personality and *process* of creation. In considering the creative process, psychologists went beyond the visual arts to establish commonalties of experience among all types of people involved in solutions to creative problems.

Creativity was, and is, no longer the private preserve of the art room, but as a result of discovering how the creative process served the teacher of mathematics, for example, ideas were beginning to emerge that would permit art teachers to view their profession with new understanding. Art teachers have always suspected that art, taught under proper conditions, is capable of promoting values that transcend the boundaries of the art lesson. Since Guilford's famous address in 1950, many beliefs of art educators have been verified in psychological studies of such quantity and significance that it is impossible for non-art educators to ignore them. Indeed, the movement to examine creative behavior has been a key factor in the current educational reform and the ferment in learning theory of the post-Sputnik era.

One effect of the new research was the serious questioning of the validity of the I.Q. test. Scholars such as Jacques Barzun[57] were concerned about the limitations of a test that relied so heavily on cognitive learning. Barzun felt that whole areas of a child's intellectual makeup were ignored by objective, machine-scored tests. It is precisely the nonverbal capabilities, neglected by the I.Q. test, that most research in creativity has concentrated on. Belated attention has been given to the speculative, intuitive factors in problem-solving; indeed, the nature of the problems themselves has undergone dramatic change.

Researchers in creativity are still investigating an entire range of problems—such as the relation of creativity to intellectual ability, the relationship between home environment and aesthetic response, the role of humor among creative types, and the effect of classroom environment on productive thinking. J. P. Guilford,[58] in working with highly creative

[55] New York: Appleton-Century-Crofts.
[56] Paris: F. Alcan, 1888.
[57] *Teacher in America* (Boston: Little, Brown, 1945).
[58] *Personality* (New York: McGraw-Hill, 1959).

people, has constructed his own tests to define particular abilities that could be identified with his subjects, and Sidney Parnes[59] has developed a course of study designed to promote creative power in college students.

One way to characterize creative behavior is to project a composite picture of the kind of adults we might want our children to be. In this manner we can identify as creative those children who are flexible in coping with new problems, who are not intimidated by the unknown, and who, in later years, can maintain the spontaneity of childhood. The teacher's task, then, is to teach for such characteristics. But this becomes difficult if instructors themselves do not value creative behavior as defined by psychologists or if, as teachers, they are highly structured persons, wedded to a subject rather than a process. Asahel Woodruff views the situation as follows:

> The creativity problem transcends the field of art, and it seems to me its significance can be enhanced by looking at it as part of the broader concept. I am not sure how best to approach it, so I will just start listing some of the elements of the problem. . . . [C]reativity is often associated with rebellion, delinquency and social disruption. Studies of creative people tend to support this notion by showing that creativity is associated with preference for change rather than stability; tendency to delay closure rather than to structure ideas; tendency to challenge old structure; tendency to let incoming perceptions dictate their own patterns, rather than to force preconceived patterns on them, and so on. Opposed to these tendencies are the overwhelmingly dominant tendencies of most people to maintain structure, and to find security in the maintenance of an unchanging environment. This tendency is deep-seated in the facts of human adjustment. It is perfectly natural, then, for most people to resent those who are unstructured and who are responsive to freshness and differences because they are threats to security.[60]

It is difficult to separate concern for creativity from philosophical belief, and so it comes as no surprise that the leading figures in the study of creativity range from empirical researchers such as Jacob Getzels and Philip Jackson,[61] whose works read in many instances like philosophy, to psychologists such as Laura Zirbes,[62] who views creativity as a door to a rich, fully realized life. The art teacher should welcome the support of what has become a formidable array of intellects from areas outside the discipline of art. The teacher must use their findings and theories to make the art room a laboratory wherein theory and statistics provide the

[59] *Instructor's Manual for Senior Course in Creative Problem Solving,* 1960. (A syllabus created for the course taught at the State University of New York at Buffalo.)

[60] Quoted in R. C. Burkhart and H. M. McNeil, *Identity and Teacher Learning* (Scranton, Pa.: International Textbook, 1968), p. xvii.

[61] *Creativity and Intelligence* (New York: Wiley, 1962).

[62] *Spurs to Creative Teaching* (New York: Putnam, 1959).

basis for more sophisticated instruction. Let us take a specific example. In planning an art program for the fourth grade it would be helpful for the teacher to know that one early study found some causes for recession in this grade to be (1) effects of competition; (2) segregation of groups; (3) ostracism; (4) social subordination; (5) ridicule of offbeat, unusual ideas. Numerous studies of this kind pertain to all grade levels, but some art educators have yet to learn to apply pertinent research data to the teaching situation.

The conscientious teacher realizes that although personal conviction and experience can occasionally be a valid basis for curriculum planning, it can just as easily limit the program. It is imperative, therefore, that competent art teachers look beyond their own experiences to the expertise of others. That is the reason for the existence of professional literature, graduate programs, and those periodic get-togethers known as conventions.

Table 1.1 represents an attempt to relate the findings of several research psychologists to some specifics of art instruction. The chart has been purposely left unfinished in the hope that readers will relate it to their own problems in curriculum planning.

THE OBJECTIVES OF CONTEMPORARY ART EDUCATION

The main objective of art education today is to assist in the intellectual, emotional, and social growth of their learners according to needs and capacities. In addition to this general objective, art education today has certain specific objectives.

Art is included in the school program so that children may:

1. Gain insight into and identify with the nature of creative, artistic acts.
2. Acquire artistic skills in relation to activities involving their emotions and intellect.
3. Learn some of the possibilities that accompany freedom of thought and action in relation to artistic pursuits.
4. Be brought to understand what the word "environment" means so that as adults they can assume responsibility for its improvement.
5. Acquire knowledge of and insight into art as cultural history.
6. Learn to look on the art of *seeing* as an active perceptual process capable of clarifying all visual phenomena.
7. Acquire the ability to note and describe formal relationships between the elements of a work and consequently to sense how such relationships relate to the meaning or content of the work.

Table 1.1

HOW THE ELEMENTARY ART PROGRAM MAY BE RELATED TO CHARACTERISTICS OF CREATIVITY

Researcher	*Attributes of Creative Behavior*	*Related Art Learning Activities*
J. P. Guilford	The thinking of unusually creative people is characterized by:	
	(1) *Flexibility.* The ability to adapt, redefine, reinterpret, or take a new tack to reach a goal. Flexible thinking is demonstrated in tests of creativity when respondents suggest unusual uses for bricks and other common objects.	*Boxes* may be used instead of bricks—children may paint them, collage the six surfaces, combine them sculpturally, or play interior against exterior surfaces. Children create solutions with materials rather than listing possible solutions in words. (Grades 3–6)
	(2) *Fluency.* The ease with which ideas are generated. Fluent thinking is demonstrated by the number of ideas suggested within a given period of time.	*Printmaking* may combine both *fluency* and *elaboration.* If the children work with a module of design, such as a soap eraser, they may stamp out varying combinations involving color switches and background changes, progressing to adjustment of the surface of the eraser by subtracting sections (square to circle, circle to linear division). (Grades 3–6)
	(3) *Elaboration.* The degree of development of ideas. Elaborated thinking is demonstrated by the richness and complexity of detail shown in the performance of verbal or visual tasks. (See Figure 1.18.)	
Donald W. MacKinnon	Highly creative people are *discerning, curious, receptive, reflective,* and *eager for experience.* They make finer distinctions and seek deeper meanings than do less creative individuals.	*Eagerness for experience* is a direct outcome of motivational effectiveness, long a concern of the art teacher. *Receptivity* and *curiosity* are attitudes that cut across all ages and activities, and on which art teachers base all studio relationships.
Abraham H. Maslow	Secure children are apt to be *spontaneous, natural,* and	Action painting, activities in calligraphy, preliminary

Table 1.1 (Cont.)

Researcher	Attributes of Creative Behavior	Related Art Learning Activities
Abraham H. Maslow (cont.)	*uninhibited.* The unknown, the mysterious, and the puzzling are not very frightening for such children; indeed, they are often attracted to these qualities. They do not cling to the familiar.	drawings for projects, and maintenance of a sketchbook are some activities that help to develop *spontaneity.*
Carl R. Rogers	Creative people are *open to experience.* They are alive to the possibilities of the moment and do not distort experience to make it consistent with predetermined concepts.	*Openness to experience* is related, among other things, to visiting galleries and to art appreciation in general. The art teacher prepares the children for experience by utilizing visual referents drawn from a spectrum of professional works of art.
Calvin W. Taylor	Creative people do not seek quick and easy solutions. They are able to resist premature closure but have a strong need for ultimate closure.	In working with cut paper or collage in a particular task, children learn to "resist premature closure." Changing the relationship of color and texture many times prior to pasting makes the students aware of many options, thus discouraging settlement for the first "easy solution."
Lawrence Kubie	Creative people are capable of using free association of the subconscious levels of operation as a basis for ideas that emerge "artistically" or free of stereotype.	If children move a pencil or crayon freely over a large sheet of paper (18″ x 24″), they will eventually have a complex of spatial divisions from which they can develop nonobjective designs for printmaking. The final selection of designs may be made by shifting a paper "window" over the design, and this in turn may be elaborated on. Although the

Table 1.1 (Cont.)

Researcher	Attributes of Creative Behavior	Related Art Learning Activities
Lawrence Kubie (cont.)		latter stage brings thought and judgment into play the basis for the design is the initial stage of spontaneous, subjective activity.
Graham Wallas	The creative process is a process with a beginning, a middle, and an end resulting in a new idea. The four stages of the creative process are: (1) *Preparation.* This first stage refers to early, deliberate attempts at discovering the answer to a particular problem. As individuals assemble and begin to ponder the ideas that are clearly relevant, the residue of all past experience is brought into play. If a satisfactory solution is not achieved immediately, the problem is set aside while the individual pursues other activities. (2) *Incubation.* This is the period during which attention is not focused directly on the problem. It is a period of subliminal absorption. (3) *Illumination.* It is at this stage, when individuals are working on another problem, engaging in physical activity, or just daydreaming, that the solution comes to them as if it were "out of the blue." The explanation for this phenomenon is that the subconscious mind remains at	*(Space is allowed here for the art teacher to fill in personal experiences with related art learning activities.)*

A *"Bugs and
butterflies"*

B *"My sister's
wedding"*

Figure 1.14 *These works by a Japanese third grader* **(A)** *and an American sixth
grader* **(B)** *demonstrate how Guilford's characteristics of creativity may apply
to painting. Factors such as flexibility, fluency, and elaboration are given form
through the handling of detail, the relation of wholes to parts, the wide range
of color, and the development of complex visual relationships. The second-hand
thinking of borrowed clichés has been avoided through an intense and extended
period of visual problem-solving.*

Table 1.1 (Cont.)

Researcher	Attributes of Creative Behavior	Related Art Learning Activities
Graham Wallas (cont.)	work until the solution is arrived at. It then notifies the conscious mind, whose attention has been directed elsewhere. (4) *Verification.* At this point the solution is tested to ensure that it works.	
E. Paul Torrance	Creative people are attracted to the baffling, the mysterious, and the difficult, and are independent in thought and judgment. They are questioning, receptive to new ideas, constructive in criticism, energetic, willing to take risks, preoccupied with a problem, persistent, intuitive, sensitive to the external world, and not afraid to regress.	

In Conclusion Every teacher attempts to give students a "map" with which they may orient themselves to the world. The teacher uses the language arts to instruct the students in linguistics and verbal communications and guides them in social studies by describing how people have operated on a social and political level. The mathematics teacher concentrates on the logic of computation. In the sciences children are made more aware of their physical surroundings by being encouraged to use their own sense experiences in creating models of the world in which they live. The art teacher hopes that as a result of instruction children can be brought to view life in personally expressive and visual terms—moving at various times from observation to intuition, from feeling to memory, and from the creation of symbols to meaningful responses to the works of others.

Art today is a field of study that can help to develop a more aware citizenry—people who enjoy intellectual and emotional control, people with skill and initiative, and people who are aware of the rich possibilities of the full life. Perhaps no other field of study can quite equal art in the flexibility with which it can accommodate itself to the most divergent types of personalities. Obviously, art has always challenged the most gifted. Contemporary teaching methods, however, have demonstrated that all normal children can find success in this work. There has been recent proof that children of retarded mental development can also engage profitably in art activities.[63] Art has been used successfully for therapeutic purposes with children suffering from various psychoses, and it is claimed that some unfortunate mental conditions have been corrected with the aid of creative artistic activities.[64] In short, as the following chapters of this book will show, art is a worthwhile activity for nearly all children.

ACTIVITIES FOR THE READER

1. Study a group of children enrolled in (a) a kindergarten or first grade and (b) a fifth or sixth grade. As you observe the children at work and at play make a note of what you consider to be their creative acts.
2. Study an art session under the supervision of an expert teacher. Make observations of: (a) the ways in which the children develop artistic skills; (b) the ways in which freedom of thought is encouraged: (c) some of the experiences the children use as bases for expression.
3. Compare the methods of G. Stanley Hall and Walter Smith as they might be applied to a drawing lesson for sixth graders.
4. Select a reproduction of a well-known painting or some other professional art form and discuss the nature of the artist's reaction to experience that the work exhibits.
5. Select reproductions of two art objects that are limited to being expressions of beauty and compare them with two that are not.
6. Observe an art lesson and describe it, making particular note of any Postimpressionistic or Expressionistic influences on the teaching methods.
7. Describe any attempts at dictatorial control in any area of the arts that you may have experienced personally and explain their ill effects.
8. Outline an art lesson according to the "five Herbartian steps." Appraise it for its strong and weak points.
9. Devise an art lesson based on the S–R theory of learning. Explain how it might fail.
10. Thinking of your own pupils, would you make any additions or corrections to the beliefs and objectives listed in this chapter? If not, could you establish an order of priority to the items listed on p. 43 that has more meaning for you?
11. Study the chart on creativity on pp. 44–48. From your own experience in art or other areas, fill in the third column for Wallas and Torrance.

[63] See for example C. D. and M. R. Gaitskell, *Art Education for Slow Learners* (Peoria, Ill.: Bennett, 1953).

[64] See Emery I. Gondor, *Art and Play Therapy* (New York: Random House, 1954), an excellent book for the layman. See also Viktor Lowenfeld, ed., *Art Education for the Exceptional Child,* Research Bulletin of the Eastern Arts Association (Kutztown, Pa.: April 1956). This phamphlet does not pretend to offer much information, but it reviews the scope of the subject.

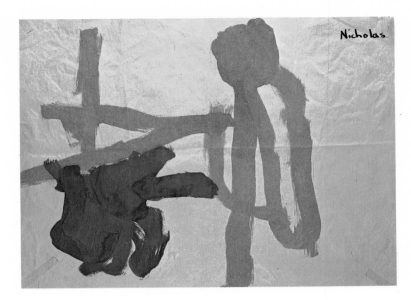

A *"Pipes under the sink," kindergarten*

Figure 1.15 *Two examples of "taking a close look at things," one of the signs of creative behavior set forth by Torrance. Sink pipes* **(A)** *and tables and chairs* **(B)** *are part of a young child's environment.*

B *"Tables and chairs," grade 1*

12. Teachers should realize that creativity can be developed in all areas
of the curriculum. The following signs of creative behavior have been
taken from Paul Torrance's observations of his own classes at the
University of Minnesota.[65] Indicate the ways in which Torrance's observations might apply to the teaching of art.

Intense absorption in listening, observing, doing
Intense animation and physical involvement
Challenging ideas of authorities
Checking many sources of information
Taking a close look at things
Eagerly telling others about one's discoveries
Continuing a creative activity after the scheduled time for quitting
Showing relationships among apparently unrelated ideas
Following through on ideas set in motion
Manifesting curiosity, wanting to know, digging deeper
Guessing or predicting outcomes and then testing them
Honestly and intensely searching for the truth
Resisting distractions
Losing awareness of time
Penetrating observations and questions
Seeking alternatives and exploring new possibilities

[65]From "Nurture of Creative Talents," in Ross L. Mooney and Taher A. Razek, eds.,
Explorations in Creativity (New York: Harper & Row, 1967), p. 190.

When children are well-motivated they can work with enthusiasm for a sustained period on a large project, as in this block-print fabric design made by sixth graders.

TEACHING METHODS
IN ART EDUCATION

[A] description of my teaching seems to me poor compared with what actually happened. The tone, the rhythm, the sequence of words, place and time, the mood of the students, and all the other circumstances which make for a vital atmosphere cannot be reproduced; yet it is the ineffable which helps form a climate of creativity. My teaching was intuitive finding. My own emotion gave me the power which produced the student's readiness to learn. To teach out of inner enthusiasm is the opposite of a mere preplanned method of instruction.*

Art as a field of study in the elementary school can be either beneficial or harmful to the learners. What determines in no small measure the value of art instruction is the teaching method employed. Faulty teaching can create in children a thorough dislike for art that may remain with them for the rest of their lives. A feeling that any artistic activity is wasted effort, a resentment against original thought in all forms of artistic endeavor from architecture to literature, a sense of insecurity when called on to make choices involving aesthetic judgment or taste—these are but a few of the possible effects of faulty teaching. Added to these may be a thorough disrespect for the school that forces on learners a subject in which they can see no value and find no personal challenge, and from which they derive no knowledge of lasting worth. Likewise, as a result of inappropriate teaching methods, more than one teacher in the past has experienced "discipline problems" during art sessions because of an insensitivity to children's preferences in materials and subject matter.

On the other hand children may be enthusiastic about art as a school activity. When such is the case, art can influence the whole atmosphere of a school, and other fields of study seem to benefit by its good effects.

---

*From *Design and Form* by Johannes Itten, Copyright © 1964, by Reinhold Publishing Corporation, p. 7.

Figure 2.1 *Schools can be changed from drab to exciting environments simply through the exhibition of children's art. The school in this photograph maintains an ongoing display of its pupils' work in the reception room adjoining the principal's office.*

Thinking becomes more lively, and children take a greater interest and pride both in their school and in themselves. School halls, classrooms, and the principal's office can be changed from drab areas into places of real interest. Children proudly bring their parents to school to see exhibitions of work. Principals report a greater degree of cooperation not only among the children themselves, but also among members of the teaching staff, and between the public and the school.

Since the degree of success achieved in an art program depends largely on teaching methods, it will be useful at this time to discuss some of the successful contemporary methods. No formulas, of course, can be offered for the details of teaching, since teaching must take account of individual situations and allow for wide variations in method. As well as discussing recommended teaching practices, this chapter will describe some methods that appear to be either ineffective or actively harmful to the artistic development of children. First, however, it will be well to consider just what type of teacher can teach art.

WHO CAN TEACH ART?

The teacher who has sufficient ability, tact, and liking for children to teach, say, language, arithmetic, or social studies may be capable of teaching art as well. Like any other subject, art of course requires of the teacher some specific knowledge and skills—such as a knowledge of pictorial composition and other forms of design, an acquaintance with professional art work, and some ability to use materials such as paint, wood, and clay. With relatively little effort, however, a competent teacher may gain the knowledge and master the skills associated with art education. The problems in teaching art, including classroom management and control, discipline, presentation of lessons, assistance of pupils, and appraisal of the success of the program are, broadly speaking, not different from the general school program. One may assert, therefore, that it is possible for a proficient teacher in an elementary school to be a capable teacher of art.[1]

The taped discussions of classroom teachers at work in Manuel Barkan's *Through Art to Creativity*[2] clearly demonstrate that a teacher's ability to communicate with children can compensate for a lack of professional art training, at least in the lower elementary grades. In a policy statement for the Commission on Art Education, Barkan wrote as follows:

> At the kindergarten and early elementary grade levels almost any truly good classroom teacher who accepts the commitments of the basic components of general education for young children can learn to teach art well. At the middle and upper elementary grade levels, however, special background and knowledge about the nature of art is essential.[3]

The National Art Education Association's publication seems to have greater confidence in the role of the classroom teacher, because it states:

> . . . Many people consider that it is the classroom teacher who knows the child and can best relate art experiences to the other areas of learning that the child is encountering in his daily program. They feel strongly that through such relationships and understanding, art becomes a means for expression and communication which is needed for every other learning experience in the daily class program.[4]

Pauline Johnson feels that "Every elementary school should have at least one person trained in the visual arts who can give leadership and assistance to the program. This person will be in a position to contribute a great deal to the effectiveness of the school in general and to become a unifying force."[5] Even if every elementary school were suddenly to be allotted its own art teacher, however, there would still be the problem

[1]See Luella Cole's summary of the characteristics of a good teacher in H. J. Klausmeier and K. Dresden, *Teaching in the Elementary School,* 2nd ed. (New York: Harper & Row, 1962). The trouble, of course, with many such summaries is that most frail humans cannot measure up to the list of excellent traits suggested by the authors. In real life, however, these same frail humans often make good teachers.

Marion Richardson unconsciously reveals in her book *Art and the Child* (Peoria, Ill.: Bennett, 1952) the qualities of a great teacher, among them tact, sympathy, knowledge of subject, sensitivity to art and children, and a number of intangibles.

Probably the most distinguished general teacher of our time is Natalie Cole, whose books *The Arts in the Classroom* (New York: John Day, 1940) and *Children's Arts from Deep Down Inside* (New York: John Day, 1966) are avidly read by art teachers eager to approach children, teaching, and art on an intuitive basis.

[2]Boston: Allyn and Bacon, 1960.

[3]In Jerome J. Hausman, ed., *Report of the Commission on Art Education* (Washington, D.C.: National Art Education Association, 1965), p. 84.

[4]Mary M. Packwood, ed., *Art Education in the Elementary School* (Washington, D.C.: National Art Education Association, 1967), p. 28.

[5]In W. Reid Hastie, ed., *Art Education,* Sixty-fourth Yearbook of the National Society for the Study of Education (Chicago: University of Chicago Press, 1965), p. 84.

of finding hours in the week for each child to be reached by his single specialist. The realities of the situation are such that, at best, the classroom teacher will serve as a partner to trained art personnel in planning and will take on a significant share of the program.

The fact remains that most elementary schools in this country do not have the arts personnel Johnson described. We therefore must assume that the average classroom teacher with the will to conduct an art program is capable of providing art activities of value. American art teachers can look to Japan and England as examples of countries that abound in exemplary art programs and that have comparatively fewer art teachers than does the United States.

SOME SOUND TEACHING PRACTICES IN ART

The following discussion about teaching methods contains nothing novel.[6] Almost anyone who has taken a course in methods of teaching will be familiar with the ideas presented below. They are outlined merely as a reminder of certain facts about pedagogy that any teacher, whether in service or in training, would do well to keep in mind.

One important lesson learned from past experiences is that a *teacher* is needed while elementary-school children are engaged in art activities. As mentioned previously, some teachers who conducted a laissez-faire

[6]Earl C. Kelley and Marie I. Rasey, *Education and the Nature of Man* (New York: Harper & Row, 1952), makes excellent generalizations about teaching and learning and is highly recommended for reading in conjunction with this chapter.

Figure 2.2 *As a guide and counselor, the teacher has a vital role to play in the art program. (Photo by Anthony Lupo.)*

type of program failed to play a sufficiently strong role in the classroom. As a result, their art programs, although largely founded on commendable ideas, failed through lack of suitable teaching methods. The contemporary program, on the other hand, rests on the foundation of a strong belief in the need for both positive guidance and a reasonably consistent methodology.

A good teacher begins where the child's natural creativity ends. During the Progressive era teachers were apt to accept everything children did as evidence of their optimal potential. We now recognize the fact that much of what children do on their own without guidance, motivation, or special material is repetitive and not a clear indication of the children's true capabilities. The teacher, weary of seeing the same array of peace symbols, cartoon characters, and other stereotypes, obviously must teach for the capability of the child. (Note pp. 76–77 on laissez-faire teaching practices.)

Children must be motivated by their experiences to produce art. As children live from day to day, they have many experiences that arise from life at home, at play, at school, and in the community in general. They bring to each new experience the insight they have acquired from previous experiences. If the new experience arouses their interest, and if it is sufficiently reminiscent of former experiences, learning should occur. If they lack interest in the new experience, on the other hand, they will probably fail to profit from it. The majority of experiences that children enjoy, however, do arouse their intellect and stimulate their feelings, and so may be considered suitable subject matter for artistic expression. Indeed, no other subject matter is worthy of a place in art education.[7]

Motivating Children in Art

The primary source of motivation, then, is the children themselves. The teacher who can regard students as thinking, feeling organisms who function intimately with both the world of the senses and that of fantasy, imagination, and dreams, will have greater insight into the possibilities of motivation. Because the *total* makeup of the child provides sources for motivation, the teacher must go beyond sensory experience and probe to a certain extent what might be called the children's "inner landscape"—that is, their dream world, their fears, their desires and reveries, even their nightmares. A very real function of the art program is to provide visual objectification for internal as well as external experiences.

In general, the teacher makes a distinction between *extrinsic* moti-

[7]Paul R. Mort and William S. Vincent, *Modern Educational Practice* (New York: McGraw-Hill, 1950), has good sections on motivation and "motivational devices" in general. See, for example, the section called "Stimulating Situations and Problems." Also included in the book are excellent summaries under the title "Reasons Why . . ." in which the authors give succinct statements derived from psychology and sociology to justify their suggestions about method. Every statement of this type might profitably be read by art teachers.

vation, which consists of outside forces (such as contests and grades) that influence the child's level of motivation, and *intrinsic* motivation, which capitalizes on internal standards and goals that the child recognizes as having value (such as the desire to perform well). The teacher should avoid striving for the short-term gain of the former, and work to bring out the latter kind of motivation, which is far more valuable in the long run to the child's development.

The teacher, having decided on the source of motivation, must consider this question: "What are the most effective means of getting the children to use their experiences with the materials I have provided?" At this point the teacher must be sensitive to the variables of the situation, linking subject to materials with techniques capable of capturing the attention of the class. The teacher may decide to focus on the excitement of untried materials, introduce the lesson with a new film, or set up a bulletin board using materials from outside the classroom. The teacher may engage the class in a lively discussion or bring in an animal or unusual still life, plan a field trip, invite a guest speaker, or demonstrate how a particular skill might be used. In some instances several such ideas may be combined.

When discussion is to provide the basis of motivation, the teacher should master the techniques of dialog, involving more children than the usual number of bright extroverts and letting the class members do most of the talking until *they* have come up with the points to be emphasized.[8] The teacher may find it wise to promote intimacy in the classroom by seating the children close by. In this kind of instruction the teacher's personality, enthusiasm for the task, acceptance of unusual ideas, and flair for communication all play an important role. When energy level is low and the class has to be "brought up" to a productive level, the motivational phase can be enhanced by a touch of "showmanship."

It is important to remember that children do not normally connect their experiences with artistic acts. If a teacher tells children to paint a picture of any item of experience that appeals to them, or, in other words, "to do whatever they like," the results are usually disappointing. Under such circumstances the children are often at a loss as to what to paint or make. A well-known cartoon of children looking up at a teacher and asking with rueful expressions, "Do we have to do anything we want to?" illustrates the point.[9] It was not that the children in the cartoon lacked experiences suitable for expression, but rather that they had not connected them with expressive artistic acts.

The teacher's task is to help children to recall an experience for expression. To do so successfully, teachers must be well aware of the areas

---

[8]For some good examples of dialog, see Barkan, *Through Art to Creativity.*

[9]"No competent and responsible educational leader has ever said anywhere at any time that the pupil is to do what he wants to do." William H. Burton, *The Guidance of Learning Activities,* 3rd ed. (New York: Appleton-Century-Crofts, 1952), p. 65.

of interest of the children with whom they are working. What these interests are will be discussed in some detail in subsequent chapters, especially Chapter 6.[10] At this point the varying interests of children at different levels of development can be briefly summarized. The most immature children are interested more in the manipulation of materials than in expressive representation. As they grow older they begin to depict subjects that are egocentric in character. Later, a number of physical features in the environment catch their attention. Still later, the relationship of the children to their associates becomes more significant for them, so that themes related to their social group are given expression.

What the teacher does for children with regard to motivation, adult artists do for themselves. Artists select those items of experience that they consider suitable for their particular kind of artistic expression. In their mind's eye, they visualize the finished work, perhaps not completely, but clearly enough for them to set a goal that they strive to reach. This goal carries them forward in their undertaking and is the real motivating force for all their endeavors.[11] In resorting to educational techniques of motivation, therefore, the teacher is in no respect departing from a traditional artistic process, but rather, accepts the nature of childhood and by means of acceptable pedagogical devices draws it closer to the nature of the artist.

Isolating and Defining a Theme. Although it may seem obvious that motivation is most effective when built on the child's existing interests, the teacher should not overlook the possibility of *creating* the situation that will motivate a pupil. For instance, a fifth grader whose interest in sculpture does not go beyond modeling in clay will need another kind of motivation should the teacher feel assembling scrap wood is a worthwhile activity. The means for establishing motivation in this case may include a discussion of some aspects of animal physiology in terms of scrap shapes, an examination of reproductions of Calder's scrap animals, or a demonstration of how color can unify scrap material.

With the most immature children the teacher may rely entirely on materials themselves as a motivating force for creative activity. It is not long, however, before the children require assistance in defining themes for expression. Then the teacher must begin to observe carefully children at school, at play, and, when possible, at home and in the community in general. Once the teacher has discovered a theme that seems to have general interest and, of necessity, one in which all the children have had

---

[10]See also Viktor Lowenfeld and W. Lambert Brittain, *Creative and Mental Growth,* 4th ed. (New York: Macmillan, 1964), for children's art interests; and Arthur T. Jersild, *Child Psychology,* 5th ed. (Englewood Cliffs, N.J.: Prentice-Hall, 1960), for general interests.

[11]"When an organism is ready to act, it is painful for it not to act." Mort and Vincent, *Modern Educational Practice,* p. 38.

some experience, the task is to define it so that the children are motivated to give expression to it.

Let us take one commonplace example. Thanksgiving provides themes broad enough to suit any pupil, and in which all children have probably participated in one way or another. Usually, a series of well-chosen questions followed by discussion serves to focus the pupils' attention on the experience. The questions should touch on many aspects of the Thanksgiving season, such as shopping for Thanksgiving dinner, table decorations, guests who come for dinner, and the significance of the day. The discussions that take place between the teacher and the pupils are a powerful means of recalling not only the facts of the experience, but also the feelings connected with it.[12]

Sometimes the establishment of motivation requires rather extensive preparation—such as visits to a farm, a dairy, a museum, a park, or a zoo. The teacher should, of course, plan any trip well in advance. It is well to discuss the expedition with the principal, so that all arrangements may be made through the proper channels. Then the teacher should make a preliminary survey of the ground subsequently to be covered by the children. Before the trip the class should discuss some of the salient features to be observed. On return from the expedition the class benefits from another discussion, after which expressive work should immediately begin.

The highly educative nature of these procedures will be readily recognized. Mere experience is of little value to the learner. It is only when one resolves experience into coherent form that it has significance. The definition that children give to events in their lives by performing expressive acts allows them to face the challenges of their environment and to profit from their contact with it. For this reason alone, art may be considered an extremely valuable part of general education.

Formulating Goals

Students and teachers may differ in their goals, striving consciously or unconsciously to achieve them. Teachers would be advised to define their own objectives, let the children voice theirs, and then proceed with all the skill at their command to lead the children to successful attainment of those ends they feel are worthwhile. The establishment of goals is perhaps the most complex task of teachers because it represents the articulation of their philosophy as it relates to their knowledge of the children's capacities and desires. In addition, teachers must take into account such considerations as class size, budget for materials, and scheduling. Goal formulation is thus a key area of decision-making in the

[12]See Daniel A. Prescott, *Emotion and the Educative Process* (Washington, D.C.: American Council on Education, 1938), for a detailed study of emotion and learning. See also Jersild, *Child Psychology,* in which some of the positive as well as the negative values of the emotions in learning are described.

art program. Kenneth Lansing refers to the problem of goal classification when he states:

> Another thing that makes the formulation of goals difficult is the fact that some of them must be cognitive, while others must be affective and psychomotor. In other words, youngsters must know and understand certain things about art; they must have relevant attitudes and values; and they must possess certain skills. Their knowledge must cover life in general, artistic procedures, composition, art history, and aesthetics. Their attitudes must include an interest in the making and appreciating of art, confidence in their own ability to make and appraise art, tolerance of the various forms that art might take, and a willingness to work hard. And their skill must center around the efficient manipulation of art tools and materials.[13]

If one accepts Lansing's statement, then goals may be seen as existing in both broad and limited categories. An art program may be conceived of as having a design, that is, as being composed of a series of learning units, the components of which all contribute to the sense of wholeness. The teacher must discriminate between the broad goal and the subgoal, for distinction between the two can be difficult. A lesson in color mixing, to cite one instance, does not fulfill the goal of "establishing color sensitivity"—an objective so inclusive that color mixing is obviously just one step in a sequence that might also include color matching from magazines, color identification in paintings, using color to express a mood, and finding color parallels to music and other sounds.

Goals for a particular lesson will, of course, vary with the nature of the task. If the class is drawing pictures to send to a school in Europe or another part of the country, one goal might be to present as much specific information as possible, so that the recipients can determine from the drawings how Americans in Idaho, for example, dress and live. If the community has just experienced a hurricane, snowstorm, or torrential downpour, the goal could be to "create new colors that might show what it was like." Or, if sixth graders are having their first lesson in contour-line drawing, the goal could relate to the amounts of variance in the line as evidence of clearly observed edges. Goals should thus be presented in "manageable segments" and in clear, meaningful terms for the child.

Unless some sort of goal, however general, has been discussed in the early phase of the lesson, evaluation cannot be effective at the conclusion of the art period. The more specific the statement of the goal, however, the more effective the evaluation. The teacher who tells students, "Today we will concentrate on bright colors" does not help the students during the critique period as much as one who says, "Today let's see how much variety we can get out of a single color by changing it through the use of black, white, or its complement."

---

[13]In Packwood, ed., *Art Education in the Elementary School*, p. 72.

Planning through behavioral goals or performance objectives is used increasingly as the preferred method for achieving educational goals.[14] This method, which is related to the more general concept of accountability in education, was examined in several conferences organized by the National Art Education Association with the assistance of Professor Asahel Woodruff of the University of Utah. It is considered by many teachers to be the most efficient way of planning and is based on the assumption that any behavior can be noted, described, and if need be, evaluated. Since the first conference proceedings in 1968, most art teachers have used Woodruff's vocabulary. The most widely accepted interpretation of the terminology is as follows:

A "performance objective" is a positive goal, stated as a declarative sentence. Example: "The student will be able to select, discuss, draw, center, and so on." In the case of a single activity, such as centering clay, the goal is specific; in the case of a sequence of activities, such as making a one-minute animated film, the goal is broad. It is also possible to set a goal for a group. Example: "The class will be able to conduct the cleanup period without teacher intervention."

A "set" is a cluster of performance objectives that the student will have to accomplish in order to complete the "carrier project," which is the end product.

A "concept" precedes the choice of the carrier project and is a statement about art, such as, "Styles in painting vary with time." Concepts may ultimately be transformed into "overt" perceptual acts, such as asking the student to sort chronologically the work of a cave painter, Giotto, Manet, and Rauschenberg.

Behaviorists in art education also recommend that the three major domains of learning be maintained. These domains, or classifications of learning, are discussed in Chapter 18 and deal with cognitive (knowledge, facts, intellectual abilities), affective (feelings and attitudes), and psychomotor (ability to handle specific processes involving physical coordination) skills.

A teacher, instead of suddenly deciding on Friday that drawing would be a good way to begin the week on Monday will go through a considerable sequence of antecedent steps:

Think about the philosophy of art education.
Decide on the goals for the year for a particular age level. (This means considering what the art program can do to convert the

[14]Two major educational agencies that utilize performance objectives are CEMREL (*Central Midwestern Regional Educational Laboratory*) in their publication, *Guidelines for Aesthetic Education,* and the National Assessment Program in Art.

philosophy into a realistic life process.)
Select both broad and specific strategies based on areas of art learn-
ings to be covered.
Determine the sets for each carrier project.
State the performance objectives within sets.

In outline form the process might look as follows:

1. The teacher's philosophy of art education
2. Goals for the art program
3. Selection of areas of art learning experiences
4. Selection of carrier projects
   a. Determination of sets, or tasks
   b. Determination of performance objectives based on learning
      outcomes
      NOTE: Evaluation is implicit in the objective.

Essential Elements.   In developing performance objectives, program
planners should consider five essential elements.

1. Identification of the individual or group that will perform the
   desired behavior.
2. Identification of the behavior to be demonstrated through the
   product to be developed: the behavior should be described as
   precisely as possible as an action that can be followed, or similarly, the product should be described precisely as an object that
   can be observed.
3. The primary conditions under which the performance is expected
   to be measured: conditions might include restrictions placed on the
   project during the performance of specified objectives.
4. Establishment of the minimum level of acceptable performance.
   This step is the critical phase and the one that poses the most
   problems. What is the criterion for success?
5. Establishment of the means of assessment, which will be used to
   measure the expected performance or behavior. What form will
   the assessment take: check list, informal observation, anecdotal
   record?

One way for teachers to get their thoughts on paper is to use a matrix
as a kind of graphic guide for the listing of ideas. The matrix is simply
a grid that indicates where key issues intersect. The example shown below
demonstrates how basic concerns can be related: What will be studied
(art content)? To whom will it be taught (kinds of students)? In what order

*Setting Up
a Matrix
for Curriculum
Planning*

Table 2.1

MATRIX A—THE FIRST STAGE

	Art Content Areas		
	Art History	Art Appreciation	Design Awareness
Upper Grades	X	X	X
Middle Grades		X	X
Primary Grades			X

(sequence)? Before these questions are answered, the teacher should have given some thought to the two principal concerns that must precede the issues mentioned above: the philosophy of the teacher (What do I believe?) and its attendant goals (What do I hope to accomplish?).

This fairly ambitious program is but one instance of a wide variety of possibilities. It would also be possible to organize a program around one particular content area. For example, one could subdivide design awareness so that the study of color would be a major area of activity for all grades. Sawyer and de Francesco plan their matrix around five basic "needs"—communication, industry, personal living, society, and commerce.[15] Just as good a case, of course, can be made for the awareness of design as for communication, and obviously the latter cannot succeed without the former. The difference is one of emphasis, and in articulating goals the teacher justifies the content and emphasis selected.

The table shown above is the first stage of planning. The subdivisions of each content area must now be indicated so that more specific information can be accommodated.

The second stage provides the heart of instruction and should deal primarily with concepts (statements about art, which Eisner describes as "principles or generalizations to be used by the teacher as a focus for subsequent work with students"[16]). The "Objectives" column translates the concept into a performance objective. The "Activities" column lists the major tasks that are designed to engage the child in the concept. The next column deals with materials, support, or resources that may be needed to fulfill the performance objectives that serve to realize the idea in the "Concept" column. The final column contains suggestions for evaluation, although this information could be reserved for the third, or lesson plan, stage.

[15]John R. Sawyer and Italo de Francesco, *Elementary School Art for Classroom Teachers* (New York, Evanston, and London: Harper and Bros., 1971), p. 143.
[16]Eliot Eisner, *Educating Artistic Visions* (New York: Macmillan Co., 1972), p. 174.

Figure 2.3 *Variations on a theme. A class of fourth graders create their own sun faces after a slide show on the sun image in the history of art.*

To cite one example, the content area of "art appreciation" can be schematized as follows:

The creation of a lesson plan for one unit of activity, whether for a day or a week, is the final stage of planning. This final plan is a more detailed description of the activities shown in Table 2.2. It could include information such as that given in the following example of a two-lesson unit on contour drawing.

Lesson Plan
    Subject area: Drawing
    Concept statement: Contour drawing is one way for an artist to

Table 2.2

MATRIX B—THE SECOND STAGE

Art Appreciation				
Concept Statements	Objectives	Activities	Media and Resources	Evaluation
"Styles vary with time and artist."	"The student will be able to recognize and distinguish between the works of Surrealists, Expressionists, and Cubists."	Sorting postcard reproductions of works of artists	Slides Films Filmstrips Games Packages File Material Postcard reproductions	After examining Cubist paintings of Braque and Picasso with the aid of the teacher, pupils can assign a painting by Juan Gris to the Cubist School on their own.

become aware of the variety of edges of shapes and the overall structure of a form.

Time: Two lessons

Objectives: The students will be able to make a continuous contour drawing of a group of simple objects selected from around the room or from their own pockets. (Several arrangements will be set up for those who prefer groups of large objects.) The students are to demonstrate their handling of detail and edges of the subject, both characteristics of contour drawing.

Concepts and processes to be stressed at the introduction of the lesson: Drawing will be defined as "a record in line of forms in space." Contour drawing will be defined as "a record of the edges of shapes," as opposed to drawing that uses lines and tones to suggest volume or mass.

Materials to be used: Soft pencil or crayon on white paper

Perceptual processes to be emphasized: The ability to focus on the edges of shapes and to see the shapes that are constituents of an object. The students may accomplish this by covering their hands with a sheet of paper so that they will not be tempted to compare object and drawing.

Group evaluation: The drawings of students and professional artists will be pinned up so that successful parts may be noted.

Questions for consideration in a group evaluation:

"How does contour drawing differ from other kinds we have done?"

"What did you notice in your subject that you had not seen before?"

"Let's take a look at some contour drawings by professional artists. How have they handled the edges of things?"

The plan that covers the three stages discussed above is an exercise in relating wholes to parts. If the teacher begins with a broad conceptual frame, then the art lesson has a clearly stated context. The novice teacher, however, too often begins at the other end of the scale, and as a result the students receive a potpourri of scattered experiences without any underlying logic.

Obviously planning a program can be arduous and time consuming if the teachers feel they must do the entire job themselves rather than consult existing models. Most teachers, in any case, will not be expected to plan entire programs on their own. The system described above is intended as a brief introduction for readers who suddenly find themselves on a team that is required to produce a total art program in depth and detail.

The idea of approaching art instruction in a disciplined manner may seem rather extreme to the teacher who feels that art lies beyond careful planning. But every teacher, regardless of philosophy or field, must face

Table 2.3

FLOWCHART SHOWING STAGES IN PLANNING PERFORMANCE OBJECTIVES

I Subject and Grade

Art Content Areas			
	Art History	Art Appreciation	Design Awareness
Upper Grades Middle Grades Primary Grades			

II Breakdown of content into broad concepts

Art Appreciation				
Concept Statements	Objectives	Activities	Media and Resources	Evaluation

III Breakdown of broad concepts into activity lesson plan

Activity Lesson Plan: Subject area, concept statement, time, objectives, processes, materials, perceptual processes, evaluation

the results of classroom work, and planning for art simply requires that the instructor consider the end results before beginning to teach.

Planning, however, should never be so tight that attention cannot be given to any child who is unable to begin work. One difficulty may be that the child has not found the assigned task sufficiently interesting to become involved. A teacher may find it necessary in this case to help the child work on another task that is compatible with the goal. For example, the teacher might eventually suggest variations of the assignment, or if need be, depart from the original plan in order to motivate the child. The solution may lie in a change of medium or subject matter. Vicarious experiences, such as stories from literature, films, radio, or television, may capture the reluctant child's interest and provide sufficient motivation to begin work. In any event, new bases for expression, from either actual or vicarious sources, must be explored until the child is prompted to action.

When
and How Much
to Teach

Teaching in art is the technique of helping children to say what they want to say in the terms in which they want to say it. Teaching is concerned, therefore, with the development of a task (once the main theme or subject has been selected), with the use of tools and materials, and with composition or design. Since the child must remain in control of the ideas being expressed and of the tools, media, and composition used to express them, the teacher should in no way resort to dictatorial methods. It will be shown later how disastrous are the results if a child is subjected to dictatorial pressures. Two important problems facing a teacher are the timing of teaching and the amount of teaching to be done.

Timing of Teaching.   Teaching must be timed so that it occurs neither too soon nor too late. Once each child has accepted an idea for expression and has selected the tools and medium, there comes a period of hesitation or doubt that any creating person, whether child or professional artist, experiences.[17] Although the teacher has assisted the child in selecting a topic and setting up as a goal a particular act of expression, the child's thoughts about both the theme and the goal tend to be nebulous. It would be a most extraordinary child who knew exactly what the subject matter, composition, and handling of media were to be. Should children have stereotyped answers to all these aspects of their work, their efforts would no longer be creative, and they would be better employed in some other activity. Once children have settled on a theme, therefore, they should be allowed to think about it and to explore it, both mentally and physically, with the medium they have selected.

[17]Described in detail by John Dewey in *How We Think* (Boston: Heath, 1933). In his *Democracy and Education* (New York: Macmillan, 1916), p. 182, he says: "The most significant question . . . which can be asked . . . about any situation or experience proposed to induce learning is what quality of problems it involves."

Figure 2.4 *In producing art, children are confronted with many kinds of visual problems, which they may be expected to solve themselves. (Photo by Rick Steadry.)*

The experimentation that occurs at this time should not consist of random activity; it should be determined by the problems and goals previously established. Although some of the child's ideas may lead to blind alleys, false moves resulting from controlled experimentation are not a waste of educational time and materials, since they narrow the number of choices the learner has as to the best means of arriving at a satisfactory solution to problems and the achievement of goals. The testing and retesting of ideas, the sifting, discarding, and coordinating that go on, are all traditional functions of a creative act and, at the same time, are highly educative. An activity undertaken without a period of personal struggle does not fall within the definition of art. It is safe to say, in fact, that no real art has ever been produced without it.

Artists accept the necessity of this period of exploration, for they must rely on their own initiative to arrive at a satisfactory solution to their problems. Children, on the other hand, are immature and cannot be expected always to solve their problems and to reach their goals to their own satisfaction. Sometimes they must rely on the teacher for help. The most important question, therefore, arises: when should a child receive help? The answer must be dictated largely by common sense.[18] When the child, because of limited experience, has exhausted the possibilities of experimenting and can proceed no further without help, the teacher must offer assistance. Because each child is different from the others, each requires individual treatment. One child may show need of assistance soon after work has begun, while another may not need help until well into the project.

In deciding when to offer assistance, therefore, the teacher must constantly study every child engaged in art work, making note of such problems as: John is not wiping his brush free of excess paint and hence is spoiling his page with superfluous drops of paint; Mary is making her main figures too small; Elizabeth is unable to draw a house; the background in Peter's picture interferes with the center of interest he has established. When children have reached the end of their resources, when they have struggled to the full extent of their capacity with the problem at hand, they must receive help. There is no formula or rule of thumb the teacher can follow. Only a personal knowledge of every member of the class, together with good judgment, can indicate when help must be forthcoming. Assistance given too soon will take away the child's initiative; given too late it will leave the child frustrated.

Amount of Teaching. The teacher has noted John's difficulty with the brush, Mary's trouble with small figures, Elizabeth's dilemma with the house, and Peter's problem with the background. The children need help,

[18]Principles are involved, of course. See Burton, *The Guidance of Learning Activities,* for a good summary.

but how much assistance should they have? If too much help is given, the teacher will be thinking for the children; if too little is offered, the children will still be unable to proceed. The amount of assistance offered must be such that the child is helped to overcome the immediate difficulty and at the same time is left free to face further problems as they may occur. Moreover, whenever practical and possible, the help provided should ideally lead the child to the position of solving the problem independently.

Obviously, the amount of help must be governed by the stage of development of the child receiving assistance. Because John is only six years old, he must be shown precisely how to dip a brush in paint and how to wipe it free of excess drops. He may require several demonstrations of this process before he can use the brush successfully. Mary is seven, and the teacher can ask her to observe her work from a distance and tell why it is difficult to see the figures. Then Mary may be asked how she would change the picture so that everyone in the class may enjoy looking at it. Some of her classmates may help her arrive at a satisfactory solution. Elizabeth is ten, and she may be asked to observe houses closely, and perhaps make some sketches of them. Peter, who is twelve, may have his attention drawn to the work of others so that he may study how they overcome difficulties in painting backgrounds. Later, he may be taught how to mix tints and shades of color for use in the background. Occasionally, the teacher may observe that many members of the class have the same difficulty and that a short general lesson to the group is needed. Unless the majority of the class will profit from a group lesson, however, this type of teaching should be offered on an individual basis.

Selecting the Media and Tools of Expression

Media are the materials that a pupil employs in art activities. Their proper use in class depends on the teacher's knowledge of certain facts concerning them that affect teaching methods.

Different types of media suit various stages of physical development of the pupils. At certain stages of development, for example, children have difficulty in using soft chalk and require instead a harder substance such as wax crayon. Too hard a medium, however, makes it difficult for children to cover paper readily and will interfere with their expression.[19] Very young children, who have not learned to use the smaller muscles with dexterity, require large surfaces for painting or assembling large objects. Yet children of all ages periodically have a desire to render detail, and there should be occasions when pencils are permitted for small-scale work, in which case the lead should be soft and the paper not too large.[20]

---

[19]See Chapter 7, "Drawing and Painting," for further discussion of suitable media.

[20]Rudolf Arnheim, in *Art and Visual Perception,* 4th ed. (Berkeley: University of California Press, 1954), and Dale Harris, in *Children's Drawings as Measures of Intellectual Maturity* (New York: Harcourt Brace Jovanovich, 1963), both state the case for encouragement of detail

As the children mature and gain greater muscular control, the size of surfaces and objects with which they work may be smaller. Some children, however, may wish to work on a large scale, no matter what stage of muscular development they have reached.

Children often show marked preferences for a particular medium. One child may find greater satisfaction in using clay than in using cardboard; another may prefer colored inks to tempera paint. Unless these children are given reasonable, although of course not exclusive, opportunities to employ the media of their choice, their art output may be inadequate.

Children may also have preferences as to tools. A certain size and type of brush may suit one child, but not another. A fine pen-point may appeal to some, while coarser nibs may be right for others. Teachers should be sensitive to the relationship between tools and paper size, bearing in mind that small tools (pencils and crayons) inhibit design on paper larger than 12 by 18 inches, and that large brushes limit detail and observation on smaller sizes of paper.

The teacher who makes an effort to provide a variety of materials and tools is following an accepted practice in art. Nearly every artist develops preferences among the many media and tools available, but this does not prevent exploration of further possibilities of favorite materials, or testing of new materials.

SOME FAULTY TEACHING PRACTICES IN ART

A number of sound teaching practices in art have been presented above. Now let us examine some hypothetical cases of teachers whose teaching practices are faulty. A study of these examples may serve not only to clarify the principles of good teaching practice but also to assist the student in avoiding some of the pitfalls of faulty teaching methods.[21]

---

as a means of clarification of concepts. On p. 168, Arnheim states: "Unquestionably the modern methods have given an outlet to aspects of the child's mind that were crippled by the traditional procedure of copying models with a sharpened pencil. But there is equal danger for *clarifying line observations* of reality and for learning to concentrate and create order." (italics added)

[21]Mildred Landis, in viewing approaches to art teaching, comes to the conclusion that most instruction falls into three categories, but that a fourth is the one to be recommended. She rejects what she calls (1) the "directing" method, because it settles for short-term goals and allows for no degree of "emotion or reflection"; (2) the "free-expression" method, because of its formless, random quality; and (3) the "eclectic" method, because, in borrowing from the first two, it suffers from their shortcomings. She suggests that a fourth method, "meaningful methodology," be adopted, because it takes a broader view of means and ends and of purposes and goals. Its ultimate aim is to encourage value formation as well as art skills, and it places a greater reliance on what she terms "esthetic principles." See Mildred Landis, *Meaningful Art Education* (Peoria, Ill.: Bennett, 1951).

*The Teacher
Who Advocates
Copying*

Every year when spring approaches, Miss L, a conscientious second-grade teacher, provides the class with yellow and green construction paper. She has designed a pretty pattern of a daffodil in which the leaves are green and the flower yellow. She demonstrates first how to cut the petals and then shows how to make the leaves. "The children," says Miss L, "love to make a daffodil. It provides a most effective art lesson."

Miss L is correct in saying that the children love to make a daffodil. Spring is in the air and the bright new paper is fascinating. Motivation of the children is not difficult for Miss L, a friendly, likable, sympathetic person, who has timed her activity well. Miss L is incorrect, however, in saying that the work constitutes an effective art lesson. The activity is not art; it is "busy work." In producing the flower, no one but Miss L has done any planning. She has not only done all the planning and solved all the problems, but any expression of feelings about the flower is hers alone. The children may have developed some skill, but they have done so without engaging in thought and feeling. The pupils, in other words, have been subjected to a mechanistic form of teaching.

The children's liking for a particular activity does not necessarily mean that the work is art or even an educationally sound pursuit. With very little motivation, children may be led to break windows or to chop down trees in public parks. Given sufficient approval, they will like these activities even more than they do making daffodils according to Miss L's directions. Actually Miss L has wasted good educational time and materials in this work. Among the basic teaching principles discussed earlier, she has failed to observe those requiring that children establish their own goals and that they face the problems that arise during their work. Miss L has taught dictatorially, and not according to the children's needs.

*The Teacher
Who Places
Undue Emphasis
on Neatness*

Miss G is a tidy person; she presents a neat appearance and her classroom is a model of order. "I like things to look right," says Miss G, as she goes about her duties in a fourth-grade classroom. "I have no use for sloppy work," she asserts, "in drawing, painting, or any other subject, for that matter." Miss G encourages neatness so vigorously that her pupils have grown afraid to experiment. Those who first tried to experiment with ideas and media ran into difficulties with both the media and Miss G. Now they hold fast to thoroughly familiar materials and well-tried clichés in artistic thought, which pleases their teacher.

Sometimes even under these conditions Miss G is not altogether satisfied with the neatness of the children's work. In these cases, with bold application of chalk or paint she "touches up" the youngsters' work. She is so clever at this that the output of her class occasionally wins prizes. Only an expert in children's art could tell where the work had been doctored, and very few such experts judge children's art work on a competitive basis, because well-informed art educators are skeptical about competition of this kind.

The children's mural work must also be neat. Sometimes in this activity, too, the children do not meet Miss G's standards of neatness, and this embarrasses her, particularly when the principal visits her. However, she has developed what she considers a "good" system of mural-making. Now the children draw and paint only the backgrounds, in which work they cannot be too untidy if properly supervised. They then cut out figures from magazines and glue them into place. The new system is much easier because no real effort is required, but the children scarcely want to draw or paint at all now.

Although no one would advocate untidiness for its own sake in a classroom, children must be allowed to experiment freely with ideas and media. Lack of skill in the organization of both subject matter and materials makes it inevitable that their art production is often untidy. Tidiness in the execution of artistic activities will occur only after the skills associated with them are mastered. To demand extreme neatness at all times is to handicap children in producing creative work. Among the basic principles of teaching neglected by Miss G are the following: expression must arise from personal experience; the products of expression must be the children's own; teaching must be built on the children's interests; mental exploration, even if it leads to blind alleys of thought, is valuable.

Mr. W is a vigorous teacher of history. Following one of his excellent lessons, he discussed with his class of boys the possibilities of picture-making in connection with the historical theme in question. After the boys suggested the aspects of the theme that most appealed to them, Mr. W, amid great enthusiasm, sent them about their research. The boys collected many clippings from magazines and from the classroom's well-stocked library of books and periodicals. Before long each boy found a suitable picture, which he copied with great care. Mr. W commended the boys on their close attention to detail and their painstaking efforts to make their work look "real."

The Teacher Who Does Not Understand Art

Obviously, Mr. W understands the technique of motivation and can arouse enthusiasm over a theme for expression. If he enjoyed as much understanding of art as he does of history, Mr. W's teaching would be most effective. But he lacks even a rudimentary knowledge of the nature and place of art in general education. The moment that copying begins, education, not only in art, but also in history, ceases. If he were to guide the boys into creative work related to the historical theme, art would probably be produced. Moreover, because recall of a historical experience would be effected creatively, the pupils would probably gain greater insight into Mr. W's favorite field of study. In short, Mr. W has failed to observe the following important principle of teaching: learners must think for themselves, testing and retesting their own ideas through controlled experimentation.

Down the hall from Mr. W's classroom is Miss deP. She is tall and dark and looks "artistic" because she wears extraordinarily large pieces of jewelry. Miss deP spends each summer studying with painters and is a supporter of all forms of avant-garde art. It is rumored that she and Mr. W do not get along.

Miss deP says she is a lover of freedom to the extent that she is reluctant to interfere with any form of childlike expression in art. "Art is the free expression of an untrammeled spirit," she says. The output of her pupils seems to be lusterless. The principal claims that the pupils are noisy and inattentive and inclined to be rude to Miss deP. Quite often, when not obstreperous, the pupils are listless. They say that they often do not know what to do. The situation is unfortunate, for Miss deP has much to offer. Her feeling for art is apparently deep, but she has failed to understand the meaning of teaching. She would have more success as a teacher if she recognized the following basic teaching principles: the pupils must be assisted in establishing personal themes for expression; teaching is most effective when the situation indicates a need for it; the teaching of art should not be used as a vehicle through which frustrated artists may satisfy their own egos.

Miss Z, the teacher of a third-grade class, is clever at mathematics. One of her favorite art lessons consists of having the children resolve objects into triangles, squares, oblongs, and circles. She admires the precision resulting from this activity. "The children are learning to handle basic forms," she explains. Thus the children are taught to draw houses by means of a triangle supported by a rectangular oblong; a chicken by using two circles; a young girl, strangely enough, by resorting to triangles and squares.

Miss Z is another example of a teacher who prevents children from expressing themselves in their art activities. Moreover, the designs she insists on are false in relation to the objects depicted. The forms of houses, chickens, and girls cannot be successfully arrived at through mathematical shapes supplied by the teacher. They can be depicted adequately only by means of personal experience and experiment on the part of the children. Miss Z's system is, in reality, a false and rather ugly one using someone else's pictogram shorthand; it is certainly anything but art. Miss Z should recall at least two basic principles of teaching: personal experience is the basis of learning, and skill (precision in the use of tools and materials) is best gained when closely connected with expressive acts engaging the thoughts and feelings of the learner.

THE EFFECTS OF INAPPROPRIATE TEACHING METHODS

The teaching methods described above are based on practices inappropriate to artistic development. Study of both art and children reveals that these methods are either ineffective or harmful. But exactly how ineffective or harmful are they? There have been numerous experiments attempting to find an answer to that question. Two are described below.[22] The first of these is concerned with dictatorial teaching practices, the second with laissez-faire practices.

The Effects of Dictatorial Teaching Practices

The first experiment was performed with 250 children between six and eight years of age, all of whom had enjoyed a creative program of art up until the time of the experiment. They were in what is known as the "symbol" stage of expression and were able to relate symbols to their environment.[23] In brief, they were capable of creatively producing pictures about their experiences. The children were paired according to their mental ages into two groups called Group A and Group B.

For Group A, consisting of 125 children, the creative program in picture-making was brought to an abrupt halt. In its place the teachers substituted ten activities of a restrictive or dictatorial nature: cutting a triangle and a square from colored paper, to be pasted on paper to form a house; drawing an apple in the form of a circle, which the teacher had previously drawn on the blackboard; copying the outline of a tree that had been drawn on the blackboard; coloring a flower that had been drawn by a teacher and mimeographed; copying a drawing of a bird from a mimeographed outline; drawing a snowman according to the teacher's verbal directions; tracing the outline of a car prepared by a teacher; copying a drawing of a girl from the blackboard; drawing a tulip according to visual demonstrations on the blackboard; and following verbal directions in the use of circles to draw a cat.

While Group A was engaged in this work for ten days, Group B, consisting of the remaining 125 children, continued to make pictures creatively. On the eleventh school day, both groups were taken to a firehouse where the firemen had consented to act as hosts. After the children had explored parts of the building and the equipment, they were given light refreshments by the firemen. The excursion was an obvious success and a stimulating experience.

The next day all the pupils were subjected to the usual forms of motivation. Then they were asked to develop a picture from their experiences. All the children in Group B were, in varying degrees, successful

[22]These are part of a research program directed by C. D. Gaitskell and sponsored by the Ontario Department of Education.
[23]The symbol stage and other stages of development are discussed in detail in Chapter 6.

in this work. Their drawings and paintings illustrated personal reactions to their observations and were produced in a variety of media and with different techniques. In Group A, however, 44 percent (fifty-five of the children), instead of presenting their reactions to the outing, resorted to drawing houses, birds, and the like, as they had been taught during the previous ten schools days. Others reverted to manipulation of the media, a stage of development that precedes production of symbols.

The children in Group A were studied intermittently thereafter for a period of two years. At the end of this time, no fewer than 8 percent (ten children) were still inclined to produce the stereotyped work they had been taught during the ten days. If only ten days of dictatorial work in art[24] interfere to this extent with their artistic expression, one may well wonder how inhibiting, say, a whole year of this kind of teaching may be on the minds of children, and how durable may be its effects.

A related study is Heilman's investigation of the influence of work-book exercises on the art productivity of second-grade children.[25] His evidence shows clearly the retrogressive effects of copying and points out how severely limiting such activity can be on the wide range of symbolization among primary-school children. But it is well to bear in mind that children can be just as inhibited by copying and working from a teacher's model as they can be by using coloring books and other stereotypes.

The Effects of Laissez-faire Teaching Practices

In order to discover the extent to which children can get along without art instruction, 200 children were selected for observation and divided into two groups. One hundred of them, whose ages ranged from five years to six years and three months, with an average chronological age of five years and eight months, were in the first group studied. Sixty-two of these children were still in the manipulative stage; the remainder were making symbols to represent some objects in their environment.

For five days their teachers provided a variety of materials already familiar to the children, including tempera paint, clay, plasticine, and construction paper and glue. No aid in motivation and no teaching assistance were offered. During the first day and largely during the second, the children got along well. They kept themselves busy either manipulating materials or forming symbols. On the second day sixteen children showed a lagging interest in the work, and on the third, fifty-nine indicated this tendency. On the fourth and fifth days nearly every child indicated lack of interest in the activities, and all the work produced lacked vitality. It is interesting to note that the older children in the group seemed

---

[24]We must not forget to take into account also the effects of variable interval reinforcement that usually accompanies such a program.

[25]Horace F. Heilman, "An Experimental Study of the Effect of Workbooks on the Creative Drawing of Second Grade Children," unpublished doctoral dissertation, Pennsylvania State University, 1954.

to miss the attention of the teacher to a greater extent than did the younger. Perhaps this was because they had grown more used to motivation and guidance than had the younger pupils and because the symbolic stage of expression requires more help from the teacher than does the manipulative stage. Of further interest is the fact that about 22 percent of the children who originally had reached the symbol stage reverted to the manipulation of materials and failed to produce any symbols.

The above procedures were repeated with the second group of 100 children. The ages of these children ranged from seven years and two months to nine years and one month, with an average chronological age of eight years and three months. The results of this study were similar to those obtained with the first group with the exception that from the first day there was a noticeable lack of interest in the work. This attitude was almost universal on the second and subsequent days.

It was concluded that the youngest children, particularly those in the manipulative stage, may apparently benefit from an occasional art period in which the teacher does not attempt to provide motivation or assistance. Too many such sessions in sequence, however, rapidly have adverse effects on the art activities of all children, but particularly on the work of those children who have advanced beyond the manipulative stage of development.

Teaching art can be far more complex than most new teachers realize. The following list is composed of significant factors that could bear on the success of a teacher. This evaluation instrument has been provided so that teachers can get a "profile" of their own style. Note that this form is not descriptive; it merely asks whether any of the factors listed were present, not present, or present in some exemplary way. Description of any one item could be elaborated if desired. The lesson is divided into five segments: preparation, presentation, the class in action, evaluation, and teaching style. Obviously no one lesson could possibly encompass all the items listed. The instrument also provides some indication of the possible variables in teaching.

Analyzing the Teacher

Preparation for Instruction and Classroom Management
1. Display areas:
   a. Display pupils' work
   b. Relate materials to studio activity
   c. Relate materials to current events in art, school, community
   d. Show design awareness in the arrangement of pupils' work
2. Supplies and materials:
   a. Organized so that the room is orderly and functional
   b. Organized so that the room is orderly but inhibiting
   c. Organized so that the room is disorderly but functional
   d. Organized so that the room is disorderly and nonfunctional

e. Distributed systematically
3. Resource material (aids, art books, art magazines, file materials, live art, film loops and other audio visual support):
   a. Provided by school system and school
   b. Not provided by school system and school
   c. Derived from teacher's reference file
   d. Not provided by teacher or school
4. Nonobservable data:
   a. (pupil's work) Kept in portfolio for reference
   b. (reference file) Made available for student use

Presentation of Lesson
1. Objectives are clearly stated
2. Objectives are arrived at through dialog
3. Discussion is related to topic or objective
4. Discussion is related to levels within group
5. Interaction between pupils and teacher:
   a. Teacher interrupts pupils
   b. Teacher welcomes disagreement
6. Demonstrations are oriented toward multiple solutions
7. Demonstrations are convergent in nature
8. Class is flexible:
   a. Chairs are easily reorganized for viewing demonstrations
   b. Children can come to teacher freely for additional material
   c. Several projects are in operation at same time
   d. Children can move freely from project to project

The Class in Action
1. Teacher:
   a. Listens to pupils
   b. Asks open questions
   c. Asks closed questions
   d. Praises work of pupils in general terms
   e. Praises work in specific terms that are relevant to the problem
   f. Uses other forms of verbal reinforcement
   g. Is able to reach pupils who request consultation
   h. Talks at length to some pupils
   i. Relates comments not only to objectives but to pupils' frame of reference
   j. Motivates those who have become discouraged
   k. Remotivates those with short attention spans
   l. Is flexible in permitting deviation from assignments
   m. Uses art vocabulary
   n. Is competent in handling discipline problems
2. Pupils:
   a. Are self-directive in organizing for work

b. Are self-directive in organizing for cleanup
c. Use art vocabulary

Evaluation Period (For final group evaluation)
1. Evaluation bears relation to goals of lesson
2. Pupils are encouraged to participate
3. Pupils do participate as a group
4. Only one work is evaluated
5. Several works are evaluated
6. There is no final evaluation
7. Pupils do not feel embarrassed or threatened by public evaluation
8. Pupils are generally negative to evaluation process

Teaching Style (Personality)
1. Teacher takes positive attitude toward instruction
2. Teacher shows rapport with pupils' age group
3. Teacher demonstrates sense of humor
4. Teacher has sense of pace: controls flow of lesson
5. Teacher is innovative in following respects:
   a.   c.
   b.   d.
6. Teacher is aware of language (vivid phrasing, imagistic speech, clarity of expression)

ACTIVITIES FOR THE READER

1. Describe any situation you have experienced in which children disliked art. Explain how the dislike arose and indicate the means you might use to alter the children's attitude.
2. Describe the traits of a personal acquaintance whom you consider to be an effective teacher of art.
3. Observe some art lessons given by expert teachers and note especially (a) the motivational devices employed; (b) the manner in which themes are defined; (c) the way in which goals are established; (d) the problems that arise and the means by which a solution to them is found. Can you add any items to the analysis instrument at the end of this chapter?
4. Describe how you would motivate a class for a lesson in increased sensitivity to color based on fall colors in nature.
5. Take a close look at your personality and try to project your teaching "style" from it.
6. Describe the steps you might take to improve the following situations: (a) a third-grade art class whose members are outrageously untidy and wasteful of materials; (b) a class of fifth graders who have always been taught to copy during their art sessions and feel they are unable to create; (c) a group of sixth-grade boys who think art is "sissy"; (d) a group of kindergarten children whose parents or older brothers and sisters have given them formulas for the drawing of objects.

Large, simple forms often make a most effective design.

DESIGN AS A BASIS
FOR ART ACTIVITY

To perceive a visual image implies the beholder's participation in a process of organization. The experience of an image is thus a creative act of integration. Its essential characteristic is that by plastic power an experience is formed into an organic whole. Here is a basic discipline of forming, that is, thinking in terms of structure, a discipline of utmost importance in the chaos of our formless world.*

Design is not a separate and distinct area of art. Design is an integral part of any art form. The message a creating person wishes to convey is made apparent by means of the formal organization produced. Whenever any work of art is being produced, whether by a child or an adult, design is automatically included in the production. A piece of clay sculpture by a child in the first grade, a Sung stoneware vase, a painting by Cézanne, a symphony by Beethoven, or a play by Arthur Miller all involve design, structure, and the relation of component elements to a unified whole. Design, therefore, is presented in all art forms and may be intuitively achieved, as in the case of some mental patients, or consciously worked with, as in the case of most professional artists. One function of art education is the development of a child's awareness of design.

This chapter will discuss design largely as it applies to visual forms of expression. The discussion includes an analysis of the parts, or elements, that make up a design, together with an outline of the methods employed by artists and others to bring about a satisfactory coherence in the use of these elements. The teacher who lacks a knowledge of design suffers a handicap. The information to be found in this chapter, however,

*From Gyorgy Kepes, *Language of Vision* (Chicago: Theobald, 1945), p. 13.

like that in the first and second chapters, is presented only as professional background knowledge. Chapter 7 will deal directly with the application of this knowledge in the classroom.

THE ELEMENTS OF DESIGN

Design is an organization of integrated elements in a work of art. The designs of accomplished artists should convey the feeling that nothing could be changed without violating their structure. Lines, colors, textures, masses and spaces, patterns of light and shade should form a complete and, as far as can be judged, harmonious whole. This final organization has been called "form," and Lascelles Abercrombie says of it:

> Whatever art gives us is given as an instance of a world of unquestioned order, measure, government, a world in which experience occurs with perfect security, knowing that the firm inter-relationship of its process can never be dislocated by chance—a world which is the desire of the mind.[1]

Abercrombie continues by stating that "form," as he calls it, is the chief excellence of art:

> It is because art presents its matter as Form that it effects this profoundly desirable impression of coherence, of inter-relation, and so of significance both of parts and of whole.

As Abercrombie suggests, the act of designing is common to all human beings. The primitive tribesman brings about some order and coherence in the jungle while constructing a village; the homemaker follows the "desire of the mind" in rearranging furniture in the living room. The lawmaker brings order to a parliamentary session and the gardener to the garden. Because the desire for order is universal, artistic acts, which demand that we achieve a form, composition, or design, have potential significance for us all.

Design, if we are to follow the Gestaltists, may be related to the factor of "closure"—that is, "behavior that signifies pattern completion, goal realization, the resolution of tension, or the process of effecting a balance."[2] Our psyches are probed even deeper when our response to design is homeostatic in nature, arising from the organism's need for stability and order. John Dewey likens design to an essential seeking for order, for reason and structure out of chaos.[3]

[1] *An Essay Toward a Theory of Art* (London: Secker, 1926), pp. 105–07.
[2] Carter V. Good, ed., *Dictionary of Education*, 2nd ed. (New York: McGraw-Hill, 1959), p. 102.
[3] *Art as Experience* (New York: Putnam, 1958).

Figure 3.1 *Exploring space through simple materials. This requires the use of the entire body. Activities of this sort are similar to dance and sculpture and suggest new possibilities for design education. (Photo by Karen Gilborn.)*

Philosophers have long been fascinated by the faultless organization of good design, and have attempted to analyze it. Repeatedly the question has been asked: What are the parts or elements that make up these splendid organizations? These philosophers, however, know full well that any intellectual dissection of a particular work can never adequately account for the significance of the entire design. From observations of life in general, people have sensed for a long time what the Gestalt psychologists stated a relatively short time ago, that the whole is greater than the sum of its parts, and that to separate the whole into parts can destroy the object we attempt to analyze. Any form of intellectual analysis when applied to design threatens to destroy the organization we study.

Even with the realization that by intellectual analysis it is not possible to arrive at a complete understanding of design nor an adequate formula for its production, one is nevertheless justified in searching for its elements. The physiologist who probes into a corpse and dissects nerves and organs knows that that body is less than the living being.[4] The chemist who analyzes a drug realizes that the individual elements cannot produce the healing effects of the compound. In both instances, however, those engaged in the research of the parts feel that from their study an insight may eventually be gained into the nature of the complete object. In other words, although the original object can be fully understood only in terms of itself and not its parts, the partial knowledge acquired may be helpful later when considering the object in its entirety.

Those who have attempted to isolate the elements of design have

[4]A figure used by Benedetto Croce in his *Aesthetic* (New York: Noonday, 1956).

reached only a partial agreement.[5] At the present time, nevertheless, a number of elements have been defined that appear to be acceptable to the majority of writers in this field. These elements of form or design are line, mass and space, light and shade, texture, and color. They will be discussed individually below so that teachers may not only acquire some insight into design as it appears in the work of children, but also develop a vocabulary for this segment of art education. We will see in Chapter 17 how even a rudimentary knowledge of the vocabulary of design can provide a basis for the discussion of works of art.

Contemporary artists, particularly the Abstract Expressionists, have worked against what they feel are static effects such as symmetry, balance, and classic proportion and have instead placed a premium on accident, stridence, and deliberate avoidance of a "closed" image. Despite this change in the concept of design, the elements of form exist in all styles, and for purposes of elementary instruction we can still use our design vocabulary in referring to both the child's work and the work of professionals.

[5]For example, compare the following: Ray Faulkner and Edwin Ziegfeld, *Art Today,* 5th ed. (New York: Holt, Rinehart and Winston, 1969); Roger Fry, *Vision and Design* (New York: Meridian, 1956); and Viktor Lowenfeld and W. Lambert Brittain, *Creative and Mental Growth,* 4th ed. (New York: Macmillan, 1964). A good system of analysis of pictorial composition may be found in Erle Loran, *Cézanne's Composition,* 3rd ed. (Berkeley: University of California Press, 1963). See also Edmund Feldman's *Art: Image and Idea* (Englewood Cliffs, N.J.: Prentice-Hall, 1967); Nathan Knobler, *The Visual Dialogue* (New York: Holt, Rinehart and Winston, 1967); and Helen Gardner's *Art Through the Ages,* 5th ed., rev. by Horst de la Croix and Richard G. Tansey (New York: Harcourt Brace Jovanovich, 1970).

Figure 3.2 *As Kepes notes, "Here is a basic discipline of forming, that is, thinking in terms of structure. . ." These third graders are involved in flexible design activities. The adjustable components of geometrical shapes permit an unlimited number of arrangements. (Education Development Center.)*

Line, the path traced by a moving point, is perhaps the most flexible and revealing element of design. If we are angry and "doodle" a line, our anger is clearly revealed in the marks we make. If we are placid, calm, or pleased, our scribbling takes on a different character. Artists readily express their feelings by means of line. In communicating hatred of war and brutality in general, an artist may use slashing, angular, abrupt lines, as Picasso did in his *Guernica*. In presenting feelings about the soft beauty of a summer landscape, the artist's lines might be gently undulating, flowing, rippling.

Line, Director of the Viewer's Eye

Line may be used strongly and directly. In Figure 3.3A Käthe Kollwitz uses line as a primary means to achieve her end; the strong, powerful line supports her anger at society and her compassion for its victims. Harold Altman creates form and integrates figure and background through his use of line (Figure 3.3B). Artists may also imply line, that is, convey it indirectly by forming edges of contrasting tones that move from one part of a painting to another.

Notice the implied line used by Cézanne in his painting of the *Card Players*, reproduced in Figure 3.4. In the line diagram in Figure 3.5 one can see how the linear movement begins over the back of the card player on the right, then swings down over his arm, only to be caught up by the line across the back of the center player. Swirling around this center card player's hat, it moves up over the arm and around the back of the standing man and, falling across the shoulders of the player on the left, ends in the sweep of the chair. Folds in the draperies and shadows in the background augment the sweep of Cézanne's expressive line.

Just as most people eventually develop a personal style of hand-writing, so artists develop a line peculiar to themselves. By skillfully commanding line artists can make the element speak of their experiences. Study of line, therefore, is a worthwhile pursuit, for line lets us know something of what its creators think and feel, and helps us respond to whatever they have in mind. In fact, line has sometimes been called the "nervous system" of a work of art.

There are generally two kinds of line—the free-flowing, and the measured. The upsurging line of a Gothic cathedral or of a modern skyscraper and the lines found in a formal Italian garden are the results of mathematical measurement. Because these lines follow mathematical rules, they may be less personal than lines that are created freely. They are, nevertheless, selected by human judgment and taste and, because of this, constitute an aesthetic element.

The study of line is particularly effective with elementary-school children because they have a linear rather than a mass or volume orientation to picture-making that derives from their earliest pre-school drawings. Lines are, therefore, a natural subject of artistic study even in the lowest elementary grades. The children will find their own words to distinguish between the "scratchy" lines of Ben Shahn, the "funny" lines of Paul Klee, or the "squiggly" character of Oriental calligraphy. This sort of exercise provides a basis on which to build the grammar of art. But the study of line need not be limited to drawing or painting, for line can be observed and enjoyed in architecture and sculpture and, in many instances, in nature.

A Germany's Children Are Starving, *lithograph, 1924.*

B Desdemona, *woodcut. (Courtesy of Kennedy Galleries, N.Y.)*

Figure 3.3 *Line may be used directly for expression of feeling and creation of form. Käthe Kollwitz* **(A)** *and Leonard Baskin* **(B)** *achieve these goals through their distinctive use of line.*

Figure 3.4 *Paul Cézanne's Card Players—a significant organization of the elements of design. (The Metropolitan Museum of Art, New York. Bequest of Stephen C. Clark, 1960.)*

Figure 3.6 *As this portrait by a sixth grader illustrates, contour-line drawing is effective in the upper elementary grades, for it utilizes the child's natural linear orientation in drawing*

Figure 3.5 *A diagrammatic indication of the movement of the lines in the Card Players.*

Mass and Space

Mass refers to the volume or bulk of objects in a work of art, and space to the areas that surround mass. The aesthetic effect of mass is perhaps most readily grasped in architecture and sculpture. The great mass of an office building and the delicate mass of a soaring church spire have the power to move us. In sculpture we are equally affected by the weight, shape, and balance of the masses created by the sculptor. The depiction of mass in a good painting or drawing affects us similarly, of course. But in painting and drawing, in contrast to sculpture and architecture, the creation of volume is an illusion. Furthermore, the word "mass" in painting and drawing refers to the large, generalized shapes on the flat surface into which the artist subsequently introduces differentiating detail. In traditional painting the artist first "massed" in the figures and background, and later put in the individual features that distinguished one figure from another or one background object from another.

Every mass is surrounded by the element of space. In a work of art

Figure 3.7 *Four examples of "exploding" design created by sectioning paper and pasting the pieces on a contrasting background. These are by fourth and fifth graders.*

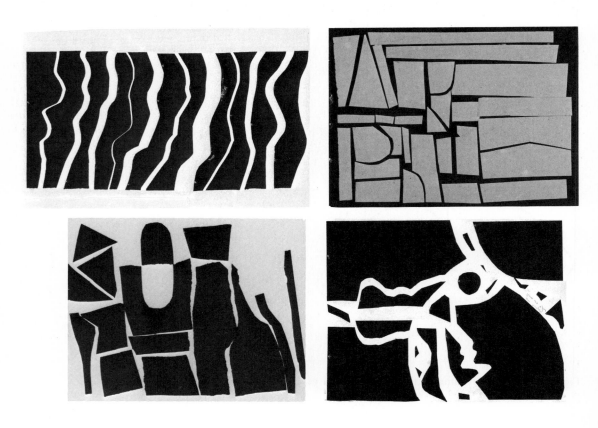

Figure 3.8 *A diagrammatic indication of the distribution of masses and spaces in the* Card Players.

space exists as a potential that is realized through the action of the artist. Then it becomes an element that interacts with other elements. As an example of the use of space in architecture, consider the courtyards separating the buildings in a modern housing development. Here the architect has carefully planned the amount of space that should be provided between one building and another. If the spaces had been planned smaller, the buildings might appear to be huddled together; wider, the buildings might not appear to belong to a coherent plan.

The artist working in two dimensions must also regulate the spaces between masses. In a Ben Shahn drawing, for example, the intervals between the volumes have their own qualities, ranging from confined to open areas. Children can learn to appreciate these qualities when they create designs by dividing dark paper on a white background (see Figure 3.7). In paintings and drawings with figure-ground relationships the artist must provide sufficient space for the objects to give coherence to the design. In doing this the artist may give an illusion of depth or of a third dimension, although not all painters wish to make use of this effect. If a three-dimensional effect is required, however, the artist may overlap masses, make use of linear perspective, adjust the color, and so on.

Children should be made aware of the action that takes place among all elements of a picture, and one way to call their attention to it is by showing them how artists solve the problem of mass and space.

Figure 3.8 is a diagram of the masses and spaces in Cézanne's *Card Players*. The masses formed by the players, the table, and the draperies are presented in a sculptural unity relieved by variations in light and shade, texture, and color. The simplicity of the spaces offers a significant contrast to the detail of the masses.

The creating person may make use of the elements of light and shade in art work. In drawing with chalk the pressure applied to the medium regulates the degree of lightness or darkness of the marks produced. By adding black or white to a standard hue of paint the degree of light and

Light and Shade

Figure 3.9 *A diagrammatic indication of the distribution of the chief areas of light and shade in the* Card Players.

shade is regulated. Architects and sculptors control these elements by a variety of devices. A building may be designed with deep recesses to produce shadows in contrast to a façade that catches the light. Sculptors likewise take great pains in controlling the hollows (negative areas) and bumps (positive areas) they make so that light and shade may be used to their best advantage.

Figure 3.9 diagrams the arrangements of light and shade in the *Card Players.* Every dark area seems to have a corresponding light area that gives it significance. Notice, for example, the contrast of the white face of the player at the left against the dark clothes of the standing figure, or the dark hat and profile of the player at the right against the light space of the background.

Figure 3.10 *This cut-paper collage shows how a sixth grader differentiated the light and dark areas in the accompanying photograph. (Photo by Margaret Bourke-White.)*

The dramatic effects that light and shade are capable of producing have been well demonstrated in black-and-white films, where, if the elements are used effectively, we may be quite content that color is absent. The etchings and paintings of Rembrandt and the work of Caravaggio move us largely because of the skillful handling of these elements. Light and shade, then, when well controlled, are powerful elements to which we may react strongly.

Texture may be thought of as the degree of roughness or smoothness of any surface. Every surface has a texture; a pebble on the seashore, a veined leaf, the wrinkled face of an old man, a brick wall, a sheet of glass, all display varying kinds and degrees of texture.

Texture and Textural Effects

Very often we derive a sensuous enjoyment from texture. We like to run our hands lightly over the surface of a tweed jacket or a fur coat. We may enjoy holding a smooth stone lightly in our hands or gently stroking a baby's hair. When we go to bed we may take delight in the smoothness of the sheets or, on the other hand, in what Rupert Brooke called "the rough male kiss of blankets."

Texture appeals to people, of course, for aesthetic as well as sensuous reasons, although it is doubtful if the two can be entirely separated. The texture that artists use may be actual or simulated. Paper for watercolor paintings is carefully chosen for its actual textural qualities. Some painters stipple a surface with gesso before painting on it with tempera or oils. The paint itself may be applied with careful regard for its textural effects. Paint applied thickly has a degree of roughness, but it can also be put on with silky smoothness. Cutting tools allow children to create texture on such surfaces as linoleum. Sometimes artists devise textural effects that are not actually rough or smooth, but only appear so. In some parts of a drawing, for example, lines may be crisscrossed or a pattern of dots may be devised so that the area has a rough appearance. Other areas may be left untouched or washed in with smooth or flat color to create a textural contrast.

The delight children take in surface quality provides the basis for activities involving collage (see Figure 3.11). Again, teachers can develop tactile sensitivity by discussing the treatment of texture and surface in the work of such artists as Schwitters, Marca-Relli, Picasso, and William Harnett, who simulates rather than uses real textures.

Because of the complexity of color, both artists and scientists have for years been attempting to arrive at a theoretical basis for its use. Feldman has noted:

Color, a Powerful and Complex Element

Color theory provides speculative answers to questions which are not often asked in the course of examining works of art. Some color systems seem

Figure 3.11 *Problems in collage may alert children to the possibilities of texture. This work by a fourth grader combines collage with painting.*

related to the physiology of perception more than to the aesthetics or psychology of perception. Others may have evolved from industrial needs for the classification and description of dyes, pigments and colored objects. At any rate, artists work with color—pigment to be exact—more on an intuitive than a scientific basis.[6]

In teaching children about the nature of color the teacher may vary the methods, using intuitive approaches[7] in the primary grades and gradually moving toward teaching color terminology and its application in the middle and upper grades. (Chapter 7, "Drawing and Painting," discusses the properties and definitions of color that may provide the basis for more effective color activities and picture-making.)

It must be emphasized that color is a powerful element. Its misuse can be disastrous in any design. A room, no matter how good the furnishings may be, can be ruined by painting the walls the wrong color or tone. The design of a painting likewise can fall apart if the colors have not been chosen wisely. Color serves to emphasize the extent to which the elements are interdependent. Although the elements have been discussed here separately, in reality they cannot be dissociated. The moment we make a mark on paper with black crayon, light and shade are involved. If paint has been applied, color is present. As soon as a shape is drawn it functions as a mass. Only for the sake of convenience, as was pointed out above, have we treated elements as separate entities. Color can be understood as functioning on two levels. On the cognitive level, color conveys information (1) in purely descriptive terms, as when leaves change color in the fall or one dog is tawny and another brown and (2) in symbolic terms, as in the case of flags and traffic signals. On the affective level, color works on psychological associations and thereby creates

[6]Feldman, *Art: Image and Idea*, p. 248.
[7]These may include the use of associative frames of reference, such as "happy" or "sad" colors, painting to music, or any exercise that allows children to translate their emotional state into color terms.

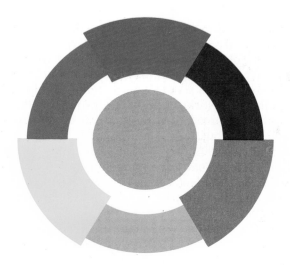

Figure 3.12 *Color wheel and value scale.* **A** *The color wheel is chiefly valuable because it provides a standardized vocabulary for discussion of art. The primaries are red, yellow, and blue. The secondaries result from mixing two primaries and are green, violet, and orange. The tertiaries result from mixing primaries with their opposing secondaries and refer to a variety of grays. The complementaries refer to the relationships of the primary and secondary colors on the wheel; they are red opposite green, yellow opposite violet, and blue opposite orange.* **B** *The value scale is a gradual progression of tones from white to black. White is the highest value and black is the lowest; the intermediate tones are made by mixing white and black in appropriate amounts.*

moods and feelings. As any industrial design consultant is aware, color affects us physiologically as well as psychologically and can be discussed in terms of the wavelengths of light as legitimately as in terms of the interaction of pigments. Indeed, so pervasive are its effects that the vocabulary of color theory can be used metaphorically in a wide variety of contexts, as in music, when we refer to tone color, or in writing when we speak of purple prose.[8]

The Language of Color. Scientists may define color as an effect of physical forces on our nervous system through their impact on the retina. Color, however, is far more complex to painters: to them it is a vital pictorial element that is closely related to all the other visual elements at their disposal. The sensitivity with which color is used can convey a personal

[8]The relationship between color and music has intrigued musicians and artists for a long time. Color and sound "organs" were developed as early as 1730. Using Newton's optical theories as a basis, these "organs" related seven colors to the seven tones of the diatonic scale. Charles Parkhurst discusses the terminology of art and music in his pamphlet "Light and Color" in Bernard S. Meyers and Trewin Copplestone, eds., *Art Treasures of the World* (New York: Harry N. Abrams, 1955), p. 6.

style and the meaning of a particular work. Ultimately it can influence the varied responses of viewers to a work of art.

The painter's color terminology also differs from the physicist's, whose primary reference is light rather than pigment. In art, a consistent terminology has come to be accepted as a means of discussing and using color, both in looking at works of art and in producing them. The following definitions provide some guidelines for instruction in painting, design, and the appreciation of art.

HUE is another word for "color," as in the phrase "the varied hues of the spectrum." Scientifically, a hue is determined by the wavelength of light reflected from an object. As the wavelengths change we note those distinct qualities that we call hues. Hues, therefore, are identifiable segments of light waves.

To the scientist working with light, the primary colors are green, yellow, and red, since these are the irreducible hues from which all other colors can be derived. To the painter working with pigment, on the other hand, the primaries are red, yellow, and blue. Most children can recognize and work with the painter's primaries as well as violet, green, and orange, known as secondary colors because they can be created by mixing the primaries. The tertiary colors result from mixing primary and secondary colors and may be more difficult for children to achieve since they require a greater control of paint. The tertiaries are also called "grays" and provide richer hues than the simple mixing of black and white will yield. The use of a color wheel on which the above discussion is based, should be deferred usually until the upper grades, except for teacher demonstration in the lower grades.

VALUE, or "tone," refers to the degree of darkness or lightness of a hue. The lighter a color, the higher its value, the darker a color, the lower its value. Hence, if white is added, the value is heightened, if black is added, the value is lowered. Hues also may be changed by the use of a *glaze,* or a veil of thin transparent color, which is brushed over the hue. This method of changing a color was much favored during the Renaissance but is rarely used today.

SATURATION is sometimes used interchangeably with "intensity" and indicates the freedom from admixture with another color—in other words, the ultimate purity of a color. Any hue that has not been mixed with another color is considered to be at its maximum saturation, although the purity of color can be enhanced or neutralized by adjacent colors in a painting. Some artists hesitate to use the word "intensity" as a synonym for saturation because, although a color can be made more intense by the addition of another color (as in the addition of some oranges to some reds), the original color may lose its distinctive identity if mixing is carried beyond a certain point.

COMPLEMENTARY is a term that refers to the relationship between primary and secondary colors on a color wheel. On the wheel, these colors are in opposition to one another, as red to green, blue to orange, and yellow to violet. The complementaries are antagonistic in the sense that neither color in a pair possesses any property in common with the other. Mixing such colors, therefore, will neutralize them and create a wide range of grays, which, as noted earlier, are potentially more interesting than grays composed of black and white.

ANALOGOUS colors are intermediate hues on the color wheel and may be explained to children in terms of families of color. All colors are conceptually on a continuous spectrum, thus allowing analogous colors to be likened to a family in which, for example, a red man and a blue woman produce a violet child. Analogous colors always get along; it is the complementary colors that often disagree.

WARM and COOL refer to the psychological properties of certain colors. We normally associate reds, yellows, and oranges with warm colors, which we generally perceive as coming forward, or "advancing," in a field of color. Blues and greens are usually identified as cool, "receding" colors. The movement forward or backward of any color, however, depends entirely on its relationship to the surrounding hues. A red with a touch of blue can appear even cooler than otherwise when placed next to an orange in full saturation and may well recede behind it, while yellow with a touch of green, normally warm, will seem very cool when placed next to red-orange, which will advance. Experimentation with recession and advancement of color, in Hans Hoffman's terms "push and pull," is of special interest to the Hard-Edge and Color-Field painters.

TONALITY refers to the generalized color effect in a painting and may be achieved by children through the use of analogous colors. Even children in primary grades can identify works from Picasso's Blue or Rose periods as demonstrating tonal consistency.

COLOR WHEELS, referred to in the preceding definitions, are chiefly useful as guides to understanding color relationships. They can be, and often are, compared to compasses. And like compasses, they need further refinement if painters are to navigate successfully the treacherous waters of art toward a safe haven. No teacher should ever restrict pupils to the schematized set of relationships shown on the wheel. If color wheels have any virtue at all, it is to enlarge the options available to pupils rather than narrow them.

Despite the power, complexity, and appeal of color, it is one element that is not a primary feature of design. Many art forms are produced in which this element is lacking—black-and-white films, most forms of sculpture, many of the etching processes, drawings in which black-and-white media are used. Any design, moreover, to which color is applied before due consideration is given to the arrangement of the other elements would probably be unsuccessful. Color, then, is a complex element—at once dependent, powerful, and very moving in its sensual appeal. As for

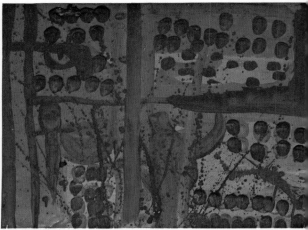

Figure 3.13 *These two paintings by children in the second grade illustrate the moving and powerful quality of color and convey the children's delight with its possibilities.*

the interests of children, teachers will discover that color has an appeal far in excess of the other elements of design.

ORGANIZATION OF THE ELEMENTS

The structure of a work of art consists of an arrangement of the elements. The design is successful when the arrangement is coherent and complete in itself so that the observers respond favorably to it and can continually return to it with interest and approval.

It would be convenient to offer a formula for the production of satisfactory designs, but, of course, if designs could be subjected to rules and regulations, art would cease to exist. The truth of the matter is that every good design is different from every other design. All artists, moreover, have unique ways of producing designs, just as every good design is distinct from all others.

We may ask, however, whether there are any common denominators in all satisfactory designs. Can we discover some general principles broad enough to allow for the variations to be found between one good design and another, but without which no design could be considered satisfactory? What, in other words, makes a design successful?

Unity of Design

The highly integrated nature of design was mentioned at the opening of this chapter. Design was described in terms of order and coherence and was made analogous to a world of stability. These are the most obvious

Figure 3.14 *Playing card redesigned by a fifth grader. Children like reversing flat, hard shapes on a large scale. They also enjoy redesigning postage stamps, flags, and dollar bills.*

characteristics that result from a successful organization of the elements, and they may be found in any successful art form, whether musical, dramatic, literary, or graphic. Each element is so arranged that it contributes to a desirable wholeness, or oneness. In a drawing, a line ripples across a certain area to be caught up elsewhere; masses and spaces set up beats and measures in a kind of visual music. Colors, textures, areas of light and shade, all contribute to the orchestration of the visual pattern. This oneness or wholeness we call "unity," and unity of design seems to be the first characteristic of all successful art.

At the risk of oversimplifying and placing too great a reliance on the intellectualization of a process that is largely one of feeling, we may analyze to some extent how unity is achieved in a visual design. Three interdependent devices, or arrangements of the elements, may be observed in a unified work of art—rhythms, centers of interest, and balance.

97

Rhythms. The controlled movements that are to be found in all good design are called rhythms. They may be established through the use of any of the elements—lines, areas of light and shade, spots of color, repetitions of masses and spaces, and textured surfaces. For example, in a particular work of art a line may ripple in one direction, then undulate in another. This movement may be momentarily halted by an obstructive brightly colored mass before it darts away elsewhere along a pathway formed by areas of light and shade. Rhythm is used by artists to give orderly movement to the manner in which our eyes move over a work of art and to control the pace at which our gaze travels.

There appear to be at least two main types of rhythms in works of art. The first has the character of a flow, and is usually achieved either by lines or through the elongation of forms. The work of El Greco is an outstanding example of this type of rhythm. The second type has the character of a beat. An element may be used in one area of an art form and repeated elsewhere, either as an exact duplication of the original theme or motif, or only reminiscent of it. In traditional paintings we are more likely to find reminiscences of an original motif than duplications.

Centers of Interest. Many works of art—perhaps the majority—are arranged so that one center of interest has paramount importance. Georgia O'Keeffe's painting *Black Abstraction* and Giacomo Balla's *Street Light* are illustrations of the use of this type of arrangement. Particularly in recent years, however, compositions have appeared in which several centers of interest are established, as in Léger's *Propellers* or Mondrian's *Color Squares in Oval,* or dispersed across the surface as in Jackson Pollack's *Autumn Rhythm.*[9]

Just as any of the elements may be used in the development of rhythms, so also may they be used in the establishment of centers of interest. A large mass centrally placed or peculiarly shaped, a bright color area, a sharp contrast between light and shade, an area more heavily textured than its surroundings, a series of lines leading to a certain place—these are some of the means at the disposal of the artist to attract and hold the observer's attention.

Balance. A third device for developing unity of design is balance. When the eye is attracted equally to the various imaginary axes of a composition, the design is considered to be in balance.

Many writers, particularly those who were connected with the Postimpressionist movement, attempted to explain balance in terms of physics, usually referring to the figure of a seesaw. Unfortunately, the

---

[9]*Black Abstraction* and *Autumn Rhythm* may be seen at the Metropolitan Museum of Art, New York; the other paintings mentioned in this paragraph may be seen at the Museum of Modern Art, New York.

concept is not quite accurate, since physical balance and aesthetic balance, while probably related, are not synonymous. Balance in aesthetics should be considered as attraction to the eye rather than as simple gravitational pull. Aesthetic balance refers to all parts of a picture—the top and bottom—and not only to the sides, as the seesaw analogy suggests. Size of the masses, moreover, while having some influence on aesthetic balance, may easily be compensated, and indeed outweighed, by a strong contrast of elements. A small, bright spot of color, for example, has great visual weight in a field of gray, as does an area of deep shade next to a highlight.

In many books on art there is still some discussion about "formal" *versus* "informal" balance. The arrangement of a composition with one well-defined center of interest placed centrally and with balancing elements placed on either side of this center, as in Duccio's *Maestà* or Fra Angelico's *Coronation of the Virgin,* is called "formal," or "symmetrical," balance. All other arrangements, such as in Miró's *Painting* or Orozco's *Barricade,* are called "informal," or "asymmetrical." In recent writings these terms appear to be disappearing from the vocabulary of design, largely, it appears, on the grounds that balance, like other aspects of design, must under all circumstances be considered in terms of the expressive needs of the artist. The distinction between formal and informal appears to be, in short, largely an artificial one reminiscent of the Post-impressionists' formulas. The more dynamic concept, emphasizing the artist's expressive requirements, will no doubt be of greater service to education.

Attraction to one kind of balance or another seems to be dictated by the ebb and flow of artistic fashion. The history of art shows us that most civilizations (including Hindu, Aztec, and Japanese) have gone through a symmetrical-design phase. The High Renaissance prized symmetry and was followed by the Mannerists, who rejected the limitations of two-point perspective. The Dadaists of the 1920's and the Abstract Expressionists of the 1950's discarded all semblance of conventional visual order; yet, during the 1960's, many Hard-Edge painters and Pop artists revived it for the simplicity and directness of its impact on the viewer.

The elements of design, then, must be unified if the resulting work is to be successful. It is possible, however, to produce a design that has all the attributes of unity but is neither interesting nor distinguished. A checkerboard, for example, has a rhythmic beat, a series of centers of interest, and a balance, but as a design it is unsatisfactory because it is monotonous and lacks tension. Likewise, a picket fence, a line of identical telephone poles, and a railway track are as uninteresting as the ticking of a clock. A stone wall, however, has great design interest because of

Variety of Design

Figure 3.15 *In this painting Edward Hopper develops subtle variations on the same basic shape. (Edward Hopper,* Early Sunday Morning, *1930. 35″ × 60″. Collection Whitney Museum of American Art.)*

the lack of similarity among its units. Even in a brick wall, in which shapes are similar, people generally prefer the variety of color, tone, and texture found at random in old, used brick.

Painters like Edward Hopper and Charles Burchfield have used house gables, telephone poles, and railway tracks as subject matter for their work. But while maintaining an overall unity, they have introduced subtle variations into the delineation of these objects, as Figure 3.15 illustrates. Mondrian has even gone so far as to use a single basic shape, the rectangle, as the foundation for his post-Cubist compositions. He has, however, varied the size, color, and relationships of this shape sufficiently to generate considerable visual interest.

While the perceptual process, as we have noted, seeks closure, or completeness, educated vision demands that in art, at least, a degree of complexity be attained if our attention is to be held. Every element, therefore, must be employed to bring about a desirable variety within unity.

This variety within unity is, in fact, an expression of life. Philosophers have postulated that design, or form, is a manifestation of people's deepest and most moving experiences. In the designs they produce, people are said to express their relationship to the universe. In *Art as Experience,* Dewey mentioned the mighty rhythms of nature—the course of the seasons and the cycle of lunar changes—together with those movements and phases of the human body, including the pulsing of the blood, appetite and satiety, and birth and death, as basic human experiences from which design may arise.

Sir Herbert Read, commenting on Platonic doctrine, tells us that

the universality of the aesthetic principle is Plato's philosophy: the fact that it pervades not only man-made things in so far as these are beautiful, but also living bodies and all plants, nature and the universe itself. It is because the harmony is all pervading, the very principle of coherence in the universe, that *this principle should be the basis of education.*[10]

Dewey, Plato, and Read would, then, seem to assert that the search for order, which the design impulse seeks to fulfill, is important not only for an individual's art work, but also as a reflection of that person's larger integrative relationship with life itself.

THE ATTITUDES AND MENTAL PROCESSES OF THE ARTIST

What do artists think and feel when they produce a design? How do they know when their work is "right"? There are divergent views on this subject. Some feel that the act of designing is a feat of intellect; some hold that it is an emotional adventure. The Gestalt psychologists point out, however,

[10]*Education Through Art,* rev. ed. (New York: Pantheon, 1958), p. 64. (italics added)

Figure 3.16 *In this self-portrait in oil crayon by a fifth grader, various shapes are used to enhance the design qualities of the image.*

that the human organism acts in totality: when people are occupied with an act of artistic expression, both their feelings and intellect are involved.

It is true that creative people tend to have a particular orientation: architects and industrial designers lean toward an intellectual approach to design, whereas painters and poets generally favor an intuitive approach. Nevertheless, both intellectually and intuitively inclined artists apparently alternate between feeling and thinking. "I feel that this should be done" is followed by "I think that this is right," or vice versa. Thus, emotion enlivens an artistic statement and intellect tempers it. Exactly when intellect is the dominant force in artistic acts, or precisely when feeling replaces intellect, is difficult to detect. Often creative people themselves are unable to analyze their approach.

While developing their design, artists manipulate the elements until they arrive at a unity and a variety of composition that satisfy them. This manipulation is performed creatively and is never the result of adherence to a formula. Whatever is produced is unique.

In producing a design for functional purposes, such as a design for a building, a piece of pottery, or an item of furniture, some consideration for practical requirements is called for. In such a case designers must let their decisions be governed by an honest respect not only for the materials used but also for the purpose to which they are put.[11] Efficiency cannot, of course, always be identical with aesthetic quality since extreme functionalism, as required in, say, high-speed airplanes, must eliminate the personal choices that are necessary to artistic acts.

Thus, one important difference between "fine" artists and industrial or commercial designers is the amount of autonomy enjoyed by the former. Unless their work is commissioned, fine artists answer only to themselves; they are members of no team, responsible to no board of directors, and subject to no limitations of time or budget imposed by others. The blessings of freedom, needless to say, place other burdens on them, but it is only through this state of freedom that artists periodically produce works that are unique, authentic, and innovative.

PRINCIPLES OF DESIGN

Art does not lend itself readily to rules and regulations, and any statement concerning principles must be outlined with caution.[12] Nevertheless, it

[11]See Robert C. Niece, *Art: An Approach* (Dubuque, Iowa: Brown, 1963).

[12]"The emergence of many systems of theory dealing with formal elements in art is, I believe, an indication of a not altogether healthy state in art education. In periods of confusion as to standards . . . the purely formal theory seeks certainty and safety."—Robert Iglehart, "Theories of Design: An Evaluation," *Art Education Today*, 1941 (New York: Teachers College, 1941), p. 26. Iglehart goes on to point out that in clinging to the "safety" of theory, the artist can no longer explore. Ralph M. Pearson, in *The New Art Education*, rev. ed. (New York: Harper & Row, 1953), shows the unfortunate results that occur when the so-called classic or scientific principles are applied blindly by children.

Figure 3.17 *In this combine painting Rauschenberg has mixed three-dimensional objects with two-dimensional forms. Children respond enthusiastically to mixed-media approaches. (Canyon, 1959. 86½″ × 70″ × 23″. Courtesy of Leo Castelli Gallery. Collection Mr. and Mrs. Michael Sonnabend, New York/ Paris.)*

is helpful from time to time to set down principles of design. There are dangers, of course, attendant on the enunciation of general principles. Should learners come to rely on the principles they have developed from their experiences to such an extent that they cease to look for new, deeper truths in art, their thinking will become stale. Whatever universal beliefs we may hold about art must, it seems, be subject to continued revision and further inquiry. General truths about art, in short, must always be regarded in a pragmatic light. Following William James, we should say to ourselves: "This principle appears to be true about all art because at the present it works for us. Tomorrow the principle may not be adequate because by then we shall have enjoyed new experiences and gained new insights into design."

The current attitude toward honesty in the use of materials reflects what James advocated. If we are still to hold to the idea that artists must respect the integrity of their materials and work from the accepted definitions of painting and sculpture, what are we to say of George Sugarman, who paints his sculpture, or of Marisol, who adds drawing to the same combination? Should we adhere to the "rules" and reject their work, or should we keep ourselves open to the element of surprise and amusement when confronted with such combinations? Obviously, today's children should be prepared for the art of their time, and there is no reason why there cannot be room in their life for both the "integrity" of a fresco by Michelangelo and the multi-media combines of Robert Rauschenberg's work. (Bear in mind that in the opinion of many of his contemporaries, Michelangelo violated the integrity of the human figure through his distortion of human proportions.)

Each learner arrives at a personal statement of principles that reflects personal experience and its resulting insights. If the pupil has worked thoughtfully with all the elements of design and has mastered, with some degree of success, problems related to unity and variety of composition, two principles of design somewhat like the following may be arrived at:

Every successful design exhibits unity of composition.

Within its unity, every successful design exhibits variety in the use of its elements.

The learner who has studied and worked with many materials will probably enunciate a third principle:

In a successful design the character of the materials must be utilized for ends that are consistent with the nature or function of the final product.

The learner who has studied and produced some functional objects might state:

The successful design of a utilitarian object is largely governed by the function for which it is produced.

In considering experiences with all types of design activities the learner will probably advance a principle as follows:

All successful design in art bears the stamp of the personality of its creator.

To these principles, some readers will wish to add others that have emerged from their own thinking. No matter what principles one may formulate, however, they should be employed only as temporary working hypotheses.

ACTIVITIES FOR THE READER

The preceding discussion about design consists of a verbal and intellectual analysis of a process that is visual and, in considerable measure, intuitive.

At best, such a discussion can afford the reader only a partial insight into the nature of design concerns. It would be well, therefore, for the reader to attempt the production of some works to experience directly what designing actually involves. Accordingly, several activities that the reader may try are described below.

ACTIVITIES EMPHASIZING LINE

1. Select black chalk and a sheet of inexpensive paper, such as newsprint, measuring about 18 by 24 inches and having a natural color. Play some stimulating music and begin to draw a line, not to depict an object but rather to develop a nonobjective arrangement. Draw the line freely, without attempting to produce a particular effect. Repeat the operation, but in this second case consider the variety of the line. See that it swoops and glides, ripples and pauses. Repeat again, this time thinking of the unity of the composition produced. Play music of a completely different mood and produce some further compositions in line.

2. Cover your hand with cloth or paper. With a short pencil draw an object under observation, such as a park bench, a person, or a flower. "Blind" contour drawing of this type tends to place more emphasis on line than on any other element. Analyze your handling of edges and do not worry about the relationship of parts. After doing several such drawings, select the most successful and draw it again, referring this time to your paper to "connect" parts to wholes. Continue this exercise, progressing to more complex forms—fruit to houses, boxes to people, stools to bicycles.

3. Study the paintings and sculpture of such recognized masters as Picasso, Rembrandt, and Henry Moore. Make a line analysis of one of the works. Such an analysis should emphasize the main flows of line in the composition without copying the objects themselves. Pen and ink, soft lead pencil, and crayon are suitable media.[13]

4. Take a subject that is small, such as a bit of crumpled paper or nuts and bolts. Using a brush, try to blow the detail up on a sheet of mural paper that measures at least 3 by 4 feet. Consider the space between the lines and how the figure (the object) relates to the ground (the surrounding space).

ACTIVITIES EMPHASIZING MASS AND SPACE

1. Cut some rectangular shapes from paper of various tones but generally neutral in color. Move these shapes on a piece of white cardboard until a satisfactory arrangement of the masses and spaces has been found, then glue them into place. Using similar shapes, drop them from above the cardboard so that they fall in an accidental pattern. Continue this procedure until you come upon an arrangement that pleases you. Compare the "found" design with the planned one. Which do you prefer and why? Does the accident offer an element of surprise that the planned design seems to need?

2. Take toothpicks or balsa strips and glue them together to form a non-

---

[13]See Ray Bethers, *Composition in Pictures,* 2nd ed. (New York: Pitman, 1962), for some interesting analyses of the elements in pictorial composition.

objective three-dimensional construction having interesting internal space relationships.

3. Using pieces of cardboard or wood scraps, make the same type of construction described in 2. Concentrate on the way flat planes work with internal space relationships—confirming them, allowing one space to flow into another, and so on. If this sculptural approach to mass and space has caught your interest, try combining the lines of the balsa strips with the planes of the cardboard. You can further articulate your space by connecting one area to another with string and by cutting the cardboard for a colored-glass or cellophane insert.

4. Study the drawings and sculpture of such artists as Maillol, Lachaise, Lehmbruck, Zorach, and Brancusi for the manner in which they have arranged masses and spaces. Make a drawing that emphasizes these elements.

5. Work a mass of clay (of about 8 lbs.) into a good-sized block. With simple tools, scoop out sections of the clay and then note how light and shade can be manipulated. When you have established a relationship between shallow and deep areas and the surface of the clay, take a flashlight and study how the character of your work changes with the light source. Think of this in relation to architecture as well as to sculpture. Notice how this problem overlaps with the category below, light and shade.

6. To investigate line and space, try the exploding design. Divide a sheet of dark paper into sections and place the sections on a white background. Observe how pulling the sections apart creates everything from a thin white line to a dominant segment of white. Do this also with curving lines that bisect the paper. (See Figure 3.7.)

ACTIVITIES EMPHASIZING LIGHT AND SHADE

1. Paint six or seven containers found around the house (cereal boxes, tea tins, cigar boxes, soup cans) a single unifying tone of white. After grouping these before you on a table, draw them with black chalk on gray paper, using white chalk for highlights. Let the color of the paper play through for middle tones and reserve the white and black for the extreme values. Try one view with the flat side of your chalk and another with the point, carefully building your tones by massing strokes and lines.

2. Place the three pieces of sculpture produced to illustrate problems of mass and space in the path of a strong light. Manipulate them until the shadows and highlights on the objects themselves, together with the shadows cast from one object to another, form an acceptable unity. Observe the pattern of the shadows cast on a light surface behind the sculpture.

3. Analyze the work of several well-known artists, such as Cézanne, O'Keeffe, and De Chirico, for their arrangements of light and shade. Make an analytical drawing of one of the paintings to emphasize the use of these elements.

4. Project a slide of a group of buildings on a sheet of light paper. Forget that you are dealing with buildings and fill in the image with dark and light patterns. As a follow-up, take your sketch outdoors and see if this exercise in concentration on pattern and mass and light and shade has aided you in seeing (and drawing) an actual building.

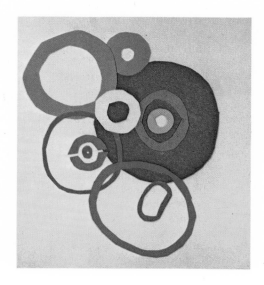

Figure 3.18 *Example of a design in which variety is obtained from a single geometric shape. Grade 4.*

ACTIVITIES EMPHASIZING TEXTURE

1. Cut pieces from printed pages that utilize various kinds and arrangements of type. Paste the pieces on cardboard or paper so that an interesting textural arrangement is developed.
2. With pen and ink draw a continuous line in such a way that enclosed spaces are formed. By using dots, crossed lines, small circles, and the like, create a design having an interesting textural quality.
3. Repeat 2 using a sheet of aluminum foil, but this time merely press the foil with a pen.
4. Roll out a slab of clay and cut it into various shapes—square, round, rectangular, triangular. Create textural patterns on the surface by pressing found objects (coins, scissors, nuts, wood scraps) into the clay. With softer materials such as sponge, burlap, combs, and string, make patterns even closer to the surface. Use your imagination to think of items other than the ones suggested above.
5. Crumple a piece of paper and spray it with black paint from one angle only. Let the paper dry and press it flat. Notice the startling dimensional quality of the texture.
6. Create a collage that changes texturally in one direction from glassy smoothness to extreme roughness. Feel it with your eyes closed and compare it with those of your classmates. Vary the feel by adjusting the size and location of your textural samples.

ACTIVITIES EMPHASIZING COLOR

1. Paint freely with a large brush, noting the apparent changes in hues as one color is placed next to another. How do the adjacent colors affect each other? Cut out various-sized windows in black paper and move them about your painting, noticing the variety of compositions and color interactions that are possible.
2. Dampen a sheet of heavy white drawing paper and drip tempera paint or watercolors so that different hues run and blend. Note the new colors so formed.

3. Study the work of such great colorists as Rembrandt, Tintoretto, Rubens, Van Gogh, Seurat, and Matisse. Study the color effects obtained by Hard-Edge and Op Art painters.

4. Join the class in bringing in a swatch of color you think is red. When placed next to one another, the swatches of paper, paint, and cloth will produce a surprising range of tone and value in a subtly modulated monochromatic collage. Try other colors as well, including black and white. Notice in each case how the surface texture contributes to the effect.

5. Cut out six squares of any single color and paste on them circles of six different colors. Notice how each of the circular background colors changes the nature of the constant foreground color. Is color a fixed entity or does it have relative characteristics?

ACTIVITIES RELATED TO FUNCTION AND TO ADEQUATE USE OF MATERIALS AND TOOLS

1. Collect for study pictures of "families" of similar objects such as automobiles, chairs, yachts, and kitchen equipment. Compare one brand with another from the point of view of function. How does a Jaguar car, for example, compare with a Buick or a Jeep in this respect? What concessions have the manufacturers made to "style" at the expense of function? Why have they done so? To what extent are they justified in so doing? Start a scrapbook of "horrors," which concentrates on the most poorly designed products.

2. Find a number of objects in which a certain material has been processed to resemble another, such as cardboard to resemble leather, or plastic to look like woven cloth. Why has the manufacturer resorted to such practices? What are the opinions of designers and critics about them?

OTHER ACTIVITIES

Emphasizing analogies. Working from photos or observation of familiar objects, draw another object that the first one appears to resemble. Thus a fence may remind you of teeth, a fireplug of a Martian, and a rock of a loaf of bread.

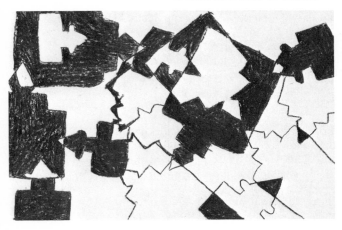

Figure 3.19 *The overlapping shapes of an India-ink bottle treated in black and white show a balance of positive and negative areas. Grade 4.*

Emphasizing positive and negative patterns of dark and light. Draw an overall pattern using the shape of a common object like scissors, tableware, or an ink bottle. Where the forms overlap, switch back and forth from black to white, so that the objects are fragmented and the viewer becomes engaged in reestablishing the form of the object (see Figure 3.19).

Emphasizing variety within a single form. Select any geometric shape as a working module. Using any media you like, create an arrangement based on your shape, obtaining variety in the design by adjustment of the size or color of the shape, by overlapping, and other effects (see Figure 3.18).

Emphasizing change in a single pattern. Design, cut, and paste on paper a simple pattern of dark and light geometric shapes. As a window, cut out of a piece of paper curved vertical shapes that do not repeat themselves. Move the cutout over the design from right to left and notice how the patterns change as the shapes grow and diminish in size.

Their own interests and experiences will often provide children with highly suggestive themes, as in this chalk drawing of a playground. Grade 4.

DEVELOPING A PROGRAM
OF STUDIES IN ART

4

The central task of curriculum development is to (a) anticipate what levels of learning groups of children may be capable of achieving in relation to the common goals for the teaching of art and (b) select curriculum components to provide the experiences that can bring forth the intended learnings. Whether the curriculum components are in the form of studio activities, reading or observation, discussion or analysis, the teacher's attention must be fixed on the teaching goals. The activities selected are valuable only to the degree that they provide experiences through which the intended goals are realized.*

WHO DESIGNS THE ART PROGRAM?

Procedures vary from one educational system to another as to the delegation of responsibility for developing the art program. In some systems curriculum makers and general administrators at the highest levels of administration are concerned with art education. These officials may even supervise the writing of courses of study and ensure that the courses, once designed, are effective. In the past, some city and state educational authorities have set down exact statements of what to do from fall to spring, or during January, or for Easter, or in preparation for the Fourth of July. The teacher who attempts to follow directions closely usually discovers, however, that much of the work prescribed may be unsuitable for the particular class. It is difficult, if not impossible, for anyone who is remote from the classroom situation to prescribe an adequately detailed art program.

*From Manuel Barkan, "Art in the Elementary Schools," in Jerome J. Hausman, ed., *Report of the Commission on Art Education* (Washington, D.C.: National Art Education Association, 1965), p. 81.

General administrators, especially in parts of the United States, Canada, and the United Kingdom, are giving tangible evidence that they accept this fact. The former tendency for central offices to set down a detailed program of art has largely changed in recent decades. Pamphlets and booklets about art are still published by large administrative bodies in the United States, but these publications now deal with the broad aspects of art education—philosophy, general pedagogy, and sometimes a few general directions for the production of two- and three-dimensional art forms.[1] Mere hints about how to perform a project rather than detailed, step-by-step instruction are offered. In this way the teacher not only is encouraged to gain information about materials and processes through first-hand experience and exploration but also is reminded that art experiences demand such exploration, as opposed to the slavish copying of directions. In Canada there appears to be a tendency for provincial departments of education to provide not one but a series of publications for the schools of a province. In some respects these bulletins are more detailed than those of United States origin, but they do not prescribe a program to be followed rigorously.

In most educational systems today, only those directly engaged in art instruction—the local teaching and supervisory staff—attempt to determine in any detail the nature of the program to be followed. If the local art supervisors, or consultants, and school principals are up-to-date, they will allow the art program to develop according to a number of educational circumstances peculiar to the classroom in which art is taught. To ensure that this idea prevails locally, some state departments of education are issuing attractive pamphlets urging that superintendents of education rely on the local art specialists and teachers to devise art programs to suit local conditions.

Classroom teachers are the key figures in the development of an effective art program, for only they can know the needs and capabilities of the students who are to benefit from the program. The teachers' concerns are both philosophical and psychological in determining what values to seek and in deciding what can reasonably be expected of the pupils. On these values and expectations they build an art program, working in concert with local art consultants.

---

[1]A few of the more interesting elementary guides to examine are: *Art Curriculum Project for Mifflin Schools 1–6,* prepared under a United States Office of Education Title III Grant, 1969; *Art in the Elementary School* (Miami, Fla.: Dade County Public Schools, 1965); *Art: Creative Experiences* (Long Beach, Calif.: Long Beach Unified School District, 1962); *Art Teaching Guide: Hawaii—K–12* (Honolulu: Division of Instruction, 1960); Manuel Barkan and Laura Chapman, *Guidelines for Art Instruction Through Television for the Elementary Schools* (Bloomington, Ind.: National Center for School and College Television, 1967); and *The Visual Arts in Illinois* (Springfield, Ill.: Office of the Superintendent of Public Instruction, 1969).

A large part of the success of any art program depends on the type of working relationship established between the classroom teacher and the art consultant. In one school system,[2] an attempt was made to determine the nature of this important relationship by varying not only the *structure* of the relationship (art teaching as opposed to art consulting) but also the *ratio* of teachers and schools to art specialists. In some situations the art personnel did all the teaching on a scheduled basis; in some they served as advisors rather than teachers; and in other cases they maintained a balance between scheduled teaching and nonscheduled "open," or flexible, use of time. The strong and weak points of these combinations are described below.

The Teacher–Consultant Relationship

Scheduled Teaching. This approach lends itself to systematic and structured program planning. The art teacher who can count on a planned number of art sessions per year can teach sequences of activities with the assurance that certain minimal programing will be carried out and continuity will be given to the activities. The disadvantage in scheduled teaching lies in the tendency of the classroom teacher to abandon the role of art teacher, leaving the burden of the entire program on the art specialist. If the classroom teacher is prepared to offer follow-up activities between the art teacher's classes, the possibilities of the program are greatly extended.

Open, Flexible Consulting. A system of flexible consulting assumes that the classroom teacher accepts the primary responsibility of conducting the art program and calls on the art teacher to solve problems that require special help. It is a good concept in theory, but it does not always work in practice. Often those teachers who do not place a value on art activity never call on the art teacher, while others, who do not need help, call on the art teacher's services either to bolster an already strong program or to supply themselves with a "free" period.

The dilemma posed by these two situations would suggest that no relationship is going to work unless the classroom teacher assumes a planning role in working with the art teacher/consultant. The fact remains that the majority of art instruction in the United States and Canada is still carried out by the classroom teacher. The principal and art specialist should impress classroom teachers with the importance of the art program in the school curriculum and offer opportunities for improving their skills and attitudes. Until the public schools have reached the enlightened stage of having one art teacher for each elementary school, the art specialist and classroom teacher must work together to provide the children with the range of art activity to which they are entitled.

[2] Newton Public Schools, Newton, Mass.

KEY DECISIONS IN PLANNING AN ART PROGRAM

The development of the program of studies must, like other aspects of art education, be considered a creative endeavor. It requires the planner to take account of such factors as (1) the learning situations related to the goals; (2) media, tools, and techniques; (3) the social setting of the class; and (4) standards of accomplishment as they relate to growth expectancies. As the art program unfolds in the classroom, the successful teacher learns to anticipate difficulties in carrying out the program and is prepared to employ alternate procedures. No plan should be so rigid that it does not allow for change at any point.

Selection of Themes

The opening chapter pointed out that although a mature artist may select from a whole range of experience particular themes suitable for expressive acts, such is not usually the case with children. Children who are told to do "anything they like" in art often are reluctant to express themselves artistically, simply because no specific stimulus prompts this expression. The teacher should provide a limited number of specific stimuli strong enough to motivate expression, but the pupils must have full freedom to select those aspects of the ideas that interest them. The problems[3] and themes chosen by the teacher, although they may be limited to a specific rousing experience, must always allow the children to select their own subject matter. Thus a distinction is made between activities that focus on *perceptual situations,* which are most often planned by the teacher, and "thematic," personally expressive pictorialization, which most often comes from the life experience of the child. For example, the teacher might provide the theme "We Went to the Aquarium" for a class of third graders, but the expression of this theme might range from a painting of an octopus to a drawing of a group of children listening to an official of the institution.

Selection of Media, Tools, and Techniques

Just as controlled freedom appears desirable in the child's selection of a subject for expression, so may it often be recommended in choosing media and tools. Most themes can be given expression in a number of different media and with a variety of tools. The trip to the aquarium could be depicted in a painting by means of watercolor, tempera paint, chalk, or wax crayon; it could be shown in sculpture employing paper or clay; it could be developed in a textile design, carved in linoleum, or even

---

[3]The term "problem" refers to an art-learning situation as opposed to picture-making. (The design and drawing activities at the end of Chapter 3 are "problems.")

woven in colored yarns. Obviously, the simultaneous use of all these media and their attendant tools would create an impossible teaching and administrative burden in the classroom. But because each of these materials provides valuable educative experience for most children, the art program should be developed so that a wide range of media and tools may eventually be selected for classroom use.

Another area of decision-making is that of technique. In working with each medium the chidren are able to use more than one method of manipulation. They may stipple with a paintbrush as well as employ it in a stroking fashion.[4] They may use thin paint over a "resist" area where wax has been placed. They may "add to" a basic body of clay or "draw out" from it.[5] They may work with or without an inner support for the clay mass.

Generally the child will have time to use only one technique in a single art session, but in the evaluation period the teacher may describe other techniques for handling materials. For instance, the child who has worked with wood should know that printmaking can be accomplished with vegetables, cardboard, and linoleum as well; that a print can be treated as a single image, as a repeat pattern, or as a dominant pattern that may be printed over a picture clipped from a magazine, a collage, or a painted surface; that one effect can be achieved when two plates are made for color separation, and an entirely different effect will result when a single plate is moved around for an overlapping image. Multiple solutions apply also to activities in sculpture, drawing, and painting.

In preparing the art program, the teacher must look closely at the social requirements of the class. Should the art work be performed by a group, providing valuable social learning or by an individual, providing valuable experience at independent work? Sometimes a type of work like mural-making, a light show, or puppetry demands that the children pool their efforts to ensure the project's success.[6] Other art activities demand solitary efforts, in which a group of people cannot profitably work together.

The Social Setting

Finally, the teacher must make decisions about standards, based on expectations according to age. How "excellent" must the children's work be?[7] Children are experimenters, and sometimes as a result of experiments the artistic quality of their work deteriorates. How much should one encourage experimentation at the expense of an artistic standard? Although unnecessary untidiness, undue lack of completeness, and similar

Standards of Accomplishment

[4]See Chapter 7 for a description of drawing and painting techniques.
[5]See Chapter 9 for a discussion of work in clay.
[6]See Chapter 12 for a discussion of group activities.
[7]See Chapter 18 for a discussion of the appraisal of children's work in art.

shortcomings in artistic production are detrimental to the finished expression, too great an emphasis on neatness may not only inhibit experimentation, but may also damage artistic standards themselves. The selection of suitable standards is perhaps the most crucial decision of the art program. Criteria will vary with the task. Obviously there will be greater consensus on the success in centering a pot than in the more subjective areas of picture-making.

The Child's Role in Decision-Making

Children who are subject to the carefully developed strategy of a teacher are evidently capable of making a wise choice in their art activities. Some years ago, an experiment was conducted in which children were allowed to participate in the development of an art program.[8] At that time, many teachers were expected to follow a fairly rigid art program, often designed by a central committee. However, in this four-year experiment, every child in a representative experimental group of pupils from the first to the sixth grade was allowed a certain freedom to select an art activity. The choices that the pupils could make were necessarily restricted so that the teachers could offer adequate stimulation and assistance.

At the beginning of the experiment only two choices each of theme, tools, media, and technique were open to the children. Thus a child in the first grade could, for example, either work at picture-making in paint or construct objects out of boxes. Soon, however, four choices were allowed, and this range of choice was maintained in all classes for the remainder of the four-year study. The teachers were careful in arranging the choices that the children could make at any one time. The four available activities always included at least one involving two-dimensional work, while the other three might require work in three dimensions. Occasionally, activities involving historical or theoretical work, such as a study of local architecture or a survey of the output of local painters, were included, particularly in the higher grades. Also in the higher grades, group activities were frequently introduced.

The results of the four-year testing period showed that the children had selected for themselves a broad and comprehensive art program. Every child had included both two- and three-dimensional work and, when offered, activities involving both individual and group effort. From time to time the children had even selected work of a theoretical or historical nature. A comparison of the art output of the children in the experimental group with that of the pupils who were more restricted revealed that the freedom of the experimental program appeared to have beneficial effects. The experimental group's work exhibited a greater

---

[8] In the Powell River and District Schools, British Columbia, Canada, 1940–43, during which time one of the authors was the Supervisor of Art for this area. About 150 pupils in grades 1 through 6 participated. No kindergartens operated at that time in the publicly supported educational system of British Columbia.

variety of techniques, a wider range of subject matter, and surprisingly, superior qualities of design.[9]

It was concluded, therefore, that children should be given considerable freedom to select their art activities. Under conditions of freedom, modified only by a necessary pedagogical strategy, they appeared to select a reasonably broad program of art and to improve the artistic standard of their output.

INFLUENCES ON DECISION-MAKING

As the development of the art program progresses, a variety of choices in many different situations will be apparent to both pupils and teacher. The best choice in any given case is more likely to be taken if the following influences are given adequate attention.[10]

Every major area of learning has developed traditional attitudes and subject matter as well as a series of activities and a historical background peculiar to itself. The traditional attitudes of art—that is, freedom of expression with respect to subject matter and design, willingness to work to capacity, and the like—have been discussed previously. An earlier chapter also has suggested that the sources of art have remained constant throughout the centuries, in the sense that the subject matter has always reflected the reactions of the artist to the environment.

The Tradition of Art

The activities that have engaged people in this capacity are similarly traditional. In the educational background of many artists will be found experience in both two- and three-dimensional art forms, although most artists tend to reach eminence in just one form. Expression in drawing and painting is often more powerful if the artist has enjoyed some experience in three-dimensional output. Sculpture and ceramics also have tended to be more successful if the artist has worked in two-dimensional fields. Every child should thus be given an opportunity to produce pictures as well as various types of sculpture and modeling.

Study of the historical background of art cannot begin too early in the elementary school. Even kindergarten children have much to gain merely by being exposed to carefully chosen works. Naturally, the limited understanding of the children will restrict their insight into the nature of the work on view. If, however, examples are related to the children's

[9]This experiment was also conducted in grades 7 through 12, with similar results.

[10]Some criteria that can help determine the adequacy of the teacher's plans are listed in Harold G. Shane and Wilbur A. Yauch, *Creative School Administration: In Elementary and Junior High Schools* (New York: Holt, Rinehart and Winston, 1954), p. 273. Although these criteria refer to education in general, rather than to art in particular, the art teacher will find them interesting.

Figure 4.1 *The comparison of Henry Moore's drawing* Two Seated Figures in a Shelter *with his sculpture* Family Group *illustrates the value to the artist of having experience in both two- and three-dimensional art forms. (City Art Gallery, Leeds, England; Collection, The Museum of Modern Art, New York. A. Conger Goodyear Fund. 1948–49. Bronze (cast 1950), 59¼ × 46½", at base 45 × 29⅞".)*

current expressive work, a beginning may be made in acquainting them with their vast cultural heritage in art.[11]

So flexible is the subject matter of art that it may be accommodated to a learner of practically any age, personality type, or experience. Competent teachers realize that just as no two children are alike, so also classes or groups of children differ. A program of art suitable for the class of a year ago may not be suitable this year.

Readiness of the Learners

The previous educational background of children has an important bearing on the art program. Sometimes a group of children may have enjoyed little creative work in art, but instead may have been taught according to dictatorial methods. Then the teacher's task must be to help the pupils think for themselves and not place too much reliance on their teacher. Other children may have had an exceptionally rich background of experience, in which case the teacher must offer a more challenging program. In former classes, children may not have been given sufficient group work in art, with the result that they are at a loss as to how to proceed in an activity involving a number of individuals. Other children may not have mastered sufficiently the technique of working individually. Some children may have suffered from an overemphasis on certain types of art work at the expense of other types. A former teacher, for example, may have laid undue emphasis on "craft," or three-dimensional, projects at the cost of providing opportunities in picture-making. The teacher must be prepared continually to modify the nature of the program so that a balance of art experiences is offered to the children.

The capacities of the children to learn will obviously influence the art program. Variations in intelligence, contrary to popular opinion in some quarters, may affect art output as well as general learning about art. Slow learners in academic fields of study are often also slow to profit from art activities—especially when they have an insensitive teacher—and because of this their program must be arranged so that the wrong things are not expected from them. Intelligent children, on the other hand, will usually profit from art work that continually challenges their creative energies. Children who vary in temperament also require different and carefully arranged degrees of stimulation.

The needs, capacities, and dispositions of the children, therefore, demand diversification of art programs. In addition, it is strongly recommended that the children be encouraged from time to time to select the activities that most appeal to them, even at the kindergarten level. As the children grow older and gain more experience with art media they require an increasing latitude. All art programs should be designed to allow the children some voice in the activities.

[11]Chapter 17 discusses in detail the development of an appreciation of art.

The effectiveness of any art program is also linked to the skill and preparedness of the teacher. The teacher of art who knows materials and tools and the techniques associated with them can provide pupils with adequate assistance and sponsor an efficient and stimulating program. Teachers who feel inadequate in handling some tools and materials can readily acquire skill through practice after school hours, often with the assistance of a supervisor or another teacher. The feeling that "I can teach a little picture-making, but when it comes to crafts, I'm hopeless," soon disappears after relatively little experience with crafts.

The necessarily limited experience of beginning teachers will tend to restrict the art program until they enlarge their knowledge of media and methods. As time goes on they should make it their business to explore more and more activities that can be added to the art program. Attendance at art workshops and conventions, together with the continued assistance of an art consultant, if one is available in the school system, will help young teachers to expand their capabilities in art.

A teacher should have had *some* experience with any medium, tool, or technique to be introduced into the classroom. Even if it is a simple medium such as wax crayon, the teacher should experiment with it beforehand, however briefly. The various types of paint and the materials lending themselves to three-dimensional work, such as clay or folded paper, should similarly be tested and subjected to experiment. In this way the teacher not only anticipates difficulties in the classroom, but also gains insight into the potentialities of the media. Preparation of this nature is as necessary for the teacher as reading a poem, working out a mathematical problem, or performing an experiment in science before presenting it to the class.

Sometimes a teacher will develop enthusiasm for a specific type of work, such as the silk-screen process or wood sculpture. This enthusiasm is often catching, so that many pupils may also take delight in the activity. When such is the case, teaching tends to be inspiring. Enthusiasms in teaching are to be encouraged, but two cautions are in order. First, the enthusiasm should arise in relation to an activity that is of reasonable importance in art education and that is suited to the pupils' level of development. If painting in polymer catches the attention of a sixth-grade teacher, the subsequent classroom activities could be extremely practical and beneficial. If making shell-work pictures of old-fashioned ladies and roses becomes a passion with the teacher, it is better to suppress this enthusiasm and present other work in the classroom. Second, it is common sense for the teacher to guard against inflicting any enthusiasm for particular work beyond the point of interest and capability of the class. No matter how strong the feeling for the chosen activity, the teacher should always make adequate provision for optional activities.

A strong but subtle influence on an art program is that of the teacher's artistic taste. Exactly what good taste is and how it is acquired are difficult factors to determine.[12] Just as we all enjoy different kinds of cooking, so also do we all exhibit different preferences in art. There is a minimum aesthetic standard, however, by which each of us determines whether or not what we observe or produce is art. Those who recognize this standard will not countenance that which is shoddy, insincere, or trite. A reasonably good standard of taste can be acquired partly through an acquaintance with good art and can be improved by attempts to produce art. The development of artistic taste is said to begin in childhood and to continue throughout one's life. Some people seem to improve their taste more readily than others, but all can do so to a considerable degree.

If the teacher's taste is reasonably sensitive and aesthetic standards sufficiently high, every art activity in the classroom will tend to be acceptable, and praise or some other manner of emphasis should be given to the admirable aspects of the students' work. The teacher's taste, influenced by personality and cultural background, will also be reflected in critical comments on the works of art selected for study. Such decisions set the aesthetic "tone" of teaching and have ensuing effects on the pupils.

The necessity of maintaining high standards of taste in general education has never been stated more forcefully than by Clive Bell:

> If standards go, civilization goes. To hear people talk you might suppose there had never been such things as dark ages. . . . Besides taste in art there is such a thing as taste in life; a power of discerning and choosing in life's minor matters; and on this taste in life, this sense of the smaller values, is apt to flourish that subtler and more esthetic sense. Without this taste no civilization can exist.[13]

Manifestly the art program is greatly affected by the school setting. The climate of opinion in the school with respect to art education, the classroom accommodation, the supplies and equipment available, will all have a bearing on what the teacher can hope to accomplish. A wide variation exists in these respects from one locality to another. Sometimes, but fortunately not often, the school authorities may be of the "old school" type and resent monetary expenditures on anything but the most "basic" subjects. In some schools, virtually no special provision is made in classrooms for art, and little money is allocated for the purchase of supplies and equipment. Occasionally the teacher is in a school where the schedule is inflexible, and art has to be taught at certain periods and deal with specific themes. By integrating art with other subjects the teacher may offer even more art than by adhering to the hourly period once a week.

The School Setting

No matter how discouraging the situation may be, with determination and ingenuity, the teacher can always find a way to develop a

---

[12]This topic will be discussed in greater detail in Chapter 17.
[13]Clive Bell, *Since Cézanne* (New York: Harcourt Brace Jovanovich, 1922), pp. 149–50.

Figure 4.2 *If few materials are available for the teacher to use as a stimulus for subject matter, then perhaps the teacher and pupils can bring in objects from the home and the environment. Here a child studies an object on a still-life table composed of a varied assortment of toys, antiques, junk, billboard segments, and the like. (Photo by Roger Graves.)*

reasonably acceptable art program. If themes are specified, then the children must become sufficiently conversant with them and excited about them to express themselves in a creative manner. If sufficient supplies cannot be purchased, then they must make use of scrap materials. Various conveniences may be built in the classroom at little or no cost. Although an initial lack of supplies and accommodation may limit an art program, these conditions need not prevent art from being taught.[14]

The Community Setting

As has been pointed out previously, the substance of art is to be found in the immediate environment. Artists have invariably discovered subject matter in those experiences peculiar to the part of the world they know. In this sense, art is always local. The art of children, of course, will always be greatly affected by their community, and this is fitting. Only thus will their art activities rest on the sole reliable foundation for aesthetic expression.

In the past, some teachers have felt that art should arise from an event romantically remote from the humdrum local scene. Children living in an eastern seaboard city might draw pictures of the Rocky Mountains, and those in a rural community might depict the skyscrapers of some mythical metropolis. The strength and vitality of children's expression do not, in the long run, arise from objects and events remote from their lives. Such attributes are more likely to come from their own immediate

[14]Subsequent chapters will indicate how a teacher may improve on conditions for art education with regard both to supplies and accommodation. See Chapters 5 and 7–11.

environment. It is the teacher's responsibility to encourage artistic expression derived from personal experience.

The community served by the school not only can provide much of the subject matter for an art program but can perhaps supply materials

A *"My neighborhood,"* *grade 2*

Figure 4.3 *The community setting provides rich subject matter for children's art.* **A** *is part of a mural done in tempera;* **B** *is a drawing done in chalk.*

B *"Playground,"* *grade 3*

for expression. In the most populous cities any original local materials have largely ceased to exist, and supplies must be purchased or gathered from scrap. Business and industry can provide various kinds of surplus scrap material such as cartons, wood trimmings, and cardboard tubing. In rural areas suitable woods for sculpture, clays for modeling and ceramics, grasses for weaving, and so on, may be found locally. These materials, of course, should be exploited fully, and their use will have bearing on the development of the art program.

Sometimes the general character of the community will influence the art program. In Oregon, the author observed a far greater use of wood in the art program than in Miami, where sand casting seemed to be of greater popularity. Communities in which there is a well-defined interest in local history might again influence some of the activities in the art program. In certain locations, ethnic groups still maintain a few traditional arts and crafts of which they are proud.

The teacher and students will do well also to study physical aspects of the community, noting distinguishing characteristics of trees, architecture, public squares, and places of recreation. Perhaps the class can go on a field trip to observe the community. Is the area hilly or flat, old or contemporary, cluttered or open? Answers to such questions can provide rich teaching material for the art program.

PLANNED <u>VERSUS</u> IMPROVISED PROGRAMS

The art teacher today has a great number of options as to how to approach curriculum planning. A basic decision to be made is whether to take a planning approach or an improvised approach; to completely avoid planning in the hope that spontaneity and improvisation among the students will determine the course of the year's work, or to take the initiative in deciding what the priorities must be, establishing certain plans as "organizing centers" intended to bring about specific art learning.

Since the class time allocated to art is generally limited, most teachers want to be selective as to the activities used, setting their own priorities according to their long-range goals. For example, a teacher may decide that although blowing paint through straws is fun and the results are occasionally exciting to look at, an extra session on contour drawing would move the children closer to a goal of increasing their ability to observe analytically. This book provides ample material for various kinds of planned programs. An example of a planning approach, recommended as an "organizing center" for the unit on color, is given in Table 4.1. This plan considers the character of the children and what can be expected of them in art before the content and activities of the program are decided on.

Table 4.1

PLANNING A PROGRAM ON COLOR FOR THE THIRD AND FOURTH GRADES*

Character of the child:
The pupil begins to ask for reasons; requires that praise be specific; is beginning the process of self-evaluation; is capable of increased attention; sticks to own group and sex; enjoys group activities; is a collector; is physically coordinated; has ambivalent attitude toward adults.

Expectancies in art:
The student will be able to master most art processes involving physical manipulation; sharply increase color perception; relate art vocabulary to art problems; enjoy work with a group in making murals, dioramas, and other group activities; recognize formal elements of design.

Content	Activities	Materials	Art References
1. *Color:* The distinction between primary and secondary colors	Creation of a design, based on a still life, that utilizes primary and secondary colors	Tempera	
2. The meaning of tints and shades	Creation of a design based on flower forms, using one color as a base and shades or tints of that color on top	Tempera	Cubist paintings
3. The emotive power of color	Creation of a nonobjective painting that reflects a mood or state of mind	Watercolor	Kandinsky, German Expressionists Film: *Fiddle-de-dee*
4. How color neighbors affect each other	Formation of a large group collage from samples of an assigned color chosen by each child	Colored paper, clippings from advertisements, and fabrics	
5. Difference in function between mixing colors and selecting colors	Matching of colors in a painting, first with paint, then by pasting colors from magazine advertisements	Magazine advertisements and tempera paint	
6. Difference in effect between broken color,† mixed color, and flat, pure color	Painting of one tree in a painterly manner and another in a hard edge manner	Tempera	Impressionists such as Monet and Pissarro, and Hard Edge painters such as Stuart Davis, George Ortman, and Frank Stella
7. How color behaves in relation to light	Experimentation on acetate or old slides	Tempera, hole punchers, nail polish, acetate, and slide projector	
8. Selecting as opposed to mixing color	Creation of a "warm" or "cool" design utilizing colors taken from magazine advertisements and illustrations	Colored magazine clippings	

*"Color" is one of several units planned for the semester. Other organizing centers for art learning might be "Forms in Space" and "Printmaking."

†Broken color refers to the Impressionistic manner of painting an area in short, flickering strokes of different hues.

Figure 4.4 *"Downtown," a chalk drawing by a sixth grader in a ghetto school, is an honest portrayal of the urban environment.*

CASE HISTORIES OF THE DEVELOPMENT OF AN ART PROGRAM

By now it must be obvious that the development of an art program demands much strategic thinking on the part of the teacher. Many local factors affect the character of the program. At the same time the teacher must keep in mind the traditional nature of artistic effort, so that whatever work is produced in the name of art will have the attributes of art.

Many teachers have been eminently successful in developing a program of art in keeping with these concepts. It is instructive to study the efforts of some of them, to observe how they have coped with the various factors affecting the program. Accordingly four case histories are presented to illustrate the manner in which these teachers solved, to the general satisfaction of all concerned, the problems associated with the development of an art program.[15]

A School in a Depressed Urban Area

Mr. G is an art teacher in a school situated in an old and deteriorated section of an American East Coast metropolis. The buildings of the district are dirty and monotonous, housing conditions are poor, and heavy trucks rumble continually to and from the adjacent docks. Four blocks away

[15]Should the reader consider some of the settings somewhat unusual, it must be pointed out that often an unusual problem more clearly demonstrates an educational strategy.

is the glitter of the city's world-famous amusement area. There is neither a playground nor a public park within convenient reach of the school.

Mr. G enjoys his work because he senses a great need for it. His own classroom is a model of neatness, order, and attractiveness. He has sponsored the formation of a pupils' committee that is responsible for hanging attractive displays of art work in the halls of the school. Because the school board has had the halls and classrooms painted in attractive colors, entering the building after leaving the drab street is a happy experience.

The program followed by Mr. G is in some respects similar to that found in many other situations. The pupils make pictures related to their lives and intersperse this type of activity with some of the usual three-dimensional projects. If some of the pupils' output displays negative interests resulting from a sordid environment, their expressions at least have the saving graces of honesty, clarity, and a sharp perceptual response. Indeed Mr. G is quite aware of the special perceptual problems of his pupils. He devotes much of his time to discussions and activities that deal with sharpened visual awareness, size and color discrimination, relation of parts to wholes, filtering out of irrelevant details, and study of symbols in the environment.[16]

The most outstanding feature of the art program under Mr. G's guidance is the attention given to home and community planning. The members of his class work at problems related to this theme—such as designing a park, an apartment, or a recreation center. On one occasion, the pupils reconstructed in miniature the entire neighborhood. Some of the boys and girls have planned a "dream house" and other individuals have designed the bedroom or kitchen each would like to occupy. As frequently as possible Mr. G takes the pupils on expeditions to see the layout of the city parks, new housing developments, or other building projects worthy of note.

Mr. G was faced with grave problems arising from the choice of theme and the social setting. Should the pupils continue to express sordid things, or turn to another type of subject matter remote from their present world? Fortunately Mr. G had sufficient insight into art to realize that expression must arise from what the pupils knew, even though what they knew was often far from socially desirable. He realized that reliance on artificial subject matter would probably only adversely affect the pupils' artistic taste. Therefore, he made sure that the pupils had some socially commendable experiences that they could employ as themes. The discipline of art was still operative, expression was still within the artistic tradition, but now it embraced the "real" world. This was the objective of his strategy, which he felt succeeded as far as was artistically expedient.

---

[16]See the design activities at the end of Chapter 3.

Mr. Y accepted his first teaching position in an isolated community in the Tennessee mountains. Only seven families supplied the twenty-six children enrolled in his school. Mr. Y noticed that many of the parents had little good to say for their neighbors and that their conversation about them contained many unkind references. No social gatherings in the community had occurred for some years; instead, the people were in the habit of seeking their entertainment in the small town some fifteen miles away. In summer, the people were able to drive to this town, but in winter traveling became almost impossible because of snow or mud.

Mr. Y was young and liked people and he determined to begin his program by defining art in its social function. He organized a dance to take place in the schoolhouse. Two hired men—one who played a fiddle and the other a guitar—consented to make the music, and each family was asked to bring food.

The children were excited about the forthcoming dance. The drab appearance of the classroom, however, had escaped their notice. Indeed, in that area no one seemed to be concerned with interior decoration, at home or elsewhere. Mr. Y brought the matter before the class. "What could we do to make the classroom pretty for the dance?" he asked, producing a few art supplies. After much discussion a theme for decoration was agreed on: Summer in the Mountains. The children drew or sculpted in paper the flowers, birds, and trees of the surrounding country. They painted a mural depicting a trip to the neighboring town. They made paper doilies to place under the food, and finally, they modeled paper hats and funny faces from papier-mâché for the guests.

When the parents and a few visitors arrived at the schoolhouse on the night of the dance, not many words were passed concerning the gay appearance of the schoolroom. But the decorations were nevertheless noticed. "That teacher's a smart artist," a parent commented. When they learned that the work was entirely that of the children, the parents could scarcely credit the fact. Later, after they realized that the children had been responsible, some small bickering developed as to whose children were the "smartest" artists.

Let us examine how the five influences discussed earlier affected Mr. Y's decisions. The tradition of art exerted itself largely from the standpoint of the "function" of the project. Since the community was primitive artistically and otherwise, nothing but a "practical" or functional form of art, such as the project clearly proved to be, would probably have been acceptable to the parents. The problem was well within the understanding of the children, and they were ready for the activity; the art activities being of a simple nature largely because of the lack of supplies, the young teacher needed no special training to be able to assist the pupils. Finally, the community setting provided a theme for decoration. A local theme was the logical choice to appeal to the parents and to evoke real artistic responses from the children.

Mr. Y, as well as doing the community a social service, had cleverly launched an art program in a region where art, if it had ever been considered at all, had been relegated to outsiders and highbrows. He had demonstrated to the people that school art was practical and acceptable. As a result of this strategy, the considerable attention he gave to the development of an art program met with local approval.

On the seaboard of the northwestern part of the state of Washington is a thriving settlement of some 20,000 people. Here lumber and other wood products are produced in a number of large sawmills. The district is wealthy, and no reasonable expense for the school system is refused. Art rooms are models of efficiency; supplies are abundant.

A School in a Well-to-do Scenic Area

Miss A accepted a position in one of the large elementary schools in this town and was assigned to teach art in the fourth, fifth, and sixth grades. In studying the art output of children under the guidance of her predecessor, she was disappointed to discover that the program had been extremely rigid. Its nature was evidenced by still-life drawings of flower arrangements, exercises in perspective and in color theory, and a few illustrations based on literary themes.

Miss A is a competent painter whose work is sensitive rather than powerful. She is, furthermore, an experienced art teacher and is thoroughly familiar with contemporary ideas in art education. Her former home in North Dakota was a complete contrast to northwest Washington. As she looked about her Miss A was deeply impressed by her new environment. At her back rose the great mountains, before her was the sea, and in the distance the peaks of an island mountain range showed their caps of snow. At night she could hear the rumble of the mills and watch the moving lights of the ships as they came and went with their cargoes. She became familiar with the native art of the local Indian tribes. Deeply moved by all she saw, Miss A recognized that here was all manner of inspiration for art.

The people of the settlement went busily about their affairs, apparently giving little aesthetic attention to their environment. The children also seemed unaware of their surroundings. Miss A, however, was enthused. Somehow, she decided, she must make the pupils really see and feel this place.

She began her program simply. The pupils were asked to produce pictures based on the usual happenings in their lives. Their first work was neither more nor less inspired than one would find in many other schools. Gradually, however, she introduced them to the folklore of the coastal Indian tribes. She showed them the artifacts of the Indians, pointing out their strength and originality. She played music of the sea—not the tinkly kind, but powerful compositions, like Britten's "Sea Interludes" from his *Peter Grimes,* Mendelssohn's *Fingal's Cave,* and the majestic tonalities of Sibelius. Occasionally she read them excerpts from Conrad and Masefield. After the children had produced some pictures on sea themes she showed them reproductions of works by Marin, Mattson, and Ryder, and a print of *The Great Wave* by Hokusai.

Following the motivation related to the sea she introduced the subjects of the mountains and valleys, and later the forests and the lakes. In each case she made use of related literary and musical interpretations of these subjects. Then she told her classes stories of the explorers of the West Coast. Finally she turned to the mills and to the drama of heavy industry.

As time passed the art program expanded in many directions. Miss A discovered, for example, a local wood that was suitable for carving. Later she introduced various kinds of textile printing and encouraged the children to use motifs inspired by the local environment. She helped the children organize fist-puppet shows, for which they wrote scripts about life, either past or present, on the West Coast.

As an artist Miss A knew intimately the nature of art as a discipline. She possessed many artistic skills and her taste was impeccable. Her pupils also possessed some skills and a reasonably developed taste. Her strategy, then, was first to make the local scene acceptable to the pupils as a basis for expression; second, to get the pupils to use the abundance of two- and three-dimensional materials wisely in expressing their reactions to the locality; and third, to make use of important historical facts having artistic significance.

She carried out her strategy by exhibiting the work of artists and artisans who had lived in, and had been moved by, similar surroundings and by inspiring the pupils through her own deep and commendable enthusiasm. Perhaps the most important change Miss A brought about was to reveal the environment to the children.

Art
in a British
Open Classroom

Someday a situation may arise in which the art program may have to be rethought in terms of a national philosophy. For some years, the primary schools of Great Britain have been moving toward the "open classroom" or the "integrated day," as the new approach to teaching is called. This new approach has affected the methodology as well as the content of teaching and has, in general, improved art instruction. Art, under the new practices, has been extended from consideration as a separate subject to integration into the rest of the curriculum. A comparison of educational practice—both structured and open is listed in the table on the next page.

The case study discussed below describes the way in which a classroom teacher might handle art activities within the context of an open classroom.

Table 4.2

COMPARISON OF EDUCATIONAL APPROACHES

Structured Education	*Open Education*
Graded Organizational Pattern	Nongraded Organizational Pattern
One Teacher	Team Teaching
Group-Paced Learning Experiences	Self-Paced Learning Experiences
Group Instruction	Individualized Instruction
Restricted Space	Flexible Use of Open Space
Systematic/Logical Learning	Discovery Learning
Subject-Centered Education	Life-Centered Education
Direct Teaching	Indirect Teaching

Mrs. H teaches a primary-school class in an industrial town in Yorkshire. Unlike her American counterpart, she has had only three years of professional preparation rather than four, and like her American colleague she has had little or no training in art to prepare her to conduct competently an art program. Mrs. H does not have an art specialist to consult, but she does have two advantages over an American teacher: she is part of a movement that strongly endorses not only the role of visual art but of all of the arts and she has a strong in-service program to assist her in filling the gaps of her background. She looks on professional development as an on-going process rather than as ending with the completion of her schooling. If strong in-service training is not offered, she and her colleagues will most likely demand it.

Despite the disadvantages of a limited budget and a large class (well over thirty children), Mrs. H manages to carry on an art program on two levels. One might be called "art for art's sake," where the children have a set time of the week or day to work in a medium or subject of their choice, and the other is an integrated program where art is used in conjunction with other subject areas—illustrating stories, making scale models, creating decorative maps and charts, and the like. Mrs. H cannot be a master of every material with which her students elect to work, but there are other staff members who can help, and one day she might send someone to a teacher who knows fabric printing while the following week she in turn will help students from another class with lino-cuts, a special interest of hers. The "head," or principal, is particularly strong in ceramics and has a weekly class on an informal basis for those students who are interested.

Mrs. H's school is quieter than an American one; there is a seriousness about the way work is carried on, and this shows in the care and

Figure 4.5 *Children select their own materials and work at their own pace in a British open classroom. (Photo by Neil Jacobs.)*

time that the students bring to their art. One girl has been working on a large painting of the school playground for several weeks while a team of boys are taking considerably longer to create a life-sized diorama of underwater life. Some enjoy doing outdoor sketches of the school grounds, and if ideas run out there are always the ever-present but changing still lifes that both Mrs. H and the class are arranging. These may center on a particular idea such as a color, a specific geometric shape, objects used by local workers such as coal miners, or the still lifes may consist of interesting bits of junk or cast-off pieces of machinery collected along the way to school. The children are thus urged to use their environment in as many ways as possible as a source of ideas for art. Whatever the children draw or paint is mounted with care, exhibited in an organized way, and carefully labeled. It is obvious from visiting Mrs. H's school that art is considered very much a part of general education and that, far from being a special case, her class reflects the philosophy of the school, which in turn is part of a national trend in education.[17]

The programs of the four teachers just described, although varying

[17]This description is a composite of impressions taken during the author's visit to four "open" schools in Yorkshire. For greater insight into the subject, read the articles on art in *The Open Classroom Reader,* Charles E. Silberman, ed. (New York: Vintage Books, 1973).

in detail, have several characteristics in common. Each teacher, while stimulating and helping the pupils, allowed them sufficient freedom of expression and choice of activity within the framework of a theme. All the programs were successful because the teachers were sufficiently competent in both pedagogical and artistic matters to make each program effective.

PLANNING FOR THE FIRST SESSION: TWO DIALOGS

All teachers must plan for the first meeting with their pupils. The taped dialogs recorded here represent two approaches to this first meeting. The first conversation depicts a teacher's attempt to get a grass-roots definition of art from disadvantaged children in the third grade, and the second demonstrates how the first planning session with middle-class children might sound.

TEACHER: My name is Mrs. D. Do any of you know who I am? (*pause*)

TOMMY: You an art teacher?

First Dialog

TEACHER: That's right. I am your art teacher. Now, can anyone tell me what an artist does?

SARAH: He paints you pictures.

TEACHER: Very good. What other kinds of artists are there? (*longer pause*)

FLORENCE: Are you going to let us paint pictures?

TEACHER: Certainly, we'll paint pictures, but we'll do things that other kinds of artists do too. Can you think of other things we can do that other artists do? (*pause*) Well, think of going shopping with your mother. Can you think of the work of artists in a shopping center?

TOMMY: (*suddenly*) I know! He can paint you a sign. . . .

TEACHER: (*enthusiastically*) Yes, yes, sign painters are artists, too—what else?

TOMMY: (*picking up the enthusiasm*) And if you had a butcher shop and you had a good—I mean a *good* artist, he could paint you a pork chop on the window. . . .

   The above conversation is a fragment of a discussion held by Mrs. D during the first meeting with a group of third graders in a slum school. The children were quite different from the upper-middle-class youngsters the teacher was accustomed to working with. The purposes of her discussion were to (1) learn the children's concept of art; (2) establish the kind of rapport that comes only through a relaxed exchange of ideas; and (3) prepare the children for the program she had planned for the year. As a result of her discussion, Mrs. D set aside quite a few activities she had planned, realizing they were inappropriate for these children. Being both a skilled and experienced teacher, Mrs. D was sensitive to the range of difference among the children; she understood that all of them came to the art class with their own ideas of what constitutes an art program. To some it represented part of social studies; to others art meant carrying out school services. For one child it was the high point of the week, while to another it was a traumatic period during which the student was constantly cautioned against making a mess, when in fact the materials at hand were (to the student) created for that very purpose. A teacher skilled in conducting class discussions can bring diverse points of view into the open—reconciling some of them, questioning others, and eventually presenting ideas in relation to those of the class. The fact that children can have a strong voice in planning the year's program should in no way, however, keep a teacher from carrying through the major part of the program already conceived.

Second Dialog

Let us eavesdrop on another discussion taking place at a meeting of an art consultant and some pupils. These pupils are fifth graders in a middle-class neighborhood. A content analysis of the pupils' comments is provided in the left-hand column.

Teacher–Pupil Dialog

MR. H: Good morning. My name is Mr. H. I'm an art teacher as well as your art supervisor, and I'd like to talk with you about some of the things you're going to be doing this year with Miss G, your regular art teacher.

SUSAN: You mean you're not going to be our art teacher?

MR. H: No, but I hope I'll be coming in now and then to see what Miss G is doing, and perhaps later on I'll take a few classes myself.

MARK: What are we going to do today?

MR. H: Well, as I said earlier, I'd like to take this time to talk about what you'd like to do this year.

Analysis of Pupil Comments

This remark may be interpreted as a sign of disappointment that Mr. H will not be their regular art teacher.

Mark is ready to go to work. In his eyes the art period (there are so few of them) is not a place to talk, but to do and make things.

If the art teacher is thinking of giving appreciation lessons that involve close looking in relation to a new vocabulary, he will find that Mark's attitude may provide a clue to the general class readiness for discussion as opposed to actual art work. The teacher has to find ways of making exciting activities of observation and discussion.

SUSAN: Will Mr. S be back?

MR. H: I don't know. Who is Mr. S? (*great commotion*) One at a time—could we please use our hands? Deirdre? (*The children had prepared name tags.*)

DEIRDRE: Mr. S illustrated books and he showed us how he did his pictures.

OTHERS: Yeah—he was cool. Boy, could he draw!

MR. H: (*going to the blackboard*) Well, we have our first request. You'd like to meet a real, artist. (*Writes this on board.*) Anything else?

MARCIA: The raccoon—the raccoon?

MR. H: The raccoon?

OTHERS: Yes—Miss G brought in this raccoon. We petted him. It climbed up the bookcase.

MR. H: All right—let me see—how shall I put it? How about "Drawing from Live Subjects"—that way we can use live fifth graders as well as other kinds of animals. (*laughter*) Very good. I think drawing from nature is a great idea—it would be even better if we could get a baby elephant in here— (*laughter—other animals are suggested that are equally unrealistic*)—All right, now, keep going— yes, Barbara?

BARBARA: I liked the field trip to the Museum of Fine Arts.

MR. H: Oh, what did you see?

BARBARA: It was Rembrandt.

PAUL: No it wasn't. (*others join in quick argument*)

MR. H: Does anyone remember the exact title of the show?

PAUL: I know! "The Age of Rembrandt," that's what it was.

MR. H: O.K. Let's put in "Field Trips." I'll write it under "Visiting Artists," rather than "Drawing." What else?

SUSAN: Are we going to paint?

MR. H: Certainly—what's an art class without painting?

DAVID: I don't like to paint.

MR. H: Why not?

DAVID: I don't know. I like making jewelry.

MR. H: Well—we can't like everything, can we? You must feel about painting the way I feel about lettering. Let me put down "Crafts," David. That'll hold the door open to other materials. Who'd like to name some?

"Mr. S" was a participant in the Creative Arts Council's program designed to bring performing artists of all kinds into the schools. The children's interest in observing professionals at work thus opens the door for potters, printmakers, painters, and the like to step into the art curriculum.

Marcia's mention of the raccoon allows the teacher to emphasize as much drawing from observation as he feels is appropriate. Should he decide to have the children do contour-line drawings from a posed figure, brush drawings of animals, or should he decide to use any of these as a basis for subject matter or point-making, he has Marcia's suggestions to which he may refer.

Paul and Barbara's suggestion has given the teacher the opportunity to plan additional field trips or a first lesson in art appreciation based on the Dutch School.

In setting up categories the teacher hopes to get the children to begin making distinctions within the arts. This is a technique that will be developed further in the informational part of the art program.

The teacher did not skirt David's dislike of painting. By acknowledging it publicly he hopes to create a threat-free environment in which differences of opinion are discussed openly.

The discussion of the function of the clay results in adding sculpture to the list of activities.

POLLY: Clay.

PAUL: Clay is sculpture.

POLLY: Bowls are clay and . . .

PAUL: Clay is more sculpture.

MR. H: Actually, clay can be either. If it is something we use, we generally refer to it as "craft"; if it's something we admire in the way that we admire a painting, we usually call it "fine arts." In any case we can put down "Sculpture" as long as you mentioned it. Can you name some other crafts?

EMMA: Batiks. We did batiks once.

PAUL: Weaving. That's crafts.

SUSAN: Are we going to do all these?

MR. H: I'm afraid not—but let's get them down anyway so we'll see what we've done. Say—I've got one for you. How about movies? We can make a movie.

OTHERS: Movies? How?

PAUL: I took pictures with my father's camera. It's an 8mm.

MR. H: Well, I had in mind another kind, something we could all do together. We can scratch designs right on the raw film, put all the pieces together, and put it to music. How does that sound?

Now that the teacher has rapport with the class he can intrude his own ideas. Others that eventually followed were activities in architecture (redesigning the school playground) and design ("making a picture or sculpture go together"). Sculpture was also broken down into several media, and printmaking was added.

The important thing to note in studying the above dialog is that the teacher knew in advance what the rough content of the year's work would be. In communicating with the pupils he could have:

1. Doled out the projects on a piecemeal basis as the year progressed without attempting to communicate the overall structure. This is an *improvised,* teacher-directed approach.
2. Described the entire year's activities to the class, providing a *planned,* directed program.

Instead the teacher chose a third approach, in that he:

3. Involved the class in the planning. In so doing, many of the teacher's own ideas were made to seem to originate in the class. By engaging their participation, he assured a climate of acceptance for new ideas that might not normally be accepted.

ACTIVITIES FOR THE READER

1. Describe in some detail the significant planning decisions that must be made in an art program developed in the following situations: (a) a sixth-grade classroom in a new, wealthy suburb of a large city; (b) a third-grade classroom in a temporary school for the children of construction workers in an isolated part of North Carolina; (c) a mixed-grade classroom (first through fourth grades) in a mission school for Indians located in New Mexico.

2. Describe how you would constructively handle a situation in which your principal was more interested in having an art program based on a rigid program of outdated concepts than on a contemporary, creative approach. Choose a classmate and do some improvised role-playing on this subject.

3. If a fellow teacher who gave evidence of atrociously bad taste in art asked you for an honest appraisal of his or her artistic efforts, what would you say or do?

4. You are elected chairman of an eight-person *ad hoc* committee in a city school system to submit ideas to a central authority for the improvement of the art program. You are expected, furthermore, to select the eight members of the committee. State the kinds of people you would choose. Describe the agenda you would draw up for the first hour-long meeting.

5. Because of negative associations with a previous art program, your fifth-grade pupils do not seem interested in helping you develop an art program. Describe how you might improve matters.

6. A former teacher had for two years taught nothing to fourth-, fifth-, and sixth-grade pupils except the copying of either comic strips or picture postcards. How would you proceed in developing an art program in your new teaching position?

7. Improvise the conversation you might have with a parent who thinks teaching art is a waste of taxpayers' money, which should be used for "more important fundamentals," Try this conversation with various types of parents: professionals, lower-middle-class factory workers, local shopkeepers.

8. Compare the features of structured and open education; list specific instances involving art under the items shown in both columns on page 131.

A third grader views the art room from a multiplicity of perspectives. Drawn directly in felt pen.

ARRANGING AND EQUIPPING
A CLASSROOM FOR ART ACTIVITIES

*To obtain a flexible, functional environment, well-designed furnishings must be utilized. A carefully planned, fully stocked, and well-equipped art room contributes far more effectively to significant educational development in art than does an inadequate, cluttered, converted classroom or a program forced to operate almost exclusively on scrap materials and tools brought from home.**

In order to conduct an art program successfully the teacher must often plan alterations and additions to the basic classroom that is provided. Accordingly this chapter will discuss some of the ways and means by which the layout of a kindergarten and of a general classroom may be modified to accomodate pupils engaged in art work. Some attention will be given also to the planning of an art room, should a teacher or principal at some time find such a room available. It might be noted here that this chapter deals only with the physical equipment and functional arrangements for art activities in different types of rooms. The general classroom might not be adaptable to our suggestions, since certain educational requirements must take precedence over artistic considerations.

A classroom, and especially an art room, is a workshop, and its design must be governed primarily by functional considerations. Fortunately, however, if functional demands remain strictly paramount in all classroom arrangements, the setting will then tend to be compatible with whatever display techniques are subsequently employed. There is little or no reason, in other words, for a functional classroom to be anything but attractive.

*From Howard Conant and Arne Randall, *Art in Education* (Peoria, Ill.: Chas. A. Bennett Co., 1963), p. 229.

Many of the problems that arise from the task of reorganizing a room for art are unique to the particular situation. The size and shape of a room, the number of children in a class, the type of activities in the program, all will modify the arrangements to be made. The making of suitable physical arrangements for art, therefore, presents a challenge that in the long run only the teacher can satisfactorily meet.

PHYSICAL ARRANGEMENT OF THE CLASSROOM

The physical arrangements in a classroom for any particular subject are dictated by the operations to be carried out. It is well at this time to consider the various important operations that occur when art is taught.

Before an art session takes place, the teacher must usually arrange the supplies. As every experienced art teacher knows, a class of eager children descends on art supplies like a flock of starlings on a cherry orchard. Things disappear fast! Unless the teacher has made adequate preparations so that the supplies are abundant and easily obtainable, much confusion and subsequent dissipation of energies may occur. The teacher must often select the supplies that the children require from a storage area. Many supplies come in bulk and should be arranged in convenient units before being put where the children can most easily reach them.

After the children learn what to obtain and where to obtain it, and how to move so that they do not get in each other's way (all of which they learn through discussion with the teacher and subsequent practice), they must have suitable places at which to work. Art supplies and processes raise special accommodation problems. Papers for drawing and painting are usually much larger than those for writing, so that surfaces to accommodate them must be larger than most school desks. Certain activities, such as wood sculpture or linoleum-block printing, demand a special surface on which the materials may be cut. Through use this surface will roughen and become unsuitable for drawing and painting and other activities. Two boards, then—a work board and a drawing board—are necessary.

After the children have worked, their unfinished and completed work will create more accommodation problems. The unfinished work may be wet, and a place must be found where it can be dried before being stored away. The finished work—two- as well as three-dimensional—must be put on display. Hence drying space, storage space, and display boards and shelves must be provided.

In summary, a classroom in which art is taught requires physical provisions for the following operations: storing bulk equipment and supplies; preparing current supplies for the class; setting out the supplies for current work; working delicately as in drawing and painting, or robustly as in cutting and hammering; drying unfinished or completed work; storing unfinished work; displaying work. The furniture these operations require includes the following:

1. A storage cupboard with some adjustable shelves, the latter at least 8 inches wide for small items and other shelves at least 18 inches wide for larger items. The outside dimensions of the cupboard will, of course, be determined by the floor and wall space available.
2. Two tables, preferably at least 5 feet long and 30 inches wide, one to be used largely by the teacher in arranging and displaying supplies and the other for children's group work.
3. A sink, or a stand for pails of water. The sink should have two faucets or spigots to hasten the clean-up activity.
4. A drying shelf or battery of shelves near a radiator or other source of heat. The shelf should be about 12 inches wide and as long as space permits.
5. Some display facilities to be discussed later in this chapter.
6. Some chalkboard space.

BASIC SUPPLIES AND EQUIPMENT

Each type of art activity, of course, demands particular tools and equipment and sometimes special arrangement of furniture.[1] The accompanying list of general tools and supplies, however, appears to be basic to nearly any art program. Miscellaneous supplies and equipment such as scissors, thumbtacks, masking tape, and paper cutter (18-inch minimum) are not listed, since they are part of general equipment for other subjects. Crafts materials are not listed because they vary so much with each teacher.

1. *brayers* available in a variety of widths from 3 to 8 inches; a soft rubber roller is recommended; a set for one class can service the entire school
2. *brushes* painting: flat, hog-bristle, one-quarter of an inch to 1 inch wide
painting: pointed, sable, large (size 6 or 7)
paste brushes
3. *chalk* soft, ten or twelve colors plus black and white; dustless preferred

---

[1]Subsequent chapters will discuss in detail the tools, media, and special features of teaching particular art subjects at the various developmental levels.

4. *crayons*   wax, soft, ten or twelve colors plus black and white
5. *oil crayons*   such as cray-pas or oil pastels
6. *pens*   felt tip marking pens
7. *cutting tools*   sloyd knives, X-acto tools, single-edged razor blades, and linoleum carving tools
8. *drawing boards*   about 18 by 24 inches, soft plywood at least "BC" grade (that is, clear of knots on at least one side), Masonite, homosote, composition board (optional)
9. *erasers*   Artgum type
10. *inks*   ordinary blue-black fountain-pen ink
    water-base printing inks in tubes for block printing
11. *linoleum*   minimum of 6 square inches per child; also available mounted on plywood blocks, but are more expensive
12. *paint*   poster: liquid in pints, or powder in pounds (white, black, orange, yellow, blue, green, and red as basic; magenta, purple, and turquoise as luxuries; probably twice the quantity of black, white, and yellow as of other colors chosen)
13. *paint*   watercolor: primary colors will do, but secondary colors recommended if available within budget
14. *paint tins*   muffin tins, with at least six depressions (baby-food jars and frozen-juice cans may also be used)
15. *paper*   roll of kraft (brown wrapping), about 36 inches wide; or "project roll," 36 inches wide
    manila: 18 by 24 inches, cream and gray, 40 pound
    colored construction: 12 by 18 inches (red, yellow, blue, light green, dark green, black, gray, and perhaps some in-between colors like blue-green and red-orange; about forty colors are available)
    newsprint and colored tissue: size optional
16. *paste and glue*   school: in quarts
    powdered wheat paste for papier-mâché
    white glue for wood joining (thinned, it works well as an adhesive for colored tissues)
17. *pencils*   drawing: black, soft
18. *printing plates*   glass trimmed with masking tape
19. *firing clay*   3 pounds per child

EXAMPLES OF CLASSROOM ARRANGEMENTS

To illustrate the manner in which arrangements for art are influenced by the age level of the pupils and by local educational conditions, four situations are discussed below: the kindergarten, the modern general classroom, the art service area, and the art room.

The problems in arranging the kindergarten arise largely from the stage of physiological development of the pupils. Because kindergarten-age youngsters use the large muscles in drawing, painting, and three-dimensional work, they need generous working spaces. They also require relatively large tools and bulky media, which create storage problems.

The teacher's preparation of art materials for kindergarten children is often quite different from that in the higher grades. Older children can usually select art materials for themselves, but the kindergarten teacher must, at least at the beginning of the school term, arrange sets or kits of materials. These vary greatly in the number of items contained. For example, for crayon drawing the youngsters need only six crayons and a sheet of manila paper. For painting they require perhaps an apron or Father's old shirt, a sheet of newspaper or oilcloth to protect the painting surface, two brushes, a sheet of newsprint, a paint cloth, and some liquid colors.

From a necessarily large and convenient storage space the teacher selects items to make up the kits and places them on a long table, cafeteria-style. The six crayons may be placed on a paper plate and set on the sheet of paper. The painting kit may be assembled in discarded "six-pack" cartons, on a metal or plastic tray, or on a wooden work board. The paint should not be included at this point because of accidents that may occur as the children transport the kit to the place where the painting is done. Paint and any other "dangerous" materials should be placed in the working area ahead of time.

The following suggestions may be helpful in storing tools and supplies to be ready for distribution:

Figure 5.1 *This kindergarten classroom demonstrates a regard for carefully arranged displays of art, interesting materials that can serve as a source for subject matter, and thoughtful placement of furniture and equipment. (Photo by Neil Jacobs.)*

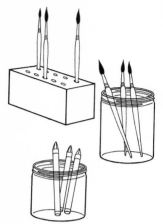

Figure 5.2 *Brushes, pencils, and crayons are easily stored in glass jars or in a block of wood with holes bored in it.*

1. Brushes and pencils should be placed in glass jars, with bristles and points up (see Figure 5.2). Blocks of wood with holes bored in them, each hole large enough to hold one item, provide another convenient way of arranging this type of tool. This manner of storage also allows the teacher to make a quick visual check for missing brushes.
2. Crayons should be separated according to colors. Each container, which might be a milk carton or a cigar or cheese box, should hold only one color.
3. Moistened clay should be rolled into balls and placed in a large earthenware jar or a tin container, either of which should have a tight lid to keep in the moisture.
4. Paper should be cut to size and arranged on a shelf in piles according to size and color.
5. Paper scraps should be separated according to color and saved in small cartons.
6. Paste should be kept in covered glass jars (or, if dry, in the bulk packages). The teacher should place paste on disposable paper plates or simply on pieces of cardboard after it has been mixed for use.

It is fortunate that the furniture in most kindergartens is movable, for the floor provides an excellent work area for art. If the floor is covered with heavy linoleum or linoleum tile, it is necessary to set down only a thin protective covering such as oilcloth or wrapping paper before work begins. If the floor is in any way rough, cardboard mats may be put over the areas where the activities are to take place. The type of work being done, whether flat or three-dimensional, often determines the kind of floor or table covering to be set down. The teacher should have available the following types of protective covers:

1. Masonite or 3-ply wood, about 18 by 24 inches, not necessarily thick, for drawing and painting.
2. Masonite or 3-ply wood, about 18 by 24 inches, for hammering, cutting, and the like.
3. A piece of waterproof oilcloth, about 18 by 24 inches, for clay work, fingerpainting, and so on.

Any of these coverings may be put with the kits, although many teachers prefer to put them in place themselves or with the help of the more responsible children.

Some teachers like to hang paintings to be dried on a clothesline with spring clothespins. Tables are often used for drying three-dimensional projects. The floor, of course, if part of it can be conveniently reserved, is an excellent place for drying all types of work. Not much unfinished work requiring storage is produced in the kindergarten, for most projects are completed in one art session.

It is desirable, of course, for all children eventually to learn how to procure and replace equipment and supplies for themselves. A start in this direction should be made even in the kindergarten. The room should be so arranged that the children can perform the task easily. In the kindergarten, as elsewhere in the art program, the cafeteria system is useful.

The children must develop the ability to obtain and replace art materials according to a plan that they themselves help to determine. The teacher should discuss with the children the necessity of learning these skills. However, in the kindergarten the children will usually follow plans willingly and treat the routine as a game. The game can even include a rehearsal or drill of the routine.

In many contemporary school plans considerable thought is being given to suitable accommodation for art activities in general classrooms. A description of the special provisions for art in the general classroom is offered here primarily for those teachers who are provided with a reasonably liberal budget for the modernization of their art facilities.

A Modern General Classroom

Because desks are not fixed to the floor in the majority of classrooms being constructed today, they can be easily arranged to suit the studies in progress. Movable desks are a great convenience for drawing and painting since they allow a pupil to use a drawing board without interfering with other children. Clusters of desks may be arranged so that large flat areas of working space are available for group activities.

In some contemporary classrooms an entire wall is provided with fixtures to facilitate the teaching of art, as shown in Figure 5.3. A counter

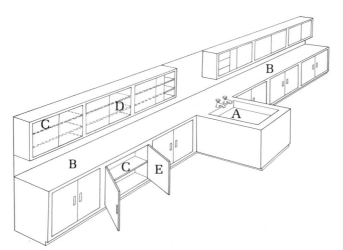

Figure 5.3 *A wall fixture for art activities in a general classroom (sketch based on an original design by the Ontario Department of Education).*

A Sink
B Counter
C Adjustable shelves
D Sliding doors
E Swinging doors

Figure 5.4 *The general classroom usually has little space for the display of children's art. Here the teacher has used the tackboard at the back of the room to handsomely exhibit the work of the class. (Photo by Neil Jacobs.)*

covered with linoleum or some other suitably processed material is built from wall to wall. This counter houses probably the most important single convenience for art activities—a large sink supplied with hot and cold water. Below the counter are several storage cupboards equipped with adjustable shelves and swinging doors where all expendable supplies may be stored. A second row of cupboards is suspended about 12 inches above the counter. These cupboards also have adjustable shelves, but the doors are of the sliding variety so that pupils will not bump their heads on them when open. Additional supplies or the pupils' unfinished work may be kept in this storage space. Electrical outlets are frequently provided at convenient intervals along the counter. The whole assemblage, which substantially resembles a work unit in a modern kitchen, occupies relatively little floor space. Sometimes an additional work counter is provided along part of the window wall; more cupboards may be built below this counter.

Because a teacher in a general classroom requires a relatively large expanse of chalkboard it is sometimes difficult to find sufficient space to display art. This is often provided, however, on the side wall to the rear of the room, and on two walls above the chalkboards, where a wide strip of tackboard is fastened. But since even these areas are usually insufficient for display purposes, many new schools are being equipped with display boards and cases in the main halls of the building.

Teachers who are fortunate enough to occupy modern classrooms of the type described seem to experience little difficulty in conducting a reasonably broad and effective program. This is especially true in buildings provided with what is known as an "art service" room.

In a growing number of elementary-school systems, the "art service" room has been developed for use by the teachers. This room serves schools where art is taught in regular classrooms rather than in an art room. The art service room is not restricted to new buildings; it can be provided in any school where space can be found. Space is becoming increasingly available as enrollments decline due to the reduction in population.

An Art Service Area: Supplies, Preparation, and Storage

The art service room performs several important functions by eliminating many of the difficulties associated with teaching art in homerooms. First, it provides a place outside of their own classrooms for teachers to experiment with art materials and equipment. Second, from a stock of tools and materials in the art service room the teachers may conveniently prepare whatever they need for art work in their own classrooms. "Art service carts," which resemble tea wagons with several trays, may easily be wheeled to the classrooms when loaded with the appropriate equipment. A considerable outlay of money, which otherwise would be spent in duplicating material in several classrooms, is saved by this central stock of supplies. This is particularly true of block-printing, weaving, and woodcarving equipment, which are not used frequently in any one classroom during a term.

Third, the art service room is equipped not only with storage shelves and cupboards for expendable materials but also with shelves for work in progress. Teachers may send such items as costumes and properties in various stages of preparation for school plays to be stored safely until needed. Clay objects may also be kept safe there before firing, and objects made from papier-mâché may be set out for drying. Classrooms are thus kept free of half-finished objects, which might be damaged in some way if they remained in the room.

Finally, the art service room serves as a depot for storing, sorting, and preparing current exhibitions of school work. Teachers may bring to the rooms those pieces of work they consider suitable for exhibition. Art shows thus may be coordinated and carefully arranged so that they are truly representative of the school. The art service room is primarily a work area for the teacher. As such, it is distinct from the art room, although in some instances they may be combined.

Let us now consider another situation in classroom accommodation. Suppose as art teachers we are asked to give advice in planning an art room in a new school. Let us make two further, rather far-fetched, suppositions: first, that no expense is to be spared, and second, that whatever the art teacher proposes will be acted on. In today's educational world, budgets are not always large enough for our needs, and the wishes of art teachers are not always respected. If not all the ideas set forth in this section can be adopted, perhaps some of them may be employed as the teachers gradually improve the working conditions in their school.

An Art Room

An art room should be placed near a service entrance on the main floor of a school building, for convenience in delivering supplies and equipment. In junior high schools it is preferable also to have the room situated reasonably close to home economics rooms and industrial arts shops in order that pupils may conveniently move from one room to another when the use of special equipment is required, such as looms in the home economics room. It is further recommended that the art room be not too far from the auditorium, since puppetry and stage craft sometimes require ready access to the stage.

The room should be large, with a minimum floor space of about 30 by 60 feet. A spacious floor can provide working centers in which many art activities may be carried out. The floor should be laid in heavy linoleum or rubber tile. Mastic tile may also be used but is rather more tiring to walk on than other types of tile.

Lighting in an art room is of the greatest importance. Fluorescent lighting is recommended and should be arranged so as to cast no pronounced shadows. Preferably the lights should be set flush with the ceiling, with the exception of spotlights for important displays. Unless the teacher has a daylight screen, blackout curtains for the windows should be provided so that films may be shown. In all matters pertaining to both artificial and natural lighting, architects and lighting engineers should be consulted. Many excellent materials and arrangements are

Figure 5.5 *First graders working on the floor around a painting center. The floor is often the most satisfactory place for activities requiring a large amount of space. It also facilitates the sharing of limited materials. (Photo by Education Development Center.)*

Figure 5.6 *This art room is planned for several work areas, each allowing for separation of activities and privacy of pupils. (Photo by Neil Jacobs.)*

available, including directional glass bricks, opaque louvers, clerestory lighting, and various types of blinds.

We may now consider the use of space around the walls. Along one of the shorter walls, storage rooms jutting into the room might be planned. Two storage areas are desirable—one to house a stock of expendable art materials and the other to store the pupils' unfinished work. Each storage room should be fitted with as many adjustable shelves as is convenient. Since the shelves may rise to a considerable height, it would be well to have at least one light stepladder available in either one of the rooms. The outside walls of these storage rooms, facing the classroom, can be faced with tackboard.

The long wall area opposite the windows should for the most part be faced with tackboard running from about 30 inches above the floor up to the ceiling. An area of about 20 square feet, however, should be reserved for a chalkboard. Space might be provided for counters and cupboards. The sink may be located on this long side of the room. Its position should be reasonably central, and it should be accessible from at least three directions (see Figure 5.3). It may be placed in a separate cabinet so that the pupils can approach it from all directions, or it may be placed at the end of a counter running at right angles from the wall toward the center of the room. However arranged, the sink should be large, deep, acid-resistant, and equipped with hot- and cold-water taps. Clean-out traps should be fitted, and all plumbing leading from them should also be acid-resistant.

Along the entire wall at the end of the room opposite the storage rooms, storage cupboards might alternate with glass-enclosed display cases. These cases should be provided with adjustable glass shelves and illuminated with hidden or indirect lights.

Beneath the windows a work counter might run almost the full length of the room. Below the counter storage cupboards could be constructed, or the space might be left open to house tools. Jutting out at right angles might be a series of small counters for delicate work. Each small counter, which might be collapsible, should be provided with a stool of convenient height. At the extreme end of this wall an area might be set aside for the teacher's desk and files.

Once the preliminary plans for the walls are complete, attention may be given to the matter of electrical outlets. This is a problem for an expert who understands electrical loads, but the teacher must be sure that outlets

Figure 5.7 *Comprehensive plan for all-purpose art room (based on a design produced by the Department of Public Instruction, Commonwealth of Pennsylvania).*

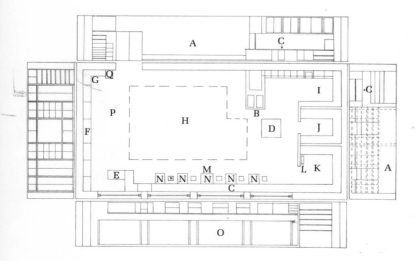

A   Tackboard and screen
B   Sinks
C   Work counters
D   Heavy workbench
E   Teacher's desk
F   Cabinets and display cases
G   Library corner
H   Central space for tables and seats
I   Clay-working area
J   Storage area: expendable art materials
K   Library corner
L   Stepladder
M   Area for 3-dimensional work
N   Solid desks for 3-dimensional work
    and individual stool for each desk
O   Windows (may not exist if room is
    air-conditioned): windows should be
    provided with blackout curtains for
    showing slides and films
P   Area for easels, posing models, etc.
Q   Filing cabinet

are placed in correct locations. As well as outlets for ceramic and enameling kilns, and service outlets in general, there should be an outlet for an electric clock. The pupils should always be aware of how much time is available to begin certain phases of their work or to start cleaning up toward the end of the art period.

Certain equipment should be placed in convenient relation to the arrangements around the walls. Such items might include an electric kiln with a firing area of not less than 3000 cubic inches, a pull-out storage bin for clay, a storage box for keeping clay damp, and a spray booth. The clay-working area should be located near the sink. A filing cabinet for storing catalogs, folders containing information about the students, and miscellaneous items useful to the teacher should be placed near the teacher's desk.

Furniture for the art room must be chosen with care. Suitable art desks come in a variety of designs, but a desk with low shelves on which the pupils may place schoolbooks would have optimum utility. Desks with movable tops, by which the slope of the working surface may be regulated, have not proved to be particularly serviceable because they tend to get out of order. For seating, chairs, stools, and benches have all proved practical. The room should be provided with one or two carpenter's benches as well as with desks for drawing and painting. The benches should be supplied with vises and have storage space beneath them for tools and other equipment.

The colors used to decorate the art room must be carefully planned. Bright colors are generally to be avoided since they rebound and confuse a painter. Tints or neutral colors such as pale grays are recommended for the walls and ceiling. The ceiling should be lighter in tone than the walls. The floor should also be neutral, but mottled. Chalkboards need not be black but may be bought in pale greens or ivory. Natural or limed wood finishes on cupboards and doors are attractive and serviceable. In general, color in an art room must not interfere with the color work in progress, and it must serve as a background for the displays of the children's work.

Before an elaborate art room of the type described can be set up successfully, much study must be given to the problem and many experts consulted. Not only should plans of the room be drawn but also a model should be made. Particular attention should be given to the grouping of furniture and equipment so that overcrowding in any one part of the room is avoided and everything necessary for any one type of work is conveniently located in one area. Obviously an art room entails costly construction, and whatever arrangements are made, good or bad, are likely to be in use for a long time. One example to study is the plan shown in Figure 5.7.

Figure 5.8 *These children are designing and making facilities for their art room, using sheets of heavy cardboard to construct storage space. (Photo by Education Development Center.)*

The Learning Environment of an Art Room.   Equipment, facilities, and storage have been considered thus far, but there are functions other than purely practical ones that must be considered. The art room can be an environment for learning about art as well as an assembly of hardware. As a learning environment it must contain many stimuli; it must be a place for sensory excitement; it is also the child's link with the world outside the classroom. Here, before painting a favorite animal, a child may have access to slides, paintings, or photographs of animal life. One day the teacher may bring in a live puppy, kitten, or turkey to study. At times the art room may resemble a science laboratory as the teacher attempts to acquaint the children with intricate, hidden forms of nature. The room may contain microscopes (now obtainable for under five dollars), aquariums, terrariums, bones, rock formations—anything that can direct the child's attention to visual cues that have bearing on the art experience.

A corner of the room might be reserved for research and supplied with art books, well-illustrated children's books, magazines on a suitable reading level, file material, slides, and filmstrips. Another part of the room might be set aside as a "serendipity corner"—a place for interesting and unusual things to draw. The more provocative these items are, the better. Each teacher creates a unique collection of objects, chosen for their shapes, colors, and associations. This collection provides its own stimulus for any lesson that employs observation as part of the problem.

Figure 5.9 *The art room should contain many different kinds of objects that can stimulate the child's imagination and interest. Here a pupil has selected a fossil for study out of a collection of natural objects. Her initial drawing will be developed into a large painting or print. (Photo by Roger Graves.)*

One way to create a learning environment in the art room is to have the children themselves design portions of the room. Orange crates painted in bright colors and units constructed of Tri-Wall board can provide flexibility even beyond purchased components. The teacher who thinks of the child as entering a laboratory of visual delight—a place for looking, feeling, shaping, and forming—will have some idea of what the art room or even a section of the classroom might be. Above all, an art room should have a special character. The moment a child enters should be one of happy anticipation.

The Classroom versus the Art Room. In kindergarten and in the first six grades of elementary school it is common for the classroom teachers to be responsible for their own art program and for the children to perform art activities in their own homerooms. The generally accepted practice of teaching art in the children's regular classroom, while not entirely convenient in all situations, has much in its favor.

Art activities in the elementary school, especially in the lower grades, should take place immediately following the motivation phase. In a situation where a special art room is provided, children who are ready to express themselves through art may be denied the opportunity because the special room is occupied by another class. When the regular classroom is used for art work, however, expression may occur as the occasion demands. By using the homeroom, moreover, the teacher tends to have greater control over the supplies and equipment required for work in art.

The choice of an art room as opposed to a general classroom as the most appropriate place for art activities is somewhat parallel to the choice of an art specialist as opposed to a classroom teacher as the ideal art instructor. Although the classroom and its teacher provide a more direct line to an understanding of the child, the special art room and teacher ensure a wider range of activity. Most classroom teachers would agree that the difficulties posed by setting up such activities as painting, sculpture, and puppetry too often lead to an indulgence in the overworked crayons. Because of the good effect that proper facilities have on instruction, it is recommended that the teacher accept an art room if a choice is offered. The presence of such a location in the school need not cut off art activity in the classroom any more than the services of an art consultant need limit the content of the curriculum.

Figure 5.10   *The general classroom can provide stimulation for its pupils as well as the art room can. This still-life display offers background material for a session in stitchery for these five- and six-year-olds. (Photo by Neil Jacobs.)*

ACTIVITIES FOR THE READER

1. Everyone who teaches art efficiently develops a number of good ideas for the distribution and collection of supplies. Jot down in a notebook any ideas you observe being put to use by art teachers.
2. Visit a number of art rooms used by children in various grades. Make notes on the manner in which "traffic" is regulated when supplies are being distributed and returned.
3. Discuss with a group of children what might be the best ways of (a) preparing supplies; (b) distributing supplies; (c) keeping supplies in good order while work is in progress; (d) returning supplies; (e) cleaning up the room after work.
4. Discuss with children some of the best ways of keeping tools in good condition.
5. Organize teams of children to look after tools, supplies, and the classroom in general. Have the children appraise the results of their work.
6. Make a cardboard or wooden model, to scale, of the art room in which you would like to work. Use twenty-five or thirty symbols (such as buttons or red squares of wood) to represent the pupils, and move them around your model to indicate the positions of the pupils during any given time in an art session. Make a note of "traffic jams" and rearrange the system to eliminate congestion of pupils.
7. Suppose you had to conduct an art program in a one-room schoolhouse. Your budget is low, but your ambitions are high; what might you and the children do to adapt the classroom to your needs?
8. Make a half dozen or so specific suggestions on changing a general classroom in which art is taught into a suitable art environment for elementary school children.

Relative size will generally indicate symbolic importance in children's art, as in this tempera-and-crayon painting by a second grader.

THE DEVELOPMENT
OF CHILDREN'S ART

The child begins to express itself from birth. It begins with certain instinctive desires which it must make known to the external world, a world which is first represented almost exclusively by the mother. Its first cries and gestures are, therefore, a primitive language by means of which the child tries to communicate with others. *

Expression in art relies on both its creator's unique personal qualities and experiences in life. Since children neither possess identical personalities nor react in wholly similar fashion to experience, their output in art must of necessity vary. Nevertheless, at certain periods of their general development children tend to pass through various stages of artistic production and consequently to adopt recognizable modes of artistic expression.[1] It is highly desirable that a teacher be familiar with the developmental stages of artistic production and with the accompanying modes of expression. Often the stage of expression that children have reached will give clues not only to the type of subject matter that may interest them, but also to the tools, materials, and activities with which they may cope successfully.

Familiarity with a child's stage of expression will also help the teacher to determine what kind of stimulation, assistance, and general educational treatment the child requires. This chapter will describe the stages and modes, or "form concepts," of children's artistic expression, including the peculiarities of design. It will also comment on how well-known writers have categorized the artistic output of children, and on

---

*From Herbert Read, *Education Through Art*, rev. ed. (New York: Pantheon, 1958), p. 108.

[1]The terms "mode," "schema," "scheme," "form concept," and "formula" have all been used synonymously by various writers. The words denote the overall means by which a child tries to make clear to us his artistic intention.

the various ways that children's art is related to traditional artistic expression.

It is difficult to indicate precisely at which grade level or age each stage of artistic development occurs. Lowenfeld attempts to do this but urges flexibility in relating activities to expectancies. Some writers, probably in attempting to steer away from too rigid a classification of developmental stages, present so general a list of "expectancies" that their statements tend to become meaningless. Although this chapter attempts to be as definite as possible in describing the developmental stages and modes of expression, the reader should understand that human behavior, perhaps especially in art, is more often unique than it is uniform.

DEVELOPMENTAL STAGES AND MODES OF EXPRESSION

Scholarly interest in the art of children has been manifest for a surprisingly long time. Read indicates that it probably began with John Ruskin in his book *The Elements of Drawing,* which appeared in 1857.[2] As Read notes, the "first documents in a long and increasingly complicated process of research" were published in 1885 and 1886. These were articles written by an English schoolteacher, Ebenezer Cooke, for the *Journal of Education* (London).[3]

Read then lists at least a dozen writers, from James Sully[4] in the 1890's, who defined some of the stages of development in terms similar to those we use today, to Helga Eng,[5] who in the 1930's made a searching analysis of the modes of expression, or *schemata,*[6] to be found in children's drawings.

The interest of psychologists in the nature of children's artistic production and a desire to classify it has grown in the last century. The methods of psychologists, however, vary considerably. (Kellogg developed her ideas from the study of 100,000 drawings while Eng and Piaget felt it necessary to study only a very few children.) It is therefore difficult to arrive at a scientifically validated, comprehensive theory regarding the psychology of early drawing; one can infer general concepts from a

---

[2] Read, *Education Through Art.*

[3] Read says, "These articles . . . are . . . remarkable as an anticipation of subsequent theories."—*Education Through Art,* pp. 169–70. Extracts of the articles may be found in the appendix of that book.

[4] James Sully, *Studies of Childhood,* rev. ed. (New York: Appleton-Century-Crofts, 1903).

[5] Helga Eng, *The Psychology of Children's Drawing,* trans. by H. Stafford Hatfield (New York: Harcourt Brace Jovanovich, 1931).

[6] According to Read in *Education Through Art,* the word "schema" (pl. "schemata") was first used by Sully and later given great significance by the German psychologists. It is interesting to note the contemporary revival of the word, largely as a result of Lowenfeld's writings. See, for example, the latter's frequent use of the word in *Creative and Mental Growth,* 4th ed. (New York: Macmillan, 1964).

consensus among the major theorists. Today numerous classifications are to be found, but basically they all agree on the existence of at least three main stages that occur before adolescence.

The first stage is one at which children manipulate materials, initially in an exploratory and random fashion. Later in this stage the manipulation becomes increasingly organized until the children give a title to the marks they make. During the next stage the children develop a series of distinct symbols that stand for objects in their experience. These symbols are eventually related to an environment within the drawing. Finally comes a preadolescent stage at which the children begin to become critical of their work and express themselves in a more self-conscious manner. The fact that these stages appear in the work of most children in no way detracts from the unique qualities of each child's work. Indeed, within the framework of the recognized stages of expression the individuality of children stands out more clearly.

The first stage of artistic production is that of manipulation. It is also known as the scribble stage, but whereas the word "scribble" implies a distinct early phase of image development, "manipulation" implies a general stage of initial exploration and experimentation with any new materials or ideas. The manipulative stage may begin earlier in life than many people realize. When children are little more than a year old they may reach for something that will make a mark, such as a pencil or a crayon, grasp it in their fist, and make a few hesitant scratches. This scribbling is the beginning of the manipulative stage and, indeed, of all artistic expression, and usually lasts until the children are in kindergarten or the first grade.

The Manipulative Stage

The period of producing scratches lasts several days, weeks, or months, depending on the child's muscular development, intelligence, general health, and the time devoted to practice. As time goes on, the scratches are increasingly controlled; they become more purposeful and rhythmic. Eventually many children tend to resolve their marks into large circular patterns, and they learn to vary their lines so that they are sweeping, rippling, delicate, or bold.

The great variety of circular patterns, or "mandalas," according to Rhoda Kellogg's analysis of thousands of children's drawings,[7] appears as a final stage between scribbling and representation. Carl Jung and Rudolf Arnheim both view the mandala as a universal, culture-free symbol that evolves out of a physical condition (that is, as a basic property of the nervous system) as well as a psychological need (the quest for order on its simplest level). It is interesting that the mandala, like other mani-

---

[7] *What Children Scribble and Why* (Palo Alto, Calif.: National Press, 1959).

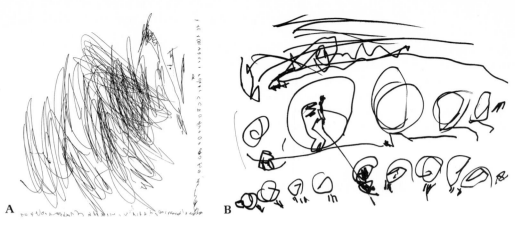

Figure 6.1 *This pair of drawings demonstrates how abruptly change can take place. Here, a three-year-old went from manipulative scribbling* **(A)** *to more structured arrangements* **(B)** *of symbols in less than a month. Transitions of this sort are usually more gradual.*

festations of children's early drawing, can appear as readily among Nigerian children as in nursery-school children in an upper-middle-class American suburb. Ultimately the children's growth in language and their growing awareness of the specifics of their culture provide the differences that enable us to distinguish between their drawings. Read[8] describes how a secondary-school teacher obtained a rich variety of mandala structures by having his students close their eyes to receive "mind-pictures." From his description we may assume that the mandala as a form of expression is not unique to young children. One may also point to the widespread use of the mandala in the psychedelic art of the youth of our own generation.

When children are given paint, in kindergarten if not before, definite changes are to be seen in their output. Usually they begin by handling the brush as they do the crayon; that is, they produce lines rather than areas of color. Later, particularly if they are given a broad, flat brush, they are likely to paint masses of color, and sometimes they may outline these masses with lines of contrasting color. Many children become fascinated with the various effects to be achieved with a brush and attempt stippling, "dry-brush" painting, and sometimes even a controlled splashing of paint by shaking the brush. Someone has recommended that children at this stage be permitted to paint only in a bathtub.

The child from about two to kindergarten age goes through a similar process of manipulation with three-dimensional materials. Clay may at first be squeezed through the fingers in a relatively uncontrolled fashion. Later the clay may be rolled into thin lengths, or pommeled, or shaped into balls. In box sculpture, the units may first be stacked, knocked down, and restacked into arrangements that display little order. In time, however, the child may develop a system of stacking so that the larger boxes are

[8]Read, *Education Through Art.*

used as a base for the smaller ones. When scraps of wood are used for sculpture, the same process is often observed.[9]

After perhaps five or six weeks of work with several art media most children gain sufficient skill to repeat shapes, either in line or in mass, with paint, clay, boxes, or scraps of materials. The painting may, for example, take the shape of an oblong not unlike a window, or boxes may be crudely arranged to resemble, say, a bridge. Clay may be rolled to appear snakelike.

Up to this point children have neither established a theme of expression nor given a title to their work. Eventually, however, the pupils lift their eyes from their work and say, "It's me," or "It's a window," or even "That's Daddy driving his car." The manipulative process has at last reached the stage at which the product may be given a title. This development very often occurs within the first month of the child's school life.

We may assume that in general the children up to this stage share a number of other characteristics:

1. The work of art is primarily instrumental in nature, in other words, it is an adjunct of another thought process rather than an end in itself. This does not preclude, however, drawing as a self-rewarding act.
2. Early drawings are general rather than specific; that is, they deal with dominant impressions as opposed to differentiation. (Noses may be more significant than the roundness of the head.)
3. For reasons known only to themselves, children always know when the drawing is finished. The sensitive parent, therefore, does not force the child beyond this point.
4. Each stage of development is usually accompanied by a period of retrenchment, often regression, during which time the schemas are repeated in a seemingly mechanistic way. Eng calls this "automatism."[10]

The nature of the thinking that goes on during the naming of the manipulated material is not known. It appears that the child does not begin work with a theme in mind but rather that the naming occurs after the material has taken shape. The child rolls clay, for example, mainly for the pleasure of rolling it. When the clay suggests some object, the appropriate title, which is always related to an experience, is attached to it. Sometimes a title appears to arise from manipulative work because of kinesthetic or muscular associations. In such cases a child may pick

Figure 6.2 *Much information can be conveyed in early symbolic drawings. In this three-year-old's drawing of his neighborhood the symbols represent a street, an apartment building, two kinds of vehicle, and the child himself.*

---

[9] All these media, together with large crayons and large soft pencils, are most suitable at this stage. Chapters 7 to 11 will comment in detail on the subject of suitable media at different stages.

[10] Helga Eng, *The Psychology of Children's Drawings from the First Stroke to the Coloured Drawing* (New York: Humanities, 1931).

up a brush loaded with paint, proceed to make rhythmic marks, say "choo, choo, choo," and subsequently inform the teacher that the paint marks represent a "ride in a train." Here, the movement of the arm has reminded the child of motion in the train. Unless present when the painting is being produced, the teacher will no doubt experience difficulty in seeing the connection between the title and the marks set down.

As we have seen, the manipulative period in artistic expression includes three overlapping but recognizable phases: (1) scribbling, or random manipulation, (2) controlled manipulation, and (3) named manipulation. Although it is impossible to assign any stage of expression to any age group, or to predict how long each learner will take to pass from one stage to the next, certain generalizations can be made about rates of development. Much depends on the children's preschool or nursery-school experience with art media and on their muscular development. If the children are provided with materials and encouragement, they may begin random manipulation during their second year and reach the stage of relating symbols to an environment before they enter kindergarten. Other children, who have been given no practice in using art media, may be capable only of random manipulation when they enter kindergarten. Children with poor muscular coordination may spend a year or more learning to control their manipulation of art media, whereas better developed children may pass through the whole manipulative stage and enter the symbol-making stage within a few weeks of beginning kindergarten or first grade.

The teacher of the early elementary grades must be prepared, then, to find pupils at many stages of development and to see pupils progress at different rates. In the case of most normal children, however, the teacher might expect satisfactory progress through the three phases of the manipulative period to take about six weeks to two months. At the end of this period most children will be entering, or ready to enter, the symbol stage.

Actually, no one leaves the manipulative stage entirely. Confronted with an unfamiliar substance or a new tool, we are likely to perform some manipulation before we begin to work in earnest. After buying a new pen, for example, we generally scribble a few marks with it before settling down to write a letter. The artist who purchases a new kind of paint will in all likelihood experiment with it before he paints seriously. Indeed, the manipulation of paint has been one criterion of art since the Venetians during the Renaissance and most recently was one of the chief values among the Abstract Expressionists. Moreover, the painterly surface is one of the hallmarks of all Romantic art much as the repression of painterly effects is a distinguishing characteristic of classicism. Surface manipulation plays the same role in sculpture (Rodin in contrast to Canova). One might think of the visible manipulation of surface qualities as representing the pleasure found in working the materials of art.

The teacher should realize that manipulation is not a waste of educational time and materials; it is a highly educative process. The control of tools and materials that the children gain through manipulation allows them to enter the symbol phase of expression.

The Emergence and Development of Symbols. To produce symbols, the children must be able to give their marks or shapes desired characteristics and must be able to reproduce these forms at will. The production of symbols demands a relatively high degree of precision, because a symbol, unlike most of the results of manipulation, is a precise statement of a fact or event in experience.

The Symbol-Making Stage

Before a symbol proper appears in children's work, they usually have produced many consistently similar marks or shapes. Circular shapes may have appeared in paint or clay, for example, or an elongated, enclosed form may have been invented and repeated in paper sculpture. Some children may produce dozens or hundreds of marks or shapes having a close resemblance. Eventually, as was noted above, the children relate the result of this manipulation to a specific object. Pointing to a circular mark in paint, they may say, "That is a man." A symbol has then been established.

We have no precise knowledge as to how they arrive at this pictorial-verbal statement. It has been suggested that the shapes they produce in their controlled manipulations remind them of objects in their environment. On the other hand, the dawning realization that marks or shapes can convey meaning, together with a newly acquired skill to produce them at will, may prompt them to plan symbols. Perhaps the symbol appears as a result of both mental processes, varying in degree according to the personality of its author. Whatever the process may be, the ability to produce symbols constitutes an enormous advance in the child's educational career. The kindergarten child has now developed a new means of expression and communication with associates that is definitive, personal, flexible, and artistically effective.

The first symbols to appear in children's output vary from one child to another. The subject matter seems to be determined by the objects in the pupils' experience that have most forcibly impressed them. These objects may be flowers, animals, furniture, or people, but the symbol that appears most frequently represents "human being."

Once children have arrived at a symbol they work hard with it, repeating it or producing many others in the same category. To a casual observer, all symbols within a given subject category may appear to be a mere repetition of its predecessor. Such, however, is not usually the case. As the children work, they apparently think about the objects they are delineating, so that the symbol becomes increasingly recognizable in form (see Figure 6.3). For example, the first symbols for a human being

Figure 6.3 *Diagrams showing some symbols that represent person, tree, and house. These diagrams, proceeding from simple to complex, were all taken from the work of kindergarten children.*

are crude. To an elliptical or circular shape may be attached one or two appendages denoting legs. Later, marks may be included to indicate arms, and circular shapes may be added to represent buttons or eyes. Still later perhaps, marks are added for hair and other features. Little by little, with each addition giving clarity to the statement, the symbol takes form. After much thought and labor the symbol becomes unmistakably human and cannot be confused with symbols for other objects.

Differentiation of the symbol progresses further. Once the symbol for, say "human being" is firmly established, the categories within the human race begin to appear. The marks or forms for hair may be varied to depict "man" or "woman." Items of clothing may serve to portray particular people. In time the children can produce to their satisfaction

Figure 6.4 *Symbols vary in originality and complexity with each child. In* **A,** *the child uses lines to make a complex symbol of a flower pot; in* **B,** *powerful black masses are utilized to represent storm clouds.*

A "Flower pot," *kindergarten*
B "Rain is to fall," *grade 1*

not just a human symbol but one to depict any particular person they have in mind.

Children do not usually concentrate on fully developing any one category of symbols. Many diverse objects receive their attention simultaneously and are developed in symbolic form at a rate that is governed by their knowledge of and interest in the objects depicted, together with their skill in portraying these objects. Between kindergarten and the second grade two or more symbols delineating different categories of objects will appear in their output. This development may sometimes occur almost simultaneously with the appearance of the first symbols, although it may occur some days, or even weeks, later. When the development occurs, however, the children have made an advance into a second phase of symbolic expression.

The symbol is a form of shorthand that children create for their particular needs. As such, it will vary in complexity and originality, as will their later efforts. When, on entering school, children take the Goodenough-Harris "Draw-a-Man" test, their ability to recall detail will be used as one index of their reading readiness. The seeds of their ability to recall such details as facial features, number of fingers, and details of dress lie in the symbolic stage.

Relating Symbols to an Environment.   Whenever pupils produce in the same composition two or more symbols related in thought, they have demonstrated an advance in visual communication, for they have realized that a relationship of objects and events exists in the world. The problems that confront them at this point revolve around a search for a personal means of expressing satisfactory relationships between symbols and their environment. In striving for such a means of expression, normally by the age of seven, they are engaged in the main task of all artists.

This development can occur only if educational conditions are right. Unfortunately, during these delicate developmental stages havoc may be perpetrated by adults who view children's art as a crude version of adult work rather than as an entity unto itself. The child's work up to now exhibits to the eye of the uninitiated an untidiness, a disorder, and often an unintelligible appearance. To make children's work neater or clearer, adults sometimes use certain "devices"—such as outlining objects for them to color, allowing them to copy and trace the work of others, and providing kits of circles, squares, and triangles from which they are to shape the forms of people, birds, and the like. All these activities, often designed by well-meaning people, have been proved beyond doubt to interfere with the developmental processes mentioned earlier.[11] In performing the prepared activities the children begin to rely on them and

---

[11]For further discussion, see C. D. and M. R. Gaitskell, *Art Education in the Kindergarten* (Peoria, Ill.: Bennett, 1952).

cease to exert themselves in a search for adequate modes of personal expression.

Left to their own devices, the children in the primary grades are self-accepting. True primitives, they approach art as though it were their private discovery, working freely and unself-consciously, despite the profusion of visual influences around them. Allowing children in this stage to use a coloring book opens the door to self-doubt because they are dramatically confronted with the gap between an adult's image and their own. In attempting to draw a clown at a later time, they may recall a "grown-up" clown they had once colored and either try, unsuccessfully, to emulate it or suddenly become dissatisfied with their own rendering. A study by Horace Heilman[12] of the effect of coloring books on children demonstrates the inhibiting effect of adult images superimposed on the art of young children.

Let us return, however, to the normal pattern of development as a result of creative effort. Children may begin relating a symbol to its environment by simple means. They may render in paint, clay, or some other suitable medium two similar symbols for human beings to which they give the title "Me and My Mother." Soon they begin to put together symbols for diverse objects that have a relationship in their thought. Their work may be given such titles as the following:

[12]An Experimental Study of the Effect of Workbooks on the Creative Drawing of Second Grade Children," unpublished doctoral dissertation, Pennsylvania State University, 1954.

Figure 6.5 *The first grader who painted this has not yet completed the transition from drawing to painting, but she has begun to relate symbols to an environment. Note the clearly defined skyline and the obviously commanding position she has given herself at the family barbecue.*

Me and My Friends
Our House Has Windows
My Dog Is in the Sun
I Am Riding on My Wagon
Daddy's Car Bringing Me to School
The Postman Bringing Me a Valentine

Expression based on vicarious experiences—stories told or read to them or events they have seen on the television or in the movies—may appear in their output, with such titles as:

These are the bears and this is Goldilocks
Here is a wolf going to blow a house down
This is a little mouse who lives in a house
The Indians are running

Even in these early years a difference in preference for subject matter is to be found between the sexes. Boys, for example, produce three times as many symbols for mechanical objects as do girls. Boys also depict animals more often, but girls use a larger number of symbols for human beings. Whether the current trend toward antisexist education will change this differentiation in choices remains to be seen.

Although children may first depict nothing but the objects they mention in the titles of their output, they soon begin to provide a setting or background. Certain children in an early symbolic stage seem to consider the paper on which they are drawing or painting as an environment for the symbols being delineated. To emphasize this concept and thus define the limits of the environment, children have been observed to paint a border around the edges of the paper and to give the resulting work a title such as "I am in a room" or "I am in a garden." In the early stages of symbol-making the child quite frequently uses this convention (see Figure 6.7).[13] Sooner or later, however, most children use a "base line" as an indication of a floor or ground on which another symbol may stand. The base line may be placed away from a symbol or it may touch the symbol. It may take the form of a line drawn from edge to edge of the paper, or it may be painted in a mass. Sometimes children paint several base lines when they wish to depict two sides of a street or different events in a story that are closely connected in thought but remote in space. The child may extend the meaning of the base line by using it to depict such items as steps, hills, sidewalks, or railway tracks.

Another symbol arising from the environment is that of the sky line.

[13] Viktor Lowenfeld and W. Lambert Brittain, in *Creative and Mental Growth,* have made some penetrating observations of this and other schematic representations. See in particular their Chapter 26, "The Achievement of a Form Concept."

Figure 6.6 "I am skipping." *Approaching the age of seven, the girl who painted this has added many details to her symbols. Notice that she makes herself much larger than her playmates.*

Figure 6.7 "My tooth is frozen. He put a needle in my gum." *The five-and-one-half-year-old girl used a border to establish an environment for the symbols in her tempera painting.*

Sky is usually indicated at first by a line drawn across the upper portion of a working surface, with most symbols below it. Often accompanying this symbol is that of a sun, which is depicted as a circular shape with radiating lines. Starlike shapes are sometimes added as a further indication of sky. These symbols often persist for many years, and the sky does not appear as a solid mass of color touching the earth until the child has developed greater maturity of expression, probably between the eighth and tenth years.

As the children's use of symbols broadens and their expression consequently grows in complexity, the task of finding adequate modes of expression to make their meanings clear becomes increasingly difficult. Their strong desire to express themselves with clarity leads them to adopt many curious artistic conventions. The ingenuity exhibited by the children in overcoming a lack of knowledge of technical devices, such as linear perspective, and in substituting acceptable and expressive devices of their own is nearly always interesting and, indeed, is sometimes little short of miraculous.

Let us consider some of the means that children may adopt to make their artistic expressions clear. One of the most obvious devices is to vary the relative sizes of the symbols used in their work. A symbol having emotional or intellectual importance to the pupils may be made larger than others related to it. "Mother," for example, may be depicted as being larger than a house, or, perhaps more frequently, the children, who are generally egocentric at this stage, will delineate themselves as towering over their associates. The children will employ this device in connection with all the familiar art materials, but it is especially noticeable in their painting, as illustrated in Figure 6.6. When they use paint, they not only give a greater size to the object that appeals most to them but also may paint it in a favorite color. Color is often chosen for its emotional appeal rather than for its resemblance to a natural object. Soon, of course, the children's observation of the world affects their choice of color—sky becomes blue and grass green. When this happens, at about seven years of age, their paintings tend to lose some of their naiveté.

Even though young children lack the technical ability to express themselves through visual forms, they are extraordinarily inventive in devising relatively complicated modes of composition through which to present their emotional and intellectual reactions to life. Young painters, for example, do not hesitate to use an "X-ray" approach in developing their images. Frequently they weave into one composition events that occur at various times. In a sense, they may treat the subject of a painting as they do that of a written composition. For example, in a painting entitled "Shopping with Mother," they may show themselves and their mother driving to a shopping center, making various purchases, and finally unpacking the parcels at home. Here we have, as it were, a story in three paragraphs with all the items placed on one painting surface. Some of these compositions may be arranged aesthetically, while others may contain items that tend to be pictorially unrelated. If not always related aesthetically, however, the items are at least related in thought.

Another interesting device adopted by many children passing through the "symbol-and-environment" phase of visual expression frequently arises from their inability to use linear perspective. In a picture of a hockey game or of people seated around a table, for example, some of the participants may appear to be lying flat or to be standing on their heads. The many children who produce compositions of this type usually do so by moving their picture in a circular fashion as they delineate objects or people. Thus, a child may draw a table and place Mother or Father at the head of it. Then, by turning the paper slightly, the child may place Brother in the now upright position. This process continues until all are shown seated at the table. As an alternative to moving the drawing or painting surface, children may walk around the work, drawing as they go. Figure 6.10 shows several different ways children will render circle games.

The preceding examples illustrate not only that children are highly inventive when they are moved to express themselves artistically, but also that they tend to use reason in solving their problems. A careful study of the compositions of children at this developmental stage usually reveals a logic as well as an aesthetic quality.

Lowenfeld refers to this stage as the *schematic* stage. Other observers of children's art have applied their own terminology to it. While the labels may vary, most agree that around the age of seven, children settle on their own symbolic rendering of objects. If the children do not progress beyond their symbol-schema after a period of a year or so, the teacher is faced

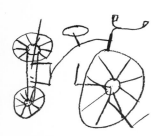

Figure 6.8 *The first grader's multiple view of a tricycle is not unusual for that age group. Multiple views will persist until a more mature spatial orientation is developed.*

with a new task—that of encouraging the children to regard the object with a fresh eye so that they may progress beyond what has become a convenient visual cliché. Second- and third-grade children's individual treatment of such subjects as houses, figures, and space tells us much about their knowledge of that subject and what their concept of reality is. Thus the schema for a nose may be a straight line for one child and a ball for another. The children can move out of the schematic stage only if their attention is directed elsewhere by the teacher, through questioning, or by encouraging them to observe and comment on the subject of the schema. In the cases of extremely prolonged use of the schema these methods may be advisable.

The manipulative stage in particular provides a basis for the work of certain professional artists, such as some artists of the Abstract Expressionist school, whose random, manipulative techniques are a means of achieving spontaneous, accidental effects in their painting. Untrained observers often fail to see the value of such experimentation because it appears to lack structure and coherence and it looks too much like play. Only recently have educators begun to place a value on the potential seriousness of play activity. It has been said—perhaps rightly—that understanding physics is child's play compared with understanding child's play.

Figure 6.9 *In the lower grades children often combine interior and exterior views of subjects to make "X-ray" pictures. Grade 2.*

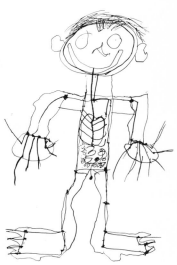

Figure 6.10 *After they played circle games (**A**), first graders were asked to draw their favorite games. Note the treatment of people in a circle. Note also the wide range of expression as each child extracted from the experience that which had most meaning. To **B**, it was a fashion parade; to **C**, the game "Rabbit Run" was meant to be taken literally. **D**, evicted from the games for misbehavior, shows himself sulking on the Jungle Jim, while **E**, likewise ostracized, was obviously less disturbed by the situation. **F** is interested in the problem of shifting views of people standing on the playground.*

172

From our point of view, the preadolescent stage includes children from approximately the third to the sixth grades. The older children's approach to expression in art is different from that of the young children. Although the older children are still naturally inquisitive and creative they have learned to be more cautious in what they do. Younger children go about their work in art with a fine, free abandon; they "try anything once," often regardless of the consequences. To them practically every experience in art is a new one, and they enjoy working on unfamiliar ground. The older children, on the other hand, have learned that one is, to some extent at least, held responsible for one's actions, and that whatever one does will probably affect other people. The older children, in other words, are beginning to learn what we all must realize eventually: we live in an organized society that has little room for completely egocentric behavior.

The Preadolescent Stage

The art teacher in the middle grades faces a special problem, for the new social awareness of the third and fourth graders tends to make them dissatisfied with their work. Their critical sense has developed far in advance of their ability to render in ways that are satisfactory to them, and other forms of communication, both verbal and written, that they have learned to control have supplanted the excitement of the language of art. Furthermore, the potency of the visual symbol leads them to unrealistic expectations. They accept the fact that they cannot read or write or speak on an adult level, but the shock of seeing their immaturity in visual terms is often hard to accept. An important task of the teacher at this time is to find ways that will lead the children to self-acceptance. In extreme cases it might even be wise to concentrate more on spatial-

Figure 6.11 *The elements of design such as tone, color, space, and line are used by older children to give their work as much a sense of "realism" as possible. Here a ten-year-old Parisian boy has painted his neighborhood church, Notre Dame des Champs. The skillful employment of linear perspective, tonal variations on gray, and overlapping forms lends the painting considerable depth.*

Figure 6.12 *The older child becomes increasingly aware of adult standards of representational accuracy in art. This pair of drawings by two fifth-grade classmates clearly demonstrates the wide range of perceptual acuity within the same age group. It is precisely as the child's skill in drawing increases that frustration grows also.*

constructing activities than on the more expressive areas of drawing and painting.

The preadolescent's work tends to be relatively complete in statement. Central objects are depicted with increasing reality so that details of features and clothing appear. Backgrounds are given attention, sometimes to such an extent that they become confused with the main objects in the composition. Light and shade and textural effects are employed, not so much for aesthetic ends as to give the work greater authenticity or "reality." In the same way, color, becoming refined through the use of tints and shades, tends to approximate the actual hues of the objects depicted. Instead of presenting a flat appearance, the output of older children often displays depth. This effect is achieved by overlapping objects, toned color, and linear perspective, devices that are taught to the children as their need and readiness become apparent.

In later childhood young people often band together in groups of the same sex. In Western culture this is the only period in life when the sexes willingly and consciously draw apart, and the division immediately precedes the marked commingling of the sexes during adolescence. Expression in art is affected by activities and interests arising from the group and peculiar to the sex of the child. Certain tendencies in subject preferences are apparent. Boys gravitate toward machines and speed symbols, acting out heroic masculine roles in their drawings, whereas girls, apparently more introspective, are less interested in detail and structure and more positive in their identification with sentiment, animals, and what strikes them as "pretty." Children should be encouraged to avoid sexual stereotyping as well as any other kind of attitude that inhibits a variety of expression. There is no reason why both boys and girls cannot draw subjects that have a wide appeal, such as sports events or domestic scenes.

174

The cultural backgrounds of the children account for variations in sex differences from one geographical region to another. In a study of East Indian children it was found that girls drew work tools more frequently than did boys, who preferred spirits and flowers.[14] Differences in choice of subject matter also hold true when American children select topics from vicarious experiences (A Hero's Welcome, Lost in Death Valley, The Last Desperado) or real-life situations (Camping Out, My First Party Dress, Open House for the PTA). No one can deny the catholic taste of the preadolescent.

As adolescence draws closer, a few pupils exhibit some further developments. Sometimes a student may show an interest in design for its own sake and welcome activities that allow insight to grow in this direction. Portraiture and life drawing may also have appeal. In some drawings produced by pupils at this stage, one may find that considerable attention has been given to anatomical detail. The advanced preadolescent has, however, many distinct problems that demand sympathetic and skillful teaching practices from the art teacher.[15] But few pupils reach this stage within the first six grades of the elementary school.

THE DEVELOPMENT OF A SENSE OF DESIGN

As with professional artists, the design output of children is inseparably linked to their general expressiveness. Thus the physical, mental, emotional, and social development of the learners, which of course influences the subject matter of their expression, governs also the designs they produce. Let us now examine the relatively consistent development of design that occurs in children's work.

It was noted earlier that picture-making in general comes naturally to children at a surprisingly early age. Some children will grasp a crayon and make marks with it before they are fifteen months old. The fact is that the bodily movements of all young persons are overall movements, and these result in a broad rhythmic action.[16] When very young children paint, they do so from their fingertips to the ends of their toes. Not until they grow older and gain control of the smaller muscles do their muscular actions in art become localized to the arm and hand.

Even up to the age of nine or ten, children treat pictorial space almost entirely intuitively. As far as one may observe, little conscious thought is given to aesthetic structure before the child enters preadolescence. The

---

[14]Cora Dubois, *The People of Alor* (Cambridge, Mass.: Harvard University Press, 1960).

[15]The characteristics of preadolescence and early adolescence have been described in some detail in C. D. and M. R. Gaitskell, *Art Education During Adolescence* (New York: Harcourt Brace Jovanovich, 1954).

[16]See the interesting study by G. E. Coghill, *Anatomy and the Problems of Behavior* (New York: Hafner, 1929).

work is nevertheless often pleasant to look at and presents a naive, uninhibited appearance of great charm. Moreover, the paintings of primary-school children are strikingly integrated. It would be difficult to interchange sections from one painting to another because the choice of color, the grouping of shapes, the very brushstrokes all provide a consistency of form that is not easily attained at the upper elementary level.

As well as exhibiting an ability to design in two dimensions, the preschool child often learns to produce three-dimensional designs. By the time some children have reached the age of three, they have experimented with sand and—sometimes to their parents' horror—mud. They are capable of joining together scraps of wood and cardboard boxes or using building blocks to bring about the semblance of an organized three-dimensional form.

On entering kindergarten at the age of four or five, those children who have had practice at home with art materials and who have produced pleasing designs tend to lose the ability to design in a natural and charming manner. Sometimes their work becomes deficient in visual unity because of a lack of balance and rhythm. Often children at this level show little feeling for space as an element of composition. Variety in the use of the elements and particularly of line may eventually produce only a state of confusion.

The causes of these conditions are not hard to find. In the first place the children are passing through a period of adjustment in a strange social setting. Many of them are removed for the first time from the protection of their parents and their homes. Unfamiliar faces and situations surround them, and a new and powerful adult in the form of a teacher must sometimes be placated. The confused state of their art is simply a reflection of a slightly upset personality. A second reason for the deterioration of their design at this period is the fact that many are passing through a new phase of artistic development. From the scribble or manipulative stage they are progressing into that of symbols. As was mentioned earlier, in this latter stage marks can no longer be placed at random on a sheet of paper but rather must be set down with greatly increased precision. In their attempt to achieve greater command of symbols the children tend to lose their natural sense of freedom. Not until the young learners feel more at home in their new environment will qualities of spontaneity and directness return.

A two-year study of the designs produced by kindergarten children who had been enrolled in class long enough to have become accustomed to their new environment revealed some interesting facts about their artistic production.[17] Through experience in handling media and organizing ideas, and through the normal progress of orientation in the classroom,

[17]Research sponsored by the Ontario Department of Education, 1949–52. Some 9000 children enrolled in 425 kindergartens were studied. See C. D. and M. R. Gaitskell, *Art Education in the Kindergarten.*

the children's designs rapidly became more coherent. The aesthetic qualities of their output developed naturally and improved rapidly.

Even kindergarten children can produce designs displaying a considerable degree of unity. Most frequently they achieve this unity by establishing a center, or centers, of interest. Of the pictures studied, about 57 percent had one clearly defined center of interest, about 42 percent had none, and the remainder had more than one. Most of the children developed their centers of interest by making their central symbols large or by embellishing a central figure with copious detail.

Kindergarten children seem to have greater difficulty in maintaining variety in their designs than they have in developing unity. The large brushes and the standard size of crayons used seemed to prevent the children studied from varying the thicknesses of line. Their method of working with full pressure of the brush, as well as their marked preference for delineation of objects in solid outline, also tended to interfere with variety in their designs. Some variety, however, was achieved by changing the directions of the lines drawn. Even the youngest children apparently have the ability to produce lines that change from straight to curved and from rippling to flowing.

Regressions in ability occur with each child, of course, from time to time and may be observed at any level of development. Absence from school, illness, or temporary emotional upsets are clearly reflected in the design output of any child in the elementary school. The quality of design deteriorates, furthermore, if the child is subjected to dictatorial teaching techniques, related not only to design itself but also, as indicated earlier, to the symbols of expression and to any other general ideas being stated. Regressions may also occur whenever the child is attempting to solve a new problem such as, for example, the delineation of an object never before attempted or the most effective uses to which a new medium may be put. Immature children are more subject to regression in these respects than are the more advanced pupils.

The period of most marked regression in the design ability of children may be found during preadolescence. Regression, as we have already mentioned, can occur in the third, fourth, fifth, or sixth grade but is most common in the third and sixth grades. In these grades some children tend to become intellectually critical of their artistic efforts, and consequently their output begins to lose some of its naive properties. The mental attitudes that are developed at this time are forerunners of those in adolescence, when the critical abilities of young people often develop far in advance of their productive capabilities in art.

The obsession with realistic detail exhibited in the preadolescent period can lead to the weakening of design quality.[18] One sure sign for

[18]Chapter 7, "Drawing and Painting," treats the problem of working from observation in greater detail.

Figure 6.13 *If the emotional basis of a drawing or painting is sufficiently powerful, the quality of the design will not suffer from the normal course of regression that affects children from time to time.* **A** *is by a sixth grader who witnessed riots in his neighborhood;* **B** *is by a seven-year-old Polish girl who watched her father exercise in an internment camp.*

B

the teacher to observe is the abuse of the eraser as the child hunts vainly for the "perfect" line. Unless the teacher is careful, the pupils will become worriers rather than artists. The demand for photographic accuracy in delineation of objects is often accompanied by a self-critical, self-conscious, and hence inhibited approach to art work. Lines, for example, that in former years were produced with a joyful rhythmic freedom may become broken and hesitant, color that was once gay may grow muddy, spaces may lose their interest because of background crowded with detail. The plunge into adolescence is beginning.

CLASSIFYING CHILDREN'S ART

Personality Types

We have already noted the difficulties involved in explaining the developmental stages of children's art. The classification of personality types is even more hazardous because more inferences must be made from more uncertain data than is available in the developmental studies.

Certain writers have classified children into personality types largely according to the art work they produce. Perhaps the best known of these authors are Herbert Read and Viktor Lowenfeld. Their writings on this subject have aroused wide interest and their theories—especially those of Lowenfeld—appear to have exerted a great deal of influence on art education in the United States.

In *Education Through Art,* Read classified children's drawings into eight categories: Organic, Empathetic, Rhythmical Pattern, Structural Form, Enumerative, Haptic, Decorative, and Imaginative. In compiling his list of types, Read claimed to have been influenced in particular by two writers, Edward Bullough and C. G. Jung.[19] Read also expressed admiration for the work of Lowenfeld.[20]

A preliminary analysis of children's drawings left Read tentatively with twelve categories. Bullough, after investigations related to the perception of single colors, had listed four "types of aesthetic appreciation," and Jung described eight "psychological types." By an extraordinary feat of intellectual gymnastics, which nevertheless did not fail to be logical, Read was able to reduce his original twelve types to eight, so that he could both relate them readily to the categories listed by Bullough and Jung and support Lowenfeld's ideas. He then demonstrated a parallel between their classifications and his own.

Lowenfeld is concerned with a greatly reduced number of categories. He says: "We can now clearly distinguish two types of art expression both by the end product and by the attitude toward experience."[21] These types he calls "visual" and "haptic."[22] The visual type, as was mentioned in Chapter 1, is an observer and "usually approaches things from their appearance," while "the main intermediary for the haptic type of individual is the *body-self*—muscular sensations, kinesthetic experiences, touch impressions, and all experiences that place the self in value relationship to the outside world."[23] Of the people Lowenfeld studied, "47 percent

---

[19]Bullough published a number of articles pertaining to psychology and aesthetics in the *British Journal of Psychology* during roughly the first two decades of this century. Of Jung's books, Read finds his *Psychological Types* (New York: Pantheon, 1959) of exceptional significance in relation to the art of children.

[20]See in particular Read, *Education Through Art,* where he mentions Viktor Lowenfeld's *The Nature of Creative Activity* (New York: Humanities, 1959).

[21]Lowenfeld and Brittain, *Creative and Mental Growth,* p. 258.

[22]"Haptic" derives from the Greek ἅπτειν, "to touch."

[23]Lowenfeld makes several differentiations in *Creative and Mental Growth,* and uses pictures to support his text. Some of the differences of his two types may be further described as follows:

a. VISUAL—feels like a spectator; sees the general shape of an object, then details; usually begins work with outline of object, then adds details; "'how it looks' is the first reaction to any object met in darkness" (p. 261); considers correct proportions and measurements of drawn or modeled human figure of prime importance; likewise, represents space according to laws of perspective (true according to camera).

b. HAPTIC—"the self is projected as the true actor of the picture" (p. 261); "sizes and spaces are determined by their emotional value in size and importance" (p. 261); "the haptic type . . . uses the human figure as the interpreter of his emotions and feelings" (p. 263); "the perspective of haptic space is a perspective of values" (p. 268).

were clearly visual, 23 percent were haptic, and 30 percent . . . were . . . not identifiable."[24]

Many teachers who work intimately with children may question the apparently static quality of personality that the classifications of Read, and in particular of Lowenfeld, seem to imply. Barkan points out that while Read's "interpretation is somewhat more fluid than Lowenfeld's . . . his effort to categorize individual creations according to personality types seems to confuse his primary emphasis on individual uniqueness."[25] Because Lowenfeld is much more rigid in defining static typological categories of personality, Barkan finds his ideas even less acceptable than those of Read. Lowenfeld's error, intimates Barkan, lies in his apparent failure to recognize the "potency of social experience as an agent for the development of personality."

Can it be that experience—especially art education—has so little effect on the basic personality that one who works at art may not exhibit a change in type? Actually, no indisputable evidence that the personality remains static exists, and there is much evidence to indicate that change in personality can result from experience. It is known that psychologists can modify personality by planned experience and that general experience may markedly alter a person's pattern of overt behavior.

Partly in order to learn the apparent effects of artistic activity on the behavior and output of children, a study was begun in 1948 with a group of seventy pupils ranging in age from nine to fifteen years.[26] These pupils showed special interest in art, and some appeared to give promise of talent. Each year new children were enrolled, but thirty of the children were studied for a period of six years.

Because Lowenfeld, unlike Read,[27] clearly differentiated between his categories, it was not difficult in the study to sort the children's output according to visual and haptic characteristics. Although the haptic, visual, and undetermined cases did not appear, in the opinion of the Ryerson staff, in percentages similar to those discovered by Lowenfeld, a working differentiation of types was achieved. By comparing the work of each child from one year to another, certain peculiarities became manifest:

1. Nearly every child produced work in each year that sometimes appeared haptic and at other times visual in conception.
2. The longer a child worked at artistic pursuits, the greater seemed the tendency to produce pieces having the haptic characteristics.

[24] *Ibid.*, p. 259.

[25] Manuel Barkan, *A Foundation for Art Education* (New York: Ronald, 1955), p. 168.

[26] Ryerson Institute of Technology, Toronto, in art classes for children sponsored by the Ontario Department of Education. The staff was composed of educators and artists; consultations were arranged at irregular intervals between members of the staff and other types of specialists such as psychologists.

[27] Of his eight types, Read says: "It must be emphasized . . . that none of these types . . . is found in a pure state, . . ." *Education Through Art*, p. 150.

The following deductions were accordingly made. Children who, during a given period of time, produce various pieces of work, some of which have haptic characteristics and others visual, are reflecting varying responses to unlike experiences. If they feel personally involved with a subject so that their emotions and intellect are noticeably aroused, they may give expression to their subject in a seemingly haptic manner. If the subject does not excite them—and certainly not every subject is equal in its appeal—the work may appear more visual in character. However, as the children gain facility with the media and tools of expression, as they mature through adolescence, and as they become more selective in their choice of subject, they tend to feel their way into the expressive acts engaging them. With their materials under control and their insight developed, they can give greater attention to the inner nature and meaning of their subject matter. Perhaps for this reason some of the work of the children in the study seemed to swing toward the type of expression associated with Lowenfeld's haptic category.

The incomplete research described above does not invalidate the opinions of the writers who have seen fit to type art production and the children responsible for it, but neither does it support the permanence of the categories under discussion.[28]

The danger, if one exists, arising from a typology such as Lowenfeld or Read devised lies in its possible effect on teaching methods. In the words of Barclay-Russell (who, incidentally, believes there are fourteen varieties of expression to be found in the art of adolescents): "It is probably much more important in practice for art teachers to use such comparisons as approximate guides rather than to think of children's art in terms of psychological labels which may well be only partially understood." [29] While a teacher may find interest in the opinions of those who wish to place children and their work into categories, to base a system of pedagogy on such opinions might not be an altogether wise course of action. A sounder and more practical viewpoint in the business of art education is to consider each child a dynamic individual, capable of personal growth and of unique artistic output.

The psychologists' analyses of children's art have led to a number of theories that attempt to interpret artistic behavior as well as to account for changes in modes of expression. Harris and Goodenough[30] have developed a drawing test often used by elementary-school personnel to

Psychological Theories

[28]The research included a study of the effects of stimuli, media, and teaching methods on artistic output. Further cases are required to clarify the problem of the effects of the pupils' physiological maturity on their work.

[29]A. Barclay-Russell, "Art and the Adolescent," in *Education and Art* (Paris: UNESCO, 1954), p. 47.

[30]Dale Harris, *Children's Drawings as Measures of Intellectual Maturity* (New York: Harcourt Brace Jovanovich, 1963).

spot retardation and to determine general intellectual maturity. This instrument differs markedly from the I.Q. test and analyzes children primarily in terms of their sense of visual recall. Taking a quite different approach, Rose Alschuler and La Berta Hattwick[31] researched the ways in which children's art products, their choice of materials, and their behavior during art work relate to their personalities. This elaborate study of 150 children also drew attention to the ways in which choice of media and the personality of the child were related to realistic and abstract modes of expression. Viktor Lowenfeld's[32] theories of child art are based on his belief in the value of children's experiences and their sensory and imaginative awareness; he views the creative process as the most effective basis for the total development of the child.

Rudolf Arnheim[33] challenged the "intellectualist" view (children draw what they *know*) with his own view that children draw what they *see*. Dale Harris,[34] in one of the most comprehensive reviews of research in the entire field, mentions several studies that present another variant of how the preschooler operates—children draw what they *feel*. June King McFee[35] has allied herself with Arnheim by concentrating in her perception-delineation theories on those environmental factors that *precede* and *condition* artistic output. Sir Herbert Read,[36] drawing from the ideas of C. G. Jung,[37] has pointed out the universal character of preschool art, as evidenced by the recurrence of symbols that are part of every person's subconscious self.

Recent research into the human brain[38] suggests that the two halves—or hemispheres—of the brain bear a direct relationship to nonverbal artistic behavior. The *corpus callosum* connects the two hemispheres, and by severing it psychologists have been able to isolate and study the effects of each side of the brain on human behavior. As a result of their studies, these psychologists have come to believe that the left hemisphere controls one's aptitude for verbalization, analysis, and speech and the right hemisphere deals with spatial ability, imagination, competence in music and drawing, and the recognition of Gestalt patterns. Since most of the school's curriculum deals with the powers of the left hemisphere the child who learns best through the powers of the right hemisphere is obviously at

[31] Rose H. Alschuler and La Berta Weiss Hattwick, *Painting and Personality: A Study of Young Children,* Vols. I and II (Chicago: University of Chicago Press, 1947).

[32] *Creative and Mental Growth.*

[33] *Art and Visual Perception,* 4th ed. (Berkeley: University of California Press, 1954).

[34] *Children's Drawings as Measures of Intellectual Maturity.*

[35] *Preparation for Art* (New York: Wadsworth, 1961).

[36] *Education Through Art.*

[37] *Man and His Symbols* (New York: Doubleday, 1964).

[38] Some of the research leaders in this area are: Dr. Roger Sperry, California Institute of Technology; Dr. Ronald Myers, Laboratory of the National Institute of Neurological Diseases; Dr. Jerome Bruner, Harvard Graduate School of Education; and Dr. Philip Vogel and Dr. Joseph Bogen, White Memorial Medical Center at Los Angeles.

a disadvantage. As one brain researcher noted, "Excellence in one [hemisphere] tends to interfere with top-level performance in the other, . . ." and as two others observed, "When the habit of always using the same side of the brain becomes too pronounced, it can narrow one's personality."[39] This, of course, has vast implications for the teacher who tries to maintain a balance between verbal and nonverbal modes of learning. It also suggests a closer look at various activities within the arts themselves. (Are there not verbal, or left-hemisphere, components of nonverbal experiences that should also be dealt with? Most art teachers do feel that children, in addition to creating paintings, should be encouraged to discuss and perhaps even read about art.) A well-rounded art program, while utilizing the strengths of the nonverbal right hemisphere, should also contain verbal and analytic material that can be dealt with by the opposite side of the brain.

Assumptions regarding the psychological significance of children's art are held by everyone interested in the subject. While some beliefs represent a valid consensus among psychologists, others are so speculative and theoretical as to be of limited use in their application. Until more complete scientific verification is achieved, art educators will derive their assumptions from a body of experience that is commonly accepted and cannot be ignored. Harris[40] has listed what he believes to be the most significant assumptions. They are as follows:

1. Interpretation of children's art is most valid when based on a series of a subject's drawings rather than when based on a single example.
2. Drawings are most useful for psychological analysis when related to other available information about the child.
3. Free drawings are more meaningful psychologically than drawings of assigned topics.
4. When a human-figure drawing is assigned, the sex of the figure first drawn relates to the drawer's sexual self-image.
5. A child adopts a schema or symbolic way of portraying objects that may be highly significant psychologically.
6. The manner in which certain features are portrayed in drawings may be used as a sign of psychological states or conditions in the artist.
7. Drawings must be interpreted as wholes rather than segmentally.
8. The use of color in drawings can be significant for studying personality.

[39]Maya Pines, *The Brain Changers: Scientists and the New Mind Control* (New York: Harcourt Brace Jovanovich, 1973), pp. 150, 152.
[40]Dale Harris, *Children's Drawings as Measures of Intellectual Maturity,* p. 52.

Figure 6.14 *The Maestà altarpiece by Duccio (c. 1255–1319) illustrates an enlargement of the important figures. Compare the use of this convention seen here with that found in Figure 6.6. (Alinari. Museum of the Duomo, Siena.)*

ARTISTS AND CHILDREN'S ART

To the uninitiated, children's art may appear unrelated to traditional artistic expression. A careful study of their work, however, reveals the interesting fact that many of the devices employed by the very young resemble expressive modes of highly esteemed professional output. The child's treatment of sky areas, for example, has its counterpart in some Oriental paintings. The flat painting of children finds its sophisticated echo in contemporary Hard-Edge paintings. The enlargement of important figures in painting and sculpture has been used expressively by many great artists, for example by Duccio in his *Maestà* painted for the cathedral of Siena (see Figure 6.14). The "X-ray" type of picture, so common in the work of young children, is found frequently in professional work, not only in painting but also in theater stage settings. As a means of depicting movement, space, and time, Marcel Duchamp, in his well-known *Nude Descending a Staircase,* produced an art form reminiscent of the space-time compositions developed intuitively by children.

The relationship between the artistic style of the child and that of the adult artist may be an unplanned one as in the case of "primitives," such as Grandma Moses, Horace Pippin, and Henri Rousseau, whose works contain distinctively childlike qualities. The fact that primitive painters and children both lack professional training and enjoy a kind of independence from the mainstream of art accounts for such common pictorial traits as crude perspective, hard edges, flat patterning, a preoccupation with detail, and an arbitrary use of space.

184

There are also some professional painters who consciously use one characteristic or another of children's art as a determining factor in their own work. The potency of color and boldness of line of the group of German artists known as Die Brücke was in part the result of an awareness of these elements in children's painting. Others, such as Paul Klee, saw mystical "interiors"—values that were quite different from the more painterly qualities prized by Die Brücke. Klee's pursuit of what is seen by the innocent eye, uncorrupted by a technological society, has left us a body of work noted for its remarkable range—humorous, delicate, mystic, and fey—drawing its strength from the shapes and symbols of the four- to six-year-old child. If Klee entices us into a delicate world

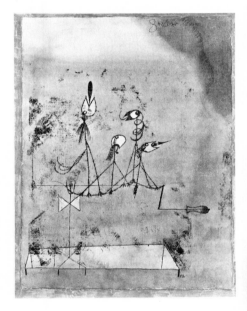

B *Jean Dubuffet,* Portrait of Henri Michaux, *1947. Oil on canvas, 51½ × 38⅜". The Sidney and Harriet Janis Collection. Gift to The Museum of Modern Art, New York.* © *ADAGP 1975.*

A *Paul Klee,* The Twittering Machine (Zwitscher-Maschine), *1922. Watercolor, pen, and ink, 16¼ × 12". Collection, The Museum of Modern Art, New York. Purchase.* © *1974 by SPADEM PARIS.*

Figure 6.15 *Both Klee and Dubuffet display the directness of expression found in children's art, but with very different results. Where Klee coaxes and invites, Dubuffet assaults the viewer; where one invites contemplation, the other commands participation.*

of quiet fantasy, then Jean Dubuffet jars us with raw, brutal forms reminiscent of graffiti left by children on sidewalks and walls. Dubuffet establishes an "antiart" attitude by utilizing the crude, tactile aspects of children's art, thus reflecting the child's independence from the traditions of aesthetic value and technique.

The value of children's art varies according to the point of view of the observer. The educator may view it as one route to the development of personality, the psychologist as a key to understanding behavior, and the artist, placing a higher value on it than either of the others, sees it as the child's most direct confrontation with the inner world of sensation

Figure 6.16 *"The Twittering Machine," grade 3. This drawing illustrates the similarities between the art of Paul Klee and that of children. It is in fact inspired by Gunther Schuller's musical study on Paul Klee's painting* The Twittering Machine.

and feeling. But educator, psychologist, and artist would all view children's art as a "reflection of the unconscious and as a non-verbal and pre-verbal mode of expression providing a direct access to the unconscious and pre-conscious processes."[41]

ACTIVITIES FOR THE READER

1. Collect from a kindergarten and a first-grade class a series of drawings and paintings that illustrate the three phases of the manipulative stage.
2. Collect some drawings or paintings by a single child to illustrate the development of a symbol, such as that for "person," "toy," or "animal."
3. Collect from several children in the first to third grades a series of drawings and paintings that illustrate developments in symbolic expression.
4. Collect from pupils enrolled in the third to sixth grades drawings and paintings that illustrate some of the major developments in the pre-adolescent stage.
5. Make one collection of drawings and paintings that is representative of artistic development from kindergarten to the end of the sixth grade.
6. Collect work in three-dimensional materials, such as clay or paper, from the pupils in situations identical with, and for purposes similar to, those mentioned in the five activities above.
7. Make a collection of children's work to illustrate the normal development in design from kindergarten to the end of the sixth grade.
8. Attempt to classify a number of sixth-grade drawings and paintings according to Lowenfeld's "haptic" and "visual" types.
9. Over a period of at least one school term collect drawings and paintings of individual children who have been subjected to many art experiences. At the end of the period analyze the work of each child according to Lowenfeld's categories. What, if any, evidence do you find of both categories in the work of any one child? Explain your findings.
10. Make a note of any art teaching you may observe that is based on a typology (or strict classification of pupils according to personality type). Comment on the effects that this type of teaching seems to have on: (a) the attitudes of the pupils and (b) the work produced.

[41] Elliot Eisner, *A Comparison of the Developmental Drawing Character of Culturally Advantaged and Culturally Disadvantaged Children*, Project No. 3086 (Washington, D.C.: U.S. Office of Education, September 1967), p. 9.

PART TWO

TEACHING ART

This first grader's watercolor, produced by using resist techniques, exploits the design possibilities offered by calligraphy.

DRAWING AND PAINTING 7

Duplicating the outward appearance of a thing as exactly as possible is no longer a job for the artist—if it ever was. The camera can do this well enough if such a record is required. The artist must occupy himself with something far more important than mere "recording"—he must interpret, penetrate, reveal—say something meaningful. He must show the spectator more than "what is there." *

As was pointed out in Part One, drawing and painting in school at one time referred to manual activities demanding great dexterity "of hand and eye" but little personal expression. Children were taught the mechanics of drawing and painting, rather than encouraged to explore them as expressive activities. This was the era of mechanical drawing, of drawing chalk boxes and railway tracks, and of laying down watercolor washes. Today children produce drawings and paintings that say something about their reactions to experience or heighten their abilities to observe. Indeed many art educators are now inclined to believe that these activities, often called picture-making, are the most important work in the entire art program. Certainly, when taught effectively, drawing and painting activities are universally enjoyed and provide a very flexible and practical means of expression for the young at all stages of artistic development.

This chapter describes the tools and materials for drawing and painting and comments on their use at various developmental levels. Reference is made to certain problems related to the teaching of drawing and painting, such as working with color and form; dealing with space; producing figure, landscape, portrait, and still-life compositions; using mixed media; and, finally, improving pictorial composition.

*From Robert C. Niece, *Art: An Approach* (Dubuque, Iowa: Wm. C. Brown Co., 1963), p. 69.

Figure 7.1 *Picture-making is an important early step toward self-expression. Here a group of fourth-grade pupils have painted self-portraits outdoors.*

THE MANIPULATIVE STAGE

The chief purpose in encouraging beginners to draw and paint is, first to allow them to become familiar with the materials associated with picture-making, and second, to help them develop sufficient skill so that they can produce symbols easily when they reach the symbol stage.

Media and Techniques

In selecting media for children in the manipulative stage the teacher must keep in mind their working methods and their natural inclination to work quickly and spontaneously. Paints or crayons should be easy to handle and should yield a rich and satisfying sweep of color when applied to a surface. For beginners, soft chalk and charcoal are rather too dusty and tend to smear and break too easily. These media are more acceptable when the child has progressed well into the symbol stage, about grade two.

Young children who are beginning to draw seem to prefer felt pens and wax crayons to other media. Crayons are sold in boxes containing varying amounts of sticks of colors; they should be firm enough to resist breakage but soft enough for the color to adhere to the paper without undue pressure. Felt pens, although expensive, are especially popular because of their vivid colors and ease of handling. The paper to be used with wax crayons should be about 9 by 12 inches in size. The effort to color surfaces much larger than this tends to be too tiring for most young children. Manila paper is inexpensive and has sufficient "tooth" for crayon. Newsprint is also suitable, but although it has the advantage of being even less costly than manila, it has rather too smooth a texture and tears easily.

Children in kindergarten should learn to work with paint, a splendid, exciting medium attractive to all children. The most suitable paint for the beginner is an opaque medium usually called "tempera," which may be purchased in several forms, the most usual being liquid or powder. The powdered variety is somewhat less expensive than the liquid but must be mixed with water before it is used.[1] (With beginning pupils the teacher

---

[1] Some brands tend to turn sour in time. This souring may largely be prevented by adding a few drops of oil of cloves to the mixture.

must mix all the paint.) It has one advantage over the liquid paint in that its textural qualities may be varied as desired. The liquid paint tends to go on with a uniform smoothness, whereas the powdered variety may be applied with varying degrees of roughness or smoothness depending on how much water is mixed with it. The textural advantages of powdered paint, however, are of more importance to children who are producing symbols than to those in the manipulative stage.

The broad, muscular fashion in which young children naturally work is even more noticeable with paint than with crayon. It is necessary therefore to provide paper for painting that is at least 18 by 24 inches. Both newsprint and manila paper are suitable, as are the thicker papers such as "bogus," and "kraft."[2] Newspapers and colored poster paper may also be used.

Brushes for painting should be broad, with long handles. Hog-bristle brushes with handles about 10 inches long are recommended. The brushes may be either round or flat, although the former seem for many children to be easier to handle. If flat, the brushes should measure about one-half inch across the bristles. After use the brushes should be washed in cold water and stored in jars with the bristles up.

A medium lending itself readily to manipulation but of decidedly limited artistic value is finger paint. To start work in this medium the teacher should place several spoonfuls of the paint on a well-dampened sheet of paper having a glazed surface. After the children have spread the paint over the dampened surface of the paper they use their fingers, knuckles, and the palms of their hands to create rhythmic patterns. They can quickly erase a pattern by smoothing the paint with the flat of their hand before proceeding to produce another pattern.

Children must exercise some care in finger painting to keep from spilling the paint on their clothing or on the desks and floor. The painters should wear aprons, and the painting surface should rest on a protective covering such as oilcloth, cardboard, or absorbent paper. Newspapers make a good covering for the working surface and, because of adhesion resulting from excess paint, have the added advantage of keeping the sheets of finished work flat.

Of all painting methods, finger painting provides the most fun in the doing, in the actual process, so much so that children are seldom critical of the results. The most sensuous and muscular of "flat" activities, it lends itself to a total physical involvement more than tempera painting does. It is, however, inappropriate for subjects that require handling of detail. Choice of medium thus affects how the subject matter is handled: crayon bestows linear qualities to the child's work, finger paint allows broad sweeps, and tempera enables the child to make use of both line and mass.

[2]The teacher should ask the supply firm to submit samples.

Teaching   The very young children are usually anxious to experiment with the media that confront them and will often do so merely by using the crayons, paint, and paper they find within reach. Their attention span, however, is short, so that within five minutes or so they may exhaust their interest in this work and seek a new activity. The more children experiment with art media, however, the longer their attention span becomes.

When children first use paint it is a wise practice to offer them only one color. When they have gained some familiarity with the manipulation of the paint, two colors might be provided, then three, then four. They can learn to handle as many as eight colors by the end of one school year of painting. If more than one color is supplied, the teacher should provide contrasting hues. The paint should be put in small containers such as glass jars, milk cartons, or orange-juice cans. To prevent accidents these containers should be placed firmly in a wire basket or a cardboard or wooden box. Very young children should have one brush for each color because they cannot at first be expected to wash their equipment between changes of color.

From the beginning of the children's experience with paint the teacher should attempt to enlarge their color vocabulary. This may be done naturally by naming colors as they are used. The use of "coloring drills," often seen in some kindergartens, seems unnatural and hence is to be avoided. The children learn about color most effectively by using it and talking about it.

Because children come to school with a linear orientation to picture-making, the first experiments in painting in both the manipulative

Figure 7.2   *These illustrations by kindergarten and first-grade pupils show the primarily linear orientation they first bring to both drawing and painting.*

and symbolic stages are likely to be brush drawings. Picture-making in its early stages is generally a matter of enclosing mental images with lines rather than the more sophisticated work of placing areas of color next to each other. Even if they begin as painters, the children will often complete the work by going over it with black lines to lend greater clarity to the masses. At first the teacher should accept whatever strategies the children happen to use but should keep an eye on the children's work habits and handling of materials and should get them to talk about their work during the evaluation period.

When the children have become familiar with crayons, paints, and brushes, the teacher may try a few simple teaching methods to encourage them and perhaps to help them improve their technique. Sometimes background music helps children improve the rhythm of their lines or color areas. When certain children in the group make discoveries, such as stipple or dry-brush effects, the teacher might draw the attention of the class to these discoveries. The teacher should also, in a general way, praise each child's industry or some other broad aspect of the pupil's endeavor. Actually the work the young children produce has little meaning for them since it is in the activity itself that they find delight.

When the children reach the phase of named manipulation the teacher should encourage them to talk about the subject matter of their painting. In so doing, the pupils tend to clarify their ideas and thus progress into further stages of development. The relation between ideas, language, and images is very intense at this age and should be encouraged. Whatever learning takes place at the stage of manipulation, however, depends largely on the children. The teacher, in other words, has little actually to teach, but must simply be encouraging. To a certain extent this principle applies to all art teaching, but it is particularly true at the manipulative stage. A pleasant working environment and one in which suitable materials are readily at hand are the main ingredients of a successful program during this stage of expression. The teacher must give much thought to preparing and distributing supplies and equipment and must work out satisfactory procedures for collecting work and cleaning up after each session (see Chapter 5).

THE SYMBOL-MAKING STAGE

When the children begin to produce symbols in their work the media and tools may remain the same as those used during the manipulative stage. As children add details to their symbols, however, they frequently require several types of brushes in various sizes. If rounded-bristle brushes were first used, some of the flat type should also be made available. The sizes of flat and rounded brushes may vary from about one-eighth to one-half inch in width. Some large sable brushes (sizes 6 to 10) and a wide range of colors in tempera paint should also be provided.

Media and Techniques

Figure 7.3 *At the symbol-making stage the child becomes increasingly involved in descriptive detail, as in this pencil-and-crayon drawing's treatment of clothes, mouth, and hair.*

In earlier art sessions little or no chalk is used, but in this stage, with their newly acquired skills, the children will probably be ready to use soft chalk, or "pastels," as they are sometimes called, which may be purchased in sets of ten to twelve colors. "Dustless" chalk, while somewhat lacking in color potency, leaves less residue on the children's clothing. Charcoal is another medium that might be used. Pressed charcoal in hard sticks is better than the "willow vine" variety, which breaks easily. Chalk and charcoal may be used conveniently on manila and some newsprint papers, which should measure about 12 by 18 inches in size.

The use of transparent watercolor before the third grade is in most cases not recommended because the medium is difficult to control. The features that are prized in watercolor—its transparent, fluid, accidental qualities—seem to work against the primary-school children's need to work through their own clearly established set of concepts. As Lowenfeld and Brittain state:

> . . . the transparency of watercolor serves best to paint atmosphere. . . . Its running quality introduces many accidents that do not lend themselves to repetition. . . . Since in his painting the child is more concerned with expressing his own ideas than with visual stimuli, such accidents would only frustrate him in his feelings of mastery.[3]

Teaching   In the symbol-making stage drawings and paintings represent subject matter derived directly from the children's experiences in life. The teacher may thus from time to time assist the children in recalling the important facts and features of the depicted objects. For example, for those children developing symbols for "man" or "woman" the teacher should draw attention to such activities as running, jumping, climbing, brushing teeth, wearing overshoes, combing hair, and washing hands. If the children will

[3]Viktor Lowenfeld and W. Lambert Brittain, *Creative and Mental Growth,* 4th ed. (New York: Macmillan, 1964), p. 38.

196

act out these activities, the concept inherent in the symbol may be expressed more completely. Judicious questioning by the teacher concerning both the appearance of the symbol in the children's work and its actual appearance as observed by the children in their environment might also take place. These teaching methods, it should be noted, are not suggested for the purpose of producing "realistic" work, but rather to help the children concentrate on an item of experience so that their statements concerning it may grow more complete.

When two or more symbols appear in the children's output, the teacher must be particularly careful to ensure that they are inspired by topics that seem worthy of expression.[4] At this point vicarious as well as actual experience may be used effectively. In addition to discussion of topics related to home, parents, school, companions, and the like, such stories as "Little Red Riding Hood," "Jack and the Beanstalk," and those by Dr. Seuss will provide children with opportunities to relate pictorially two or more symbols having differences in appearance. Current television shows can also serve as a source for characters and settings.

When the children relate their symbols to an environment, their chief difficulty often arises from an inability to make the symbol sufficiently distinct from the background of a picture. The following dialog between a teacher and a third-grade pupil relates to such a problem.

TEACHER: Mark, it looks as if you're about finished. What do you think?
MARK: I don't like it.
TEACHER: What's the matter with it?
MARK: I don't know.
TEACHER: You know, there comes a time when every artist has to stop and look at his work. You notice things you don't see up close. (*Tacks painting on easel.*) Now look at it hard.
MARK: You can't see it too clear—
TEACHER: You mean the tent?
MARK: It doesn't show up.
TEACHER: What we need is a way to make the subject—that is, the tent— stand out. What can you do? I can think of something right off.
MARK: I know—paint stripes on it.
TEACHER: Try it and see what happens. You can paint over it if you don't like it.

There could have been other solutions, such as using an outline or increasing the size of the tent. The important point of this dialog is that the teacher got Mark to discover his own solution without requiring him to give a single correct answer. The problem of developing contrasts between figure and ground, especially in color, light and shade, and

---

[4]See Chapter 6 for a more complete discussion of this important topic.

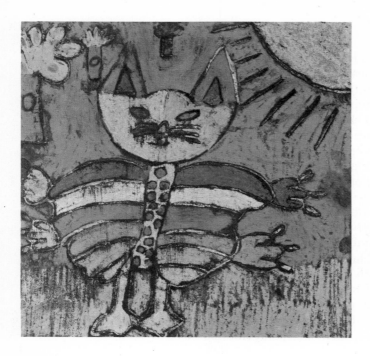

Figure 7.4 *Children at the symbol-making stage often display considerable inventiveness. In this mixed-media drawing a fifth grader has created a composite beast from many animal forms. Despite the inventiveness of the beast, however, the convention for the sun symbol is retained.*

sometimes texture, is an important one that the pupil should be helped to solve at this time.

THE PREADOLESCENT STAGE

Media and Techniques

By the time children reach the fifth and sixth grades they will probably have enjoyed a considerable amount of experience with art media and will have developed many skills in their use. A brush or a crayon should now do for the children generally what they want it to do.

A wide variety of brushes should be provided, ranging from about size 4 to size 10 of the soft, pointed type made of sable or camel hair. The hog-bristle type should also be available in long-flat, short-flat, and round types and in all sizes from one-eighth of an inch to 1 inch in width. Since children at this stage will sooner or later use tints and shades of color, it is sometimes good to provide a neutral-toned paper so that the tonalities of color may be more effective. Some pupils avoid pure white papers because of their confusing glare. Pupils in this stage will require not only the standard opaque and transparent paints, but also inks, crayons, pressed charcoal, pastels, and drawing pencils of reasonably good quality. Conté crayon, which is available in both black and sepia, makes an excellent drawing medium and may be used effectively with white chalk on gray paper. Crayons might have a range of some twenty colors. Soft lead pencils should range in weight from about 3B to 8B.

198

A

B

Figure 7.5 *As the child grows older the approach to painting becomes less intuitive.* **A***, by a second grader, exhibits exciting, "painterly" qualities, but* **B***, by a fifth grader, seems less spontaneous.*

Figure 7.6 *Children should learn to express their feelings by experimenting with the emotive power of color, as in this painting from life by a fifth grader.*

The discussion that follows will focus on several important techniques that preadolescents are expected to develop at this stage—techniques involving facility in the use of color, understanding space, skills in drawing from observtion, and ability to mix media. Because the teacher's role is central to the process of developing these techniques, comments on how to teach them are incorporated into this discussion, rather than set forth in a separate section.

Developing Facility with Color.   In the early preadolescent stage, children may become concerned with the relationship of background to foreground. This concern, together with their interest in the effects of light and shade, involves them in problems related to the tonalities of color. Up to this point, the teacher has probably been supplying most colors ready-mixed, including some deviations from the standard hues. But when the teacher considers the pupils mature enough to mix colors on their own, no time should be lost in encouraging them to do so. Most pupils can begin mixing some of the opaque pigments at least by the time they reach the third grade.

Once it is decided that the mixing of color is to be performed by the pupils, the physical arrangements in the classroom for the distribution of pigments must again be carefully planned. The cafeteria system allows the pupils to select their colors from jars of powdered or liquid tempera. Using a spoon or wooden paddle, they place the desired quantity of each color in a muffin tin. The mixing of paint and water and mixing of colors can be done right in the tins. Because children tend to be wasteful of paint they should be told to help themselves to only enough pigment to meet their requirements, and they should be cautioned not to mix too large a quantity. By adding colors, such as blue to yellow to make green, or red to white to make pink, a quantity of paint may often be saved.

Color may be altered from the standard hue in a variety of ways. To mix black with the standard tempera color results in a *shade,* while the addition of white produces a *tint.* If watercolor is used, the addition of black results in a shade, but the water itself creates the tint. The ability to mix tints and shades and thus arrive at different values greatly broadens the pupils' ability to use color. Children in the elementary school can also alter hues without undue difficulty by mixing the standard hue with its complement. Hence, when green is added to red the character of red alters; the more green added, the greater the change in the red, until finally a brownish gray results. Grays achieved by this means are various in character and different from those achieved by mixing black and white. When used in a composition, they give dramatic emphasis to the areas of bright color.

By the time the children have gained some ability to mix colors, they should have a reasonably broad range of standard hues, including black, white, red, yellow, blue, light and dark green, violet, orange, magenta, turquoise, and brown. Because the choice of colors is so wide, however, the teacher may find it necessary from time to time to caution the pupils against using too broad a palette. Children often attempt to use too many colors; in fact, they sometimes try to use every available color in one painting. They may then find it difficult to build a unified composition.

Children in the upper elementary-school grades are capable not only of looking analytically at how color behaves, as in the color wheel, but also of using what they learn about color in their paintings. This is not as true of children who have not yet reached the preadolescent stage, for young children tend to work intuitively—the works of first graders often exhibit exciting, "painterly"qualities. But the upper grader, being more cautious and less spontaneous in expression, requires stronger and more specific motivation (see Figure 7.5). Color activities built around problems posed by the teacher enable the student to learn more about the interaction of color as well as to arrive at a more personal, expressive use of color.

Here are some problems and questions for the pupils to consider:

1. Questions about sensitivity to color in the environment:
    How many colors can you see in this room?
    Would everyone who is wearing red please stand together?
    Name the colors you see outside the window. Can you grade them according to brightness or dullness?
2. Problems relating to color investigation:
    How much can you do with few colors?
    First make a painting with just three primary colors—red, yellow, and blue. Mix them any way you like. In a second painting, add black and white to the three colors.
    Compare the brown in the bottle with a brown of your own, made by mixing black and red. Which do you like better?
    Mix your own orange and compare it with the prepared orange.
3. Problems relating to the nature of pigment:
    What happens when you use color on wet paper?
    What happens when you use color on black paper?
    What happens when you combine painting and collage? Notice how a separation of color and texture appears. How can you bring the painted part and the collage section together?
4. Problems relating to the emotive power of color:
    How can you think of color in terms of feelings?
    Mix a group of colors suitable for a painting about a hurricane, a picnic, a carnival.
    Prepare little "families" or related groups of color around specific ideas and see how close you can get to what you are trying to express. For example, for a blazing house, you might group red, black, and orange; for an autumn scene, yellow, red, brown, and orange.

Such problems may be viewed as ends unto themselves or as preliminary stages to more complete picture-making. They lead into the area of art appreciation when the children are asked to relate their class activities to the solutions developed by artists. Thus, in conjunction with exercises in the emotive power of color, the teacher may refer to El Greco's *View of Toledo,* Léger's series *Le Cirque,* and many of Picasso's "Blue Period" paintings.

Coping with Space.   The older child will often be frustrated by the problem of rendering space and will require the help of the teacher. Teaching perspective is similar to teaching sensitivity to color in that in neither case does an *intellectual* approach assure the teacher that personally expressive use will follow. Children can have their attention directed to the fact that distance may be achieved through overlapping, diminution of size, consistency of vertical edges, atmospheric perspective or neutralization of receding color, and convergence of lines. This knowledge, however, has only limited value if the children are not able to see the many ways in which perspective may be used; indeed, effective pictorial expression may occur without recourse to linear perspective. Such painters as Feininger, Picasso, De Chirico, Marin, Dali, and Braque should be studied as examples of artists who have distorted, adjusted, and exaggerated the laws of perspective for particular artistic ends (see Figure 7.7).

The teacher's job is not so much to decide that a particular treatment of space is to be used in the children's work as it is to keep the children moving by helping them through any phases of dissatisfaction. Calling the children's attention to perspective as seen in the natural world and the realm of painting can help the students in such cases. It is wise, therefore, to have on hand several examples of the different ways space may be treated. Such examples might show:

1. The Oriental placement of objects, which usually disregards the deep, penetrating space of Western art.
2. The Renaissance use of linear perspective, with its vanishing points and diminishing verticals and horizontals.[5]
3. Cubist dissolution of Renaissance-type space, with its substitution of multiple views, shifting planes, and disregard of "local" (realistic) color.

[5]Although found in paintings as old as those preserved on the walls of Pompeii, linear perspective has been used for relatively limited periods in art history. It was not extensively developed in Western art until the early Renaissance in Italy. The prevailing artistic mode prior to the Renaissance—the Gothic tradition—largely ignored linear perspective, although it did appear from time to time, notably in the unique and powerful art of the Florentine, Giotto (1276–1337). By the fifteenth century, or *quattrocento,* of the Italian Renaissance, many painters became interested in this artistic convention and used it effectively. Masaccio (1401–28), Uccello (1397–1475), della Francesca (c. 1420–92), and other experimenters made marked advances in this direction, so that by the High Renaissance linear perspective had become the accepted device in Western painting and remained so until today.

Figure 7.7 *(left) Georges Braque's painting The Table (1928) almost completely lacks depth, although it contains the favorite Renaissance symbol of linear perspective, the checkered floor. Oil on canvas, 70¾ × 28¾″. (The Museum of Modern Art, New York. Acquired through the Lillie P. Bliss Bequest. © ADAGP 1975.)*

Figure 7.8 *(right) Hans Hofmann's Cathedral (1959) exemplifies his use of color tensions to create pictorial rather than object-oriented space. Some colors come forward and some recede in what Hofmann calls a "push-and-pull" process. (Mr. and Mrs. Albrecht Saalfield.)*

4. Photographic techniques using aerial views, linear perspective, and unusual points of view in landscape subjects.

Space may also be studied through examining color in abstract paintings in which very few familiar associations come between the viewer and the painting. Children can describe which colors seem to come forward and which recede, which ones "fight" with each other and which are harmonious. Hans Hofmann refers to the tensions of color as a process of "push and pull." Discussing color in such terms gives children a sensitivity to the difference between *pictorial* space, achieved primarily through color, and *object-oriented* space, achieved through the relationships between color and objects.

Under no circumstances should perspective be taught by such mechanical means as drawing complicated diagrams of chalk boxes or cylinders in various positions. Indeed, the pupil should be fully aware that to follow the laws of linear perspective blindly, without due regard for aesthetic considerations, will interfere with a successful outcome in picture-making.

In teaching perspective, as in teaching color, it is necessary to observe the fundamental principles of good pedagogy. Only when the children are ready for help and when they themselves are aware of a need for help should assistance be forthcoming. The teacher should keep in mind that the children may produce successful paintings without using linear perspective. Should elementary-school children not exhibit any inclination to adopt linear perspective to develop depth, they should be encouraged to master such alternate modes of composition as the overlapping of planes and the toning of colors. On the other hand, should pupils show an interest in this type of perspective, judicious teaching concerning it may allow their expression to grow in clarity and power.

Developing Skills in Drawing from Observation.   Sir Herbert Read makes a distinction between three categories of activity—the activity of *self-expression,* the activity of *observation,* and the activity of *appreciation.*[6] In terms of child development, self-expression has greater implication for the lower elementary grades, and observation is more relevant to the capabilities of elementary-school children in the upper grades. Although opinion among art educators is still divided as to when drawing from observation should begin, a growing number feel that directed perception satisfies a strong desire among older children to depict subject matter.[7]

One area of misunderstanding that accounts for division of opinion is the assumption by some educators that any form of directed vision implies a staunch devotion to realism, a violation of the "creative, expressive" self, or both. Any teacher who has ever asked a class of thirty children to draw the same object knows it is erroneous to assume that such instruction automatically robs children of individual responses. Unless instruction is of an aggressively inhibiting nature, the child's "self" will be asserted. What is not certain is whether the self will attempt to enrich and expand its vision in specific directions. The art teacher is needed to direct this operation.

Concerning the problem of realism, is "realistic" drawing necessarily "bad" drawing? The issue of good or bad exists apart from any particular style, for values in drawing, as in painting, reside chiefly in form rather

[6]Herbert Read, *Education Through Art,* rev. ed. (New York: Pantheon, 1958).

[7]Pauline Johnson questions drawing from observation: "Young children when asked to draw from models may be confused by working from direct observation. They may produce some skillful results and the teacher may be proud of the products, but he is overlooking the value of an experience in the child's total development."—in W. Reid Hastie, ed., *Art Education,* Sixty-fourth Yearbook of the National Society for the Study of Education (Chicago: University of Chicago Press, 1965), p. 80. Pearl Greenberg, on the other hand, recommends the use of models, still life, and landscape as early as the second grade (*Children's Experiences in Art* [New York: Reinhold, 1966]), and Helen Merritt devotes a full chapter to the problem in *Guiding Free Expression in Children's Art* (New York: Holt, Rinehart and Winston, 1964). Miriam Lindstrom, in her detailed description of the art program of the De Young Memorial Museum in San Francisco, emphasizes the use of observation as a primary basis for art activity (*Children's Art* [Berkeley: University of California Press, 1957]), as does Adelaide Sproul in *With a Free Hand* (New York: Reinhold, 1968).

Figure 7.9 *This eleven-year-old girl demonstrates a deep concern for detail as she works on a still life. (Photo by Neil Jacobs.)*

than in the degree of realistic representation. "The painter may . . . imitate what he sees," says L. A. Reid, in an attempt to find a place in art for realistic drawing, "but he imitates what he sees, because what he sees fulfills and satisfies his needs."[8] Good drawing necessarily occurs, then, when the artists select, interpret, and present in a personal, aesthetically coherent composition those items of experience that move them, regardless of whether or not the presentation is realistic. Weak drawing occurs when the forms used are drawn merely to fill gaps in the pictorial surface, without regard for the unity of the composition. In accomplishing the feat of organization, an artist may purposely depart from nature to varying degrees in the interest of design.

There is little merit in encouraging children of any age to draw with photographic accuracy, if for no other reason than that this is hardly possible. But a distinction must be made between requiring children to work for realism in drawing and using certain drawing techniques to heighten their visual acuity. Few teachers who use nature as a model or have the class work with contour line really believe that they are forcing their students to conform to photographic realism. In the first place this kind of professional facility is impossible to achieve on the elementary level, and secondly, there would be very little point to such a goal, even if it were possible to attain. The argument that working from nature is inhibiting to children is no longer accepted by most art educators. As Roettger and Klante point out:

> Play with line leads logically to a fresh way of looking at nature. Today this is often thought outmoded, because some blinkered minds will not realize that it does not need a great effort of imagination to break nature's spell. Observation and imagination thus merge inextricably, as when children (whether from imagination or memory is immaterial) try to draw objects, flowers, animals or their own reflections in the mirror.[9]

[8] *A Study in Aesthetics* (New York: Macmillan, 1931), p. 236.
[9] Ernst Roettger and Dieter Klante, *Creative Drawing* (New York: Reinhold, 1964), p. 3.

A

B

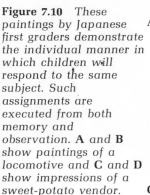

Figure 7.10 *These paintings by Japanese first graders demonstrate the individual manner in which children will respond to the same subject. Such assignments are executed from both memory and observation. A and B show paintings of a locomotive and C and D show impressions of a sweet-potato vendor.*

C

D

The question a teacher must inevitably ask is, "What can the child learn from drawing activities?" Obviously, there is not enough time for some children who lack the perceptual development required of drawing to master it. Nor is mastery of any one skill a definable goal of an elementary art program. Drawing activities can, however, serve to:

1. Provide pleasurable art activity that allows children to attain a degree of success.
2. Direct children away from stereotypes.
3. Provide children with usable skills that may be employed in other art activities.
4. Offer an opportunity to study works of outstanding professional artists.
5. Provide a process of observation that can reveal such factors as the structure and texture of objects and the relation of parts to wholes.
6. Develop in children a sensitivity to design and to the structural uses of line.

Sources of Observation. Good drawing depends in no small measure on the producer's experience of the things drawn. Such experience, it should be noted, depends not only on the eye, but on a total reaction of the artist, involving, ideally, all the senses. Often in the fifth and sixth grades good drawing may be developed through the use of some time-honored subjects that demand a comprehensive reaction to experience. Using sources grounded in experience, the child may produce drawings of the human face and figure, landscapes, and still-life subjects. The teacher should not be bound by the traditions associated with such subject matter. According to what subjects, materials, visual references, and motivating forces the teacher selects, drawing can be an exciting and pleasurable activity, or an academic and inhibiting one (see Figure 7.13). Table 7.1 compares two approaches to teaching drawing activities for a sixth-grade class.

As far as is practicable, the children should be responsible for arranging their sources of observation. For example, they should have some control in posing the model for life drawing. The teacher, of course, will have to oversee the lighting and the setting of reasonable time limits for poses. Artificial lighting by one or more spotlights can be used, and these lights must be moved until anatomical details are clearly revealed and an interesting pattern of the elements, especially line and light and shade, is visible. Models must not be asked to pose after the holding of a position becomes painful (usually for a preadolescent youngster, ten minutes is a lifetime). However, if the pose is too brief for a

Table 7.1

TWO APPROACHES TO TEACHING DRAWING

	Subject	Materials	Instructions for Visual Reference	Motivation and Historical Reference
Negative Instruction	*Still life:* A Chianti bottle, a tennis ball, and a plate on a table at the front of the room.	Hard pencil on newsprint, 8 by 10 inches, flat desk tops used as work surface.	"Draw everything you see—light and dark, lines, and so on."	None.
	Human figure: A girl posed sitting in a chair, which is on the floor.	Ballpoint pens on newsprint, 18 by 24 inches.	"Make the drawing as real as you can; make the folds really stand out."	None.
Positive Instruction	*Still life:* Four still-life centers, each composed of large shapes of interesting objects—pieces of machinery, drapery, and so on.	Dustless chalk on black construction paper, 12 by 18 inches; drawing boards used as work surface.	"Concentrate just on contour. Use a different color chalk for each object and let the lines for the shapes flow through one another."	Contour drawing demonstrated (see dialog, pp. 213–15). Line drawings by Matisse, Picasso, or good commercial illustrations shown.
	Human figure: A boy and a girl, one sitting, one standing, dressed in odd bits of costume and holding musical instruments; placed above eye level.	Black crayon and watercolor wash on 40-pound white paper (size optional).	"Balance light washes of watercolor against line. Lay in the broad directions of the figures in wash, and when it dries, work the lines over the wash."	Demonstration given; wash and line drawings by Rembrandt, Tiepolo, and Daumier shown. Lesson related to previous lesson.

complete drawing to be made, the teacher merely needs to remind the model to memorize the position in order to return to it after a rest. The teacher, of course, should also remember the pose in case the pupil forgets it. Chalk marks to indicate the position of the feet often help the model to resume the pose.

In producing life drawings and portraits, older pupils will be assisted by an elementary study both of pertinent relationships among parts of the body and of approximate sizes of parts of the figure. The pupil who is maturing physiologically often shows an interest in the human body by drawing certain anatomical details in a rather pronounced manner, especially when females are depicted. Any emphasis beyond the requirements of aesthetics may be counteracted to some degree by a study of the human body. The teacher should point out the nature of the mechanically independent body blocks—the head, the torso, and the pelvic girdle.

The human figure lends itself to interpretation. Once the children have closely examined the figure, they might be asked to interpret it in terms of fantasy or qualities of mood—joy, doom, strength, violence. Such subjects can be drawn from observation as well as imagination, for students can be posed displaying these moods.

In still-life work, the pupils should not only arrange their own groups of objects, but they should also be given the opportunity to become

Figure 7.11 *Using nature as a model does not require photographic accuracy in drawing. For this picture the child was asked to use the entire paper (12 × 18 in.) and to concentrate only on the features of the face in order to achieve a striking image. Grade 5.*

Figure 7.12 *Examples of drawing from observation:* (**A**) *continuous contour of figure, grade 5;* (**B**) *jeep, grade 4;* (**C**) *imaginative bug based on a study of a real object, grade 6;* (**D**) *drawing from model in period costume (the pupil decided to leave the face blank because of difficulty with the features), grade 6;* (**E**) *still life composed of music stands grouped in a cluster, grade 5.*

Figure 7.13 *In these two watercolors of flowers, different stages of observation are clearly apparent. The top painting is by a third grader and the bottom one is by a sixth grader.*

thoroughly familiar with each item. By handling the objects they may make note of differences in textures and degrees of hardness and softness. Sole dependence on the eye in art work limits unnecessarily the experience of the creating person.

The teacher must, of course, ensure the adequacy of still-life arrangements. They must have a challenging variety of objects, in which there are various types of contrasting surfaces, such as the textures found in glass, fur, metal, cloth, and wood. Contrast in the shapes of objects (masses and spaces) must also be arresting. The other elements—line, light and shade, and color—should also be considered for the variety they can bring to a still-life arrangement. As the objects are assembled, however, an attempt should be made to bring them together into a unified composition.[10]

The success of a still-life problem is often determined by the interests of the children. A group of fifth-graders who were asked to list objects they would like to draw as opposed to those that would not appeal to them produced the following two lists.

I Like	*I Don't Like*
Motorcycles	Models of airplanes (but I would
Pitchers	like a model of a pirate ship)
Rocking chairs	Lamps
Musical instruments	Books
Old pocket watches	Modern furniture
Old hand tools	Fruit
Old guns	
Helmets, swords	
Bottles	
Antiques	

[10] See Chapter 3 for ideas about variety and unity.

Figure 7.14 *In this still life by a fifth grader, one object has been repeated and overlapped in varying shapes and sizes.*

Selection of still-life material is another instance of the need for the teacher to plan a program with the pupils' preferences in mind.

Once the objects of the still life have been selected and arranged, the teacher must establish some visual points of reference with which the pupils can work. These might include getting them to:

1. Search for size relationships among various objects.
2. Concentrate on the edges of objects (contour drawing).
3. Use crayon to indicate shadows.
4. Use one object (an ink bottle, a wine bottle, a hammer) to arrange repeated shapes, overlapping portions of the object to obtain a pleasing flow (see Figure 7.14).
5. Concentrate only on shape by drawing the forms, each on a different color of paper, cutting them out, and pasting them on neutral-toned paper in overlapping planes.
6. Relate the objects to the size and shape of the paper. Students will find they can work on rectangular surfaces (12 by 18 inches), on squares, and even on circular shapes; they can draw small objects many times their size and reduce large objects to paper size.

In general, landscapes selected for outdoor painting or for preliminary studies to be finished in the classroom should have a reasonable number of objects in them that can be used as a basis for composition. Hence, a scene with a barn, some animals, a silo, and some farm machinery is preferable to a sky and a wheatfield, or a lake and a distant shore. By having many objects before them, the pupils may select items that they think will make an interesting composition. The wheatfield or the lake may not give them enough material to draw. Children can be sent outside the classroom to bring back sketches of the environment for their classmates to identify. A simple homework assignment is to have the students bring in drawings of their homes that show the surrounding landscape.

The work in these activities need not be of long duration. Some pupils, however, may wish to produce a more finished work and, of course, should be encouraged to do so.

Contour Drawing as a Basis for Observation. Contour-line drawing, which can be applied to landscape, figures, or objects, is considered by many educators to be a sound basis of perception. The contour approach requires the children to focus their visual attention on the edges of a form and to note detail and structure; they are thus encouraged to move away from visual clichés to a fresh regard for subjects they may have lived with but never truly examined. The following teaching session demonstrates how one teacher went about introducing this method of drawing.

Figure 7.15 *In these tempera-and-ink paintings a thirteen-year-old Tunisian boy depicts his city. The pupil was presented with several design problems by his teacher in addition to the representational one of producing a cityscape. The design problem involved the development of surface patterns through the use of line as well as color.*

TEACHER: . . . I need someone . . . to pose. Michael, how about you? (*Michael is chosen because he is the tallest boy with the tightest pants. He will do very well for the purpose of the lesson. The teacher has him sit above eye level in a chair placed on a table.*) Now listen carefully. First, is there anyone here who is not able to draw a picture of Michael in the air by following the edge of his body with his finger? . . . Then let's try it. (*He closes his right eye and slowly follows the outer edge of the subject in the air. The class follows, feeling fairly certain of success, at least at this stage.*) Very good. That wasn't too bad, was it?

PAUL: But that's not drawing.

TEACHER: Let's wait and see. Now, suppose I had a pane of glass hanging from the ceiling and some white paint. Couldn't you *trace* the lines in Michael's body right on the glass? (*They think about this for a moment.*) After all, it's the next thing to drawing a line in the air, isn't it?

ALICE: We don't have any glass.

TEACHER: True. I wish we did. But if we did you could do it, couldn't you? (*All agree they could.*) O.K.—then if you can follow the lines through the glass, you can see them. If I ask you to put them on your paper instead, what will your problem be?

ANDY: How can we look at Michael and at our paper at the same time?

TEACHER: Andy is right. We can't do it, so we just won't look at our paper. . . . May I show you what I mean? (*The class heartily approves of this. The teacher goes to the blackboard.*) Now, I'm not going to

Figure 7.16 *Two examples of line drawings made from models by* (**A**) *a fifth grader and* (**B**) *a sixth grader.*

look at the blackboard because I'm more interested in training my eye than in making a pretty picture. I'm going to concentrate just on following the edge. Do you know what the word "concentrate" means? Who knows?

ALICE: To think very hard about something.

TEACHER: Exactly. So I'm going to think very hard—to concentrate—on the outside edges of Michael. We call this "contour-line drawing." (*Writes it on blackboard.*) Contours are edges of shapes. You don't see *lines* in nature as a rule. . . . What you see mostly are dark shapes against light shapes, and where they meet you have *lines.* Who can see some in this room? (*Among those mentioned are where walls meet the ceiling, where books touch one another, and where the dark silhouette of the plants meets the light sky.*) Very good, you get the idea. We start with edges—or contours—then. Another example is my arm. (*He puts it up against the blackboard.*) If I ask you to draw my arm from *memory,* you might come up with something that looks like this (*draws several schematic arms—a sausage shape, a stick arm, a segmented form divided into fingers, hand, forearm and upper arm divisions, and so on. The class is visibly amused*). Now, watch this carefully and see what happens when I concentrate on the contour of my arm. (*With his right hand he follows the top contour and the underside of his arm. As he removes his arm from the blackboard*

214

the class is delighted to see a line drawing of the teacher's arm remain on the board.)

VERNON: I used to draw around my fingers that way.

TEACHER: Well, it's kind of hard to trace around every object you'll ever want to draw, and even if you could, would that teach you how to look?

VERNON: But you just did it on the blackboard.

TEACHER: What was I trying to show you?

ALICE: You were trying to show what the *eye* is supposed to do.

TEACHER: Exactly. I showed you what the eye must do *without* a subject to feel. What did the eye show me about my arm? (*The class notes wrinkles, the separation of shirtsleeve and wristwatch and hand.*) I'll bet you didn't realize there were so many dips and squiggles in just one arm, even without shading—that is, without dark and light. Once a contour drawing is finished, the eye fills *in between* the lines. Now, let me try Michael. (*As he draws he describes what is happening.*) Now, I'm starting at the top of his head, working down to his toe. I'm going up over the ear, down to the neck, and on to the collar. Now I move away, along the shoulder, and here the line turns down the arm. (*He continues in this manner until the line reaches the foot of the model and starts the process over again, moving the line down the opposite side of the figure.*)

The discussion points made by the teacher in the dialog were arrived at after careful study of the kinds of problems children face when attempting contour-line drawing. Their confusion arises in part from the necessity to coordinate eye and hand in analytic drawing skills. Because the contour-line drawing focuses on only one aspect of form—that of the edges of the subject—it cannot be expected that the relationship of parts will follow. This problem should be taken up as a second stage in the activity of contour-line drawing.

Developing Methods of Mixing Media.   Children can mix media from an early age, so that by the time they reach the higher elementary grades they may achieve some outstandingly successful results by this means. The use of resist techniques, for example, is practical for preadolescents and tends to maintain their interest in their work. Scratchboard techniques may also be handled effectively by older pupils.

The technique of using resists relies on the fact that waxy media will shed liquid color if the color has been sufficiently thinned with water. A reasonably heavy paper or cardboard having a mat, or nonshiny, surface is required. Ordinary wax crayons are suitable and may be used with watercolor, thinned tempera paint, or colored inks. The last are particularly pleasant to use with this technique. In producing a picture, the pupil first makes a drawing with wax crayon and then lays down a wash of color or colors. To provide accents in the work, thicker paint or India ink may be used. The ink may be applied with either a pen or a brush, or with both tools.

In using a scratchboard, the pupil scratches away an overall dark coating to expose selected parts of an under-surface. Scratchboard may be either purchased or made by the pupils. If it is to be made, Bristol board is probably the most desirable to use. The surface is prepared by covering the Bristol board, or other glazed cardboard, with a heavy coat of wax crayons in light colors. A coating of tempera paint or India ink sufficiently thick to cover the wax should then be applied and left to dry. Later, the drawing may be made with a variety of tools, including pen points, bobby pins, scissors, and so on. A careful handling of black, white, and textured areas has highly dramatic effects.

The techniques described above are basic and may be expanded in several ways. For example, white wax crayon may be used in the resist painting, with paint providing color. Another resist technique is to "paint" the design with rubber cement and then float tempera or watercolor over the surface. The next day, the cement can be peeled off, revealing broken white areas against the color ground.

Lines in dark ink or tempera work well over collages of colored tissues, and rich effects can be obtained by covering thick tempera paintings with India ink and washing the ink away under a faucet. The danger of mixing media lies in a tendency toward gimmickry, but often the use of combined materials can solve special design problems. One should not consider these techniques as merely child's play. Many reputable artists have used them to produce significant drawings and paintings. Some of Henry Moore's sketches, for example, produced with wax and watercolor

Figure 7.17 *Painting need not be flat. This girl is "wrapping" her painting around a box, changing the colors as she moves from one surface to another.*

A   **Figure 7.18** *This pair of self-portraits show how an idea can be enriched through*   B
several stages. In **A** *the idea was first stated in a pencil drawing and later
transferred to a second sheet,* **B**, *where it was developed in a mixed-media
approach through the use of tempera and oil crayons. Grade 5.*

in the London air-raid shelters during the Second World War, are particularly noteworthy.[11]

Other forms of mixed media are as follows:

India ink and watercolor. The child may draw in ink first then add color or reverse the procedure.

Watercolor washes over crayon drawings. This is a way of increasing an awareness of "negative space" or background areas.

Black tempera or india ink over crayon or colored chalk. Here the black paint settles in the unpainted areas. The student can wash away the paint, controlling the amount left on the surface of the colored areas.[12]

[11] See Henry Moore, *Shelter Sketch Book* (New York: Wittenborn, 1946) and *Sculpture and Drawings*, 3 vols., rev. ed. (New York: Wittenborn, 1957–65).

[12] The most thorough treatment of mixed media processes is to be found in Frank Wachowiak and Theodore Ramsay, *Emphasis: Art,* (Scranton, Pa.: International Textbook, 1965).

THE DEVELOPMENT OF PICTORIAL COMPOSITION

Some assistance in pictorial composition must occasionally be offered if the children are to realize their goals of expression (see Chapter 3). This means that children should be helped toward an understanding of design and a feeling for it, largely in connection with their general picture-making. As they gain experience with the elements of design, the children should be praised for any discoveries they make, and any obvious advances might be discussed informally by the class. There is no reason why some professional work emphasizing certain elements of design should not be brought to the attention of even those pupils who are still in the early symbol stage. The works of Picasso, Matisse, Gauguin, Klee, Chagall, and others may be viewed by children with much pleasure and considerable profit if related to their own acts of expression.[13] The teacher should also use slides and originals of work by the children to demonstrate the possibilities of design on their own level.

As they grow older, children tend to become more concerned with certain elements of design than others. Somewhere between the third and fifth grades, for example, preadolescents begin to incorporate shadow effects in their pictures and to pay some attention to background details. It is then that they require assistance in arriving at suitable tonalities of color.

From time to time some children need help in arriving at a successful composition. In cases of this kind the teacher must resist the impulse to supply formulas for the designs of pictures. It would be a simple matter, for example, to tell children who are having difficulty in creating a center of interest to draw a central object on a large scale. Children instructed to do this would undoubtedly establish a desirable focal point, but in so doing they would be following an ultimately stultifying formula. Instead they should be exposed to discover for themselves through carefully arranged activities many various means of developing centers of interest. No single method should receive undue prominence.[14]

Questions directed at the children are valuable for yielding visual information that can lead to more satisfactory picture-making. When this technique is used, the teacher should try to establish the connection between *ideas* and *pictorial form*. This can begin when the children are at an early age by playing a "memory game." Here the teacher simply draws a large rectangle on the chalkboard and asks someone in the class to draw a subject in the center, say a turtle. The teacher then draws a second rectangle next to the first and puts the same subject in it. What

[13]See Chapter 17 for a detailed discussion of this topic.
[14]See Chapter 3 for the means of developing centers of interest, rhythms, and balances.

then follows is a series of questions about the turtle. The children answer the questions by coming up and adding details to the turtle in the second rectangle. As shapes, ideas, and forms are added, the picture becomes enriched and the space *around* the turtle is filled as a result of the information acquired. When the picture is finished the first one looks quite barren by comparison. The questions surrounding the subject of a turtle might be posed as follows:

Q. Where does a turtle live?
A. In and around the water.
Q. How will we know it's water?
A. Water has waves and fishes.
Q. How will we know there is land next to the water?
A. There is grass, rocks, and trees.
Q. What does a turtle eat? Wheaties? Canned pineapple? Peanut butter? What does he eat?
A. He eats insects, bugs.
A. He can eat his food from a can, too.
Q. Think hard now: Where are there interesting designs on a turtle?
A. On his shell. . . .

Composition is thus approached through the grouping and arranging of a number of ideas. As each answer provides additional visual information, the picture takes on a life of its own by the relation of memory to drawing. The teacher can play this simple game with third graders, and it can provide a way of thinking about picture-making.

Another important task for the teacher is the development of a vocabulary of design terms. In all other subject areas, attention is paid to the exact meanings of words. This has not always been the case in art education, partly because the vocabulary of art in general has tended at times to be nebulous, and partly because teachers have not always attempted to build for themselves a precise vocabulary of art terms.

Some teachers have been eminently successful in assisting children to use words about design with precise meaning. They have done so, of course, with due regard for the fact that art learning should not be primarily verbal but rather should consist largely of visual and tactile experiences. These teachers have made sure that, if not at first, then eventually the terms are used with understanding and precision. Thus, although the teacher might at first compliment a child on the rhythmic flow of lines in a composition by saying that the quality of line was like the "blowing of the wind," later the teacher would use the word "rhythm." In this incidental but natural manner the vocabulary of even the youngest child may be developed.

If continual attention has been paid to such informal vocabulary-building, pupils may leave the elementary school with a reasonably adequate command of art terms that will enable them to participate later

Figure 7.19 *Memories of a first trip to the circus. Sometimes distance from a striking personal experience can help in concentrating on design problems. Careful attention to shape, symmetrical composition, flat decorative pattern, and color distinguish this work in felt pen done by a ten-year-old Egyptian girl.*

Figure 7.20 *Scratchboard and crayon was the medium chosen by an eleven-year-old Austrian boy for his portrayal of an automobile junkyard.*

in a more formal program of composition and art appreciation. It is necessary for pupils to have a working vocabulary in art by the time they reach adolescence. At that period in their development, they are often ready and in fact eager to approach design in a more intellectual manner. Without at least a rudimentary vocabulary, they are handicapped in engaging in the type of art work their stage of development requires.

ACTIVITIES FOR THE READER

The teachers should be thoroughly familiar with the tools, media, and techniques that they will use in the classroom. The following activities are suggested to help them gain this familiarity. Because knowledge of the processes of art, in this instance, is more important than the art produced, teachers should not feel hampered by technical inabilities. Experience with art media is what counts at this stage.[15]

[15]See Monroe Wheeler and John Rewald, *Modern Drawings* (New York: Museum of Modern Art, 1944), for a variety of drawing techniques; also for line work, see Wheeler's *Modern Painters and Sculptors as Illustrators* (New York: Museum of Modern Art, 1946). Also interesting from the point of view of drawing is Thomas Craven, ed., *A Treasury of American Prints* (New York: Simon and Schuster, 1939). For landscape work, a good book for the beginner is Kenneth Clark, *Landscape Painting* (New York: Scribner's, 1950).

1. Using a large hog-bristle brush for broad work, paint in tempera an interesting arrangement of color areas on a sheet of dark paper. Try to develop varied textural effects over these areas in the following ways:

   a. BY USING DRY-BRUSH
   Dip the brush in paint and rub it nearly dry on a piece of scrap paper. Then "dry-brush" an area where the new color will show.

   b. BY STIPPLING
   Holding a nearly dry brush upright so that the bristles strike the paper vertically, stamp it lightly so that a stipple pattern of paint shows.

   c. BY BRUSH DRAWING
   Select a sable brush and load it with paint. Paint a pattern over a color area with wavy or crisscrossed lines, small circles, or some other marks to give a rougher-looking texture than is found in surrounding areas.

   d. BY USING POWDERED PAINT
   Apply liberal amounts of powdered paint mixed with very little water to your composition to obtain some rough areas (add sawdust or sand to liquid tempera if you have no powdered tempera).

   e. BY USING A SPONGE
   Paint the surface of the sponge or dip it into the paint and rub the sponge on your composition.

   f. BY USING A BRAYER
   Roll the brayer in paint and pull it over cut-paper forms. Experiment with the roller by using the edge or by wrapping string around it. Place small pools of color next to each other and pull the brayer over them, changing directions until you have blocks of broken color that lock into each other.

2. Select a small segment of a landscape and make a preliminary sketch with Conté crayon or 5B to 8B pencil on drawing paper. Keep working at your sketch, rearranging the positions of items until you think you have an interesting variety and unity of masses, spaces, light, and shade. With watercolor or thin tempera, paint over parts of your drawing to form an interesting color pattern. In another composition, try limiting your dark areas to just black or brown for dark wash tones.

3. Select some objects you think are interesting and use them to make a still-life arrangement. Sketch the arrangement with wax crayons, using light, bright color where you see the highlights at their brightest, and using dark-colored crayons where you see the darkest shadows.

4. Place some finger paint on dampened, shiny-surfaced paper. Smear it around with your thumbs, fingers, and the flat of your hand to develop an interesting pattern. Wash your hands and then try another painting, this time using two colors. The colors should be ones that mix well together. In a third composition, smear one color all over the sheet of paper and wash your hands. Then dip your fingers or the side of your hand into a second color and begin creating rhythms.

5. Using heavy drawing pencil, try to draw the following subjects in a strictly accurate, photographically correct manner. (Remember that lines

below the horizon line rise to this level; lines above fall to this level; all lines meet at the horizon line.)

a. A sidewalk or passageway as though you were standing in the center.

b. A cup and saucer on a table below your eye level.

c. A chimney stack, silo, or gas storage tank, the top of which is above your eye level.

d. A group of various-sized boxes piled on a table or on the floor. (It is easier to draw if you first paint the boxes one unifying color, such as gray or white.)[16]

6. Sketch a house or a collection of houses or other objects with crayon or heavy pencil, following the rules of linear perspective. In another drawing, rearrange the areas you drew to change the patterns of masses and spaces. Carry the lines through each other, taking liberties with the spaces between the lines. Notice how this freedom gives your picture more variety.

7. Have a friend pose for you. On manila or newsprint measuring at least 12 by 18 inches, make contour drawings in Conté crayon or heavy pencil. Draw quickly, taking no longer than three to five minutes for each sketch. Do not erase mistakes—simply draw new lines. Make many drawings of this type based on standing, sitting, and reclining poses.[17]

   Now begin to draw more carefully, thinking of places where bones are close to the surface and where flesh is thicker. Heavy pressure with the drawing medium will indicate shadows; the reverse will indicate light areas. Think also of the torso, the head, and the pelvic region as moving somewhat independently of each other. Begin to check body proportions.

   Later make drawings with ink and a sable brush. Always work quickly and fearlessly. Try using some of the suggested visual references for drawing listed in the section "Sources of Observation."

8. Place yourself before a mirror for a self-portrait. Study the different flat areas, or planes, of your face. Notice the position of prominent features (especially eyes, which are about halfway between the top of your head and the bottom of your chin). Quickly draw a life-size head in charcoal, crayon, or chalk. When your features have become more familiar to you, try some other media, such as ink or paint. Try a self-portrait that is many times larger than life-size.

9. Make scratchboards. In scratching out your drawing, be sure that you have a pleasant distribution of white, black, and halftone (lined) areas. Practice scratching with many different implements, from razor blades to bobby pins.

10. The formal exercises listed below express nothing and are valueless for children, but they can help you develop technique.

   a. Draw about a dozen 2-by-2-inch squares, one below the other. Paint the top square a standard hue; leave the bottom one white. Make

---

[16]Good problems are to be found at the end of each chapter of Ernest R. Norling, *Perspective Made Easy* (New York: Macmillan, 1940).
[17]See Kimon Nicolaides, *The Natural Way to Draw* (Boston: Houghton Mifflin, 1941).

a gradation of color areas ranging from the standard hue to white by progressively adding white to the standard hue. The "jumps" between areas should appear even.

b. Repeat (a), using some other hues. Use transparent watercolor as well as tempera for some exercises, adding water instead of white paint to the watercolor pigment.

c. Repeat, this time adding the complementary color to the first one chosen. Now the gradations will go from standard to gray rather than to white.

d. Add black progressively to a standard hue to obtain twelve "jumps" from standard to black.

e. Try shading about six 3-inch-square areas with Conté crayon, charcoal, or heavy pencil so that you progress from very light gray to very dark gray.

f. Draw textures in four 3-inch-square areas so that each square appears "rougher" than the next. Crisscrossed lines, wavy lines, circles, dots, and crosses are some devices to use. India ink and a writing pen are useful tools in this exercise.[18]

g. Using the side of a crayon, take a series of "rubbings" from such surfaces as wood, sidewalks, rough walls, and so on. Create a design using the rubbings you have collected.

11. With the insight into drawing and painting gained from performing activities such as those suggested above, make the following plans for the classroom (see Chapter 5).

a. Draw plans for setting out materials for children in the grade or grades in which you are interested for the following activities: painting in tempera; painting in watercolor; working with a variety of media. Show arrows on your plan to indicate the flow of children.

b. Draw plans complete with arrows to indicate how children would return equipment for each of the above activities.

c. If possible, test these plans in a classroom. Take note of overcrowding or any other difficulty that may arise. Revise your plans accordingly and test again.

12. List in one column the art terms that you think children should become familiar with at each developmental level. In a second column list activities for which the terms might be appropriate, and in a third column list examples of painting, sculpture, and architecture that exemplify the vocabulary.

[18]See Ralph L. Wickiser, *An Introduction to Art Activities* (New York: Holt, Rinehart and Winston, 1947).

"Stop," grade 2. Both cutting and tearing were used in this picture.

WORKING WITH PAPER

Tear it. Fold it. Rip it out and bend it. Slash it. Mend it. Twist it or crumple it. Tape it, glue it. Dissolve it. Score it, scratch it. Emboss it. Toss it away. "It," of course, is paper. *

Paper has achieved a new primacy in our time. Technological advances now permit us to think of paper in terms of furniture, clothing, and even sports-car bodies. In recent years, paper and its derivatives have become increasingly important as expressive media in art education. Children should be encouraged to test paper and to get some sense of its special qualities of strength, tension, and resilience. The children should learn that if they tear paper, it offers little resistance; yet if they pull it, another kind of force is involved, exerting tremendous strength. By capitalizing on this factor, the children could design a paper bridge to carry their own weight, or, if they prefer, a tower.

Because paper has so many uses as a medium of art expression there is no rule as to when paper work should be offered in the art program. Sometimes paper work will introduce art activities; sometimes it will supplement expression in paint. Sometimes it will serve as the major activity, for, among other things, paper can be used in sculpture or as part of a mixed media process.

Not all types of paper work are suitable for children in all three stages of development, however. Picture-making with paper is practical at the manipulative, symbol, and preadolescent levels, but box sculpture may lose much of its appeal as the child enters preadolescence. Other kinds of freestanding paper sculpture, however, provide welcome activities for children in the symbol stage through preadolescence. Forms in space may be enjoyed at all levels of development.

*From Robert Munaff, "Think Paper," *Craft Horizons,* Vol. 27 (November–December 1967), p. 11.

This chapter will describe the use of paper and its derivatives in picture-making, modeling, and general construction work, together with ways of using paper as a plastic medium.

PICTURE-MAKING WITH PAPER

Media and Techniques. Every child from kindergarten through the sixth grade may profit from picture-making with paper. The paper provided for this purpose should be varied in color, texture, and weight and should be available in several shapes and sizes. If cartons containing odds and ends of paper, from newsprint to corrugated cardboard and including metallic and transparent papers, are provided, the pupils may select the type of paper they want. The very fact that children are able to select from many types of paper is stimulating for those working in this medium, whatever their stage of development.

Ordinary school paste, which may be purchased in either the powdered or the more popular liquid form, may be used to fix the papers to a background. The teacher will find it necessary to dip out small quantities of paste for the youngest children. The paste may be placed on cardboard pie plates, saucers, or even on a scrap of cardboard. Several children may share one small supply. Individual jars of paste fitted with a small brush in the lid are easy to use but are more costly than paste purchased in bulk. Children who are older and more experienced in handling art materials can use the glues that come in tubes. Rubber cements and various chemical plastics are readily controlled but are more expensive than paste and should be used only when a considerable degree of precision is required. Pastes with a high mucilage content are also more expensive than school paste but have greater strength. White acrylic glues,

Figure 8.1
Arrangement of supplies for picture-making with paper.

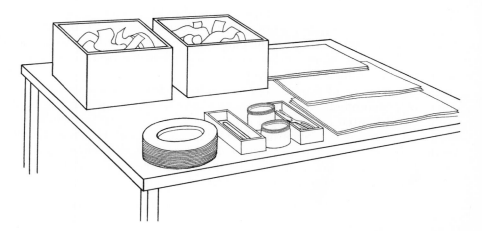

the most expensive of all, can be diluted for tissue overlays and collages or used full strength for joining wood.

Children may spread the paste with their fingers or with popsicle sticks. Some teachers like children to use strips of cardboard, which can be discarded afterwards. Brushes, of course, may be used to spread paste, but paste spoils a brush for further painting. The bristles stick together and the hot water that must usually be used to remove the paste takes away the "life" and spring of the bristles.

Children in the early manipulative stage can create pictures merely by tearing paper. Very soon, however, they will wish to use scissors, and these should be chosen with care. For young children, the scissors should be short and light; for more experienced pupils, they may be heavier and have longer cutting edges. Although their cutting edges may be kept sharp, the scissors should not have pointed tips; these may be convenient to use, but they are dangerous. As well as being provided with scissors, the pupils in the preadolescent stage might also be allowed to use knives for cutting paper. These also have their dangers, but most pupils in about the third grade and up can learn to handle them safely.

Cutting out shapes is related to drawing in that in both activities the children record events by focusing on the edges of their subject. They are not discouraged by the fact that cutting calls for greater manual skill than does line drawing. They settle for less detail in return for the pleasant sensation of working with multicolored silhouettes. One advantage of paper work is its flexibility: shapes and spaces can be evaluated and shifted before the final design decision is made. In this sense, picture-making with paper is opposite to painting, which requires a direct commitment to what is put on paper.

The sources of subject matter for picture-making with paper are identical to those mentioned earlier for drawing and painting. The child

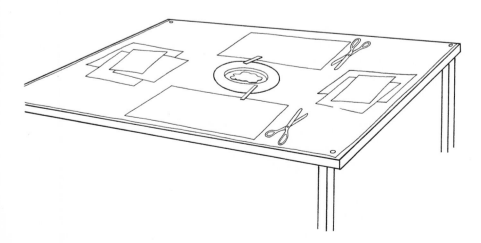

Figure 8.2
Arrangements for two children to do picture-making with paper.

Figure 8.3 *In this picture by a third grader, the family Christmas is recorded in cut paper. To the child, cutting a shape is related to drawing it.*

in the early manipulative stage will experiment with the paper without attempting to produce a composition based on a theme related to experience in life. As time goes on, the work of these young children tends to become more organized. Symbols develop that are similar to those found in drawing and painting, and in due coarse the symbol-and-environment phase appears. Eventually the characteristics of pre-adolescent art emerge. The problems of depth, tonality of color, pictorial composition, and more exact representation of objects arise in paper work just as they do in painting. Paper work, however, tends to move the child away from a concern with realism toward a greater awareness of the vivid effects of pattern and shape.

Teaching. Children who work with paper to make pictures seem to find that the new medium and tools do not present insurmountable difficulties. The stimulation and counsel offered by the teacher are like those given for drawing and painting. The use of paper, however, entails a few mechanical problems not found in painting.

Young children often use too much paste, with the result that when pressure is applied, ridges of excess paste form along the edges of the paper. The children must learn to be economical with paste, particularly in applying it along the outside edges of the paper. Beginners also frequently have difficulty in holding scissors in a cutting position. The teacher will have to use considerable judgment in determining whether or not the children possess sufficient muscular coordination to use scissors.[1] Until the children are ready to use scissors, the teacher should

[1] According to the Vineland Social Maturity Scale (Edgar A. Doll, Director of Research, The Training School at Vineland, New Jersey), ability to use scissors comes between the

encourage them to tear paper. At first, the pupils tear robustly and therefore with little control, but with practice they learn to be more exact. Teachers should also be sensitive to left-handed pupils and have appropriate scissors available.

Teaching picture-making with paper will help the pupils expand their ideas about design. As children in the manipulative stage become familiar with this medium, they find it possible to develop many interesting effects peculiar to it. The teacher should encourage the children to play not only color against color but also texture against texture, metallic surface against the usual paper surface, and mat finish against glazed finish. Transparent papers might be used to add more variety to the design; having two or more transparent papers overlap both themselves and ordinary papers of varying hues produces particularly interesting effects. The children might be encouraged to make use of various textiles, string, and thin wood in their compositions.

Eventually children, particularly those in the symbol stage, should learn how to build up their paper compositions from a support, thus developing three-dimensional effects. In working on the theme, "My Flower Garden," for example, the child may first glue the paper flowers flat to the support. The teacher may then demonstrate how petals can be curled by running the paper between thumb and scissors and gluing the center portion of the flower. Three-dimensional effects can also be achieved by scoring, say, the center veins of the leaves or petals. Other three-dimensional effects are obtained by bending, folding, twisting, cutting, and stretching. Figure 8.5 illustrates relief forms of a sculptural nature. The surfaces of the forms rising from their support catch the light in patterns that are determined by the manner in which the paper is cut, scored, and folded.

Although the teacher will have to demonstrate certain techniques, demonstration as a teaching device should be used with restraint. Demonstration is a necessary and effective practice, but wrongly used it is very inhibiting to all children, especially to those in the manipulative and symbol stages. Classes have been observed in which the paper work displayed an unfortunate uniformity resulting directly from an overeffective lesson on "how to work with paper." The folds and cuts that the teacher carefully demonstrated were observed by the class to be practical; as a result, the children tended to rely on the teacher's thinking. Since children do have the ability to develop suitable methods on their own, it seems a pity for them to cut short the struggle for mastery of the medium in order to arrive at quick results. Significant development in paper technique is made largely as a result of a personal conquest of the medium. Unless demonstrations are offered sparingly and with strict regard to the needs of the pupils, paper work may easily become stereotyped.

ages of two and three years. Observation in kindergartens leads one to believe that not until they are over five years of age are many children able to use scissors effectively.

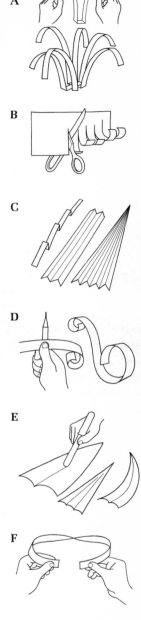

Figure 8.4 *Some ways of developing three-dimensional forms in paper:* (**A**) *folding and bending,* (**B**) *frilling,* (**C**) *pleating,* (**D**) *stretching,* (**E**) *scoring, and* (**F**) *twisting.*

Actually, successful pictures in paper result from many teaching devices other than demonstration. In the initial phases of manipulation, most children will stick the torn or cut paper to a background without much help or suggestion from the teacher. The bright paper and the natural curiosity of children are sufficient motivations to start the production of pictures. Praise merely for being adventurous will encourage further experimentation. As children progress from manipulation to the production of symbols, the teacher's pleased and vocal recognition of well-established centers of interest, rhythms, and balances in the work of some individuals tends to help the class generally to improve design. When children exhaust their own ideas, the teacher may demonstrate some of the ways of treating paper mentioned above.

As preadolescence approaches, problems arising from the pupils' desire to make more realistic statements will occur. Ranges of color of paper should then be expanded so that the pupils may employ tints and shades for depth and emphasis. The teacher should also see that papers having many different types of textures are readily available. If the pupils appear to feel handicapped by having to rely entirely on cutting and tearing, they should be allowed to draw or paint over some areas requiring detail.

BOX SCULPTURE

Media and Techniques. Activities involving the use of paper and cardboard to produce freestanding three-dimensional objects may be used in all stages of the child's development. As a preliminary type of three-dimensional work to complement the picture-making discussed above, box sculpture is highly effective.

The only supplies necessary are an assortment of small cardboard containers and some school paste. Tempera paint and suitable brushes may also be supplied. The containers should vary in shape and range in size from, say, about 1 inch as the largest dimension to 1 foot on each side. If possible, cardboard tubes of different diameters and cut into various lengths and perhaps a few empty spools should also be provided.

Teaching. Young children delight in pasting the containers together to build shapes at random, and later they like to paint them. As one might expect, they first build without apparent plan or subject matter in mind. In a matter of a week or so, however, the children begin to name their constructions. "This is a bridge," says five-year-old Peter to his classmates, describing an object faintly resembling such a structure. "This is my dad's factory," says Arthur, who has placed a chimneylike object on top of a box. "I guess it's a castle," says Mary, describing a gaily painted construction. This parallels the "naming" stage in drawing, which occurs at an earlier age.

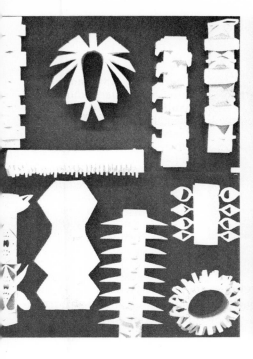

Figure 8.5 (left) Fifth graders achieved these three-dimensional effects by cutting, scoring, and folding. (Photo by Rick Steadry.)

Figure 8.6 (right) These third graders are assembling a class "totem pole" from curved and scored paper forms. Paper is used as a group art project. (Photo by Rick Steadry.)

Eventually the pupils begin to make plans before starting work. One child might decide to make a boat; another, to construct a house, paint it red, and build a garden around it. Thus children, when working in box sculpture, tend to progress through the usual stages of manipulation and symbolic expression. This, however, is about as far as they go in box sculpture. The preadolescent usually loses interest in it and looks for another kind of paper work in three dimensions. For children in the manipulative stage, little teaching is required apart from the usual general encouragement and an attempt to keep the children free of paste and paint. In the symbol stage, the children should have ample opportunity to discuss their symbols with the teacher and with one another. In this way their work will grow in clarity and completeness. The teacher should encourage children in this stage to add significant details in cut paper and in paint.

OTHER FREESTANDING FORMS

Media and Techniques. Children in upper elementary grades find other freestanding forms of paper sculpture more challenging than box sculpture. The supplies required for such sculpture include the usual scissors, knife, construction paper and cardboard, odds and ends of colored paper, paste, and a vast array of miscellaneous articles such as drinking straws, toothpicks, and pins with colored heads.

The chief problem for the children in developing freestanding forms

Figure 8.7 *Any manufactured containers that are readily available may be used in box sculpture. The items used in these sculptures include shoe boxes, toilet-tissue rolls, egg cartons, and packing tubes. The children who created these works chose to make animals; they could just as easily have created a city. (Photo by Rick Steadry.)*

in paper lies in the necessity to develop a shape that will support the completed object. A tentlike form is perhaps the first such shape children will devise. Later they may fashion a paper tube or cone strong enough to support whatever details they plan to add. In constructing a figure of a clown, for example, the children might make a cylinder of paper for the head, body, and legs. The arms might be cut from flat paper and glued to the sides of the cylinder. A hat could be made in a conical shape from more paper. Details of features and clothing might then be added with either paint or more paper.

For preadolescent children the technique of employing rolled paper to construct objects is also practical. Old newspapers may be used together with paste, string, and sometimes wire. The child who begins this work obviously must possess some ability to make plans in advance of production. Plans must include an idea of the nature and size of the object to be fashioned. Will it be a man or a bear, a chicken or a giraffe? What will be its general shape? This shape will largely govern its basic construction.

The underlying structure is easily developed. Arms, legs, body, and head may all be produced from rolled newspapers. A chief component— say, the body—should be tied at several places by string, and other components may be fastened to this one, again with string. Should one part of the creation tend to be flimsy because of extreme length—perhaps the giraffe's neck—it can be reinforced by wire or strips of cardboard or wood.

When the main structure is complete, it is strengthened by carefully wrapping 1-inch-wide strips of newspaper dipped in paste around all parts of the object until it looks like an Egyptian mummy. While it is still wet, the pupil can add details such as ears, tails, and the like, made of buttons, scraps of fur, and other odds and ends. When dry, the creation may be painted and covered with shellac or varnish.

Preadolescent children may use heavy construction paper or thin cardboard to fashion miniature buildings; also required are a ruler, scissors, a knife, and strong glue. Although children in kindergarten and perhaps the first grade also construct buildings, these are very simple and symbolic in character. Usually only the façade is produced, which, in order to stand upright, must be supported by a small box to which it is glued. Preadolescent pupils generally wish to develop more realistic four-sided structures. After folding the four sides of a construction-paper house into a hollow square, the child puts on a roof, which at first may be flat but later will have a peak. Little by little the pupil improves on the structures and in time learns to plan in advance even the details of cutting and folding (see Figure 8.9). Tabs are left for gluing and peaks are arranged for a pitched roof. Details such as windows, doors, and porches may be painted on or cut from other paper and fixed in place. To the basic structure, furthermore, wings, garages, and so on will probably be added. Drinking straws, tongue depressors, swab sticks, wire, and string are among the items that the child may eventually use to enlarge on architectural ideas.

Teaching. The teacher will often find it necessary to resort to demonstrations of the techniques involved in general freestanding paper sculpture, rolled-paper sculpture, and miniature architectural work in paper. But in order to keep the work as creative as possible, the stages and possibilities of construction in each of the three techniques should always be fully discussed with the pupils. Solutions to the problems brought up in the discussion should, as far as possible and practicable, be suggested and acted on by the pupils.

When basic forms are being produced the teacher should keep a

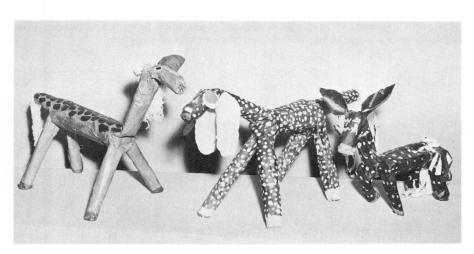

Figure 8.8
Rolled-paper animals made by fifth-grade pupils. (Photo by Royal Studio.)

close eye on each pupil and be ready to make suggestions in time of need so that an otherwise impractical improvisation in a paper technique can be successfully altered or compensated for. For example, the pupil may have forgotten to leave sufficient paper to make tabs for fastening two pieces of paper together. Sticky tape might then be suggested. If a horse's head in rolled paper is so heavy that it droops, a thin stick of wood, wired to the neck from body to head, might be suggested as a solution to the problem.

The teacher may also find it necessary, at least with the less experienced pupils, to offer many suggestions concerning the finishing of the articles. After studying a pupil's rolled-paper figure of a clown, the teacher might suggest, for example, that absorbent cotton from the scrap box would make a good beard, or that small buttons be glued to the main paper figure.

As the pupils gain experience, the teacher must emphasize the necessity of making reasonably detailed plans in advance. The pupils might make sketches of the basic shape of a figure so that it may be accurately cut. Even a sketch of a rolled-paper figure in which some indication of proportions and reinforcement points is given is occasionally helpful. In fact, the pupils and teacher together might well go through all the stages of using a medium in advance of individual construction.

Architectural construction sometimes requires even more detailed plans in which every tab and fold, together with each component of the planned assembly, is decided on before starting work. Such details, however, need not always be planned in advance. Much of the fun in this, as in other art work, comes from improvisation. Nor should perfection be expected in the children's work. They must be permitted to develop

Figure 8.9 *A diagram of detailed plans for a cardboard house based on the work of a sixth grader:* (**A**) *roof,* (**B**) *walls and base with tabs,* (**C**) *structure with chimney and garage being added, and* (**D**) *completed structure.*

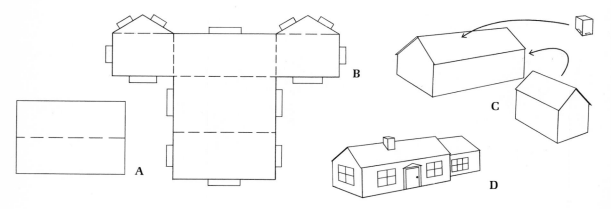

both their thinking and skills at their own pace. Preadolescents are usually no more ready to construct, say, a well-made model of a house than to produce a professional painting. Their first architectural efforts, while possessing charm, will lack precision. Walls will lean, roofs will not fit, and chimneys will tumble. The same kinds of flaw will be found in other early paper construction. Only time, experience, and effort will allow them to master the difficult feat of constructing in paper. The teacher must accept the learners' initial efforts until their skill grows more exact.

PAPER IN PLASTIC FORMS

Two types of paper work in which the material is sufficiently plastic to be molded and modeled will be described in this section. The first type uses dampened paper; the second, mashed paper, or as it is more commonly know, papier-mâché. Dampened paper is suitable for children in the advanced symbol stage; papier-mâché may be used by pupils in all stages.

Media and Techniques. For molded paper, old newspapers, school paste, tempera paint, shellac, perhaps some clay, scissors, and a willing pair of hands are the necessary items for production.

The technique consists of building a substructure over which strips of paper thoroughly dampened with school paste are laid and pressed into place. After drying, the paper strips, which form a hard shell, may be removed from the underlying form and are usually finished with paint and shellac.

Model igloos, tunnels, mountains, and the like may be readily produced by covering different types of substructures with the sticky strips of newsprint. The substructures may be made with fine wire netting, clay, balls, or slightly dampened newspaper that has been pressed into the desired shape. A life-size mask is slightly more difficult to construct. A detailed description of the process will suggest practicable ways of making not only the mask itself but also the miniature objects mentioned above.

In producing a mask, newsprint is used first to establish a suitable size. The pupil should fold the paper into a strip about 3 or 4 inches wide, then fit the strip under the chin and over the head. When glued, the oval of paper indicates the outside dimensions of the mask. The oval may then be stuffed with wads of slightly dampened newspaper until a mound is formed within the oval. Pinching the dampened newsprint will make a lump for a nose, and pressure in the right places will form eye sockets. Small pieces of wax paper should be placed over the mound so that the next layers will not adhere to the mold just completed. The entire assembly should then be covered with strips of newsprint that have been dipped in paste. Each layer of paper should be laid down in the opposite direction from the preceding layer. The crossing of the strips adds strength to the construction. By using papers of different colors, the pupil can distinguish one layer from another. When the paper has dried into a hard shell the inner wads of newsprint can be removed. Holes may then be cut for the eyes and nostrils (see Figure 8.10). Features such as ears, hair, and nose may be developed further from paper or various scraps of materials. Paint and shellac give color to the finished product.[2]

Modeled clay, the surface of which has been thoroughly greased or covered with wax paper before the strips of paper are set down, may also be employed as a base for much of this type of work. Firing clay or oil-based plasticine is particularly recommended for children who possess special ability in art, because it lends itself to a greater variety of modeling effects. If plasticine is in short supply, a substructure of scrap wood can be used to support the sculpted surface. Earth clay must be kept under plastic to preserve dampness from one day to the next. When using either, the pupil should keep the substructure smooth and free of undercuts so that the paper "skin" will come off easily.

Mashed paper, or papier-mâché, has been used as a modeling medium for centuries. Chinese soldiers of long ago are said to have made their armor with this material. Mashed paper is strong and may be put to many uses in school. To prepare this plastic medium, newsprint is torn into small pieces. (Magazine paper with a glazed surface should not be

[2] See Matthew Baranski, *Mask Making*, rev. ed. (Worcester, Mass.: Davis, 1966). The work described in this book is often too difficult for young children, but the techniques will be of interest to teachers.

Figure 8.10 *Diagram of the steps in mask-making taken by a fifth-grade girl: (**A**) measuring for size, (**B**) filling paper oval with balls of paper and molding features, (**C**) applying lengths of paper, (**D**) removing base, (**E**) cutting features, and (**F**) adding trim. The face could also have been modeled in clay, covered with oil, and then covered with paper strips. This method allows for greater detail.*

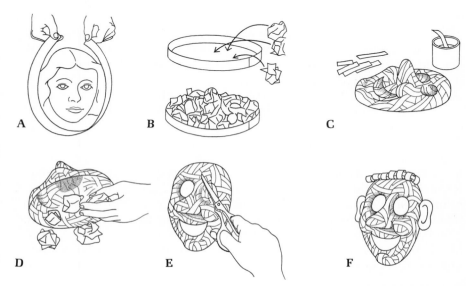

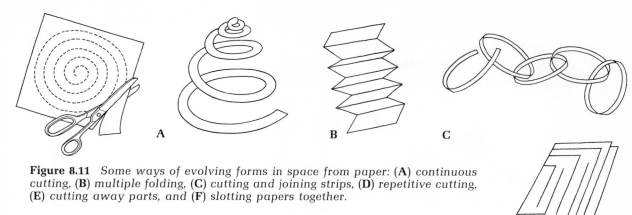

Figure 8.11 *Some ways of evolving forms in space from paper:* (**A**) *continuous cutting,* (**B**) *multiple folding,* (**C**) *cutting and joining strips,* (**D**) *repetitive cutting,* (**E**) *cutting away parts, and* (**F**) *slotting papers together.*

used.) The torn paper is left to soak overnight in water. The excess water is then drained off, leaving a pulp. The pulp is wrung dry in a cotton cloth so that there is less likelihood of excess moisture deteriorating the paste, which must be used next. About a cup of school paste or wheat flour is thoroughly mixed with approximately five cups of pulp. The mash is then ready to be used as a modeling medium.

Children in the manipulative stage will roll it and pommel it; in the symbol stage they produce three-dimensional symbols with it, usually fruit forms. Preadolescent pupils learn to control it further and model sculptured pieces. After the mashed paper has dried—a process that takes about a week—it may be worked with hand tools. The dry substance can be sandpapered, holes can be bored in it, it can be carved, and it can be painted. Painted objects should be shellacked if possible. Acrylic can also be used, both for its brilliant color and its protective qualities.

Teaching. The remarks made earlier about teaching other techniques involving paper will, of course, apply to molding and modeling in this medium. One additional teaching device might be employed to good effect here. Because a kind of metamorphosis occurs in the medium between the beginning and end of modeling or molding, the pupils may become confused unless they have a clear picture of the entire process before work begins. It is recommended, therefore, that the teacher prepare in advance a step-by-step display of paper as it changes from a flimsy newspaper to a hard, painted shell resulting from the papier-mâché process.

FORMS IN SPACE

Media and Techniques. The creation of forms to be displayed in space, or "mobiles," either for their own sake or to be used for practical purposes (such as holiday ornaments), is a challenge to the children's ingenuity. In general the paper for this work should be of "construction" weight

Figure 8.12 *Example of form in space.*
See text for description of Mary's work.
(Photo by Royal Studio.)

(80 lb. paper) and available in black, white, and a full range of colors. The only tool necessary for young children is scissors; older children who are capable of more precise output may wish to use a wooden or steel ruler as well as a razor-type knife and a hole puncher. For fastening papers together, rubber cement, paste, glue, and a stapler are required. As will be seen later, stiff wire or string in several colors is useful.

Forms in paper may be evolved by the following means: multiple folding or pleating; cutting strips of paper and joining them in various ways; continuous cutting in a sheet of paper to form, say, a spiral; folding and making related or repetitive cuts; cutting away parts of the paper; and cutting slots into two or more pieces of paper and pushing the pieces together (see Figure 8.11).[3] Which of these means of treating paper the pupils attempt depends on their stage of development. Most children in the early manipulative stage make use of pleats and strips and soon learn to make a continuous cut. The ability to make related cuts and to produce forms by cutting slots in paper and by cutting away areas of paper often follows before the close of the manipulative period.

Teaching. Children in all stages of development, even preadolescents, have much to gain from this work by approaching it in a spirit of experimental play. Working from predeveloped plans might militate against such a desirable experimental attitude. The paper should be approached with the idea, "Let's see what happens!"

Since the type of paper work being discussed in this section ranges from the very simple to the complex, the problem of suggesting suitable

[3] See Toni Hughes, *How to Make Shapes in Space* (New York: Dutton, 1955). This book will interest teachers, although the activities are in general too advanced for elementary-school children. Another text worth examining is Pauline Johnson, *Creating with Paper* (Seattle: University of Washington Press, 1958).

teaching techniques is more difficult than usual. As an example of the duties of a teacher while forms in space are being produced, and perhaps as a summary of teaching methods for any type of paper work, let us examine some children at work.

It is party time, and the children want to make paper ornaments for the classroom. The teacher has placed some strips of paper about 1 inch wide and 20 inches long in front of them. John, aged six, is still in the manipulative stage. With no suggestions from anyone, he picks up a strip, makes a hoop with it, opens the hoop, twists the paper, and makes a twisted hoop. At the teacher's suggestion, he pastes the ends of the hoop together. Repeating these maneuvers, he manages to place a second hoop inside the first. He repeats this process after being complimented by the teacher. The teacher gives him some colored string. Without hesitation he ties more hoops together and holds up his mobile to be admired.

Mary, in the symbol stage, is seven. She has in her hands a 7-inch square of paper. Using scissors, Mary first trims the paper so that it is no longer square but irregular in shape, and then starts on a trip with her scissors through the shaped paper. With encouragement from the teacher, she cuts, traveling in a circular fashion toward the center. Finally she can cut no longer, so she picks up the paper and a "snake" ripples away from her fingers. Then, having seen a classmate do likewise, she takes a piece of wire or cane. Experimenting, she thrusts it upward through the dangling shape and at the teacher's suggestion fixes it by means of rubber cement to the top of the ornament.

Susan, a resourceful child, is a sixth grader and in the preadolescent period. The teacher suggests that she devise a paper form in space. After the teacher advises her merely to experiment with folding followed by cutting, Susan folds in half a sheet of paper measuring about 5 by 8 inches. Taking her scissors and still experimenting, she makes a cut from the folded edge and parallel to the short side. With a knife she slices down from the first cut and at right angles to it. She repeats these maneuvers several times to form similar cuts. Then she opens the paper and twists it to discover the various effects she may achieve by means of the repetitive cuts, until she is satisfied with the results.

Arthur wants to make a mobile. The teacher tells him that he should try first fixing one piece of cardboard to another and then build on this technique. The teacher demonstrates and Arthur repeats the demonstration, cutting slits into two pieces of cardboard and notching them together. He continues to build in this manner, later adding some curved shapes, and all the while watching the play of the various colors. Finally he attaches a string to his design so that it can be suspended. Arthur has thus constructed a simple mobile. He continues to produce this type of art form and expand his ideas by employing pliers and wire to construct more complicated mobile forms. Occasionally he goes to the teacher for help and advice. He learns that it is not a simple matter to arrange the physical balances necessary in the suspension of the mobile. He also experiences difficulty in maintaining an aesthetic balance of the elements once the physical balances have been established. These problems he discusses with the teacher. The teacher comments on his design and says that he must guard against a floating composition and try instead for an aesthetic composition, interesting to observe in its movements and in the relationships of its elements as they shift from one position to another. Because Arthur is resourceful, he succeeds. Many pupils in the elementary grades, however, find the problems associated with the making of mobiles like this rather too advanced and must first master the simpler cardboard constructions described earlier in this section. Others, however, are able to progress into even more complicated moving forms.

Where did the ideas for these techniques originate, once motivation had occurred? Obviously some of the children came across them entirely through experimentation. Other children required timely suggestions from the teacher, as well as demonstrations. Whatever the source of their inspiration and insight the children all had the satisfaction of feeling that they were in command of the situation. As a result the children developed paper work with the stamp of originality.

ACTIVITIES FOR THE READER

1. Make some pictures with paper:

   a. With a range of colored papers (including some light, dark, and middle grays, and black and white) and rubber cement or paste, make a nonobjective picture on a piece of heavy paper or cardboard no smaller than 18 by 24 inches. You might start by developing a colorful center of interest out of an irregularly shaped area cut from a bright piece of paper. Thin strips of paper in contrasting colors, acting as a contrast to this center, could be used to develop interesting and useful rhythms. Watch the balance of your composition as the background becomes covered up. Stop before the work becomes cluttered.

   b. Cut pieces of paper from the colored, the halftone, and the black-and-white pages of a magazine. Make a picture using these pieces, recutting them where necessary. Use the differences in texture of the various scraps to good aesthetic effect. Your theme may be realistic, abstract, or completely nonfigurative.

   c. Set up a still life and base a paper picture on the arrangement. Watch tonalities of color and other aspects of general composition.

   d. Make a collage using a subject like a portrait of an old man or an old house. Use such materials as absorbent cotton, felt, and printed cottons, as well as paper, in your work. Absorbent cotton might suggest hair or eyebrows, for example; felt or sandpaper, a man's beard; printed cloth, a background. For the house use such textures as sandpaper, painted paper, wallpaper, and so on. Use a

Figure 8.13 *A method for constructing objects from rolled newspaper.*

little paint for details if you wish. Try to be imaginative, but be restrained in achieving variety in your design.

2. Prepare a chart showing paper that has been scored, twisted, frayed, stretched, curled, torn, and so on, until you have included all the ways you can think of for treating paper for picture-making.
3. Make a collection of papers to develop a graduated range of textures from roughest to smoothest.
4. Make a collection of gray papers and show their gradations in tone. Do the same with a range of papers in one hue.
5. Collect some cardboard boxes and wooden spools. Select a relatively large box for the body of some animal. Add smaller boxes or spools for the legs, neck, and finally the head. Add paper, felt, or cloth ears; a string or paper tail; paper, button, or large pin-head eyes. Paint with tempera color, and when dry, cover with one or two coats of varnish, shellac, or acrylic polymer. A brush 1 inch wide is useful for applying the acrylic, varnish, or shellac. After shellacking, wash the brush in methyl alcohol (which is a poison). After using varnish, wash the brush in turpentine or a turpentine substitute. The brush used to apply the acrylic polymer can be washed simply in water.
6. Make freestanding figures of animals or people based on each of the following basic forms: (a) a tent made with one simple fold; (b) a cylinder; (c) a cone that may be cut to shape after twisting and gluing. Heads and legs should be devised by cutting and shaping paper and gluing it in place. Add features and details of clothing by gluing cut-paper pieces to the basic shape.
7. Make an object out of rolled newspaper. Roll the newspaper into a tight cylinder for the body and tie it with string in three or four places. For arms and legs, make thinner cylinders of newspaper tied with string as above. Tie the arms and legs to the body. Next the neck and head should either be modeled separately and attached to the body or be bent under as an extension of the body cylinder. Dip strips of newspaper

241

or paper toweling about 1 inch wide into paste and wrap them around the figure. When the object is dry add details with colored paper, scraps of fur, and so on. Finish with paint and shellac. (See Figure 8.13.)

8. Make a model building out of cardboard. Sketch your plan beforehand, working out the position of tabs. Draw the plan accurately on cardboard. Cut away excess cardboard and score the cardboard with the back of a pair of scissors where the folds are to be made. Fold and glue. Add details such as drinking straws for veranda posts and cut paper for windows. Prepare a landscape for the model, perhaps using green and gray paper for lawns and paths, twigs with green paper leaves for trees, and paper in bright colors for flower beds.

9. Make a mask over a clay base. On a workboard, model a mold for the mask in clay. Leave the clay to dry overnight; then cover it with cooking oil or small pieces of wax paper. Dip 1-inch strips of newspaper into paste and lay them over the clay mold, pressing them gently to the wax paper (or oil) covering the clay. Crisscross paper strips until they make four or more layers. To help keep track of the layers, alternate layers of the Sunday comics with black-and-white newsprint. When dry, lift the shell away from the mold, trim the edges, cut holes for the mouth and eyes, paint, shellac, and add other features from a "junk" collection, such as curtain rings for earrings, fur for hair, and so on.

10. Practice laying a shell of newspaper strips over a mold made of wads of dampened newspaper. After doing the preceding exercise, the reader will find the directions offered earlier in the chapter sufficient.

11. Prepare papier-mâché according to the directions on page 235. While it is wet, model some of this plastic medium on a workboard into a nonobjective form. With the rest of the pulp, model a representational form. Be sure to keep these objects solid and chunky rather than spindly; the solid form will more readily stay in one piece as it dries. When the objects are dry, try making one of them smoother by rubbing it lightly with fine sandpaper. Paint both the smooth and the rough object with tempera paint to enhance the designs already created.

12. Using pieces of decorative wrapping paper in a wide variety of patterns, make a collage of a city scene, showing architectural forms; unite the different patterns with paint or create an abstract design.

13. Prepare an attractive and easily understood exhibit for display in a classroom, to show the whole papier-mâché process from newsprint to finished object.[4]

14. Make four simple paper or cardboard forms in space, using each of the processes described earlier in the chapter. Carry your exploration as far as you can until you have some satisfying suspended or free-standing forms.

15. Make a mobile with wire and cardboard. Obtain some wire of the weight and type used for coat hangers (coat hangers themselves will serve the purpose) and a pair of long-nosed pliers with a built-in wire cutter. Snip off a piece of wire about 4 inches long and another about

---

[4]See Victoria Betts, *Exploring Papier-Mâché* (Worcester, Mass.: Davis, 1955).

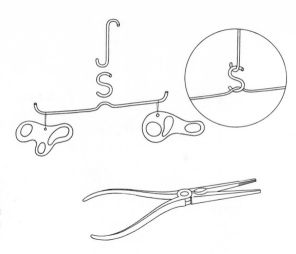

Figure 8.14 *Some techniques used in making a mobile sculpture from wire.*

6 to 8 inches long. Curl up one end of the short piece, put a hump in the middle of the long piece, and join the first to the second with an S-shaped link. Squeeze the open parts of the S together. Curl the ends of the long piece so that anything attached at either end will not slip off. Use thread to attach some cardboard pieces of interesting shapes and colors to either end of the long piece of wire. This is the first unit of a simple wire and cardboard mobile (see Figure 8.14). Try making some more mobiles with additional units.[5]

16. Bring into class yesterday's newspaper. As a class project, change the character of an entire wall. Change the total room environment through the use of your newspapers, using some of the shaping techniques suggested, plus your own ideas.

17. Take one issue of the daily paper and, using only scissors, paste, and stapler, create a costume for yourself.

[5]See John Lynch, *How to Make Mobiles* (New York: Viking, 1953).

This sculpture was made of plaster of Paris by a fifth grader.
(Harbrace photo)

SCULPTURE AND POTTERY: MODELING, CARVING, AND CONSTRUCTING

*Essentially sculpture means taking possession of a space, the construction of an object by means of hollows and volumes, fullnesses and voids; their alternations, their contrasts, their constant and reciprocal tension, and in final form, their equilibrium.**

Carving and modeling include the fashioning of three-dimensional art forms, either in relief or in the round. Although the definitions are not always strictly adhered to, in art education *carving* usually refers to a process by which part of a material is removed to form the finished product; *modeling* is performed by building up from a mass of material and often by adding even more material to that which is being formed. Thus to produce a piece of sculpture in wood one whittles away the wood until the desired form appears. In modeling a piece of clay, on the other hand, one shapes the form from the mass of clay and later adds subsidiary forms, such as noses or ears to a head.

Today's art requires a rather broad definition of sculpture, one that takes into account the mixed-media approach and the interrelation of art and technology. "Shaped canvases" can be viewed as painted sculpture or as painting that moves into space. The assemblage artists create unusual contexts for mundane "found objects," and the Pop artist Marisol combines whimsical and traditional forms of drawing with carved and geometric forms. Jean Tinguely animates his constructions with intricate mechanical devices; others are experimenting with sound and light as components of the total sculptural experience. Because children respond positively to many of the concepts inherent in sculpture today, problems of both a traditional and a contemporary nature should be considered

*From Henri Laurens, quoted in Andrew Carnduff Ritchie, *Sculpture of the Twentieth Century* (New York: Museum of Modern Art, 1953), p. 43.

245

when planning activities that are built around forming, shaping, and constructing.

In the traditional sense, carving and modeling are activities in which raw materials from the earth and forest are directly manipulated by the artist. In modeling, the pupils may approach the clay with no tools other than their bare hands, while in wood and other types of sculpture, a tool as primitive as a knife allows them to pit their skill against the material. If the worker shows respect for the substance, the primary characteristics of the original material remain in the finished product. Wood remains wood, clay remains clay, and each substance clearly demonstrates its influence on the art form into which it was fashioned.

Children in all stages of development can work successfully in modeling clay and in one form or another of wood sculpture. Only older preadolescents, however, are able to carve wood and plaster of Paris, since the skills involved are beyond the ability of younger children, and some of the tools required are too dangerous for them to use. It is important in considering the appropriateness of art activities for various grade levels to make a distinction between *media* and *concepts*. Instead of arbitrarily relegating any one type of material to a particular grade level, the teacher

Figure 9.1   *"There are many ways of creating form."* (**A**) *(left) This sculpture was made of slotted cardboard that was joined, painted, and attached to boxes. Grade 5.* (**B**) *(right) A ten-year-old girl applies the finishing touches to a painted sculpture she has assembled from scrap material. (Photo by Troy West.)*

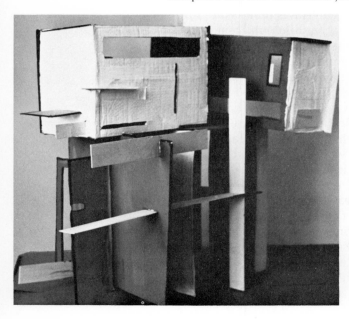

should examine the material in terms of the specific problem to be explored. It is true that the range of manual control varies with the age of the children, but for every grade level there are some concepts associated with a particular medium that are within the children's capability. For instance, even primary-grade children engaged in making animal figures can be encouraged to "pull out the shapes" and to "piece the figure together so that the parts don't fall off." They can also practice maintaining uniform thickness of the side of a pinch pot and can press patterns of found objects into clay tiles. These concepts might be presented to the children with such remarks as:

"There are many ways of creating form. As all artists do, choose the one that is most comfortable for you."

"Some kinds of modeling (or sculpture) require practice, just like learning a musical instrument or handling a ball. It may not be fun at first, but later it may help you to make something that you will want to keep."

"Even a flat piece of sculpture (relief) can be made to catch light and thus make interesting surface patterns."

"There is an animal form trapped in this piece of clay. Can you help it emerge so that we can see what it is?"

Sculpture has a universal appeal; the problem of creating forms in space and wedding materials and processes to ideas engages the interest of people of all age groups. Indeed the ideas discussed in this chapter are as useful to senior high school or even college students as they are to elementary-school pupils. The child who is making the first papier-mâché mask and the team of teen-agers involved in carving totemic figures out of discarded telephone poles can equally benefit from the practical suggestions found here.

Other materials of sculpture, such as cardboard, string, and papier-mâché, are discussed elsewhere in this book. Since repetition seems unnecessary, we will deal mainly with the more basic sculptural materials of clay, wood, and plaster of Paris here.

SCULPTURE IN WOOD

Children can handle wood in many ways. Odd shapes can be glued into structures just as they are, or their sizes and shapes can be adjusted by carving, sawing, and planing. The surface of the wood, in turn, may be left as is, or it may be painted or stained. Surfaces can also be sanded smooth or "pebbled" with carving tools; edges can be rounded with a file or plane. The options for design in wood, as in painting, are many, the only limitations being the manual control of the child and the tools that are available.

Using Scraps of Wood

Media and Techniques.   If access to an industrial arts shop in a nearby secondary school is available, the teacher may obtain from there scraps of wood varying in shape and size. These scraps of wood should be inspected to see that they have no dangerous splinters. In addition to scraps of wood the children might be supplied with tongue depressors, swab sticks, and wooden spools. To fix pieces of wood together, a particularly strong glue (white vinyl is the best), which may be purchased at any hardware store, is necessary.

Children in the manipulative and symbol stages put together pieces of wood much as they put together the boxes and tubes in box sculpture. Two pieces of wood are selected, both are smeared with glue along the edges to be stuck, and they are then pressed firmly together. The process is continued until several pieces of wood form one solid structure. A swab stick or a tongue depressor may be used to apply the glue. After assembling the pieces the children often like to paint their structures. Although combining wood with paint was once considered to be poor art practice, sculptors for some time have successfully combined the two media. This method may have positive advantages for children if the design possibilities of both painted and unpainted surfaces are discussed beforehand. A complex piece, composed of eight or nine wood scraps varying in size and shape, can be given unity through the addition of a single color or through color patterns that correspond to sharply articulated planes. Whereas the older child may use paint and sculpture to solve a problem in design, younger children may color surfaces only for decoration.

The distribution of supplies causes few special problems. Scraps of wood may be placed in cartons from which each child can select a number of pieces. The glue is best distributed by the teacher, who should place a dab of it on paper or cardboard set before each child. Paint is handled in the usual manner described for picture-making.

Sculpture in the Round

Media and Techniques.   Only older preadolescent children, usually in about the fifth and sixth grades, will be able to produce wood sculpture in the traditional manner. Traditional wood sculpture consists of carving bumps and hollows in a piece of wood that is suitable, or, as sculptors sometimes say, "sympathetic," for this purpose. Neither very hard woods like oak nor very soft woods like balsa are suitable for children. The hard woods, of course, demand more strength than the children possess, while the soft woods fail to offer the resistance that the developing muscles of the young require.

Wherever possible, woods from the local environment should be selected. By using local wood children explore their immediate environment and capitalize on their own resources. Seasoned woods of some of the cedar and cypress families are excellent for sculpture because they cut cleanly without splintering and do not demand too much physical

Figure 9.2 *One of Picasso's many sculptures from wood scraps, Musical Instruments 1914. His playfulness as well as his inventiveness led Picasso to discover surprising uses for castoff materials. (Owned by the artist's estate. Photo by John Webb, FRPS. © 1974 by SPADEM PARIS.)*

exertion. Unfortunately they have all but disappeared from most parts of our landscape. However, wood from poplars, pines, birches, and many other varieties, when seasoned, have excellent qualities for sculpture. Lumber merchants often sell suitable scraps of these woods. If the wood is damp, it should be stacked under cover out of doors until it dries. Wind dries the wood, and stacking prevents it from warping.

City children often have to depend on scraps of wood from discarded objects, such as old boxes or broken furniture, or from friendly fruit dealers and building contractors. If a source of discarded wood is not available, the school can usually purchase sufficient wood for its needs at reasonable cost. A call to the local telephone company can often yield free telephone poles, sometimes delivered directly to the schools.

Wood can be worked to a considerable degree of satisfaction with merely a strong, sharp pocketknife. Sets of carving tools may be bought, however, that allow the worker to produce a wide variety of cuts. These tools are obtainable in a number of shapes, such as straight-edged knives, V-gouges, and U-gouges. All tools should be kept sharp by constant honing on fine oilstone. In addition, some files, rasps, and sandpaper, from coarse to fine grain, may be required.

Wood can be cut on a 5-ply workboard placed over a school desk, but wood sculpture is best performed on an industrial arts (carpenter's) bench. These benches usually are fitted with vises that allow the worker to place both hands on the cutting tools. (Without a vise, the pupil must hold the wood with one hand, which may easily be injured unless great

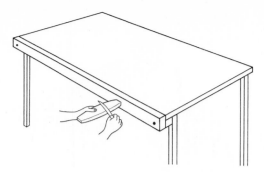

Figure 9.3 *Protective strip of wood bolted to edge of table for wood carving.*

care is exercised.) In general, the wood should be cut in a direction away from the body. Rough two-by-four strips bolted to the side of the work table will provide a protective surface against which pupils who work without a vise can carve. This permits the pupils to sit while carving (see Figure 9.3).

One method of working in wood that is often suggested in books for art teachers is not recommended here. By this method, the pupils are supposed to cut with a saw, first, a side profile, and second, the top and bottom of the subject in wood. The method recommended here is that of "roughing-out" the subject from all sides. The wood is held in one hand and pressed against the bench, or is placed in the vise if one is available, while the carving tool is applied along the grain. Turning the piece and cutting, the pupil gets rid of excess wood until the desired shape begins to be formed. Rasps—very coarse files—may be used at the close of the roughing-out process if the vise is used. The sculpting-in-the-round approach allows the pupil to create a solid, chunky piece of sculpture that is attractive in its "woodiness"—a desirable feature in this type of sculpture and difficult to achieve by the other method.

The article must be finished with some care so that neither the design nor the inherent quality of the wood is spoiled. For a smooth finish the student can use a rasp followed by a file and later by sandpaper on the surface. Wood usually requires the application of a preservative; perhaps the most acceptable is wax. A thin coat of solidified wax can be applied with a cloth and then polished vigorously. Successive coats should follow until the wood glows. A thin oil stain might occasionally be employed to enhance the wood, but this preservative should be used with caution. For one thing, it is often difficult to maintain a desired uniformity of tone because of the effect of the grain of the wood. Also, a bright stain may distort the natural appearance of the wood. Too often one sees a fine white wood spoiled by the application of what is fondly called a "mahogany" stain. Other than wax, perhaps the safest and most satisfactory finishes for wood are clear varnish and colorless shellac, both of which may be applied with a brush. Even with these coverings, however, there is a danger of making the wood look like toffee. In short, nothing is better than the quality of wood itself.

Teaching.   Sculpture in wood affords many opportunities for effective teaching; in particular it calls for discussion and demonstration. Wood is a medium with many excellent qualities that must not be destroyed through clumsy and inappropriate working techniques. The teacher's first task is to discuss with the class the fine qualities of wood—its color; its grain; its various surface qualities enhanced by different finishes, including sanding, waxing, and painting. Studies might be made of the various uses to which wood may be put and of how people have often relied on it to develop civilization.[1] Included in this study might be examples of faulty as well as successful treatment of wood.

Because most tools for working with wood are dangerous, the teacher should demonstrate the correct ways of handling them and, perhaps, discuss safety in using tools and the procedures for giving first aid for a cut. The teacher should give lessons concerning the sharpening and care of tools, emphasizing the pride good artisans have in their tools. A class trip to a sculptor's studio would be very worthwhile at this time.

The teacher will also find it necessary to discuss the subject matter suitable for wood sculpture. Reference to sculpture in wood from medieval German sculptors to the moderns, such as Louise Nevelson, will indicate to the pupils that sculpture is a form of expression as personal as painting.[2] Above all children should be helped to avoid clichés (such as the "Sleeping Mexican" and the "Noble Dog") and to express their own experience in their work.

As well as suggesting expression based on representational themes the teacher might encourage the pupils to do some nonobjective work. In this way they can concentrate on troublesome aspects of technique

[1] See Lewis Mumford, *Technics and Civilization* (New York: Harcourt Brace Jovanovich, 1963).
[2] See William Zorach, *Zorach Explains Sculpture,* rev. ed. (New York: Tudor, 1960); *Art in Our Time* (New York: Museum of Modern Art, 1939); Reginald H. Wilenski, *The Meaning of Modern Sculpture* (Boston: Beacon, 1961).

Figure 9.4 *This wood sculpture by Louise Nevelson shows the rhythmic possibilities of the medium. (Case with Five Balusters, 1959, white wood. Courtesy of Martha Jackson Gallery.)*

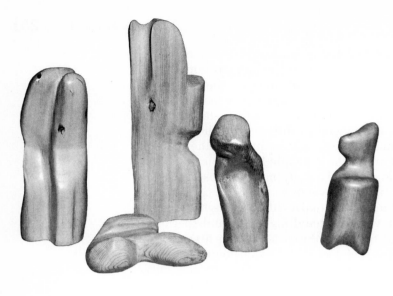

Figure 9.5 *Wood sculpture made by sixth graders. These objects are similar to the "feelies" of the Bauhaus school. (Photo by Royal Studio.)*

without being bothered by subject matter. A suitable project at this point might be the making of "feelies," small, highly polished carved objects designed to feel good in the hand (see Figure 9.5).[3] Before working with the wood itself it might be a good idea for the children to experiment with clay and soap to find out how material can relate to the hand. Because the "feelie" is hand-sized, the student has no difficulty in bringing a high degree of finish to the wood by sawing, filing, sanding, polishing, and waxing.

The child who works with wood in the round should learn that the chunky appearance of this sculpture is a natural outcome of the technique. The teacher should emphasize the fact that flimsy protuberances of any kind are not in keeping with wood sculpture and tend to affect the design adversely. The child should also be taught that any detail that is cut into the main contours must be developed with some restraint lest the distinctive wood quality of the piece be lost. Such insights into the technique will come, of course, to a great extent, through practice.

As the children work in wood they should be taught that the bumps, hollows, and textures they have carved must be studied for the patterns of light and shade they produce. By holding a child's sculpture in a reasonably strong light coming from one source, the teacher can demonstrate how to study the highlights and shadows. As in other art forms, it is far more important for pupils to learn to judge the quality of sculpture from the point of view of design than to judge it from its "realistic" appearance.

Figure 9.6 *A method for wood carving in relief.*

[3]The Bauhaus included such exercises in its design course. The artist began by rolling the wood over and over again in his hand until a certain shape began to suggest itself. His experimentation often led to solution of such varied industrial problems as developing handles for gun stocks and designing refrigerator doors.

A constant challenge to the teacher of sculpture is to select and employ only those teaching methods that develop the pupils' artistic integrity and taste. The search for excellence of craftsmanship will show clearly in wood sculpture as will the growing mastery of tools. Any subterfuge in the treatment of wood soon becomes evident. For example, pupils should not be obliged to obliterate the tool marks from the surface of their work if they do not wish to do so. Tool marks may add greatly to the design quality and particularly to the texture of a sculpted piece.

SCULPTURE IN PLASTER OF PARIS

Media and Techniques. For most children in the preadolescent stage a suitable medium for sculpture is plaster of Paris. A child who is capable of using any kind of cutting tool safely can use this material successfully. Sculpted pieces displaying satisfying qualities in either relief or in the round can be produced with plaster of Paris.

The plaster is usually bought in sacks. It should be mixed by sifting handfuls of the plaster into a pail of water until the plaster reaches the water level. The mixture should then be activated by sliding the hand in the water under the plaster and moving the fingers around at the bottom of the pail. By this means, a creamy consistency without lumps is attained. If the plaster tends to dry too quickly, the rate of drying may be slowed by adding about a teaspoonful of salt for every two cups of plaster.

After being mixed with water the plaster must be poured quickly into a mold to dry and harden. Children will find that small cardboard containers make suitable molds. (Pupils may also create their own molds by taping sections of heavy cardboard together.) The container is selected according to the type of work intended; a shoe box, for example, might have the right length and height for a plaque on which a relief sculpture is to be carved, and a carton that held a large tube of toothpaste would serve to mold plaster to be carved in the round. When the plaster dries, which it does with extraordinary rapidity, it contracts slightly so that the cardboard is easily peeled away.

Plaster may be combined with other materials, thus allowing for a choice in the degree of density. Students can mix, in various proportions, plaster, vermiculite, pearlite, sawdust, dirt, and sand. Samples of these aggregate combinations might be prepared and records kept of the degrees of hardness, kinds of texture, and so on, that are obtainable with the different proportions. The students might want to add some tempera for color and thus create truly personalized carving media.

The techniques used in cutting plaster are rather less robust than those used with wood. Almost any cutting tool may be used on plaster— pocketknives, woodworking tools, or linoleum cutters. Even worn-out dentist tools can be used. No special accommodation is necessary for this

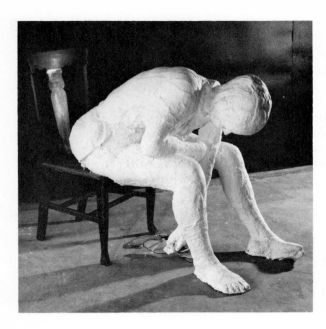

Figure 9.7 Girl Putting on Her Shoe, *one of George Segal's plaster body-castings placed in its own environment. (Plaster, wood, plastic, 37 in. high. Collection of Mr. and Mrs. William Paley, New York. Courtesy of Sidney Janis Gallery.)*

work; the cutting can be done on an old drawing board. When cutting is satisfactorily completed, the plaster should be lightly rubbed with fine sandpaper to obtain smooth surfaces where they are desired. A preservative finish is not necessary and would in fact spoil the attractive appearance of the medium.

Another method of working with plaster is to dip surgical bandages or strips of cloth into plaster and drape them over armatures or other substructures. The sculptor George Segal has been responsible for a whole new direction in art with his body-castings placed in complete environments (see Figure 9.7).

Plaster is one of the most versatile and least expensive of all art media. It does require more preparation and cleanup than many other activities, but it lends itself to working out of doors, weather permitting. Plaster and wood are in themselves two very good reasons for the establishment of art rooms in all schools.

Teaching. Because this medium is less difficult to cut than wood, demonstration need occupy relatively little time. Pupils often require more assistance in preparing the plaster than they do in working with it. The teacher should be sure that the children know what their subject matter and technique are to be before they mold their plaster. Low relief requires a flat slab, while sculpture in the round requires a block of plaster. Obviously once the plaster is molded the children are committed to work that suits the shape of the material. As for carving, the suggestions made earlier in connection with the teaching of wood carving are generally applicable to the problems that arise in working with plaster of Paris.

254

MODELING WITH CLAY

Modeling is another activity in which children in all stages of development may participate. Clay has been a standard modeling medium in the schools for many years because it is inexpensive and easily manipulated.

Media and Techniques. Clay may be purchased or it may be found in the ground in some localities, especially along lakes, bays, or small creeks. Any slippery, soapy earth having a red, blue, or whitish tinge and adhering tenaciously to the hands is probably clay. Working with the earth, however, will soon reveal whether or not it is suitable for modeling. Natural clay must usually be refined before it can be used as a modeling medium.

Three-Dimensional Modeling

Figure 9.8 *Carving may begin in the primary grades, as evidenced by this second grader's handling of soft soapstone. Tools are simple rasps, files, and cut pipe. (These items are from a kit developed by the Education Development Center in Newton, Massachusetts.) (Photo by Education Development Center.)*

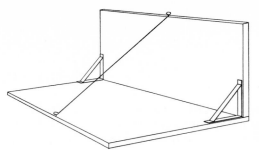

Figure 9.9 *A wedging table for "working" clay.*

If dry, it should be powdered and put through a sieve to remove lumps, pebbles, and other foreign matter. If wet, it must be rolled and kneaded on a porous slab, or "bat," and any lumps or foreign substances removed by hand as they come to the surface. A suitable porous bat can be made of plaster of Paris prepared in the manner outlined on page 253.

When purchased, dry standard clay (always cheaper than prepared clay) is usually packaged in 50- or 100-pound bags. In preparation for use, water should be poured over about half a pail of clay and mixed in with a spoon. It takes about 5 quarts of warm water to thoroughly soak 25 pounds of dry clay. A tablespoon of vinegar added to the water will neutralize any alkaline content and make it easier on the hands. After the clay has settled overnight, any excess water can be poured off. Clay also comes in a plastic state, usually in 25- to 100-pound bags. It is more expensive than dry clay because of the shipping charge for the added water content, but it is still relatively inexpensive, costing about ten or twelve cents per pound. One pound of clay makes a ball the size of an adult's fist, and this is a good average amount for a child to work with.

The youngest children are not able to prepare the clay for modeling and must depend on the teacher to perform this task. For this reason some teachers have turned to the commercially prepared oil clays (such as plasticine). While substances can be substituted, nothing can entirely replace natural, water-based clay as a modeling medium.

Before modeling can be successfully performed, the refined and dampened clay should be kneaded and rolled on the porous surface until it is almost rubbery. When a coil of it can be twisted and bent so that it neither breaks readily nor adheres unpleasantly to the hands, it is ready for modeling. To assist in working the clay to this necessary condition, an apparatus called a "wedging table" is useful (see Figure 9.9). The wedging table consists merely of two boards about one-half an inch thick, or 5-ply wood, fixed at right angles to each other with screws. Brackets strengthen this assembly. The measurements of each board should be at least 18 by 24 inches. A length of fine but strong wire should be attached from the top center of the upright board to the outside center of the lower board. "Wedging" makes the clay uniformly moist and free of air bubbles. A lump of clay is cut by pressing it into the wire. The resulting two pieces are then thrown with force onto the surface of the wedging table or slapped together. If the slapping of clay gets out of hand, the children should be encouraged to *knead* the clay from a standing position. This entails folding the clay back into itself, without trapping any air in the folds, until it has the proper rubbery texture. This process is continued until no tiny bubble holes are to be seen in the cut clay.

A reasonably large quantity of clay for modeling may be prepared in advance and stored for a short time in airtight tins or earthenware containers. Indeed, this storing tends to make it more workable. Small pieces of clay for each pupil may subsequently be cut away by means of a wire. Used clay can often be reclaimed by soaking it in water for about forty-eight hours. When the clay appears workable again it may be put back in the covered container.

Before the children work with clay or other modeling materials the working surfaces should be protected with newspapers, cardboard sheets, clear plastic, or oilcloth. The children will find it convenient to model the clay on a board placed on the protective covering. While working, the children can turn the board to view the sculpture from all sides. Plaster bats provide both a working and a kneading surface.

Modeling in clay and other materials is essentially an activity for the hands and requires no tools. Sets of tools are available, however, to assist more experienced children in producing details in their pieces. A small pointed stick, about the size of a lollipop stick, is also handy for this purpose. A damp sponge or cloth is useful to moisten the fingers and partially clean them at the close of the activity. The teacher should resist the temptation to use the sponge to smooth out objects. The surface of the clay is a record of the children's individuality, as is the texture of their crayons or the marks of their brushes and, as such, should be preserved as part of their total response.

The child's stage of development in pictorial work is reflected in the output in clay. The youngest and most inexperienced children are satisfied with a short period of manipulation, after which the clay is left in a shape resembling nothing in particular. Later, the children may give a name to shapes of this kind. Still later, the symbols associated with drawing and painting may appear in the clay in three-dimensional form (see Figure 9.11). Finally, the preadolescents refine their symbols, aiming at greater detail and realistic proportion. The younger children are less concerned about permanence of their objects than are the older ones, who want to see their pieces fired and carried to completion through the use of glazes.

There is no one technique recommended for modeling. Children begin to model naturally with considerable energy, enthusiasm, and, generally, dexterity. Given a piece of clay weighing from half a pound for kindergarten and first-grade pupils to 2 pounds for those in higher grades, the child will squeeze, stroke, pinch, punch, and pat it to get a satisfactory result. Whereas younger children may pull out their subject

Figure 9.10 *These fifth-graders are creating architectural structures for clay figures in a lesson on architectural space.*

from a central mass of clay, they seldom draw this way, preferring to assemble objects out of separate parts. In clay, however, they will use both methods and should be encouraged to proceed in any manner they find satisfactory.[4]

The finished product in clay must be a solid, compact composition. If the children, as they gain confidence in the medium, attempt to form slender protuberances, these usually fall off and they quickly learn not to draw out the clay too far from the central mass. They may add little pellets of clay for, say, eyes and buttons, but even these must be kept reasonably flat if they are to adhere to the main body of the clay. The use of watery clay, or "slip," may help them to fix these extra pieces. Slip is prepared by mixing some of the clay used in the modeling with water until the mixture has the consistency of thick cream. The worker scores, or roughens, the two surfaces to be stuck together with the teeth of a comb, a knitting needle, or a pointed stick, and then paints or dabs on the slip with the fingers before pressing the pieces together.

If worked on too long, clay becomes too dry to manipulate. In order for the clay to be kept sufficiently moist from one day to the next, it should be wrapped in a damp cloth over which is wrapped a rubber or plastic sheet, and, if possible, the whole should be placed in a covered tin until it is to be worked again. When the work is finished and left on a shelf to dry it should be dampened from time to time with water applied with a paintbrush. The small protuberances will thus be prevented from cracking or dropping off before the main body of the work has dried.

In some forms of advanced modeling, malleable wires called "armatures" are sometimes fixed to a base and then twisted into the general outline of the object as it is conceived in the mind of the artist. These devices are a convenience to the experienced person because once they have been arranged, the clay can be built up around them to form a more

[4]Viktor Lowenfeld and W. Lambert Brittain, in *Creative and Mental Growth,* 4th ed. (New York: Macmillan, 1964), suggest that such differences of approach depend largely on the type of thinking of the worker. Lowenfeld and Brittain, however, appear to neglect the influence on technique of the characteristics of the material being used and of the personal changes in the pupil as a result of maturation.

delicate, open type of work. For most elementary-school children, how-ever, the use of armatures is too difficult and should be avoided, except in cases where the child exhibits a marked ability in clay work. The simple, solid mass of unsupported clay is challenging enough for most young children and results in a wide variety of significant output. Occa-sionally, however, a small pointed stick can be thrust up from the base of the partially completed object to assist in keeping, say, a head erect.

Teaching. The teacher must be concerned with the preparation of the clay, the physical arrangements for handling it in the classroom, and the subject matter selected by the children.

For the youngest children the teacher must prepare the clay. For the older children, step-by-step instructions and then careful supervision of their preparation of the medium is needed. The clay must be prepared correctly if the work is to be successful. The room and its furnishings must be adequately protected from clay dust and particles. The teacher should ask each child to spread newspaper on the floor under the work area. Desks or tables on which the work is performed should be covered with oilcloth, rubber, or plastic sheeting, or with more paper. Many cleaning cloths dampened with water should be readily at hand, and the pupils should be taught to use them both when the work is in progress and when it is finished. The pupils must also learn to pick up the protec-tive coverings carefully so that clay particles are not left on the desks or floor.

Good teachers will see that adequate shelves are provided for storing clay work. They should carefully supervise as each child stores the work and make sure that the products are in no way damaged during the storage process.

Subject matter for modeling in clay is somewhat restricted. Usually it involves one person or thing, or at the most two persons or things resolved into a closely knit composition. Only objects or shapes that are chunky and solid can be successfully rendered. Thus the human figure and certain animals such as owls, squirrels, or pigs, which can be suc-cessfully stylized into a solid form, are more suitable subjects than natu-rally spindly creatures such as giraffes, spiders, and flamingos. Discussion regarding the need to select a subject in keeping with the nature of clay must take place in the classroom before the pupils begin work.

Working from a posed figure has recently become accepted as a desirable adjunct to drawing activity, yet relatively few teachers apply this idea to sculpture. Positioning the human body and interpreting its proportions can be exciting art experiences when carried through in both the flat and in-the-round approaches. The upper-grade child can establish a basic standing figure without too much difficulty, but to make the figure sit, crawl, sleep, and perform other such activities, often requires a posed model.

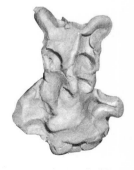

Figure 9.11 *Symbols in clay by first-grade pupils.*

Figure 9.12 *The human face may be used as a subject for modeling. In this face by a fourth grader the unglazed clay was fired to give the effect of terra cotta. (Harbrace Photo.)*

Often, before the actual modeling occurs, the teacher will be obliged to demonstrate some of the techniques of handling clay, especially for preadolescent pupils, who generally wish to arrive at an exact representation of the objects they are fashioning. Included among the demonstrations should be the two chief methods of modeling—pulling out from a central mass, and shaping or welding, in which prepared pieces such as arms and legs are scored and treated with slip. The use of some modeling tools to produce details may also require demonstration.

There is no reason why modeling in clay cannot be used to reinforce other learning in art. If fifth and sixth graders sketch the human figure, they can sculpt it as well, working either for heightened observation or for purposes of personal expression. If texture is being examined through collage, the children can study texture further by impressing found objects—bark, string, burlap, and the like—into the responsive surface of clay. Plaster casts can be made of such exercises and then combined into attractive wall panels for the school.

Long-Range Planning in Clay

One teacher who used clay as a major medium planned a complete sequence of activities as follows:

Early Grades

Make a flat slab of clay with the palms of the hands.

Roll the clay into a thick coil, a thin coil, a big clay ball, and several small clay balls.

Make a bird out of one lump of clay using a particular texture for feathers.

Make a pinch pot out of one small ball of clay.

Middle Grades

Join two pieces of clay together.

Show a film, slides, or books illustrating the clay process and finished clay objects.

Make a mother and child sculpture of one kind of animal.

Make a prehistoric creature, embellishing it with natural textures from imprinting objects such as leaves or fir cones.

Make a clay figure showing a particular emotional state.

Make a clay figure showing physical action.

Make a fantasy clay world or an imaginary environment.

Allow a small group of the most advanced students to be responsible for firing clay objects under the supervision of the teacher.

Figure 9.13 *Clay modeling activities can make use of posed models just as drawing does. In* **A**, *a teacher calls attention to the "action" of the figure. In* **B**, *a group of completed figures, about to be fired, generates an aura of mystery. Grade 6. (Photos by Rick Steadry.)*

A

B

Upper Grades

Make a large pinch pot.

Make a coil pot container. Decorate it with a pattern consisting of either an incised texture or added bits of clay.

Make a relief slab puzzle using a drawing or painting as the subject matter.

Make a ceramic slab wall hanging as a group project.

In addition to the activities listed above, the teacher's clay curriculum also included suggestions of a more general pedagogical interest. Wanting to provide the children with adequate motivation, the teacher showed them photographs of animals and other subjects. To determine the relevant characteristics of the children at a given stage of development, the teacher noted their growing awareness of differences within classes of objects. To emphasize the formal elements of the art form the children were working in, the class discussed the specific properties of clay and glazes. Above all the teacher worked to establish measurable performance criteria, such as "the pupil will be able to give a subject personality by understanding the drama of body movement."

STABILE CONSTRUCTIONS

Media and Techniques.   Stabile constructions are sculptures made of one material, such as wire, straws, or balsa-wood strips, or of combinations of materials, such as string, wood, and cardboard (see Figure 9.15). Although the subject matter may be real—animals, buildings, or people— these "stabiles" are most effective when designed abstractly, with empha-

Figure 9.14 *This fifth grader is using a block of styrofoam as a base for her stabile. (Photo by Rick Steadry.)*

A

B   C

Figure 9.15 *Various forms of stabile constructions, using string combined with portions of boxes* (**A**), *straws* (**B**), *and thin balsa strips* (**C**). *(Photos by Education Development Center.)*

sis placed on balance of line against plane, transfer of space into solid areas, relation of parts to wholes, and so on. The mechanically minded pupils may include moving parts in their constructions, and creative individuals may incorporate such materials as ping-pong balls, feathers, and colored cellophane into their work.

The wire construct is a practical activity for all children but those in the manipulative stage. Wire lends itself to the creation of a composition that depends largely on a continuous line. When bent into any position the wire should stay there. Copper or aluminum wire, or wires made of alloys of these elements, are suitable. The necessary tools include snips to cut the wire, long-nosed pliers to manipulate it, and a drill to bore holes in a base for the sculpture to stand in. The wire may also be attached to the base by stapling and by bending a nail around the end of the wire.

Teaching.   These sculptures are appropriate to our time, since they allow for an open approach to materials and a wide latitude of personal style. The children should therefore be strongly encouraged to approach the activity experimentally. A teacher might demonstrate how a length of wire can be bent and then leave the children to make their own discoveries. The first bends may be made with the hands; later the details might be added with pliers. When the desired shape is attained the teacher might suggest that either one or both ends of the wire be placed in a base sufficiently heavy to support the sculpture. After further experimentation children may use two separate pieces of wire effectively. By polishing the wire with an appropriate metal cleaner and the wood with wax the pupils learn to finish the sculpture so that it shines in an attractive fashion.

This craft is a relatively delicate one. It requires no special equipment and makes little mess, except perhaps in the preparation of the wooden bases, and the teacher meets no outstanding problems in arranging the classroom for the work involved. The activity allows the teacher to isolate a single idea or material for study; for instance, the manipulation of wire is a logical way to study line in space. Slide reproductions of the works of Calder, Gabo and Pevsner, early Giacometti, or Gonzalez will demonstrate to the children that a new kind of space can be controlled and unity and movement can be obtained through constructions as well as paintings.

MAKING POTTERY

Media and Techniques.   Pottery is a form of clay modeling in which the children in the symbol stage usually make play dishes by hollowing a solid lump of clay. Preadolescents are capable of what are called the "coil" and "slab" methods. A simple pinch pot is a good project on which to start a child at any age. Children may begin by shaping the clay into a ball and working the thumb of their right hand into the center. They then rotate the ball slowly in the palm of one hand, gently pressing the clay between the thumb and the fingers of the other hand to expand the wall. The wall should be thick and the pot periodically tapped on the table to maintain a flat base. If the walls are thick enough, they may subsequently be decorated by incising lines or pressing hard-edged objects into the surface.

In producing coil pottery (see Figure 9.16), the child will find it convenient to work on a plaster bat. A ball of clay is flattened on the bat until it is about half an inch thick. Then it is trimmed with a knife to the desired size, usually about 3 to 5 inches in diameter. A coil of clay about half an inch in diameter is next produced by rolling the clay. The coil is then applied to the edge of the base, which should be scored and dampened with slip so that adhesion is assured. The coil should then be pinched to the base. A second coil is built on the first in the same way. No more than four or five coils should be made in one day lest the assembly collapse under its own weight. After allowing the clay to dry for a day the pupil may add another four or five coils. This goes on each day until the bowl has reached the desired height.

The position of the coils determines the shape of the bowl. Placing a coil slightly on the outside of the one beneath it will flare the bowl; placing it toward the inside will diminish the bowl in diameter. Although a perfectly uniform bowl is not expected, nor indeed altogether desirable, it is necessary to examine the rising edges from all angles to see that the shape of the object is reasonably symmetrical. A template, or contour, cut in cardboard may be applied to the side of the bowl, but this shaping technique is frowned on by many people for the very good reason that it is mechanical and rather extraneous to the process of coil pottery.

When the outlines of the bowl are formed the pupils should either smooth both the inside and the outside with their fingers or smooth just the inside for support and allow the exterior coil texture to show. Dipping the fingers in slip facilitates the smoothing process. The lip of the bowl should be flattened or tapered and perhaps trimmed with a wire tool or knife. The bowl should then be cut away from the slab with a wire. Its edges may then be gently smoothed with the fingers.

The slab method shown in Figure 9.17 involves the assembly of a number of flat pieces of clay to form a box. Well-prepared clay is rolled flat, like pastry, with a bottle or rolling pin that rests on wooden guides. The base of the object being made is then cut to size, as are the sides. The bottoms of the sides and edges of the base are scored and dabbed with slip where they are to be joined. A coil of clay, also dabbed with slip, is applied to all sides of the base just inside the edge. A side is put in place and reinforced on the inside by the coil. This process is repeated until all four sides are pressed firmly in place in an upright position. Fine sandpaper or a damp sponge may be used to make the sides smoother once the object is dry.

The box is only one product of slab construction. Slabs have many uses: they can be slotted and joined, and flat and curved sections can be combined. Unbroken surfaces can offset textured sections, and large areas can be created by interlocking slabs, which may, in turn, have smaller sections cut away. Slabs that bisect and interpenetrate one another can result in pleasing nonobjective sculptural forms. Slabs can also be alternated with coils to attain greater variety in constructing containers.

Teaching.   Two important demonstrations peculiar to the slab method of construction are necessary. First is the method of rolling clay flat. The

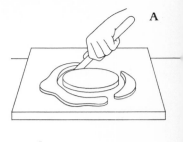
A

B

C

D

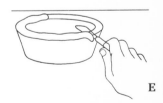
E

Figure 9.16   *The coil method of pottery-making:* (**A**) *trimming the base,* (**B**) *rolling the coil,* (**C**) *applying the coil,* (**D**) *smoothing the coil, and* (**E**) *trimming the lip.*

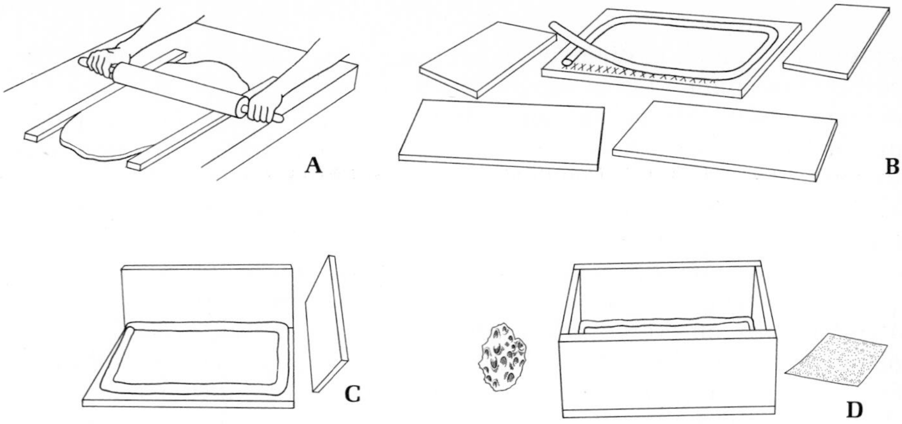

Figure 9.17 *The slab method of making pottery, showing* (**A**) *preparation of the clay,* (**B**) *placement of the supporting coil,* (**C**) *application of the sides, and* (**D**) *sponge and sandpaper for smoothing the sides.*

teacher should take a ball of well-prepared clay and flatten it to about three-quarters-of-an-inch thick on a piece of rubber sheeting or plastic. Two pieces of wood about one-quarter- to three-eighths-of-an-inch thick should be placed parallel to each other along two opposite boundaries of the flattened clay. A bottle or rolling pin should travel over these pieces of wood until the clay has been rolled to a thickness equal to that of the strips of wood.

The second demonstration involves fixing the sides of the box to its base. This process has already been described above and illustrated in Figure 9.17.

Finishing Processes

Media and Techniques. Several techniques may be used to decorate objects made of clay. These include glazing, incising, painting with engobe (colored slip), pressing with various objects, and a technique of incising through engobe known as "sgraffito."

The successful glazing of clay requires skill and experience. First, the raw clay must be very carefully wedged to remove air bubbles. Next, after the modeling is done, the object must be dried thoroughly, often in an artificially heated cabinet. Then a kiln or oven must be skillfully stacked with the pieces for preliminary firing, or what is called the "biscuit" during which varying temperatures must be maintained before, during, and after the firing. When the first firing has been successfully completed, one must apply the glazes (of which there are at least five distinct types), stack the kiln in such a way as to prevent the glaze on one object from touching another, and go through a second process of firing and cooling. Although it produces lovely results glazing is a formidable process, and few people can learn how to do it merely by reading a book on the subject. To learn how to glaze competently, one should enroll in a workshop under the guidance of a ceramics expert. Under such conditions, glazing is not too difficult to master in a reasonably short period. A month's course at night school or at a summer school allows ample time to become reasonably proficient at glazing.

Incising involves scoring the clay with various objects. The clay must be partly dry before incising can be done. Any one of a number of objects, ranging from nails and knitting needles to keys and pieces of comb, can be repeatedly pressed into fairly moist clay to make an interesting pattern, particularly after the second firing.

Engobe, or colored slip, is underglaze pigment, a teaspoonful of which is added to twice that quantity of finely powdered dry clay. The same clay used in the main body of the piece must be used in the engobe. After the dry pigment and clay have been well mixed, water is added until the mixture resembles a thick cream. A few drops of glycerine make the engobe flow readily. Commercially prepared engobe is available from school-supply houses. The engobe is painted on almost dry clay (called "leather-hard" clay) with a sable brush. When the painted clay is dry it must be fired twice as described earlier.

Sgraffito combines both incising and painting with engobe. Engobe is painted onto the partially dried object. In order to get thorough coverage and avoid streaks, two coats should be applied, the first by brushing consistently in one direction, the second by brushing consistently in another direction. When the engobe coats have almost dried, lines are incised through them—usually with a stick—to the clay before firing the object.

Following the lead of some professional potters, a number of teachers are experimenting with new approaches to surface decoration, which may include polymer acrylics or even tempera paint. In the latter case, when the paint is dry it may be left mat (nonglossy) or covered with a protective coating of shellac. The new polymer paints, unlike tempera, will not come off when the object is handled. Shoe polish gives a pleasing surface tone and may be used in place of paint; it comes in a surprising range of colors. In all cases the clay should be completely dry before a coating is applied.

Figure 9.18 *Some ways of making designs in clay, using a comb, a spoon, and a piece of fire-brick. (Photo by Royal Studio.)*

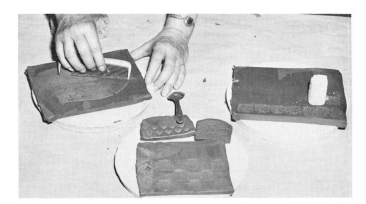

Teaching.   Finishing clay objects produced by elementary-school children places the teacher in an educational and artistic dilemma. As Victor D'Amico says in speaking of pottery, glazing is the "crowning experience" of the craft.[5] More than that, glazing is the only really acceptable finish for clay. Although clay will take paint, which may in turn be covered with shellac or varnish to give it a shine, such a finish is not suited to clay and tends to make even the best work look cheap and tawdry. On the other hand children can paint clay easily enough, but most of them cannot successfully fire it without help from the teacher. So much help is required, in fact, that the children must usually surrender their control of this activity to an adult.

Teachers have attempted to solve the dilemma arising from the finishing of clay products in several ways. Some tell the children that it is impossible for them to fire and glaze their work at the present time, but that they might instead try pressing or incising a design into it. The decorated object is then preserved in its natural form. Often teachers glaze for each child one or two products finished in engobe, sgraffito, or another technique that the teacher has demonstrated. Others show the children how to coat the work with shellac and explain that this is merely a makeshift process. Still other teachers, having explained that not all the steps in glazing can be taken by the children themselves, go ahead with glazing but take every opportunity to let the children do whatever lies within their competence. Thus a young child might at first only paint a bowl with engobe but later might help to stack the kiln. None of these alternatives is wholly satisfactory, but perhaps the last provides the children with the most insight and experience into the craft of pottery.

THE EMERGENCE OF A NEW AESTHETIC IN SCULPTURE AND CERAMICS

The art teacher will occasionally be unable to relate sculpture and ceramic activities in an elementary program to the work of professionals. Materials and methods are difficult to duplicate in fields where contemporary artists work with such diverse means as synthetics, electricity, and control of the atmosphere. In general, teachers should be cautioned against concentrating on any extreme approach for the sake of living out their own personal interests. A teacher's indiscriminate pursuit of the avant-garde may have as little meaning to fifth graders as a stubborn reverence for traditional forms.

Sculpture and ceramics, like any art form, should challenge a child within the boundaries of enthusiasm and capability, providing experience

---

[5]*Creative Teaching in Art,* rev. ed. (Scranton, Pa.: International Textbook, 1966), p. 140. This book contains excellent chapters on sculpture and pottery.

Figure 9.19 *Aesthetic awareness can be developed by linking sections of playground equipment with rope in a weaving activity that will produce a patterned arrangement of colors and spaces.*

Figure 9.20 *Sculpture may now include "environments" built to the scale of the child. It may become a place to live in as well as an object designed to be observed and contemplated, as these sixth graders discovered.*

in depth and breadth. There is a time to work from observation and a time to work from one's imagination; a time for ideas that move quickly and a time for sequential approaches. Children may carve and model as artists have done for ages or they may combine assembled constructions with light and motion, as is currently practiced. In a broad sense sculpture in particular may be said to encompass many kinds of volumes and masses organized within a spatial context. It can be created with boxes or junk, clay or plaster. During the course of six or seven years in an elementary school, a child should have the pleasure of working with many approaches.

Although a conscientious teacher plans for most of the activities, a portion of the program should be left open for the unexpected. A windfall of unusual materials, a trip to a gallery, a magazine article, or acquaintance with a great artist could capture the interest of both students and teacher in a new activity.

ACTIVITIES FOR THE READER

1. Survey the district around your school for materials suitable for sculpture and pottery. Is there any clay, wood, or wire to be had? Test the materials according to the suggestions found in this chapter under the subheadings "Media and Techniques."

2. Seek out an efficient industrial arts teacher who should be only too happy to talk about wood. Ask questions about the types of woods and their various properties, seasoning wood, hand and power tools for woodworking, the care of tools (including sharpening), and finishes for wood. Ask for demonstrations of some of the processes associated with woodworking. Seek advice about brands of tools and types of sharpening stones. Exchange a picture you have made for scraps of wood (sanded ones, if possible).

3. Go to a good furniture store and make a note of the different types of finishes. Speak to an industrial arts teacher in one of your secondary schools if you do not understand how some of the finishes are obtained.

4. Glue scraps of wood together to form a piece of sculpture. Smooth the surfaces of the sculpture with medium and then fine sandpaper. Wax the sculpture and polish it with a soft cloth until it glows. Ordinary solid floor wax is suitable.

5. Experiment with various kinds of woods by cutting them with a heavy pocketknife. (Keep the knife sharp by rubbing it gently over a fine oilstone.) When you find wood that you like to cut, plan, either in your mind's eye or in a pencil sketch first on paper and then on the wood, a nonobjective design that you intend to cut. Start cutting, turning the wood from time to time so that you cut from all angles. Cut away from you and keep your other hand behind the cutting edge. Study the developing design for unity and variety of the elements. If you would like to put some holes in the wood to get three-dimensional effects, you will have to use a large drill or brace-and-bit. When the carving more or less satisfies you, put it gently in a vise and start filing it smooth. Sometimes sculptors protect their work from the jaws of the vise by placing pieces of wood between the sculpture and the jaws. Let the file "bite," by pushing it away from you. Finish with medium and fine sandpaper and, finally, polish with about a dozen coats of wax.

6. Select a flat piece of solid gumwood or pine. Practice using gouging tools by making some V-cuts with two strokes of a knife, making a vertical cut and removing pieces of wood by gouging toward this cut, gouging out a circular depression, and creating many different textural effects by cutting, chipping, and gouging.

7. Cast a plaque about 6 by 9 inches in plaster of Paris. Carve a nonobjective design in the plaque based on overlapping oblongs and squares. In some areas devise textural effects by cutting or gouging.

8. Cast a block of plaster of Paris about 2 by 2 by 8 inches. Plan a representational subject (a torso is excellent) and carve it out of the block.

9. Model a nonobjective shape in clay; model a representational form in clay.

10. Try a life-size self-portrait in clay. Imagine yourself in an unusual

role—a king, a slave, a dreamer, or a prophet. Use a soda bottle filled with sand as an armature to control the weight of the clay.

11. Enroll in a clay workshop under the guidance of an expert in ceramics. Learn something about pottery of various kinds, decorating pottery, firing, and glazing.[6]

12. Roll a slab of clay big enough to wrap around an oatmeal box. Press rows of designs into the clay with hard-edged objects such as seed pods, coins, tools, wood ends, and the like. Keep a balance of large and small shapes and deep and shallow marks. When the slab is covered with designs, wrap it around the oatmeal box and seal the joined edges by pinching them. Remove the oatmeal box. Add a clay base and fire the object. You will have a unique container.

13. Cut a rectangle measuring at least 18 by 20 inches from a half-inch-thick slab of clay. With a nail file, begin cutting out a family of shapes, both curved and angular. Use some linear shapes as links in your design. As you cut out the shapes, place them on a board covered with sand, dirt, or dried clay. (This will keep your forms from sticking.) Make sure that the forms overlap or touch one another. After sprinkling the design with more sand or dried clay, place a second board on top of the pieces and press down hard. (You can even jump up and down on it.) Lift up the board and notice the subtle play of edges and the unifying surface quality attained by the pressure of the board. You can cut the design into sections and begin all over again.

14. Go to a hardware store and ask to see samples of malleable wire. Buy a few feet of different sizes and types. Using only your hands, bend the wire into nonobjective shapes. Then, with pliers, try to fashion the outline of some objects in wire such as flowers, leaves, or animals. Instead of working from section to section, keep in mind the overall rhythmic flow of the piece.

15. Plan a piece of nonobjective wire sculpture in which you use some fine copper wire screen as well as at least two types and sizes of wire—say, heavy copper and fine aluminum wire. Work out the main rhythms with the wire. Then add some screen areas to the composition. The screen pieces may be cut with shears or heavy scissors and fixed in place with a clear plastic cement or by weaving the wire through the screen. Work for balance of line (wire) and plane (wire screen).

16. Create a piece of "junk" sculpture—either a wall section or freestanding composition. Scour a basement, an alley, or an empty lot for odd bits of wood, fruit crates, picture frames, discarded toys, loose wheels, and so on. Select them on the basis of their design potential or their relationship to one another by association. Assemble your "construction" by nailing or by binding with wire or string. Will you leave it as it is? Will you paint it one unifying color, or use color to accentuate the movement of the shapes?

17. Study a "jungle gym" in a nearby elementary-school playground. Imagine it to be an armature—how would you convert it into a piece of sculpture?

[6]See Julia Hamlin Duncan and Victor D'Amico, *How to Make Pottery and Ceramic Sculpture* (New York: Museum of Modern Art, 1947).

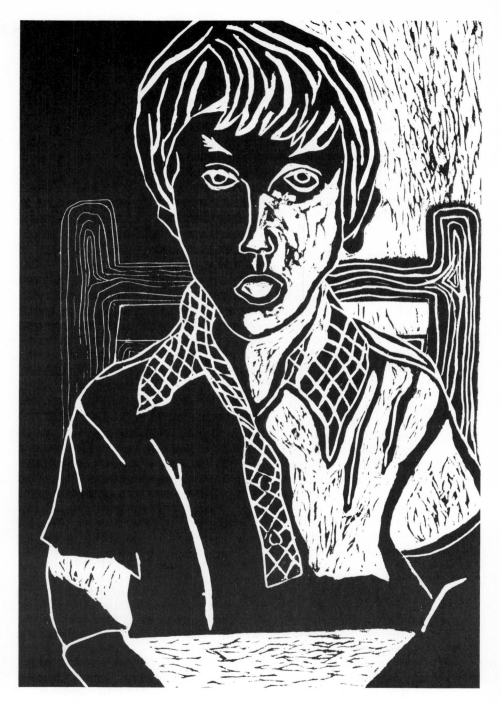

Linoleum prints can provide strikingly dramatic images, as in this self-portrait by a sixth grader. The original print is 12 x 18 in. Large prints require an ability to maintain interest over an extended period of time.

PRINTMAKING

A fine print may be produced lovingly and patiently, or violently and impetu-ously—dependent upon the "climate" of the printmaker. From a fleeting idea wrested from the complex of human experience, worked through to the final visual image on paper, the print is employed as a medium in its own right. It is utilized by the printmaker for what it alone can accomplish in serving his particular needs. This precious sheet of paper bears the autographic trace of the printmaker on its surface; in his own "handwriting," then, we read the record of his dreams, his hopes, aspirations, play, loves, and fears.*

$\mathbf{T}$his chapter concentrates largely on the printing process in which an image is transferred from an inked plate to paper. The process may produce multiple prints, as in the case of woodcuts and linoleum-block prints, or a single transfer, as in the case of monoprints. In contrast to drawing and painting, paper work, and sculpture and pottery, which are largely direct activities, printing is an indirect process; something is done to one substance in order to produce an effect on another substance. Between the child and the finished print, in other words, lies a whole series of moves with intermediary materials that must be completed successfully before the final image itself appears.

It is this emphasis on process that intrigues the preadolescents to the extent that they often lose their self-consciousness about the quality of the end product. Why worry about the shape of the house when it is so much fun to gouge the wood, roll on the ink, and transfer the image?

The subject of a print can be a single image, as in pure design, landscape, and figure studies, or complex images developed from a num-ber of motifs. However, because the printing processes exert especially strong influences on the design, the treatment of subject matter often

*From Jules Heller, *Print Making Today* (New York: Holt, Rinehart and Winston, 1958), p. xiv.

requires considerable modification to suit the technique. Children will soon discover that details and shading are more appropriate to drawing than to printmaking and that a successful print makes a strong impact through simplification and contrast.

It is clear, then, that printmaking can be a relatively complicated process for the young and raises a number of questions about the treatment of subject matter and the influence of technique on design. Printing techniques, however, do lie within the capabilities of most schoolchildren. These include monoprinting and vegetable and "stick" printing, which children at all stages can do successfully. Even the intricacies of linoleum-block printing can be mastered by fourth graders, and sixth graders are perfectly capable of handling woodcuts.

This chapter includes a description of all these types of printing. In addition, stenciling is discussed, since, although this is not strictly a form of printing, it is closely allied to it and makes use of many of the materials required to produce repeated art forms. Experimental printmaking with such unorthodox materials as corrugated cardboard, collographs, collage, and clay, is also discussed. The search for new solutions to traditional problems is as much a part of contemporary printmaking as of painting, and every public-school art program should provide for some degree of experimentation in basic art forms. For example, if a press is available the class can experiment with scratched acetate prints.

MONOPRINTING

Media and Techniques.   The printing technique most closely allied to drawing and painting, and to which any child may transfer some picture-making ability, is called monoprinting.

The supplies required are a sheet of glass with the edges taped so the children cannot cut their hands. Instead of glass, a piece of linoleum may be used, measuring about 6 by 8 inches and preferably glued to a slab of wood. In the lower elementary grades, finger paint may be used directly on the table, since it is easily cleaned with a damp cloth or sponge. Also required are a brayer about 2 to 6 inches long, some water-soluble ink in as wide a range of colors as is available, and newsprint or other reasonably absorbent paper. Brayers and water-soluble inks made especially for this work are sold by several school-supply firms.

To begin the process, the ink is squeezed from the tube onto the surface of the glass or linoleum and then rolled evenly over the surface. More than one color may be used if desired. If two colors are used, for example, they may be dabbed onto the glass and then blended with the brayer. Another method is to mix the colors lightly with a palette knife before rolling. Each technique produces its own effect.

The drawing can be produced with almost any implement capable

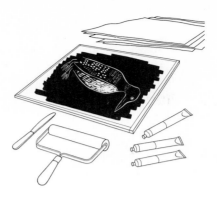

Figure 10.1 *Arrangements for making a monoprint.*

of making a strong mark directly into the ink. The eraser end of a pencil, a piece of cardboard, and a broad pen point are but a few of the suitable tools. The drawing, which is made directly in the ink, must be kept bold because the inked surfaces do not show fine details. Only the ink that is left on the surface will be recorded in the final printing.

For the printing, a sheet of paper should be placed gently over the prepared inky surface and pressed to it with the tips of the fingers. A clean brayer rolled evenly over the paper also produces a good print. The completed print may then be gently peeled away. Sometimes two or three impressions may be taken from one drawing. By using papers with varying textures an interesting variety of prints can be obtained. Although newsprint is recommended because it is cheap and absorbent, other papers should be tried also, such as colored tissue, construction and poster papers, and even the coated stock found in magazine advertisements.

Another method of monoprinting is as follows. The glass is covered with ink in the usual manner. The paper is then placed gently over the inked glass. Next the pupil draws with a pencil on the upper side of the paper, taking care not to drag the side of his hand on the paper. The resulting print is a composition of dark lines with some imprint of ink on the background areas.

Drawing in monoprint creates an arresting line quality—soft, rich, and slightly blurred. Because of this, it is particularly appropriate as an adjunct of contour-line drawing in the upper grades.

Another variation of monoprinting is the "paper stop out" method. Paper forms are cut or torn and then placed in a desired pattern on the inked plate. The impression is made by putting fresh paper on the arrangement and rolling it with the brayer. The cut-paper forms beneath serve to "stop out" the ink, and the areas they cover will appear as a negative pattern (that is, as the color of the paper) in the finished print.

Prints may also be produced by arranging objects such as string, a piece of wire screen, burlap, or scraps of rough-textured cardboard on a clean glass. Newsprint is placed over the arrangement and an inked brayer is run over the paper to obtain a print. These techniques may be

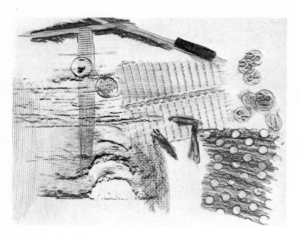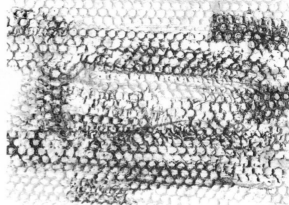

Figure 10.2 *Crayon rubbings of various objects may be used to investigate surface textures. Objects can also be glued to a hard surface and inked in order to make collage prints.*

used as a preliminary for collage prints, which are made by gluing objects to a cardboard base and coating the assembly with shellac. Literally dozens of prints can be rolled off on such a plate. (The shellac keeps soft materials such as yarn and burlap from shedding onto the brayer and paper.) Variations of the same print can be obtained by pulling a second impression that is slightly off register, as in Figure 10.4.

Teaching.   Four main tasks confront the teacher of monoprinting. The first is to arrange furniture, tools, and supplies so that printing may be done conveniently; the second is to see that the ink does not get all over the children and the room; the third is to give stimulating demonstrations and continued encouragement; and the fourth is to make certain that there is a cleared area for wet prints to hang or otherwise be stored until dry.

Printing should be done on a long table covered with newspapers or oilcloth. At one end or at several points on the table the teacher should arrange the glass, brayers, and inks. Because it would be uneconomical for each pupil to have a separate set of printing tools, the pupils should be given an order in which to work. Those who are not printing should know what other activities are available. As each print is completed the student should place it carefully on the remaining table space. When all the children have finished, the teacher should encourage them to select the prints they consider most interesting. When wet, the prints can be hung with clothespins on an improvised clothesline and then when dry pressed between the leaves of a heavy book such as an almanac or a telephone book. When possible, a wall should be cleared to mount new prints for drying.

As can be imagined, a large amount of ink comes off on the children's hands. The teacher should make sure that the pupils either wash their

276

Figure 10.3 *This print was made by arranging string, cut-paper shapes, and cut-paper sculpture of a fish on a clean surface and then inking the paper. Grade 4.*

hands often or at least wipe them on a damp cloth. Unless the classroom has a sink the teacher must provide pails of water, soap, and towels or damp cloths.

The teacher should demonstrate efficiently all methods of mono-printing. Although the techniques are simple enough, it would be wise to practice before the lesson; monoprinting can be very messy unless one

Figure 10.4 *String monoprints are an effective follow-up activity for contour drawing. The string is glued along the lines drawn in the ink before the print is made. Note that a double image is achieved by slightly altering the position of the plate for the second printing. Grade 4.*

has had some previous experience with the work. If the teacher appears clumsy during the demonstration there may be a very inky classroom once the children begin to experiment.

Pupils find monoprinting challenging and stimulating. Once they know how to begin they are eager to discover all the possibilities of this technique. It is a valuable activity not only because it permits spontaneous work but also because it gives children a reasonably accurate idea of the printmaking process in general. Any form of printmaking works well for small groups, especially when they try it for the first time.

VEGETABLE AND STICK PRINTING

Media and Techniques. All children can produce work in the technique called vegetable printing, and nearly every child at the symbol stage can print with sticks.

For vegetable printing the children should select pieces of vegetable with a hard consistency such as cabbage, carrot, potato, or celery. The pieces should be large enough for the children to grasp easily and should be cut flat on one side or end. All the children need do is dip the flat side of the vegetable into watercolor, tempera paint, or colored ink and then dab it on a sheet of newsprint. The child in the manipulative stage at first dabs at random but later controls the pattern and develops a rhythmic order of units. Fruit rinds or scraps of sponge of various kinds may also be used in printing (see Figure 10.7).

The next step in technique is to control the design by cutting into the end of the vegetable. The best vegetable for this purpose is a crisp potato, but carrots are also suitable. The potato should be sliced in half and the design cut into the flat side with a knife. If a design of a different shape is wanted, the printing surface can be trimmed into a square. Tempera may then be painted over the designed end, after which printing on paper may begin.

Sticks to be used for printing should be selected from any soft wood such as pine and should measure from half an inch to 2 inches square at the end by 6 inches long. Beginners will use only the uncut stick. When children can prepare sticks for themselves, sometimes in the first grade and usually in the second grade, they should do so. The design for the printing end of the stick may be made with a three-sided file. The end of the stick may be left square, of course, or may be made round. These end shapes can be altered by filing either the sides adjacent to the end or the end of the stick itself, or by cutting grooves in the end with a knife (see Figure 10.6).

The technique of stick printing is similar to that of vegetable printing and may be done on paper or textile. Newsprint is suitably absorbent and reacts favorably to tempera or watercolor, but any dark-toned paper

Figure 10.5 *Stick printing in two colors done by a fifth grader. Cuts were made in the stick with a knife after careful directions were given.*

makes a striking background for the printing. The stick may be loaded with color by dipping the end in paint or ink, the paint may be applied to it with a brush, or the end may be pressed against a piece of sponge or rag soaked in paint or ink. Some experimenting may have to be done before the right consistency of paint is found. Usually tempera paint must be thinner for stick printing than for picture-making. Oil-based printer's ink should be used only if the teacher is willing to cope with clean-up problems requiring cleansing solvents such as turpentine. Water-based inks are now manufactured with sufficient potency to be used on cotton. However, if the cloth is to bear repeated washings, the oil-based ink is recommended.

In addition to cutting sticks, interesting shapes may be obtained by using a variety of wood scraps. If the wood is soaked for an hour or so, the grain swells and creates circular patterns. The wood scraps may then be dipped in paint and applied to the printing surface. In such cases, the design rests on the arrangement of odd shapes and colors rather than on the broken surface of one piece of wood. The two techniques might be combined.

An easily manipulated material to use instead of vegetables or sticks is the square soap eraser. The surface is soft enough to be cut by a pin, yet the edges can hold up for dozens of impressions. The six available sides also allow for a variety of imprints. When the class is finished with the project, the teacher can glue all the used erasers to a board, run a brayer of paint over the group, make an impression on paper, and thus have an interesting wall piece for the room.

Teaching. Printing on textile with sticks necessitates the preparation of a printing surface. A suitable surface would be a table covered with felt. The edge of the covering should be tacked to the underside of the table to prevent it from slipping. If papers are used, they might be covered with cotton sheeting, also tacked to the table (see Figure 10.8).

Because the techniques involved in vegetable and stick printing are appealing in themselves, the teacher should have no problem motivating

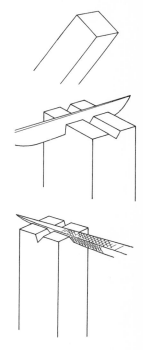

Figure 10.6 *Sticks for stick printing: plain, cut, and filed.*

279

Figure 10.7 *In this mixed-media print, the red and yellow cut-sponge shapes were used to set off the background of colored chalk. Grade 4.*

the children. The chief task is to encourage every child to explore the numerous possibilities of the process. The children should be encouraged to find and use many kinds of vegetables and other objects suitable for printing. When controlled cutting is used the teacher could suggest that not merely a knife, but forks, fingernail files, and other implements may

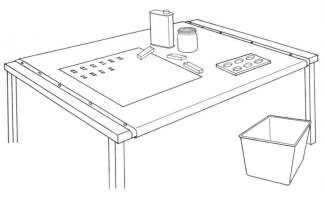

Figure 10.8 *Arrangements for stick printing on textile with printer's ink.*

also be used to cut the ends of vegetables so that different designs may result. The teacher should also suggest that background papers for these types of printing can be specially prepared with thin color laid down with a wide brush. Also, the teacher should note that backgrounds may be prepared with a large vegetable, such as a cabbage sliced in half, over which a potato or a smaller vegetable with the controlled cut may be used for printing in a contrasting color.

Eraser and stick printing should be made equally challenging. The pupils should use several sticks or erasers with different designs on one printing surface. Also, combinations of colors should be tested. Backgrounds might be painted with thin watercolor or patterned with vegetables, sponges, or even crumpled balls of paper that have been dipped in thin paint.

Few, if any, problems will arise over subject matter. Only non-objective or highly abstract patterns can result from this work, and the techniques lend themselves to repeated patterns rather than to picture-making.

LINOLEUM AND WOODCUT PRINTING

Media and Techniques. A linoleum or woodcut print results when the linoleum or wood has had pieces cut out of it, has been inked, and, finally, has been pressed to a suitably absorbent surface. The raised surface parts create the pattern. The technique requires the use of sharp tools, some physical strength (particularly in the fingers), and an ability to perform several operations of a relatively delicate nature. Only the more mature students in the fourth, fifth, and sixth grades will be capable of this work.

The usual heavy floor covering with a burlap backing is suitable linoleum to use for cutting. It may be purchased from furniture and hardware stores or from firms that lay floor covering. Linoleum comes in large sizes, but scraps of it may often be obtained at a reduction from the standard price. Small pieces may be cut from a larger piece by scoring the linoleum with a knife and then bending it.[1] The linoleum snaps apart where it is scored and then only the burlap remains to be cut through with a knife. The pupils will find it convenient but not entirely necessary to glue the linoleum to be carved to any wood scrap that is the exact size of the linoleum. The burlap side of the linoleum should be smeared with a strong carpenter's glue, then pressed against the wood and held firmly in a press until the glue is dry. Linoleum may be bought already affixed to wood blocks, but it is quite expensive.

Sets of linoleum cutters and short holders for them are needed. These

---

[1] For beginners, pieces measuring 3 by 4 inches are satisfactory; later, pieces as large as 6 by 8 inches can be used, and for sixth graders, pieces can be even larger.

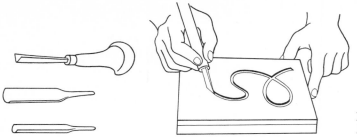

Figure 10.9 *Some tools for linoleum cutting.*

sets consist of straight knives, V-shaped tools, and U-gouges of varying sizes. The knives and gouges are perhaps the most effective tools, although the V-tool is capable of producing some highly sensitive lines and interesting textural effects. It is especially important to keep the tools sharp, and for this purpose a specially shaped oilstone may be bought.

The same tools are necessary for woodcutting. The best woods to use are maple, pine, and apple.

Almost any reasonably absorbent paper is suitable for receiving the impressions, from inexpensive newsprint to the costly but delightful Japanese rice paper. Generally it is found that paper thinner than newsprint tends to stick to the block, and paper heavier than 40-pound bond or construction does not have enough resilience to pick up all the details of tool marks. Many textiles, including cottons, linens, and silks, will be found practical for printing if their textures are not rough. For printing

Figure 10.10 *Close observation of the structure of trees aided a sixth grader in establishing this rich design for a block print.*

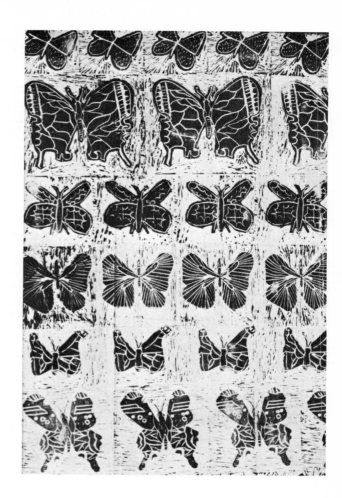

Figure 10.11 *A linoleum-block print of butterflies made by a group of fourth graders. Water-based ink was used on a discarded cotton sheet, which then served as a window curtain.*

on textiles an oil-based or printer's ink is necessary to obtain a lasting color; otherwise a water-based ink may be used. A few other supplies are also necessary—rubber brayers, a sheet of plate glass to be used as a palette, and, for printing on textiles, a mallet.

In cutting the linoleum, many people use the V-tool to make a preliminary outline of the main areas of the composition. When using this tool, it is often more convenient to move the block against the tool than the reverse. After the outlines have been inscribed the white areas in the design may be cleared away with the gouges. If any textural effects are desired in these areas, the linoleum should be gouged so that some ridges are left. If, however, the worker wishes the areas to print pure white, the linoleum should be gouged out almost to the burlap backing. Various kinds of textured areas may be made by cutting parallel lines, crosshatching lines, or removing "pecks" of linoleum with the V-tool.

Cutting in wood calls for greater manual control and sharper tools. A woodcut generally does not allow for as much detail as a linoleum cut.

Figure 10.12 "Noah's Ark," *linoleum-block print by a fourth grader. Several preparatory drawings preceded the cutting.*

To make up for these limitations, it offers a grained surface for dark areas. If the stark black-and-white qualities are combined with a surface of a good grain (complete with knots), a more powerful print can be obtained than with linoleum. During cutting the block should be steadied with a vise or cutting board and turned frequently for curved cuts (see Figure 10.14). Naturally, the softer the wood, the easier it is to cut; pine is ideal for this task. The student should learn how to take care of the tools and keep them sharp. However, even the sharpest gouge may require the use of a hammer to move it along the surface; wood offers much greater resistance than linoleum.

The pupils generally will find it helpful to take rubbings of their work from time to time to appraise their progress. To do this, they should place a thin sheet of paper over the working surface and, holding it firmly, rub soft pencil or crayon across the paper.

Although no formula can be offered for making a successful cut, it may be observed that a composition that displays a balance between white, black, and textured areas will prove to be particularly interesting.

284

Blockprints are distinguished by the distribution of light and dark masses across the surface. Because of the relative difficulty in producing detail, these masses tend to be more prominent than in other forms of the plastic arts. Evidence of tool marks lends great vitality to the surface and gives the print the look and feel of the material. A print from a linoleum cut or woodcut should not be mistaken for a pen-and-ink drawing.

When the pupils find the cut satisfactory, they are ready to pull an impression of it. Before printing on paper it is wise to dampen all but the softest tissues with a sponge. After the paper has been dampened it should be placed between pieces of blotting paper to remove any excess moisture. Then the pupils coat the brayer by rolling it evenly in water-soluble ink on the glass palette. Next, working in several directions with long sweeps of the brayer, they coat the linoleum or wood evenly with ink. The dampened paper (or dry tissue) should then be placed over the block and in turn covered with a sheet of blotting paper. This covering should be pressed and rubbed gently with the hands until enough contact between the block and the paper has been made to make an impression. In order to pull ink up from the block onto the paper a considerable amount of pressure has to be applied. This is usually done by a press or by prolonged rubbing with the back of a large spoon. The spoon must be used with great care lest the paper tear or become crinkled. The print may then be peeled away from the block. To prevent it from wrinkling

Figure 10.13 *One way to mount a print.*

Figure 10.14 *When composing a block print the pupil would do well to strive for a balance between the black, white, and textured areas. In working on this linoleum cut the pupil had to turn the block to achieve the curve of the elephant's trunk and back. Grade 5.*

it should be tacked to a drawing board and allowed to dry before it is removed and perhaps mounted.

For exhibition purposes a mount for the print (see Figure 10.13) may be constructed by folding in half a sheet of paper of appropriate size and color and then cutting a "window" in one of the halves through which to display the print. The print may then be fixed in place behind the window by means of rubber cement or tape. If the paper on which the print is taken is translucent, as in the case of certain tissues, an interesting effect may be obtained by fixing colored papers behind it. The "window" approach may also be used without the backing and is as satisfactory with heavy white or black paper as with mat board.

When printing is to be done on textile the cloth should be spread over felt or newspapers. The block should be inked in the manner just described for paper, except that, as mentioned previously, an oil-based ink should be used to obtain permanent color. The ink may be thinned with turpentine. Printing can be done with the hands, although much pressure must be exerted. A small wooden mallet is the most effective tool for this job. The block should be tapped smartly, first in the center and then on each corner. Each time the block is used it should be freshly and uniformly inked.

Teaching.   The chief problems in teaching wood and linoleum cutting and printing concern the printmaker's treatment of subject matter and the development of skill in cutting. Organization of the classroom, of

Figure 10.15 (*left*) *A woodcut print by a sixth grader. Although wood is much more difficult to work with than linoleum, it can often be more satisfying because the quality of the raised surface is usually richer.*

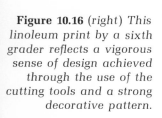

Figure 10.16 (*right*) *This linoleum print by a sixth grader reflects a vigorous sense of design achieved through the use of the cutting tools and a strong decorative pattern.*

Figure 10.17 *Wood investigations undertaken as a preliminary stage to making a final woodcut. Portions of the grain are cut away while other sections are retained for their textural effect. Grade 6.*

course, raises problems, but these are similar to the organizational problems that arise with stick printing.

Linoleum and wood cutting have often given rise to some unfortunate teaching methods concerning the selection of subject matter. Even teachers who have emphasized the importance of developing original subject matter in the direct processes have allowed pupils to copy designs for their work in linoleum and wood so that they may concentrate on technique. Such a teaching practice, however, proves in the long run to be as ineffective when applied to cutting as it does when applied to other types of art. No matter what the art form being produced, design and technique must develop in close relationship to each other.

The suggestion was made earlier that sculpture in wood might begin with experimental play with the wood (see Figure 10.17). This method is practical for linoleum and woodcut work as well. At first the children should work directly with the material. Rather than attempting to follow a drawing they should explore the many ways of cutting out pieces of the linoleum or wood. After becoming acquainted with the cutting methods they can follow the teacher's suggestion of making some preliminary sketches with India ink and a brush. By that time they will have insight into the limitations of the medium and will realize to what extent a plan may help them in their work. The students should be encouraged to think in terms of print qualities rather than characteristics associated with drawing and painting. Because the children are working in media that do not permit a great amount of detail or halftones, their preliminary sketches and planning should be done in a single tempera or ink tone rather than pencil or crayon.

Linoleum and wood cutting lend themselves to picture-making as

Figure 10.18 *These linoleum prints by fifth graders were enhanced by the use of magazine advertisements for printing surfaces.*

Figure 10.19 *A black-and-white linoleum print compared with the same print on a surface prepared with watercolor washes. Grade 6.*

288

Figure 10.20 *Art history can provide good examples of woodcuts. Note the balance of dark and light areas and the use of tool marks in this portrait by Ernst Kirchner. (© Roman Norbert Ketterer, Lugano, Switzerland)*

well as pattern-making, so that the problems arising from the selection and treatment of subject matter are varied. The teacher must, of course, help the children to select suitable items from their experience and observations. Beyond that, the work produced is modified both by the children's artistic level and by the technique itself. The children's output in using these media, in other words, while strongly reminiscent of their painting and drawing, is not identical to them because of differences in the media and tools. Nevertheless, whatever emerges must, of course, be the children's personal expression. Often a display of the entire process of making a cut is helpful in starting the children to work. After that, further demonstrations of technique may be necessary from time to time. These, however, should be kept to a minimum so that children can develop their own methods of working. Linoleum in particular, unlike some other substances, is a medium that allows many variations of approach to be discovered through experience.

The possibilities for exploration of block cutting and printing are endless.[2] The various types of cuts, the selection of different papers, the use of two or more colors on the same block, the placing of units on the textile, and, for sixth-grade pupils, even the use of two or more blocks to form a pattern may all be challenging to pupils working in this art form. As follow-up activities, students may make their impressions on such varied surfaces as magazine clippings, colored-tissue collages, gift wrappings, sections of the Sunday comics, and painted backgrounds (see Figures 10.18 and 10.19). These backgrounds may be used for random

[2]See Robin Tanner, *Children's Work in Block Printing* (Peoria, Ill.: Bennett, 1936).

effects, or they may be planned with the design of the print in mind.

Some artists whose work in linoleum and wood the children will enjoy are Antonio Frasconi, Pablo Picasso, Leonard Baskin, Sidney Chafetz, and several of the German Expressionists. Mexican folk art and medieval and Japanese woodcuts are also rich background sources for appreciation of printmaking.

OTHER FORMS OF PRINTMAKING

Collography

The making of collographs involves cutting shapes out of cardboard, gluing them to another board for backing, inking the entire surface, and printing. The collograph permits the worker to obtain interesting light areas around the edges of the raised surfaces, where the brayer cannot reach. It is best to shellac the plate before inking, since cardboard will weaken with washing.

Corrugated cardboard allows the child to work on a large scale, for this material can be obtained in sizes as large as refrigerator cartons. It provides three surface areas to print: (1) the flat exterior surface; (2) the striated pattern of corrugation, which is between the surface "skins"; and (3) the negative areas—sections of the cardboard completely cut away to reveal the paper on which the print is transferred. Figure 10.21 shows how these three areas actually print.

Figure 10.21 *Printing from corrugated cardboard allows the child to work on a large scale. In this print a "counterchange" problem is applied to a still life. Grade 5.*

STENCILING

Media and Techniques. Stenciling allows the child to print repeated units of design with considerable control. The activity demands a reasonably high degree of skill and an ability to plan in detail before production. For these reasons, it should be performed only by the more experienced preadolescents. In stenciling, shapes are cut out of paper, after which paint is applied to a surface covered by this paper. Only where holes have been cut will paint appear on the under-surface, and thus a controlled design is established. The pieces removed by cutting may also be used as "masks" in the stencil process, as shown in Figure 10.22.

Strong waterproofed or special stenciling paper should be used. Such paper may be purchased, or it may be prepared by coating a heavy paper with shellac, varnish, or wax (if wax is used, the paper should later be smoothed with a hot iron). Knives are required for cutting the stencil paper, and although a sharp pocketknife or single-edged razor blade will serve, for more detailed work special knives made for the purpose should be bought. Hog-bristle brushes may be used to apply the paint, but inexpensive stencil brushes are obtainable. If stenciling is done on paper, tempera and watercolor are suitable; for stenciling on textiles, ordinary oil colors in tubes may be used. Special stencil paints, however, are available and are very satisfactory to use. Almost any surface, provided it is not too rough, will receive a stenciled pattern. Evenly woven cotton cloth is perhaps the most suitable textile for children to use, and most types of paper for drawing and painting are serviceable.

The paper being cut for the final stencils should be laid over a glass plate or a piece of hard building board. Care must be taken to be exact in cutting, so that a cut stops where it is supposed to stop and joins exactly

Figure 10.22 *Techniques for (**A**) cutting stencil and (**B**) applying color. (**C**) Both the hole and the cutout piece may be used to create a stencil pattern.*

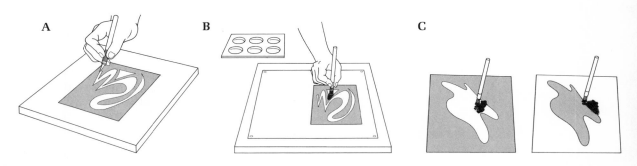

Figure 10.23 *For this stencil, a fifth grader cut out a bird form and used both positive and negative sections of the design. Color and overlapping of images were also used to achieve variety.*

with another cut. The worker must leave "ties," or narrow bands of paper, to hold parts of the design together. Hence the design must be simple. To perform this relatively delicate cutting, some people find it convenient to push the knife away from themselves in the Japanese manner; others prefer to draw it toward the body.

When paper is being stenciled, it should be pinned to a drawing board. Textile, on the other hand, must be stretched tightly over newsprint or blotting paper and then pinned firmly in place. The paper underneath the textile will absorb any excess paint that might otherwise run and spoil the work.

Paint should be thick enough not to run, yet not so thick as to form an unpleasantly heavy coating on the painted surface. Tempera paint for printing on paper can be placed in a muffin tin. After being dipped into the paint the brush should be scrubbed slightly on scrap paper to rid it of excess paint. Oil paints for textiles should be squeezed from the tube onto a palette, which might be a piece of glass. The amount of paint picked up by the brush can be controlled by gently dabbing the brush on the palette.

Paint should be applied to the holes in the stencil with some care: if the brush is used too vigorously, the stencil may be damaged. For an even spread of color over the entire cut-out area the paint should be applied with a dabbing motion. Stroking from the edge of the stencil into the cut-out area will give a shaded effect.

Teaching. Clean equipment is necessary if smooth work is to result. The brushes in particular should be kept scrupulously clean. While cool water will suffice to wash brushes used with tempera paint, turpentine is the solvent for oil-base colors. Brushes that have been cleaned in turpentine should be washed again with soap and cool water. After the brushes have been washed they should be placed in a container with the bristles up. It scarcely needs to be added that the pupils should be taught to clean their palettes after using them. Should the pupils wish to preserve the stencils from one day to another, the teacher should direct them to wash the stencils carefully with water or turpentine, depending on the type of paint used, after which the stencils can be suspended from a line strung in a storage cupboard for the purpose.

A second task for the teacher is to assist the pupils in becoming familiar with the stenciling technique as a means of personal expression. As in the case of linoleum and wood cutting, the children should be given ample opportunity to experiment with the technique. Preliminary practicing may be done on ordinary paper or cardboard. Following the teacher's demonstration, and after practice in cutting, the children will discover how to leave the "ties," or small bands, to hold parts of the design together. Largely through practice accompanied by the teacher's comments they will learn that a stencil design must be kept simple and that intricate shapes are generally to be avoided.

Finally, the teacher should encourage experimentation, for which stenciling provides many opportunities. Experimental arrangements may be explored when placing the design units on textile or paper. Various colors may be used both separately and blended. A good effect is achieved if the stencil is moved slightly when a second color is used. Furthermore, two or more stencils may be used on the same surface.

ACTIVITIES FOR THE READER

1. Produce a monoprint contour-line drawing by using one color and drawing directly in the color after you have applied it to a sheet of glass. Repeat, using two colors lightly blended with the brayer.
2. Produce a monoprint contour-line drawing by drawing on the paper after it has been laid down over the inky glass. Experiment by using several colors of ink at the same time.
3. Produce a nonobjective design in monoprint by laying down an orderly arrangement of string, burlap, and cut cardboard on the inky surface before applying the paper for the impression.
4. Experiment with a number of vegetables, suitably cut, to produce various printed textural effects on paper. Over these effects print an orderly design with a potato or carrot into which you have cut a pattern with a knife.
5. **a.** Experiment with a potato, scoring it not only with a knife but also with a fork or a spoon. Try printing a sheet of paper with an overall pattern that repeats the unit exactly.
   b. Prepare two soap erasers with different designs ("a" and "b") and print the units as follows:

   a, b, a, b, a
   a, b, a, b, a
   a, b, a, b, a
   a, b, a, b, a, etc.

Figure 10.24 *Fifth graders used cans of spray paint in this stencil mural based on a class study of jungle life. The shapes were cut and pinned into place before spraying. The forms were then moved about for a second and third spraying.*

    c. Now print as follows on black paper:

        a, b, b, a
        b, a, a, b
        a, b, b, a
        b, a, a, b, etc.

    d. Print, turning "a" or "b" upside down.
    e. Print, overlapping "a" and "b."
    f. Print with varying space between the "a"'s and "b"'s:

        a a a
          b b
        a a a

    g. Create some different arrangements, perhaps eventually using three and four motifs, or units. In all cases, the pattern should be repeated exactly.[3]
    h. Combine some of your printed arrangements with interesting backgrounds prepared experimentally.
  6. Cut sticks so that they will print a unit and experiment on paper as indicated in 5a–h, above. Combine cut ends with scrap ends of found pieces of wood.
  7. Select the arrangement you like best and print it on textile.
  8. Experiment with a piece of linoleum, making a nonobjective design to obtain many different types of textures. Take several rubbings of your work as you progress. Finally, print it on paper.
  9. Cut a 2-inch square of linoleum and glue it to a block. Cut a nonobjective unit of design in this piece of linoleum. Print the design on paper in

[3]See R. R. Tomlinson, *Picture and Pattern Making by Children* (New York: Viking, 1950).

repeated patterns in the manner indicated in 5a–h, above.

10. Print the pattern produced according to activity 9, above, on textile rather than paper.

11. From a landscape, still life, life drawing, or some other representational work you have produced, plan a picture to be cut in linoleum. Make an India-ink drawing the exact size you intend your cut to be, say 5 by 8 inches. Cover the linoleum with a thin coat of white tempera paint and then redraw your sketch on the linoleum. Start cutting, taking as many rubbings as you require, and later make some test prints to give you an idea of your progress. When the design is ready, print it in several single colors. Then try printing with two colors simultaneously.

12. Take a plank of wood and make a print of the grain. Use light colors and overlap the grain or turn the wood to create patterns. If the pattern of the grain suggests anything to you, cut away a few sections of the wood to make the movement of the pattern even stronger.

13. Make a collograph by cutting out cardboard shapes, gluing them to a base, inking the surface, and taking a print. The thicker the cardboard, the greater the play of light around the edges of your shapes in the print.

14. Make a corrugated cardboard print at least 18 by 24 inches. Try one print on a surface that is covered with a colored tissue collage.

15. Cut a stencil, using a nonobjective design no smaller than 3 inches square and print it on paper. Experiment on paper as indicated in 5a–h, above.

16. Obtain a styrofoam meat tray from the local supermarket. Using a ballpoint pen or blunt pencil, draw on the tray. Then, using a brayer, ink the drawn area and print the image on paper cut to fit the tray.

Examples of inked designs on film. The designs were created without regard to content or timing. Grade 3.

11
NEW MEDIA: COMMUNICATION AND DESIGN

Adventure and intrigue await the experimenter in design as he improvises with line, form, texture and sometimes with color, for the aesthetic delights he can create. The inherent feature of designing with light is the freedom to improvise, to invent subject matter and to produce an art form in the contemporary idiom.*

MEDIA AS A MEANS OF INSTRUCTION

Art teachers customarily associate the word "media" with such accepted materials as paint, clay, and charcoal, and may be unaware of the development of another context—one that refers to the technology of instruction. Instructional media encompass television, films, slides, tapes, and other similar means of communication. The term "media" in this sense implies a rather sophisticated approach to the teaching-learning situation and is associated with advances in learning theory. Lanier offers a conception of the uses of media that may seem grandiose to the teacher who has not progressed beyond an occasional use of slides or reproductions. He suggests using "prepared units presenting specific content both verbally and visually." [1] Instructional media in Lanier's view are much more than support material; they can provide the very basis of a curriculum. In Lanier's units, content is broken down into its most manageable segments and sequenced in a logical progression with a wide range of visual materials suggested for each step.

The hardware of media are considerably more than mechanical gadgets for presenting information; they are linked to the very shape and structure of the content being imparted and thus represent many different

*From Robert W. Cooke, *Designing with Light on Paper and Film* (Worcester, Mass.: Davis, 1969), p. 5.
[1] Vincent Lanier, "The Language of Education," *Arts and Activities*, Vol. 58, No. 1 (September 1965), p. 37.

Figure 11.1 *An example of the use of the media as a means of accelerating perception. The first two drawings* (**A**) *were pretest assignments for the topic "Draw anything you like that will include a landscape and clouds." The next two* (**B**) *are from the same class a week later. Films of clouds and landscapes followed by discussions were used as motivation. Grade 4.*

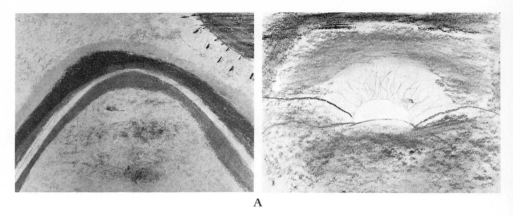

A

ways of learning. Let us consider for a moment the many ways by which instructional media are able to extend students' perceptions of a subject such as painting:

A *film* about a particular artist can show something of the process of change and maturation in an individual.

A comparison of *slides* of works of art can lead to a group discussion of likenesses and differences in style, content, and the like.

Packets of small *reproductions* allow students to investigate at their own pace the visual components of a series of paintings.

A set of four-minute *film loops* can give children a closeup of various painting processes that they may want to incorporate in their own work.

A *filmstrip* can provide an inexpensive collection of slides centered on a single idea. For commentary the students can use an accompanying record, read the lecture notes, or work from their own impressions.

A *live television* lesson can bring a professional artist to the class for a single performance.

A portable *video tape* machine can play back a demonstration by a visiting artist for future reference or for classes that could not attend the original performance.

A *tape recording* of an interview with a local artist can be stored for future reference.

It is improbable that any teacher would have access to all of the above modes of instruction, but with time, knowledge, and equipment, teachers can significantly extend their own style of teaching (for both groups and individuals), the pupils' style of learning (through discussion, listening, observing), and the range of subject matter (painting skills, perceptual skills, the creative process).

Let us examine briefly one of the devices mentioned above: television. Here is a perfect example of an instructional tool that has its roots

B

in the life style of the child; yet teaching art through television does not automatically assure a teacher of success. A number of questions regarding its use must be considered. How relevant is the lesson in relation to what the teacher has planned? Who can vouch for the quality of the lesson—that is, the validity of its content, the professionalism of the production staff, the choice of the art objects? Is the level of the dialog suitable for the class scheduled to receive the lesson? Does the classroom teacher have the materials required for a successful follow-up? The advantages and the hazards of art instruction via television may be summarized as follows:

> The television lesson can rarely be geared to the specific instructional needs of a particular classroom and is therefore not a substitute for regular teaching. It is a basically inflexible medium with regard to timing. Color, moreover, has not yet been perfected to the point where one can safely study the quality of color in art works presented on television. On the other hand, television can support the existing art program by presenting what the average teacher cannot provide: guest artists; closeups of processes such as jewelry-making, pottery-making, and use of tools (although this advantage also has its limitations in that the closeup seems to encourage a "how-to-do-it" approach); access to original works of art from local museums; the opportunity to work with a master teacher who has a great amount of time and a number of production facilities available.[2]

No authoritative theory of media instruction exists at this time. While teachers await such a theory, C. R. Carpenter, a leading media researcher, asks them to consider the following:

[2]Obviously there must be some liaison established between the studio and the classroom. The school systems of San Mateo, California, Dade County, Florida, and Denver, Colorado have created programs worthy of viewing, as has Pennsylvania State University. Publications such as Manuel Barkan and Laura Chapman, *Art Instruction Through Television for the Elementary Schools* (Bloomington, Ind.: National Center for School and College Television, 1967) attest to the growing concern for quality in this medium.

No coherent audio-visual theory seems to have been derived from the behavioral sciences. There have been a few spurious attempts to formulate such theories. The basic, nontheoretical facts are that humans have sensory-perceptive capacities which permit responses to different kinds of energy changes such as heat, sound and light waves, contact, pressure and kinesthesis, and the chemical senses of taste and smell. The many senses of the human being, acting as separate modalities or in combination, depend on the characteristics of the stimulus situation; they provide possibilities and also limits to the ways the individual can react to his environment or to materials which are formed as arts.[3]

Instructional media require advance planning. A plan may call for a single student studying slides, or it may involve an entire system of instruction in which large segments of the curriculum are related to the equipment deemed most appropriate. The plan may be directed toward exploration of one idea or toward anticipated behavioral changes for the whole class, involving provisions for feedback and evaluation of learning performance. It is unlikely that systems approaches, programed learning, or other instructional packages that require extensive media will reach the average elementary art program. As a rule, these media are expensive to operate, need intensive planning, and imply to most art teachers too great an abrogation of their teaching responsibility.

Art teachers are, however, making increasing use of manageable media, such as those described above for instruction in painting. Yet even on this level the teachers will not accommodate themselves to instruction via media if they have the art teacher's traditional suspicion of mechanical gadgets, or if the school budget will not allow for support materials such as slides, tapes, and rented films.

MEDIA AS A BASIS FOR ART EXPERIENCES

Media, it appears, have a twofold role to play in the current ferment of education. One has already been discussed—the utilization of communication facilities in instruction. Teachers should also utilize the carriers of information as art forms in themselves; that is, they should place the equipment in the hands of the students for them to make use of its creative potential. In many school situations, such an approach is no longer new. Children are making both live and animated films as well as studying the cinema as an art form. Even first graders are working directly on raw film and projecting images they created. Children in the fourth, fifth, and

[3]*Final Report of the Uses of Newer Media in Art Education Projects*, NDEA Project No. 5-16-027, Vincent Lanier, Project Director (Washington, D.C.: National Art Education Association, 1966), p. 12.

sixth grades are capable of running tape recorders, handling cameras, and combining several modes of projection in the production of their own "light shows." These activities are described in detail below. First, however, we shall consider how the child's environment today fosters experimentation with the new media.

Children today are both eager and prepared to engage in media activity. The factors that stand in the way of such activity are the teacher's ignorance of media and unwillingness to recognize media as a valid basis for art instruction. The children, unaware of their teacher's reservations, continue to develop in their own environment. Their visual sense is oriented to motion because of early exposure to television and films. They accept condensed time/space concepts because they view live coverage of news events, and they have never doubted, for instance, that they could breakfast in one part of the world and lunch in another. The camera is probably not a novelty in the family. Many children would rather study structure, perception, and color with a camera than with a box of crayons. The objections of those adults who hold the traditional art activities in high esteem are just academic quibbling to the child with an avid multisensory curiosity.

Environmental Influences

The art teacher who is truly sensitive to what is happening outside the art room will give serious thought to incorporating media activity into the existing program, recognizing the fact that these media are probably the most direct link to the nonschool culture of the child. Society has created the climate for working with media today just as the numerous art movements of the 1920's liberated contemporary conceptions of painting and helped shape the pattern of many of the art programs of the Progressive education movement. If hesitant art teachers take a fresh look at media they will have to admit that there is no inherent contradiction in goals or philosophy between creating in either the new or the traditional media. Both kinds of materials provide excitement and challenge in the areas of design, including color, and drawing; both elicit original solutions on the part of the child and call for a high level of creative ingenuity. Newer media have simply added such increasingly relevant ingredients as time, motion, and light to the elements of color, space, mass, line, texture, and shade. Teachers will be shortsighted, indeed, should they fail to capitalize on the built-in motivations provided by the excitement of matching sound to light or image to movement. They will also deprive themselves of a logical means of combining other arts such as music, dance, and choral reading.

The activities described in this chapter have been tested in elementary schools. They range from simple projects that can be carried out in one learning session to more complex operations requiring several sessions. In most cases, the amount of time spent on the project depends on how deeply the teacher wants to probe the subject.

Projected Images

Media and Techniques. The creation of designs on slides that can be projected gives the child an opportunity to experiment with light. The materials are not expensive, and the activity can be correlated with music and language arts. The slides should be 2 inches square and made of glass or heavy acetate. These provide the base, or "ground," for the transparent materials that carry the design. As for these materials, any that permit

Figure 11.2 *Various ways of treating glass slides.*

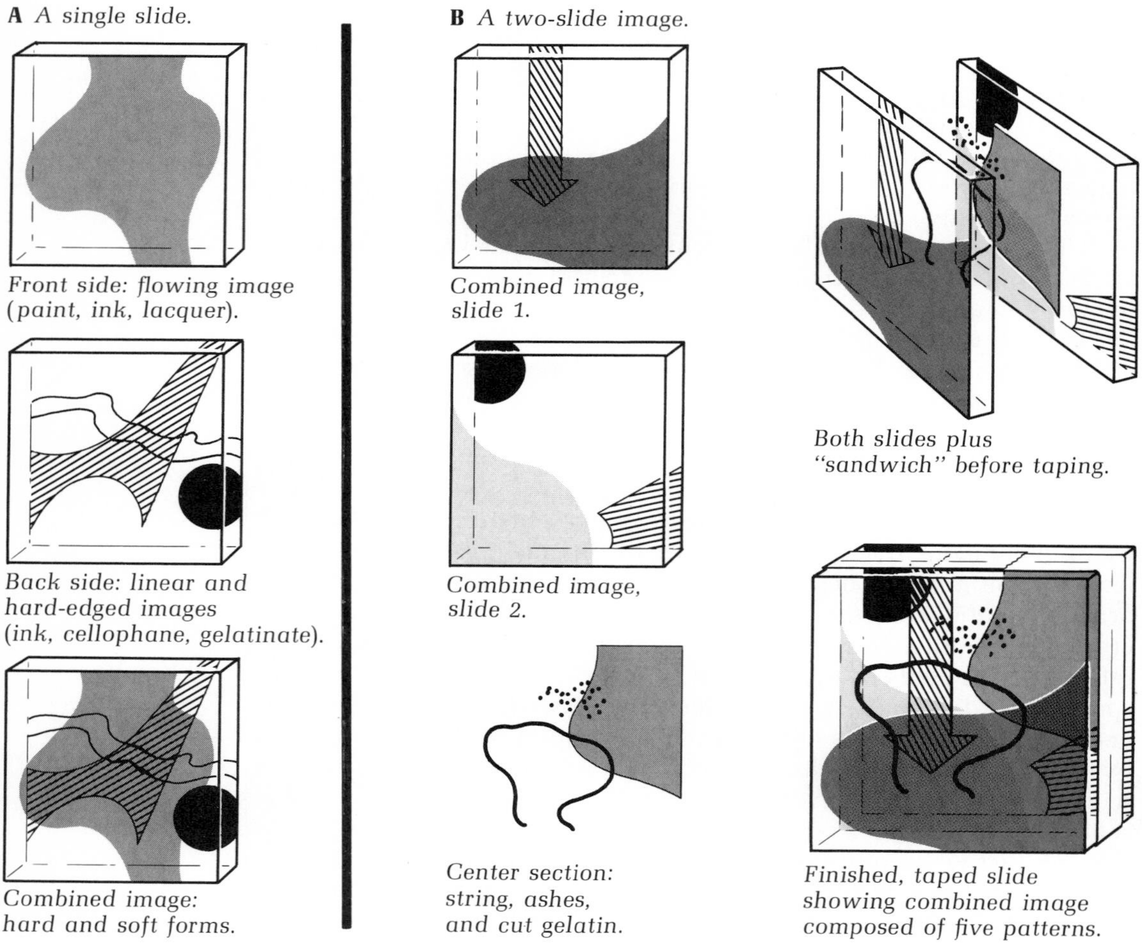

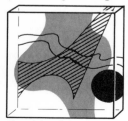

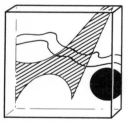

A A single slide.
Front side: flowing image (paint, ink, lacquer).
Back side: linear and hard-edged images (ink, cellophane, gelatinate).
Combined image: hard and soft forms.
B A two-slide image.
Combined image, slide 1.
Combined image, slide 2.
Center section: string, ashes, and cut gelatin.
Both slides plus "sandwich" before taping.
Finished, taped slide showing combined image composed of five patterns.

the passage of light are acceptable—colored cellophane, crystallizing lacquers, theatrical gelatins, colored lacquers, nail polish, and so on. Or the slides may be covered with India ink or tempera paint and sections scratched away to allow passage of light. Applying the color is a simple matter. Nail polish, crystallizing lacquers, and colored lacquers can be painted on with cotton swabs or detail brushes. Colored cellophane and theatrical gelatins can be applied to the slide with white plastic glue that has been thinned out with five parts water to one part glue.

The children should design both sides of the slide; one might be used for solid color and the other for linear effects with India ink. In such a case the design problem would be to combine the elements of mass and line into a satisfactory whole. Another variant might be to design soft shapes on one side and hard-edged forms on the other. If children want to make a two-slide image, they have not only four sides to plan but also the area between the slides. Here, they may choose to add such "stop outs" as sand, ashes, and thread to create silhouette effects. The edges of the plates should be taped to keep the center of the "sandwich" in place (see Figure 11.2). Because of the limited size of the slides an abstract design is a more appropriate subject than a realistic image. Slides of art works, landscapes, buildings, and family groups make interesting raw material for photo-collages (provided the owners have decided to discard them).

The slides can be projected through a standard school projector. Two projectors allow for overlapping of images. It is safe to say that the more projectors going at once, the larger the image, and the darker the room, the more exciting the possibilities. The projections are often as effective when the images are diffused as when they are sharply in focus. A musical selection that the class enjoys might be used as an accompaniment for the designing of the projections. When the slides are run on two projectors in conjunction with the music the class has a novel program for a school assembly or a PTA (Parent-Teacher Association) meeting.

Teaching. One way to begin instruction is to let the class manipulate color and light on an overhead projector. If time is limited, the teacher can move about colored cellophane on a sheet of acetate while the class discusses how such movements affect the image. This activity may be followed by some wet mingling of colored lacquers on the acetate. The discussion may then focus on how such activities can be transferred to the smaller confines of a glass slide. The class might list materials that block the passage of light and those that permit light to pass through. If the teacher has any finished slides on hand, the class can look at them and speculate on how the effects were achieved. By this time the class will be more than ready to begin their own slides. The teacher might want to select music for the class to listen to as they work and, later, help organize a light show to project the finished slides.

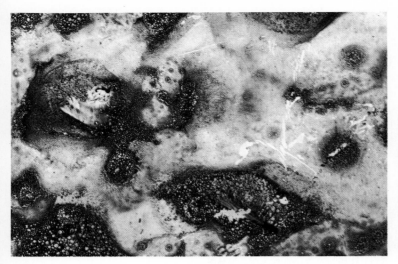

A   B

Figure 11.3 *The design of colored slides appeals to students at all levels. Often the identification of age levels becomes difficult as experimentation and investigation become more important than obtaining a "finished" product.* **A,** *by a sixth grader, was made with watercolor, liquid soap, and felt pen;* **B,** *by a student in the eleventh grade, was made with colored lacquer.*

Filmmaking Without a Camera

Media and Techniques. Filmmaking without a camera is accomplished by painting or drawing directly on the actual segments of film, as the student shown in Figure 11.4 is doing. Thus the basic materials for this activity are strips of 16mm film—clear leader or black with an emulsion side—and inks or paint to apply to the film. White leader may also be used; it offers a soft gray background for color. It is also possible to purchase transparent colored leader film.

The most elementary technique is to draw a black line on the clear film. India ink may be used, but it has a tendency to flake off while being used in the projector. The best ink for this technique is Pelikan (K) black, a plastic ink that adheres permanently to the acetate of the film. When black emulsion-type leader film is used, the design consists of white line on a black ground. The white line is produced by scratching through the emulsion with a needlelike tool. Simple etching tools can be made by fixing sewing needles in pencils or sticks. Because it is rather difficult to see the scratched lines, it is advisable to work over a sheet of white paper or on windowpanes. Care should be taken that the lines are not etched too deeply, for the film can be weakened in this way. Another variation of the scratching technique is to punch out a series of holes in varying sizes, thus creating a pattern of flashing lights when the film is projected. Rotating leather punches, which have six or eight sizes of holes, are good to use for this purpose.

304

Colored lines may be drawn with felt-tip pens, which are available in a variety of colors. These pens can also be used to make free nonobjective color patterns to serve as background for more controlled black-line exercises. If a flat color treatment is desired, a material called Cutacolor is effective. Cutacolor is a transparent acetate sheeting with an adhesive surface. After being cut with an X-acto knife, scissors, or a single-edged razor blade into any desired shape, the backing is peeled off and the piece is placed directly on the film. The material may be used alone or it may be incorporated into one of the linear techniques. If the student wants to work with color materials of a more plastic nature, two that give excellent results are transparent lacquer and transparent acetate ink. Transparent lacquer is a thick liquid, so it must be applied to the film with a small brush rather than a pen. Because it has a penetrating odor it should be used only in rooms with proper ventilation. Perhaps the best color medium is acetate ink. It has the brilliant color qualities of transparent lacquer without its offensive fumes, and it can be applied to the film with a pen.

The student should experiment with a variety of pen points or brushes. If the ink resists flowing onto the film, it is possible that the surface has become greasy as a result of being touched by oily hands. The film can be cleaned quickly with a rag dampened with alcohol. Sufficient drying time should be allowed before running the film through an editing machine or projector.

The length of the filmstrips need not pose problems as to where to work. The children may work standing up, hanging their strips vertically on the wall or blackboard; they may tape segments of film to cafeteria-type tables; or they may move the film along their desks. It is recommended that white paper be used as a backing for the section of film being worked on.

Figure 11.4 *The camera is not needed for filmmaking in the elementary grades. Here a third grader is drawing directly on film with pen and ink, (Photo by Rick Steadry.)*

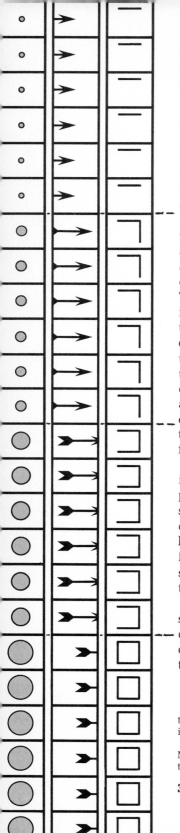

Figure 11.5 *Three basic control activities in painting film segments. All three require the child to maintain a distinct stage of size or motion for six frames. (Left): making an object advance toward the viewer; (center): making an object travel horizontally; and (right): metamorphosis of a shape.*

Teaching. Before the actual creative work on the film begins the teacher should explain how motion is achieved in filmmaking. The student should understand that twenty-four frames will pass through the projecting lens in one second at "sound" speed.[4] Since twenty-four frames comes to about 7 inches of film, about 2 feet of film per child will allow three seconds of animation.

Because most students have difficulty understanding the frame and time relationship, it is advisable to present them first with some simple activities exploring fundamental paths of motion—horizontal, vertical, and spatial. One basic activity is to have the student develop a series of dots, circles, stars, crosses, or some other objects that advance or recede.[5] To make them advance, the objects should begin very small and gradually increase in size until they take up most of the frame. The objects seem to recede when they gradually diminish in size. At least six frames for each stage of growth should be allowed, for it takes this long for the eye to accommodate a distinct unit of motion (see Figure 11.5 left). In order to have a shape travel horizontally from left to right, the student should draw the forward part of the object on the left-hand side of the frame for a six-frame segment. Every time the object is advanced toward the right of the frame the position should be held for six frames until finally only the last portion of the object is visible from the right-hand edge of the frame (see Figure 11.5 center).

Another activity develops the ability to make a shape grow or change into another shape. This task requires that the student think of the finished product first and then break the design process down into manageable segments that develop logically out of each other. In order to make a line draw itself into a square, for instance, the student might first draw a horizontal line, repeat it for six frames, next draw a connecting vertical line in another six frames, and thus continue until the four sides of the square are completed (see Figure 11.5 right). This method can be applied to drawing a triangle or even a face.

Ideally, the children should have access to a film-editing machine so that they can view their work immediately. With such a machine, the child can see clearly that each frame is a single discrete image. The flow of one image to the next is controlled in much the same way one controls the movement of "flip" books—by speeding up or retarding the controlling

[4]"Silent" speed slows the film down to sixteen frames per second. But it is recommended that sound speed be used as the basis for designing the film sequence, in case the final result is worthy of having a sound track added.
[5]An excellent film to study in relation to this spatial effect (and others) is Norman McLaron's *Fiddle-de-dee* (Canadian National Film Board, 1947; distributed by the International Film Bureau).

mechanism (see Activity 5 at the end of this chapter). By observing how their films work in this machine the students can understand how the movies they see on Saturday afternoons function.

Unless the whole class works in shifts on one large segment of film, it will be necessary to purchase a film splicer to join the segments. There are usually two or three mechanically inclined children in most fifth- and sixth-grade classes who can be taught to use the splicer. At least 5 feet of leader should be reserved for splicing at the beginning and at the end of the completed film; this amount is needed to get the film into the projector.

THE LIGHT SHOW

In the light show media are used for both their communicative and their creative potential. In addition the light show allows the children to combine many forms of media. For example, consider how a class might treat a subject like the Fourth of July in a light show. The class not only has available the traditional performing arts (readings, songs, period music, dramatic scenes) but it also has fresh visual opportunities supplied by the medium of the light show; projection of "fireworks" drawn on clear film, slides of American patriots flashed against a background of moving patterns of stars and stripes.[6]

Given a number of multimedia devices to explore for the first time, children will engage in manipulative activities very similar to their first reaction to clay or any other new art material. During this initial stage the children should be encouraged to experiment freely with the tools of light and motion; they should be allowed to combine fixed and moving images, blend sounds, and work light with color in a random fashion. However, to abandon the challenge of ultimately obtaining some sort of content and meaning in their work would be like cutting off the painting experience after a session or two of dripping and splashing. Ideally, the light show should be planned with some degree of structure around a central idea. If children can be taught to plan a light show with as much care and thought as they bring to the creation of a puppet show or mural, their range of learning can be considerably extended.

There is a very popular but misguided notion that a light show is a psychedelic experience. The term "psychedelic" in its popular sense lacks validity here, for it implies the use of drugs, from which elementary-school children are still largely exempt. The light show does, however, have the effect of extending the sensory awareness of its participants and as such definitely has a place in today's art program.

---

[6]The multimedia treatment of national holidays is an effective way of breaking away from stereotyped school programs that no longer hold any excitement for many of today's students.

Figure 11.6 *Preschool children watch their teacher set up an environmental light show in which they will participate. (From a project "The Space Place" developed by CEMREL Laboratories in St. Louis, Mo. This is a mobile environment developed for the use of museums.)*

No single successful way to prepare a light show can be set forth. Much depends on the equipment to which the class has access. The teacher should first take an inventory of the audio-visual equipment in the school. The following items allow students a wide range of effects to work with:

1. *35mm slide projector*[7] For use with prepared and original projections.
2. *16mm film projector* For use with both commercially prepared films and drawings and paintings on clear or black leader film.
3. *Overhead projectors* Overhead projectors may be used to manipulate transparent colored theatrical gels and cellophane or paper cutouts and grease drawings on acetate, which are placed over the colored transparencies. Interesting effects are obtained by connecting segments of cellophane and pulling them slowly under and over the light. Pieces of colored glass or plastic in a bowl of water, when placed under the light source and stirred, project shifting patterns of color. Similar effects may be had with colored varnish, oil, and water mixed in a bowl or pan; these patterns vary with the ways in which the ingredients are combined. Water prisms, magic reflectors,[8] and convex and concave lenses moved in front of the light source project dancing light images.
4. *Record players* The tendency today is to use mostly rock music to accompany a light show, but other varieties of music should be investigated—and at decibel levels that are kind to the human eardrum. Of the classical composers, Bach is a favorite. Music poses a problem: the degree to which its style and mood should

[7]The Kodak Carousel model offers flexibility in timing.
[8]Available from Creative Playthings, Princeton, N.J.

be accommodated to the visual images. A natural means of achieving consistency of sound and image is to have the children draw or paint to music, take colored slides of the results, and incorporate them as part of the projections.

5. *Tape recorders*   The students can create their own sound effects by collecting the sounds of the street, birds, traffic, playground, and the like on a battery-powered recorder. They can blow into bottles, snap their fingers, or run a block of wood over a series of objects to produce special sounds. Even within the four walls of their classroom there are surfaces such as glass, metal, and wood that yield interesting aural patterns when combined in varying rhythms. The school's music specialist could be prevailed upon to serve as consultant for such investigations in developing awareness of sound.

Before preparing a light show the teacher should check with the principal or custodian to determine the maximum carrying power of the source of electricity. For best results the room in which the show is projected should be blacked out as completely as possible, and there should be three basic areas of projection. Because a class will rarely have access to more than one large screen, the children should improvise other screens with sheets or large sections of cardboard that have been painted white. When the surfaces of the improvised screens are covered with paper that is rumpled, scored, bent, or curved, the sculptural effects thus derived can add greater variety to the projection. Parachutes and white sheets may be added to the "hard" shapes so that further variety within the images may be obtained. Certain images are even more interesting when taken off the conventional projection screen—the ceiling and the audience itself can be exciting projection surfaces.

Figure 11.7 *Materials used in creating this light modulator were colored cellophane and strips of cardboard stapled together.*

Figure 11.8 *A class uses the Video Tape Retrieval system. (Photos by Roger Graves.)*

(A) *Improvised scene in an improvised setting. Members of the class rehearse before appearing before the camera.*

(B) *Everyone takes a turn at the camera.*

(C) *Teacher critiques class production on the monitor.*

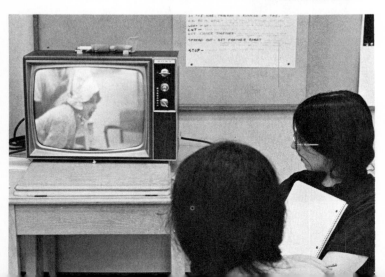

VIDEO TAPE RETRIEVAL

The portable Video Tape Retrieval (VTR) unit is gaining popularity in the schools at a rapid rate. However, the VTR has still to gain wide acceptance as part of the art program, and its position at this time is similar to that of the camera a generation ago. If one examines the creative possibilities of the VTR dispassionately, one must admit that a truly revolutionary instrument is at hand. To the children it means that they can, in a sense, control the very machine that for so many years has dominated their leisure hours. Their new domain is a television studio in miniature, consisting of camera, television monitor, and tape deck for sound and storage of video tape. The tables are suddenly turned, and the viewer is in command, becoming producer, director, or actor. It is now possible for formerly passive observers to control the camera, create the image, and get immediate feedback on the monitor. Nor do they have to limit their activities to the school; they can extend their control to the playground, the neighborhood—anywhere the VTR can be carried.

The operation of the VTR is far too complex to describe within the limits of this chapter. As with photography, its technical aspects are best learned in a workshop. It is, however, worth noting some of the ways one art teacher with special training went about building a sequence of activities around the VTR. By the end of a summer workshop[9] the children, working in rotating groups had:

designed and presented their own commercials. This involved designing the package, writing copy, and delivering the "message," as well as recording the entire experience on tape.

designed and assembled several settings for short plays, which were developed from a series of improvisations. Sets were constructed of large sheets of cardboard and included castoff furniture.

studied the effects of light and change of scale by examining miniature sets on camera.

criticized commercial programing viewed on the monitor.

role-played various social situations derived from their school and home experiences.

behaved as television art teachers by demonstrating a simple process such as potato printing, stenciling, or collography.

took turns as cameraman, director, performer, switcher, designer, and producer. They also learned the basic operation and nomenclature of the equipment.

---

[9]This special workshop for fifth and sixth graders was offered by the Newton Creative Arts Summer Program.

There were still many activities that the children did not explore. Some techniques planned for the second year are as follows:

Projected Slides on Rear Screen. Slides can be integrated into a tape by recording them with the vidicon camera. Enlarged projections can be scanned by the camera for closer examination.

Projected Movies. Films made by the class can also be incorporated in the same rear-screen-projection technique used for showing slides.

Off-Air Recording. Personal reactions can be taped and replayed to provide voice-over content from groups or individuals.

Still Images. By starting the "still" control on the recorder, children can stop visuals and frame them for analysis of any desired special effects.

Infinity. The camera is aimed at the monitor, and the monitor shows the monitor, showing the monitor, on ad infinitum. With controlled manipulation, interesting wave forms, patterns, and mandalas can be viewed and explored.

TV Animation. By using cardboard figures and inserted tabs, parts of the anatomy, such as mouths, eyes, and hands, can be made to move in interesting ways. Movement can be enhanced by using the figures against both painted and projected slide backgrounds. Puppets and simple objects may also be animated.

The use of television in the art program is still a relatively new and unexplored area. A review of the activities listed above must surely make a curious teacher speculate about the many possibilities offered by the VTR as a means of extending the children's visual awareness.

ACTIVITIES FOR THE READER

The chapter itself describes many activities to try with the instruments of light and motion. Included here are some more activities of that type.

1. Run two films simultaneously but eliminate the sound of one and the image of the other. Now try to create connections between the image of the one film and the sound track of the other.
2. Using an overhead projector, improvise a series of shifting color patterns by manipulating colored gels and string. Draw on clear acetate with a grease crayon; note how the scale seems to change when the drawing is projected on the screen.
3. For immediate feedback of projected movement, work directly on those parts of the film that are exposed to view while in the projector. With felt-tip pens or hole punchers, work on a section, advance the film, and

work on another part; then watch the results by reversing and advancing the film.

4. Obtain films that have outlived their usefulness and are about to be discarded. Work over the images with marking pens or with watercolor mixed with liquid soap, dyes, and inks. Parts of the image can be scratched away with a razor blade or knife. The work may be done randomly (without regard to content) or with some structure (by relating changes to the content of the film). Old film can be made clear by soaking it overnight in half-strength bleach.

5. Any series of still pictures will give the illusion of motion when viewed in sequence. Create a sequence of "flip cards" by working on one side of a group of index cards. By slightly changing the position of the image from card to card, it is possible to create the illusion of a ball flying off the page, a ship sinking into the sea, a smile appearing on a face, or Dr. Jekyll turning into Mr. Hyde.

6. Experiment with methods of correlating music and media. Select some music and create abstract images on glass slides in any manner suggested by the music. Such elements as line, color, and mass should all reflect the mood of the music. The slides can be grouped according to their relation to the changes in the mood and pace of the music. A roughly synchronized slide production can be made if two projectors are used and the image of one is faded into the image of the other by adjusting the focusing mechanism of the projectors.

Young teenagers create "Street Dragon" for their neighborhood in Pittsburgh. The structure was assembled out of discarded junk under the guidance of Troy West, a local architect.

GROUP ACTIVITIES IN ART 12

A group of children around a conference table setting up goals, making plans, assuming responsibilities, or evaluating achievements represents an essential prelude to intelligent, responsible citizenship. Children learn from one another through sharing ideas; group action is more effective when several individuals have shared in the planning; individuals find a place in group projects for making contributions in line with special talents; and morale is higher when children work together cooperatively on group projects. This is not meant to imply that there is no place in the modern classroom for individual effort; there should be a time for both individual and group activity.*

In his book *Democracy as a Way of Life,* Boyd H. Bode says that "teaching democracy in the abstract is on a par with teaching swimming by correspondence."[1] This is why he feels that "the school must undertake to exemplify in its organization and procedures its conception of democratic living."[2] In a democratic community, Bode says, there is provision for all people to share in the common life according to their interests and capacities. A democratic school promotes the doctrine that people are "free and equal" by taking proper account of individual differences and by reliance on the principle of community living. Such a school neither excuses the individual from a responsibility to the group nor replaces one set of fixed ideas about living with another, equally static, set. The children in a democratic school enjoy a free play of intelligence, and they emerge from this school with their own set of conclusions. The children, asserts Bode, must acquire something "other than a docile acceptance of a point of view."

*From William B. Ragan and C. B. Stendler, *Modern Elementary Curriculum* (New York: Holt, Rinehart and Winston, 1966), p. 192.

[1]*Democracy as a Way of Life* (New York: Macmillan, 1937), p. 75.

[2]*Ibid.,* p. 77.

It is the purpose of this chapter to enlarge on the role that art can play in giving children some understanding of social processes as they operate in the art program. We shall study some artistic activities that are especially suitable for the development of the children's social insight. Among these activities are various forms of puppetry and mural-making. We will also discuss new concepts of group art that have emerged in recent years.

THE ROLE OF THE TEACHER IN GROUP ACTIVITY

While realizing the desirability of including group activities in an art program, the teacher may have certain questions concerning the mechanics of this technique. How does group activity work? How should the activity be chosen? What should be its scope? What is the role of the teacher?

A number of years ago, Kilpatrick outlined the steps in what he called a "purposeful activity." These steps, which have stood the test of time, he called *purposing, planning, executing,* and *judging.*[3] Kilpatrick's

[3]W. H. Kilpatrick, *Foundations of Method* (New York: Macmillan, 1925), pp. 203ff. See also Frances Pauline Hilliard, *Improving Social Learnings in the Elementary School* (New York: Teachers College, 1954), p. 68, in which the author discusses "the process of cooperative planning and working." Her ideas will be clearly seen to be an elaboration of those of Kilpatrick.

Figure 12.1 *Rag tapestries provide effective opportunities for group work. Here several pupils are working on a tapestry based on the Gilgamesh myth of ancient Babylonia.*

steps were to be verified much later in the many descriptions of the creative process that came to light as a result of research into creativity. Creative minds in both the sciences and the arts were found to work in a progression of thought and action similar to Kilpatrick's steps.

Group activities, like those of an individual, must begin with some end in mind. This sense of purpose, Kilpatrick says, supplies the drive necessary to complete the project. Moreover, it is the children who share a role in the "purposing." The teacher, of course, may make suggestions, but before these suggestions can be effected, the children must accept them wholeheartedly. Both the "planning" and the "executing," which are outcomes of the purposing, must also be controlled by members of the working group. Finally, the children themselves must ask the general and the specific questions concerning the outcome of the activity. Did they do what they planned? What was learned in the doing? What mistakes were made? How could the activity be done better next time?

The functions of the teacher in a group activity in art are parallel to those associated with individual learning.[4] The methods of motivation, isolating and defining themes, establishing artistic goals, and selecting media and tools of expression now must be applied to those pupils, whether few or many, who make up the art group.

In the collective life of the school or classroom, occasions requiring group effort in art invariably arise if goals are to be reached. "Let's have a play," the children say, "Let's run a puppet show. . . . Let's make a big picture to go in the hallway. . . . Let's do a light show." Very little suggestion need come from the teacher to set in motion a desirable group project. The children themselves, who are usually quick to realize when working together will get desired results, are often the first to suggest to a teacher that a group activity be considered.

No matter how desirable it may be to encourage children to work cooperatively the teacher must realize that art is a matter of individual concern and will always remain so. An art form should never be produced by a group unless the size and scope of the work is such that an indiviual could not possibly master it. Only when a work requires for its successful completion a diversity of skills, a fund of energy, and a span of attention exceeding those of any one child, is the need for group endeavor indicated.

Before encouraging children to proceed with a group project the teacher must judge not only whether it is sufficiently challenging to occupy the attention of several people but also whether it may be too large for successful completion by a group. In their enthusiasm for art, children are sometimes willing to plunge into a task that they could never complete. Once fired with the idea of a mural, for example, a group of fifth graders might cheerfully embark on the enormous task of designing

---

[4]See Arthur D. Hollingshead, *Guidance in Democratic Living* (New York: Appleton-Century-Crofts, 1941), p. 120, for the necessary "personal qualifications" of a successful teacher in a group activity.

murals for all four walls of a school gymnasium. One or even two murals might be made successfully, but production of many more would exhaust the pupils. A group activity in art that comes to a wavering halt because the children have lost interest or lack competence to complete it reflects not only on the group techniques but also on the teacher's judgment. When failure looms the teacher must help the pupils alter their plans so that they can achieve success.

Having a greater maturity and insight into group processes, the teacher must fill the role of counselor with tact, sympathy, and skill. As soon as the need for group work in art is apparent, the children must be urged to elect leaders and establish committees necessary for "purposing, planning, executing, and judging" to take place. As stated earlier, the teacher should see that as far as is practical the children control these steps. Although having the power of veto, the teacher should be reluctant to use this power. If at times the children's decisions seem to be wrong, the teacher should nevertheless allow them to proceed, unless, of course, their chosen course of action would only lead to overwhelmingly disastrous results. It is part of the learning process for people to make mistakes and, profiting from them, subsequently to rectify them.

To one aspect of counseling the teacher must give special attention. Since group procedures depend for success largely on the maximum contribution of each participant, the teacher must see that every child in the group is given a fair opportunity to make a suitable contribution to the project. A good group project should include a wide enough range of tasks to elicit participation from every member of the class.

GROUP ACTIVITIES FOR BEGINNERS

Media and Techniques.   Often beginners at school, either kindergarten or first-grade children, are not mature enough to participate fully in a group enterprise. Nevertheless, a beginning may be made early in their school careers. This takes the form of a quasi-group activity in which children pool work originally completed as a result of individual effort.

The activity requires little or no group planning and does not appear as cooperative endeavor until its close. Teachers make use of the quasi-group activity even with children who are still in the manipulative stage. For example, in one kindergarten enrolling children at this stage, a small Christmas tree was successfully decorated. Each child twisted and curled colored paper into a gay decoration and later hung it on a branch of the tree.

The quasi-group activity may be based on any theme that interests young pupils and may make use of any medium and technique that the children are capable of handling. If a kindergarten class happens to be talking about the subject of spring, for example, each child who has

Figure 12.2 *This mural of a monster by slow learners is the result of quasi-group activity. Two of the children drew the outline, and each participant in the activity filled in a particular section of the work. Children enjoy seeing a single image emerge from seemingly unrelated parts. (Photo by Rick Steadry.)*

reached the symbol stage may select one item of the season to illustrate. The children may draw and paint symbols of lambs, flowers, birds, trees, and other springlike objects. After drawing or painting each item the children cut away the unused paper around the symbol. Then the drawings and paintings are assembled on a tackboard.

Many other suitable topics could be treated in a similar fashion. Among them might be included the following:

1. "Shopping with Mother," in which the various stores may be drawn and painted, together with people and automobiles. This subject could also be handled as an interior scene showing the articles on display in a supermarket.
2. "Our House," in which pictures of houses are eventually assembled to form a street.
3. "My Friends," in which the outlines of boys and girls are assembled to form a crowd of children.

Three-dimensional output also lends itself to quasi-group activity. For example, the children can assemble on a table modeling and paper constructions to depict scenes such as "The Farm" with barns, cows, and so forth, and "The Circus" with clowns, elephants, and so on.

Teaching. The teacher begins the group activity in the same way as individual picture-making or three-dimensional work. Motivation and teaching take place as they are required. Eventually, when the children have produced their work, the teacher, who has reserved a display space

319

in the room, asks each child to bring a piece of work to the board and pin it in place. At first, a rather disorganized arrangement may result. A short discussion with the class, however, will elicit a few suggestions for improving the placement of the individual drawings. Some of the largest and brightest work can be located near the center of the panel while smaller drawings of the same symbol drawn by several children might be grouped or arranged in a rhythmic line. When the "mural" is made with cut-out shapes, even a first grader can begin to think of subject matter in relation to organization of masses in space. In such cases, it may facilitate matters to do the initial planning on the floor where shapes may be more easily adjusted than on the wall.

The finished composition will, of course, have a pattern with many small areas of interest reminiscent of some of the output of Grandma Moses and other so-called primitive artists. Teachers should not attempt to improve the layout by adding any of their own work. If they are tempted to provide a fence or road in perspective, or even a horizon line, the temptation should be resisted on the grounds, first, that the children should learn to depend only on themselves in developing a group activity and, second, that only a muddle could result if adult work (however naive) and children's work were assembled on the same panel. Children should not be used as surrogate artists for the teacher.

The main aim of conducting the quasi-group activity is to lead children to the point at which they can control Kilpatrick's four steps. Therefore, even in this beginning stage, all the teacher's actions must be governed by this aim. The teacher should solicit themes from the children so that "purposing" may develop. Later the children should be urged to decide as a group which items of any class of objects each child should draw. For example, at first all the children might draw lambs for the spring picture, but later the group might decide that certain children should draw chickens, ducklings, and so on. This would lead to better "planning." Then group decisions about, say, media or subject might begin to improve design. Finally, such a simple question as "Could we have made the picture better?" could begin the stage of "judging" even in these early years.

Following practice in quasi-group work the children may exhibit an inclination to band together from the start of a project and work with even a minimum of cooperation. They are then ready for group activities proper. A "group" may be defined as a team ranging from three students to a complete class, depending on the nature of the project. Small groups work very well on dioramas, middle-sized groups can work in the sandbox, and larger groups can take on constructions like shopping centers and housing communities. Other projects include decorative maps and a mural that transforms the entire classroom into a medieval environment, complete with mullioned windows and stone walls.

According to most writers, group development should be fostered at some point in the kindergarten and should occupy more and more school time as the child matures. Encouragement of group work becomes much easier for the teacher as the child's age increases. In the third or fourth grade the child becomes especially interested in associating with peer groups. Interests in the "gang" are evident in the children's drawings and paintings. The teacher may capitalize on this interest to promote art activities that lead to a greater social maturity of the young participants. Among the group activities suitable for this purpose and selected for the major part of the discussion here are puppetry and mural-making.

PUPPETRY

Perhaps some of the most effective group activities lie within the several fields of puppetry. Unfortunately puppetry has been a casualty in the war between the advocates of a basic education that emphasizes academics and the supporters of a child-centered program that concentrates on activities. Because it is more complex than most art activities, puppetry is often seen as a threat to other priorities in the curriculum. It is therefore neglected in favor of art experiences that require less time and planning and fewer materials. This is to be regretted because, properly conducted, puppetry can carry the children into language arts, computation, and history as they go about gathering information, preparing scenarios, and planning and constructing a theater and settings. Work in puppetry is a natural focal point for the various learning styles that educators are currently investigating, and no child should go through elementary school without at least one experience in it. Moreover, puppetry is enjoying growing popularity with language arts as well as visual arts teachers.

To produce a successful puppet play the group as a whole must reach decisions, and each member of the group, although maintaining personal identity, must give full cooperation if the enterprise is to succeed. Puppets range in technical complexity from the very simple to the very intricate, so that groups of children at any particular stage of development may select techniques compatible with their capabilities. The three major types of puppets that elementary-school children in one stage or another may select are fist puppets, string puppets (or marionettes), and shadow puppets.

Media and Techniques. Simple stick puppets—the type operated directly with one hand—may be produced in a variety of ways. The beginner can draw a figure on cardboard and later cut away the excess background. The cut-out figure is then attached to a stick. In place of a cut-out figure, the pupil may use a bag stuffed with paper or absorbent cotton, decorated with paint or cut paper, and tied to the stick.

A paper bag may also be used for a puppet that moves its head. A

Fist Puppets

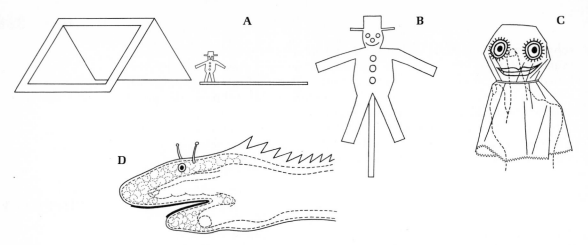

Figure 12.3 *Diagrams of stick puppets (**A** and **B**), a puppet made from a paper bag (**C**), and a puppet made from an old stocking (**D**).*

string is tied about the middle of a paper bag, leaving just enough room for inserting the index finger above the middle. A face is painted on the closed upper portion of the bag. To operate the puppet, the hand is thrust into the bag up to the neck and the index finger pushed through the neck to articulate the head (see Figure 12.3C).

An old stocking, appropriately decorated with buttons for eyes and pieces of cloth or paper for hair, ears, and other features, also makes an effective puppet when slipped over the hand and arm. Animals such as snakes or dragons may be formed by this means. They become especially fearsome if a mouth is cut into the toe of a sock and cloth is stitched to form a lining to the throat so formed. Both top and bottom jaws should be stuffed with a material like absorbent cotton. The jaws are worked by inserting the fingers in the upper section and the thumb in the lower. The attractiveness of this creation can be enhanced by making a lining of a color contrasting with the sock, or by adding teeth or a tongue made from bright materials.

A fist puppet may be constructed from a wide variety of materials. Some of the modeling media mentioned in earlier chapters, including papier-mâché, are suitable for the construction of heads; plastic wood may also be used. The bodies of the puppets may be made from remnants of most textiles. These more advanced fist puppets should be capable of articulation in both the head and arms. The thumb and little finger are usually employed to create movement in the arms, while the index finger moves a modeled head (see Figure 12.4).

To model a head, the pupils should first cut and glue together a stiff cylinder of cardboard (preferably light Bristol board) large enough in diameter to fit their index finger loosely. The modeling medium, which tends to shrink the cylinder slightly, is then worked directly around the cardboard until the head, including all features, and neck are formed. The neck of the puppet modeled over the lower part of the cylinder, or "fingerstall," should be increased slightly in diameter at its base to hold in place the clothes, which are attached by a drawstring. When the modeling medium is dry, it should be smoothed with sandpaper and then decorated with poster paint. An attractive sparkle can be added to eyes, lips, or teeth by coating them with shellac or, better still, clear nail polish. In character dolls, attention can be drawn to outstanding features by the same means. Most puppets tend to be more appealing if the eyes are considerably enlarged and made conspicuous with a shiny coating. Hair, eyebrows, and beards made from absorbent cotton, yarn, cut paper, or scraps of fur can be pasted or glued in place.

The clothing covers the operator's hand and arm and forms the body of the puppet. The outside dimensions of the clothing are determined by the size of the operator's hand. The hand should be laid flat on a desk with the thumb and index and little fingers extended. The approximate length of the puppet's arms will be indicated by the distance from the tip of the thumb to the tip of the little finger, and the neckline should come halfway up the index finger (see Figure 12.3). To make clothing, one folds a single piece of cloth in two, makes a cut in the center of the fold for the neck, and then sews the sides, leaving openings for the fingers. Small mitts may be attached to the openings to cover the fingertips. If the pupils wish their puppets to have interchangeable costumes, a drawstring can be used to tie the clothing to the neck. If they plan on designing only one costume for their puppets, the pupils can glue it into place, as well as tying it for extra security.

Figure 12.4 *Diagram showing how a fist puppet may be manipulated.*

Lively puppet costumes can be made with bright textiles; men's old ties are valuable for this purpose. The lining of the ties should first be removed and the material ironed flat before being folded over and sewn to make a garment. Buttons and other decorations may be added, of course, as they are required.

When children make puppets they expect to use them in a stage production. In presenting a fist-puppet show, the operators work beneath the set. This means that the stage must be elevated so that the puppeteers can stand or crouch under it while the show goes on. A simple stage can be constructed from a large topless cardboard carton with an opening for the stage cut in its base and two sides removed. The carton is then placed on a table with the opening facing the audience. The operators stand or crouch behind the table and are concealed from the audience by a curtain around the table legs.

Pupils in about the fifth and sixth grades may wish to construct a more elaborate stage using lumber. A good general plan is a three-panel screen covered with wrapping paper or cloth, with an opening for the stage at the top of the center panel. The frames for the three panels of the screen are formed from 1-by-2-inch lumber, each panel measuring about 3 by 5 feet. Each panel is braced by crossbars of the lumber; the

Figure 12.5 *A puppet head modeled over a cardboard fingerstall.*

center panel is made so that the crossbars do not interfere with the stage opening, which measures about 2 by 3 feet. The panels are assembled with screws (not nails) so that they can be dismantled easily and are joined by three hinges each. A wire from which to hang the curtain is strung above the stage opening. The three panels are covered with kraft paper or old sheets dyed a dark color. When the screen is set in place for a stage production, the wings of the assembly are held in place by a long piece of the 1-by-2-inch lumber screwed to the top members of the two wings.

The stage settings should be simple. In most cases they may be approached as large paintings, but they should have strong "carrying" power and be rich in a decorative sense. The costumes and backdrops should be designed to provide a visual contrast with each other. Because the stage has no floor, the background is held or fixed in position from below or hung from a frame above. On it may be pinned significant items such as windows and doors. Separate backdrops may be prepared for each scene. Likewise, stage properties—tables, chairs, and the like—must be designed in two dimensions. Spotlights create striking effects and bring out the features of the presentation. Occasionally it may be worthwhile to experiment with projected materials like slides.

The manipulation of fist puppets is not difficult; the pupils can teach themselves the technique merely by practice. One should remember, however, that when more than one puppet is on stage, the puppet that

Figure 12.6 *A fifth-grade class brought King Arthur's England to life in puppets representing knights (shown here), magicians, and peasants. A puppet show was then presented in connection with a class study of medieval life.*

is "speaking" should be in continual movement, so that the audience may know exactly which puppet is the speaker. The other puppets should be still.

A more flexible puppet, but one that is somewhat more difficult to make and operate, is the string puppet, or marionette. This type of puppet moves by means of strings and, if desired, every member may be articulated. Some puppets constructed by professionals may move even mouths, eyes, and eyebrows. Children in the elementary school, of course, could not even start to construct such puppets, let alone manipulate them. Nevertheless, they are able to make and manipulate marionettes that can walk, wave their arms, sit down, shake their heads, and perform a whole series of other interesting maneuvers.

String Puppets (Marionettes)

Media and Techniques.   Children in the symbol stage, but no younger, can produce simple string puppets. A stuffed paper bag, with a head formed by tying the top of the bag with string and with features drawn, painted, or glued on, forms the main part of the puppet. Arms and legs can be cut out of heavy paper or cardboard and pasted to the body. Only two strings, attached from each end of a 6-inch wooden crossbar (called the "control") to each shoulder, are required. A small screw eye at each end of the control and adhesive tape stuck on the paper body serve to anchor the strings. An equally simple marionette may be fashioned in a similar manner from a stuffed sock or stocking.

   After the children learn to control these simple puppets, they can modify them so that more strings can be added. For example, arms can be constructed of two pieces of cardboard joined at the elbow with a paper fastener; then strings from the control can be attached to the hands. The child now has to control the shoulder strings and the arm strings. More strings may be added as the operator's skill grows.

   Preadolescents in the fourth, fifth, and sixth grades who have practiced puppetry earlier will be able to make much more elaborate marionettes. Perhaps the most practical of these puppets has a modeled head and moving arms and legs made from cloth. The head of the string marionette is modeled and finished in a manner similar to that described for fist puppets, but here the fingerstall is replaced by a solid piece of wood of a similar size. The body is constructed on a different principle. A convenient material for making the body is cloth. Two cutouts of the puppet's body—one for the back and the other for the front—are made from the cloth. The two pieces are then sewn together, leaving a small opening at the bottom through which to insert the filler. Absorbent cotton is a good filler, although paper may also be used. Before the body is filled, a weight should be sewn inside the body at the base of the spine. Lead fishing sinkers are convenient to use, especially those that have loops at either end. Two-ounce sinkers are sufficiently heavy. When the body is weighted and firmly stuffed, an oval of cloth should be fitted over the bottom opening to provide an area to support the puppet when it is in a sitting position.

The arms and legs are made from rectangular pieces of cloth, which, like the body, are sewn, weighted, and stuffed. The weights should be placed near the heels and on the bottom sides of the forearms just above the hands. At this time, joints must be made at elbows, wrists, knees, and ankles. These may be made merely by working a "channel" in the stuffing with the fingers and then stitching the channel. The arms are joined to the shoulders by sewing. To make them flexible, it is a good idea to gather the cloth with a thread before it is fixed to the shoulder.

In order that their movement may be more readily controlled, the legs should be pressed flat at the hip so that their full width may be attached with a horizontal joint to the base of the body. So that the legs will not bend in the wrong direction at the knees, a cloth hinge should be sewn behind the knees on the outside of the leg at points slightly above

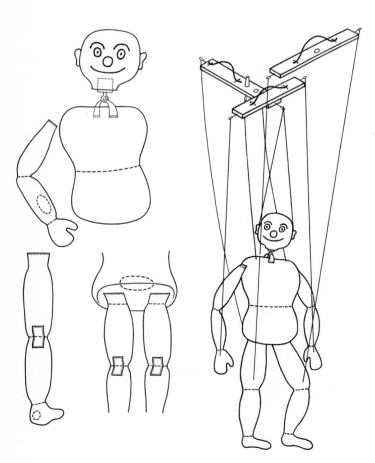

Figure 12.7   *Head, body, leg, and control assemblies of a string puppet.*

and below the joint. A final joint may be put at the waistline. The completed body should be attached to the head assembly with a cotton tape. The wooden neck should be rounded at the end and have a screw eye fastened there. The tape is sewn to the front of the puppet's body and runs from the chest through the screw eye to the back of the puppet where it is again sewn. This arrangement allows separate articulation for the head assembly (see Figure 12.7).

As with the simple marionette described earlier, strings attached to certain parts of the marionette and leading to a control direct the movement of the puppet. The control is made of wood, and the strings are cut from fine fishing line or heavy linen thread. Ordinary string is not suitable because it tangles. Strings should be tacked to the puppet's ears, and should be sewn securely to the shoulders, the wrists, the tops of the knees, and the base of the spine. Nine strings are about the maximum number an elementary-school pupil can control efficiently.

A simple control for this type of puppet consists of three pieces of wood as thin as one-quarter of an inch and about 1 inch wide. The main control is about 6 inches long, and to this, at one end, the first crossbar, measuring about 4 inches, should be tacked. The strings leading from the ears should be fixed to a screw eye or a tack placed at the crossbar end of the main control. The length of these strings, which determines that of all others, should allow the puppet's feet to touch the floor when the operator holds his arms horizontally with his elbows resting in their normal position close to his body. Next the strings from the puppet's wrists should be tied to screw eyes at the extremities of the crossbar and should be long enough to allow the arms to fall downward at almost, but not quite, full length. Then the strings from the shoulders should be tied to screw eyes placed on the main control just behind the crossbar. The string from the base of the spine should be fixed to the main control at the end opposite the crossbar. Only the strings to the tops of the knees remain to be attached to a control. Since these strings are used for walking movements, they must be fastened to an independent crossbar, which the operator should hold in front of the main control. When the leg control is not in use, it can be rested on the main control on the point of a nail; for this, a hole is bored through the leg control so that it fits loosely over the nail. If the leg control is about 2 inches longer than the crossbar, it can be identified quickly when it is needed during a performance (see Figure 12.7).

Once the puppet is strung, the pupil will find it necessary to practice manipulating it. The technique of manipulation is so personal that one can identify the operator by the way the puppet moves. The infinite number of basic movements of which the nine-string marionettes are capable may be discovered only through practice. Because they are fascinated by this aspect of puppetry the pupils will practice during any spare moment.

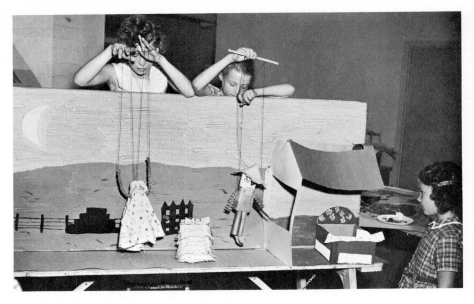

Figure 12.8 *A simple string puppet stage, arranged by fourth-grade pupils using a table and cardboard. (Photo by Royal Studio.)*

After making a human figure for a puppet the children may want to experiment with bird and animal forms. The controls for birds, whose wings merely replace arms, are similar to those used for humans. Animals, however, require controls to operate four legs, and these are usually made with two fixed crossbars attached at either end of the main bar.

When not in use puppets should be carefully protected lest their strings become tangled. Handles made of twine or string stapled to each control are useful for hanging up the puppet. When the puppet is stored, however, the strings must be carefully gathered together and twined around the crossbar.

A simple puppet stage, more for practice than for finished performances, may consist only of a sheet of cardboard, or even paper, with a hole cut in it for a stage opening. It should be propped up on a large table. The pupils stand on the table while manipulating the puppets. (See Figure 12.8 for another form of a simple stage.)

For a finished performance, it is more satisfactory to have a carpenter build a real puppet stage, such as that illustrated in Figure 12.9. This stage consists of a framework of 2-by-4-inch finished wood strong enough to support the weight of the operators who lean against it. The stage opening, which must be high enough to exhibit the puppets, is located at about 2 to 3 feet above the floor of the classroom. Above the stage opening, the wall of the stage usually extends high enough to hide the operators. Some stages allow the audience to see these people, but unless suitably strong lighting is beamed on the stage, the antics of the operators will greatly distract from those of the puppets. Directly behind the backdrop of the puppet stage is a platform on which the pupils stand. They are separated from the stage proper by a partition supporting the backdrop decorations over which they lean to animate the marionettes. Steps leading up to this platform are often convenient. Stage curtains and at least two spotlights to be beamed on the stage are refinements that add to the effectiveness of a production. Costuming and décor may be arranged in ways similar to those described for fist puppets. Since the marionette stage has a floor, unlike the fist puppet stage, properties are usually three-dimensional; they can be constructed from cardboard suitably decorated with poster paint.

Media and Techniques. Although shadow puppets are not difficult to make, successful operation of them demands some finesse. In this technique a silk or nylon screen is set up between the operators and the audience. Strong spotlights on the operators' side are then beamed on the screen. The puppets, consisting of cardboard figures[5] attached to a thin control stick, are held close to the screen in the direct path of the light, thus casting a shadow on the screen. Because the puppet appears to the

Shadow Puppets

[5]The Javanese, who are expert at this type of puppetry, use leather.

Figure 12.9 *The frame for a marionette stage. "A" is the floor of the stage, and the area enclosed by the beams marked "X" is the stage opening. The board marked "B" is the bridge, on which the performers stand; they lean over the beam marked "C" to work their puppets. All parts of the frame except the stage opening should be covered by cloth or wood. The backdrop hangs between "C" and "A."*

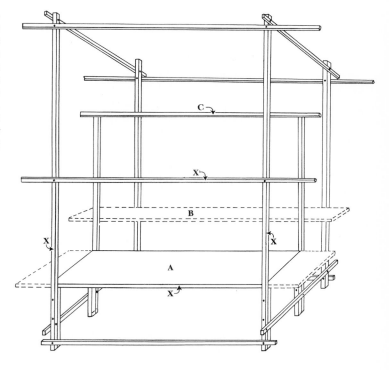

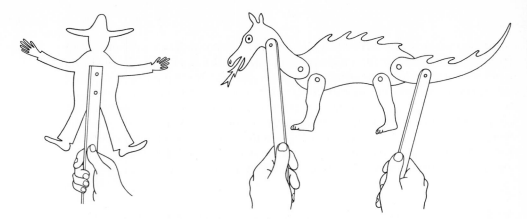

Figure 12.10 *Simple shadow puppets of a human figure and of a dragon with moving head and tail.*

audience only as a shadow silhouette, the figure needs no painting or decorating. The technique of operating is similar to that used with fist puppets, so that the stage for the latter may also be used for shadow puppets.

Children in the earliest phases of the symbol stage can be taught to make shadow puppets. The child simply cuts out a figure drawn on thin cardboard and glues it to a stick. As the children develop their ability to produce symbols and as their skill in using cutting tools improves they can make much more elaborate puppets. Outlines will become more subtle so that such features as shaggy hair, heavy eyebrows, or turned-up noses can be suggested in the silhouette. By punching holes or cutting inside the puppet, the pupil can depict, say, buttons, eyes, and frilly clothing.

Still more experienced pupils can make shadow puppets with moving parts. To make a dragon, for example, a number of small sections of cardboard are joined with paper fasteners. Two sticks are attached to the assembly. With practice, a child can make the creature wiggle in a highly satisfactory manner (see Figure 12.10).

All properties, from tables to houses, must be cut from cardboard, placed on sticks, and also shown in silhouette.[6]

Teaching All Types of Puppetry. As indicated earlier, it is not difficult for a teacher to arouse pupils' interest in puppetry to the point where they desire to produce a play. Most children today are familiar with puppets; some puppets have even gained national interest and affection.

[6]It is recommended that some of the following be studied at this time:
Marjorie Batchelder, *The Puppet Theater Handbook* (New York: Harper & Row, 1947); Winifred H. Mills and Louise M. Dunn, *Marionettes, Masks and Shadows* (New York: Doubleday, 1927)—this contains an excellent section on shadow puppets; Joseph S. Kennard, *Masks and Marionettes* (New York: Macmillan, 1935); F. J. McIsaac, *The Tony Sarg Marionette Book* (New York: Viking, 1930); and Waldo S. Lanchester, *Hand Puppets and String Puppets* (Leicester, Eng.: Dryad, 1948).

Short educational films that show puppets in action are available. The screening of such a film in the classroom is often enough to launch a puppetry project. A demonstration by the teacher is another effective way of stimulating interest in puppets.

Cooperative planning of the project is more difficult. Many teachers begin by holding a general discussion of the problems involved. After viewing a film, children are asked to analyze the various tasks that must be done before a show can be successfully produced. Eventually the main items of work are listed: selecting or writing the play; making the puppets; making the stage scenery and properties (sometimes making a stage if one is not available); lighting the stage; practicing manipulation and general stagecraft.

Next, committees should be listed to carry out the various tasks. Such committees might include a selecting committee for the play with the duty of recommending suitable plays to the general group; a coordinating production committee, or stage committee, to recommend suitable stage properties and backdrops for each scene, the general size of the puppets, and the costumes; and a stage-building committee (if required).

Often the chairmen of the committees are elected with the understanding that they will form a "cabinet" with the duty of overall coordination of the project. Either the members of the cabinet or all the children elect a head chairman, or president, of puppeteers from among the cabinet members, whose duty is to report from time to time to the children about progress and to seek suggestions for improvement.

The teacher's task during these proceedings is to see that elections take place smoothly. The work intensifies when the "executing" stage is

Figure 12.11 *This fifth-grade boy is fortunate in having an authentic Javanese puppet to study during a unit on shadow puppetry. (Photo by Education Development Center.)*

reached. Often demonstrations, short lessons, and informal advice are needed. The teacher must be particularly careful to keep in constant touch with the chairmen, often through the president, to see that they are successful in their efforts. Exactly what a teacher does at this stage, however, would be difficult to define for all cases.[7] Each situation brings its own problems and suggests its own procedures.

Puppetry, like any theatrical activity, culminates in the inevitable presentation of a performance for an audience. The teacher should help the class as a whole to decide who will review the performance—the PTA? the class next door? all the sixth-grade classes? and so on. Once the audience has been decided on, publicity must begin; this may involve preparing posters for bulletin boards, a story for the school paper or PTA bulletin, and mimeographed programs, that final testimonial to all who have had a hand in the production.

It is most important that group evaluation or judging take place both as the production proceeds and after the show is finished. With the head chairman presiding, questions should be brought up for discussion. Each chairman's report should be analyzed and suggestions for improvement made. After the performance, the time-honored question must be raised: "How can we improve the show next time?"

MURAL-MAKING

Media and Techniques.   The term "mural" in its strictest sense refers to a painting made directly on a wall. In many schools, however, it has come to denote any large picture, and this is the meaning of the word as it is used here.

What are the technical requirements of this art form? Although the youngest pupils may not understand the significance of all these requirements, the teacher should know about them and, when advisable, teach them. The first technical requirement arises from the architectural quality of a wall. A plain undecorated wall possesses some fundamental architectural characteristics, which it should retain once the mural is in place. The wall is obviously solid and flat rather than undulating. In a mural a wide diversity of depths achieved by linear perspective, or an extreme range of colors tends to interfere with these basic characteristics of the wall and many people find such interference unpleasant. The design of the mural, therefore, must be kept reasonably flat if the wall is to maintain its architectural qualities.

A mural should be considered as part of a scheme of interior decoration and should be integrated with it. The color relationships already

---

[7]For an amplification of this discussion, see Hollingshead, *Guidance in Democratic Living*, especially Chapter 7.

A   B

Figure 12.12 *Groups can also function constructively outside the classroom.* (**A**) *The youngsters here are working on a large group drawing of their neighborhood in rural Georgia (Photo by Marvin Grossman).* (**B**) *This mural, painted with flat, exterior house paint, was produced to decorate the front of the children's school with scenes from books they had read.*

established in the interior in which the mural is placed should be echoed in the new work. Furthermore, since door and window openings create a design in a room, the mural should be placed so that it does not violate the architectural arrangement of these elements but rather tends to maintain the existing plan or even to improve on it. The architectural limitations of classrooms are so consistently severe that most murals will probably be no larger than 4 by 8 feet—a size convenient for resting on the ledge of the blackboard. Homosote or composition-board backing, which can be purchased at lumberyards or building-supply stores, may be used as a light, portable background for direct painting or as a backing for mural paper.

Despite the technicalities involved in the successful production of a mural, most children find that the activity is generally within their capabilities, and the experience of mural-making is a happy and rewarding one for them. Children in primary grades will have difficulty in preplanning their work and will probably see mural-making as an activity that allows them to paint large pictures on vertical surfaces. But those who have reached a stage of social maturity that allows them to work with a degree of cooperation and preplanning should find little difficulty in making a mural.

The subject matter for murals may be similar to that used in individual picture-making, or it may derive from a broader frame of reference such as social studies. The most successful murals reflect the children's own experiences and interests. A subject such as "The Western Movement," though not a part of the child's personal background, can still be worthwhile if due attention is given to motivation by creating the environment of the early settlers with folk music, old prints, posters, and films. Whatever subject is chosen must be sufficiently broad in scope to allow several pupils to elaborate on it. A still-life composition, for example, would not be an appropriate subject for a mural.

The distinction between a painting with a limited focus of attention and a mural with multiple focuses must be made. A subject in which there are many objects of related but differing appearance, such as houses, factory buildings, or crowds of people, would be most suited to group activity. An example of a subject that offers a great variety of shapes is "Spring in the Garden." Members of a third-grade class thought of the following ideas for inclusion in the subject: plants, flowers, butterflies, bugs, turtles, birds, clouds, and grass. The following are examples of themes that elementary-school pupils have successfully developed:

From the Experience of the Child	*From Other Areas of the Curriculum*
Our School Playground	The Year 2000
A Trip to the Supermarket	The Western Movement
A Circus That Came to Town	Books I Have Liked
Playing Outside in Winter	The Meaning of Freedom
Shopping at Christmas	How People Differ from Animals
The Easter Parade	Our Town in History
The Seasons Change	Acting My Age in Ancient Greece

Figure 12.13 *Children often like to work as a team if the project demands it. This painting of a seventeenth-century harbor scene was in its second week of work when photographed. (Photo by Neil Jacobs.)*

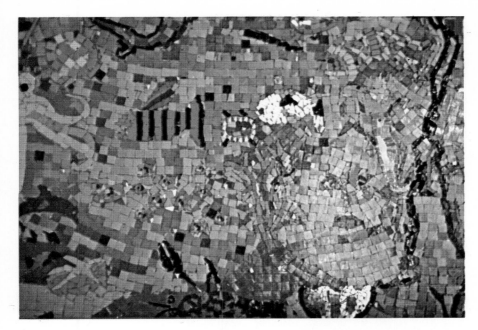

Figure 12.14 *Children who have reached a degree of social maturity can work together on large projects. These are details from a large mosaic mural produced by fifth and sixth graders.*

Figure 12.15 *A group of primary-grade pupils paint a mural in one session. The work was done spontaneously, without pre-planning.*

Most of the picture-making media can be used in mural production. The paper should be sufficiently heavy and tough to support the weight of the finished product. Kraft paper, the heavy brown wrapping paper that comes in large rolls, is suitable. Many school-supply houses offer a gray mural paper that is pleasant to use. When ordering paper, a 4-foot width is recommended. The most effective coloring medium for young children is tempera paint. This should be applied with the same wide range of the brushes suggested for picture-making. Some especially wide brushes should be available for painting the large areas of the mural. In applying tempera paint excessive thickness should be avoided, since the paint will flake off when the mural is rolled up for storage. Chalk may be used, but it tends to be dusty and to smudge badly when several children are working at one time. Colored cut paper is another medium by which effective results can be achieved from the first grade on; the cut paper can also be combined with paper collage. Wax crayons are not suitable because they require too much effort to cover large areas, but crayons may be used in some areas as a resist with thin tempera.

The technique of planning and executing the mural varies with the child's social and artistic stage of development. The kindergarten child may begin by working side by side with classmates on the same long strip of paper. Beginners all paint on the same topic suggested by the teacher and use the same medium, but each child actually creates an individual composition without much reference to the work of the others. Not until they reach the third or fourth grade are some children able to plan the mural cooperatively. When they develop this ability they may begin by making sketches lightly in chalk on the area allotted for the mural. Considerable discussion and many alterations may occur before the design satisfies all the participants. By the time they reach the fifth or sixth grade, many pupils are ready to plan a mural on a reduced scale before beginning the work itself. They prepare sketches on paper with dimensions proportionate to those of the mural. These sketches are made in outline and in color. Later, when the mural paper has been laid over a large table or pinned to tackboard, the final sketch is enlarged on the mural surface. Usually this is done freehand, but sometimes teachers suggest that the squaring method of enlargement be used. By this method the sketch and the mural surface are divided into corresponding squares. A pupil redraws in the corresponding area of the mural what is in a specific area of the sketch.[8] Such a procedure, while common practice with professional muralists, may easily become inhibiting with elementary-school children and should be used with caution. Only the most mature children are capable of benefiting from this technique.

After the drawing (or "cartoon," as it is sometimes called) has been satisfactorily transferred to the mural surface, the colors are applied. If tempera paint is to be used, it is usually mixed in advance in a relatively limited number of hues. Tints and shades are also mixed in advance. All colors should be prepared in sufficient quantity to complete all areas in the mural where they are to be used. In this way time and paint are saved, and the unity of the mural created in the sketch is preserved in the larger work. If colored chalk or cut paper is used, the problem of running out of a color is not likely to occur, of course.

When pupils use cut paper, the technique for producing a mural is less formal than when paint or chalk is used. The pupils can push areas of the colored paper around on the mural to find the most satisfying effects. Thus plans may undergo even major revision up to the final moment when the colored paper is stuck to the surface. Colored construction paper is recommended for the main body of the mural because it gives the background areas added interest.

In carrying out the plan of a mural the pupils quickly discover that

---

[8]This mural-making technique has been developed by Vige Langevin and Jean Lombard, *Peintures et Dessins Collectifs des Enfants* (Paris: Éditions du Scarabée, 1950). The members of the class produce small paintings. One painting is selected and divided into squares, which are numbered. Each child in the class is assigned one square to copy on a large scale on another piece of paper. Eventually the large squares are assembled to form a very large picture. Although the children are encouraged to develop details in their copied area, the necessary emphasis on using someone else's idea limits the activity. Considerable work of this kind may be seen in some Paris schools.

they must solve other problems of design peculiar to this work. Because the length of a mural in relation to its height is usually much greater than in paintings the technical problem arises of establishing a satisfactory center of interest. Although one center of interest may be developed it must not be so strong that the observer finds it necessary to ignore portions of the work at the extremities of the composition. On the other hand, if a series of centers of interest are placed along the full length of the composition, the observer may consider the result too jumpy and spotty. In general, the composition should be dispersed, the pupils being particularly careful about connecting the rhythms they establish so that no part of the mural is either neglected or unduly emphasized. The balances in a mural made by children, furthermore, have a tendency to get out of hand. Not infrequently children become intrigued with subject matter in one section of the work, with the result that they may give it too much attention and neglect other sections. Profuse detail may overload a favored part, while other areas are overlooked.

One problem of design that rarely occurs in mural-making is lack of variety. Indeed, with many people working on the same surface the problem is usually too much variety. Once they become aware of this difficulty, however, children are usually able to remedy the defect.[9]

Teaching.   As with puppetry, it is not difficult to interest children in making murals. Showing a film and slides or going to see a mural in a public building are two fairly practical ways of arousing their interest. Children are also motivated by seeing the murals that other children have made. Perhaps the most effective method is to discuss with the class the needs and benefits of making murals as decorations for specified areas of the school, such as the classroom, the halls, the cafeteria, or the auditorium.

Although in puppetry there is often enough work to be done to permit every member of the class to participate in the endeavor, this is not so in mural-making. The pupils may all discuss the making of murals, including the various media, the most suitable subjects, and the probable locations in which the work might be placed, but eventually the pupils must divide into small groups, probably not to reunite until the final evaluation period. In the elementary school, the small groups may comprise from three to ten pupils each, depending on the size of the mural.

Preadolescents should be able to organize their own mural-making. First, all the pupils in a class interested in mural-making assemble to discuss what the theme should be. After the pupils' suggestions for the main theme have been written on the blackboard, each pupil selects some aspect to work on. Those pupils interested in the same aspect form a team to work on that particular mural. If too many pupils elect one aspect,

[9]See Arne W. Randall, *Murals for Schools* (Worcester, Mass.: Davis, 1956).

two teams can be created, each to work separately on the same subject. The teams are finally arranged and each elects its chairman.

Discussion then takes place within each team concerning the size and shape of its particular mural, the medium, and possible techniques. Sketches are then prepared, either cooperatively or individually. The teams can either choose the individual sketch most liked by all or prepare a composite picture, using the best ideas from the several sketches. The cartoon is then drawn, usually with the chairman supervising to see that the chosen sketch is reproduced with reasonable accuracy. Next the color is added. From time to time the chairman may find it necessary to hold a team consultation to appraise the work so that some of the pitfalls of design in mural-making are avoided. This process goes on until each team's mural is completed. Finally, under a general chairman, all the mural-makers meet to review their work and to discuss the usual topics that arise in the "judging" stage.

During these proceedings the teacher acts as a consultant. If the pupils have previously made individual pictures, the teacher need give few demonstrations. The teacher's tasks consist for the most part in seeing that a working area[10] and suitable materials are available, providing the initial motivation, outlining some of the technical requirements of a mural, and demonstrating the "squaring" method of enlarging, if it is to be used.

A completely different approach allows the children to develop the mural spontaneously. In this approach the children choose only the colors beforehand in order to assure some harmony. The group then gathers around all four sides of the paper that is placed on the floor and begins to paint. If the group is too large to do this comfortably, then it is divided into smaller units. The first children paint whatever comes into their minds and succeeding groups of children try to relate their shapes and colors to those that have preceded them. The entire experience should be as open and the children as immediately responsive as possible.

The teacher should take advantage of the mural-making activity to introduce the children to some great murals in art history. They should be acquainted with the splendor of Michelangelo's Sistine Chapel ceiling, the richness of Chagall's painting in the dome of the Paris Opera House, the massive forms of Diego Rivera, and the dramatic contrasts of José Orozco. Although elementary-school children cannot use oil or do frescoes they can at least gain familiarity with the terms used in discussing these media. They can also observe how mural materials have changed with the advancement of technology: muralists now use such materials as welded metals, fired enamel plates, ceramics, and concrete. David Siqueiros, for example, has used automotive lacquers as well as other industrial materials in his murals. Gyorgy Kepes has produced murals

---

[10] It is often difficult to find space in the classroom for mural work. See Chapter 5 for some possible solutions to this problem.

using illuminated glass and John Mason has used clay. Many muralists today are more likely to be sculptors than painters; children who are exposed to their work may want to make a relief mural rather than a painting in their class activity.

OTHER GROUP ACTIVITIES

Dioramas,
Panoramas,
and Peep Shows

A *diorama* re-creates in minature a three-dimensional subject involving complex spatial relationships. A diorama is usually set into a three-sided container for support and for ease in representing the background. When the diorama is prepared on a flat surface, it is usually referred to as a *panorama,* and when the entire scene is enclosed in a box, except for a viewing aperture, it is a *peep show.* Making panoramas is an excellent extension of mapping exercises, and peep shows lend themselves to experimentation with lighting effects when the walls or ceiling of the container include sections of colored cellophane. The subject matter for these activities is most often derived from social studies and language arts.[11]

All three activities call on the ingenuity of students as they search for materials whose qualities approximate those of the objects they are to represent and that are in scale with one another (thimbles for tables, bits of dyed sponge for bushes, stippled plasticine for grass, sandpaper for roads). Use of ready-made objects such as toy soldiers and model cars is not a recommended practice; the children should learn to create their own symbols, leaving the plastic toys to their model railroads. These activities, which may be performed by groups or individuals, are capable of uniting fantasy and reality: in their creations the children can renew their neighborhoods, plan a city of the future, or speculate about the living patterns of the past. Dioramas test the pupils' ingenuity in finding materials to carry out ideas.

Books

Printmaking activities can lead to the production of books. The class begins the project with individual efforts in making the prints (the contents of the book) but carries the project through as a group in putting the books together. Each child ends up with a copy of the project.

There are two basic methods of book construction. For an *open-fold booklet,* the interior sheets are attached to the folded cover by stapling or by threading heavy yarn through punched holes. The outer cover can be made of cardboard decorated with an overall vegetable- or eraser-print pattern, or it can be covered with cloth or decorative wrapping paper.

---

[11]See Chapter 15 for a fuller discussion of the nature of subject matter and for some illustrations of the activities.

Figure 12.16 *Example of an accordion book.*

(Construction paper is not recommended for covers because folded edges will not lie flat unless taped.) The second method involves the *accordion book*. Here, the contents are pasted to both sides of pieces of cardboard. The boards are then connected with yarn and binder tape; like an accordion, it can be folded flat or extended, as the child wishes. When extended, the booklet can be displayed to advantage (see Figure 12.16).

TOWARD A NEW AESTHETIC: GROUP ART

Group art, like any art, is more than the sum of its parts. The final product comes into being through the efforts of a group of individuals working with visual materials toward some end that ultimately reflects the perceptions of all the participants. All forms of contemporary group art assume that the participant can function both as an individual and as a member of a collectivity; they also assume that the end result of a group activity can be something that by its very nature is beyond the capabilities of any one individual.

Some group activities are spontaneous (chalk-ins, graffiti covering city walls), while others are planned (theater pieces, parades, parties, celebrations). Group activities can be cheap or expensive, and they can cross over, sometimes disconcertingly, into other categories of expression (group drama can become group dance, the delicate art of calligraphy can have a boisterous resurgence in subway graffiti).

The general educationist is, as has been mentioned, interested in group activity because it provides one entree into a broader social process and is a vivid means of enlivening the study of geography, history, the language arts, or any other field. The youth of the 1960's, disregarding accepted views of education, embraced the idea of communal art, with its concomitant belief in the shared values of creative social action, and

341

rejected what was felt to be the egocentricity represented by the individual work of art. In many ways they have made possible new attitudes toward group art in the public schools.

Let us examine the major direction from which group art may develop. Random events allow every participant to work independently, yet, through interaction with others, to have a marked impact on the environment. The popular chalk-in, carried on by a group of young people, can make any parking lot take on new life. Inner-city students who decorate walls around building sites are using the cumulative effect of random design to alter the nature of an entire street. These examples are simultaneously random and planned in that functions, such as the use of a particular color, are clearly defined and that no one can completely anticipate what the final result will be.

When enlarging an image, randomness moves closer to control. In this situation, students work strictly on their own but within certain limitations in the knowledge that a surprise awaits them. For example, a junior-high school art teacher wanted to celebrate Washington's birthday in an unusual and memorable way. He cut up a reproduction of Leutze's *Washington Crossing the Delaware* into one-inch squares. Each student received a square and a large sheet of paper cut to a proportionate size. The class then "blew up," or enlarged to scale, the small segments and transferred them to the large paper. No attempt was made to match colors since Day-Glo paint was used instead of standard materials, such as tempera, watercolor, or chalk. Hence individual students used whatever colors they wanted to without regard for Leutze's painting or to the choice of other students. A wall was selected for mounting the project. When the completed pieces were assembled in proper order and fixed in place, a black light was turned on the wall and the effect was overwhelming. The teacher's behavioral goal was reached: "Neither teacher nor students will ever forget Washington's birthday."

The "transformation" activity described by Laliberte is considerably more random than the preceding example in its open-endedness, but it also requires more interaction within the group.

> The instructor or teacher leaves the room for 15 minutes. In his or her absence the students are asked to do something to dramatically alter the physical appearance or change areas of space within the room—i.e., stacking furniture on top of cabinets, everyone standing on top of each other in a corner of the room, all furniture upside down on the floor as if the entire room was now upside down. Variation: cover all the objects in the room with colored paper (or glossy paper, colored cellophane, aluminum foil, newspaper) to create a different mood or atmosphere.[12]

[12] Norman Laliberte, Richey Kehl, et al., *One Hundred Ways to Have Fun with an Alligator and One Hundred Other Involving Art Projects* (Blauvelt, N.Y.: Art Education Inc., 1969), Project 78.

One could refine the activity even more by requiring that only one material, such as string, old newspapers, or aluminum foil be used. Or one could use the room for a series of daily changes that involve a sequence of materials.

Another example of a transformation activity that combines both preplanning and spontaneity is the "Woven Playground Sculpture." In this activity, the teacher prepared the students by using the jungle gym as a three-dimensional loom. The boundaries between weaving and sculpture disappeared as the entire class used the boxlike structure of the gym to create all manner of volumes and spatial divisions with yarn. When the activity was completed, the class had used a simple craft technique to transform wholly an object for which they held an entirely different set of associations. Once the students sensed their power of transformation, the second stage was begun. This involved a consideration of how one could go about using the entire playground—swings, chinning bars, slides, horizontal ladders—as a dispersed armature for a unified structure. Preplanning required listing the techniques and materials needed. Improvisation occurred when objects such as large paintings and pieces of cardboard sculpture were added as the occasion arose and as a spontaneous response to design requirements occurred. The completed product consisted of units of playground equipment linked together by clotheslines holding planar divisions of sheets and old clothes soaked in plaster of Paris plus the art work produced for the occasion. Color was added here and there as a final touch.

Group art leaders are intrigued by the promise of more effective communication between individuals and the possibility that numbers of people can produce and share the experience that we normally associate with individual creativity. John Cage sees it as follows:

> Art, instead of being an object made by one person, is a process set in motion by a group of people. Art's socialized. It isn't someone saying something, but people doing things, giving everyone (including those involved) the opportunity to have experiences they would not otherwise have had.[13]

Since group art operates on the levels of both individual and group effort, it is difficult to define. Kultermann,[14] in discussing the roots of the intermedia movement (itself a form of group art), lists a number of influences on it and then states that it is impossible to explain the developments within the movement as an outgrowth of the history of any one medium. According to Kultermann, "different threads come together in each case," cross traditional boundaries, influence and enrich each other, and ultimately result in a new art form.

---

[13]John Cage, *Year from Monday: New Lectures and Writings* (Middletown, Conn.: 1967), p. 151.
[14]Udu Kultermann, *Art and Life* (New York: Praeger, 1971), p. 33.

Kultermann's conclusions could be applied to group art, but with certain differences. The intermedia movement borrows heavily from technology and is synaesthetic in nature (involving total sensory awareness). It draws on the more traditional movements within the arts themselves as sources of form. Group art, as it is currently practiced, does not rely on traditional artistic forms and owes much of its existence to social forces that function outside the arts. Part of it comes from social and political theory, part of it comes from consciousness-raising exercises, and part of it derives from the heightened sensory perception of the past decade. We might recall the felt need for deeper interpersonal relationships among the youth of the 1960's. Radical changes in the theater, which were formal as well as political in nature, also contributed to the development of group art.

The range of group-art activities is limitless. Dioramas, murals, and puppetry are examples of how the term has been traditionally understood. Light shows and random events are examples of the contemporary understanding of the term. The differences between these understandings of the term reflect the differences that exist in the field of art generally.

Group art is also an act of faith, a gesture toward growth through involvement on a large scale; it requires an ability to minimize the desire for "success," what people *gain* from an activity, in exchange for the values people *bring* to a situation for which nothing in their past may have prepared them. Group art thus comes closer, not to art proper, but to what art ought to be—a model for life. If one can transfer the regenerative power of life to art, then one can ignore the Cassandras who announce the death of art. But if art is not to die, it must redefine itself periodically in order to maintain its vital sense of being. The leader of group art thus redefines art by shifting his attention from the private product to the public process.

ACTIVITIES FOR THE READER

1. Study a group activity in a classroom and analyze it according to Kilpatrick's four stages.
2. Describe three quasi-group activities not mentioned in this chapter.
3. Make three fist puppets: a simple stick puppet, a more complicated paper-bag puppet, and, finally, a cloth puppet of an animal whose jaws will move. Improvise dialog around a situation with a fellow student's puppets.
4. Practice manipulating each of your puppets. When skillful, give a short performance for some of your younger friends and see how they react.
5. Make three string puppets: the first from a paper bag, with two strings; the second from cloth, with three strings; the third from cloth, with a modeled head and at least seven strings.

6. Practice manipulating your string puppets and eventually give your friends a performance.

7. Study any professional murals in your locality. Make a note of their subject matter in relation to their location, their design, and the media used.

8. Design a mural on a small scale that you think might be suitable for the interior of your local post office, the foyer of a local theater, or the entrance of the local high school. Choose subject matter of local interest.

9. Create a panorama depicting a mythical island or kingdom. Using the top of a card table as a base, turn your panorama into a game in which players race for a buried treasure by throwing dice and drawing directional cards.

10. Select an occasion and plan a party. Think of it as an art work, unique in conception, compelling in its visual possibilities. Involve the entire class and be sure you have some participatory element. It must not cost more than fifty cents per person and should include something to eat and drink.

Retarded children often exhibit exceptional sensitivity to line, color, and space, as in this abstract painting reminiscent of the work of Jackson Pollock.

SPECIAL EDUCATION: ART ACTIVITY FOR SLOW LEARNERS

Indisputably, drawing provides for the retarded child possibilities to which he can measure up . . . a path of liberation. In terms of humanity, what blossoming! In spite of the definitive weakness that stands in the way of normal development . . . the child who is incapable of assimilating intellectual concepts . . . retains an elementary possibility of unimpaired humanity . . . through his art work.*

Every modern educational system takes pride in the attention it gives to individual pupils. In recent years, many special education programs have been developed for abnormal and atypical children—the blind and partially sighted, the deaf, the retarded, the extremely mal-adjusted, and the physically handicapped. It is well that this should be so, for classroom teachers who lack training in how to treat these exceptional children will find themselves in difficulty. With many handicapped and retarded children, art activities are used in highly specialized ways for specific and, in an artistic sense, narrow ends. Art is frequently employed, for example, not as a means of artistic expression in the traditional sense, but as a device by which children reveal their difficulties to a therapist. Whatever progress is made by these children occurs as a direct result of highly skilled diagnoses and subsequent clinical treatment, not necessarily because of participation in art activities *per se*.[1]

A distinction should be made, however, between the exceptional child who receives special schooling and the slow-learning child who is capable of functioning within the framework of a normal school situa-

---

*From: *Les dessins des enfants,* by J. Boutonier, Éditions du Scarabée, Paris, 1953. Quoted in Betty Lark-Horovitz, Hilda Present Lewis, and Mark Luca. *Understanding Children's Art for Better Teaching* (Columbus, Ohio: Merrill, 1967), p. 143.

[1]See, for example, Emery I. Gondor, *Art and Play Therapy* (New York: Random House, 1954), a booklet written in simple language by a sensitive clinician.

347

tion.[2] "Slow learners" are simply those pupils who make considerably lower than average scores on intelligence tests and who progress in academic subjects at a pace manifestly slower than that displayed by the majority of their fellow students. But if Henry Schaefer-Simmern's experiments with what he terms "mental-defectives" are any indication, a sensitive and deeply committed teacher can attain remarkable artistic results with the slow learner. His case study of "Selma" demonstrated that the subject's personality, as well as the visual quality of her work, showed remarkable progress under his supervision.[3]

The slow or retarded learner is but one of the many types of handicapped children that the art or classroom teacher is likely to encounter in the course of a normal teaching situation.

The current tendency is to move handicapped children out of specialized schools and into the more normal environment of the regular school. As a result, there is an increasing likelihood that all teachers will have to reeducate themselves, at least to some degree, in order to serve the handicapped student more effectively. Teachers will have to reexamine their particular subject area in search of more effective means than were used in the past for dealing with the gifted, the emotionally disturbed, the physically impaired, and the mentally deficient.

This area of concern for the nonaverage child is known more generally as "special education." Its growth as a branch of art education has been very great in the past decade and probably will continue to grow as the therapeutic role of the arts is more fully understood and appreciated. We should also note that there has been new legislation on both state and national levels that is intended to vastly increase the quality of services provided for the handicapped with less attention paid to the gifted.

This chapter will concentrate on the slow learner rather than children with other types of handicap because of the greater likelihood that

[2]For a detailed analysis of the intellectual characteristics of mentally retarded children, see Karl C. Garrison and D. G. Force, Jr., *The Psychology of Exceptional Children,* 4th ed. (New York: Ronald, 1965).

The reader is also directed toward the following at this time: Hollis L. Caswell, ed., "Teaching the Slow Learner," in *Practical Suggestions for Teaching,* rev. ed. (New York: Teachers College, 1951); Christine P. Ingram, *Education for the Slow-Learning Child,* 3rd ed. (New York: Ronald, 1960); Arch Heck, *The Education of Exceptional Children,* 2nd ed. (New York: McGraw-Hill, 1953), Chapters 23–25; Florence L. Goodenough, *Exceptional Children* (New York: Appleton-Century-Crofts, 1956), especially Part 3, "The Intellectually Inadequate"; Maida Abrams and Lori Schill, "Art in Special Education," *Art Education, Elementary* (Washington, D.C.: National Art Education Association, 1972).

The reader should be warned that not one of these authors mentions art education for children of low mentality. However, they give a good general background for the subject. Art education for slow learners so far seems to be a neglected area, if one may judge from the lack of worthwhile literature on the subject.

[3]Henry Schaefer-Simmern, *The Unfolding of Artistic Activity* (Berkeley: University of California Press, 1948).

these learners will be encountered in the average classroom.[4] First the characteristics of the art of slow learners and the subject matter they are likely to select will be considered. Then the teaching methods and art activities especially suitable for these children will be discussed.

CHARACTERISTICS OF THE ART OF SLOW LEARNERS

The causes for retardation should be noted. While some children may indeed be suffering from cerebral or neurological dysfunctions, the deficiency of others may be due to sources of deprivation such as lack of family (loving, touching, and playing) or of general sensory and environmental deprivation. Both Uhlin[5] and Lindsay[6] therefore view the concrete, sensory nature of art experiences as vital to the development of a sense of self in the child. Art experiences, crafts in particular, can involve the student in learning situations that are tactile, sensory, and stimulating physically as well as mentally. Identifying the causes for retardation are best accomplished through a team approach when the art or classroom teacher has a psychologist, physician, or psychiatrist to consult.

The classification of mental ability by I.Q. varies according to different systems. Table 13.1 gives some indication of differences suggested by four major agencies. Any child who functions below 70 I.Q. can be considered a slow learner as dealt with in this chapter.

Slow learners enrolled in a regular classroom begin their artistic career, like normal children, by manipulating art materials rather than by drawing or modeling recognizable objects.[7] They are sometimes slower than normal children to play with the materials given to them and may not explore their possibilities fully. Having been given a box of twelve wax crayons of various colors, for example, they might use only one color. Once they have begun manipulating a medium they are often reluctant to branch out into the use of symbols. If given a second type of material they frequently prefer to manipulate the original medium, with which they apparently feel more secure. In some cases, they seem to be content to watch other children play with the new materials. If familiar toys are

---

[4]Much of the subject matter of this chapter is condensed from the statements made in C. D. and M. R. Gaitskell, *Art Education for Slow Learners* (Toronto: Ryerson Press, and Peoria, Ill: Bennett, 1953), by special permission.

[5]Donald Uhlin, *Art for Exceptional Children* (Dubuque, Iowa: Wm. C. Brown Co., 1972), Chapter 3, "The Mentally Deficient Personality in Art."

[6]Zaidee Lindsay, *Art and the Handicapped Child* (New York: Van Nostrand Reinhold Co., 1972), pp. 18–45.

[7]The study on which this and the following statements are largely based included 514 children enrolled in fifty-five schools. The I.Q. range was 50 to 89, with a median I.Q. of 70 and a C.A. range of 7 years, 6 months, to 16 years; they produced 3,674 pieces of art for analysis.

available in the classroom, furthermore, they often prefer to play with them rather than to work with art materials.

Whereas a normal five-year-old child may arrive at the symbol stage within a period of time ranging from three weeks to six months, the five-year-old slow learner who has an I.Q. of about 70 may not reach this stage for a year or more. In time, however, slow learners arrive at the symbol stage in a manner resembling that of normal children. Once the symbol stage has been reached, several symbols may appear in their output in quick succession.

Because of their greater chronological age, the mentally retarded children often possess powers of physical coordination superior to those of normal children of the same mental age. These physical powers, of course, help them to master drawing skills more readily and allow them to repeat a recently developed symbol without much practice. Repetition that requires little thought suits slow learners and gives their work a characteristic rhythmic quality. Their tendency to repeat a discovery interferes with their creation of new symbols and at the same time retards their development of the symbols already discovered. In other words, they are as slow to make progress in the stage of symbols as they are to pass through the period of manipulation. Nevertheless, a slow learner, like a normal child, will sometimes surprise a teacher with a burst of progress.

As noted in an earlier chapter, regression from the symbol stage to that of manipulation will sometimes occur in the work of all children as a result of such factors as fatigue, ill health, temporary emotional disturbances, periods of intense concentration, interruptions of various kinds, absence from school, or faulty teaching methods. Reversion of this kind occurs more frequently with mentally retarded children than with normal children.

Gradually, slow learners begin to spend more time on their work

Table 13.1

**COMPARATIVE SYSTEMS OF
CLASSIFYING RETARDATION BY I.Q.**

U.S. President's Panel on Mental Retardation		English System	National Association for Retarded Children and American Association on Mental Deficiency
I.Q.	Classification		
50–70	Mild	ESN (Educationally subnormal)	70–85 mildly retarded
35–49	Moderate	SSN (severely subnormal)	below 70 moderately retarded
20–34	Severe	SSN	
Below 20	Profound	SSN	

Figure 13.1 *Slow learners sometimes continue in the manipulative stage longer than normal children. This painting by a retarded eight-year-old displays considerable spontaneity and improvisation.*

and thus begin to add details to their symbols. Sometimes they may learn to relate their symbols to one another. The progress they make depends largely, of course, on the attention they give to their work. Slow learners' attention span tends to increase with both their chronological age and their mental age. Of 342 mentally retarded children studied for their retention of interest in making a picture, some lost interest in their work within a few minutes, but others worked as long as an hour and a half. The older children tended to work longer than the younger. Moreover, many of the older children were willing to return to the same picture for days on end.

The forms used by slow learners to extend the meaning of their symbols have some peculiar characteristics. The length of limbs in a human symbol may be greatly exaggerated, for example, if children feel such distortion is necessary to tell their story. Although this type of distortion may be seen in the work of normal children, it seems to be more pronounced in that of slow learners. Details added to the symbols may fail to show uniform development. An otherwise crude symbol of a human being might include a most detailed and relatively accurate delineation of facial features or of certain small particulars of clothing that have special significance for the children. Because of their concern only with details that hold their interest and because of their limited powers of concentration, slow learners may omit some items that normal children would probably include in their symbols.

A type of symbol or mark used more frequently by slow learners than by normal children of the same mental or chronological age is an artificial, conventionalized notation like that found in professional car-

351

Figure 13.2 *"The telephone men," crayon drawing by a boy, C.A. 10, I.Q. 68. Note the lack of uniformity of development in the delineation of symbols.*

toons. Lines, for example, may be employed to show noise emanating from a particular source—a flow of music from a radio or a rush of air from a window. Sometimes feelings of excitement or happiness ascribed to a symbol of a human being are also represented by this type of notation. Slow learners also sometimes employ writing with their symbols in an attempt to clarify their pictorial statement.

A few observations must be made concerning the general composition and aesthetic qualities of the pictorial output of slow learners. These children often use the usual childlike conventions, like X-rays, series, and fold-over pictures, but they adopt these relatively complicated conventions only after much practice in art. Even when retarded children use one of the above conventions, they do not, as a rule, use it throughout their composition, but apply it only to some selected point of emphasis.

Slow learners often fail to achieve unity in their compositions. The rhythms they adopt become monotonous; centers of interest that may appear as they begin work are later destroyed, and almost half the work they produce fails to establish a reasonable balance. Slow learners, however, are usually successful in achieving variety in their use of the elements of design, although it is rarely as interesting as that found in the work of normal children. They appear to have most success in their use of color, although they make relatively little use of tints and shades, and rely instead on unmixed colors. In fact, rarely will light and shade in any form be found in their output. Some slow learners use line quite successfully. Occasionally the lines are either vigorous or delicate enough to be very interesting. Textural effects achieved by means of drawing occur extremely infrequently in any of their work.

Sometimes a retarded child may produce work that has some extremely attractive detail. On even rarer occasions, a slow learner may develop a composition both charming and original either in its pattern or in its subject matter, or in both. Art work is significant, however, largely in relation to the child who produces it. The art activities may be serving primarily therapeutic purposes. The quality of the finished work is not as important as the feeling of well-being and stability that attends the working process.

SUBJECT MATTER SELECTED BY SLOW LEARNERS

As indicated earlier, all children who have the aptitude to do so pass through the normal stages of pictorial expression mentioned in Chapter 6—the manipulation, symbol, and preadolescent stages. The child with a mental age of around three and a chronological age of six will not go beyond manipulating materials; however, the child with the same chronological age and a mental age of four or more may begin to enter the symbol stage. With a mental age of five, the child will even place symbols within their environment.

Figure 13.3 *An example of graphic design that combines printmaking, poetry, and typography. This picture comes from a publication of the Dr. Francis Perkins School in Lancaster, Massachusetts.*

Music stands around me
While I stand alone .
Birds flutter back and forth
From here to there
Until they're tired ,
Then they go home .

The trees stand sturdy and strong
While the leaves blow along .
The people move here and there ,
The waves toss everywhere .
Music stands around me
While I stand alone .
                              Perry Hunkins

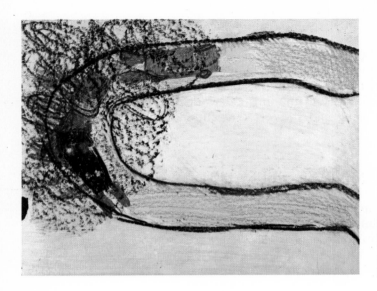

Figure 13.4 *"Accident in my neigh-borhood," crayon drawing by a boy, C.A. 12, I.Q. 80. Slow learners are capable of exaggeration for expressive purposes.*

Once they progress beyond the stage of manipulation, slow learners, like normal children, discover subject matter for expression in their own experiences. Many of the titles they give to their works are little different from those selected by normal children. The titles describe events that occur at home, at school, at play, or in the community. The following are representative:

> We are working in the garden
> Our class went to visit a farm
> I saw a big fire
> I helped my Dad wash the car

Titles such as these are usually selected by those slow learners in the late symbol or preadolescent stage of expression with the highest I.Q.'s. The titles are concise and in most of them the children have identified themselves with their environment. The less able the slow learners, the less inclined they are to relate themselves to the world in which they live. In other words, an ability to identify oneself with the environment seems to vary directly with intelligence.

The themes that many slow learners select are often closely connected with little intimate events in life. A normal child might overlook them, or, having touched on them once or twice, would then find other interests. Many slow learners, on the other hand, seem to find constant interest in pictures of this nature. Some representative titles are as follows:

> I sat on our steps
> The birds are in the trees
> I am walking to school

354

In some of their titles, slow learners seem to place considerable emphasis on authoritarian actions, either their own or those of others. This emphasis may indicate the child's desire to assume command, or conversely to see those in authority as oppressive in a world in which the child finds few opportunities to be a leader. Examples of such an apparently compensatory attitude may be found in the following titles:

The guard is telling those boys when they can cross the street
The soldiers are keeping the kids back as the parade goes by
Dad only lets me decorate the Christmas tree
There were two children in our tree; I told them to come down or
   I would fight them

Frequently, the various objects or actions depicted in the work of slow learners have little or no clear and logical connection. Their titles may illustrate their general inability to organize thoughts or to cope with strong emotional experiences. When the child shows deep concern about the subject matter included in this type of expression, the teacher must take the work especially seriously. The following titles are illustrative of this class of expression:

The car went bang and I was eating candy and then I cried
I wish I had a doll and maybe Lucy is coming over to my house
   and I guess she is mad

In some of their titles, slow learners anticipate future consequences of the actions depicted in their illustrations. Here the statements are usually logical and serve to complete a little story begun in the picture itself. These titles sometimes appear to illustrate the child's confusion between present and future action. The following indicate this form of anticipatory statement:

This boy is going to be hit by a car
This is my uncle; he has a big farm and I am going to visit him
Our school is playing hockey and we are going to win

Like normal children, mentally retarded children frequently like to depict their reactions to vicarious experience, even though they are more attracted to actual experience. Dramatized versions of familiar stories and events shown on the movie or television screen may excite them to visual expression. However, the teacher should, whenever possible, connect the physical experiences of the children and their drawings. Situations that deal with personal accidents ("falling down," "bumping my head") make effective sources for drawing as do activities such as rolling or bouncing balls and using playground equipment. If there is any clear agreement among authorities it is a belief in the need for motor experiences to develop a sense of space and relationships between objects.

Adolescent slow learners with an I.Q. of at least 70, no matter what their grade level, tend to use some of the subject matter found in the art work of the normal adolescent. Their work often exhibits a growing interest in social events at which both sexes are present. Boys, especially, make pictures about sports and sporting contests, deeds of daring, and many kinds of mechanical objects. Considerable attention is often given to anatomical detail of human beings shown in the pictures.

METHODS OF TEACHING

The fact that mental retardation usually affects the whole personality makes the task of the teacher of slow learners difficult. Often, as the result of external pressures, a mentally retarded child suffers from emotional disturbances. Thus each slow learner, not only because of the mental handicap but also because of unfortunate accompaniments, may exhibit behavior that makes extraordinary demands on the teacher's understanding.

To teach slow learners one must possess a number of commendable personal qualities and professional abilities. The teacher must, above all, be patient, for these children progress slowly in their work. The work may be exasperating and discouraging enough to make the life of any but a patient teacher unbearable. The teacher of slow learners must, furthermore, be able to stimulate these children so that they are kept as mentally alert as is possible, while, at the same time, not hurrying them into work beyond their abilities. Finally, the teacher must treat every slow learner as a unique being and not as the possessor of some sort of standard type of personality. The fact that all such pupils suffer from a similar

Figure 13.5   *"Chance"-effect work by a girl, C.A. 11, I.Q. 75, using string dipped in paint and pulled across paper.*

handicap does not mean that they lose identity as individuals. A study of their output in art offers a striking illustration of the fact that the personalities of slow learners differ widely.

Bryant and Schwann were interested in seeing if the design sense of retarded children could be improved, and developed a test to assess sensitivities to five art elements: line, shape, color, value, and texture. Based on these elements, fifteen lessons of half an hour each were provided over a period of time. Their study suggests that children with substandard I.Q.'s (23–80) can learn design concepts through systematic teaching. They discovered that children can

> learn art terminology by direct exposure to concrete objects, which they are able to observe, examine, manipulate, verbalize about, react to, and put together in some artistic way. They can get involved in producing art, which they understand and enjoy. The materials needed in the art lessons do not have to be expensive or elaborate; rather, they can be readily procured from the home, the school supply room, and the local community store.[8]

If the teacher finds in an otherwise normal class one or two particularly slow learners in art who require special attention, this should not create problems. Obviously the teacher should in no way indicate to other members of the class the deficiencies of their mentally retarded classmates. Since all successful teaching in art rests on a methodology that demands that the teacher treat all pupils as individuals, the fact that the slow learners are afforded certain special attentions should in no sense make them unique in the eyes of their fellows. Every child in the class, whether handicapped, normal, or gifted, will require individual treatment. If the teacher is placed in charge of a whole class of slow learners, the same educational principles apply. Although every member of the group is a slow learner, no two children will react in an identical manner to art. Here, as elsewhere, every child must be offered an educational program tailored to individual needs and capacities.

Some teachers of mentally retarded children have been tempted to obtain more skillful-looking results by mechanical busywork. Exercises in tracing, copying, and coloring the work of others constitute one such type of work. Activities involving "chance" techniques constitute another type, and activities that are taught step by step tend also to become busywork.

As stated earlier, the educational values of copying, even for normal children, are dubious; such work is, therefore, not recommended. Copying also interferes with the ability of mentally retarded children to participate in a creative art program. Indeed, research has indicated that undesirable as this busy work may be with normal children, it appears to have even

---

[8]Antusa P. Bryant and Leroy B. Schwann, "Art and Mentally Retarded Children," *Studies in Art Education,* Vol. 12, No. 3 (Spring, 1971), 56.

more inhibiting effects on less robust minds.[9] A child generally does enjoy a certain sense of security in such activities as copying and tracing; however, the teacher who tries to encourage original thinking later will find it difficult to wean the child away from what can only be described as emotional and visual crutches. The benefits to be achieved from approaching art as a thinking, feeling process should be available to children of all mental ages.

Busywork that produces results that are original but derived by chance rather than by planning poses a different educational problem.[10] To include much of this work in the art program for normal children cannot be recommended because it fails to provide the stimulation inherent in creative work. For slow learners, however, these activities may be of some value. Since the mentally handicapped children cannot profit from some of the more difficult activities found in the art program for normal pupils, their program may lack variety unless there is recourse to several chance activities. Although activities that depend on chance are artistically problematic, they may well become artistically acceptable if the pupils gain control of them through experimentation (see Figure 13.5). If the limitations of this kind of work are recognized, it may profitably be included in the art program for slow learners as a means of broadening it. Indeed, chance activities might be occasionally included in the art work of normal pupils, provided they are recognized as having limited value.

Finally, step-by-step teaching practices, while rarely of value to normal pupils because they present no real challenge, may often give the slow learner a valuable and necessary sense of achievement. Frequently this teaching method, if used wisely, may lead slow learners into more creative endeavors.

The approved methods now used with normal children are to a large extent also practical and effective when used with slow learners. The handicapped children, however, require more individual attention than their normal counterparts, and the pace of teaching often has to be slowed. Motivation, classroom arrangements, and appraisal of the effectiveness of the program in progress, nevertheless, require little or no modification in principle when applied to retarded pupils.

Teaching the slow learner does not require as much of a reorientation on the part of the teacher as one might suppose. It does require teaching in concrete terms hence the importance of demonstrating craft processes,

---

[9]Some of the harmful effects of busy work on normal children are outlined in Viktor Lowenfeld, ed., *Workbooks and Art Education,* Research Bulletin of the Eastern Arts Association (Kutztown, Pa.: 1952–53).

For a report on similar effects of this work on slow learners, see C. D. and M. R. Gaitskell, *Art Education for Slow Learners.*

[10]See Carl Reed, *Early Adolescent Art Education* (Peoria, Ill.: Bennett, 1957), which emphasizes chance methods. The same applies to large sections of *A Guide for the Teaching of Art* (San Francisco: San Francisco Unified School District, 1956).

simplifying, slowing down verbal instructions, having the patience to repeat directions, and, above all, breaking down the learning experience into manageable stages. These few suggestions are also recommended for teaching certain types of emotionally and physically handicapped children.

SUITABLE INDIVIDUAL ACTIVITIES

Having discussed the characteristics of slow learners, as well as effective methods of teaching them, we may now consider in detail some art activities especially suitable for them. Most art activities have proved to be sufficiently flexible to be performed by slow learners either in special classes or in regular classrooms. These activities include some types of drawing and painting, some forms of paper and cardboard work, a certain amount of sculpture and pottery, and some types of printing, all of which have been described earlier and hence require only brief mention here. Little additional comment about teaching these activities will be offered since the reader may refer to other chapters where teaching methods were discussed at length.

Other activities, including certain kinds of weaving, stitchery, and bookcraft, are particularly valuable for slow learners. These activities and methods of teaching them are described in some detail below.

Media and Techniques. In drawing and painting, slow learners may use the standard tools and equipment recommended for other pupils. Hence, wax crayons, tempera paint, the usual types of brushes and papers, and so on may be employed. Nearly all slow learners are capable of producing

Basic Activities

Figure 13.6 *"Robin Hood," chalk drawing by a boy, C.A. 11 years, 4 months, I.Q. 65.*

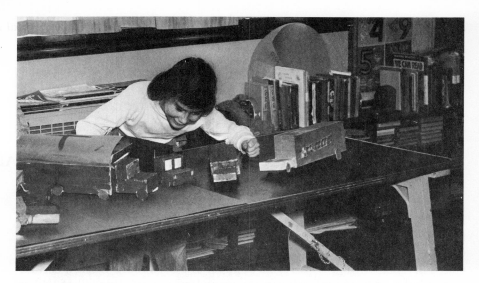

Figure 13.7 *Work in box sculpture by pupils ranging in C.A. from 9 years to 12 years, 5 months and in I.Q. from 60 to 75. (Photo by Royal Studio.)*

creative paper work. Most of these pupils achieve greatest success when cut paper is used as a medium for two-dimensional pictures. Some pupils, however, may begin to build their pictures into three dimensions. Nearly all these children enjoy box sculpture, and many of them seem capable of doing some freestanding paper sculpture. Many slow learners can use molds to make simple masks, and nearly all of them can work successfully with papier-mâché if it is prepared in advance for them.

Carving in wood and other substances is not recommended for most slow learners. The tools required in much of this work are too dangerous for them, and the technique is beyond their ability. Simple forms of modeling and pottery, however, are recommended. The direct nature of modeling pleases these pupils, and the repetitive character of most pottery makes this craft highly suitable. Both stick and vegetable printing are also useful techniques largely because they are repetitive, whereas stencil and linoleum work may be too difficult to master.

Teaching. With all the basic activities mentioned above the teacher of slow learners must modify classroom techniques to suit the creative abilities of these pupils. A step-by-step approach becomes necessary not only in the work itself but also in the selection of tools and media. If their I.Q. scores fall below 70, preadolescent slow learners usually experience difficulty when confronted by a wide range of color or by the problems of mixing tints, shades, and even secondary hues. The teacher will therefore often find it necessary to supply all colors ready-mixed. Chalk and charcoal also create difficulties for many of these slow learners, as does the mixing of media.

360

When three-dimensional work such as pottery or box sculpture is being taught to slow learners, the teacher would be wise to analyze the process from start to finish in terms of separate operations. Then, before the pupils begin work, they should be shown a finished object so that they know what to expect at the end of their work. After that, however, demonstrations and general teaching should be performed only in relation to one operation at a time. The pupils should select the tools only for the one operation, complete the operation, and then return the tools. This process should then be repeated until all the necessary operations have been mastered.

The length of each operation depends on the class. Pupils of lower I.Q. scores are able to master only very short and simple operations. Perhaps the greatest challenge facing the teacher of slow learners is to judge correctly the length and complexity of a unit of work so that each pupil is stimulated but not confused. An example of a step-by-step analysis of work is set forth in the section that follows.

Media and Techniques. To replace some of the activities that slow learners may have difficulty with, one may turn to certain weaving techniques. Because weaving is an extremely flexible technique and depends largely on a repetition of movement, it is especially suitable for slow learners.

Card-Loom Weaving

The process called "card-loom weaving" allows children to produce a number of practical articles such as mats or baskets without too much difficulty. To make a container, for example, one should draw on fairly heavy cardboard a circle having a radius of 3 to 6 inches and inside that circle, a smaller circle having half that radius. Spokes about three-quarters of an inch to 1 inch wide should be drawn from the circumference of the smaller circle to the circumference of the larger circle. A space about one-eighth of an inch wide should be left between the spokes. It is recommended that an uneven number of spokes be drawn at first. The space between the spokes should be cut out and the spokes should then be bent upward (see Figure 13.8).

Weaving may now begin with wool, string, or raffia—a grasslike substance having a long fiber. Starting from the base circle, the weaving material is simply taken over one spoke and under the next until each is entirely covered except for about one-quarter of an inch of cardboard at the outside extremity of the spokes. This may be doubled over from the inside to the outside to form an edge to the container. Any ends of weaving material that are sticking out should be cut off.

To finish the base of the article, one may glue felt to the center, both on the inside and the outside. The base may also be woven. With a large needle, one takes one strip of weaving material from the inside extremity

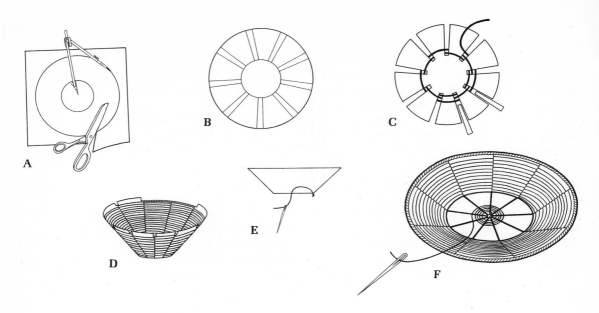

Figure 13.8 *Processes in card-loom weaving:* (**A**) *drawing and cutting the cardboard base,* (**B**) *marking the spokes,* (**C**) *weaving,* (**D**) *finishing the rim of the basket,* (**E**) *sewing in strips of material for weaving base, and* (**F**) *weaving the base.*

of each spoke to the center of the base; over-and-under weaving may then be done with the needle. This technique may be used, of course, only in a basket with an uneven number of spokes. The rim of the article may be finished by binding the edge with the same material as was used for weaving. If holes are first pierced through the edge of the spokes before binding begins, the task will be easier. Binding is done by sewing over and over the edge.

To make a mat, one should cut a circle of cardboard of convenient size, and then cut out a small circle from the center of the cardboard. The rim of the cardboard should be notched; then the weaving material is looped repeatedly from the rim to the center of the cardboard. Binding the edge in the manner mentioned above completes the mat.

Many slow learners will eventually be able to try some simple experiments with card-loom weaving. Various colors of weaving material may first be introduced; later perhaps, material with a variety of both texture and color might be used. The shape of the cardboard might be altered; an oval may be used instead of a circle. An even number of spokes may be used, in which case two weaving materials of different colors can be used simultaneously to produce an interesting design. Handles for objects can be made by running a strand of weaving material over and under three long strands of the same material. Such handles may be attached merely by sewing.

Teaching. Suppose the teacher plans to have a class of very slow-learning pupils make woven containers. To arouse interest and to make sure that all members of the class realize what the finished object should look like, the teacher exhibits and talks about three containers. These objects are finished identically at the edges and centers but are made in different colors. The following separate operations and demonstrations are considered to be necessary for this group of children.[11]

OPERATION A. *Preparing the cards*

Demonstration 1. Obtain cards, scissors, and compasses
2. Describe inner and outer circles; cut away excess cardboard
3. Draw spokes
4. Cut away cardboard between spokes

OPERATION B. *Weaving*

Demonstration 1. Select weaving material
2. Begin weaving
3. Weave
4. Finish weaving

OPERATION C. *Finishing center*

Demonstration 1. Obtain felt and glue jar containing brush
2. Measure center with compasses, transferring measurements to paper; cut out paper as guide for cutting felt; cut felt
3. Glue cut felt to center
4. Return compasses

OPERATION D. *Finishing edge*

Demonstration 1. Obtain large needle and binding material
2. Pierce cardboard
3. Sew edge over and over
4. Sew between spokes, through weaving material
5. Finish binding, knotting, and cutting material

OPERATION E. *Returning all tools*
(no demonstration, but verbal reminder to be orderly)

OPERATION F. *Picking up scraps and general tidying up*
(no demonstration, but verbal request to do a good job)

In another class the teacher might combine some operations, should the intelligence of pupils allow this. Also, more choice in materials and techniques might be permitted.

----

[11]This lesson was planned for a class of boys, I.Q. range 50 to 70, C.A. range 11 years to 15 years, 5 months.

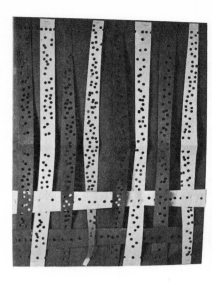

Figure 13.9 *Slow learners might profit from experimenting with paper weaving. A hole puncher was used to decorate these strips of colored paper. (Photo by Rick Steadry.)*

Box-Loom Weaving

Media and Techniques. The more advanced preadolescent slow learners—usually those who score over 70 on an I.Q. test—are able to weave successfully on a simple "cradle" or "box" loom. The loom is so simply constructed that the pupils may easily make it themselves. It consists of what look like two sets of miniature goal posts joined by four dowel rods, which can be made from old broom handles. At one end of the apparatus, slots should be made in the posts for a tension bar (see Figure 13.10).

Three items of equipment are required before weaving can begin. The first of these is what is called a "heddle." This is a frame of metal or wood about the same width as the loom, containing bars pierced by holes. The heddle is the mechanism that allows the cross threads to be put through the warp threads. Since heddles are made with considerable precision, they must be bought rather than made by the pupils. Most school-supply firms sell heddles of various sizes, with differing numbers of bars to the inch. The number of bars determines the texture of the woven cloth. The second item is called a "shuttle." This is a flat piece of wood with notches cut at each end to hold the weaving material, which is wound lengthwise around it. Pupils will find it a simple matter to make shuttles. The third item is known as a "warping frame," a piece of wood with a nail at each end. It is used to measure yarn, and can be made by the pupils.

The first step in the actual weaving process is to mount on the loom the threads running lengthwise (called the warp threads) and at the same time to thread the heddle. To make the warp threads the pupil must first tie the weaving material to one nail on the warping frame and wind several turns around both nails. Then, with a pair of scissors, the threads should be cut where they meet one of the nails, thus providing a number of warp threads of equal and correct length. The mounting of the warp threads and the simultaneous threading of the heddle may now begin. First the tension bar should be placed in the slots at one end of the loom.

364

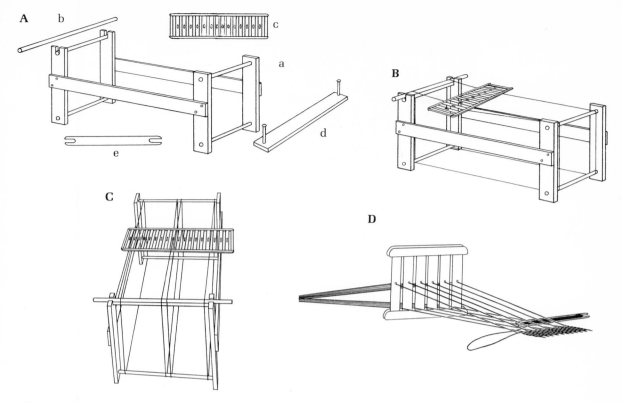

Figure 13.10 **(A)** *The equipment needed for box-loom weaving: the loom itself (a), showing the tension bar separate (b), the heddle (c), the warping frame (d), and the shuttle (e).* **(B)** *The loom with the tension bar in place and the heddle resting on the supporting threads.* **(C)** *The first two warp threads in place.* **(D)** *The shuttle passing through the warp threads.*

Next, two strings should be tied from the ends of the top dowels, so that the pupil may rest the heddle on them. Next, taking one warp thread already prepared on the warping frame, the pupil passes it through the center hole of the heddle and around all the dowel rods and the tension bar of the loom. The ends of this encircling warp thread should be tied together at the top dowel rod opposite the end supporting the tension bar. This process must be repeated with another warp thread, this time passing the thread through the adjoining space on the heddle instead of through the hole. The pupil must continue to thread the loom in this fashion, working on each side of the center of the heddle and passing the warp threads alternately, first through a hole in the heddle and then through a space, until the desired width of the material to be woven is reached. The function of the heddle will now be clear. By either pulling up or depressing the heddle, the pupil will observe that "sheds" are made, through which the shuttle may be thrust with the cross weaver or "weft" thread (see Figure 13.10).

To weave, the pupil should first wind the yarn thread around the shuttle. Then the heddle should be raised and the shuttle passed through the shed on the near side of the heddle. With the heddle, the weft thread should then be pressed to the end of the loom (beaten) toward the operator. Next, the pupil must press the heddle down and again pass the shuttle through the shed. This process is continued with the sheds being formed by the alternate raising and lowering of the heddle, the shuttle going from side to side, until the desired length of cloth is produced.

A certain degree of skill is necessary, of course, to perform well on a loom. The weft threads must be placed at equal distances from each other. If they are beaten too vigorously with the heddle, the weaving will be bulky. If the weft is not pressed closely enough, the cloth will be flimsy in places. Again, skill is required to keep the edges of the woven material straight and tidy. If the weft thread is pulled too tight, the edge will have a wave; if the weft is not pulled tight enough, the edge will display unsightly little loops. Difficult though the skill of weaving may appear to the beginner, the technique can soon be mastered satisfactorily on the loom described above.

Once the learners have developed an ability to use this loom, they will no doubt become very fond of weaving, and may wish to make articles such as scarves or place mats requiring the full length of the warp thread. In such cases, they must learn to move the weaving around the loom so that they may continue to use the heddle in its normal place. To move the weaving, they need merely to remove the tension bar, and then, using the heddle, to ease the woven material around the dowel rods until only warp threads are visible. After they have replaced the tension bar, they may continue weaving as described previously.

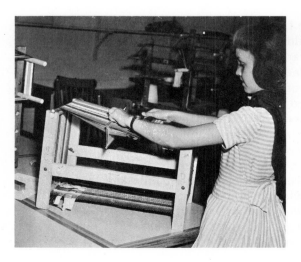

Figure 13.11 *Weaving on a box loom. (Photo by Royal Studio.)*

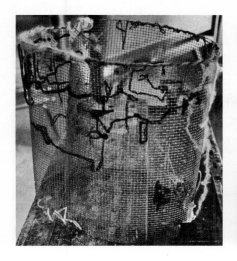

Figure 13.12 *The environment provides many opportunities for unusual forms of weaving to which slow learners will respond. A cylinder of wire mesh permits circular weaving patterns, and an unused entranceway allows the creation of string and yarn patterns on a grand scale. Screweyes were placed at 1-inch intervals along the sides and top of the door frame. (Photos by Rick Steadry.)*

To finish the edges of an article after they have cut it from the loom, the pupils may knot together the warp threads by twos and then trim the strands to form a fringe. To make the edge more secure, they may also sew the last two or three strands of weft to the warp threads.

Experimentation in weaving is within the capabilities of many slow learners. Although 4-ply wool is perhaps the best material with which to learn weaving, various types of both warp and weft material may eventually be used. Interesting patterns may be developed by using materials of different colors and textures.

Teaching. Before slow learners are taught to weave on a loom the teacher should analyze the operations and list the demonstrations as was done above for card-weaving.

Loom-weaving creates storage problems, since both the loom and the wool are bulky. These problems may be partially solved by having collapsible looms that can be dismantled when not in use. Another solution to the difficulty, of course, is to have only a few looms that are used by the pupils on a rotation basis.

Good weaving depends on the tension of the strands. One learns to control tension largely through feeling, in the same way that one learns to skate or ride a bicycle. Before attempting to teach, the teacher should practice maintaining an even tension until it is almost automatic. Because each type of loom has its own peculiarities, the teacher should practice on the type of loom that the pupils will use. As each step of setting up the loom is taught, the teacher should inspect the assembly of every pupil. The warp threads should be tapped with the palm of the hand to see that each strand is secure and that tension is right. The tension should be such that tapping the threads causes a vigorous rebound of the hand.

When everything is ready for weaving, the teacher can often help

Figure 13.13 *In this excellently appointed art room slow learners have ample space to explore the possibilities afforded by weaving, stitchery, and knitting. (Photo by Bradford Herzog.)*

slow learners by standing behind them, lightly holding their hands, and going through the motions of using heddle and shuttle until the pupils can acquire the correct rhythmic motion.[12]

Stitchery

Media and Techniques. Another activity that need not be confined to slow learners but is especially suitable for them because of its repetitious character is stitchery. Stitchery need not mean commercially stamped products depicting old-fashioned ladies or forget-me-nots; it can be as stimulating and original as many other contemporary art forms. In one form or another stitchery is popular with children in all grades. The products of their work can be purely decorative, such as wall hangings, or they can be practical, such as pillow covers, purses, and aprons. The subject matter of the designs may be nonobjective or representational. Appliqué techniques are also possible with stitches. Stitchery is a good activity for a group or for the individual child.

To a large extent this activity makes use of scrap materials. Cotton and burlap are very good materials on which to work. If colored burlap is not available, potato or apple sacks will do just as well. Needles may be purchased in almost any five-and-ten-cent store, as may embroidery cottons in many colors. Yarns in different weights and colors add variety to the work.

Many kinds of stitches are used in this activity, among them the simple running stitch and the more complicated stitches such as the blanket, buttonhole, chain, daisy, outline, and feather stitches (see Figure

[12]Recommended references for weaving are Harriette J. Brown, *Handweaving: For Pleasure and Profit* (New York: Harper & Row, 1952), and Mary Kirby, *Designing on the Loom* (New York: Viking, 1955).

13.14).[13] The design, which can be planned in advance or created on the cloth, is outlined with a simple stitch, and areas are given texture with the more complicated stitches. Buttons, beads, and brightly colored felts may be incorporated into the design for accents. As in any design, too many conflicting patterns in the same piece should be avoided; it is advisable to work for a few "balances"—line and mass, pattern and solid, large and small. When the work is completed, it may be mounted in a picture frame for display.

Teaching. The most practical way to teach stitchery is to treat it as a form of picture-making. With the simple materials mentioned above, even mentally retarded children may immediately set to work. There is no need at first to show them a number of complicated stitches, because what is known as the "running stitch" comes quite naturally to them. Mariska Karasz says:

> If you have ever held a needle in your hand you know how to do this stitch without being told. It . . . consists simply of running the needle in and out through the fabric at fairly regular intervals. It is the simplest kind of stitch with which to draw a line or outline a shape. But you will be missing its best use if you don't try it also as a filler.[14]

Thus, children may use the needle directly as a means of expression. After

[13] A good introductory booklet on embroidery is Mildred Ryan, *Needlecraft Handbook* (New York: Arco, 1954). A good general source book is Lili Blumeneau, *Creative Design in Wall Hangings* (New York: Crown, 1967).
[14] "Creative Arts of the Needle," *House Beautiful,* January 1952, p. 85.

Figure 13.14 *Diagrams of some embroidery stitches:* (**A**) *one kind of running stitch,* (**B**) *blanket stitch,* (**C**) *buttonhole stitch,* (**D**) *feather stitch,* (**E**) *daisy stitch,* (**F**) *cross stitch,* (**G**) *chain stitch, and* (**H**) *long and short stitch.*

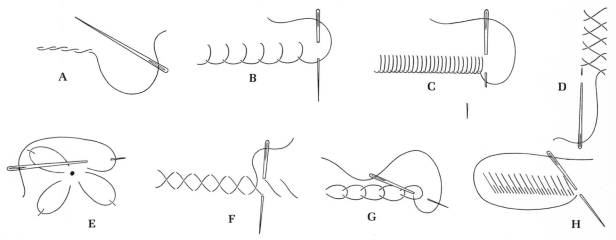

Figure 13.15 *Stitchery, for slow and normal learners, begins with line, as another form of drawing. Grade 2.*

selecting their cotton or burlap background material, they may start working without drawing lines. When they have gained experience in the technique, they might later sketch some ideas in pencil before they begin the actual stitchery. After this they may be taught the more complicated stitches, some of which are rather easy to learn.

Slow learners have little difficulty in acquiring the skills needed for stitchery and are generally very creative in this activity. They can experiment with using threads and backgrounds of varying colors, weights, and textures, or explore the potentialities of a newly discovered stitch.

The pedagogical case for weaving and stitchery has been stated by Schill and Abrams in their discussion of the role of manipulation of media in teaching retarded children.[15] They state:

> Various forms of conceptual thinking can be initiated for these children through art. Color, perception, size and shape discrimination and light and dark, over and under, around and through, and numerous others can be integrated into the total art program. However, the retarded child will not develop them unless they are consciously and overtly taught.

[15]Abrams and Schill "Art in Special Education," p. 164.

370

"Conscious" and "overt" teaching, as has been stated, imply simplification, concrete presentation, and above all, repetition.

Media and Techniques. Bookcraft has been mentioned as one possibility for group work. But it is also suitable as an individual activity for children of all ages. Most slow learners can learn to make books, which may be used as attractive scrapbooks or notebooks, with decorated covers and end pages. Much of this work appeals to slow learners because the techniques used to decorate the books are simple and yet result in quite spectacular designs.

Bookcraft

First, the pupil decorates the front and back of the cover paper. This may be done by stick or vegetable printing, finger painting, or some "chance" effects. Some of the techniques depending on chance are as follows.[16]

1. Tempera colors are splashed over paper that has been dampened with water. The colors will run and blend in a pleasing manner.
2. A few drops of thin oil paint of various colors are placed in a shallow pan of water. By gently blowing on the surface of the water, the pupils develop a swirling pattern of color. Paper should then be slipped into the water at one end of the pan, submerged completely, and then raised gently. The oil paint will adhere to the paper to form a unique pattern.
3. A toothbrush loaded with tempera paint is held over a sheet of

[16]These techniques are also suitable for producing gift-wrapping papers or for backgrounds for various forms of printing.

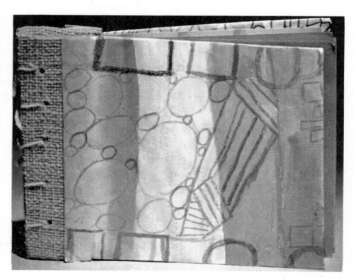

Figure 13.16 *In this open-fold book made by a slow learner several materials were used. Yarn holds the spine in place; heavy cloth remnant and a crayon and watercolor resist provide the cover decoration. Both the picture and cloth were pasted to heavy cardboard backing with white plastic glue. The book contains prints made by the pupil's classmates.*

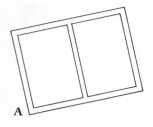

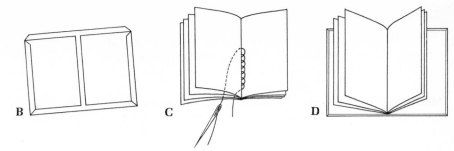

Figure 13.17 *Processes in making a simple booklet: (A) placing cardboard on treated cover paper, (B) mitering and folding the cover paper, and (C) sewing the page inserts. The finished booklet is shown in D.*

paper. Using a scraper such as a knife, the pupils draw the blade toward themselves over the toothbrush, thereby spraying the paper. Several colors may be used. This technique can be controlled by using a "mask," or covering paper, to block off areas where the spray is not desired.

4. Tempera paint in two or more colors is placed thickly on paper. The sheet is folded in half with the painted surface inside. When drawn apart, the paper displays a bisymmetrical pattern.

To make the cover of the book, pupils place the prepared cover paper on the desk, with the reverse side of the cover paper facing them. Next they cut a sheet of stiff cardboard slightly smaller than the cover sheet. They then cut the cardboard into two pieces of equal size and lay the two pieces side by side over the cover paper, leaving a small gap between them to form the spine of the book. The cardboard and cover paper are pasted together; the corners are carefully folded and, if the pupils are capable of doing so, mitered (see Figure 13.17). The pupils then fold the edges of the cover paper over the cardboard.

To prepare the inside of the book, sheets of paper about one-quarter of an inch smaller than the cover are folded to form pages. These are lightly stitched together with a needle and thread along their spine. The front and back pages of this assembly are then pasted and pressed to the covers. To complete the book, the pupil may shellac the cover.

Many other types of bookcraft are possible, of course, but most of them are too exacting to be considered for slow learners.[17]

Teaching. Although the exact steps of making a book must be taught to slow learners, the teacher can employ a creative approach both in the "chance" effects of decorating paper and to some extent in the actual making of the book. The techniques leading to a chance pattern should be demonstrated one at a time so that the pupils will not become confused

[17]The following references are recommended: Chris Groneman, *General Bookbinding* (New York: Taplinger, 1958); Lawrence Town, *Bookbinding by Hand* (New York: Pitman, 1952); Douglas Cockerell, *Bookbinding and the Care of Books,* 5th ed. (New York: Pitman, 1953).

by a multiplicity of materials and ways of using them. Maximum and minimum size limits for the book should be established, but the pupils can decide on the exact dimensions they want to use within those limitations.

SUITABLE GROUP ACTIVITIES

Whether in special classes comprising only slow learners, or in classes in which there are only one or two slow learners, the mentally retarded require thoughtful consideration when group activities take place.

Most retarded pupils have difficulty participating in class or group art activities largely because of considerable differences to be found in the mental and chronological ages of individual members of the group, even among pupils in special classes for the retarded. Group activity presents many difficulties for normal people; for the mentally retarded,

Figure 13.18 *A quasi-group activity suitable for slow learners is the making of a tapestry. Each pupil contributes his own square of weaving. All the pieces are then sewn together and attached to a frame.*

who have usually suffered to some extent from frustrations in life and hence are often emotionally volatile, the group activity must be very carefully chosen and supervised if it is to succeed.

A highly recommended group activity for classes of slow learners is puppetry. This activity allows the child to work both as an individual and as a member of a group. Only the simplest of puppets described in Chapter 12 need be made for a successful group performance. Stick and fist puppets are suitable for most slow learners, but string puppets are beyond their ability to build or to manipulate. The child's own symbols, cut in cardboard and tacked to sticks, or doll-like creatures made from old socks or paper bags and manipulated with the fingers, will serve as suitable characters for a play. A large cardboard carton provides a simple stage. The spoken lines and the action of the play may be derived from a well-liked story or based on some experience in the children's lives.

Because mural-making demands a high level of group cooperation and organization, this activity as handled in conventional situations is not generally recommended for slow learners. The quasi-group activity, however, in which the general plan is discussed and decided on by a group but in which each child works independently on a section of the display, is more practical for slow learners, as it is for young children. Slow learners may not be able to grasp the design concept of a mural, nor is it important that they do. What they do know is that working on a large scale is a pleasurable experience. Many partly cooperative activities of this type may be carried out in clay or in other modeling or building materials, including empty boxes and odd pieces of wood. A service station, a farm, a village, or a playground are subjects that slow learners might be interested in developing.

When only one or two noticeably slow learners are found in a class of normal children, the difficulties arising from group work are greater, since these pupils must participate and attempt to hold their own with their classmates. The problem of having these pupils purposefully occupied is not too great when the whole class is engaged in a group activity such as puppetry. That activity involves a variety of tasks, such as assembling the stage or hemming curtains, to which slow workers can contribute if given some guidance. In the more difficult activities involving only a few major tasks, such as, say, mural-making, the slow learners' relative lack of ability tends to become conspicuous. Obviously they cannot be asked to do only such menial jobs as washing brushes or cleaning paint tins. They must be given more important jobs if they are to retain their self-respect.

A solution some teachers have found is to arrange privately with one of the more intelligent and sympathetic class members who have been chosen as leaders to elect a slow learner to the team. This leader provides the slow learner with some aspect of the drawing and painting and coaches and supervises the slow learner carefully. The contribution of the slow learner in the mural activity may range from filling in areas of color, outlining areas, creating repeat borders—tasks that can be undertaken with the knowledge that they contribute materially to the activity.

THE VALUE OF ART EDUCATION FOR SLOW LEARNERS

Slow learners will display difficulty in working on some art projects, especially those that involve a high risk of failure. Nevertheless, wherever possible they must be stimulated by work of a creative nature rather than lulled by copy work. Most art activities are sufficiently flexible to engage their attention profitably.

Many teachers feel that process-oriented activities provide the slow learner with much needed specific, concrete operations. Schaefer-Simmern's comments on the learning process of the mentally retarded may have some relevance here. He states: "Creating order and organization in the realm of concrete, visual experience is a discipline thoroughly suited to the nature of mentally defective individuals. . . . These patients who are taught embroidery, weaving, rug making and the like, often surprise one with the accurateness of their work." [18] Schaefer-Simmern also cautions against falling into the trap of providing such children with packaged designs, stating that "for the sake of their inner stability and satisfaction, for the sake of their own enjoyment in the realization of their own world, they should be led to create their own cultural pattern."

For this reason the activities involving fabric design and construction have been left to this chapter. It must be remembered, however, that bright children, in their own way, gain even more from weaving or stitchery than do slow learners. One difference between the two groups is that slow learners have a tendency to enjoy an activity for the pleasure of the process, whereas the above-average child uses technical knowledge more readily as a means to an end. In addition, the bright child has a greater ability to pursue and develop ideas in art activity. The bright child can, moreover, deal consciously with the problems of design.

Art education may have considerable significance in the general education of most slow learners. There is wide agreement that a child who is adversely affected in one area of personality is likely to be adversely affected in other areas. It is reasonable to suppose that this process could operate in reverse, and that a slow learner who profits from art activities might undergo desirable changes in personality. Whatever progress in art is made by slow learners depends primarily on the patience and sympathetic understanding of their teacher.

The gains to be derived for slow learners working in art may be summarized by the following six points:

[18] *The Unfolding of Artistic Activity,* p. 187.

Figure 13.19 *The art room of the Dr. Francis Perkins School can serve as a model for children in any school situation. Here one pupil works on a loom while another is at a printing press. (Photo by Bradford Herzog.)*

1. Through art activity slow learners may create a product that is not necessarily inferior to that of their neighbors. Their efforts need not suffer by comparison.
2. The process of concept-formation through symbolization takes place for slow learners as it does for average and above-average children. Through art, slow learners can present ideas that may be denied expression because of limited ability in handling language skills.
3. For the trained observer, the drawings of slow learners may provide diagnostic clues to emotional difficulties that sometimes accompany retardation.
4. Art activity can function as therapy, providing a source of satisfaction and stability to children who have a history of failure.
5. Working in art provides vital sensory and motor experiences that involve the total mental and physical capabilities of the workers. The integration of physical and mental operations in turn facilitates the union of thought and feeling. In this respect, art serves the same unifying function for subnormal children that it does for normal ones.
6. Artistic activity provides slow learners with experience in decision-making and problem-solving—socially useful skills.

OTHER KINDS OF HANDICAPS

Although this chapter has concentrated on art and retardation, teachers may be faced with other kinds of handicaps as children with disabilities are moved from special learning situations into the regular classroom. Teachers cannot be expected to become instant authorities in the many problems that may confront them, but a study of the following chart may

Table 13.2

SUGGESTED TEACHING METHODS FOR VARIOUS HANDICAPPED LEARNERS

Identification	Characteristics	Appropriate Approach	Suggested Activities
Mentally Retarded	Slower to learn and to perform. Short attention span, impaired self-image. Limited spatial perception. Difficulty in socialization. Lack of desire for experimentation. Poor body awareness.	Overteaching and repetition. Specific instruction in specific skills. Regular follow-up is imperative. Simplification of concepts and skills in lessons. Gradual addition of steps in sequential order.	Direct manipulation of materials: finger paint, fabrics, clay, and so on. Body sensory awareness through motion and tactile experiences. Simple puppets (paper bag, paper plate, sock). Unconventional media (shaving cream, vanilla pudding, chocolate syrup) on formica surfaces. Painting on a mirror. Self-adornment (costumes, hats, jewelry, body paint). Thickened tempera paint (with soap flakes). Sand casting, Play Dough, simple weaving, papier mâché. Tactile boards and boxes. Junk and body printing. Constructions, stuffed shapes.
Physically Impaired (blind or partially sighted)	Limited or no visual field. Uncomfortable in unfamiliar physical setting. Difficulty in perceiving total image. Learn through tactile experiences. Lack of environmental awareness.	Organize materials so child has same place to work each time. Develop familiarity with environment. Develop tactile sense to the fullest. Develop sense of rhythm, patterns, motion sequencing, body awareness, and sense of space.	Tactile experiences. Matching and sorting textures, texture boards, texture walls, aprons with textures. Feely boxes. Clay. Collages of wide range of textures. Sand casting. Construction and junk sculpture. All tactile media as above. Weaving, macramé. Shape discrimination games.
Perceptually Handicapped (extreme reading disability)	Lack of form discrimination. Lack of spacial orientation. Hyperactive, especially in periods of frustration. Poor eye-hand coordination. Impaired visual reception. Poor kinesthetic performance. Distractable. Failure syndrome.	Keep visual distraction to a minimum. Repetition. Develop sense of rhythm, pattern, motion.	Body awareness exercises, calisthenics and movement to music. Sequencing activities. Matching colors, sizes, shapes. Letter, number, and shape collages. Use of tactile media to develop eye-hand coordination. Construction. Hammer and nail letters. Pencil drawings. Drama, puppetry. Stuffed letters.
Deaf or Partially Deaf	Limited language. Difficulty in communication. Lack of conceptual language. Limited environmental	Develop nonverbal communication. Instruct through demonstration and illustration of work. Emphasize visual and	Drawing or painting based on bodily movements. Drawing on blackboard. Any activity based on clear, well-trained

Table 13.2 cont.

Identification	Characteristics	Appropriate Approach	Suggested Activities
Deaf or Partially Deaf cont.	awareness. Tend to withdraw. Difficult to motivate.	tactile experiences. Develop sense of rhythm, pattern, motion, sequencing, body awareness, and space.	demonstration by teacher (clay, sculpture, collage, and so on). Color discrimination. Weaving, sewing. Printing, painting.
Orthopedic Problems (cerebral palsy)	Spastic, rigid, jerky, involuntary movement. Impaired eye-hand coordination, impaired speech and general communication. Lack of muscular control.	Extend art time. Secure materials and sufficient space. Teach through actual manipulation, direct tactile experiences before using tools. Build up handles on tools with plasticene or foam rubber. Attach drawing instruments to wrists.	Built-up felt tip pens provide emphatic lines and bright colors. Thickened tempera paint. All tactile media as above. Water play. Any activity that uses the hands and body in a physiotherapeutic manner.
Emotionally Disturbed	Short attention span and easily distracted. Failure syndrome. Lack of self-confidence. Hyperactive. Poor self-image. Egocentric.	Create a code of acceptable behavior. Limits are imperative. Provide security through repetition of activities and single tasks. Experiences should be "open." Encourage expression of feelings.	Stuffing precut shapes. Making media such as Play Dough, papier mâché pulp. Construction (glued). Body awareness. Costumes and puppets. Painting. All tactile media as above. Water play. Paint with thickened paint. Book making.

provide a guideline for beginning to deal with some of the problems that may arise. This chart was organized by a group of art teachers who were interested in preparing themselves for those exceptional children they might be teaching the following year. The chart, while incomplete, reflects not only their own experience and judgment, but that of others cited in the bibliography. It can also provide readers with a format within which to add their own observations and findings.

ACTIVITIES FOR THE READER

1. Collect drawings and paintings done by slow learners in various grades and with various I.Q.'s. Compare the work of each group of slow learners with that of a group of normal children (a) in corresponding grades and (b) having corresponding chronological ages. List the differences between the work of slow learners and that of normal pupils in each instance.
2. Compare the work habits of the slow learners with those of the normal pupils in the instances described in the activity above.
3. From a collection of work by slow learners select pieces of art having some pleasing aesthetic qualities. How would the number of pieces

selected compare with the number obtained from a collection of equal size comprising the work of normal children in corresponding stages? List some of the chief characteristics of the work chosen from the slow learners' collection.

4. Make a list of titles that slow learners give to their drawings and paintings. Can you give any explanations for the titles?

5. Describe the personal characteristics of a teacher of slow learners whom you know well.

6. In preparing to teach a class of slow-learning boys and girls (I.Q. range 50 to 70, C.A. range 11 to 15), analyze the *operations* and *demonstrations* considered necessary for successful outcome of each of the following activities: (a) making a rolled-paper animal; (b) making a small clay bowl by the coil method; (c) making a tempera painting.

7. Build a small box loom as described in this chapter and, using heavy weaving material, weave two place mats.

8. On a piece of burlap or cotton about 12 inches square, create a non-objective design in stitchery. Using a lightweight cotton and a running stitch, make an interesting line arrangement that has a variety of enclosed areas. Using wools, cottons, and yarns of different weights and colors, create textural effects in some of the outlined areas. If you are satisfied with your work, frame it under glass as you would a drawing.

9. Using materials similar to those suggested in 8, above, make a represen-tational picture in stitchery. Choose subject matter from life, such as a still life or landscape.

10. Observe an art class that has one or two slow learners at work on group activities. Note the techniques used to assist the slow learners. Describe any opportunities missed to help the handicapped children. Suggest practical steps that might have been taken to assist them.

Precocity of drawing and design mark this view of an art lesson as the work of a gifted child. (Eleven-year-old Japanese boy.)

ART ACTIVITIES FOR GIFTED CHILDREN

While every child, regardless of where he stands in his development, should first of all be considered as an individual, the gifted child makes us doubly aware of this responsibility. In fact, his highly developed sensitivity within his special field of interest not only makes him often appear different from others but may also keep him from participating in general activities less important to him. To do justice to the gifted child is not only vital to this society, but is an important educational principle.*

In considering the gifted or talented child[1] we are confronted with something of an educational mystery. Strangely enough for a society that looks to the gifted for its leaders, the gifted child was until recently perhaps the most neglected of all types in the public schools. This neglect cannot be excused on the grounds that gifted children are able to make satisfactory progress without help. On the contrary, there is much evidence that cases of failure, delinquency, laziness, and general maladjustment easily occur among gifted children as a result of educational neglect.[2] Since the Sputnik crisis in 1957 the lot of the academically talented has improved through the addition of special programs, grouping arrangements, the reorganization of faculty into teams, teaching aids, and paraprofessionals. The child who is gifted in art, however, is to a large extent still not adequately provided for.

A cautionary note must be sounded at this point. Even if artistically talented children are singled out and supported, it must be recognized

---

*From Viktor Lowenfeld and W. Lambert Brittain, *Creative and Mental Growth*, 4th ed., p. 384. Copyright, The Macmillan Company, 1947, 1952, 1957, 1964. Used by permission.

[1] In some educational writing "gifted" refers to children with a high general intelligence, while "talented" refers to a special capability in one field of endeavor. This differentiation of meaning is by no means universal and has not been adopted here. In this chapter the words are used interchangeably.

[2] An excellent general reference is Paul Witty, ed., *The Gifted Child* (Boston: Heath, 1953).

that discontent may yet arise. The intensity of the children's preoccupation with art may lead them to view other school obligations in a negative light, and the fact that they are singled out for attention may cause them to withdraw from art activity. De Francesco cautions against "exhibitionism, exploitation, and pressures. Public performances for their own sake . . . contests," while at the same time pointing to existing "inadequacy of the regular instruction, or even of the special instruction." [3]

Art educators have ambivalent attitudes regarding the gifted in art. An examination of art education literature shows that many writers do not even discuss the gifted. There is, undoubtedly, a mystique surrounding artistic talent. Even the students, echoing the attitudes of their parents, may profess to have misgivings about art activity, protesting to the teacher that "I can't draw a straight line," or "I'm no artist." It is important that students, administrators, and the public alike recognize the fact that all children are capable of creative activity, and that the benefits obtained from the study of visual things should be available to all children. It is desirable, therefore, that not too much fuss be made over the gifted, who constitute a relatively small minority among those studying art. But talent does exist, manifesting itself as early as the kindergarten; when it shows itself the teacher should be prepared to deal with it constructively.

This chapter deals with three main topics: how to identify the gifted children, how best to educate them, and what art experiences they should have. Connected with each of these topics are problems as yet unsolved, but recent research offers at least partial solutions for them. [4] The educational and artistic importance of arriving at satisfactory solutions to these problems will be realized when one considers that on this solution probably depends the blossoming of much talent that otherwise might never be developed.

IDENTIFYING THE GIFTED CHILD

It seems to be more difficult to identify the artistically gifted child than the generally gifted. With the latter, investigators can rely to a very large extent on the I.Q. scores that the pupils make. [5] The determination of artistic talent is not so simple. While the results of one study indicate that every child who seems to be gifted in art also scores above average

[3] Italo de Francesco, *Art Education: Its Means and Ends* (New York: Harper & Row, 1958), p. 404.

[4] Betty Lark-Horovitz, Hilda Present Lewis, and Mark Luca, *Understanding Children's Art for Better Teaching* (Columbus, Ohio: Merrill, 1967), offers the reader forty-two research references in Chapter 6, "The Exceptional Child." See also Robert J. Havighurst, Eugene Stivers, and Robert F. De Haan, *A Survey of the Education of Gifted Children* (Chicago: University of Chicago Press, 1955).

[5] Among psychologists, L. M. Terman applied the term "gifted" to all those with I.Q.'s of 140 or over; L. S. Hollingworth suggested 130; H. H. Goddard, 120.

Figure 14.1 *A sixth-grade boy drew this fruit stall. His pencil drawing is an example of acute observation and very personal handling of the medium.*

on I.Q. tests, not every child with a high I.Q. score possesses artistic talent.[6] Some, indeed, with exceptionally high I.Q.'s appear to be lacking in even normal artistic skills and sensibilities.[7]

One of the greatest difficulties in discovering artistic talent arises from the fact that no reliable measures exist to judge either art production or appreciation. Whatever beliefs we may hold about a particular child's abilities in art are necessarily based on personal appraisal rather than on data gathered objectively (see Chapter 18). Most experts hold that subjective appraisals are not so important in such academic fields as reading, spelling, and number work, where certain fundamental abilities may evidently be measured fairly accurately and, as a consequence, talent in them identified. One suspects, however, that the expressive and appreciative aspects of even these academic fields are no more amenable to a reliable measurement than they are in art.

Since most teachers depend on purely subjective means to identify artistically talented youngsters, their estimate of the children's artistic future can be relied on only with reservations. Nevertheless, the pooled

[6] In the classes sponsored by Ontario Department of Education, the lowest I.Q. among the children gifted in art was 112; the lowest C.A. was 9 years, 3 months.

[7] Adding a further difficulty, some writers maintain that artistic talent appears to have a slower rate of maturation than other talents, particularly musical talent. See Florence L. Goodenough, *Exceptional Children* (New York: Appleton-Century-Crofts, 1956). The author cites Catharine Morris Cox, *The Early Mental Traits of Three Hundred Geniuses*, Vol. 2 (Stanford, Calif.: Stanford University Press, 1926), which discusses thirteen great artists and intimates that their early work did not compare in stature with that of young musicians of similar chronological age. The differences in rate of maturation in the two artistic fields might be questioned, as Goodenough rightly suggests, on the grounds that we do not possess suitable measuring devices for artistic talent.

Figure 14.2 *"Pennsylvania," drawn from memory by a fifth grader a year after he left the scene. Gifted children "demonstrate unusual attention to detail and precocious representational ability." This child later attended an art school.*

opinion of informed people has frequently led to surprisingly accurate judgments concerning artistic talent.[8]

Characteristics of Gifted Children

Several authorities have made the study of artistically gifted children a special concern. One of the earliest efforts to characterize the special capacity for art was made by Norman Meier, a psychologist whose interest in the subject led to the design of tests that were intended to assess the degree and kinds of artistic talent among children. Meier claimed that gifted children derive their artistic ability from superior manual skill, energy, aesthetic intelligence, perceptual facility, and creative imagination. His study of gifted and average children led him to conclude that, since youngsters with the greatest artistic aptitude had a greater number of artists in their family histories, the genetic factor played a major role in determining artistic abilities.

[8]Pooled judgments have been important in Goodenough and Harris' "Draw-a-Man" test, the Cleveland Studies, and Eisner's *A Comparison of the Developmental Drawing Characteristics of Culturally Advantaged and Culturally Disadvantaged Children.*

384

Let us compare the conclusions of some other writers as they describe the phenomenon of talent among elementary-school children.

According to Miriam Lindstrom,[9] an art teacher, gifted children:

1. Are extraordinarily perceptive in both objective fact and subjective effect.
2. Are better able to indicate a clear sense of structure in the interrelationships of parts.
3. Show deeper appreciation of significant expressive gesture or attitude.
4. Possess a generous unspoiled readiness to respond to the challenge of new experience.
5. Enjoy a relative freedom from the ordinary frustrations of most children.

According to Howard Conant,[10] educator, painter, and writer, gifted children:

1. Possess heightened visual acuity and interest in both idea and detail.
2. Are better able to see the underlying artistic structure of realistic subject matter.
3. Are characterized by a level of persistence and interest far beyond their classmates.
4. Demonstrate unusual attention to detail and precocious representational ability: possess a photographic mind, acute powers of visualization and draftsmanship.

According to Lark-Horovitz, Lewis, and Luca,[11] art educators and psychologists, gifted children:

1. Are usually beyond the norm of their age group in developmental status, technical skill, and aesthetic judgment.
2. Excel in compositional arrangement: enrichment in decorative and aesthetic qualities.
3. Show great ease in working with media.
4. Present a commonplace subject more imaginatively and with a greater variety of detail.
5. Possess a richer storehouse of images.
6. Show greater facility with the "true to life" appearance level.

[9]*Children's Art* (Berkeley: University of California Press, 1957), p. 49.
[10]*Art in Education* (Peoria, Ill.: Bennett, 1959), p. 183.
[11]*Understanding Children's Art for Better Teaching*, Chapter 6, *passim*.

7. Are both original and fertile in their fantasies; possess imaginative ability to an extraordinary degree.
8. Can more readily depict movement.
9. Can better handle symmetry.
10. Can use color with subtlety as well as brilliance; are able to achieve contrast by well-balanced and integrated coloring.
11. Are more eager to explore media for original effects.

Figure 14.3 *The rich variety of forms and ideas in this drawing by a sixth grader shows the range of interest and conceptualization of a gifted child.*

12. Display effective interplay between selective visual observations and a strong visual memory; retain impressions of things seen long ago.
13. Have a stronger desire to learn; ask for explanation and instruction.

Any discussion of the differences of art products of average and

Figure 14.4 *Gifted children "can use color with subtlety, as well as brilliance,"
as the gifted sixth-grade girl whose work is represented here demonstrates.*

talented children must include mention of the studies conducted at the
Cleveland Museum. In these studies, art products, rather than behavior,
were analyzed; it was concluded that gifted children surpass their classmates in portraying motion, grouping objects (composition), effectively
using media, handling line, and in representational skills such as perspective.[12]

Using the points on which there was greatest consensus, one might
construct a profile of a gifted child as follows:

> A gifted child observes acutely and has a vivid memory, is adept at handling
> problems requiring imagination, and is open to new experiences, yet can
> delve deeply into a limited area. The child takes art seriously and derives
> great personal satisfaction from the work. Indeed, the gifted child may
> sometimes be obsessive or compulsive about art work, often neglecting other
> areas of study for it.

Thus stated, this composite of the qualities of a gifted child reads very
much like a list of acceptable goals for any art program. If this is so, can
we not assume that the character and behavior of the gifted child provides

[12]Thomas Munro, Betty Lark-Horovitz, and E. N. Bernhart, "Children's Art Abilities:
Studies at the Cleveland Museum of Art," *Journal of Experimental Education,* Vol. 11, No.
2 (1942), pp. 97–155.

us with very definite clues as to the nature of an art program for average students? This is mentioned more as a hypothesis than as a recommendation. Yet the evidence suggests the idea is worth pursuing.

Strong indications of the nature of talent may sometimes be found in case histories of artistically gifted people, but it is often difficult to unearth actual evidence of their early work. A child's art is usually lost, and both parents and teachers are generally unable to recall accurately the child's early behavior. For some cases, however, there are reasonably detailed and apparently accurate data.

Case Histories of Gifted Children

Among these cases are the histories of two girls of the same age from upper-middle-class homes, Susan McF and Mary M.[13] These girls gave promise of talent in art very early in their lives. A study of their production shows that both of them began manipulating media just before they were a year old and that they had passed beyond the stage of manipulation before their second birthdays. Around fifteen months Susan was naming the marks she was producing in crayon. Mary did the same when she was sixteen months old. Around this age, Mary began to use some spoken words clearly, but Susan was slower to learn to speak and instead was producing sounds such as "rrrr," which consistently stood for "automobile," and "goong" for "duck." When, by the use of symbols, she depicted such objects in her paintings, she named them in this vocabulary. When she was twenty-five months old, Susan produced an attractive montage with sticky tape and colored paper. Around twenty-seven months of age, both girls could delineate many different symbols and give them some relationship in the same composition.

Both children led normal, active lives and during fine hot weather neglected their art for outdoor games. A study of their work (which their parents carefully dated) reveals, however, that inactivity in art did not seem to interfere with their continuous development. By the time both children were three years old they were overlapping objects in their drawings and paintings, and at four Mary in particular seemed to recognize texture as an expressive element of design. By six, they were skilled in a variety of techniques—toning colors, devising textural effects, and inventing outstanding compositions. Before she was seven, Mary even gave hints of linear perspective in her work. It is important to note that both girls attended elementary schools that apparently provided progressive and highly commendable art programs.

By the time Susan was ten years old and Mary ten years and eight

[13]Because each girl has highly educated parents who are especially interested in art and are knowledgeable about both child psychology and pedagogy, records of their art were preserved. The parents systematically filed the children's work after writing comments about each piece on its reverse side. Both children eventually enrolled in the Ontario classes for gifted children, at which time the parents disclosed the girls' records. The girls' I.Q.'s are as follows: Mary, 120; Susan, 130.

Figure 14.5 *The control of pictorial and realistic space, the sense of structure, and the feeling for detail in this picture are signs of one type of giftedness in children. Grade 6.*

months, their work had lost most of its childlike qualities. Each girl passed through a realistic stage in which objects were rendered rather photographically. Then Susan's work became distinctly mannered in its rhythms, and Mary's output became reminiscent of that of several artists. In quick succession, she went through an Aubrey Beardsley period, followed by one reflecting the influence of Degas and later of Matisse. When they were twelve years old, the girls first met and became friends. They attended the same art classes in high school and produced paintings in a style obviously derived from that of the Impressionists.

Fortunately their secondary-school art program proved to be almost as efficient as that of their elementary schooling. After a time their work became noticeably more personal. Eventually both girls attended special classes for children with artistic talent, where they remained for four years. Here they produced some sensitive paintings and sculpture in forms that continued to be recognizably personal. Both girls went on to attend a college of art where, according to their teachers, they gave evidence of outstanding artistic ability.

There seems to be little doubt that Mary and Susan are talented. What characteristics common to both might identify them as such? First, they are characterized by their almost lifelong preoccupation with art. Although at times their interest in art was intermittent, the production of art forms by both girls was for the most part uninterrupted. Second, both girls came from cultured homes in which the parents enjoyed artistic interests. Both environment and biological inheritance often contribute to talent. Children of artistic parents have the double advantage of artistic "nature" and artistic "nurture" often denied the children of parents who lack these interests and abilities.[14]

Third, the progress of Mary and Susan throughout the phases of their childlike expression was both richer and more rapid than normal. Although both girls developed a skill in handling tools and materials that was obviously above average, neither allowed her skill to assume paramount importance in her output. Again, at one period, the girls apparently became dominated by technique, and the work of other artists whom they admired strongly influenced their output. Fortunately, however, their insight into artistic processes and their personal integrity, intellectual vigor, and vision were sufficient to overcome these powerful influences, which can be very seductive to the gifted young person who seeks a satisfying means of artistic expression.

Witty says that "perhaps it is desirable . . . to consider any child gifted whose performance, in a potentially valuable line of human activity, is consistently remarkable."[15] This statement can be accepted in relation to a creative field such as art only if the phrase "consistently remarkable" is interpreted broadly. Because people employed in art are continually exploring new fields, they cannot always be expected to produce work of a consistently high quality. Sometimes their experiments may fail and then their efforts, however commendable, will probably result in bad art. The art careers of both Susan and Mary show ups and downs. "Consistently remarkable" must therefore allow for plateaus as well as peaks of productivity.

The Evaluation of Talent

There is no denying, however, that "gifted is as gifted does." The child whose performance in art more often than not is "remarkable" may be suspected of being gifted. Such a child will almost inevitably possess above-average intelligence, display skill beyond the ordinary, give noticeable evidence of sensitivity in organizing the elements of design, and

[14] It is interesting to observe that the classes for gifted children of the Ontario Department of Education, though situated in a low-income section of Toronto, enroll over twice as many children from distant high-income areas than from the surrounding district, in spite of the fact that every effort is made to select the talented from any level of society in which they may occur.

See Witty, ed., *The Gifted Child,* in which he discusses the "importance of home background" of the gifted, pp. 271–72. He quotes L. M. Terman and Melita H. Oden, "Correlates of Adult Achievement in the California Gifted Group," in the Thirty-ninth Yearbook of the National Society for the Study of Education (Bloomington, Ill.: Public School Publishing Co., 1940), pp. 74–89. Terman and Oden state that talented pupils have generally "the more satisfactory family background in terms of occupational status . . . parental education . . . home instruction and mental stock."

[15] Paul Witty, "The Gifted Child," *Exceptional Children,* Vol. 19 (April 1953), p. 255.

be capable of producing work bearing the stamp of a distinctive personality.

Because the data used in the evaluation of talent must be subjective to a degree, judgment cannot be made either lightly or hastily.[16] Herbert A. Carroll, in his study of teachers' judgments of children's intelligence,[17] discovered that only 15.7 percent of students suggested by 6,000 teachers were accurately assessed, a fact corroborated by another report issued by the Education Policies Commission.[18] The teacher who suspects a child of possessing unusual artistic talent might be wise to enlist occasionally the opinions of others, including artists and art teachers. Opinions of such well-informed people, furthermore, might well be sought over a relatively long period of time. A sudden appearance of talent may later prove to be merely a remarkable but temporary development of skill. Again, what may appear to be artistic talent in early years may disappear as the child develops other interests into which energies and abilities are channeled.

The problem of assessing giftedness continues throughout a child's school career. Those who are most concerned with its identification are the admissions personnel of art schools. While the traditional means of admission rests on the applicant's portfolio (which reflects the child's capabilities in drawing, color, or design), many art schools have for some time used other criteria for admission, such as problem-solving abilities, evidence of creative thinking, and personality traits that are assessed through personal interviews. In other words, an alert student with a flexible and inventive mind may now have an advantage over an applicant whose main talent lies in skillful watercolors.

The system of identification that is based on both time and the opinion of many specialists seems to function with reasonable efficiency.[19] In the Ontario experiment, pupils who, in the opinion of their classroom teachers and art consultants, had talent were recommended to attend special art classes. Recommendations were based not only on their ability in art, but also on their intelligence rating and success in other areas of school life. After pupils had attended the special classes for eight months, the staff passed judgment on their progress. If, in the unanimous opinion

[16]A discussion of objective art tests will be found in Chapter 18.

[17]*Genius in the Making* (New York: Hill & Wang, 1940).

[18]*The Education of Gifted Children,* Bulletin of the National Art Education Association (December 1957).

[19]For a description of two other systems of selection, see Havighurst and others, *A Survey of the Education of Gifted Children.* Neither the Quincy nor the Portland test described in this publication seems to be wholly acceptable. The Quincy test apparently includes such items as the drawing of "stick men," which can scarcely be described as art activity in any sense. The Portland test appears to rely to some degree either on a laissez-faire technique, in which the pupils are given "free choice" of subject matter, or on assigned subjects in which, as far as one can ascertain from the account, the pupils may have little or no real interest.

For further discussion about "identifying the child talented in art," see Witty, "The Gifted Child." What this author says seems to be borne out in the performances of Susan and Mary.

of the staff members, pupils had failed to show outstanding talent, they were usually removed from the classes so that room was made for other, more promising pupils. By these procedures the staff seemed to be able to select only the most gifted children with whom to do research.

In the special art classes offered the children of the Miami and Newton schools, the major criterion for admission was commitment to art rather than talent as such. These special classes demonstrated that skill did indeed improve in many instances once children worked in an environment of a shared enthusiasm. The classes were specifically designed for those whose hunger for art was simply not satisfied by the amount of activity the normal school could allow.

SPECIAL ARRANGEMENTS IN ART FOR GIFTED CHILDREN

When gifted children have been identified, the problem concerning suitable educational treatment for them arises. An "enriched" program may be offered by the classroom teacher or art consultant whereby the pupil is assigned advanced work, is given special materials, and is allowed to take time from other obligations to work in art. The danger here is that the classroom teacher might not be equipped to provide special help, or that excusing the child from nonart activities to work in art might arouse adverse reactions from the rest of the class. Then there is also the curious but significant situation of the teacher who is jealous of the gifted child. This situation may account for the negative attitude that many teachers take toward children who are particularly nonconformist in their creative behavior.

Another arrangement for helping the gifted is the "special class," in which only talented children are enrolled. Such classes may be offered during school hours, after school, or on Saturday mornings. Educators believe these classes provide the best solution to the problem of meeting the needs of the gifted. Teachers can be engaged who possess capabilities in special artistic fields. Much as a sympathetic teacher of general subjects may help a gifted child in art, a specialist can provide even more assistance. In the special classes the need to provide for individual differences will be even more apparent. According to David Manzella:

> These classes should be taught by producing and exhibiting art educators or by professional artists. They should be real studio experiences with a real aura of art about them—not ersatz . . . fabrications. These would not be general art classes in which a little of this and a little of that was presented, and a ceramist taught painting, and a painter, weaving. My recommendation would be to secure the services of good artists who love to teach and are sympathetic with and have an understanding of children and young people. And I would have these artists teach in whatever medium and in whatever way they found most satisfactory. . . . The nature of the

particular medium is not important. A youngster's abilities can be challenged and nurtured by good teaching in all forms of the visual arts.[20]

Whatever special arrangements are made for the child with artistic talent, two considerations of paramount importance to the child's future development must be kept in mind. In the first place, on no account should the child's artistic development be unduly hastened into adult forms of expression. In the elementary school, the talented youngster is still a youngster, and artistic growth must occur with due regard for this fact. "Overstimulation, growing from the drive of eager adults . . . has often killed the child's urge for artistic expression."[21] Even so, in the second place, every talented child must be provided with sufficient challenge to work to capacity. Unless this condition prevails, the gifted pupil may lose interest in the work, and considerable energies and abilities may be dissipated in less worthwhile ways.

Under what circumstances will talent flourish? To begin with, the home should, at best, encourage an interest in art and, at worst, not discourage it. While it may be true in some cases that "genius will out" no matter what the circumstances, it nevertheless seems that a sympathetic home environment is extremely stimulating. The home that provides suitable art media, a library of art books, and a convenient place to work, together with loving and intelligent parents to admire the work being produced and to encourage further production, will aid substantially in fostering talent. Next, the elementary and secondary schools that the gifted pupil attends should provide a sufficiently stimulating and challenging art program. Finally, somewhere along the line of artistic progress, the gifted pupil should be afforded special opportunities for the cultivation of talent and should have the opportunity to encounter a supportive teacher who is sensitive to any capabilities that set the gifted child apart from other pupils.

The unique and precious artistic gifts can flourish under the cooperative efforts of parents, teachers, artists, and departments of education. After all, "talents ask little—the opportunity to show and know themselves, a little space and light and air to grow in, a little leisure to bloom."[22]

SUITABLE ART ACTIVITIES

It is unwise to offer the gifted a curriculum that is oriented primarily toward media. The talented child can be challenged by ideas as well as by materials in special classes. Moreover, there should be opportunities

[20]*Educationists and the Evisceration of the Visual Arts* (Scranton, Pa.: International Textbook, 1963), pp. 91–92.

[21]Viktor Lowenfeld, *Your Child and His Art* (New York: Macmillan, 1954), p. 176.

[22]Donalda Dickie, *The Enterprise in Theory and Practice* (Toronto: Gage, 1940), p. 86.

for students to work in one area in depth.[23] A conceptual approach to art activities begins with an idea and then asks the child to use materials merely as a means of solving a problem. The problem may be stated as follows: "One characteristic of human beings is that they design their environment for pleasure and for aesthetic purposes as well as for function and utility. In creating your own environment take into consideration purpose, scale, and materials. Decide whether you wish to work as part of a planning team or as an individual." Stating the problem in this manner opens up a number of choices for the student and encourages decision-making that is different from the kind that results when the child is given such directions as: "On the table you will find cardboard, pins, knives, and rulers. These are the materials to be used in making a scale model of a vacation home."

A series of sculpture lessons might be used as a focal point for the idea of *opposition*—that is, of hard and soft forms, of open and closed forms. The children are encouraged to obtain an understanding of this concept through their own investigation of the materials. This approach obviously offers greater opportunity for growth in problem-solving than is allowed by concentrating only on how to use a particular medium. The gifted children in the special class, then, can be guided away from object-making into the kind of visual thinking that might not occur until a later stage.

The teacher of the special class or the art consultant teaching in an after-school program may want to take an inventory of art activities offered prior to the special class in order to plan better the new program. Thus a child who is interested in sculpture but has worked only in clay might try a large-scale plaster or wood carving. In printmaking, a child who has worked only in linoleum may try a woodcut, or one who has handled both of these could attempt a multiple-color silk screen or any other problem beyond the capabilities of the other children. These activities extend the range of the child's experience and serve to compensate for the relatively limited exposure to the art in the regular school program.

Figure 14.6 *Sculpture in wood by a gifted girl, C.A. 13, I.Q. 120. (Photo by Royal Studio.)*

Gifted children demonstrate a number of peculiarities in their selection of art activities. Their interests in such basic types of art work as life, still life, landscape, portraiture, and sculpture develop early, and they appear to find greater challenge and deeper satisfaction in these than they do in some of the craft fields such as weaving and paper construction. While they may occasionally turn to these for their novelty, they generally

General Activities

[23]The Saturday morning classes in the Newton schools, Newton, Mass., offer in-depth approaches to such activities as drawing, painting, and filmmaking. Student interest has been high over the year—95 percent of those attending elected to remain in the area they first chose rather than change at the semester break.

return with renewed interest to what might be described as the more classic, or traditional, art forms, possibly because these art forms afford the children an opportunity to display their special brand of precocity.

Gifted children usually prefer to work at art by themselves rather than participate in group endeavor. Although as a group the gifted are socially inclined they seem to recognize in art a subject that demands individual deliberation and effort. They are not entirely adverse to participating in puppet shows, mural-making, and other art forms requiring a pooled effort, but most are happiest when they are submerged as individuals in artistic problems.

Although gifted children find a ready challenge in the usual media and activities suggested for normal children, a few special materials and techniques are especially suitable for them. The expense and technical difficulties associated with these materials and processes forbid their wide use in the general elementary-school art program, but they are recommended for the gifted enrolled in special classes. Since in the heterogeneous classroom no hard and fast divisions can be maintained between an art program for normal children and one for the gifted, teachers might also occasionally apply some of the following suggestions to their general classes.

Figure 14.7 *A twelve-year-old Italian girl depicts a scene of student protest observed in her native Milan. Her handling of proportion, detail, and depth is far in advance of her age group.*

Figure 14.8 *"Tower Bridge." A gifted fifth-grade boy found oils to be a suitable medium for conveying the feeling of a foggy day in his native London.*

Painting in oils is a good example of a special activity suitable for the gifted. It offers the student an effective means of identifying with "real artists." The oils are rich and sensual in color and are far more versatile than most water-based paints. The slow-drying quality of oil paint makes it suitable for art projects undertaken over a period of time. By the time they reach preadolescence, gifted children should have had an opportunity to work with it. However, not even the most gifted children can use it effectively until they have had experience with many other types of paint. Only a few ways of using oil paint can be mentioned here; to list them all would require a disproportionate amount of space.[24]

Painting in Oils

The surface to which the oil paint is applied, usually called the "support," is traditionally made of wood or canvas. The pupils can use shellacked paper tacked to a drawing board to practice. Later they can buy commercially prepared canvas boards or stretched canvas. They can also make supports simply by coating a strong building board or one-quarter-inch plywood with either thick oil-ground titanium white paint

[24] See Ralph Mayer, *The Painter's Craft,* 2nd ed. (New York: Van Nostrand, 1966); Frederic Taubes, *The Technique of Oil Painting* (New York: Dodd, Mead, 1946); Max Doerner, *The Materials of the Artist,* rev. ed., trans. by Eugene Neuhaus (New York: Harcourt Brace Jovanovich, 1949); W. G. Constable, *The Painter's Workshop* (New York: Oxford University Press, 1954).

These publications are clearly written and cover the subject in sufficient detail. Before holding classes in oil painting a teacher should not only be able to paint but also be familiar with at least one of these books.

or zinc white paint. After about a week of drying,[25] these prepared boards may be rubbed with sandpaper if their surfaces are too rough.

Oil colors have many peculiar characteristics. Those that fade in light are called "fugitive"; those that do not fade are called "permanent." Those that can be mixed together safely are called "compatible"; others that set up chemical reactions when mixed are called "incompatible." The cost of colors varies widely because of differences in manufacturing processes and in the raw products used. The cheapest colors, called "students' quality," are not reliable because they are fugitive. They are suitable for practice, however, so that the pupils might use them while learning to paint. It is recommended that, in general, paints and supports of a better quality be supplied as soon as the pupils master some of the basic techniques of oil painting.

Painters develop their own "palette," or range of colors, which they usually consider indispensable. Taubes recommends seventeen pigments, which he says "are all permanent . . . and most of them are compatible with each other." The following list is adapted from Taubes.[26]

White	1. Zinc or titanium white
Blue	2. Prussian blue
	3. Ultramarine
Green	4. Chrome oxide green (transparent)
Yellow	5. Yellow ochre
	6. Naples yellow
	7. Cadmium yellow light
	8. Cadmium yellow medium
	9. Cadmium orange
Red	10. Cadmium red
	11. Venetian red
	12. Indian red (or Mars violet)
	13. Alizarin crimson
Brown	14. Burnt sienna
	15. Raw umber, or
	16. Burnt umber
Black	17. Ivory black

A beginner should not use this rather extensive list in its entirety before learning how to paint. A basic palette for a young pupil might consist of the following pigments in Taubes' list: 1, 3, 4, 5, 7, 10, 16, 17. The pigments are bought already ground in oil and packaged in tubes.

---

[25] For absolute permanence, six months are usually required for drying. This, of course, is not necessary when young children are using the boards.

[26] *The Technique of Oil Painting,* p. 25.

The 12-ounce, or "studio," size is economical for all but white, which should be bought in 1-pound tubes.

Before one begins painting, small amounts of paint should be squeezed from the tubes onto a palette, which may be a sheet of glass resting on a table. If the glass is placed over a sheet of light gray or white paper, the colors will show clearly; this procedure is especially recommended when using mixed colors. Another type of palette is the traditional wooden board held in the painter's hand. This is a convenient piece of apparatus for outdoor painting. No one way of arranging colors on the palette is recommended. Each pupil should develop a personal system to follow consistently until the selection of pigments during painting becomes automatic. Any painter should be able to reach for the desired color on a palette as automatically as one selects a control on the instrument panel of an automobile. One convenient method of arranging colors is to place black and white side by side at the far edge of the palette, and then to place the yellows, browns, and reds on the white side and on the black side, the blues and greens (see Figure 14.9).

Painting tools consist of flat bristle brushes, from about size 6 up, and a palette knife. Easels are a convenience but not entirely necessary. Before beginning to paint, the pupil should outline the subject on the canvas with a pointed brush dipped in an oil color diluted with turpentine. This outline will often show after a painting is finished. Some painters use scarlet so that the outline will materially affect the design. Others use neutrals or near-neutrals—grays or earth colors—so that the outline will not become prominent.

The most familiar and most convenient method of painting that children can use is called *alla prima*. In this method one paints spontaneously, trying for the final effect from the start. If corrections are made later, the first coat of paint must be scraped off while wet rather than

Figure 14.9 *An arrangement for a palette of oil colors.*

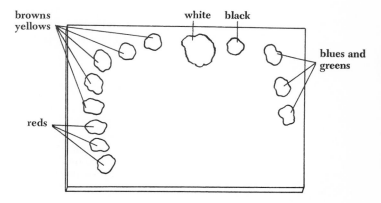

covered when dry with another coat. Usually the pigments as squeezed from the tube are of suitable consistency for application on the support and need no oil or turpentine added to them. Indeed, it is an unwise practice for beginners to dilute their paint except when they outline the subject; they have a tendency to thin it too much to make it approximate tempera or watercolor. Painting should generally be done with the largest possible brush for the area being covered. As a rule the paint should be laid on with reasonable thickness. Many painters like to use thin paint in areas of shade and thick paint where light is depicted, but this is a matter of personal choice. The palette knife can be used to load paint onto the support where a bold thick covering of pigment is desired. The end of the brush handle may be conveniently used to draw lines through the wet paint.

When finished painting, the pupils should thoroughly clean their brushes, palette knives, and palettes. Turpentine can be used as a cleaning agent, although some of the commercially prepared cleaning fluids are easier on the bristles of the brushes. Brushes should be washed in a solution of mild soap and warm water after they have been rinsed in the cleaning fluid.

Other Media for Drawing and Painting

Gifted pupils in the preadolescent stage will find several other media challenging which may not be available in the course of the regular art program. Some of the more expensive colored drawing inks, for example, might be used in conjunction with India ink or in some of the mixed-media techniques mentioned in Chapter 7. Work with steel pens and pointed brushes might be explored. Charcoal and Conté crayon in black and brown can also be used fairly extensively, either in quick sketching or in more deliberate drawing. Some of this line drawing might lead to a consideration of etching and other graphic processes like dry-point, aquatint, and mezzotint.[27]

Some gifted children in the preadolescent stage become proficient in the use of various types of watercolor. In the opinion of many painters, transparent watercolor is one of the most subtle and difficult of media. It must be used with precision and speed, and its "wetness," or watery character, should be reflected in the finished work. Good watercolor paints, brushes, and especially papers are relatively expensive. The pigments in tubes are more convenient to use than those in cake form. When gifted pupils begin to paint seriously in watercolors, they should be

[27] See Victor D'Amico, *Creative Teaching in Art,* rev. ed. (Scranton, Pa.: International Textbook, 1966) for a description of these processes. Before exposing gifted children to any of these processes, a teacher should, of course, be skilled in the use of all tools and materials associated with them. Furthermore, the teacher should have a well-equipped room in which the children can explore the processes.

provided with materials of a higher quality than is usually found in the school art program. The many acrylic paints on the market offer colors as intense as oils as well as quick drying properties. Gouache is similar in handling to oils and acrylic paints; it dries quickly and, unlike tempera, is both water soluble and, when dry, waterproof. The use of these media may require demonstrations, which specialists are usually more capable of handling than classroom teachers.

A craft that is suitable for gifted children is silk-screen printing, a technique in which ink is squeezed through a prepared screen to leave a design on a paper or textile surface. Although not particularly difficult it involves the use of considerable quantities of oil textile ink that might create difficulties in a crowded regular classroom. This activity, however, seems to challenge gifted pupils sufficiently to produce some interesting results.

Silk-Screen Printing

The activity requires the use of a light wooden frame measuring approximately 1 foot square and covered with silk-screen bolting cloth, nylon, or a good grade of organdy. The cloth is stretched tightly and tacked to the outside of the frame with carpet tacks. It must then be treated in

Figure 14.10 *Methods of preparing the silk screen, using wax paper* (**A**) *and tusche* (**B**).

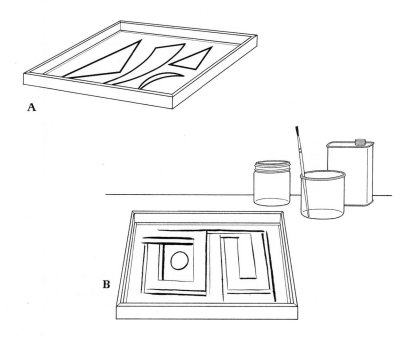

such a way as to prevent paint from passing through some areas of the screen while allowing it to pass through other areas (see Figure 14.10).

Any of three methods of preparing the design on the screen (cloth) might be considered for classroom use. The simplest of them is to put masking tape on the reverse, or downward, side of the screen. Another is to glue wax paper on the screen. A more complicated method, but one that leads to more controlled results, makes use of what is called "tusche"—a heavy black liquid. Using tusche, the pupil paints a design on the upper side of the screen. To prevent paint from running under the frame, paper tape is stuck around the inside of the screen where the screen meets the frame. After this, a mixture of one part ordinary glue and one part water is spread thinly with a piece of cardboard over the entire screen, covering tusche and all, so that not even pinpoint openings are left. When this glue solution is dry, the tusche and the glue covering it are washed out with turpentine. To do this, the pupil should place the screen upside-down on newspaper and pour turpentine over it. Gentle rubbing with a cloth removes the tusche, leaving areas in the screen through which color will pass.

Whatever process is used, the printing from the screen should be done on a long table covered thickly and evenly with newspapers. First, textile ink is poured into the screen. Then a rubber-edged scraper, or "squeegee," about as long as the inside width of the printing frame, is drawn across the screen, pulling and squeezing the ink as it moves. The ink passing through the unglued areas makes a design on the paper or textile beneath. Before printing on textile the pupils should try printing on paper.

Many experiments may be performed in silk-screen printing. The screen can be placed in various positions on the textile to form different types of overall patterns; two or more colors may be used; more than one technique of preparing the screen can be used to give different effects; two or more screens could be prepared for use on one printing project. Transparent "gel" for mixing with pigment should be investigated for the number of color overlays it allows. Found objects, such as masking tape, torn newsprint, paper stars, and legal seals, can be used as quick stop out materials by merely pasting them to the screen.

TEACHING THE GIFTED

The young gifted child will, of course, make use of the usual materials and perform the basic activities mentioned in earlier chapters in connection with the general art program for normal children. Since the gifted can be recognized only over a period of time they must obviously take part in the art program designed for all until their talent is discovered. When it is clear that individuals possess gifts above the ordinary, the teacher, using the teaching principles suggested in Chapter 2, can help the children to progress at their optimum level of accomplishment. This may be done through any art form. In drawing and painting, it means more drawing and painting; in sculpture, more sculpture. Progress in art occurs when the worker keeps producing art. Mere quantity of production or repetition of forms previously created is not progress, but production that leads to improved skill, more penetrating insight, and greater mastery of media will help to develop a child's talent.

The principle of teaching in response to the needs of the learner has been emphasized throughout this book. The preceding chapter observed that in order to profit from art at all some slow learners need to be subjected to a step-by-step method of instruction. With the gifted the reverse is necessary. Here the teacher is faced with the necessity for what might be described as "under-teaching." Every attempt must be made to challenge the greater abilities of gifted children. Whenever they can learn a fact or a technique for themselves they should do so. Assistance must in general be withheld until the children have explored every possible avenue for a solution to their problems. Gifted pupils who are given this type of educational treatment thrive on it, and so does their art.

Whether in a special classroom or as individuals in a normal classroom, artistically gifted children must be continually challenged with drawing and painting and three-dimensional media of all types and with examples of fine production in these media. Artistically gifted children are normally motivated to express themselves with drawing and painting media. They should always have access to fine works of art in the media of their choice or, failing the actual works, good reproductions of them. The teacher should suggest certain outstanding works for them to study at art galleries and museums. Talented children can be assumed to be capable of extending their passion for creating works of art to the appreciation or criticism of art. Art works should be discussed—both for their own sake and for the problems they pose as regards the work currently in progress.

The teacher will have to make special efforts with gifted pupils from underprivileged homes to encourage them to see the best art and to read good books on art. Gifted children from cultured homes generally have many opportunities to add to their knowledge of art. Underprivileged children enjoy few, if any, such opportunities. Indeed, their gift must often be an especially vital one if it is to survive. In their case, the teacher's duty is to supply the inspiration and sources of knowledge that their home environment has denied them.

It was noted earlier that gifted pupils, evidently sensing the importance of personal expression in art, tend to prefer individual to group activity. However, when gifted learners are found in general classrooms, their classmates often elect them to important positions in the committees established to perform group work. Indeed, they are frequently elected to chairmanships of various enterprises. With their special abilities in art, these children are thus placed in a position to do much of the difficult work, thereby depriving their classmates of tasks that they should do themselves. Gifted children, however, should not be encouraged to dominate the activities of the class. Fortunately, gifted pupils tend to be well adjusted in other ways, and a teacher can appeal to their reason and good judgment with better than average results. Hence, when gifted pupils appear to be assuming more than their share of responsibility in group work, a short, forthright, and friendly discussion about the situation usually results in their relinquishing some tasks to their fellow classmates.

In cases where a group of gifted pupils shows a disinclination to perform group work in art, it seems reasonable to suggest that the teacher respect their wishes. After all, the pupils are probably well adjusted socially without group work. Whatever further practice they need in working cooperatively can be assigned in other areas of learning, thus leaving them free to exercise their remarkable individual talents in art— the area best suited for a personal contribution.

ACTIVITIES FOR THE READER

1. Study some children considered to be artistically gifted. Make a note of their outstanding personal qualities, work habits, and their attitude toward their contemporaries.
2. Make a collection of drawings and paintings by artistically gifted children. Analyze the work for its subject matter, design, and technique. Compare this collection with one composed of the work of normal children of the same chronological ages as those in the gifted group.
3. Study the home environment of several artistically gifted pupils. How does this environment rate culturally and economically?
4. Set up a still-life arrangement and sketch it on paper in pencil or ink. Then outline the general composition in thin paint on canvas and begin to paint with oils. It is wise to keep to a few pigments at first—say, one bright one, like yellow, and umber, black, and white. Paint bold strokes with medium thick paint on the areas having middle light values. Later add highlights in thicker paint, using a palette knife if desired. Paint the shadow areas in thinner paint.
5. Paint a landscape or portrait in oils, but continue to keep the number of colors restricted.

6. Prepare silk screens according to the directions given in this chapter. Experiment with all three methods of preparing the screen. Practice printing on paper, using some of the pattern arrangements suggested in Activity 5a-f at the close of Chapter 10. Finally, print your favorite pattern on textile.

7. Contact some artists and request that they lend you a drawing from their school days, if one still exists.

8. Get a copy of the Advanced Placement course description in studio art. How is giftedness implied in the description of the course requirements?

Correlating art to the general school curriculum can provide much stimulation to children. After studying Oriental culture, a fourth grader produced this lovely, free-flowing calligraphic design.

RELATING ART
TO THE GENERAL CURRICULUM

Teachers often think if history is illustrated, or interpreted in the art lesson, integration of the two subjects takes place. This is by no means true. In such a superficial situation neither is history explained nor does a creative experience become meaningful. . . . Integration does not occur from the outside; integration is not "made" by "assembling" two subjects; integration happens from within. This shows clearly that integration can only take place by self-identification.*

Stimulus for valid artistic expression may derive from any area of a child's life. If a child is genuinely moved by an experience, it makes little difference from an artistic standpoint what the source of stimulation is. Since children live a large part of their lives in school, one might expect that many situations found in play or study at school can promote expression. Such, in fact, is the case. Life at school may and, indeed, should be the source of many and varied significant artistic statements.

THE NATURE OF CORRELATION: ART AS AN INTEGRATIVE FORCE

That other subjects should serve as a basis for children's art work is educationally sound in principle. It will be remembered from Chapter 1 that whereas the mechanistic psychologists believed that learning can best occur when school subjects are broken down into their smallest parts, the Gestalt psychologists disputed this assertion and proved that just the reverse is true. Wholes, not parts, are primary, they asserted. Learning occurs best, not when subjects are dissected, but when they are combined.

*From Viktor Lowenfeld and W. Lambert Brittain, *Creative and Mental Growth,* 4th ed., pp. 49–50. Copyright, The Macmillan Company, 1947, 1952, 1957, 1964. Used by permission.

Figure 15.1 *In relating art to their study of Indians, a class of slow learners painted a mural, built a model, and demonstrated two kinds of weaving. (Photo by Rick Steadry.)*

Through the practice of correlation, school subjects formerly considered discrete are closely related. Reading, composition, spelling, grammar, and handwriting, for example, have become one area of study known as the "language arts," and history, geography, and civics are called "social studies." As a result of such groupings of subject matter, the pupils are said to gain greater insight into all the areas of learning involved.

Further grouping occurs in the unit (or "area," or "experience") curriculum. Here, the broad areas of learning that result from correlation of subjects are superseded by even broader themes. In place of "language arts," "social studies," and "general science," one may find in some school curriculums such items as "living together in the home," "how people make a living," or "how we are fed, clothed, and sheltered."[1] In working on these themes children are able to learn many facts related to various subject areas and to develop the necessary skills in such areas as spelling, computing, and penmanship. A large part of the day is spent in doing research on the main theme and the problems associated with it, during which time the pupils may draw, write, read, sing, build, and measure. A part of each day is set aside not only for the evaluation of products and procedures but also for the practice of skills that the learners need to improve. In a well-conducted unit, pupils are able to develop skills in a functional manner that rivals in efficiency the methods of developing skills by drills used when subjects are studied independently. As well as serving as a means of learning facts and developing skills, the unit approach provides ample opportunities for pupils to develop social skills in group activities. The children must cooperate with one another for the successful outcome of their efforts (see Chapter 12). "During the course

[1]These units are quoted from Donalda Dickie, *The Enterprise in Theory and Practice* (Toronto: Gage, 1940). See also Lavone A. Hanna, Gladys L. Potter, and Neva Hagaman, *Unit Teaching in the Elementary School* (New York: Holt, Rinehart and Winston, 1955), and A. Gordon Melvin, *The Activity Program* (New York: Reynal & Hitchcock, 1936).

of a unit of work children . . . have continuous experiences in democratic living whereby they develop . . . characteristics so desired in democratic individuals. The very nature of unit teaching makes it the best method so far devised for children to have these experiences."[2]

The schools of the future may some day place art within a broader context of a "related arts" division so that art, music, dance, and drama can have perhaps the same status that nature study, biology, physics, and chemistry now enjoy under the more general heading of "science." The number of articles, conferences, and grants devoted to combining art with other areas of learning clearly indicates a national trend toward new liaisons for art specialists.[3]

Three main directions seem to be followed by the many new programs now being developed. These are (1) integration within the various arts, (2) the use of art to develop varieties of sensory awareness, and (3) the integration of art with academic subjects. The conscious seeking of relationships between separate disciplines is assumed to be educationally desirable in any discussion of art beyond its customary function. If one examines the "grass roots of art," to borrow Sir Herbert Read's evocative phrase, the distinctive qualities of visual art become less apparent as one compares the formal characteristics of art to those of its neighbors. As an example, design features, such as line, rhythm, and pattern, have their counterparts in music, drama, and dance. For this reason design components are often used as the basis for many related art programs. The visual arts all involve perception, emotion, and the creative processes: a love of manipulation (of both forms and materials), a delight in sensations, and considerable pleasure in the contemplation as well as creation of structured experiences.

Correlations in Art

It is precisely because of the shared characteristics of art that it is so suitable to other subject areas. Since the major interest in the correlation of art with the general curriculum lies in its integration with academic subjects, this chapter will focus on that area. Before we examine this direction, however, let us look at a few examples of the way art is employed in the two other areas mentioned above.

Art and Sensory Awareness.   In this instance, art is used to enhance a process that gives children a more vivid awareness of some aspect of themselves than it is an attempt to achieve a product goal. In many cases,

[2]Hanna, et al., *Unit Teaching in the Elementary School*, p. 72. See also L. Thomas Hopkins, *Interaction: The Democratic Process* (Boston: Heath, 1941), especially Chapters 1 and 2.

[3]Two indications of interest in this area are the NAEA's sponsored "mini conference" on "Art in Interdisciplinary Contexts" (Boston: October 1973) and the projected NAEA national conference on the same theme (Miami: April 1975). See also Al Hurwitz, "Integrated Arts in the Public Schools," in *Issues in Art Education*, Vol. 1, No. 5, 1970–71, Gordon Plummer, ed.

Figure 15.2 *A clear, direct response to an experience is an important feature in the production of art, as can be seen in this painting of a clown produced by a first grader after a visit to the circus.*

however, a sensory exercise can be a vivid preliminary to the creation of a painting or sculpture. Below are listed a number of activities based on the theme, "Receiving and Responding Through Art."

1. Speaking the Pattern

    The class is divided into pairs. Partners then sit back to back, each with a set of matching cut paper shapes. One member of the pair (**A**) builds a composition using the design units, while the other (**B**) attempts to build the same pattern using only **A**'s verbal directions. When the design is complete, **A** and **B** look at their designs and discuss any mismatching. Question: Was mismatching the result of a failure in communication on **A**'s part or in listening on **B**'s part?

2. Surrogate Artist

    A draws slowly with a finger on **B**'s back. **B** then attempts to reconstruct with chalk or crayon the image **A** has developed. Questions: Is **A** going too fast? Is **B** attending closely enough to the image produced by **A**?

410

3. Blind Sculpture

Both **A** and **B** are blindfolded and are not allowed to speak. Thus, neither knows the identity of the partner. A piece of clay is placed between the partners, and they are asked to create together a piece of sculpture using only the cues communicated through the clay and each other's fingers. Music may be played throughout the experience. Question: Are **A** and **B** responding to the changes in the clay produced by each other?

The above exercises are intended to encourage children to pay careful attention to each other and to develop powers of concentration. In all cases the process is indeed the product, with the end result simply emerging as a record of the process.

Relationships Within the Arts. In a situation in which the different arts interrelate in a broad context, some principle or concept is selected because it is a part of the artistic experience, while at the same time existing separately from a particular art category. Let us take one concept that many artists face at various times in their careers—"improvisation"—and examine its possibilities as a "connector" between several art forms.

As a rule, improvisations do not allow any preplanning. They are spontaneous acts that are created from moment to moment, using some stimulus in the immediate situation as a point of departure. Improvisations always call on the inventiveness of the participants, thus developing such creative attributes as flexibility, fluency, and imagination. Participants in improvisational situations learn to respond to the moment at hand and to trust in their ability to embellish, expand, and develop an idea. Below are several suggested improvisational activities organized by category.

1. Visual Arts

Graphic Improvisation: **A** draws a line, **B** counters with another, and **C** follows suit. The idea is to work from the previous image, relating new images as intimately as possible to the preceding ones, thus provoking each pupil to respond immediately to the partners' work. Have each pupil use individual colors, or have all of them use one color as a means of gaining cohesiveness. The criterion for success is the sense of unity that is attained.

Musical Improvisation: Select two or three violently contrasting musical pieces (such as Mozart's "Eine Kleine Nacht Musik" and Ravel's "Bolero"). While listening to each, pupils allow their crayons to roam freely over sheets of paper. They should allow themselves to respond completely to the suggestiveness of the music, especially in terms of color and rhythm. When the music has ended, set up a section of the wall on which to hang the pictures for class criticism and discuss differences and similarities in structure, choice of colors, and the like.

Word Images: The teacher calls out words with strong emotional overtones, and the pupils improvise drawings suggested by the words. As an alternative, pupils can respond with their bodies, thus reacting either physically or pictorially to such words as "explosion," "piston," and "eggbeater."

2. Drama

Situational Improvisations: Select several pupils and ask them to imagine themselves in the following situation. Two people are making camp in a deserted place. At some point, two unknown people appear on the scene. The pupils should decide for themselves what roles or characters they are playing and why they are in this place. All players should agree on where this place is, but neither pair of participants should know in advance the roles the other pair has decided to adopt. What would the members of each pair say? Does a plot or "situation" develop out of the dialog? An infinite number of variations on this scene can be developed.

Another improvisation can be developed by setting the scene at the departure gate of an airport near which a number of people are waiting. At some point the teacher interjects an unexpected occurrence: announcing that the flight is cancelled or that there has been an accident; or instructing another student to play a hijacker, to become violently ill, or to behave in some eccentric manner. The participants should know nothing of the teacher's plan in advance of the scene; they should respond to the incident as they would in a life situation.

After dramatic improvisation has been completed the class can draw or paint their visualization of the setting. The children should try to be as spontaneous in their art work as in their acting.

3. Movement and Music

Sculpture Machines: The class is divided into four groups. A leader is selected for each group and creates a "living sculpture," designing the team for visual interest as well as for the possibility of movement. Each member of the team should adopt a frozen posture showing movement of the torso, arms, or legs. Working from a Sousa march, for instance, the sculpture should activate itself in time to the musical beat. The basic form of the sculpture (the position of the pupils) will remain in place while the separate parts (their bodies) will move.

The preceding descriptions of improvisational activities are a very brief introduction to the kind of thinking that has arisen from a growing desire to extend the base of art education and is reflected in new approaches to team teaching. The art teacher of the future may be expected to think and function beyond the immediate demands of the art program. There is also evidence that the education of art and classroom teachers is beginning to include art electives drawn from fields outside the visual arts. Additional knowledge of related arts is easier for the prospective art teacher to acquire than is some expert familiarity with academic subjects, yet it is in the academic areas of language arts and social studies that the new art teacher is often asked to contribute special skills. Therefore, the major portion of this chapter discusses the correlation of art with the existing academic curriculum of the schools.

Many of the claims art teachers make for their subject are parallel to goals in other subject areas. Recently a group of social studies specialists specified the goals for which they teach. Their choices indicate some very obvious analogies to art. Listed below are eight points they felt were vital for any current social studies program. These assumptions may be similar to those made for an art program, but the teacher should be cognizant of the art program's unique features, as the comments in parentheses indicate.[4]

Overlapping Goals

1. Man in relation to his natural environment and cultural environment is a proper subject for the elementary-school social studies curriculum. (This is also proper subject matter for art activities.)
2. Contrast is a powerful pedagogical tool: look at unfamiliar cultures to understand one's own; look at animal behavior to understand what characteristics man and animals have in common and what differentiates them. (As Chapter 16 points out, the art teacher utilizes the contrasts found in works of art to reinforce learnings in criticism and appreciation. Polarities of style and technique are stressed to heighten the child's perceptions of likenesses and differences in artworks.)
3. "Ways of knowing" are important, such as the way of the anthropologist, the archeologist, and others. ("Ways of knowing" in art implies understanding not only the functions of critic, historian, and artist, but also of the kinds of "knowing," perceiving, and experiencing that differentiate the painter from the sculptor, the architect from the potter.)
4. Studies in depth provide a thorough foundation and a point of reference around which later learnings may cluster. (An art program that included in-depth studies would give a great deal of time to a few selected concepts deemed important, such as draw-

[4]The list of goals is taken from "Curriculum Study Group: Social Studies" (Newton, Mass.: Newton Public Schools).

Figure 15.3 *Cooperation in the creation of a work of art provides valuable social skills that can be used elsewhere in the general curriculum. In **A** one student tries to draw "through" another. Both partners must cooperate closely to achieve success. Close cooperation is also needed in "blind sculpture" (**B**), which involves working sensitively with an "invisible partner." (Photos by Roger Graves.)*

ing, color, and painting, rather than skip to a different activity each week without making any connections among the activities.)

5. Discovering how things are related and discovering how to discover are the ends of learning; the end should not be just mastery of the subject matter. (Discovery is a part of the process in art as well. Sensitive teachers are aware of the importance of the changes that may occur when children are taught for discovery as well as for adult-inspired goals.)

6. The student is a participant; he can be a self-motivated inquirer rather than just a passive receiver. (The taped dialogs included in this book testify to the value of interactions between teacher and pupil in discussions of art activities.)

7. The student should find his own meaning in the material, some of which should be "raw data." (Raw data have always been at the heart of the art program. The raw data the art student should encounter are creative studio experiences and original works of art, be they buildings, paintings, or craft objects.)

8. The gap between current research in curriculum and methodology in social studies should be narrowed. (No one has yet assessed the effects of research on art education in the classroom. The results obtained from doctoral dissertations are rarely read by classroom teachers, and much research is unfortunately too limited in nature to be of use. Art teachers need the kinds of broad curriculum investigation that have taken place in mathematics and physics; these are slow in coming to the humanities. A gap does exist and it must be narrowed if the teacher is to reflect the findings of the researcher.)

A

Figure 15.4 *Literature can almost seem a "natural" source of subject matter for art. In* **A** *a fourth-grade girl illustrates a favorite story. In* **B** *a fifth grader creates a picture in watercolor and ink from a line of poetry.*

B

The eight points have been included here to emphasize the need for art teachers to define the special nature of art, even when art appears to be close to other subjects in its ultimate objectives.

In any case, the teacher who correlates art with other subjects will have to determine when an activity ceases to be art or when it may even go against the very nature of art. When in doubt, a teacher should ask a few basic questions:

Does the activity allow for freedom of decision in interpretation, design, and choice of subject?

Does the task call for strong personal identification with the subject, or does it rest primarily on someone else's solution?

Can the pupils take the information beyond the source material and add something of their own?

It is instructive to study both some of the developing techniques involved in correlations between art and other subjects and some of the results of using art activity as part of a larger unit of study.

CORRELATIONS BETWEEN ART AND OTHER SUBJECTS

The Need for Motivation

The teaching of art has, of course, been affected by both the correlation of subjects and their fusion in the unit curriculum. In certain circumstances art education has benefited from the grouping of areas of learning; in other circumstances, however, it has suffered.

As has been noted on several occasions in earlier chapters, artistic expression is based on a series of delicate circumstances (see Chapter 2). Not the least important of these is a definite reaction to an experience on the part of a person prior to expression. The production of art, therefore, does not occur automatically as a result of correlation or a general fusion of school subjects. Only a child who is emotionally and intellectually moved by an experience in another area of learning is in a position to relate artistic expression to other school subjects. Then the fusion of art and other subjects may be said to be strong, and learning, both artistic and academic, is gratifying.

Many educators feel, however, that art is often abused in the process of integration—that in serving the rest of the curriculum, the creative drive necessary to art becomes diluted, and means are often confused with ends. Many activities, such as copying maps and model construction, are labeled "art" simply because art media are used. In these instances, the art teacher should say to the colleague in the classroom, "It is your right to have them color in mimeographed maps of the Western movement, but let's not call it art." Activities correlated with social studies, for example, involve art

Figure 15.5 *Current events provided the motivation for this fifth grader's drawing of Richard Nixon and Rosemary Woods.*

only if the lives of the pioneers and Indians can be linked to some sort of life experience, personal identification, or visual problem-solving of the child. To copy Indian designs in crayon is not art, but to study the design style of the Indian and to weave one's own pattern on a loom that one has assembled comes much closer to being art.

Figure 15.6 *After an intensive study of Lagos, Nigeria, a fifth grader did this illustration for stories about life there in a class project on the country.*

The Language Arts

Experiences in the language arts can lead to strong correlations with art. Stories and poems may encourage children in the symbol or later stages of expression to make two- and three-dimensional illustrations. The media associated with picture-making or paper work serve best in this type of work, although modeling materials may also be useful. Either the stories and poems the children read and study in class, or in some cases those they write themselves, may be used as the basis for pictorial or three-dimensional expression. Certain teaching precautions must be observed if the correlation is to be successful. In illustrating published stories, the children's experience is vicarious. Only when the literary source has aroused them to the extent that they strongly wish to express something about it is the vicarious experience suitable subject matter for art. If they have failed to respond sufficiently to the work under consideration, they cannot be expected to react artistically to it, and hence no correlative output of this kind should be encouraged.

The same is true of the children's own literary expression. Only when the youngsters retain a strong interest in the experience suggested in their written work can they be expected to express a similar reaction in art. Should their interest remain high after written expression, a further expressive act in another medium might lead to further clarification of their reaction. In such a case the teacher may safely encourage a correlated activity.

A strong interrelationship exists between puppetry and other theater arts on the one hand and spoken and written English on the other. The subject matter of a puppet or stage play may be derived, first, from a play already written by someone else; second, from one the children prepare after reading a narrative poem or a story; and finally, from one written entirely by the children. All three sources demand the use of English spoken in a natural, functional setting. The last two require, furthermore, a high degree of ingenuity and creative effort, which is not beyond the capabilities of most groups of children in the elementary school. Drama for children is after all a form of make-believe that occurs frequently in their free play.

Social Studies

For children, social studies begin in their immediate environment. The geography, history, and civics they first consider are found close to home. Because children are naturally interested in what goes on around them few problems arise when they base their art on this area of learning. Their paintings, murals, and three-dimensional work may depict such themes as "Our Neighborhood," "The People Who Call at Our House" (baker, milkman, or laundryman), "Our Waterfront," "Families Who Haved Lived Longest in Our District," "What Our Firemen Do," "How We Travel in Our City."

In the lower grades a topic frequently related to social studies is

Figure 15.7 *This mask in papier mâché reflects the pupil's examination of African sculpture. Grade 3.*

"Our Friends and Neighbors in Other Lands" or "Boys and Girls in Faraway Places." Here the subject takes the children away from the environment they know, and as a result their art work often deteriorates. The chief reason for this deterioration is that the children frequently do not know enough about the remote region to express much about it, with the consequence that the teacher may substitute stereotyped symbols for true information. How often have we seen such ethnic stereotypes in children's work as a tulip, a windmill, and a boy in baggy trousers to represent the Netherlands; a man sleeping under a cactus plant for Mexico, or a mounted policeman in a red coat for Canada. These banal symbols—a species of adult pictogram—give so restricted an idea of a country that they interfere with the child's understanding of the true character of the foreign land. Granted that the Netherlands has tulips, that Mexicans sleep, and that Canada maintains the Royal Canadian Mounted Police, such images do not represent the heart of these lands.

Before children can be expected to give expression in art to a theme based on remote regions, they must gain a wide knowledge of them, and they must be stirred by some aspects of this knowledge. By reading books and looking at moving pictures, by singing songs of the countries, by studying the work of their artists, and so forth, in course of time they may gain a body of knowledge and a sense of the true character of distant places that will allow them to express something worthwhile.

The same principle applies to the output of pupils in the higher

Figure 15.8 *A scientist would call these constructions models of molecular forms; an artist, sculpture. Both would be correct.*

elementary grades. Frequently more mature pupils may be inspired by events and conditions remote in time and place. In their national history, for example, they may be stirred by events in the American Revolution, the Civil War, the winning of the West, or the exploration of the Antarctic, and may be ready to give expression to them. If, for the lack of knowledge, they find it necessary to copy the work of others, they are not engaging in art and are probably learning little about history. Their time could be more profitably occupied elsewhere. If, on the contrary, they have equipped themselves with a sufficient background of the period that interests them and are thereby capable of giving a knowledgeable account of it, they are in a position both to gain historical knowledge and to produce art of some consequence.

Mapmaking is not art but science. It is an extraordinary fact that even today a few teachers seem to consider the making of maps, either drawn and painted or molded in flour and salt mixtures, to be a form of artistic effort. If a map is to be of any use at all, it must be scientifically accurate and allow no liberties of form for artistic purposes. No personal statement, therefore, can be permitted to influence the outline being produced. It is possible, however, to make an art experience of map-making if the task is divided into two clearly defined phases: the *scientific,* wherein accurate boundaries, coastlines, rivers, and so on, are located, and the *imaginative,* wherein the children add their own pictographs or symbols for trees, ships, physical features, decorative titles and borders, and legends. Children also enjoy "aging" the paper by crumpling it, shellacking or oiling it, or tearing and, under the teacher's supervision, singeing the edges. Purely imaginative maps can also provide the basis

420

for creative writing in the language arts. Maps can, and often do, evoke fantasies in addition to providing information.

Although artists like Audubon and da Vinci have been able to bring art and science into close proximity, it is generally recognized that scientific drawings and artistic expressions differ in intent. Like a map, a scientific drawing is an exact statement of fact, allowing no deviation from the natural appearance of an object.

Science

   Many years ago, art programs gave considerable importance to the drawing of natural specimens. The pussy willow was a favorite theme, as were daffodils, tulips, and bunches of grapes. These objects were drawn even by the youngest children with strict respect for photographic accuracy. We now know that children should make use of their own symbols to represent objects. For children a natural object evokes feelings and holds meanings that a scientific statement could scarcely express. To ask children in an art session to draw scientifically serves merely to curb their

Figure 15.9 *This imitation of an ancient parchment map led to a written composition describing the dramatic events that took place on the island here depicted. Mapmaking can be exciting if a clear distinction is made between scientific and imaginative functions.*

Figure 15.10 *The uses of a microscope: this is a ceramic relief based on a drawing of cellular structures viewed in a science class by a fifth grader. (Harbrace Photo.)*

expression. However, the objects in the science corner of the classroom, such as fossils, shells, and rocks, can provide the basis for inventive drawings.

Most elementary-school children, of course, are incapable of drawing with scientific accuracy. This does not mean that they should not be exposed to natural objects or that they should not use them for expressive purposes. On the contrary, flowers, birds, seashells, fish, and animals, as stated previously, may be used with excellent effect in art. Any natural object may be employed as the basis of design, provided the children are given freedom to depart from the scientific form they observe.

The fact that this freedom is allowed does not retard the children's growth in scientific knowledge. In looking at natural objects and experiencing them in other ways they come close to nature. Later, should they be of a scientific turn of mind, their art experiences with the natural world will provide them with valuable insights that may lead to scientific inquiry.

The greatest care, of course, must be taken not to supply children with symbols, considered to be artistic, that tend to replace or interfere with a study of natural objects. The cutting of paper snowflakes, for example, could be approved only if the activity was introduced after a careful study of these lovely forms and was entirely creative. The drawing of evergreen trees in the well-known bisymmetrical zigzag design occurs more often in children's work as a result of a teacher's demonstration than because of the child's observation.

Music and art lend themselves to several types of correlation.[5] As an indirect correlation, a background of music is often valuable to children while they are drawing, painting, or working in three dimensions. The music appears to influence the children's visual output in a subtle fashion.

Music

The teacher may arrange direct correlations between music and art for children at any level in the elementary school. Music with a pronounced rhythmic beat and melodic line may be employed as a basis for nonobjective patterns such as that seen in Figure 15.12. The following are well-known and well-loved examples of musical selections suitable for elementary-school children:

> J. S. Bach—"Brandenburg" Concerto No. 1
> > *The Wise Virgins* (ballet, arr. Walton)
> Beethoven—Overtures: *Leonore,* No. 3
> > *Egmont*
> > *The Consecration of the House*
> Bizet—*L'Arlésienne,* Suites 1 and 2
> Borodin—*Prince Igor:* "Polovtsian Dances"

[5]The "Activities for the Reader" at the end of Chapter 3 suggest methods and media suitable for both teachers and pupils.

Figure 15.11 *A variety of musical rhythms is the basis for this large drawing project.*

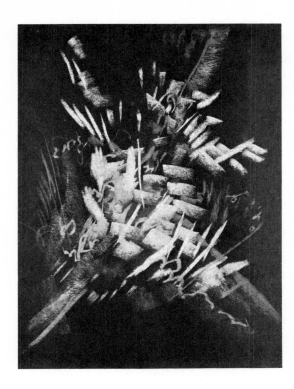

Figure 15.12 *A chalk drawing on black paper by a gifted boy in the sixth grade, based on the "Saber Dance" from Khachaturian's* Gayne Ballet, Suite No. 1.

Khachaturian—*Gayne Ballet,* Suite No. 1
Lalo—*Symphonie Espagnole*
Liszt—Hungarian Rhapsodies Nos. 1 to 7
    Mephisto Waltzes
Prokofiev—*Peter and the Wolf*
Rossini—Overtures: *The Barber of Seville*
    William Tell
    Semiramide
Von Suppé—Overtures: *Light Cavalry*
    Poet and Peasant

Music depicting a definite mood may also lead to some interesting pictures, especially in the fifth and sixth grades. Before playing the record, the teacher usually discusses the mood of the selection. After hearing the music the class may discuss possible combinations of colors, lines, and other elements of design to express the mood pictorially. Work, preferably in soft chalk or paint, then begins, with the music playing in the background. The following are selections expressing certain moods and are suitable for fifth- and sixth-grade pupils.

Bax—*Tintagel*
Borodin—*In the Steppes of Central Asia*
Britten—*Peter Grimes,* "Four Sea Interludes"

Copland—*Appalachian Spring*
     El Salon Mexico
Debussy—*Clair de Lune*
     La Mer
Elgar—*Pomp and Circumstance*, Nos. 1 to 4
Ravel—*Bolero*
Moussorgsky—*Night on Bald Mountain*
Sibelius—*The Swan of Tuonela*
     Finlandia
Wagner—*Die Walküre*, "Ride of the Valkyries"

Music with a literary theme, "program music" as it is sometimes called, may also assist in developing noteworthy picture-making by pupils in the symbol or later stages of expression. The teacher gives the outline of the story, plays excerpts from the music, and from time to time draws attention to passages depicting specific events in the narrative. Examples of program music suitable mainly for pupils in the fourth or higher grades are as follows:

Beethoven—Symphony No. 6, F Major, Op. 68 ("Pastoral")
Bernstein—*West Side Story*, Overture
Bizet—*Carmen*, excerpts
Grofé—*Grand Canyon Suite*
Humperdinck—*Hänsel und Gretel*, excerpts
Moussorgsky—*Pictures at an Exhibition*

Figure 15.13 *Danse Macabre by Saint-Saëns suggested the theme used by a sixth-grade boy in this tempera painting.*

Prokofiev—*Cinderella,* excerpts
Respighi—*The Pines of Rome*
Rimsky-Korsakov—*Scheherazade*
Saint-Saëns—*Danse Macabre*
Tchaikovsky—*Sleeping Beauty*

Mathematics   As soon as a child is capable of using a measured line, mathematics may begin to enter into some of the art work. Activities such as building model houses, making costumes for puppets, or constructing puppet stages lend themselves to this correlation.

Some teachers have attempted to combine the two fields by having the children work during art sessions with mechanical-drawing tools, such as compasses, triangles, and T-squares, to devise geometric designs. If this type of work is largely mechanical and hence not particularly expressive, there is little to recommend it. However, since children do enjoy the clarity and precision that designing with draftsmen's tools provide, in many situations the teacher may establish creative and aesthetic standards to make the design activities worthwhile. These tools might be combined with work in any number of techniques—crayon and pencil drawing, painting, crayon resist, and etching among others.

Figure 15.14 *Finnish children combine art and math by using geometric forms as a basis for collage and design.*

The preceding are examples of correlations that some teachers have consciously developed. Many other correlations may occur that are not arranged formally. Children who develop harmony of movement in physical education, a sense of balance through study of numbers, a concept of unity from some aspect of social studies, or a feeling for rhythm from poetry will find these attainments paralleled in their artistic achievements. Many of the general learnings of this nature are present in many areas of the educational program and can serve as the basis for integrating art into other subjects. So subtle are these correlations in learning, however, that the child and indeed the teacher may be unaware of what is taking place. The most the teacher can do for children is to keep all learning on the highest possible creative and aesthetic levels.

Unplanned Correlations

Many workbooks used for what is termed "seat work" in the various academic subjects are on the market. The authors of some of these seem unable to resist the temptation to make what they think is a correlation between their subject and what they consider to be art. The reader will no doubt recall many such "exercises." In a series intended to improve reading one may find this printed under a line drawing: "This is a bird; color it red." In number work: "Here is a top; draw three tops." Most other subjects are given similar treatment.

Correlations Through "Workbooks"

The authors of these books are either unaware of the expressive modes in art of young children or are determined to ignore them. The symbolic representations normal to children are never used. Furthermore, the areas in which children are supposed to do their copying of tops, rabbits, balls, and so on are too restricted to suit the child's physiological development. Finally, the drawings found in the books are usually so hackneyed as to do little for the child's taste except degrade it.

If books of this kind are of any value—a debatable point—other than for keeping children quiet, it would be a relief were some adventurous authors to attempt to place the activities on a more creative level. Until this is done, teachers would do a service to art, and probably to education in general, if they would steadfastly refrain from using them. Similar criticism can be made of coloring books, in which children learn to scribble colors over line drawings of dubious quality. As one teacher facetiously remarked "Administering chloroform to children would keep them quieter and might do less harm."

Many of the special days for religious and national observance are important civilizing influences. In the Christian calendar are Christmas and Easter, for example, and in the Jewish calendar, Hanukkah and Passover. All American children usually observe such national and folk holidays as Independence Day, Memorial Day, Halloween, and Thanksgiving.

Relating Art to Holy Days and Holidays

Symbols of great antiquity and deep meaning are associated with some of these festivals: the crucifix, the star of David, the menorah. Then there are symbols from folklore: the black cat and witch, the Christmas candle, Santa Claus, the pumpkin, the horn of plenty. Unfortunately, these symbols are often used in a standardized, uncreative way in art classes. Year after year the dreary procession of copy work appears—a lily and a cross for Easter, a witch on a broomstick and a cat with an arched back for Halloween, a horn of plenty bulging with apples and grapes for Thanksgiving.

In being limited to the mere copying of these symbols, the children are prevented from giving attention to the special significance of these events in their own lives. Thanksgiving, for example, is an important national holiday that provides an opportunity for the family to gather and eat together. These are important community events, charged with feeling and deserving thoughtful contemplation. Above all, from an art stand-point, they are eminently suitable for expressive purposes. To suggest to children that they should copy a symbol like the shopworn horn of plenty instead of offering their own impressions of Thanksgiving is to minimize their creativity. If, of course, children hold a particular symbol very dear, they might work with it, not as an isolated object but in close association with the environment in which they found it. As a result they probably will produce an original design in which the symbol is the chief motif. Picture- and mural-making, modeling, and other art activities based on the children's personal reactions to holy days and holidays should be encouraged in every grade; they can result in output rich in subject matter and artistic quality.

Figure 15.15 *"Lighting the menorah for Hanukkah," tempera painting by a sixth-grade boy.*

ART ACTIVITIES ESPECIALLY SUITABLE FOR CORRELATION

Two types of work that serve especially useful purposes in both correlative and unit activities are poster-making and three-dimensional picture-making techniques generally known as dioramas, panoramas, movies, and peep shows.

Media and Techniques. From time to time a classroom project or school activity may require some form of advertising by poster. Ways and means can be devised by which the poster is produced in accordance with sound educational and artistic principles.

Poster-Making

To be effective and useful, a poster must fulfill several well-defined basic requirements. It must be arresting, it must convey its message briefly, it should usually contain only one idea, and it should be easily readable from a distance. The children should be reminded that a poster is designed to attract attention and convey information. In order to do this, it is recommended that they (1) limit colors and emphasize contrast, (2) avoid clutter in layout (composition), and (3) avoid too much "copy" (words).

The lettering required in most poster work demands practice and provides little scope for the imagination. Letter "A" must be letter "A," and very little deviation can be allowed if the letter is to remain readable. Indeed, to produce acceptable letters and layout for a poster requires a technical competence usually beyond the capabilities of an elementary-school child.

The solution to this problem is to build on whatever abilities the children possess. Most school systems include a carefully graded program to teach writing. The youngest children frequently begin writing in what is called "print script." This is often subsequently developed into a "joined print script," and after this stage the children begin cursive writing. Competence at each stage is the result of much painstaking teaching. It is wise, therefore, for the children to use in poster work the abilities gained in the writing program. Whatever alphabet they have learned and mastered as part of the writing program seems to be the logical one to use in a poster because in both types of work they are employing the hard-earned skill of using words to convey ideas. To teach children "roman" lettering, or to encourage them to copy or to devise some curious lettering of their own, would be inefficient educational practice.

In poster-making, the beginners in writing should first use the usual large pencils and writing paper to which they are accustomed. Later they can use wax crayons and drawing paper. By the fifth and sixth grades the pupils are able to use special equipment for poster-making, such as felt-tip pens, or India ink and large lettering nibs having round, oval, and

Figure 15.16 *A cut-paper poster by a second-grade boy.*

square tips to make the writing bold enough for a poster. Following a little practice in using special pens and inks, the pupils seem to experience no great difficulty in writing in their accustomed style on the larger scale required for the poster.

Whatever drawings and paintings the children use in conjunction with their verbal message should likewise be in keeping with their developmental level and general competence. Children in the symbol stage of expression, for example, obviously should use this form in their poster work.

To make the poster more interesting the teacher can capitalize on previous art experiences in cut paper collage (for richness of texture) and montage (for arresting images of unusual juxtapositions of photos and advertisements). If posters are assembled from separate segments such as decorative letters, pictures, or other elements, the children can rearrange the shapes and spaces until they find a composition they like. Preparatory activities in lettering, aside from the styles mastered in the writing program, may involve creating designs from one's own name, printmaking activity using raised letters mounted on cardboard, and collages of letters taken from newspaper headlines and magazines.

Because all posters need to be seen and understood at a distance, it is a good idea for the student to pin letters and pictures in place and study them from a distance. In most cases, children become accustomed to scaling their work according to the distance between them and their desk tops and will not automatically make the proper adjustment for

Figure 15.17 *These playful manipulations of letter forms served as a basis for unusual posters.*

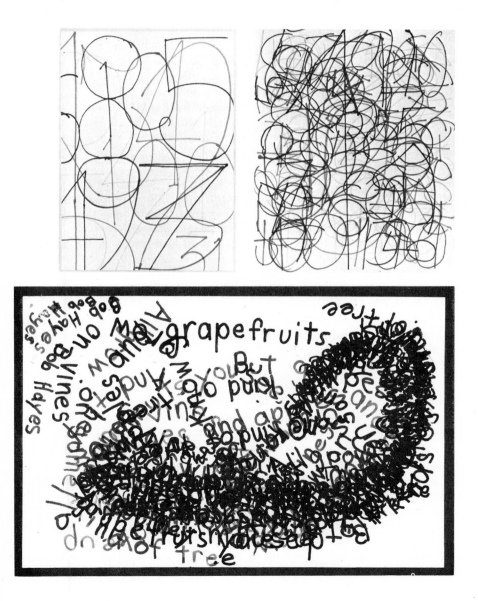

posters. The study of good professional advertisements and travel posters can help them appreciate the appropriate scale.

Teaching. Poster-making can cause problems for an elementary-school teacher because of the demands made on the school by officials of local charitable organizations who wish to advertise the worthy causes they sponsor. While picture-making teachers are contented with work of a technical competence commensurate with the child's developmental level, such is not always the case when posters are being produced for the community. In an attempt to obtain useful posters, the teacher may apply pressure so that the children are forced both to copy the drawings of others and to spend valuable educational time in outlining letters of the alphabet. All this militates against an expressive art program. Overtures from outside sources to have posters made for events unconnected with the school, therefore, should be resisted. Much as the school wishes to support the community at large, the technical difficulties involved in the making of posters for the community forbid the inclusion of this work in the art program in the elementary grades.

A poster for a school activity is quite a different matter. Then, of course, the teacher should encourage the project and offer assistance as it is required. The size of the poster, its design, the strength of color used, the boldness of the writing, and the like should be discussed. The teacher should also demonstrate the different types of lettering nibs, brushes, and pens available. Time for practice with these tools should be found before the poster is made. As pupils become more experienced in the work the teacher should encourage them to make rough layouts before beginning work on the final project.

Thus the poster, if treated as an extension of writing and picture-making, serves a limited but necessary purpose in the art program of the elementary school.

Dioramas, Panoramas, Movies, and Peep Shows

Media and Techniques. These four types of work are especially valuable for correlations between art and literature or history. Three of these have already been treated in Chapter 12 and will be reviewed briefly here.

A diorama is a display having a backdrop and wings rather like a miniature stage. It may be made from a carton or box with the lid and the one side removed. The objects placed in this setting may be made from cardboard, carving materials, or a variety of other substances. The backdrop can be painted or designed in paper.

A panorama is constructed on an open surface and may be seen from any side. The well-known "sand table" is a kind of panorama arrangement. The supporting surface is a tray of convenient size having wooden sides to prevent objects from falling off. All manner of materials and techniques may be used in the making of the panorama. Sand for deserts, glass for rivers, cardboard for houses, papier-mâché for people and animals, and paper for trees are among the items one might suggest.

A "movie" is a series of pictures attached to each other to form a ribbon. For displaying the movie, a cardboard carton may be used. An opening for the "screen" should be cut in the bottom of the carton. Two wooden rollers (old broom handles make good rollers) are then thrust vertically through the carton on either side of the screen opening. The ends of the rollers must project well beyond the sides of the carton. Pictures are stuck together in a ribbon, the ends of which are tacked to the rollers. By turning either of the rollers the pictures are made to move across the opening. The usual drawing and painting materials are used for the pictures.

The peep show is actually a variation of the diorama. An old shoe box provides a good basic unit for this technique. In a small end of the box a hole about the size of a quarter should be cut. Inside, at the other end of the box and at least halfway up the sides, a background must be painted. Figures and trees in front of the background are best made from cardboard. Other properties may be constructed of a variety of materials from straw to absorbent cotton. Interesting lighting effects can be obtained by covering the top of the box with colored plastics or tissue papers. (When the peep show is not in use, the covering should be protected by placing the box lid in position.) Moving a straight beam of light, such as that from a pencil-type flashlight, over the colored material gives the viewer many pleasant and surprising design effects.

Figure 15.18 *The panorama approach was used in this sand-table group project depicting a primitive community. Grade 5. (Photo by Education Development Center.)*

Teaching.   These four techniques essentially constitute group work involving from two to, say, a dozen pupils, in any grade and in at least the symbol stage of pictorial development. The teacher's work is chiefly that of sponsoring group activities according to the principles outlined in Chapter 12. The techniques of constructing, modeling, drawing, and painting mentioned in earlier chapters should be employed in these activities as well.

The teacher's greatest concern should be that of ensuring that the pupils give maximum attention to developing designs with artistic qualities. Unless the teacher discusses design from time to time, any one of these four types of work could degenerate into busy work. There is no need for this to happen, however, since each type of work can be an art activity in every sense.

ACTIVITIES FOR THE READER

1. Prepare detailed plans for three lessons involving a correlation between art and each of the following: physical education, reading, arithmetic.
2. Describe from your classroom observations some attempts at correlation between art and other subjects that degenerated into busy work. Explain in each case how you would have altered the lessons to ensure that art was produced.
3. Analyze a unit of work you have seen in a classroom for the art education that was involved in it. Explain how learning about art might have been improved.
4. Study some "workbooks" and list any errors made by the authors when they attempt to correlate what they consider to be art with another subject. Suggest art activities to replace those outlined by the authors.
5. List all the symbols related to holy days and holidays that children have been asked to copy in classrooms you have observed. Suggest some art work to replace this copy work.
6. Experiment with a number of lettering nibs. Use your own handwriting but try to eliminate any wiggles and squiggles. Also, in the interest of clarity, reduce the length of ascending and descending letters.[6]
7. Cut out twenty-four 2-by-3-inch rectangles and convert them into cut block letters. Cut by families or groups—those that may be folded vertically or horizontally and those that are based on circles.
8. Make a poster for a school event: (a) select a title for the headline—if a secondary heading is required keep it to three or four words; (b) make

[6]For students who wish to become especially proficient in lettering, see Ross F. George, *Speedball Text Book,* 19th ed. (New York: Landau, 1965).

The student who wishes to know more about lettering should see Oscar Ogg, *An Alphabet Source Book* (New York: Dover, 1947); this is a purely technical work. Ogg, *The 26 Letters* (New York: Crowell, 1961), is more historical than the previous works just cited. The interested student can also refer to the section on lettering in the bibliography at the end of this book.

a rough layout, including letters and illustration if any; (c) outline the poster on Bristol board; (d) paint the picture if you have included one; (e) do the lettering; (f) analyze your work from a distance of 10 feet for clarity, brevity, and design quality.

9. With the help of one or two other interested people, experiment with many materials to make a diorama, a panorama, a peep show, and a "movie." In the movie include a title page and captions as well as drawings to tell your story. Relate all four activities to some other classroom work.

When children produce works of art they are presenting themselves fully, as in this fifth-grade girl's self-portrait containing symbols representing important situations in her life. The proper display of their art is hence vital to the encouragement of children's expressiveness.

DISPLAYING CHILDREN'S ART   16

The final major responsibility of the teacher of art is to display the children's completed art. Since art is appreciated through visual activity and emotional sensitivity, exhibiting it is a necessary part of the cycle of activity involved in any art project. Children have enjoyed the creating of an art project and they also enjoy their completed work. They want to share with others a part of what is so vital to them. Realizing this need and desire for recognition, the teacher should plan to display the work of the children in whatever way best suits the particular art product.*

From the art program come tangible visual results of the learning experience; the art program in fact constitutes the only part of the school curriculum whose results are truly visible because they can be exhibited over a prolonged period. As such, art lends itself to display, which serves as the final and communicative stage of the creative process.

Several obvious educational benefits may occur as a result of effective display techniques. It is the purpose of this chapter, therefore, to discuss some of the most important aspects of presenting children's work, including the chief reasons for displaying the work, the problem of selecting pieces for display, the techniques and media involved in arranging displays, and the teaching methods appropriate to this aspect of art education.

WHY DISPLAY CHILDREN'S ART?

Perhaps the most important reason for displaying art is simply that the results of children's artistic acts are usually worth observing for their

*From Blanche Jefferson, *Teaching Art to Children* (Boston: Allyn and Bacon, 1959), p. 154.

aesthetic qualities. Children's art is often good art; for this reason alone it should not be hidden in portfolios but should be brought forth for people to see and enjoy. The production of any art form is not a casual event; it is an offering of heart and mind from one human being to another. Indeed, the whole character of expression in art has been recognized as *"an overture demanding response from others."* [1] Because children offer in their work something of their true selves, their efforts are worthy of respectful attention.

The display of children's art is an effective teaching device. One common method of display is to group the work according to topics or themes. When twenty-five or more pupils in a class present their reactions to one theme, it is highly educative for all to observe those reactions. If art is suitably taught no two children make identical statements about an experience. After viewing the various statements the children may gain a broader insight into the topic as a whole.

The display of children's art tends to develop in the pupils certain desirable attitudes toward the school. When young children see their artistic efforts on display among those of their fellows, they tend to sense a oneness with the group. Their participation brings out a feeling of belonging, which often increases the fullness of subsequent participation. Perhaps the children have stated something about a pet at home, their mother, father, brother or sister, toys, or playmates. It is comforting to them that these important aspects of their lives have miraculously found a way into their school and, furthermore, that the school is interested in them.

The display of children's art also has, of course, its decorative purposes. The classroom is usually a very barren place when the teacher enters it preparatory to the opening of school. Likewise the halls of many schools are drab caverns until suitable decorations have been arranged. Much of the art work of children has highly decorative quality that will quickly change the character of a school building. Often bold and colorful, the work lends attractiveness and an intimate feeling to even the most austere surroundings, particularly in older school buildings. But even the most delightful interior architecture of modern schools can be improved by a judicious display of children's production.

More and more, schools are serving as institutions of learning by day and as community centers by night. Parent-teacher groups, night-school classes (in which, among other subjects, art may be studied), and other meetings of interest to the members of a community are causing greater numbers of adults to visit the schools than ever before. This is a desirable development, since it provides the school with an opportunity to show the public what is being done with that sacred commodity, the

---

[1] The words are those of I. D. Suttie, in *The Origins of Love and Hate,* quoted by Herbert Read, *Education Through Art* (New York: Pantheon, 1958), p. 167.

Figure 16.1 *A student studies a wall of prints by fifth and sixth graders in his school. (Photo by Roger Graves.)*

taxpayer's money. Furthermore, it presents the opportunity of arousing or maintaining public interest in education in general and art education in particular.

SELECTING WORK FOR DISPLAY

Probably the first question in the teacher's mind is how to choose the work for exhibition. The criteria for selection should be both pedagogical and aesthetic. Although children will find interest in the art output of others, they are also interested in their own work and are usually proud of it. This means that every child in a class sooner or later during the school term should have some work on display. Since space is limited in a classroom, pupils cannot expect their work to appear very often, but they will accept this fact if they feel that their chances to have work displayed are equal to those of others. Awareness of this tends to make them more active participants in all displays that appear on the classroom walls.

As children mature, they develop an ability to appraise the standards of both their behavior and their artistic output. Most children in the upper grades can tell with some accuracy whether they "took it easy" or "worked hard." They are also capable of realizing when their output has not resulted in a success commensurate with their effort. An attempt at expression does not always result in success, as every creating person knows. When children realize that their output has not reached an accustomed standard, displaying their work would in all likelihood be an embarrassment to them. Before a particular child's work is displayed, therefore, a teacher would do well to compare it with previous performances. A deviation from the usual standard may be the result of either a decrease in effort or just an uninspired day. In either case, the normal pupil would in all likelihood not expect to find the work on display other than in the classroom.

If work for display is chosen with these ideas in mind, the child of exceptional ability will not create the problems of selection that might otherwise occur. It would be discouraging for the members of the class to see a more gifted child's work repeatedly occupying a major portion of the displays to the partial exclusion of the work of others. The gifted child exhibits a range of success in output, just as everyone else does (see Chapter 14). This being the case, only the most significant items of that child's expression need appear on display.

Sometimes—indeed perhaps frequently—the most finished and apparently competent work of particular children, no matter what their ability, may be rejected in favor of output showing an advance in some specific ability in art, such as an improvement in the handling of a medium or an element of design. On the other hand, sometimes, during what might be described as a burst of growth, children may pass from one expressive stage or mode to another (see Chapter 6). On such occasions their development may adversely affect their technique. Skills then seem to deteriorate, or rather do not keep pace with thought, so that the work appears inadequate in composition or in the handling of media. Nevertheless, because an advance has been made in other directions, the output should be displayed, provided the children are willing to have it shown.

The teacher will not have to save all the art work of every pupil during the school year to summarize the general progress of each child. While some of the work may be kept in a portfolio for reference, the teacher will be able, for the most part, to remember each child's earlier performances. The art output of each child becomes unique in the eyes of an alert, interested, and sensitive teacher.

The selection of work for display is, then, a delicate matter. It depends not only on the outward appearance of each piece but also on an intimate knowledge of every child responsible for it. The teacher must be fully aware of each child's potential and judge the work, not from some preconceived standard of attainment, but rather in relation to the pupil's personal abilities.

What part should the children play in the selection of work? This is a difficult question that the teacher will probably have to answer. It is obviously desirable that the children have some control of the selection of work. However, the teacher is probably in the best position to recognize both the aesthetic growth in individuals and the true aesthetic quality in a large proportion of the output. Perhaps a satisfactory compromise can be reached if individuals are occasionally given the opportunity to indicate their preferences for display of their own work, while committees of children are from time to time made responsible for selecting displays from the various pieces chosen by individuals. At other times, however, it may be necessary for the teacher to choose the arrangement of the display. On these occasions the teacher may still work closely with the children by explaining the reasons for the selection.

In general, it is suggested that the farther the display is removed from the classroom, the more selective should be the process of choosing the works to be displayed. When children's art goes to the front hall or to some location in the community, each piece should be selected for its ability to capture and hold the attention of the viewer. In the classroom, however, there may be times when the work of the entire class will be displayed.

ARRANGING DISPLAYS IN THE CLASSROOM

Media and Techniques for Displaying Two-Dimensional Work. The display areas should not be overcrowded. Each piece should be set apart, preferably mounted or framed. Frames should be chosen so that their color unifies the display but does not conflict with the colors used in the drawings and paintings themselves. Grays, browns, and sometimes black are usually suitable colors for mounts or frames. White is also recommended for the mounts, since it is flattering to the picture and gives a clean look to the exhibit. When the display panels are made of wood, cork, or celotex or homosote boards, both mount and picture may most conveniently be fastened to the display area by a gun-type wall stapler, or glass-head pins. Thumbtacks should be avoided because they distract the viewers' attention from the work.

Mounts or frames may be devised in a number of ways and with several materials. The simplest, cheapest, and, many think, most attractive method of mounting is to attach a sheet of newsprint, paper, or cardboard

Figure 16.2 *Some methods of mounting pictures.*

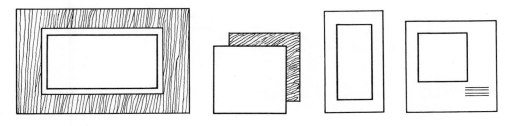

to the display board and to fasten on this a drawing or painting having smaller dimensions. A variety of effects may be obtained with this method by altering the proportion of background to picture. Another method of framing a picture is to fix the picture to the board, cut a window the size of the picture in a sheet of paper or cardboard, and then, placing the frame over the picture, attach it to the board.

Mounting and framing may also be varied by using two or more cardboard mounts or frames in different tones of one color, or by using two materials with contrasting textures, such as burlap and plywood. Sometimes a picture can be supported on a raised mount. This may be done by pinning a picture to a cardboard tray that is in turn fastened to the support.

As mentioned earlier, it is often desirable to exhibit work according to topics or themes. Sometimes a theme depicts a series of events that demand a logical order of display, for example, "Our Trip to the Dairy," which would include the departure from school, the arrival at the plant, the mechanical processes observed, and the return to school. To assist the observer in following the proper sequence of pictures, one can use a series of paper arrows. In addition to providing information, displays can invite the participation of the onlooker by asking such questions as: "What kinds of shapes does one see in a dairy?" or "How many kinds of workers bring us our milk?"

Figure 16.3 *This classroom has been temporarily converted into a gallery. Display units are dispersed to accommodate traffic and facilitate viewing. The same exhibit also provided locations for slide-viewing, kinetic sculpture, demonstrations by students, and even a puppet show. (Photo by Rick Steadry.)*

In some displays no particular logical arrangement is required, but a certain aesthetic order is desired. Those arranging a display will find string convenient in establishing patterns. If various colors and types of string or yarn, including those with a metallic finish, are strung from one place to another in a panel, some exceptionally interesting rhythms throughout the display can be achieved.

When a display is arranged, a title is usually required. Titles, of course, become part of the general design of a display. A title may be produced in two dimensions with lettering pens and India or colored inks and felt pens.[2] Although they are beyond the ability of most elementary-school children, three-dimensional titles can be made from cardboard cut-out letters. After it is cut out, each letter is stuck on a long pin that holds it away from the display board. Attractive background papers of contrasting color or texture help to make this type of title particularly arresting. Large type "primer" typewriters also produce attractive titles.

The simplest and most common arrangement of pictures on a display panel is one that follows the rectangular shape of the board. The pictures are hung so that their edges are parallel to those of the board. More often than not a formal balance is achieved so that the spectators' attention will be attracted equally around imaginary central axes of the board. The margins established between the picture frames and the outside edges of a display panel that is horizontal should be such that the bottom margin is widest, the top narrowest, and the width of the sides in between those of top and bottom. In a vertical panel, the traditional proportions to be observed reverse the proportions of sides and top: the bottom is widest, the top is second in size, and the sides are narrowest. A square panel calls for even margins at top and sides, with a wider margin at the bottom. These classic arrangements are safe, and by using them one may tastefully display any group of pictures.

If display panels are not available, it may prove difficult to exhibit works of art in the school hall because most walls are constructed of tiles. Curls of masking tape on the back of pictures are often used to attach flatwork to such surfaces, but this is far from ideal because of the expense involved and the tendency of pictures to slip. Two permanent solutions are strips of cork bolted to the wall and framed 4-by-8 foot sheets of composition board or any other material that takes staples and pins. Avoid masonite for this reason. Masonite pegboard, however, is excellent because bent metal hooks can be inserted to hang shelves, puppets, and other three-dimensional objects.

All exhibitions in a classroom must show an awareness of the display situation and should be considered as designs subject to the discipline of good taste. As each one is added, it must be considered in relation to whatever displays are already on view. In general it is a wise plan to

[2]See the section on poster-making in Chapter 15.

restrict displays to those areas especially designed for exhibits. A class-room can scarcely appear orderly if drawings and paintings are stuck to blackboards, pinned to chalk-ledges, or plastered on windows. Black-boards, chalk-ledges, and windows are functional parts of the classroom whose efficiency is impaired by displays of art. To interfere with their function through decoration is an act of bad taste.

Here are some points the teacher might keep in mind when setting up bulletin-board displays and exhibits:

1. A bulletin board has somewhat the same nature as a poster. Both must capture attention, provide information, and present a uni-fied design through pleasing relationships of textures, masses, subject matter, and lettering.
2. Pins with clear plastic heads are the best fasteners, metal pins next, and tacks last. Staples may be used if a staple remover is available.
3. Some areas of the background should be uncluttered, to give the eye a rest.
4. The eye level of the viewer should be respected.
5. Extreme "artiness," such as complicated diagonal arrangements, should be avoided.
6. Bulletin-board exhibits should seldom be on display for more than two weeks. There is no disgrace in occasionally having a blank display area.
7. If possible a well-lighted area should be used for your display.
8. Usually tops or sides of pictures should be aligned for consist-ency and order, and vertical and diagonal lettering should be avoided.
9. A supply of materials such as solid-colored burlap and corduroy should be kept on hand. These make excellent background segments to unite a small group of pictures. Any material that detracts from the objects on display should not be used.
10. When "going public," avoid supermarkets and other busy envi-ronments.

Media and Techniques for Displaying Three-Dimensional Work. Most classrooms are not equipped with display cases for three-dimensional output. It is frequently necessary, therefore, for the class to improvise other means of display. If space is available, one may place a table directly in front of a display board. The three-dimensional objects may then be set on the table and descriptions of the work or related two-dimensional work may be pinned to the board. Should it be considered necessary to link a written description to any particular piece on the table, a colored string may be fixed from the description to the piece of work.

The objects should be arranged according to their bulk and height.

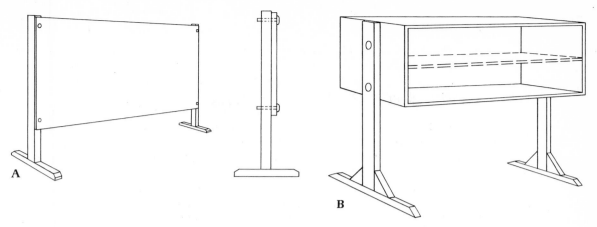

Figure 16.4 *Panels for two-dimensional objects* (**A**) *and a display case for three-dimensional objects* (**B**).

Obviously the largest and tallest objects will have to be placed well in the background so that smaller objects will not be hidden. Some groups of objects, particularly modeled or carved forms and pottery, will demand the use of pedestals. The pedestals, made from boxes or blocks of wood, may be painted or covered with textiles. By placing a sheet of glass over one or more of the pedestals, it is possible to arrange a convenient series of shelves of varying heights. Ceiling space can be utilized in many

Figure 16.5 *The arrangement of these painted paper fish stuffed with newspaper gives the effect of a mobile. The strings have been tacked to the soft celotex ceiling of the hall.* (Photo by Rick Steadry.)

unusual ways, particularly for mobiles and kites. Caution should be used, however, in hanging objects from the ceiling, for certain ceiling surfaces and lighting fixtures must be treated with care. Custodians and principals can give information in this regard.

Display boards themselves may be used to exhibit three-dimensional work. Metal brackets fixed to the boards with screws are able to support glass shelves, which make attractive display space.

In arranging three-dimensional displays, the exhibitors must give the same attention to design that they would in displaying flat work. For example, brilliantly colored pieces or those having outstanding structural or textural qualities must be well placed with respect to the centers of interest, the balance, and the rhythm of the design.[3] To bring unity to the three-dimensional display, it may be necessary to use the same background for the objects.

Some striking results may be obtained by avoiding straight rows of objects, placing them instead at different heights and at various distances from the observer, and by grouping objects within a display, yet maintaining a unity among all such groups. Objects do not arrange themselves; to present them with charm and character one must give considerable attention to the problems peculiar to three-dimensional display.

Teaching.   Because the displaying of art is an art activity in itself, it is highly desirable for children to take part in it. Even a six-year-old can see how much better a drawing looks when it is mounted and displayed. A simple act such as this can establish the connection between design and order in a young mind. Moreover, display techniques may lead to excellent group endeavors. The kindergarten is not too soon for children to begin this work. Kindergarten children may participate in quasi-group activities in which individuals bring their work to some central area for display.

As in all other art activities the teacher must continually remind the children of the importance of design in display arrangements. Whether the children are drawing up plans in advance for a display or working out a display directly on a panel or elsewhere, the teacher must encourage the pupils continually to consider the designs being formed.

The teacher should give every encouragement to the pupils to experiment with new ways of displaying their art. One method is to have members of the class report on any outstanding display techniques observed in store windows or elsewhere. Another method is to have the teacher from time to time arrange a display of children's work in which some new ideas for display are demonstrated.[4] The teacher, however, should exercise caution in arranging the display. The arrangement should

---

[3]Review Chapter 3 for a discussion of design.

[4]A good source of ideas for school displays of all kinds is George Horn, *Bulletin Boards* (New York: Reinhold, 1962).

Figure 16.6 *A large zigzag display in a school gymnasium. (Photo by Jack Engeman Studio.)*

never be so active that it draws attention to itself and thus overwhelms the work it is intended to support.

ARRANGING DISPLAYS OUTSIDE THE CLASSROOM

The problems arising from displays arranged in the halls or elsewhere in a school are little different from those related to classroom exhibits. More people and examples of work are involved, of course, so that organizational problems are intensified.

Media and Techniques. School architects today give attention to display possibilities, so it is not unusual for some elementary schools to have gallery-type walls designed adjacent to the principal's office.

If no gallery space is available, school authorities may be expected to provide suitable panels and even display cases; the cost of these is a relatively minor item in most educational budgets. When the panels and cases are being installed, those responsible for the installations must remember to arrange suitable lighting for each one.

On occasion the school may need additional display facilities. Many extra panels might be required on "Parents' Night" for example, when the school wishes to make an exceptional effort to interest the community. The design of panels for extra display facilities has become almost stan-

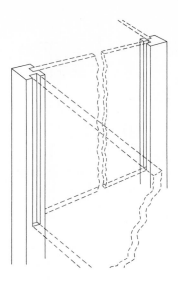

Figure 16.7 *Diagram of posts and panels for a zigzag-type display.*

dard. The panels consist of sheets of building board, usually measuring from 4 by 4 feet to 4 by 8 feet, to either end of which legs are bolted. The legs are usually in the form of inverted T's, but other ingenious and attractive designs are to be seen. For three-dimensional display a boxlike construction often having shelves takes the place of the panel.

Figure 16.8 *The units in this display arrangement can be dismantled easily and stored in a small area. Note that both the front and the back of these units may be used for display. (Designed by Pat Renick.)*

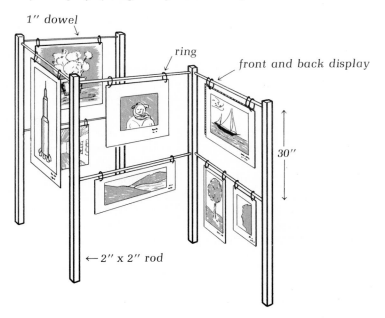

A second type of portable display board has been designed for space-saving and quick assembly. It consists of panels of building board and sturdy legs with slots cut into two adjacent sides. The panels are fitted into the slots to form a zigzag effect which is pleasing and practical. The panels are made secure by lashing the legs together with cord at the top and bottom of the panels.

Another portable display unit is illustrated in Figure 16.8. The materials needed are 2-by-2-inch wooden rods slightly over 5 feet in length, with holes bored at approximately 30-inch intervals. These rods will receive 1-inch dowels, on which hang metal rings that are attached to the pictures. The placement of the holes on the 2-by-2-inch rods determines how the units may be angled so that the flow of traffic can be controlled.

Teaching. The display of work outside the classroom can become a burdensome undertaking if too few people take on the job, but it can be a real challenge to a large group. In some schools, display committees composed of teachers and pupils are formed. These committees often decide on the themes and assign responsibility for hanging the displays. Sometimes arrangements are made in advance so that each class in the school is responsible for a display for a given period of time. Other schools select broad themes of local interest, to which each class contributes. Frequently, a combination of both types of display is used.

The teaching techniques involved in this larger display activity remain the same as those outlined earlier for the classroom display. The teachers must still stimulate the pupils, offer suggestions as they are required, and demonstrate and discuss new techniques.

THE DISPLAY AS COMMUNITY EDUCATION

The subject matter of art displays for parent and community groups may be different from that of displays for children. Parents and other adults are interested not only in the work as such but also in the pedagogical principles supporting the art program. It must be remembered that for many adults the present-day program of art in schools is completely different from the so-called art work they were forced to do in their youth. Although ignorance of the contemporary program sometimes leads to disapproval, in general parents are quick to react favorably to present-day trends in art once they understand those trends. For parents, the subjects of the exhibition of children's art might frequently emphasize some of the pedagogical and psychological implications of the activities. The themes may dramatize the overall structure of the art program or a single aspect of it. The following are a few sample topics that have proved satisfactory during Parents' Night:

Figure 16.9 *Display techniques may be very informal, as evidenced by the life-size costume parade taped to the tiled walls of a hallway. (Photo by Rick Steadry.)*

Looking at Nature
Art Education—the Old and the New
Personal Development Through Art
Variety in Artistic Expression
Group Work in Art
"How I See Myself"
The Colors of Centerville[5]
Art and the Community—An Overview of the Art Program at
   Centerville Elementary School

For each exhibition, brief but effective signs should be made to emphasize the points demonstrated by the children's work. Each show, moreover, should have a clearly marked beginning, a logical sequence of ideas throughout the body of the exhibition, and a short summary, either written or pictorial or both, at its close. The exhibit should be more than merely another chore. It is the most dramatic means of communicating the teacher's role in the school to the public, to the administration, and to other teachers.

A few last but highly important words must be said. No matter what type of exhibition is organized, whether in the classroom, in the halls, or elsewhere in the school, an art show must be kept on the move. To

---

[5]See Viktor Lowenfeld, *Your Child and His Art* (New York: Macmillan, 1954), which is written to help parents understand their children's art. Many topics that might form the core of a display for parents can be found in this excellent book.

leave it on the walls longer than is necessary is to waste an educational opportunity. Nothing becomes more bedraggled or more quickly outdated than an art show left on display too long. Perhaps, on the other hand, nothing is more effective as a teaching device or as a means of public relations than a fresh, new, attractively displayed exhibition of children's art.

ACTIVITIES FOR THE READER

1. Describe the various criteria used by teachers you have observed to select children's art work for display. Appraise each criterion according to its educational effects on the children concerned.
2. Study and compare the display techniques you have observed in various classrooms.
3. Experiment with mounting and framing a picture on a surface such as a drawing board. Try some of the ways suggested in this chapter and then devise new ways to display the picture.
4. Sketch in pencil or crayon some plans for a display of five pictures. Select the plan you like best and use it in an actual panel display.
5. Repeat 4, this time including at least twelve pictures.
6. Make some plans for the display of three pieces of pottery. Carry out the plan you like best.
7. List some subjects for an art display to be used in the main entrance of a school on Parents' Night. The entrance hall is about 25 feet long and 12 feet wide. After selecting the subject that most appeals to you, indicate in detailed sketches (a) the type and position of the display panels; (b) the number and subject matter of the pictures or three-dimensional objects; (c) the captions to be used; and (d) the route that the visitors should follow to view the exhibition and the means by which they are directed along this route.
8. Pretend you are a new teacher using a spring exhibit to acquaint the community with your art program. You have a dozen 4-by-8-foot panels on which to display the year's work in the gymnasium. What materials would you choose for your panels? How would you organize your display? Present your plan in the form of a real model made of heavy cardboard, using a scale of 1 inch to 1 foot.
9. Assume that you have completed the plans for the installation of an exhibition at your school. Now ask yourself the following questions: Should art work be labeled? Why? If the work should be labeled, what kinds of information should be included? Pupil's name? grade? medium? teacher? school? Should all, part, or none of the foregoing be included? Why?

Although copying the works of professional artists is frowned upon, the exposure of children to fine art often serves as a stimulus to creativity and as a means of increasing their awareness of aesthetic elements in picture making.

Henri Matisse. Lemons against a Fleur-de-lis Background. 1943. Oil on canvas, 28⅞ x 24¼". Collection, The Museum of Modern Art, New York. Loula D. Lasker Bequest. © 1974 by SPADEM PARIS.

DEVELOPING CHILDREN'S APPRECIATION OF ART

17

Of special interest to anyone interested in education is the question of why our college graduates or the members of the educated classes do not constitute a fairly large and powerful group of tastemakers with influence on the aesthetic life of the nation somewhat comparable to their influence on other areas of national activity. Why has this not come about? Why has the gulf between the serious contemporary artist and even the educated public remained so wide and forbidding?*

Up to this point we have considered the educational problems arising from the production of art forms. We must now turn to another aspect of art education, that of the pupils' appreciation of the work of others.

THE NATURE OF ART APPRECIATION

In considering art appreciation we face intangibles. When the pupil has produced a work of art, we have the finished product to study and to compare with the output of others. There can be no such tangible evidence of development in the pupils' ability to appreciate art. But we have good reason to believe that not only can children's appreciation of art be heightened, but that progress can be observed and, to some degree, evaluated. The validity of such a claim naturally depends on how "appreciation" is to be defined. If by the word one refers to the final act of criti-

---

*From Harry S. Broudy, "Contemporary Art and Aesthetic Education," *The School Review*, Vol. 72, No. 3 (Autumn 1964), p. 397. Published by the University of Chicago Press. Copyright 1964 by the University of Chicago.

Figure 17.1 *A pupil listens to a taped lecture at an exhibition of the posters of Toulouse Lautrec.*

cism—that is, the formation of opinions in the evaluative or judgmental stage—it may indeed be difficult, philosophically as well as practically, to attempt to chart the child's progress. If, however, one refers to the critical stages that precede judgment—that is, describing, analyzing, and interpreting what is revealed in art works—then it is possible to develop both verbal and nonverbal means of measuring and appraising the gains being made by the student.

Stated simply, art appreciation implies knowing and having information about art works and using such knowledge as a basis for discriminating, interpreting, and judging. Knowledge about art refers to information surrounding the work of art (names, dates, places) as well as to facts concerning physical details (subject matter, media, colors) taken from the work itself. Knowledge about art also involves those concepts of design, technique, and style that the teacher feels enable the student to "read" a painting, sculpture, or building with some acuity.

Knowledge about art is rooted in perception. Art appreciation rests on the skill of the teacher in developing the perceptual capabilities of the child. The development of perception is usually achieved by focusing attention on the formal aspects of the work of art and is often viewed as a preliminary phase to be followed by a valuative stage in which the pupils discuss the feelings generated by the work and whether they like the piece they are viewing or not.

454

To accept knowledge as a vital component of art appreciation is not to preclude those highly personal reactions to art that come so naturally to children. Each child is free to react spontaneously to a given art work. Some critics and aestheticians feel, however, that the children should be made aware of what is involved in the creation of a work of art.

To what do we react in a work of art and how do we react? Fry offers the argument that in all cases our reactions to works of art are reactions to relationships and not to isolated sensations, objects, persons, or events. He goes on to point out, as an example, that some of the works of the greatest colorists are built up from elements that are of no particular significance when taken separately but that through interrelationships in their composition gain the utmost significance. He carries his observations concerning our reactions to the relationships of elements into the fields of music, poetry, and architecture.[1]

An important distinction can be made between the reaction of "having a good laugh" or "a good cry" at, say, a cinema, and the aesthetic reaction to the screenplay. The former reaction, according to Herbert Read, is one of sentimentality. "Sentimentality," he states, "is a release, but also a loosening, a relaxing of the emotions; art is a release, but also a bracing." [2] Thus, in Read's view, to weep over the trials of the heroine of a play as if we were in the place of the sufferer is not to experience the aesthetic quality of the production. A work of art may lead the mind to delightful fantasies, but such a state is irrelevant if it is agreed that the work of art is the single reference for aesthetic appreciation. John Dewey sums up the matter thus: "Emotion is esthetic when it adheres to an object formed by an expressive act. . . ." [3] Fry describes the manner in which Dewey's dictum is often violated:

> Here we touch the crux of the aesthetic experience for the greater number of people who are accustomed to rely almost exclusively on their interest in, or emotion about, the persons or events called to mind by the imagery of the fine arts. Landscape for such is just reminiscence or revelation of pleasant natural scenes; portraiture interests by the beautiful . . . ladies . . . it represents; figure painting avails by its attractive and provocative nudes. . . .[4]

An aesthetic response, as distinguished from a sentimental one, seems to involve the total personality. There is probably much truth in the old saw about "a picture judging a person" rather than the reverse. What a person is—emotionally, intellectually, and socially—will determine that person's ability to appreciate art. This ability is not innate, but it seems to be built around innate qualities so that some people are able

[1] Roger Fry, *Transformations* (New York: Doubleday, 1956).
[2] *The Meaning of Art,* 3rd ed. (New York: Pitman, 1951), p. 39.
[3] *Art as Experience* (New York: Putnam, 1959), p. 76.
[4] *Transformations,* p. 3.

to acquire it more quickly than others. Art appreciation, in fact, appears to be the result of prolonged education. "As for appreciation, this can undoubtedly be developed by teaching," says Read, although "the faculty is only likely to develop as one aspect of social adaptation." [5] The problem arises in the elementary school when it wishes to help children learn to appreciate the art of others. The remainder of this chapter will concentrate on some practical ways and means of developing appreciation of art.

SOME TEACHING METHODS FOR DEVELOPING APPRECIATION

At least four points of view have been held concerning the teaching of art appreciation in the elementary school. The first suggests that there should be no teaching because children are not sufficiently mature to benefit from it. Instead the teacher should encourage the pupils to express themselves and then "can only stand over them in a kind of protective awe." [6] The second is that formal lessons should be offered from time to time, particularly with regard to "picture study."

The third view is that appreciation should be taught when such teaching appears to be expedient and when the need for it is clearly apparent. This third viewpoint implies that the logical juncture for appreciation on the elementary level may well lie in studio activity. Experience with materials may be directly related to the kinds of knowledge needed to extend the pupil's power of appreciation. The fourth viewpoint, already touched on, is that special efforts should be made to make the children, even on the elementary level, so aware of critical processes that they can apply what they have learned when confronted with works of art.

The first point of view seems to recommend a position that is practically impossible to maintain. The actions of teachers during their daily rounds of duty, their appearance, their care of the classroom, and so on must exert some effect, either good or bad, on the attitudes of children toward art. Furthermore, if expression is to receive any guidance at all, the question of appreciation immediately enters into an art activity. Whether or not teachers believe in teaching for the development of appreciation, they do so teach.

Few teachers who have ever taught for appreciation and listened to the insights that children bring to viewing would ever take this first position. The freshness, honesty, and directness that characterize the art work of primary pupils and the imaginative and intuitive capabilities of most children on the elementary level combine to provide a positive learning climate for their appreciation activities. The increased verbal

---

[5] *Education Through Art* (New York: Pantheon, 1958), p. 209
[6] *Ibid.*

Figure 17.2 *A pupil and his teacher together study a reproduction of a Matisse painting. They are examining the wide range of compositions within the total work and the way in which parts relate to wholes.*

skill of children in the upper elementary grades can compensate to a large degree for their self-consciousness in certain studio activities and can often provide academically talented children with an opportunity to excel in another area of art—critical appreciation.

The second point of view had more advocates twenty-five years ago than it has today. An extraordinary amount of nonsense has been perpetrated in many classrooms through formal lessons in art appreciation, in which questions are asked about certain works of art. Sir Joshua Reynolds' *The Age of Innocence,* for example, may be the picture chosen for study. Even when the questions are fairly pertinent to the picture being studied—"Why is the little girl placed where she is in the picture?" or, "What colors has the artist used to make us look at her?"—there is some doubt as to the value of the teaching procedure. But when, as is not infrequently the case, the questions become artistically remote from the work and include such sentimental or literary ideas as—"Isn't she a pretty little girl? Do you think she is happy? Why isn't she wearing shoes? Will it rain? What will the little girl do then?"—the appreciation of art can never occur. Such questions simply lead the children away from "the sense in which the act of expression has been defined." To offer this type of lesson in picture appreciation, even as a literary exercise, can only intensify an all too prevalent misapprehension as to the nature of art.[7]

Indeed, in recent years any formal teaching of "famous masterpieces" is held in some suspicion. "Urging people to like things, or preaching about our own likes is not the most effective way to get results."[8] As Dewey says, art can be appreciated only when there is a "hunger and thirst" for it. The formal attempt to motivate children to appreciate famous paintings is rarely as effective as its advocates maintain. But the failure in general of the formal method of teaching appreciation of art in no way obviates the necessity for children to be afforded every possible means of coming into contact with their cultural heritage.

[7]At this time the reader might profitably refer to Margaret H. Bully, *Art and Counterfeit* (London: Methuen, 1925), and, by the same author, the large and less concise but interesting *Art and Every Man: A Basis for Appreciation,* 2 vols. (London: Batsford, 1952).

[8]Thomas Munro, "Powers of Art Appreciation and Evaluation," in G. M. Whipple, ed., *Fortieth Yearbook of the National Society for the Study of Education* (Bloomington, Ill.: Public School Publishing Co., 1941), p. 340. The extent to which a child's acquaintance with pictures may be at the mercy of a teacher is well illustrated in many of the books on art appreciation that appeared about thirty-five or forty years ago. A typical example is Agnes Hammell, *Advancing in Picture Study* (Toronto: Gage, 1931). Most of the 110 illustrations chosen by this author are of the "realistic" or story-telling photographic type, by Landseer, Dupré, Breton, Alma-Tadema, Leighton, and others of similar style. El Greco is not represented, nor is Michelangelo, Gauguin, nor Matisse. Rather amazing is the inclusion of some Cézanne apples!

Figure 17.3 *Expression is an integral part of art appreciation. The Metropolitan Museum of Art uses dance movement as a means of encouraging the response to and identification with works of art. (Photo by Karen Gilborn.)*

Table 17.1

A COMPARISON OF PAST AND PRESENT METHODS OF TEACHING ART APPRECIATION

Past	*Present*
1. Emphasized immediate reactions to a work of art.	1. Defers judgment until the art object has been examined.
2. Instruction was primarily verbal and teacher-centered.	2. Instruction may be based on verbalization, perceptual investigation, studio activity, or combinations of these.
3. Relied primarily on reproductions.	3. Utilizes a wide range of instructional media—slides, books, reproductions, films, and, most important, original works of art, visits to museums and galleries, and visits from local artists.
4. Based primarily on painting, because of its "story-telling" qualities.	4. May encompass the complete range of visual form from "fine arts" (painting, sculpture) to applied arts (industrial design, architecture, and crafts). May also include mass media, television commercials, films, and magazine layouts.
5. Used literary and sentimental associations as a basis for discussion. Concentrated on such elements as beauty and morality to the exclusion of formal qualities.	5. Bases discussion on the formal qualities of the art work. Recognizes beauty and other sensuously gratifying qualities as only one part of the aesthetic experience, but also recognizes abrasive and shocking images as legitimate expressions of psychological and political motives.
6. Concentrated on the "great monuments" of art.	6. Avoids reverence of the past; shows respect for artistic efforts of all epochs.
7. Drew instructional material from the culture of Western civilization.	7. Allows examples of art works to encompass whatever cultures are most appropriate to represent a particular artistic point.
8. Spent much time in anecdotal accounts of artist's life.	8. Minimizes the life story of the artist and concentrates instead on the work.

If a stilted, authoritarian, excessively rigorous teaching situation is implied by the word "formal," then formal instruction is to be avoided; but if it is taken to mean instruction that pertains to the form of a thing, then the word becomes less inhibiting when applied to teaching. Table 17.1 may serve as a guide in comparing dated formal teaching methods with a more contemporary point of view.

Many teachers adopt the third viewpoint in devoting much of their time, thought, and energy to a program in which an appreciation of art is taught in close relationship to expression.[9] According to this method a teacher seizes every practical opportunity to introduce the subject of appreciation, not only of drawing and painting but also of three-dimensional work such as sculpture and pottery.

The method is based on the belief that one cannot logically divorce expression from appreciation. After working with a medium we know what to look for in similar work of others. We become conscious of the problems, needs, and goals that have influenced our own expressive acts. It does not matter how limited our present insight into artistic expression may be. As long as we have had some personal problem that has arisen from our own labors, some goal related to the activity, and some need for enlightenment, we are in a position to increase our insight by intelligently appreciating what another has done.

The fourth point of view is a species of formal analysis related to criticism and is really an extension of the third position. This approach requires the children to be thoroughly acquainted with the components of art works and the teacher to be sensitive to the children's perceptual and linguistic capabilities. Research offers relatively little information about this kind of teaching, but it represents a mode of instruction that many art educators today feel should be explored if such goals as aesthetic sensitivity and visual acuity are ever to be realized in behavioral terms.

Teaching the characteristics that provide the structure of a unified work of art is important in this approach to appreciation. Fry has pointed out the dangers inherent in the abuse of this kind of teaching—he feels that it can lead to fragmentation of the total aesthetic experience.[10] The teacher who does not abuse recognition and identification of design elements by an undue emphasis will find that children respond most favorably to the challenge of being specific in their discussion of paintings and sculpture.

In commenting on the reciprocity between the creative and critical processes in television art instruction, Manuel Barkan and Laura Chapman state:

> . . . the most sensitive making of art cannot lead to rich comprehension if it is not accompanied by observation of works of art and reflective thought about them. Neither can observation and reflection alone call for the nuances of feeling nor develop the commitment that can result from personal involvement in making works of art. The reciprocal relationship between learning to make art and learning to recognize, attend to, and understand art should guide the planning of art instruction.[11]

[9]This method is also advocated for adolescents in a report of the Progressive Education Association, *The Visual Arts in General Education* (New York: Appleton-Century-Crofts, 1940), pp. 72ff.

[10]*Transformations.*

[11]*Guidelines for Art Instruction Through Television for Elementary Schools* (Bloomington, Ind.: National Center for School and College Television, 1967), p. 7.

It cannot be assumed that children will make a connection between their own painting experience with color and that of an artist such as Monet unless discussion and activity direct their attention to such a relationship.

This type of art appreciation at the elementary level suggests processes whereby students may engage in both studio and critical activities, gaining relevant information while discussing works of art. It also suggests deferring judgment and interpretation until the art has been examined and discussed. To cite a specific example, let us take a single unit of instruction for sixth graders that would include the above activities.

STAGE I   *Studio Activity:*
   A line drawing of a figure and still life. The object is to:
   1. Vary the quality of line.
   2. Take into consideration the spaces between the lines as components of the design.
   3. Relate the lines to the contours, or edges, of the subject.

STAGE II   *Knowledge (Information):*
   Vocabulary-concepts around which the activity is built. These are listed on the blackboard and discussed prior to the activity.
      Contour
      Mass
      Weight
      Positive (line)
      Negative (space)

   Discussion of artists who reflect these qualities (using slides or reproductions); some artists for study are:
      Pablo Picasso   Edgar Degas
      Henri Matisse   Ronald Searle
      Ben Shahn   George Grosz

   It is possible, of course, to vary the sequence and begin at this stage by using the work of the artists for motivational purposes. Some teachers would question this rearranged sequence on the grounds that it could unduly influence the work of the class.

STAGE III   *Observation and Perception:*
   The children compare slides or reproductions of works by the above-mentioned artists to observe how their work reflects the concepts already discussed.

STAGE IV   *Interpretation and Judgment:*
   The children are asked to discuss the meaning of what they have seen (interpretation), then voice their opinions (likes and dislikes) of the art works.

The final stage clearly allows for personal reaction, but the responses have greater critical validity because they are based on preparation through activity and guided discussion. Such an approach to art appreciation compels the children to be aware of the aesthetic constituents of appreciation and draws them away from purely associative responses that overly emphasize subject matter.

Let us now examine the critical terminology used in the elementary-school classroom and note the kinds of discussions, activities, and learning instruments that may be employed to develop art appreciation.

CHILDREN AND CRITICISM

Criticism, as Feldman succinctly puts it, is "talk about art." [12] Its suggested inclusion in the elementary art program is recognition of the fact that children enjoy talking, arguing, and venturing opinions about art even if their opinions may be somewhat uninformed. With increasing use of the critical process, however, the children can develop a way of organizing their perception that provides a more valid basis for judgment.

Verbal skills may also be developed since critical discussion focuses the attention of the pupils on concepts that can be mentioned, pointed to, and used in the students' own activities. For instance, the phrase "symmetrical composition" may be meaningless to the children until they can point to a medieval icon and say, "This is more symmetrical than the Wyeth."

The Stages of the Critical Process

The critical process involves certain categories of discourse, which pupils may use as broad guidelines for the organization of their comments. Authorities differ in their ordering of "stages" and "taxonomies," [13] but we are safe in stating that four basic stages of discussion are possible—description, formal analysis, interpretation, and judgment. Let us examine these as they might apply to elementary art instruction.

Description.   In the descriptive stage the child takes an initial inventory of what is seen. At this first perceptual level a consensus should be reached that can be referred to in succeeding stages. Description involves noting objects, shapes, colors, and other items with which the children have probably had some prior experience. Children, like adults, will bring to a painting only what they have been prepared to bring. It is the teacher's

---

[12]Edmund Feldman, *Art: Image and Idea* (Englewood Cliffs, N.J.: Prentice-Hall, 1967), p. 446.

[13]See Feldman, *Art: Image and Idea,* and Stephen Pepper, *Principles of Art Appreciation* (New York: Harcourt Brace Jovanovich, 1949).

task to prepare them by broadening their base of experience. Obviously, children will not compare a Holbein and a Van Gogh in terms of "painterly" textures unless this term has been pointed out to them. Even fourth graders are capable of such distinctions if their attention has been called to nuances of appearance and of surface or if they have been brought to discover it for themselves. A discussion of nonobjective or abstract paintings (those of Kandinsky, for example) will almost of necessity be descriptive.[14]

Although the descriptive level focuses on factors that generally are perceived in ways that are common to most of us, it can lead to some heated discussions—what one sees as red, another sees as orange; one may see square shapes, another trapezoidal.

Formal Analysis.   Formal analysis also has a perceptual basis but it takes place at a deeper level. It takes the descriptive stage a step further by requiring the child to analyze the makeup or composition of an art work. The child who can distinguish between symmetry and asymmetry, describe the nature of the material, and be sensitive to the kinds and qualities of color and line can comment about the form of an art work.

The discourse initiated at both descriptive and formal-analytic stages brings about the intense visual concentration that is necessary if appreciation lessons are to have meaning and substance. Both stages are valuable also for the development of considered opinions about art. They do not allow for premature judgments, requiring instead that the student defer certain decisions until they can be handled with some detachment. At these two stages the teacher is asking, "What do you see?" rather than "What do you *think* about it?" What the child sees will, of course, depend on many factors. Some will know more than others; that is, they should know more if they have had some experience with such things as light, mass, color, line, and other elements of form.

Children view criticism as a visual-verbal game and will participate with enthusiasm if the discussions are not too lengthy (a half-hour seems to be an outside limit) and the art works under discussion are selected with care. Works with strong color, interesting subject matter, and clear, indeed obvious, compositional structure, seem to elicit the most positive responses.

Interpretation.   In the interpretive stage the child is asked to think about the meaning of the painting. To do this the child is required to establish some connection between the structure that can be discerned in a particular painting and the intent of the artist. For example, if the class has agreed that Orozco in his *Zapatistas* uses sharp contrasts of dark and light and strong directional forces, the next question might be "To what end?"

---

[14]The dialog on pp. 464–70 demonstrates how the descriptive stage should be handled.

Would the meaning have been as clear had the artist used Redon's colors? At this vital point the class is getting at an artist's conscious use of compositional elements for a specific end. How does Renoir's sensuous and pleasing color relate to his feelings regarding motherhood and courtship? How do De Kooning's fragmented shapes and strident color tie in with his attitudes regarding certain types of women? Such questions provide material for discussion in the interpretive stage.

Judgment.   The final judgmental phase is the most complex, since it requires students to render their opinion regarding the worth of an object, basing that opinion on what they have learned in the previous stages. Such questions as the following are asked: "Are you moved by this work of art?" "How do you feel about it?" "Would you like to own it or hang it in your room?" "Does it leave you cold?" "Do you dislike it?" Most viewers begin at this level; what the process of criticism set forth here attempts to do is to delay such issues until the matter has been given thought. With older students, the teacher may want to reverse the process by beginning with the judgmental level and then asking children to describe how they arrived at their opinions.

In essence the four stages are related to four basic questions:

"What do you see?" (description)
"How are things put together?" (formal analysis)
"What is the artist trying to say?" (interpretation)
"What do you think of it?" (judgment)

Examples of Appreciation Discussions   The transcript of a tape-recorded group critique of Picasso's *Girl Before a Mirror* has been included to clarify the distinctions between *description, formal analysis,* and *interpretation.* Although the session was conducted with art teachers, certain inferences can be made as to how the discussion should proceed with children.[15] Following this transcript of Dr. Feldman's tape is a partial transcript of an actual teaching session.

DR. F: . . . We don't have to know a great deal, we don't have to know the biographies of Picasso or De Kooning, we don't have to know the sequence in which the works were created or the dates of the works . . . What we have to build on in doing our descriptive analysis and interpretation of the work is our common sense, the basis of experience that we've had with people, things and shapes and spaces—our humanity. In this connection we need a certain amount of confidence

---

[15]The discussion was conducted by Dr. Edmund B. Feldman of the University of Georgia as one phase of an in-service program of art appreciation for elementary-school art teachers. Portions of the transcript are reproduced here with the kind permission of Dr. Feldman.

in the validity of our own judgments and our ability to draw inferences from what we see. This is so important—for teachers to have confidence in their own reactions and not to feel that there must be some authority who knows what the work means, what it ought to mean, and that they are inevitably making errors that some authority is going to correct. This is, in my opinion, what frightens many, many teachers. Let's look at this Picasso, *Girl Before a Mirror.*

Will somebody volunteer to come up here and I'll ask about what you see. . . . The first thing I want to ask is simply that you name the principal shapes and colors. Don't tell me what they mean, don't tell me whether they're good or bad, whether they're well executed or badly executed, just tell me what you see in the thing. If you see a girl and know it's a girl, tell me it's a girl. If you think it's a boy, tell me it's a boy. If you can't tell whether it's a girl or a boy, then tell me you see something human. *Description*

MR. W: I see diamond shapes, circle shapes, kinds of elliptical shapes, saucer shapes, ovals, diagonal shapes. I see shapes that remind me of fruits, of gourds, of bananas. There are obviously two females and—

DR. F: All right. That's enough. What about the colors?

MR. W: Well, the colors are what might be called lime, light or pastel greens, intense greens, several kinds of blues, yellows, reds, oranges, grays, and all of these colors are unified and separated.

DR. F: We don't have to talk about the unified—

MR. W: All right. Black. I see deep violets.

DR. F: Do you see a hand?

MR. W: Yes, I see a hand. I see hands, profiles, front faces, rear views of the body, profiles of the body—

DR. F: Do you see a mirror?

MR. W: I see a mirror by implication rather than realistic statement.

DR. F: Well, whether it's real or unreal, where is the mirror?

MR. W: The mirror's on the right-hand side.

DR. F: O.K. Now, that's as far as we have to go in making a description and identification of what is plainly to be seen in this work. . . . It is a fairly complete inventory, as I call it, of what's there, and to make this inventory doesn't require any special knowledge. You have to have normal intelligence, you have to be awake, and you have to have reasonably good eyesight, but you can see it with glasses. The next step, which is, in a way, a continuation of the inventory, is what I call formal analysis. Mr. Williams identified the forms, and the next step is, in a sense, to describe how the forms are operating, that is, *Formal Analysis* what the forms are doing in the picture. So, will somebody else volunteer and I'll ask some pointed questions so that you'll be able to do the analysis. How about you, Mrs. Gulbenkian? What are the main directions that you see in the work?

MRS. G: I think vertical lines are the main lines.

DR. F: How is this picture divided, would you say, particularly along the verticals?

MRS. G: Well, basically in half.

DR. F: Right. I say right. Does anybody disagree that the picture is divided?

MISS H: Well, I would have said three.

DR. F: Into three? Show me where there are three parts.

MISS H: Well, there is a lovely vertical here on the left, back of the diamonds, and then the center line.

DR. F: You mean as far as identifying the verticals, there is a vertical here?

MISS H: Right.

DR. F: What would you say about the quality of the color? In other words, its brightness or its dullness, its intensity or weakness?

MRS. G: I would say that most of the colors are very intense, but I don't have any feeling that there's one dominant color in the whole painting. One thing that surprises me is that the figures themselves seem to be more subdued, especially the parts that would normally be flesh, and yet I still have a feeling that the whole painting is very intense—the colors are intense and bright.

DR. F: That is, these diamonds show color relatively unmixed. Is there anything that connects the two halves?

MRS. G: The horizontal arm movement—

DR. F: This horizontal arm movement here. What is the arm doing?

MRS. G: It seems to be embracing the other half of the picture.

DR. F: "Embracing" is an inference. She is drawing a conclusion. She is interpreting. In a court of law we would say that. At this point we don't want any opinions. What also might it be doing?

MRS. G: It's crossing.

DR. F: It's crossing. What else might it be doing? Is it holding onto something there? Is it touching?

MRS. G: That's an inference.

DR. F: That also is an inference. All right. This much we know—that the arm crosses over and that so far as the picture is divided in half most of the directions are vertical. . . . Is there any other connection?

MRS. G: Connection of color through the red stripes on the other sleeve of the sweater.

DR. F: This carries across. . . . Right here. . . . Are there any other examples of a division between a left and a right half in the work?

MRS. G: The diamonds for instance—the left half is one color, the right half is another. The figures are reversed.

DR. F: Well, that's one side of the face. That is a face?

MRS. G: Right.

DR. F: Is it a girl's face?

MRS. G: Yes.

DR. F: How do you know?

MRS. G: The figure has long hair.

DR. F: O.K. One side of the face is a gray or a mauve color and the other side is a bright yellow. What is the relationship of this face—this will call for some inference—this face to that face?

MRS. G: They are the same size. They are looking at each other.

DR. F: They are opposite each other.

MRS. G: Well, one is the image of the other.

DR. F: Right. Which one is the mirror image?

MRS. G: The one on the right.

DR. F: And where is another hand?

MRS. G: There is this banana shape extending along the left side of the mirror.

DR. F: Right here. Now, we should have caught this in our description. There are really two hands in the picture. . . . This hand is holding onto the post. There are two posts, which support what?

MRS. G: The oval mirror.

DR. F: The oval mirror. . . . This is an oval mirror and this is the woman or the girl in the room and this is the girl in the mirror. Let's make an attempt now at what's called *interpretation* even though we haven't exhausted all the color and shape and space relations in there. . . . Now, what is interpretation? Interpretation involves advancing a hypothesis, a possible idea which will be a kind of basket and contain all these things that we have been talking about, that we have noticed, and that I assume you agree are there—the hands, the ovals, and so on. What we have done so far is bring out—and it wasn't hard to do—the evidence, the visual evidence, for an interpretation, and you can think of these things as visual facts. They're things, and to some extent they're relationships, and we're going to try to put them together so that they make sense, so that we can come up with a statement. "This picture means, or this picture is about, or this work of art expresses _____," a statement that has form. This is ordinary scientific thinking. Now, let us make a few modern hypotheses. A hypothesis is a kind of proposition that begins with "If," isn't it? If this is a girl and she's in the room, let's try to navigate among these forms and identify her anatomy. Maybe we should have done that earlier. If it is a girl, we have a line here, and it seems to divide the figure in half, so that we suspect we are looking at the woman through the hips. Maybe she is wearing a bathing suit—let us guess that she is wearing a bathing suit. . . . What is this shape here?

Interpretation

MISS H: Teardrop.

DR. F: Very good. It is perfect for the purpose of illustration. What do these shapes represent, do you think?

GROUP: Breasts.

DR. F: Breasts. They're in about the position on the torso where they would be breasts if it is a woman. What about these (pointing to mirror image)?

MISS N: Breasts.

DR. F: And since we have hypothesized that this is a mirror, these are probably the mirror images of these, and we notice that there are a lot of circles here. These are more rounded circles. Now what does this form here seem to be? What portion of the anatomy?

GROUP: The buttocks.

DR. F: What does this ovoid shape, do you think, represent?

MISS N: Stomach.

DR. F: Stomach?

MISS N: That could be the womb.

DR. F: Probably, the internal reproductive organ. O.K., the internal reproductive organ of a woman—the womb. Now, you can't see the womb from the outside, can you? So what we are looking at is the backbone in profile, the figure in front here, because of the profile of the leg, the breasts in profile by the front view here, and the buttocks probably from the rear view or the front view here. Let's see if evidence accumulates that we are right. . . . Now we're ready to interpret it more comprehensively. Let me try to do it this time.

The young girl in her wallpapered room, which is flooded with sunlight, is looking at herself in one of those old-fashioned mirrors that had two posts—a standing mirror. How do we know she is a young girl? Well, her face seems unblemished, rather clear-eyed, she hasn't yet developed the double chins and the sagging flesh that most of us have to put up with. It's fair to say that her face is rather a perfect oval. It might even be fair to say that she is an innocent young girl in all the meanings of the term "innocent." She hasn't known men. She's unmarried. Now you might even want to take a stab and say that she's fifteen or sixteen years old. Could be I am wrong; she could be eighteen or she could be fourteen. She is apparently looking at an image of herself, but the image of herself does not resemble her; that is, the nose is more prominent. The jaw is retracted somewhat more. What causes the jaw to be retracted? When we lose our teeth. When we lose our teeth, our skin becomes more tightly drawn over the face. What appears to be an eye seems to be, let's say, sunken. If you don't want to call it an eye socket, the area where the eye is seems to be sunken. Surrounding the image in the mirror are dark night colors as opposed to light, sunny colors. The image in the mirror is divided into two halves, top and bottom. The bottom half seems to be an accurate reflection at a different angle of what's going on here, but the upper half is not an accurate reflection of what's going on up here. It is the upper half that seems to be a person, a woman with her arm up, you see, corresponding to there. It's a woman at a different stage of life. It is not a young woman and it is not an

Figure 17.4 *Pablo Picasso,* Girl Before a Mirror. *(1932) Oil on canvas, 64 x 51¼", Collection, Museum of Modern Art, New York. Gift of Mrs. Simon Guggenheim.* © 1974 by SPADEM PARIS.

innocent woman. It is a woman who is older—you can tell that—quite old. The lower half of the woman, though, has the same emphasis on reproductive attributes that the other one does, organs of nourishment, organs of reproduction. The girl is wearing some kind of undergarment or bathing suit as she looks at herself in the privacy of her room, and, as all young people do, she studies herself and wonders what she looks like. Young people also wonder what's going to become of them, and this girl seems to be wondering about her biological role. She is wondering about what it means to be a woman, that is to say, what it means to have children and to undergo the crisis of giving birth—and here, of course, the artist has painted a picture of both what she sees and what she's thinking about—namely, she sees an old woman or possibly an image of someone who's dead. She sees herself as dead. Why does she see herself as dead? Possibly because birth-giving is dangerous, or she's scared. She knows she has a biological role and it frightens her. Well, that's a possible interpretation of the picture.

You may ask, "Is this what Picasso intended?" I don't know and I don't care. Do you think we ought to consult him? If you consulted him and he said, "That's not what it is about at all," and said, "It happens to be my third mistress when she was having our little baby.

That's what I was doing"—should we say, "I'm all wet and have gone off on the wrong track?" No, because the actual circumstances and intentions of the artist are not directly relevant to art criticism, mostly because the artist only knows perhaps 10 percent of what he's doing, like the 10 percent of an iceberg that is visible; the rest of it is underwater.

The following segment of an actual teaching session demonstrates what a renowned art historian[16] considers important in discussing painting with sixth graders. Because of limitations of space, excerpts of the tape have been interspersed with descriptions of what transpired.

Dr. Ackerman began by making the point that the basic task of the session was to talk about what was seen as well as to look, and that looking would come naturally to the children since they lived in a visually oriented society with constant exposure to television, films, and mass-printed media. He then listed on the blackboard four terms he felt were needed to discuss the paintings to be shown:

1. *Technique*   the ways in which artists use materials.
2. *Form*   the structure and interaction of components of an art work. The class seemed to understand the word "shape" as a component of "form" and the teacher accepted this.
3. *Meaning*   the intention; the ultimate significance of an art work. Because the children had some difficulty absorbing this concept, Dr. Ackerman accepted the term "subject" in its place.
4. *Feeling*   the emotive power that is elicited from a work.

Dr. Ackerman used the comparative method to develop the class discussion. On one screen he showed a slide of an Impressionist oil painting of poplars and on an adjacent screen he projected an Egyptian wall fresco showing trees framing a pool containing fish and ducks (see Figure 17.5).

DR. A: Who would like to try to describe the painting techniques of these two paintings?
STUDENT: The trees are watercolor. . . .
STUDENT: I think they're oil.
DR. A: You're right; that is an oil painting. How about the other. . . ? (*a lot of whispering but no volunteers*) Take a guess.
STUDENT: Watercolor—maybe tempera?
DR. A: Why do you say that?
STUDENT: It's flat and bright, not shaded like oils.
DR. A: Very good—flat is a good word, except that in this case the effect

---

[16]Dr. James Ackerman, former Chairman, Department of Fine Arts, Harvard University.

Egyptian fresco from the XII Dynasty. (The Metropolitan Museum of Art.)

A

Figure 17.5 *Two paintings for comparison.*

Claude Monet, Poplars. (Philadelphia Museum of Art. Given by Chester Dale. © 1974 by SPADEM PARIS.)

B

is due to a fresco technique. Anyone know what fresco is? (*silence*) Well, it was used by the Egyptians as a way of making painting part of a wall. They did this by using tempera paint on fresh plaster mixed with water and lime. Now back to your "flatness." If you've ever painted on plaster you know it gets soaked up and dries quickly. That doesn't allow for much shading or roundness of forms and instead gets the painter to work in clear, flat areas of color. How did this artist make his shapes seem clearer?

STUDENT: He put lines around them.

DR. A: Very good. Would you care to point to one part of the painting to show what you mean? (*Student points to outline of pool.*) Now, let's look at the subject. Can we say that one of these paintings is more true to life than the other. Let's take a vote. How many say the poplar trees are more "true to life"? (*The class votes as a group in favor of this one.*) Why is that?

STUDENT: Well, it doesn't look exactly like a photograph but it almost could be one.

DR. A: Which do you like better? (*The class votes for the Impressionist.*) Let's see how the painter looks at his subject. . . . Anyone care to comment?

STUDENT: Well, it's more like real life in the poplars.

STUDENT: The ducks are real life.

STUDENT: But it's mixed up in the fresco.

DR. A: I think you are trying to say that there are two points of view in the Egyptian's. Who can go to the screen and point to one point of view? (*One student volunteers and points to the bird's eye view of the pool.*) Where are we standing when we look at the pool?

STUDENT: Above—we're above it.

DR. A: How about the ducks?

STUDENT: You're in front of them.

DR. A: Good. Then we might say that in one way the Egyptian artist used his space and subjects with a lot more freedom than the other artists. But what does the Impressionist painting offer us instead of different points of view in the same picture?

STUDENT: You can see more . . . more details . . . more real . . .

DR. A: Would you agree with me that there are many ways of being "true"; that the Egyptian painting shows us the way we know things to be and the Impressionist more the way we are likely to react? . . .

Figure 17.6 *Studying by comparison. Both reproductions and actual paintings provide a basis for discovering likenesses and differences, clarification of terminology, and a close examination of such easily missed factors as the quality of edges in a painting. (Photos by Rich Steadry.)*

A *Raphael, Tempi,* Madonna. *(Scala: New York, Florence. Alte Pinakothek, Munich.)*

B *Käthe Kollwitz,* Killed in Action. *(lithograph, 1921)*

C *Willem De Kooning,* Marilyn Monroe (1954). *(Scala: New York, Florence. Neuberger Museum, State University of New York, College at Purchase.)*

Figure 17.7 *Paintings for comparison.*

D *Wassily Kandinsky,* Improvisation. *(The Solomon R. Guggenheim Museum, New York City. © ADAGP 1975.)*

In a research project in art appreciation[17] Dr. Ackerman's ideas were applied by one of the authors to a method of teaching whereby the children were led to discover for themselves a system of criticism. The children were shown four reproductions and were asked to name the differences they could detect among the works. The paintings used were Raphael's *Madonna and Child,* Käthe Kollwitz's *Killed in Action,* De Kooning's *Marilyn Monroe,* and Kandinsky's *Improvisation* (see Figure

The "Discovery" Method

[17]The material used in this section, as well as that used in the section on critical awareness, was taken from a research project in art appreciation in the Newton Public Schools, Newton, Mass. The entire project is described in full in Stanley Madeja, ed., "Exemplary Programs in Art Education" (Washington, D.C.: National Art Education Association, May 1969).

Table 17.2

RESULTS OF A "DISCOVERY" DISCUSSION

Object: To create categories that may serve as a basis for building subsequent sessions in art appreciation

MATERIALS What We Work With	SUBJECT What We Paint	MEANING Why We Paint	FORM How a Painting Is Made	STYLE What Makes Paintings Look Different from One Another
"Kollwitz uses crayons; it's more a drawing." (Teacher explains difference between drawing and lithography.) "The Raphael must be oil." "The De Kooning could be tempera or house paint." "The Kandinsky painting is thin, it could be watercolor." (Teacher explains that if oil paint is thinned with enough turpentine it can have the transparency of watercolor.)	"Kollwitz has a sad mother and hungry children." "Raphael has a happy mother and child." "The De Kooning is called *Marilyn Monroe,* but it takes you a long time to see her." "I can't recognize anything in the Kandinsky like I can in the others." (Teacher defines "non-objective" and "abstract.")	"Kollwitz's mother is worried about how she will feed her children." "Kandinsky's has no meaning; it's just shapes, lines, and colors that go all over the place." "I can't tell what the Kandinsky and De Kooning are all about." "The Raphael is a religious picture."	"I see a triangle in the Raphael and up-and-down forms painted really sloppy in the De Kooning." (Teacher: "We call this painterly, not sloppy.") "The Raphael is quiet. The Kandinsky is loud." (Teacher: What makes one picture "loud" and another "quiet"?) "Kandinsky makes you look in different "directions" up, over, and around."	"The Raphael looks so real you could walk into it." "The Kollwitz is real too but in a different way." (Teacher defines "selective realism.") Raphael "smooth" "like a photograph" "done carefully" De Kooning "sloppy" "done really fast" "more wild" "messy" Kandinsky "wild" "like a third grader's picture of space"

17.7). (They thus began with an achieved consensus—that the four pictures shown were obviously different in many respects.) As various differences were noted the teacher wrote them on the blackboard, setting them down in columns according to whether they related to materials, subject, meaning, form, or style. When the children's powers of observation were apparently exhausted the teacher wrote the categorical headings above the columns, pointing out that what the class had really done was create its own critical system. Such an ordering of concepts demonstrated to them that there were many ways to discuss a work of art. Instead of providing the pupils with answers prior to the discussion the teacher sought to elicit responses by posing questions that centered on a single conceptual problem—the ways in which artists differ in their work. In order to deal with such a problem the children had to become engaged in such processes as visual discrimination, ordering, comparison, classification, and generalization.

During the "discovery" discussion the teacher translated the crude vocabulary of the class into a vocabulary for criticism, adding some important characteristics that had been missed. When the task was completed, the comments listed on the board were those shown in Table 17.2.

The discovery discussion laid the groundwork for subsequent lessons. The "materials" column provided the background for a visiting artist to demonstrate the difference between oil and water colors; the "meaning" classification prepared the class for a lesson in comparison of styles, in which they were shown a variety of paintings, each of which took a different stylistic approach to the same theme.

The phase of art appreciation that calls for simple exposure to art is not difficult to arrange. A range of techniques is open to the teacher—audio-visual media, field trips to museums, visits by artists, and displays of original art works and reproductions. Teaching for the critical phase of appreciation, however, poses distinct problems. The role of dialog has already been mentioned; although verbalizing about art is central to criticism, nonverbal activities must also be considered. Children vary in their inclinations and abilities to speak about art, and class discussions are too often limited to participation by the articulate minority. Moreover, generally there is not enough time for each member of a class to give an opinion. Several verbal and nonverbal "testing" instruments are described below that suggest solutions to the problem of how to achieve total class involvement. Each "test" is related to what may reasonably be expected of children in the area of art appreciation, and each of the instruments attempts to reach one of three goals:

Other Approaches to Teaching Criticism

1. To enable the children to discuss art works with a knowledge of art terminology and to identify the design, meaning, and media as these function in particular works of art (verbal).
2. To extend the students' range of acceptance of art works (nonverbal).
3. To sharpen or refine the students' powers of observation of visual elements in art works (nonverbal).

One way a teacher can involve a full class in working with the first goal is to have them respond to multiple-choice questions while they progress through a series of slides. These questions should be based on the terminology and concepts the teacher deems valuable. Thus, as the children see their first Wyeth slide, the teacher may want to emphasize the uses of composition and placement of objects:

This painting is called *Christina's World*. You notice that the artist, Andrew Wyeth, has used a high rather than a low horizon line. (*points to line*) Now study it carefully. If you think he did it because the house just happened to be located there, put down A. If you think he did it because it allows for more space between the girl and the house, put down B. But if you think he did it because it would look that way if the scene were photographed by a camera, put down C. All right, how many put down A? B? C? How many put down more than one reason? Paul, I notice you didn't raise your hand at all—can't you decide? Mary, you voted for B. How about trying to show Paul why you voted that way? . . .

Because the entire class is involved in the physical process of marking and raising their hands the number who verbally participate do not appear to be such a minority. The teacher may wish to collect the papers to study the extent of the class's comprehension. It is important in using this device not to stress the rightness or wrongness of the answers. This kind of test should be used as a means of opening up discussion of what the teacher feels is worth noting (see Table 17.3).

Another way to involve the whole class in identifying components of design is to give each child a reproduction of the same painting and a sheet of tracing paper. The paper is placed over the reproduction and the class is asked to seek out and define such compositional devices as directional movement and "hidden" structure. This method is particularly effective if first demonstrated on an overhead projector.

The second goal is to extend the children's acceptance of art works. In order to assess this range of acceptance the teacher can use a simple preference test based on all the slides and reproductions to be used during the course of the year. This is a simple questionnaire that requires the children merely to check off the phrase that best describes their reactions to the art works placed before them. Using the children's manner of speaking the responses to be checked might run as follows:

Figure 17.8 *Andrew Wyeth,* Christina's World *(1948). Tempera on gesso panel, 32¼ x 47¾". (Collection, Museum of Modern Art, New York. Purchase.)*

B *Leonardo da Vinci*, The Last Supper. *(Scala: New York, Florence. Santa Maria de Grazie, Milan.)*

A *Auguste Renoir*, Lady with a Parasol. *(Courtesy, Museum of Fine Arts, Boston. Bequest of John T. Spaulding. © 1974 by SPADEM PARIS.)*

C *William Gropper*, The Senate (1935). *Oil on canvas, 25⅛ × 33⅛″. (Collection, The Museum of Modern Art, New York, Gift of A. Conger Goodyear.)*

Figure 17.9 *Paintings for comparison.*

Table 17.3

SAMPLE QUESTIONS UTILIZING THE TERMINOLOGY OF ART

Terminology	Painting	Question
Social Criticism	The Senate (William Gropper)	After a visit to the United States Senate the artist painted his idea of what he saw. In your opinion, this artist seemed to feel that:
		A. The only things senators did were read papers, sit around, or make speeches that no one cared about.
		B. All senators are not the dedicated public servants we think they are.
		C. Most senators read papers in order to know what was happening in different parts of the country.
Depth	The Last Supper (Leonardo da Vinci)	In this wall painting, what gives you the feeling of depth?

Table 17.3 (Cont.)

Terminology	Painting	Question
		A. The direction of the lines in the construction of the room.
		B. The strong and bright colors.
		C. Both A and B.
Paint Quality (Technique)	*The Bather* (Auguste Renoir)	The edges of the objects in this painting are *mostly:*
		A. Unclear and fuzzy.
		B. Sharp and exact.
		C. Both A and B.
Line Quality	*Killed in Action* (Käthe Kollwitz)	We can describe the line in this print as:
		A. Delicate and soft.
		B. Strong and bold.
		C. Both A and B.
Meaning	*Killed in Action* (Käthe Kollwitz)	Which statement *best* describes what is going on in this print?
		A. A mother is resting with her children.
		B. A mother is expressing misery in front of her children.
		C. A mother is playing with her children.
Style	*Zapatistas* (José Orozco)	The style (the artist's own way of painting) of this picture is called:
		A. Realism (looks life-like).
		B. Selective realism (partly real).
		C. Abstract (simple, unrecognizable shapes).
Composition	*Poplars* (Vincent Van Gogh)	The tree dominates this painting. Van Gogh makes it stand out by:
		A. Using bright colors and emphasizing the texture of the tree.
		B. Making the tree large and placing it in the center of the picture.
		C. Both A and B.

1. I like this painting and wouldn't mind hanging it in my own room.
2. This painting doesn't affect me one way or the other.
3. I don't like this painting.
4. This painting bothers me; as a matter of fact, I very much dislike it.

It may safely be hypothesized that initially most children will gravitate toward the familiar, that is, to realistic treatments of subjects that appeal to them.[18] By consistently exposing the children throughout the year to works that range from the representational to the nonobjective a competent teacher can open their eyes to a wider range of styles. This does not place a premium on any one particular style, but aims at an extension of taste from whatever point the child begins. If the preference test is given at the beginning and at the end of the course the teacher should be able to determine how the class has progressed—both as a group and as individuals.

The third goal relates to the child's powers of observation; the instrument to be used for this goal requires that the children choose paintings that have certain attributes or qualities in common. The preparation of materials might cause the teacher some difficulty, for each participant should have a set of reproductions. The sets may be compiled from inexpensive museum reproductions, which come in manageable sizes (postcards as a rule are too small). Six reproductions seems to be a number that children can handle; more than this tends to confuse them, and there may be occasions when just two or three are appropriate. Whatever the number of pictures the students are to examine them and make certain decisions about them. Figure 17.10 shows a few examples of choices they can make. This comparative study will also lead to the increased awareness terminology discussed in connection with the first goal. This type of study allows the children to proceed at their own rate and find the viewing distance most convenient for them. Spreading the pictures out on the floor or a table is preferable to flipping through them: the pictures are more easily compared when seen as a group.

TEACHING AIDS FOR DEVELOPING APPRECIATION

Among the teaching aids required in the program for the development of appreciation of art are prints of pictures, pictorial reproductions of other art forms, films, filmstrips, and slides dealing with a variety of art topics, and some actual works of art in two and three dimensions. No matter what field of art may be engaging the child's attention—pottery,

---

[18]Betty Lark-Horovitz, "On Art Appreciation of Children: Pref. of Picture Subjects in General," *Journal of Education*, Vol. 31, No. 2 (1937).

A Vincent van Gogh, Starry Night (1889). Oil on canvas, 29 × 36¼". (Collection, The Museum of Modern Art, New York. Acquired through the Lillie P. Bliss Bequest.)

B André Derain, London Bridge (1906). Oil on canvas, 26 × 39". (Collection, The Museum of Modern Art, New York. Gift Mr. and Mrs. Charles Zadok. © ADAGP 1975.)

C John Marin, Lower Manhattan (Composing Derived from Top of Woolworth) (1922). Watercolor and charcoal with paper cutout attached with thread, 21⅝ × 26⅞". (Collection, The Museum of Modern Art, New York. Acquired through the Lillie P. Bliss Bequest.)

D Stuart Davis, Owh! In San Pao (1951). Oil on canvas, 52¼ × 41¾". (Collection of Whitney Museum of American Art, New York. Photo by Geoffrey Clements.)

E Charles Demuth, Acrobats (1919). Watercolor and pencil, 13 × 7⅞". (Collection, The Museum of Modern Art, New York. Gift of Abby Aldrich Rockefeller.)

F *Irene Rice Pereira,* White Lines *(1942). Oil on vellum with marble dust, sand, etc., 25⅞ × 21⅞″. (Collection, The Museum of Modern Art, New York. Gift of Edgar Kaufmann, Jr.)*

G *Wassily Kandinsky,* Composition 8, *#260. 55½ × 79⅛″. (The Solomon R. Guggenheim Museum, New York City. © ADAGP 1975.)*

H *Henri Matisse,* Nuit de Noël *(1952). Maquette for stained glass window commissioned by Life, 1952. Gouache on paper, cut and pasted, 10′7″ × 53½″. (Collection, The Museum of Modern Art, New York. Gift of Time, Inc. © 1974 by SPADEM PARIS.)*

Figure 17.10 *Teaching from a packet of reproductions. Children can become acquainted with the art terms that are underscored in the activities below by matching certain paintings from a basic collection. The terms progress from simple, usually descriptive, terms to more complex ones dealing with qualities in art.*

1. *Four pictures use the* <u>circle</u> *as an important shape in the composition. (Answer:* **A** *Van Gogh,* **C** *Marin,* **E** *Demuth,* **G** *Kandinsky)*
2. *Two are painted in* <u>watercolor</u>. *(Answer:* **C** *Marin,* **E** *Demuth)*
3. *The effectiveness of four paintings rests on the use of colored objects that are* <u>flat and hard-edged</u>. *(Answer:* **D** *Davis,* **F** *Rice Pereira,* **G** *Kandinsky,* **H** *Matisse)*
4. *Two paintings have a quality of* <u>violence</u>. *(Answer:* **A** *Van Gogh,* **C** *Marin)*
5. *Two of the paintings show obvious uses of* <u>broken color</u>. *(Answer:* **A** *Van Gogh,* **B** *Derain)*
6. *Three paintings use* <u>line</u> *as an important factor. (Answer:* **C** *Marin,* **D** *Davis,* **G** *Kandinsky)*

Number 6 should lead the class into a lively discussion, some pupils claiming that the short strokes of Van Gogh are linear in nature and others maintaining that the geometric maze of the Rice Pereira is a linear device. This is to be encouraged, for the quality of the discussion is as important as finding the right answers.

Figure 17.11 *Two sixth graders confer over a "matching" problem. (Photo by Rick Steadry.)*

textiles, drawing, painting—the teacher will find it necessary to have available suitable works for reference, comparison, and study.

Much of this reference material will probably represent the contemporary period. Since the children are living in this era they are probably in a better position to appreciate contemporary than traditional art. Nevertheless, when the children are studying history they should become reasonably familiar with the work of the artists of the period being considered. Artists convey not only factual statements but also frequently emotional reactions to the epoch in which they live, both of which are important in assisting children to acquire insight into life in the past. The same, of course, may be said of artists from other countries. The teacher, therefore, requires a collection of visual aids that illustrate many aspects of art, both contemporary and historical, related to local and other cultures.

The selection of what is to be represented in the visual aids is crucial. The teacher must not only consider the appropriateness of the art work to the particulars of instruction but must have some sensitivity to the natural preferences of children. The teacher may avoid frustration at the beginning of the year by noting the following points when selecting visual material:

1. Children generally value subject matter more than elements of form and prefer realistically portrayed content to abstract or nonobjective work.
2. As a rule children prefer clearly stated spatial relationships and well-defined form to diffuse or ambiguous rendering.
3. Next to realistically rendered content, color appeals to children most. To this attraction they bring positive emotional associations.

4. Only older students are capable of recognizing design as a harmonious entity composed of interactions of parts; this recognition comes at a relatively sophisticated level of appreciation.
5. Young children prefer simple compositions; older students are able to appreciate some degree of complexity.

Pictorial Reproductions

Today any school can possess a good collection of prints of pictures and pictorial reproductions of other art forms. Never before has so large a selection of these been available. With the refinements of printing processes most prints today are acceptable, accurate, and, because of large editions, surprisingly inexpensive. Many stationery stores, bookstores, and artists' supply firms act as outlets for both American and imported prints. Books containing excellent reproductions are also available. Finally, popular magazines frequently devote pages in both color and black and white to reproductions of art works. Although the quality of the printing in these periodicals may not equal that in art books it is usually good enough for the prints to be kept on file for reference in the classroom.

The file should be constantly added to; every art and classroom teacher should develop the habit of collecting photographs of visual material from museums, magazines, and other sources. Such materials should be mounted on cardboard or stiff paper (discarded oaktag folders are suitable) and stored for future reference. One relatively inexpensive source of reproductions is an art-history book, which can be cut up for filing purposes.

Figure 17.12
Reconstruction *by Ben Shahn could be among the works studied when pupils are dealing with social themes. (Collection, Whitney Museum of American Art, New York.)*

Figure 17.13 *Works of art can be very suggestive to the young. Picasso's Girl Before a Mirror (Figure 17.4) was the basis for this painting by a fifth grader.*

One reason to seize every opportunity to add to the classroom collection is that the teacher can never be quite sure what pictures may be required. If some preadolescents are exploring color, for example, works of such painters as El Greco, Rubens, Gauguin, Van Gogh, Matisse, and Dufy might be studied. If some are considering social themes they might look at political posters and reproductions of Daumier's or Ben Shahn's drawings and paintings. If some are concerned with linear perspective they might compare the paintings of the Middle Ages with those of the High Renaissance. If a religious topic holds some pupils' interest they might see reproductions of works as diverse as the twelfth- to fourteenth-century bronzes of southern India, the figures on the west portal of Chartres Cathedral, and the paintings of Duccio, Rouault, and Stanley Spencer. A high priority should be placed on collection of large-sized reproductions because of their suitability for class discussion. But small-sized reproductions are adequate for the children to study on their own.

Not only must the collection of reproductions be extensive but the teacher must be thoroughly familiar with its makeup, so that the right reproductions may be found exactly when they are required. The teacher must also be sufficiently familiar with each item to be able to emphasize any particular aspect of a composition related to a pupil's interest.

Manifestly nothing could be more desirable than to have on hand a well-stocked library of books in which children could read about art and artists. In the past most writers of such books have given too little attention to difficulties of vocabulary so that few publications of any quality existed that could be mastered by children enrolled in the first six grades. Fortunately today children's books about art are increasing in quantity and quality; a special listing is offered in the Appendix.

Each year sees worthwhile additions to a growing library of acceptable art films for the young. These art films are designed to fulfill various purposes. Many of them are intended both to stimulate children to produce art and to assist them in mastering various techniques. Some are produced largely to develop the children's insight into the art forms of others. Some films, such as the internationally renowned *Loon's Necklace,* are not produced specifically as art films but prove to be highly effective in the classroom in both the production and the appreciation of art. *Films, Filmstrips, and Slides*

The teacher who uses films in the art program must understand what constitutes a good film. Before using a film with the class, the teacher must obviously preview it, and then decide how effective it may be. What criteria should be used in selecting art films to be shown to young children?

1. The film should be of high technical and artistic quality. Young children see expertly made films in theaters and on television.

Figure 17.14 Christ Mocked by Soldiers *(1932) by Georges Rouault might prove stimulating to pupils experimenting with religious themes. (Oil on canvas, 36¼ x 28½''. Collection, Museum of Modern Art, New York. Given anonymously.* © *1974 by SPADEM PARIS.)*

The day of slovenly work by producers of children's movies has long since passed.

2. The film must be suitable to the children's level of understanding and maturity. To show young children the highly competent but rather intellectual production, *An Experience in Cubism,* would probably bore them, but *Begone Dull Care,* although based on nonobjective and abstract forms, would delight them with its sparkling sound and movement.

3. The film should be closely related to the children's immediate interests. No matter how excellent a film may be in itself, it tends to be a poor educational device when shown out of context.

4. When a film is of the "how-to-do-it" variety it must not only stimulate the children but also leave some room for them to use their own initiative. Films in the "Creative Hands Series," for example, are specially designed not to "tell all." They attempt to stimulate production, focus attention on design, and give a few basic hints about technique. The content of the films stops there, however, and the child is left with many problems to solve independently.

Knowing the film intimately the teacher can use it at the right moment during the art sessions, either as an introduction to a topic, as an aid in teaching a topic, or as a summary for a series of experiences with a topic. Sometimes the teacher may consider it necessary to comment on the film to the class before it is shown; on other occasions a discussion might take place after the screening. Occasionally the teacher may want to cut off the sound completely so that the children can draw their own inferences or to substitute commentary in terms suitable for the class.

To obtain a film for a specific art class is often difficult. A projector and a screen must be scheduled as well as the film, sometimes as much as three or four weeks in advance. Therefore as much planning in advance as possible must be done so that the film will suit the type of art activity in progress.

The above remarks concerning films also have application to the use of slides and filmstrips. Although these visual aids lack the dynamic qualities of movement and sound they allow the teacher greater control of presentations. Whereas a film moves at a predetermined speed, the filmstrip frame or slide may be held on the screen for as long as it is required.

Filmstrips are an excellent value: they take up little space and are usually accompanied by lecture notes (of varying usefulness). They are inflexible, however, in that the images are set in a fixed order. Slides come in a wide range of prices with the best values to be purchased from the major museums. The cheaper slides should be avoided since their color suffers from being taken from secondary sources of reproductions, usually art books or other slides, rather than from the original works. Subjects such as drawing, architecture, or sculpture, which do not require color fidelity, may be of service even in the inexpensive lines. Slides may be arranged any way the teacher desires and can be used with double or multiple projectors for purposes of comparison.

Poster-sized reproductions of design elements, architecture, and sculpture are most useful, but are unfortunately in very short supply. Of particular merit is the *Reinhold Visual Series*,[19] which treats the elements and principles of art through a variety of visual references. Further sources of audio-visual material for art appreciation are listed in the Appendix.

Although we may obtain a reasonably accurate idea about many works of art by consulting reproductions of them, nothing can actually replace the work itself. How often one feels one knows a work of art through a study of reproductions, only to be overwhelmed on first seeing the original! Colors, brush strokes, textures, and sometimes the scale of the work are never adequately conveyed by a reproduction. It is most desirable, therefore, that children should have the opportunity from time to time to observe original works of art, no matter how familiar they may be with the reproductions.

Actual Works of Art

The most obvious sources of originals are art galleries and museums. Schools situated near such institutions would be remiss indeed not to make use of them. Even if a relatively long journey is necessary, the time and effort required to make the trip may be considered well spent.

Before a class pays a visit to a museum or gallery the teacher should take the trip alone in order to become acquainted not only with the building and the collections but also with such mundane but important problems as the location of washrooms for the children and the special rules and regulations of the institution concerning the general behavior of young visitors. At the same time the teacher can make arrangements with museum officials concerning the program for the children's visit and the length of time to be given to it.

Also before the pupils set off they should have some idea of the reason for their trip. They may be excited about seeing an art show, but without a focus of interest the trip could be largely a waste of time. As a general principle (but subject to many exceptions) it appears wise to organize trips to museums and art galleries only for those pupils who are sufficiently mature to be able to develop a long-range interest in an art problem. In many instances very young children should wait until they can define and retain in their minds a legitimate reason for the visit more closely related to art than to entertainment. Some museums and art galleries, however, have lecturers who are talented in talking to children and provide exhibits specially designed for the very young.

Unfortunately it is not always possible for children to handle the

[19] John Lidstone, Stanley T. Lewis, and Sheldon Brody, eds. (New York: Reinhold, 1968–69).

Figure 17.15 *An important part of any art program is the contemplation of great works of art from the past. Here a teacher in Amsterdam, Holland, is discussing with her class* The Night Watch *by Rembrandt. (Photo by Adam Woolfitt.)*

three-dimensional objects on display. The teacher might inquire as to the possibilities of allowing certain less delicate objects to be handled. Children who are allowed to touch many objects learn more about them.

On no account should young children be expected to make long reports or detailed drawings of the objects observed during the visit. If reports or scientific drawings are to be made they should be mere sketches. To ask young children for detailed reports might rob the whole expedition of its good effects.

Schools not located sufficiently close to museums and art galleries for visits by pupils will have to depend on other means for bringing original works of art to the children. Many museums and art galleries today maintain extension services by which well-packaged and adequately annotated items are shipped to responsible organizations. The teacher should investigate these opportunities; by such means, art can be brought not only to the children but also to the community at large.

Another possible source of original art forms is the area in which the school is situated, where very often creditable local painters and craftsmen can be discovered. The teacher should make an effort to find these local artists and to help them organize shows of their work for the children and others to see.

Finally, it is perfectly reasonable to expect that a school system set

A

Figure 17.16 *Direct contact with professional artists can be an exciting experience for children.* **A** *Members of a fourth-grade class watch with great interest as a painter describes his methods of working.*

B *Two fifth graders raptly watch a visiting artist demonstrate the techniques of paper sculpture. (Photo by Terry Garufo.)* **B**

aside funds for purchasing original paintings and other works of art as well as reproductions and slides. In time a school system of any size can possess a permanent exhibition of good pieces in which it can take both interest and pride.

The study of utilitarian objects—cups and saucers, kettles, knives and forks, telephones, and chairs—can do much to help children to develop an appreciation of art and to elevate their taste.[20]

Practical Objects

[20]The reader's attention is again directed at this time to the Bauhaus, the school of design founded in 1919 by Walter Gropius at Weimar and later moved to Dessau in Germany. Although painters of note, including Kandinsky, Klee, and Feininger, gathered there, the Bauhaus was an institution dealing primarily with problems related to architecture and industrial design. Here many unique experiments were performed by the students in order to gain experience with materials, tools, and techniques of an industrial nature. As a result, a disciplined and appropriate approach to art forms related to machine production made its appearance. The writings of László Moholy-Nagy and others, describing some of the work at the Bauhaus, have been carefully read by art educators, especially those in high schools and art schools and have influenced their teaching methods. See for example, László Moholy-Nagy, *The New Vision* (New York: Wittenborn, 1964) and Walter Gropius, ed., *Bauhaus 1919–1928* (New York: Museum of Modern Art, 1938) in which it is stated that among other reasons the Bauhaus is important "because it courageously accepted the machine as an instrument worthy of the artist."

Although a functional or practical object may not be as profound an artistic expression as, say, a fine painting or a superb piece of sculpture, it may nevertheless have the attributes of true art (see Chapter 3). Well-conceived practical objects, such as those illustrated in Figure 17.17, should be brought to the attention of young people as part of the art appreciation program. Every object shown should be chosen with the highest standards in mind. Usually these standards are well within the comprehension of most pupils in the higher grades of the elementary school.

A teaching difficulty occurs in the case of developing an appreciation of practical objects because appreciation can only rarely be related to production of such objects. Although children continually make pictures and produce sculpture that they can compare with professional work, such is not often the case with practical objects. Hence the teacher will sometimes find it necessary to discuss such objects as cups and saucers and television cabinets by themselves, rather than in connection with the children's work. The children, however, often find a discussion about such articles interesting because these are things with which they come in contact in their daily lives. The objects tend to have real meaning even when not associated with the children's expressive acts. Occasionally in school, especially as part of the unit curriculum, the children may be required to construct models of some practical objects. Then the teacher will strengthen the appreciation lesson by discussing well-designed examples of objects similar to the models under construction.

Figure 17.17 *China by Eva Zeisel—examples of well-designed practical objects. (Photo by Walter Civardi.)*

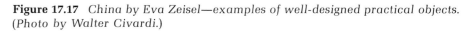

ACTIVITIES FOR THE READER

1. Select three paintings or reproductions—the first by a master, the second by a reputable but not renowned artist, and the third by an amateur—and (a) tell what the paintings all have in common; (b) explain the differences in their significance to you.
2. Describe any occasion on which you gained insight into an artist's work that previously had puzzled you. Can you account for the flash of insight?
3. Describe two paintings that deal with the same subject—one sentimentally and the other artistically.
4. Outline some teaching procedures for helping fifth-grade children to appreciate each of the following: (a) a mural by Thomas Hart Benton or some other well-known painter; (b) the design of a frying pan; (c) the design of living-room curtains; (d) a wood sculpture by Chaim Gross or some other well-known artist.
5. Create a visual reduction game by collecting about twenty reproductions and dividing them into subcategories. Directions for such a game might read as follows:
   a. Divide this group of reproductions into two piles, one nonobjective and one realistic.
   b. Now divide the nonobjective pile into two more piles, one emphasizing line and the other solid masses.
   c. Divide the realistic group into two sets, one sentimental in nature and the other aesthetic.
6. Create your own visual game or test instrument that uses perceptual judgment as its basis. The test may involve matching or sorting for a specific visual problem. In selecting your examples use a broad historical frame of reference.
7. Discuss with your class three problems with art materials that are related to some dominant concern of artists as reflected in a particular work of art.

Most children can acquire skills in representing objects that lend themselves to ready evaluation, as in this detail of a print made by a group of fifth- and sixth-grade pupils.

18 APPRAISING CHILDREN'S PROGRESS IN ART

A painter had executed a story, for which he had taken so many parts from drawings and other pictures, that there was nothing in it which was not copied: this being shown to Michelangelo, and his opinion requested, he made answer, "It is very well: but at the day of Judgement, when every body shall retake its own limbs, what will this Story do, for then it will have nothing remaining?"—a warning to those who would practice art that they should do something for themselves.*

T eachers cannot escape appraisals of some sort as the year proceeds, no matter how complex or variable the problems of appraisal may be. Evaluation of art work is a part of the ongoing teaching process, as a primary means of determining how much and when to teach. Teachers must also evaluate when it comes time for report-card grading or making progress reports. Another period of evaluation occurs during the class critiques at the conclusion of a lesson.

The basis of appraisal of a pupil's progress in any area of learning can be found only in the objectives of that area. If the objectives of a particular subject have been accurately stated, however, they will reflect not only the specific contributions that the area has to offer, but also the philosophical purposes and educational practices of the school system. An appraisal of the progress of any pupil enrolled in an educational system involves, then, a judgment of the efficiency of the school system in general and of the teacher's endeavors in particular.

---

*From *The Nature of Art* by John Gassner and Sidney Thomas, p. 284. © 1964 by John Gassner and Sidney Thomas. Used by permission of Crown Publishers, Inc.

493

HOW THE OBJECTIVES OF ART EDUCATION INFLUENCE APPRAISAL

In the opening chapter of this book a statement was given of the objectives of art education. The main objective was said to consist in helping the emotional, intellectual, and social growth of each child. Through art education it is hoped in particular that pupils will gain insight into the nature of artistic acts, that they will develop artistic skills, and that they will learn to use wisely the freedom of expression that the contemporary program allows. Through art activities it is hoped that the pupils will understand their experiences better and will develop their artistic taste. Finally, in all their art activities and general relationships with their teacher and classmates, it is hoped that they will gain insight into the social dimensions of art.

Any system of appraisal must be preceded by five basic questions:

Who will do the appraising (teachers, pupils, some outside agency)?

What is being appraised (attitudes or curriculum content such as skills, knowledge, or processes)?

Who will be appraised (elementary children, high-school art majors, retarded children)?

What is the range of the appraisal (pupil, class, entire school program)?

And finally, perhaps the most difficult,

What is the purpose of the appraisal?

Chapman lists a number of reasons for evaluation. Appraisals are intended to

inform those who are interested as to the current status of the art program,
persuade someone that changes in the art program should (or should not) be made,
diagnose strengths and weaknesses in planning for change,
predict trends and anticipate problems before they arise,
decide on priorities and select the best direction for change,
guide the step-by-step development of program changes,
confirm that certain values have been achieved through the program.[1]

[1]"Evaluating the Total School Art Program" (Papers presented at the NAEA Study Institute, San Diego, Calif., April 1973), pp. 26–27.

The teacher must consider the development of the individual children. This progress is indicated to a large extent by the art work they produce, by their reactions to the expressions of others, and by the quality of their behavior when working with others. But the teacher must not lose sight of the close connection between the progress of a pupil and the educational outlook of a school system. How can freedom of expression be judged unless freedom to express oneself exists in the educational environment? How can the development of taste be appraised unless conditions encourage such growth? It should also be borne in mind that the appraisal will be influenced not only by the attitudes of the teacher and the "learning climate" of the school but also by the home environment of the children. If pupils dislike a particular style of art, for instance, they quite probably have a mother or father who is of a similar opinion.

No child—except perhaps the gifted—will want to be graded on purely artistic grounds. Most children will be quick to proclaim, "That's not fair, Mr. Jones, I'm not an artist." But also, most will concede that they are capable of the improvement in their ability to control attitudes, to learn skills, to engage in certain kinds of self-direction—perhaps even to learn a few relevant facts! In any case, it is worth discussing the system of evaluation to be used with the class. This is one of the few aspects of art children are willing to talk about.

APPRAISAL BASED ON A TAXONOMY OF OBJECTIVES

If the teaching objectives of the art program are given a taxonomy, a system of classification, the task of evaluation is made easier. Two such systems are presented below—a study of both is recommended for the teacher who is confounded by the multiplicity of objectives within the art program. Once the objectives of a particular category are clear, the teacher will have a better idea of the type of evaluation required.

The first system utilizes three main categories based on the objectives discussed in the preceding chapters—artistic expression, art appreciation, and behavior during art activities. The lists that follow present questions connected with each of these categories, which the teacher might find useful in the process of appraisal. These lists are not intended to include all questions that might be mentioned, but, rather, are offered as examples of the type of lists that a teacher might devise.

1. *The quality of the pupils' personal artistic expression*[2]

---

[2] It will be understood that expression, appreciation, and general behavior cannot in practice be isolated from each other, and that the division has been made here only for the sake of discussion. A similar situation occurred in Chapter 3 when design was being discussed in terms of its elements.

To what extent have the pupils attempted to express their reactions to their own experiences?

To what extent have they expressed themselves emotionally and intellectually in a form commensurate with their apparent stage or phase of aesthetic development? (See Chapter 6.)

To what extent have the pupils developed a personal style?[3]

To what extent does the pupils' work show a sensitivity to functional design?

Does their work indicate that they are sensible of the effects of tools and materials on design?

To what extent does their work show ability to use each element of design: line; mass and space; light and shade; color; texture?

How successful are they in arriving at a unity of design?

How successful are they in arranging a variety in their design?

Do the pupils appear to have developed technical skills in art commensurate with their needs of expression?

To what extent are the pupils capable of: (a) relating artistic expression to other school experiences; (b) relating other school experiences to artistic expression?

To what extent has their sense of observation improved? To what extent their use of memory? Imagination and fantasy?

2. *The quality of the pupils' reactions to the work of others*

To what extent do the pupils look at the work of their classmates and of professionals, and what appears to be their attitude toward others' work?

To what extent do they consult art books?

What is their apparent attitude toward art as shown in their reactions to films, slides, talks, and visits to institutions?

What evidences of a satisfactory development of taste have they shown?

3. *The quality of the pupils' behavior as exhibited during participation in all types of art activities*

During art activities, in what respects have the pupils demonstrated personal initiative?

To what extent is there a challenge in unfamiliar art materials?

---

[3]Review Chapter 3 for this and the following questions about design.

In what respects have they demonstrated through art activities an inner discipline, worthy habits of thinking, commendable attitudes regarding a search for excellence, or other desirable personal qualities?

To what extent do they show good judgment in selecting tools and media for art work?

Once having selected an artistic goal, to what extent do they strive to reach it?

What is their attitude with regard to accepting advice about their artistic production?

To what extent do they accept the record of their past work as a basis for self-evaluation?

To what extent do they respond positively to group evaluation, allowing their own work to be discussed and joining in constructive discussion of their classmates' work?

To what extent have they demonstrated qualities of leadership in art activities?

To what extent have they shown themselves willing to cooperate generally in the worthy art projects of their group?

How willing are they to share in research work in art, in expressive work, and in the less rewarding tasks such as helping to keep equipment, supplies, and the working area used by the group clean and tidy? In general do they seem willing to share ideas about art with others?

Have they shown a reasonable attitude toward the sharing of display space?

How do they respond to new learning situations (art history and appreciation) that may not be related to their past experiences?

Obviously, children cannot be expected to show evidence of positive change in an area that the teacher has not touched on. The teacher, therefore, has as much responsibility as the pupil in the evaluation process.

Another system of classification that is useful in establishing objectives as well as criteria was developed by Benjamin Bloom and his associates.[4] The classifications, or "domains," that they chose for their taxonomy are the cognitive, the affective, and the psychomotor.

The cognitive domain includes behaviors and goals having to do with knowledge and the development of intellectual abilities. The affective

---

[4]*Taxonomy of Educational Objectives* (New York: McKay, Handbook I, 1956; Handbook II, 1964).

domain concerns itself with objectives that deal with interests, values, attitudes, and appreciations. The psychomotor domain involves the manipulative and motor skills. Bloom states:

> It was the view of the group that educational objectives stated in behavioral form have their counterparts in the behavior of individuals. Such behavior can be observed and described and the descriptive statements can be classified. . . . The process of thinking about educational objectives, defining them, and relating them to teaching and testing procedures was regarded as a very important step on the part of teachers.[5]

A brief analysis of an art program using the first two categories of Bloom's taxonomy is offered in Table 18.1 to assist the teacher in planning. The levels into which the categories are subdivided are only suggestions. It is hoped that the teacher will add items appropriate for the grade being taught.

[5]*Ibid.*, p. 5.

Table 18.1

AN ANALYSIS OF THE ART PROGRAM IN TERMS OF BLOOM'S TAXONOMY

Content and Objectives of the Cognitive Domain

Knowledge Level:
  Terminology.
  Art history: facts, names, dates, artistic schools.
  Facts about the education and career possibilities of an artist.
  Facts about processes, tools, and materials.
  Knowledge of criteria for various kinds of art products.

Comprehension Level:
  Recognition of styles and symbols of various periods.
  Ability to understand key ideas in design (unity and variety) and in art history (the hierarchical art of Egypt, the educational and symbolic art of the medieval period, the stylistic breakthroughs of the twentieth century).
  Ability to understand the various roles that the visual arts play and their concomitant satisfactions.
  Ability to direct attention to specific visual references suggested by the teacher.
  Ability to see analogies and to shift frames of reference.
  Ability to summarize.

Application Level:
  Capable of applying visual principles to studio activity; can carry ideas into practice.
  Can function in situations that require assimilation of previous experience, information, and knowledge.

Table 18.1　*(Cont.)*

Content and Objectives of the Cognitive Domain (Cont.)

Analysis Level:
　　Can identify components of an art work (design).
　　Can point to relationships between elements in a particular composition.

Synthesis:
　　Ability to unite content, design, materials, and processes into a satisfactory
　　　whole.
　　Can distinguish between the relevant and irrelevant in solving a particular
　　　problem.
　　Can point to means-end relationships in discussing the formation of objects
　　　or the creation of a painting.

Receiving Level:
　　Accepts criticism from teacher.
　　Listens to comments of classmates in group evaluation.
　　Is open to varying points of views, styles, and philosophies of a wide range
　　　of professional artists, sculptors, and architects.

Responding Level:
　　Willing to participate in discussion and respond with expressed judgments;
　　　capable of an exchange of differing opinions.

Valuing Level:
　　Willing to pursue positive, constructive criticism and appreciation of the
　　　efforts of classmates and of the works of professional artists.
　　Can distinguish between kinds of values: product values, process values, and
　　　aesthetic values in a given work.
　　Capable of immediate valuing on an emotional level.
　　Able to make a judgment about an art problem or an art work within a
　　　defined context.
　　Capable of relating criteria to judgment and of developing a personal value
　　　system in accordance with mutually accepted standards developed in the
　　　art program.

　　Bloom's taxonomy has provided theorists with much of the conceptual framework for the behavioral goals movement, particularly in art education.
　　Having sorted objectives according to various "levels," the teacher must select activities that will move the pupils to the point where they might be evaluated. Obviously, in evaluating the activities some kinds of appraisal will be more appropriate than others. Will the work of the children provide the point of reference, or will the teacher observe the children in action? Will the tests take a written or a verbal form? The children might be asked to study slides and make judgments, provide information orally or write an essay, or they might keep a notebook,

sketchbook, or scrapbook. Whatever the method of appraisal, it is the teacher's responsibility to see that the evaluation is consistent with the objectives and activities of the program.

The National Assessment of Educational Progress, operating under the sponsorship of the Educational Commission of the United States, provides one model for appraisal of achievement in learning. The National Assessment project, now underway, collects data that can help describe the knowledge, attitudes, and skills gained by American students from age nine to approximately age twenty-four. Planners who were involved in the initial phase had to state the goals for their subject area as well as the specific criteria for assessing how well the goals are being met. Brent Wilson, the major consultant to the project, appointed a committee composed of individuals with the highest professional qualifications to take the first step—the development of objectives. Feeling that this committee had produced only a summary of the educational ideas that had appeared during the previous quarter century, Wilson formed a second committee and broadened the conception of art they were to work with. The content of "art" was now to include the environmental arts, popular arts, informal art education children receive at home, while traveling, or through the media, as well as the traditional art forms of painting, sculpture, ceramics, and the like. Wilson's committees jointly produced the following objectives of art education.

1. Perceive and respond to [different] aspects of art.
2. Value art as an important realm of human experience.
3. Produce works of art.
4. Know about art.
5. Make and justify judgments about the aesthetic merit . . . of works of art.[6]

As an example of how these objectives are treated let us examine an outline of the first one:

I. Perceive and respond to aspects of art

Clarifying Definition: Aspects of art are defined as: sensory qualities of color, line, shape, and texture; compositional elements such as structure, space, . . . balance, movement, placement, closure, contrast, and pattern; expressive qualities such as mood, feeling, and emotion; subject matter, including (1) objects, themes (the general subject of a work, i.e., landscape or battle scene), events, and ideas (general presymbolic meanings) and (2) symbols and expressive content, which is a unique fusion of the foregoing aspects.

A. Recognize and describe the subject matter elements of works of art.

[6]National Assessment of Educational Progress, Art Objectives, Ann Arbor, Mich., p. 6.

Age 9. Identify themes of specific works of art.

Identify events depicted in specific works of art.

Describe how the themes of two or more specific works of art are similar or different.

B. Go beyond the recognition of subject matter to the perception and description of formal qualities and expressive content (the combined effect of the subject matter and the specific visual form that characterizes a particular work of art).

Age 9. Describe the characteristics of sensory qualities of works of art (that is, tell about colors, shapes, lines, and textures in a painting, building, photograph, etc.).

Describe the expressive character (feelings and moods) of works of art.

These behavioral objectives indicate the need for reproductions to be part of the conceptual framework. Indeed, one of the National Assessment's unique contributions has been its imaginative use of visual materials (packaging and sculpture as well as reproductions) as part of the evaluation process. Since many of the questions require varying responses, from essay-type answers and simple statements to nonverbal examples of drawings, the training of the person who makes judgments becomes a vital part of the program. The individual passing judgment may have to rely on categories of response rather than "correct" answers. As an example, in evaluating a pupil's response to Renoir's family portrait, *Madame Charpentier and Her Children,* the teacher may analyze the student's remarks according to the following classifications instead of assigning a high or low score.

Hedonism: Pleasure or displeasure.

Example: "I like this one."

Technical achievement: Skill and craftsmanship.

Example: "The hands and arms are drawn well."

Originality: Uniqueness of conception.

Example: "It's really different."

Imitation: Correspondence to reality.

Example: "You can just reach out and touch it!"

Emotion and expression: Intensity of emotion, mood, expressive qualities.

Example: "It makes me feel lonely and sad."

The preceding description is admittedly incomplete. The National Assessment of Educational Progress has undertaken the most extensive attempt so far to ascertain the level of goal achievement reached by art education. When the appraisal is completed, art teachers will have a clear indication of the progress of the field and how it is developing on a regional as well as national level.

TECHNIQUES OF APPRAISAL

Certain evaluation techniques have been employed in art education. Standardized measuring devices for the production and appreciation of art are available. Teachers also devise what are known as objective and essay-type examinations to test various aspects of the art program. Anecdotal records and observational techniques are used, as are checklists, interviews, and cumulative records. If experts in the science of testing are available, presumably even the "projective" techniques, or self-descriptive personal reports, and the "sociometric" methods of evaluation, which reveal information about the structure of social groups including the leaders and isolated children they contain, might be used in an art program.[7] To discuss in detail all these techniques would go beyond the scope of this book. Some comment, however, will be made on those devices most convenient for teachers of art and frequently used in the classroom. These include standardized art tests, art tests devised by the teacher, and less formal methods such as anecdotal techniques and checklists.

Standardized Art Tests

The decade between 1920 and 1930 witnessed extraordinary attempts to develop standardized tests to discover children's abilities both to produce art and to appreciate it. High hopes were held for the success of these tests. Thousands of children were involved; for each child, a scientific indication of ability to produce or to appreciate art forms was often set down. By the beginning of the 1930s however, those particularly interested in art education began to question the accuracy of the tests. Statements such as the following by Tannahill began to appear:

> Of all the tests in art which have been published, the most successful ones have to do with the testing of art appreciation. It is difficult, however, even in this field to reach an agreement of opinion among art teachers and connoisseurs because personal taste and style are changeable factors and artists have more or less prided themselves upon their non-adherence to a rigid standard rather than upon their adherence to one. This is true espe-

---

[7]J. W. Wrightstone, J. Justman, and I. Robbins, *Evaluation in Modern Education* (New York: American Book, 1956).

cially of creative expression, where the individuality of the artist, whether child or adult, is so important. It would seem that any attempt to test ability to create is futile. What may be a creation to one is not necessarily a work of art to another.[8]

When one studies some of the tests in question, and at the same time considers the nature of artistic acts, it is not difficult to observe some of their deficiencies. *The Scale for General Merit of Children's Drawings,*[9] for example, may be questioned as an efficient testing device, not only on the grounds mentioned in Tannahill's statement but also because its author seems to consider the exact representation of objects observed in the environment to be the chief excellence of artistic expression. Again, *Tests in Fundamental Abilities of Visual Art* [10] appears to overemphasize skills and technical details apart from the total act of expression.

One test for the purpose of measuring appreciation is the *Art Judgment Test* by N. C. Meier and C. E. Seashore.[11] Another is the *McAdory Art Test.*[12] Herbert A. Carroll says of these two, "Neither of the tests correlates to any extent with the judgment of university art instructors."[13] Actually, both tests are more a guessing game than a serious measuring device of appreciation. A more recent test is the Bryan-Schwamm Test, which is designed to measure children's sensitivity to line, shape, value, color, and texture. The test consists of examples of design elements that must be matched and identified. The test was originally intended for mentally retarded children, but may be used for any child.[14]

In spite of the fact that some writers about educational measurement seem to consider standardized art tests to be valid measuring instruments, warnings from art authorities indicate that the teacher of art should not place too much reliance on tests.[15] Under the title, "A Survey of Recent Research in Art and Art Education," Ray Faulkner lists many of the standardized art tests, but he observes: "The extent to which art abilities may be measured scientifically is still a controversial issue. Viewed objectively, few, if any, art tests have lived up to the expectations and promises of their makers."[16] With our present understanding of the human

---

[8] S. B. Tannahill, *Fine Arts for Public School Administrators* (New York: Teachers College, 1932), p. 126.

[9] E. L. Thorndike (New York: Teachers College, 1924).

[10] A. F. Laurenz (Los Angeles: Southern California School Book Depository, 1927).

[11] *Meier-Seashore Art Judgment Test* (Iowa City: University of Iowa, 1930).

[12] New York: Bureau of Publications, Teachers College, Columbia University, 1929.

[13] "What Do the Meier-Seashore and the McAdory Art Tests Measure?" *Journal of Educational Research,* Vol. 26 (May 1933), p. 665.

[14] Mankato, Minn., Campus Publishers, 1972.

[15] See, for example, Wrightstone and others, *Evaluation in Modern Education,* pp. 276–80, where it is stated during a discussion of art tests: "It is apparent . . . that knowledge about principles and skills as well as some aspects of appreciation [of art] can be measured."

[16] In G. M. Whipple, ed., Fortieth Yearbook of the National Society for the Study of Education (Bloomington, Ill.: Public School Publishing Co., 1941), p. 376.

mind and its functioning in relation to aesthetics, we lack the knowledge and ability to measure artistic qualities accurately. Writing some two decades later than Faulkner on the same subject, Lee Cronbach noted in his *Essentials of Psychological Testing*[17] that testing instruments in art ability have improved little in sophistication and reliability.

Despite the obvious hazards of objective assessment of work in an elementary art program, the problem of setting up criteria for product evaluation is still very much alive among researchers and graduate students. These researchers are attempting to isolate factors that may be recognized through a consensus of the judges. Establishing the reliability of one's judges then becomes a key factor in making judgments about art work. When one researcher wanted to analyze the drawings of advantaged and disadvantaged children, he had to be certain that his judges could "see" such elements as the horizon line, objects, and treatment of overlappings with enough agreement so that his statistics could be trusted. We can infer from this that teachers should maintain a degree of healthy skepticism regarding their own infallibility in judging works, and that criteria, if they are to mean anything to child, judge, or teacher, ought to be specific rather than general.

The trend in testing for art ability since the heyday of standardized testing several decades ago has been directed toward specific ends—that is, tests have been designed by teachers or research workers to arrive at limited kinds of information. Tests may be designed for a number of purposes, but in all cases they represent "a judgment of the adequacy of behavior as compared to a set of educational objectives."[18] Any test is a reflection of what a teacher considers important in a student's behavior, studio processes, skills, and knowledge about art. The test may be formal or informal, and it may just as easily precede instruction in the form of a diagnostic device as it may follow the instructional period to measure a student's gain. In any case, the test is but one technique among many to gauge the kind and quality of change in the student.

Formal Tests Devised by the Teacher
In addition to the standardized tests devised by experts there are tests composed by the classroom teacher. Such tests can often be useful, provided the teacher understands their significance. Sometimes the teacher may wish to use a test (usually cognitive) to discover whether or not the pupils have grasped some part of the art program. For example, it may be helpful to present a few questions based on the pupils' knowledge of a specific medium, or of facts surrounding an artist's life, or of techniques in using color.

[17] 2nd ed. (New York: Harper & Row, 1960).
[18] Elliot Eisner and David Ecker, *Readings in Art Education* (Waltham, Mass.: Blaisdell, 1966), p. 384.

The following completion-type problem could be used to test knowledge of color mixing:

Fill in the blanks:

1. To obtain a *shade* of red tempera paint add _____.
2. To obtain a *tint* of red watercolor add _____.
3. To turn *blue* into gray add _____.
4. To turn *green* into gray add _____.

An essay-type answer might be obtained from the following:

Describe two methods of mixing tempera paint to obtain gray.

Identification and multiple-choice tests are useful for younger children because they do not require written answers of any kind. For example, one item could be the following:

Which pigment, when added to red tempera paint, will result in a *shade* of red?

(a) green
(b) white
(c) black

Another recognition category might be based on slides and repro-ductions. After being shown a Rouault and a Rembrandt, a child may be asked the following items:

An art form that had a great influence on Rouault is:
(a) Impressionist paintings
(b) stained-glass windows
(c) sculpture

Which of the following methods did Rembrandt use to achieve his effects?
(a) chiaroscuro
(b) impasto
(c) glazes
(d) all the above

The items tested in these cases are merely facts surrounding art and are peripheral to art itself. Although the teacher may develop a few formal tests related to production and appreciation of art in the classroom, the essential nature of aesthetic activity will probably not be included. Any test designed to measure art itself or art appreciation will tend to be limited. We must conclude, therefore, by asserting that neither the stan-dardized test in art nor the formal test devised by the classroom teacher for specific aspects of the art program can produce a completely satisfactory indication of a pupil's real ability in this complex field of learning. At best such a test can serve merely as a supplement to less formal methods of appraisal.[19]

In the world of art, people are continually making judgments unsupported by scientific measuring devices. They assert, for example, that Seurat's *La Grande Jatte* is a masterpiece; that Leonardo is not as good an artist as the public believes; that Turner's compositions are flimsy; that Bellows was a master of concise statement with a brush. When the opinions of numbers of well-qualified people coincide about a work of art we are inclined to accept their statements as true. If numbers of such people agree for any considerable period of time that a work is excellent we begin to call it a masterpiece. By this type of informal critical appraisal, and by this alone, Westerners fill their galleries and select their masterpieces. No great work of art has ever been chosen by any other method.

The method has, of course, demonstrable limitations. The history of art is full of painters, such as Cézanne, now considered important, who during their lifetimes were either unrecognized or disliked by the critics. Then we have painters like Landseer, who were favored by contemporary critics but who, in the course of time, have lost their esteem in the eyes of reputable judges. With full awareness of the limitations of our method of selecting works of art, however, we retain this method because no better practical means of selection has been devised. Similarly, we resort to informal methods of appraising the capabilities of the judges—that is to say, their abilities to appreciate art.

Teachers should first recognize that they are subject to error in their appraisal of the children's patterns of behavior and their ability to produce and to appreciate art. Having accepted this fact, they will probably be cautious in jumping to conclusions, painstaking in their efforts to analyze the pupils' progress, and humble in the weight they attach to their opinions. Nevertheless, if they familiarize themselves with art, with the children under their care, and with an acceptable pedagogy in relation to art and children, there is nothing to prevent them from accepting with some confidence the task of appraising the progress that the children make in art education.

The Checklist. A simple method of gathering data about a child's progress in art is to keep a checklist. The most difficult part of this method

---

[19]"Any evaluation of an individual's future promise in art . . . would have to be based not only on test data, but on a summarization of his experiences in various art activities; and appraisal of his sketches, paintings, or other art products; and observation of his interests and motivation." See T. L. Torgerson and G. S. Adams, *Measurement and Evaluation for the Elementary School Teacher* (New York: Dryden, 1954), pp. 370–75. This book contains a good chapter on the construction of tests for classroom use, pp. 220–43.

Table 18.2

CHECKLIST FOR ART ACTIVITIES

The Student:	Exceptional	Average	Below Average
1. Was able to use own experiences			
2. Progressed normally through manipulative ⎫ symbol ⎬ stage preadolescent ⎭			
3. Work showed personal style			
4. Produced work that showed (a) respect for material (b) respect for function of object			
5. Used tools (a) appropriate to task (b) with dexterity			
6. Showed ability to use (a) line (b) mass and space (c) light and shade (d) color (e) texture			
7. Work showed unity of design			
8. Work showed variety of design			
9. Work showed development over period of time			
10. Successfully related (a) art work to school experiences (b) other school experiences to artistic expression			
11. Responded positively to new situations in art			

is to devise a practical list. This the teachers must do largely for themselves, because checklists made by others rarely are entirely suitable for them. It is suggested, however, that the list be based on the three general headings mentioned earlier, namely, expression, appreciation, and behavior. The subheadings might resemble the questions offered under the three general headings. Table 18.2 presents a sample of a short checklist for *expression*. It would have to be altered to suit any specific grade or type of art activity.

Figure 18.1 *Appraisal of a pupil's progress in art must be derived largely from the teacher's acquaintance with each child. (Photo by Rick Steadry.)*

The three columns can be designated by any terms the teachers deem suitable (I, II, III; excellent, satisfactory, unsatisfactory; exemplary, present, not present). Using three columns allows distinctions to be made between (1) progress that occurs in a particular area because of giftedness (exceptional), (2) the level of work of most children (average), and (3) the difficulties certain individuals experience (below average). Schoolteachers in Japan grade their pupils' pictures on a point system. The American art teacher is horrified, but the Japanese system indicates that art is considered as having the same importance as other subjects.

The "Anecdotal" Method. A second device, known as the "anecdotal" method, is also valuable. With this method the teacher periodically jots down observations about each child, based on the questions in the three categories of criteria. This method is recommended by Saucier, among others, who says of it: "A cumulative record of such specific reactions may become a rather reliable index of [the pupil's] trend and stage of development in some traits. It at least furnishes the teacher and the child with some concrete evidence of strong and weak points in his character and conduct."[20]

As an example, opposite some of the items of the sample checklist previously outlined, the following remarks might be set down for a six-year-old in first grade:

Expression	*Comments*
1. Able to use own experiences	"in general picture-making, yes, but not in correlation with social studies—copied a drawing"
2. Progressed normally through symbol stage	"normal until absence from school—then regression to manipulation for two days—after that normal—is putting in sky and ground symbols"
3. Work showed personal style	"nothing special yet"
4. (not applicable)	
5. Used tools with dexterity	"using scissors well; can literally 'draw' with them"
6. Showed ability to use line	"a nervous child—and so, nervous line—"

The teacher might also consider using a "Gestalt" anecdotal method—that is, commenting from time to time after periodic examination of portfolios. A checklist might be used as a guide in writing these comments, but need not be referred to item by item. Such records give general, overall impressions of a large body of work. The following are examples of notes about children that a teacher might write for a personal file.

John A [6 years, grade 1]

John uses a variety of personal experiences in his pictures, and he is certainly getting along well lately in trying to develop symbols of houses. It is strange, however, how his work seemed to deteriorate last week. He works hard, though, and participates well in a group.

Betty McM [11 years, grade 6]

She has always shown herself to be a sensitive child, and her paintings reflect her feelings. Her work seems overdelicate at times; to give it more character she might concentrate a little more on the use of light and shade and bright color areas. She did not seem to care for working on murals with others, but she participated well in the puppet show. She was obviously moved when she listened to music in preparation for a picture. I doubt if she will ever be a vigorous leader, but she is a fine child who must be treated gently.

[20] *Theory and Practice in the Elementary School*, p. 401.

Robert L [10 years, grade 5]

Robert continues to be careless and untidy; his paints are in a mess, his drawings all thumb-marks, his brushes unwashed. As stage manager of our play, nevertheless, he worked well. He seems to be more at home with sculpture than he is in the areas of drawing and painting. His last sculpture in clay was quite vigorous. He likes to explore new materials and last week brought to school some wood for carving.

The data derived from checklists and other notations will greatly assist the teacher in arriving at an appraisal of a pupil's progress, but it is necessary also to keep a file of the child's actual art production for periodic study and comparison with the written notations. Usually lack of space prevents the teacher from keeping any but the flat work.

These methods of appraisal allow the teacher to summarize the child's progress in only the most general of terms. Once made, however, such a summary will prove valuable to the teacher making progress reports to parents and others interested in the child's welfare. Such methods are difficult for the art teacher to follow, however, since their effectiveness rests on a day-to-day knowledge of the children being evaluated.

REPORTING PROGRESS IN ART

From time to time every school system reports to parents concerning their children's progress. This is one of the traditional and necessary functions of a school. Every aspect of the program of studies should be mentioned on a report form to parents, if only as a notice to parents that their children have been exposed to the subject. The fact that the art program does not lend itself to exact measurement does not excuse the teacher from making some sort of report on the pupils who participated in it.

In addition to informing parents of the progress of their offspring, some educators feel that reports have other functions. From the teachers' point of view, these are: (1) helping teachers to reach conclusions about their pupils; (2) assisting teachers in making plans for the future; and (3) in general, helping them to appraise the effectivenss of their teaching. From the point of view of the pupils, reports have the purpose of: (1) helping pupils to realize the progress they have made; (2) pointing out to them where they might improve in their work; and (3) indicating to them what they might do in the future to make further progress. From the point of view of some educators, if children compare their achievements with those of their fellows, reports provide an incentive for them to work harder and more efficiently.

In spite of these opinions it would seem that in relation to art the only legitimate function of a report is to let the parents know how their child is progressing in this field. A teacher of art who has waited until report time to reach conclusions about a child's progress can scarcely have acted as an efficient and sympathetic counselor in art. Furthermore, if the pupils must depend on a report card to help them understand their progress, to improve their work, and to give them clues as to future action, communication in the classroom must have reached an extraordinarily low ebb. Perhaps the worst use to which a report in art could be put, however, would be as an incentive for the pupil to work harder and more efficiently. The idea of using the report in this fashion is based on a teacher's threat and a child's fear—that the teacher will tell Mother and Father that they have a "bad" child because the child fails to perform art work to the teacher's satisfaction. No art was ever produced under these conditions, nor is it ever likely to be.

Regarding the mechanics of reporting to the parents, several points must be kept in mind. First, the method of reporting must be easily understood by all parents. Any report that makes use of complicated symbols or what is considered by some to be highly professional language (and by others to be an undesirable "pedagese") will not be appreciated by most parents. Second, the report should reflect the objectives and practices of the art program and should attempt to comment on the child, both as an individual and as a member of a group. Third, any good report should, of course, be as accurate and fair as a teacher can make it. Fourth, from the teacher's point of view the system of reporting should not demand a disproportionate amount of clerical work.

In general, since reporting in art is characterized by a number of peculiarities arising from the nature of this area of learning, it might be well for the teacher to discuss these peculiarities frankly with the parents and, in fact, with children who are in a position to understand them.

Cooperative reporting, while excellent in theory, may not always work to the advantage of art. Unless parents and others have reached a stage of thinking in which they are willing to forgo a competitive method of reporting, art education may suffer materially. Because art may be likened to a personal gift from a child to others, there is obviously no room for competition in it. To encourage competition between children engaged in art is to be at odds with the whole process of their artistic expression. When they are behaving naturally, children produce art as a result of an inner need arising from some reaction to experience, not for the sake of a prize or a mark. In the art of children we have, coupled with the need for self-expression, one of the comparatively rare human manifestations of what appears to be a desire, unmotivated by thoughts of material gain. For adults to attempt to interfere with the child's happy state of aesthetic gift-giving would be a very shortsighted and sad policy. The art work of a child, therefore, should be judged in relation to earlier work by the same child rather than in comparison with the work of peers. This view is the basis for the objection to art contests by most art teachers.

In many relationships, people appear to be competitive creatures. While many maintain that competition has its legitimate place in some aspects of our society, people cannot live by competition alone. In their artistic productions they demonstrate another side of their nature, which, in view of our modern engines of destruction, we might do well to foster. Art in the schools should be presented as a field of endeavor that depends on a love of the activity for itself and not on extraneous rewards.

The system of reporting a pupil's progress in art should, therefore, avoid any idea of competition between the children. The only means of reporting available to teachers of art are those generally called "progress reports" and "narrative reports." The progress report is based on the use of check marks, symbols, or letters. Often only two marks are used—"S" for satisfactory and "U" for unsatisfactory. Sometimes the letter "O" may be employed to signify outstanding progress. Under the heading "art" on the report form, the subheadings "expression," "appreciation," and "personal and social development" might be listed. The parent would then expect to find either S, U, or O opposite each of these subheadings. This system appears to be theoretically sound for reporting art, in that it is based on each child's individual progress, rather than on progress in comparison with that of other pupils. Children, however, will often make a competition of even these general ratings.

A teacher, not thoroughly familiar with every child, might, with the parents' consent, wish to make an initial report to them verbally during a short conference. This method tends to be time-consuming but because of its flexibility is one that has some obvious advantages over written reports to parents. It demands, of course, that the teacher have some ability to report both good and bad aspects of a child's efforts without arousing the personal wrath of a parent. No teacher, furthermore, can afford to arrange an interview of this type without first being fully prepared. For the school's permanent records, a teacher must keep on file a complete written report of each pupil, even if this report is available to the parents only on request. Of course if the child is gifted the teacher should make the parents aware of the child's exceptional ability so that it can gain the support it might not otherwise have. Many parents are completely unaware of their children's creative abilities.

ACTIVITIES FOR THE READER

1. Describe some situations in which the art program reflects the educational outlook of (a) a school principal; (b) a school board; (c) a community.
2. Devise some test items in art as follows:

    a. A true-false type to test third-grade pupils' knowledge of handling clay.
    b. A recall or completion type to test fourth-grade pupils' knowledge of color mixing.

    c. A multiple-choice type to test sixth-grade pupils' knowledge of linear perspective.

    d. A matching items type to test fifth-grade pupils' ability to use a mixed-media technique.

    e. A recognition type to test sixth-grade pupils' knowledge of art terms.[21]

3. Make checklists for (a) appreciation of sculpture by sixth-grade pupils; (b) skills needed by fourth-grade pupils while doing puppetry.
4. Study over a period of two weeks the art output of a group of ten children and write a paragraph of not more than fifty words for each child, summarizing their progress.
5. Describe any results, either good or bad, that you have observed as a result of competitive marking of children's art. How do those who have received a poor grade react?
6. Study the checklist on page 507. Try to rework a portion of it to reflect part or all of Bloom's taxonomy of educational objectives.
7. Imagine yourself to be a parent. How would you want art to change your child? List the items that in your parental view would demonstrate the effectiveness of art education. Pick a specific age level.
8. Make a checklist of items that would reflect the attitudinal change of the principal and faculty with respect to the art program.

[21]See any standard work on measurement, such as Torgerson and Adams, *Measurement and Evaluation for the Elementary School Teacher,* for definition of the types of tests.

Appendices

Appendices

I. RECOMMENDED READING FOR PREPARING TO TEACH ART

ALSCHULER, ROSE, and LA BERTA WEISS HATTWICK, *Painting and Personality: A Study of Young Children.* 2 vols. Chicago: University of Chicago Press, 1947 (rev. and abr. 1969).

ANDERSON, WARREN H., *Art Learning Situations for Elementary Education.* Belmont, Calif.: Wadsworth, 1965.

ARNHEIM, RUDOLF, *Art and Visual Perception: A Psychology of the Creative Eye,* 4th ed. Berkeley: University of California Press, 1964.

ASHTON-WARNER, SYLVIA, *Teacher.* New York: Simon and Schuster, 1971.

BARKAN, MANUEL, *Through Art to Creativity.* Boston: Allyn and Bacon, 1960.

BASSETT, RICHARD, ed., *The Open Eye in Learning: The Role of Art in General Education.* Cambridge, Mass.: M.I.T. Press, 1969.

BLAND, JANE C., *Art and the Young Child: Understanding and Encouraging Creative Growth in Children Three to Five.* New York: Museum of Modern Art, 1968.

CANE, FLORENCE, *The Artist in Each of Us.* London: Thames & Hudson, 1951.

COLE, NATALIE, *The Arts in the Classroom.* New York: John Day, 1940.

CONANT, HOWARD, and ARNE RANDALL, *Art in Education.* Peoria, Ill.: Bennett, 1963.

CONRAD, GEORGE, *The Process of Art Education in the Elementary School.* Englewood Cliffs, N.J.: Prentice-Hall, 1964.

D'AMICO, VICTOR, *Creative Teaching in Art,* rev. ed. Scranton, Pa.: International Textbook, 1966.

DE FRANCESCO, ITALO, *Art Education: Its Means and Ends.* New York: Harper & Row, 1958.

DIMONDSTEIN, GERALDINE, *Exploring the Arts with Children.* New York: Macmillan, 1974.

EISNER, ELLIOT, *Educating Artistic Vision.* New York: Macmillan, 1972.

EISNER, ELLIOT, and DAVID ECKER, *Readings in Art Education: A Primary Source Book.* Waltham, Mass.: Blaisdell, 1966.

ENG, HELGA, *The Psychology of Children's Drawing.* Trans. by H. Stafford Hatfield. New York: Harcourt Brace Jovanovich, 1931.

ERDT, MARGARET HAMILTON, *Teaching Art in the Elementary School,* rev. ed. New York: Holt, Rinehart and Winston, 1962.

FELDMAN, EDMUND, *Becoming Human Through Art: Aesthetic Experience in the School.* Englewood Cliffs, N.J.: Prentice-Hall, 1970.

GAITSKELL, C. D. and M. R., *Art Education in the Kindergarten.* Peoria, Ill.: Bennett, 1952 (5th ed., Toronto: Ryerson, 1968).

————, *Art Education for Slow Learners.* Peoria, Ill.: Bennett, 1953 (new ed., Toronto: Ryerson, 1964).

GARDNER, HOWARD, *The Arts and Human Development: A Psychological Study of the Artistic Process.* New York: Wiley, 1973.

GONDOR, EMERY I., *Art and Play Therapy.* New York: Random House, 1954.

GREENBERG, PEARL, *Children's Experiences in Art: Drawing and Painting.* New York: Reinhold, 1966.

HARRIS, DALE B., *Children's Drawings as Measures of Intellectual Maturity.* New York: Harcourt Brace Jovanovich, 1963.

HARRISON, ELIZABETH, *Self-Expression Through Art.* Toronto: Gage, 1951.

HASTIE, W. REID, ed., *Art Education.* Sixty-fourth Yearbook of the National Society for the Study of Education. Chicago: University of Chicago Press, 1965.

HAUSMAN, JEROME J., ed., *Report of the Commission on Art Education.* Washington, D.C.: National Art Education Association, 1965.

HERBERHOLZ, BARBARA, *Early Childhood Art.* Dubuque, Iowa: Wm C. Brown, 1974.

HERBERHOLZ, DONALD W. and BARBARA, *A Child's Pursuit of Art.* Dubuque, Iowa: Brown, 1967.

HOOVER, F. LOUIS, *Art Activities for the Very Young.* Worcester, Mass.: Davis, 1961.

HORN, GEORGE F., *Experiencing Art in the Kindergarten.* Worcester, Mass.: Davis, 1971.

HORNE, JOICEY, Young Artists. Toronto: Longmans, Green, 1961.

HORNE, LOIS THOMASSON, *Painting for Children: Motivation, Materials, Techniques.* New York: Reinhold, 1968.

HUBBARD, GUY and MARY ROUSE, *Art 1-6: Meaning, Method and Media.* Westchester, Ill.: Benefic Press, 1973.

HURWITZ, AL, ed., *Programs of Promise: Art in the Schools.* New York: Harcourt Brace Jovanovich, 1972.

————, and STANLEY MADEJA, *The Joyous Vision: Art Appreciation in the Elementary Schools.* New York: Reinhold, 1976.

HUXLEY, ALDOUS, *They Still Want to Draw.* New York: Oxford University Press, 1939.

JAMESON, KENNETH, *Art and the Young Child.* New York: Viking, 1968.

————, *Primary School Art.* New York: Reinhold, 1971.

JEFFERSON, BLANCHE, *Teaching Art to Children,* 3rd ed. Boston: Allyn and Bacon, 1969.

KAUFMAN, IRVING, *Art and Education in Contemporary Culture.* New York: Macmillan, 1966.

KELLOGG, RHODA, *Analyzing Children's Art.* Palo Alto, Calif.: National Press, 1969.

————, and SCOTT O'DELL, *Psychology of Children's Art.* New York: Random House (*Psychology Today* book), 1967.

KNUDSEN, ESTELLE, *Children's Art Education.* Peoria, Ill.: Bennett, 1971.

KRANZ, STEWART and JOSEPH DELEY, *The Fourth "R": Art for the Urban School.* New York: Van Nostrand Reinhold, 1970.

LANDIS, MILDRED, *Meaningful Art Education.* Peoria, Ill.: Bennett, 1951.

LANSING, KENNETH, *Art, Artists, and Art Education.* New York: McGraw-Hill, 1969.

LARK-HOROVITZ, BETTY, HILDA PRESENT LEWIS, and MARK LUCA, *Understanding Children's Art for Better Teaching,* 2nd ed. Columbus, Ohio: Merrill, 1973.

LEWIS, HILDA PRESENT, ed., *Child Art: The Beginnings of Self-Affirmation.* Berkeley: Diablo, 1973.

LINDERMAN, EARL W., *Invitation to Vision.* Dubuque, Iowa: Brown, 1967.

————, and DONALD W. HERBERHOLZ, *Developing Artistic and Perceptual Awareness: Art Practice in the Classroom.* Dubuque, Iowa: Brown, 1964.

LINDERMAN, MARLENE M., *Art in the Elementary School: Drawing and Painting for the Classroom.* Dubuque, Iowa: Brown, 1974.

LINDSTROM, MIRIAM, *Children's Art: A Study of Normal Development in Children's Modes of Visualization.* Berkeley: University of California Press, 1957.

LOGAN, FRED M., *Growth of Art in American Schools.* New York: Harper & Row, 1955.

LOUGHRAN, BERNICE, *Art Experiences.* New York: Harcourt Brace Jovanovich, 1963.

LOWENFELD, VIKTOR, and W. LAMBERT BRITTAIN, *Creative and Mental Growth,* 5th ed. New York: Macmillan, 1970.

LUCA, MARK, and ROBERT KENT, *Art Education: Strategies of Teaching.* Englewood Cliffs, N.J.: Prentice-Hall, 1968.

MacDONALD, STUART, *The History and Philosophy of Art Education.* London: University of London Press, Ltd., 1970.

McFEE, JUNE KING, *Preparation for Art,* 2nd ed. Belmont, Calif.: Wadsworth, 1970.

McILVIN, DOROTHY S., *Art for the Primary Grades.* New York: Putnam, 1961.

MANZELLA, DAVID, *Educationists and the Evisceration of the Visual Arts.* Scranton, Pa.: International Textbook, 1963.

MEARNS, HUGHES, *Creative Power: The Education of Youth in the Creative Arts.* New York: Dover, 1958.

MELZI, KAY, and WILLIAM PALMER, *Art in the Primary School.* Oxford, Eng.: Blackwell, 1967.

MENDELOWITZ, DANIEL M., *Children Are Artists: An Introduction to Children's Art for Teachers and Parents.* Stanford, Calif.: Stanford University Press, 1963.

MERRITT, HELEN, *Guiding Free Expression in Children's Art.* New York: Holt, Rinehart and Winston, 1964.

MONTGOMERY, CHANDLER, *Art for Teachers of Children.* Columbus, Ohio: Merrill, 1968.

MUNRO, THOMAS, *Art Education: Toward Science in Aesthetics.* Indianapolis: Bobbs-Merrill, 1956.

PACKWOOD, MARY M., ed., *Art Education for Elementary Teachers.* Washington, D.C.: National Art Education Association, 1962.

————, ed., *Art Education in the Elementary School.* Washington, D.C.: National Art Education Association, 1967.

PAPPAS, GEORGE, *Concepts in Art and Education:*

An Anthology of Current Issues. New York: Macmillan, 1970.

PATTEMORE, ARNEL W., *Art and Environment.* New York: Van Nostrand Reinhold, 1974.

PLUMMER, GORDON S., *Children's Art Judgement.* Dubuque, Iowa: Wm C. Brown, 1974.

READ, HERBERT, *Education Through Art,* rev. ed. New York: Pantheon, 1958.

RICHARDSON, MARION, *Art and the Child.* Peoria, Ill.: Bennett, 1952.

ROSENBERG, LILLI ANN KILLEN, *Children Make Murals and Sculpture: Experiences in Community Art Projects.* New York: Reinhold, 1968.

RUESCHOFF, PHIL, and M. EVELYN SCHWARTZ, *Teaching Art in the Elementary School: Enhancing Visual Perception,* New York: Ronald, 1969.

SAWYER, JOHN, and ITALO DE FRANCESCO, *Elementary School Art for Classroom Teachers.* New York: Harper & Row, 1971.

SCHWARTZ, FRED R., *Structure and Potential in Art Education.* Lexington, Mass.: Xerox College, 1970.

SILBERMAN, CHARLES E., *The Open Classroom Reader.* New York: Random House, 1973.

SPROUL, ADELAIDE, *With a Free Hand: Painting, Drawing, Graphics, and Sculpture for Children.* New York: Reinhold, 1968.

STEVENI, MICHAEL, *Art and Education.* London: Batsford, 1968.

TOMLINSON, R. R., and JOHN FITZMARRICE MILLS, *The Growth of Child Art.* London: University of London Press, Ltd., 1966.

TRUCKSESS, FRAN, *Creative Art: Elementary Grades.* Boulder, Colo.: Pruett, 1962.

WACHOWIAK, FRANK, and THEODORE RAMSAY, *Emphasis Art: A Qualitative Art Program for the Elementary School,* 2nd ed. Scranton, Pa.: International Textbook, 1971.

YOCHIM, LOUISE DUNN, *Perceptual Growth in Creativity.* Scranton, Pa.: International Textbook, 1967.

ZIEGFELD, EDWIN, ed., *Education and Art.* Paris: UNESCO, 1953.

Special Publications

ANDREWS, MICHAEL, "Synaesthetic Education." Four statements by members of the Department of Synaesthetic Education, School of Art, Syracuse University, 1971.

BARKAN, MANUEL, and LAURA H. CHAPMAN, *Guidelines for Art Instruction Through Television for the Elementary Schools.* National Center for School and College Television, 1967.

BINGHAM, MARGARET, "Learning Dimensions Program." Philadelphia Public Schools, 1968.

ECKER, DAVID, "Defining Behavioral Objectives for Aesthetic Education." St. Ann, Mo.: Central Midwestern Education, Inc.

EISNER, ELLIOT W., *Teaching Art to the Young: A Curriculum Development Project in Art Education.* Sponsored by the Charles F. Kettering Foundation, Stanford University, 1969.

"Evaluating the Total School Art Program." Papers presented at the NAEA Conference, San Diego, Calif., 1973.

GREENBERG, PEARL, ed., *Art Education: Elementary.* Washington, D.C.: National Art Education Association, 1972.

HOFFA, HARLAN, "An Analysis of Recent Research Conferences in Art Education." U.S. Department of Health, Education and Welfare, Office of Education, Bureau of Research, 1970.

MICHAEL, JOHN A., "A Handbook for Art Illustrators and Students." Based on Concepts and Behavior. Oxford, Ohio. 1972.

II. RECOMMENDED READING FOR TEACHING ART

Aesthetics and Criticism

ALDRICH, VIRGIL C., *Philosophy of Art.* Englewood Cliffs, N.J.: Prentice-Hall, 1963.

BEARDSLEY, MONROE, *Aesthetics: Problems in the Philosophy of Criticism.* New York: Harcourt Brace Jovanovich, 1958.

BELL, CLIVE, *Art.* New York: Putman, 1959.

———, *Since Cézanne.* New York: Harcourt Brace Jovanovich, 1922.

CASSIRER, ERNST, *An Essay on Man.* New York: Doubleday, 1956.

CROCE, BENEDETTO, *Aesthetic.* Trans. by Douglas Ainslie. New York: Noonday, 1956.

DEWEY, JOHN, *Art as Experience.* New York: Putnam, 1959.

ELLIS, HAVELOCK, *The Dance of Life.* New York: Greenwood, 1973.

FAULKNER, RAY, and EDWIN ZIEGFELD, *Art Today,* 5th ed. New York: Holt, Rinehart and Winston, 1969.

FELDMAN, EDMUND, *Varieties of Visual Experience: Art as Image and Idea,* 2nd ed. Englewood Cliffs, N.J.: Prentice-Hall, 1972.

FIEDLER, CONRAD, *On Judging Works of Art.* Berkeley: University of California Press, 1949.

FOCILLON, HENRI, *The Life of Forms in Art.* New York: Wittenborn, 1966.

FRY, ROGER, *Cézanne: A Study of His Development.* New York: Macmillan, 1958.

———, *Transformations.* New York: Doubleday, 1956.

———, *Vision and Design.* New York: Meridian, 1956.

GILL, ERIC, *Art and a Changing Civilization.* London: John Lane, The Bodley Head, 1934.

HOLME, G., *Industrial Design and the Future.* London: Studio, 1934.

MALRAUX, ANDRÉ, *The Psychology of Art.* 3 vols. New York: Skira, 1950.

MOHOLY-NAGY, LÁSZLÓ, *Vision in Motion.* Chicago: Theobald, 1947.

MUMFORD, LEWIS, *Technics and Civilization.* New York: Harcourt Brace Jovanovich, 1963.

OGDEN, C. K., I. A. RICHARDS, and JAMES WOOD, *The Foundation of Aesthetics.* New York: International Publishing, 1931.

PEPPER, STEPHEN, *The Basis of Criticism in the Arts.* Cambridge, Mass.: Harvard University Press, 1941.

RADER, MELVIN, *A Modern Book of Aesthetics,* 4th ed. New York: Holt, Rinehart and Winston, 1973.

READ, HERBERT, *Art and Industry.* New York: Horizon, 1961.

———, *Art Now,* 2nd ed. New York: Pitman, 1960.

———, ed., *The Meaning of Art,* 4th ed. New York: Pitman, 1969.

REID, LOUIS A., *A Study in Aesthetics.* New York: Macmillan, 1931.

SHAHN, BEN, *The Shape of Content.* Cambridge, Mass.: Harvard University Press, 1957.

SMITH, RALPH A., *Aesthetics and Criticism in Art Education.* Chicago: Rand McNally, 1966.

Art Appreciation

ARNHEIM, RUDOLF, *Art and Visual Perception: A Psychology of the Creative Eye,* 4th ed. Berkeley: University of California Press, 1964.

BARNES, ALBERT C., *The Art in Painting.* New York: Harcourt Brace Jovanovich, 1937.

BARR, ALFRED H., *What is Modern Painting?* New York: Museum of Modern Art, 1966.

BERGER, RENÉ, *The Language of Art.* London: Thames & Hudson, 1963.

BETHERS, RAY, *Composition in Pictures,* 2nd ed. New York: Pitman, 1962.

———, *How Paintings Happen.* New York: Norton, 1951.

BLAKE, PETER, *The Master Builders.* New York: Knopf, 1960.

CANADAY, JOHN, *Keys to Art.* New York: Tudor, 1963.

EDMAN, IRWIN, *Arts and the Man.* New York: Norton, 1939.

FAULKNER, RAY, and EDWIN ZIEGFELD, *Art Today,* 5th ed. New York: Holt, Rinehart and Winston, 1969.

FREEDMAN, LEONARD, *Looking at Modern Painting.* New York: Norton, 1961.

HAMLIN, TALBOT, *Architecture Through the Ages.* New York: Putnam, 1953.

HAYES, BARTLETT H., *The Naked Truth.* Andover, Mass.: Addison Gallery, 1949.

———, and MARY RATHBURN, *A Layman's Guide to Modern Art.* New York: Oxford University Press, 1948.

KEPES, GYORGY, *The Language of Vision.* Chicago: Theobald, 1945.

KNOBLER, NATHAN, *The Visual Dialogue: An Introduction to the Appreciation of Art.* New York: Holt, Rinehart and Winston, 1972.

KUH, KATHERINE, *Art Has Many Faces.* New York: Harper & Row, 1951.

———, *The Artist's Voice.* New York: Harper & Row, 1962.

LANGER, SUSANNE K., *Problems of Art*. New York: Scribner's, 1957.

LINGSTROM, FREDA, *The Seeing Eye*. New York: Macmillan, 1960.

LOWRY, BATES, *The Visual Experience: An Introduction to Art*. New York: Abrams, 1961.

OERI, GEORGINE, *Man and His Images*. New York: Viking, 1968.

SCHINNELLER, JAMES A., *Art: Search and Self-Discovery*, 2nd ed. Scranton, Pa.: International Textbook, 1968.

SCHORR, JUSTIN, *Aspects of Art*. Cranbury, N.J.: Barnes, 1967.

SEIBERLING, FRANK, *Looking into Art*. New York: Holt, Rinehart and Winston, 1959.

TAYLOR, HAROLD, *Art and the Intellect and Moral Values and the Experience of Art*. New York: Museum of Modern Art, 1960.

Art History

BLESH, RUDI, *Modern Art U.S.A.* New York: Knopf, 1956.

CHENEY, SHELDON, *Expressionism in Art*. New York: Liveright, 1970.

————, *A New World History of Art*. New York: Holt, Rinehart and Winston, 1956.

————, *The Story of Modern Art*. New York: Viking, 1958.

CRAVEN, THOMAS, *Men of Art*. New York: Simon and Schuster, 1931.

FAURE, ÉLIE, *History of Art*. 5 vols. Trans. by Walter Pach. New York: Harper & Row, 1921–30.

GARDNER, HELEN, *Art Through the Ages,* 5th ed. Rev. by Horst de la Croix and Richard G. Tansey. New York: Harcourt Brace Jovanovich, 1970.

GOMBRICH, E. H., *The Story of Art,* 12th ed. London: Phaidon, 1972.

GROPIUS, WALTER, ed., *Bauhaus 1919–1928*. New York: Museum of Modern Art, 1938.

JANSON, H. W., ed., *Key Monuments of the History of Art*. Englewood Cliffs, N.J.: Prentice-Hall, and New York: Abrams, 1959.

———— and DORA JANE. *The Story of Painting for Young People*. New York: Abrams, 1962.

LARKIN, OLIVER, *Art and Life in America*. New York: Holt, Rinehart and Winston, 1949 (rev. and enl. 1960).

MYERS, BERNARD S., *Art and Civilization,* 2nd ed. New York: McGraw-Hill, 1967.

————, *Modern Art in the Making,* 2nd ed. New York: McGraw-Hill, 1959.

ORPEN, WILLIAM, ed., *The Outline of Art*. New York: Transatlantic Arts, 1955.

PHILLIPS, LISLE MARCH, *The Works of Man,* rev. ed. London: Duckworth, 1956.

ROBB, DAVID M., and J. J. GARRISON, *Art in the Western World,* rev. ed. New York: Harper & Row, 1965.

ROOS, FRANK J., JR., *An Illustrated Handbook of Art History,* 3rd ed. New York: Macmillan, 1970.

SEWALL, JOHN IVES, *A History of Western Art*. New York: Holt, Rinehart and Winston, 1937.

ZUCKER, PAUL, *Styles in Painting*. New York: Viking, 1950.

Special Education

"Developing Art Experiences for the Emotionally Handicapped Child." New York: City College of New York, 1972.

FUKURAI, SHIRO, *How Can I Make What I Cannot See?* New York: Reinhold, 1973.

GREENBERG, PEARL, ed., "Art in Special Education," *Art Education: Elementary,* Chapter III. Washington, D.C.: National Art Education Association, 1972.

JAKAB, IRENE, ed., "Conscious and Unconscious Expressive Art." Proceedings of the American Society of Psychopathology of Expression. 1969.

KEPHART, N. C., *The Slow Learner in the Classroom*. Columbus, Ohio: Merrill, 1960.

KINDSAY, ZAIDEE, *Art and the Handicapped Child*. New York: Reinhold, 1972.

UHLIN, DONALD M., *Art for Exceptional Children*. Dubuque, Iowa: Brown, 1972.

Techniques and Processes

Bookbinding

COCKERELL, DOUGLAS, *Bookbinding and the Care of Books*, 5th ed. New York: Pitman, 1953.

JOHNSON, PAULINE, *Creative Bookbinding*. Seattle: University of Washington Press, 1973.

TOWN, LAWRENCE, *Bookbinding by Hand*. New York: Pitman, 1952.

Clay

BARFORD, GEORGE, *Clay in the Classroom*. Worcester, Mass.: Davis, 1963.

ROETTGER, ERNST, *Creative Clay Design*. New York: Reinhold, 1972.

SANDERS, HERBERT H., *Sunset Ceramics Book*. Menlo Park, Calif.: Lane, 1953.

TYLER, KEITH, *Pottery Without a Wheel*. London: Dryad, 1955.

Collage

BROW, FRANCIS, *Collage*. New York: Pitman, 1963.

LYNCH, JOHN, *How to Make Collages*. New York: Viking, 1961.

MEILACH, DONA, and ELVIE TEN HOOR, *Collage and Found Art*. New York: Reinhold, 1964.

Color

ITTEN, JOHANNES, *The Art of Color*. New York: Reinhold, 1961.

PASCHEL, HERBERT D., *The First Book of Color*. New York: Franklin Watts, 1959.

Crafts

COX, DORIS, and BARBARA WARREN, *Creative Hands*. New York: Wiley, 1945.

MATTIL, EDWARD, *Meaning in Crafts,* 3rd ed. Englewood Cliffs, N.J.: Prentice-Hall, 1971.

MOSELEY, SPENCER, PAULINE JOHNSON, and HAZEL KALNIG, *Crafts Design: An Illustrated Guide*. Belmont, Calif.: Wadsworth, 1962.

Design

BELVIN, MARJORIE ELLIOTT, *Design Through Discovery*. New York: Holt, Rinehart and Winston, 1970.

BLOSSFELDT, KARL, *Art Forms in Nature*. London: Zwemmer, 1936.

EMERSON, SYBIL, *Design: A Creative Approach*. Scranton, Pa.: International Textbook, 1953.

GARRETT, LILLIAN, *Visual Design: A Problem Solving Approach*. New York: Reinhold, 1966.

HURWITZ, ELIZABETH ADAMS, *Design: A Search for Essentials*. Scranton, Pa.: International Textbook, 1964.

PYE, DAVID, *The Nature of Design*. New York: Reinhold, 1964.

ROWLAND, KURT, *Looking and Seeing*. 4 vols. New York: Reinhold, 1964–66.

Display

HORN, GEORGE, *Bulletin Boards*. New York: Reinhold, 1962.

KELLEY, MARJORIE, and NICHOLAS ROUKES, *Matting and Displaying the Work of Children*. Palo Alto, Calif.: Fearon, 1957.

RANDALL, REINO, and EDWARD C. HAINES, *Bulletin Boards and Display*. Worcester, Mass.: Davis, 1961.

Drawing

ALBERT, CALVIN, and DOROTHY SECKLER, *Figure Drawing Comes to Life*. New York: Reinhold, 1962.

BOYLSTON, ELISE REID, *Creative Expression with Crayons*. Worcester, Mass.: Davis, 1954.

BRANDT, REX, *The Artist's Sketchbook*. New York: Reinhold, 1966.

BURNETT, CALVIN, *Objective Drawing Techniques*. New York: Reinhold, 1966.

DOBIN, JAY, *Perspective: A New System for Designers*. New York: Hill & Wang, 1957.

HUTTER, HERIBERT, *Drawing: History and Technique*. New York: McGraw-Hill, 1968.

KAMPMAN, LOTHAR, *Creating with Crayons*. New York: Reinhold, 1967.

KAUPELIS, ROBERT, *Learning to Draw*. New York: Watson-Guptill, 1966.

NICOLAÏDES, KIMON, *The Natural Way to Draw*. Boston: Houghton Mifflin, 1941.

PITZ, HENRY C., *Ink Drawing Techniques*. New York: Watson-Guptill, 1957.

WATSON, ERNEST W., *Gallery of Pencil Techniques*. New York: Reinhold, 1958.

WEISS, HARVEY, *Pencil, Pen and Brush*. New York: William R. Scott, 1961.

Fabric Design

ALBERS, ANNI, *On Designing*. Middletown, Conn.: Wesleyan University Press, 1971.

GUILD, VERA P., *Creative Use of Stitches*. Worcester, Mass.: Davis, 1969.

KARASZ, MARISKA, *Adventure in Stitches*. New York: Funk & Wagnalls, 1959.

KREVITSKY, NIK, *Batik Art and Craft,* rev. ed. New York: Reinhold, 1973.

LAUTERBURG, LOTTI, *Fabric Printing.* New York: Reinhold, 1959.

Jewelry

DHAEMERS, ROBERT, and HOWARD A. SLATOFF, *Simple Jewelry Making for the Classroom.* Palo Alto, Calif.: Fearon, 1958.

WINEBRENNER, D. KENNETH, *Jewelry Making as an Art Expression.* Scranton, Pa.: International Textbook, 1953.

Light-Motion Media

COOKE, ROBERT W., *Designing with Light on Paper and Film.* Worcester, Mass.: Davis, 1969.

Masks

BARANSKI, MATTHEW, *Mask Making,* rev. ed. Worcester, Mass.: Davis, 1966.

DOCKSTADER, FREDERICK, *Indian Art in America: The Arts and Crafts of the North American Indian,* 3rd ed. Greenwich, Conn.: N.Y. Graphic Society, 1966.

Materials Information

DOERNER, MAX, *The Materials of the Artist,* rev. ed. Trans. by Eugene Neuhaus. New York: Harcourt Brace Jovanovich, 1949.

Models

BASSETT-LOWKE, W. J., and PAUL B. MANN, *Marvelous Models.* Baltimore: Penguin, 1947.

Mosaics

ALLER, DORIS and DIANE, *Mosaics.* Menlo Park, Calif.: Lane, 1959.

ARGIRO, LARRY, *Mosaic Art Today,* rev. ed. Scranton, Pa.: International Textbook, 1968.

MAGDALEN, SISTER MARY I. H. M., *Mosaics for Everyone.* Los Angeles: Immaculate Heart College, 1958.

YOUNG, JOSEPH L., *Course in Making Mosaics.* New York: Reinhold, 1957.

Murals

KELLEY, MARJORIE, and NICHOLAS ROUKES, *Let's Make a Mural.* Palo Alto, Calif.: Fearon, 1958.

RANDALL, ARNE W., *Murals for Schools.* Worcester, Mass.: Davis, 1956.

Painting

BIRREN, FABER, *History of Color in Painting.* New York: Reinhold, 1965.

CHOMICKY, YAR G., *Watercolor Painting: Media, Methods and Materials.* Englewood Cliffs, N.J.: Prentice-Hall, 1968.

DAVIDSON, MORRIS, *Painting with a Purpose.* Englewood Cliffs, N.J.: Prentice-Hall, 1969.

KELLOGG, RHODA, *The How of Successful Finger Painting.* Palo Alto, Calif.: Fearon, 1958.

LALIBERTE, NORMAN, and ALEX MOGELON, *Painting with Crayons.* New York: Reinhold, 1967.

MAYER, RALPH, *The Painter's Craft.* Princeton, N.J.: Van Nostrand, 1948.

RANDALL, ARNE, and RUTH E. HALVERSEN, *Painting in the Classroom.* Worcester, Mass.: Davis, 1962.

WOODY, RUSSELL O., *Painting with Synthetic Media.* New York: Reinhold, 1965.

Paper

BECKER, EDITH C., *Adventures with Scissors and Paper.* Scranton, Pa.: International Textbook, 1959.

COX, CHRISTABEL, *Cut Paper Work.* Peoria, Ill.: Bennett, 1951.

JOHNSON, PAULINE, *Creating with Paper.* Seattle: University of Washington Press, 1966.

JOHNSTON, MARY GRACE, *Paper Shapes and Sculpture for School Use.* Worcester, Mass.: Davis, 1958.

LORD, LOIS, *Collage and Construction.* Worcester, Mass.: Davis, 1958 (rev. 1970).

ROETTGER, ERNST, *Creative Paper Design.* New York: Reinhold, 1961.

Papier-Mâché

BETTS, VICTORIA, *Exploring Papier-Mâché.* Worcester Mass.: Davis, 1966.

JOHNSON, LILLIAN, *Papier-Mâché.* New York: McKay, 1958.

Posters and Lettering

BOLLINGER, RAYMOND A., *Layout.* New York: Reinhold, 1956 (rev. and redesigned 1970).

CATALDO, JOHN W., *Graphic Design and Visual Communication.* Scranton, Pa.: International Textbook, 1966.

————, *Lettering: A Guide for Teachers.* Worcester, Mass.: Davis, 1966.

HORNUNG, CLARENCE P., *Lettering from A to Z.* New York: William Penn. 1954.

HUTCHISON, HAROLD F., *The Poster: An Illustrated History from 1860.* New York: Viking, 1968.

OGG, OSCAR, *The 26 Letters,* rev. ed. New York: Crowell, 1971.

SHAHN, BEN, *Love and Joy About Letters*. New York: Grossman, 1963.

Printmaking

ANDREWS, MICHAEL F., *Creative Printmaking*. Englewood Cliffs, N.J.: Prentice-Hall, 1963.

HELLER, JULES, *Print Making Today*. New York: Holt, Rinehart and Winston, 1972.

RASMUSEN, HENRY, *Printmaking with Monotype*. Philadelphia: Chilton, 1960.

STERNBERG, HARRY, *Woodcut*. New York: Pitman, 1962.

WEISS, HARVEY, *Paper, Ink and Roller*. New York: William R. Scott, 1958.

Sculpture

ANDREWS, MICHAEL, *Sculpture and Ideas*. Englewood Cliffs, N.J.: Prentice-Hall, 1966.

CALDER, ALEXANDER, *Mobiles*. New York: Museum of Modern Art, 1950.

LORD, LOIS, *Collage and Construction*. Worcester, Mass.: Davis, 1958 (rev. 1970).

LYNCH, JOHN, *How to Make Mobiles*. New York: Viking, 1953.

———, *Metal Sculpture*. New York: Viking, 1957.

———, *Mobile Design*. New York: Viking, 1955.

MARKS, MICKEY, *Sand Sculpturing*. New York: Dial, 1963.

REED, CARL, and JOSEPH ORZE, *Art from Scrap*. Worcester, Mass.: Davis, 1973.

RICH, JACK, *The Materials and Methods of Sculpture*. New York: Oxford University Press, 1947.

RITCHIE, ANDREW CARNDUFF, *Sculpture of the Twentieth Century*. New York: Museum of Modern Art, 1953.

SELZ, JEAN, *Modern Sculpture*. New York: Braziller, 1963.

STEVENS, HAROLD, *Art in the Round*. New York: Reinhold, 1965.

STRUPPECK, JULES, *The Creation of Sculpture*. New York: Holt, Rinehart and Winston, 1952.

WEISS, HARVEY, *Clay, Wood and Wire*. New York: William R. Scott, 1956.

———, *Sticks, Spools and Feathers*. New York: William R. Scott, 1962.

Theater Activities

BATCHELDER, MARJORIE, *The Puppet Theater Handbook*. New York: Harper & Row, 1956.

GASSNER, JOHN, and PHILIP BARBER, *Producing the Play*, rev. ed. New York: Holt, Rinehart and Winston, 1953.

JAGENDORF, MORITZ, *The First Book of Puppets*. New York: Franklin Watts, 1952.

MERTON, GEORGE, *The Hand Puppets*. Camden, N.J.: Nelson, 1958.

———, *The Marionette*. Camden, N.J.: Nelson, 1958.

ROWELL, KENNETH, *Stage Design*. New York: Reinhold, 1968.

III. RECOMMENDED READING FOR CHILDREN[1]

ADLER, IRVING, *Color in Your Life*. New York: John Day, 1962.

BALLINGER, LOUISE B., and THOMAS F. VROMAN, *Design: Source and Resources*. New York: Reinhold, 1965.

BARRY, SIR GERALD, *The Arts—Man's Creative Imagination*. New York: Doubleday, 1965.

BATE, NORMAN, *When Cavemen Painted*. New York: Scribner's, 1963.

BAUMANN, HANS, *The Caves of the Great Hunters*. New York: Pantheon, 1962.

BEAUMONT, CYRIL, *Puppets and Puppetry*. New York: Viking, 1958.

[1]For a more complete and annotated listing, the reader is referred to *A Bibliography of Children's Art Literature,* edited by Kenneth Marantz, Washington, D.C.: National Art Education Association, 1965.

BERGERE, THEA and RICHARD, *From Stones to Skyscrapers*. New York: Dodd, Mead, 1960.

BERRY, ANNA M., *Art for Children*. New York: Viking, 1952.

BORTEN, HELEN, *Do You See What I See?* New York: Abelard-Schuman, 1959.

———, *A Picture Has a Special Look*. New York: Abelard-Schuman, 1961.

BROWNER, RICHARD, *Look Again*. New York: Atheneum, 1962.

BRUSTLEIN, DANIEL [ALAIN], *The Magic Stones*. New York: McGraw-Hill, 1957.

CAMPBELL, ELIZABETH, *Fins and Tails*. Boston: Little, Brown, 1963.

CANDY, ROBERT, *Nature Notebook*. Boston: Houghton Mifflin, 1962.

CARTER, KATHERINE, *My Book of Color*. Pikesville, Md.: Ottenheimer, 1961.

CELENDER, DONALD, *Musical Instruments in Art.* Minneapolis: Lerner, 1966.

CHASE, ALICE ELIZABETH, *Famous Paintings.* New York: Platt & Munk, 1964.

COEN, RENA NEUMANN, *American History in Art.* Minneapolis: Lerner, 1965.

————, *Kings and Queens in Art.* Minneapolis: Lerner, 1964.

CORNELIUS, SUE and CHASE, *The City in Art.* Minneapolis: Lerner, 1965.

DALY, KATHLEEN N., *Colors.* New York: Golden Press, 1959.

DOWNER, MARION, *Discovering Design.* New York: Lothrop, Lee & Shepard, 1963.

EMBERLEY, ED, *The Wing on a Flea.* Boston: Little, Brown, 1961.

FORTE, NANCY, *The Warrior in Art.* Minneapolis: Lerner, 1965.

GETTINGS, FRED, *The Meaning and Wonder of Art.* New York: Western Publishing Co. (Golden Book), 1963.

GIBSON, KATHERINE, *More Pictures to Grow Up With.* New York: Viking, 1942.

————, *Pictures by Young Americans.* New York: Oxford University Press, 1946.

GILL, BOB, *What Color Is Your World?* New York: Ivan Obolensky, 1963.

GLUBOK, SHIRLEY, *The Art of Ancient Egypt.* New York: Atheneum, 1962.

————, *The Art of Ancient Greece.* New York: Atheneum, 1963.

————, *The Art of Ancient Rome.* New York: Harper & Row, 1965.

————, *The Art of the Eskimo.* New York: Harper & Row, 1964.

————, *The Art of Lands in the Bible.* New York: Atheneum, 1963.

————, *The Art of the North American Indian.* New York: Harper & Row, 1964.

GRACZA, MARGARET YOUNG, *The Bird in Art.* Minneapolis: Lerner, 1965.

————, *The Ship and the Sea in Art.* Minneapolis: Lerner, 1964.

HAMMOND, PENNY, and KATRINA THOMAS, *My Skyscraper City.* New York: Doubleday, 1963.

HARKONEN, HELEN B., *Circuses and Fairs in Art.* Minneapolis: Lerner, 1964.

————, *Farms and Farmers in Art.* Minneapolis: Lerner, 1964.

HOAG, EDWIN, *American Houses: Colonial, Classic and Contemporary.* Philadelphia: Lippincott, 1964.

HOLME, BRYAN, *Pictures to Live With.* New York: Viking, 1960.

JANSON, H. W. and DORA JANE, *The Story of Painting for Young People.* New York: Abrams, 1962.

KABLO, MARTIN, *World of Color.* New York: McGraw-Hill, 1963.

KEISLER, LEONARD, *Art Is Everywhere: A Child's Guide to Drawing and Painting.* New York: Dodd, Mead, 1958.

————, *What's in a Line.* New York: Dodd, Mead, 1962.

————, *The Worm, The Bird, and You.* New York: William R. Scott, 1961.

KIELTY, BERNARDINE, *Masters of Painting: Their Works, Their Lives, Their Times.* New York: Doubleday, 1964.

KIRN, ANN, *Full of Wonder.* Cleveland: World, 1959.

KOCH, DOROTHY, *I Play at the Beach.* New York: Holiday House, 1955.

KRAUSS, RUTH, *A Hole Is to Dig: A First Book of First Definitions.* New York: Harper & Row, 1952.

LERNER, SHARON, *The Self-Portrait in Art.* Minneapolis: Lerner, 1964.

LIFE MAGAZINE, THE EDITORS OF, *America's Arts and Skills.* New York: Dutton, 1957.

LIONNI, LEO, *Little Blue and Yellow.* New York: Ivan Obolensky, 1959.

LOVOOS, JANICE, *Design Is a Dandelion.* Chicago: Children's Press, 1966.

LOW, JOSEPH, *Adam's Book of Odd Creatures.* New York: Atheneum, 1962.

MACAGY, DOUGLAS and ELIZABETH, *Going for a Walk with a Line.* New York: Doubleday, 1959.

MANLEY, SEON, *Adventures in Making: The Romance of Crafts Around the World.* New York: Vanguard, 1959.

MOORE, LAMONT, *The First Book of Architecture.* New York: Franklin Watts, 1961.

————, *The First Book of Paintings.* New York: Franklin Watts, 1960.

MUNARI, BRUNO, *Bruno Munari's Zoo.* Cleveland: World, 1963.

MUNRO, ELEANOR, *The Golden Encyclopedia of Art.* New York: Golden Press, 1961 (rev. 1964).

NEAL, CHARLES D., *Exploring Light and Color.* Chicago: Children's Press, 1964.

O'NEILL, MARY, *Hailstones and Halibut Bones: Adventures in Color.* New York: Doubleday, 1961.

RABOFF, ERNEST, *Art for Children* series. Garden City, N.Y.: Doubleday, 1968–1971.

RAVIELLI, ANTHONY, *An Adventure in Geometry.* New York: Viking, 1957.

RILEY, OLIVE, *Masks and Magic.* New York: Viking, 1955.

RIPLEY, ELIZABETH, *Dürer*. Philadelphia: Lippincott, 1958.
——, *Goya*. New York: Walck, 1956.
——, *Leonardo da Vinci*. New York: Walck, 1952.
——, *Rembrandt*. New York: Walck, 1955.
——, *Rubens*. New York: Walck, 1957.
RUSKIN, ARIANE, *Story of Art for Young People*. New York: Pantheon, 1964.
SCHLEIN, MERIAM, *Shapes*. Hale, 1952.
SEIDELMAN, JAMES E., *The Rub Book*. New York: Macmillan, 1968.
SHISSLER, BARBARA, *Sports and Games in Art*. Minneapolis: Lerner, 1965.
SMITH, WILLIAM JAY, *What Did I See*. New York: Macmillan, 1962.
SPENCER, CORNELIA, *How Art and Music Speak to Us*. New York: John Day, 1963 (rev. 1968).
——, *Made in Japan*. New York: Knopf, 1963.
Other "Made in" titles include:
Margaret Ayer, *Made in Thailand*. New York: Knopf, 1964.
Mary Graham Bonner, *Made in Canada*. New York: Knopf, 1943.
Grace Golden, *Made in Iceland*. New York: Knopf, 1958.
Christine Price, *Made in Ancient Greece*. New York: Dutton, 1967.
——, *Made in the Middle Ages*. New York: Dutton, 1951.

——, *Made in the Renaissance*. New York: Dutton, 1963.
Patricia Fent Ross, *Made in Mexico*. New York: Knopf, 1952.
Cornelia Spencer, *Made in China*. New York: Knopf, 1952.
——, *Made in India*. New York: Knopf, 1953.
Frances Toor, *Made in Italy*. New York: Knopf, 1957.
SPILKA, ARNOLD, *Paint All Kinds of Pictures*. New York: Walck, 1963.
STRACHE, WOLF, *Forms and Patterns in Nature*. New York: Pantheon, 1973.
WEISGARD, LEONARD, *Treasures to See: A Museum Picture-Book*. New York: Harcourt Brace Jovanovich, 1956.
WEISS, HARVEY, *The Beginning Artist's Library Series*. New York: William R. Scott.
Books in this series include:
Ceramics: From Clay to Kiln, 1964.
Clay, Wood and Wire, 1956.
Paint, Brush and Palette, 1966.
Paper, Ink and Roller, 1958.
Pencil, Pen and Brush, 1961.
Sticks, Spoons and Feathers, 1962.
WOLFF, JANET, and BERNARD OWETT, *Let's Imagine Colors*. New York: Dutton, 1963.
ZUELKE, RUTH, *The Horse in Art*, Minneapolis: Lerner, 1965.

IV. FILMS

Because of the truly massive array of available films, it is impossible to include even a minimally representative list here. The reader is directed to *Films on Art*, Alfred Humphreys, ed., published in 1960 by the National Art Education Association, Washington, D.C. The publication lists 160 producers and distributors and their addresses.

It mentions over 900 titles of films on art, indicating length, grade level, and subject matter. The reader is also directed to *Index to 16mm Educational Films*, McGraw-Hill Book Co., 1967.

Offered below is an abbreviated listing of films covering areas most likely to be of concern to elementary art teachers.

Film Producers and Distributors

ACI Films, Inc., 35 W. 45th St., New York, N.Y. 10036.
American Handicrafts Co., 83 West Van Buren St., Chicago, Ill. 60605.
Arthur Baar Productions, Inc., P.O. Box 7-C, Pasadena, Calif. 91104.
Bailey-Film Associates, 11559 Santa Monica Blvd., Los Angeles, Calif. 90025.

BFA Educational Media, 2211 Michigan Ave., Santa Monica, Calif. 90404.
Brandon Films, Inc., 221 West 57th St., New York, N.Y. 10019.
British Information Services, 30 Rockefeller Plaza, New York, N.Y. 10020.
Churchill Films, 662 North Robertson Blvd., Los Angeles, Calif. 90069.

Coast Visual Education Co., 5620 Hollywood Blvd., Los Angeles, Calif. 90028.

Columbia Cinemathèque, 711 Fifth Ave., New York, N.Y. 10022.

Contemporary Films, Inc., 1221 Avenue of the Americas, New York, N.Y. 10019.

Coronet Instructional Media, 65 E. South Water St., Chicago, Ill. 60601.

Walt Disney Educational Materials Company, 800 Sonora Ave., Glendale, Calif. 91201.

Doubleday Multimedia, Box 11607, 1371 Reynolds Ave., Santa Ana, Calif. 92705.

Ealing Productions, Inc., 55 Chapel St., Newton, Mass. 02158.

Encyclopedia Britannica Films, Inc., 425 North Michigan Ave., Chicago, Ill. 60611.

Film Classics Exchange, 1645 North La Brea Ave., Los Angeles, Calif. 90028.

Francis Thompson Productions, 935 Second Ave., New York, N.Y. 10022.

Girl Scouts of America Film Library, 830 Third Avenue, New York, N.Y. 10022.

Harmon Foundation, Division of Visual Experiments, 140 Nassau Street, New York, N.Y. 10038.

Homer Groening, 301 Executive Building, Portland, Ore., 97204.

International Film Bureau, 332 South Michigan Ave., Chicago, Ill. 60604.

Jeff Dell Film Service, Inc., 1150 Avenue of the Americas, New York, N.Y. 10036.

McGraw-Hill, 1221 Avenue of the Americas, New York, N.Y. 10019.

National Film Board of Canada, 400 West Madison St., Chicago, Ill. 60606.

Portafilms, 4180 Dixie Highway, Drayton Plains, Mich. 48020.

Santa Fe Film Bureau, 80 East Jackson Blvd., Chicago, Ill. 60604.

Sigma Educational Films, P.O. Box 1235, Studio City, Calif. 91604.

Sterling Movies, 375 Park Ave., New York, N.Y. 10022.

Sturgis Grant Productions, Inc., 238 East 44th St., New York, N.Y. 10017.

Tiger Productions, 3559 Cody Road, Sherman Oaks, Calif. 91403.

University of Southern California, Audio-Visual Services, Dept. of Cinema, 3518 University Ave., Los Angeles, Calif. 90007.

Wanami Films, Japan.

Weston Woods Studios, Weston, Conn. 06880.

Yellow Ball Workshop and Newton Mini Films, 62 Tarbell Ave., Lexington, Mass. 02173.

Recommended Films

General

Adventures of an Asterisk. Brandon Films.
Adventuring in the Arts. Girl Scouts of America.
Around My Way. Contemporary Films.
Children Are Creative. Bailey-Film Associates.
Children Who Draw. Brandon Films; Wanami Film.

Architecture

Art and Architecture: Lesson 1, *What It is and Why It Is;* Lesson 2, *Art of the Middle Ages;* Lesson 3, *Chartres Cathedral.* Encyclopedia Britannica Films.
Frank Lloyd Wright. Encyclopedia Britannica Films.
My Art Is Me.
Washington, D.C.—Capital City, U.S.A. Encyclopedia Britannica Films.

Art Appreciation

Art in Action with Dong Kingman. Harmon Foundation.

Art in Our World. Bailey-Film Associates.
Behind the Scenes of a Museum. International Film Bureau.
Buma: African Sculpture Speaks. Encyclopedia Britannica Films.
The Etcher's Art. International Film Bureau.
Little Blue and Little Yellow. Contemporary Films.
Living Stone. National Film Board of Canada.
Maurice Sendak. Weston Woods Studios.
Non-Objective Art. Bailey-Film Associates.
Picture in Your Mind. International Film Bureau.
Rhythm in Paint. Encyclopedia Britannica Films.
Robert McCloskey. Weston Woods Studios.
What Is Art? Encyclopedia Britannica Films.

Art History

Beginnings of History series: Part I, *The Stone Age;* Part II, *The Bronze Age;* Part III, *The Iron Age.* International Film Bureau.
Raphael. Film Classics Exchange.
Rembrandt. Film Classics Exchange.

Art and Nature
Artist and Nature. International Film Bureau.
Birds and Etching. Bailey-Film Associates.
Eskimo Arts and Crafts. International Film Bureau.
Insects and Painting. Bailey-Film Associates.
The Zoo: Primary Activities. Coast Visual Education Co.

Art and Social Studies
Arts and Crafts of Mexico: Part I, Pottery and Weaving; Part II, Basketry, Stone, Wood and Metal. Encyclopedia Britannica Films.
Boy of Switzerland. Bailey-Film Associates.
Design and Environment. Girl Scouts of America.
Face of Lincoln. University of Southern California.
Lascaux, Cradle of Man's Art. International Film Bureau.
Loon's Necklace. Encyclopedia Britannica Films.
Portage. International Film Bureau.
Seminole Indians. International Film Bureau.
This is Britain: Old Crafts and New Graces. British Information Services.
Totems. International Film Bureau.

Design
Art in Motion. Encyclopedia Britannica Films.
Design. Bailey-Film Associates.
Discovering Art series: Color; Composition; Creative Pattern; Dark and Light; Form in Art; Harmony in Art; Ideas in Art; Line; Perspective; Texture. Bailey-Film Associates.
Light and Dark. Encyclopedia Britannica Films.
Texture. Encyclopedia Britannica Films.

Light-Motion Media
Animated films made by children can be obtained from Yellow Ball Workshop and Newton Mini Films.
Animated Cartoons: The Toy That Grew Up. International Film Bureau.
Begone Dull Care. International Film Bureau.
Dots. International Film Bureau.
Fiddle-de-dee. International Film Bureau.
Let's Make a Film. Yellow Ball Workshop.
Orange and Blue. McGraw-Hill.

Techniques and Processes
Art of Metal Sculpture. Portafilms.
Color in Clay. Encyclopedia Britannica Films.
Crayon Resist. International Film Bureau.
How to Make a Simple Loom and Weave. Encyclopedia Britannica Films.
How to Make a Starch Painting. Encyclopedia Britannica Films.
Make a Mobile. Bailey-Film Associates.
Making a Mask. International Film Bureau.
Masks and Imagination. Girl Scouts of America.
Monotype Prints. Bailey-Film Associates.
Mosaics. American Handicrafts Co.
Paper Construction. ACI, Inc.
Paper in Art. Churchill Films.
Posters. ACI, Inc.
Print with a Brayer. Bailey-Film Associates.
Rag Tapestry. International Film Bureau.
Working with Watercolor. International Film Bureau.

Nonart Films
Art teachers should not limit the choice of films to the visual arts. Often a truly fresh approach can come from areas such as the natural sciences or the language arts, or from experimental filmmakers.

Adventures of an Asterisk. Brandon Films.
Alphabet. National Film Board of Canada.
Angel. National Film Board of Canada.
Animals in Winter. Encyclopedia Britannica Films.
Animals on the Farm. International Film Bureau.
Animals and Their Homes. Coronet.
Bird Paradise. Paul Moss.
Birds: How They Live, Where They Live. Bailey-Film Associates.
Birds of our Storybooks. Coronet.
Clouds. International Tele Film.
The Critic. Columbia Cinémathèque.
The Desert. Arthur Baar Productions.
Dragons and Damsels. Kieran Kaleidoscope.
Draw Me a Telephone. Sterling Movies.
Dream of Wild Horses. Contemporary Films.
Farm Babies and Their Mothers. BFA Educational Media.
Glass. Contemporary Films.
The Great Toy Robbery. National Film Board of Canada.
The Hand. Contemporary Films.
Happy Birthday Felisa. Jeff Dell Film Service.
Horses. Sterling Movies.
Indian Ceremonials. Santa Fe Film Bureau.
Lady of the Light. Tiger Productions.
Maps Are Fun. Coronet.
New York, New York. Francis Thompson Productions.
Nittany. McGraw-Hill.

An Occurrence at Owl Creek Bridge. Contemporary Films.
Prove it with a Magnifying Glass. BFA Educational Media.
Psychedelic Wet. Homer Groening.
The Rhinoceros. McGraw-Hill.
Right and Wrong and What's in Between. Portafilms.
Secrets of the Plant World. (Time Lapse Photography) Walt Disney.

The Senses. Sigma Educational Films.
Symmetry. Sturgis Grant Productions.
Time Is. Contemporary Films.
A Valparaiso. Contemporary Films.
Very Nice, Very Nice. Contemporary Films.
The Violinist. Brandon Films.
Lively Art of Picture Books. Weston Woods Studios.

V. SLIDES AND FILMSTRIPS

American Council on Education, 1785 Massachusetts Ave. N.W., Washington, D.C. 20036.
American Library Color Slide Co., Inc., 305 East 45th St., New York, N.Y. 10017.
Art Council Aids, Box 641, Beverly Hills, Calif. 90213:
> *Children Paint Their World*
> *Emotion Takes Form*

Bailey-Film Associates, 11559 Santa Monica Blvd., Los Angeles, Calif. 90025.
Dr. Block Color Productions, 1309 North Genesee Ave., Los Angeles, Calif. 90046.
Carnegie-Mellon University, College of Fine Arts, Schenley Park, Pittsburgh, Pa. 15213.
Grolier Educational Corp., 845 Third Ave., New York, N.Y. 10022:
> The Book of Art Filmstrip Library, Sir Herbert Read, ed. Ten filmstrips intended to supplement *The Book of Art: A Pictorial Encyclopedia of Painting, Drawing, and Sculpture.* Although the books are beyond the reading level of elementary-school children, the filmstrips can be useful in a basic survey of the history of art.

Life Filmstrips, Time-Life Bldg., Rockefeller Center, New York, N.Y. 10020.
McGraw-Hill Book Co., 1221 Avenue of the Americas, New York, N.Y. 10019:

> *Arts of the United States: A Pictorial Survey,* William H. Pierson, Jr., and Mathew Davidson, eds.
> *The Color Slide Books of the World's Art*

Museum of Modern Art Library, 11 West 53rd St., New York, N.Y., 10019.
National Gallery of Art, Constitution Ave. & 6th St. N.W., Washington, D.C. 20001:
> *Survey of American Painting*

Philadelphia Museum of Art, Division of Education, 25th St. & Benjamin Franklin Pkwy., Philadelphia, Pa. 19130.
Dr. Konrad Prothmann, 2378 Soper Ave., Baldwin, N.Y. 11510.
Sandak, Inc., 4 East 48th St., New York, N.Y. 10017:
> 4000 slides of American art

School of the Art Institute of Chicago, South Michigan Ave. & East Adams St., Chicago, Ill. 60603.
Society for Visual Education, Inc., 1345 Diversey Pkwy., Chicago, Ill. 60614.
Thorne Films, Inc., 1229 University Ave., Boulder, Colo. 80302.
University Prints, 15 Brattle St., Harvard Square, Cambridge, Mass. 02138.

VI. COLOR REPRODUCTIONS

Harry N. Abrams, 110 East 59th St., New York, N.Y. 10022.
Art Education, Inc., Blauvelt, N.Y. 10913.

Artext Prints, Inc., Westport, Conn. 06880.
Associated American Artists, Inc., 663 Fifth Ave., New York, N.Y. 10022.

Catalda Fine Arts., Inc., 225 Fifth Ave., New York, N.Y. 10010.

Far Gallery, 746 Madison Ave., New York, N.Y. 10021.

Metropolitan Museum of Art Book and Art Shop, Fifth Ave. & 82nd St., New York, N.Y. 10028.

Museum of Modern Art, 11 West 53rd St., New York, N.Y. 10019.

New York Graphic Society, 140 Greenwich Ave., Greenwich, Conn. 06830.

Oestreicher's Prints, Inc., 43 West 46th St., New York, N.Y. 10036.

Penn Print Co., 572 Fifth Ave., New York, N.Y. 10036.

Dr. Konrad Prothmann, 2378 Soper Ave., Baldwin, N.Y. 11510.

Raymond and Raymond, Inc., 1071 Madison Ave., New York, N.Y. 10028.

Reinhold Publishing Co., 430 Park Ave., New York, N.Y., 10022:
Reinhold Visual Series, John Lidstone, Stanley T. Lewis, and Sheldon Brody, eds. A series of eight portfolios, each containing twenty-four prints.

Shorewood Reproductions, Inc., Dept. S, 724 Fifth Ave., New York, N.Y. 10019.

Albert Skira, dist. by World Publishing Co., 2231 West 110th St., Cleveland, Ohio 44102.

UNESCO Catalogues, Columbia University Press, 562 West 113th St., New York, N.Y. 10025.

University Galleries, Dept. SA, 520 Fifth Ave., New York, N.Y. 10036.

University Prints, 15 Brattle St., Harvard Square, Cambridge, Mass. 02138.

E. Weyhe, 794 Lexington Ave., New York, N.Y. 10021.

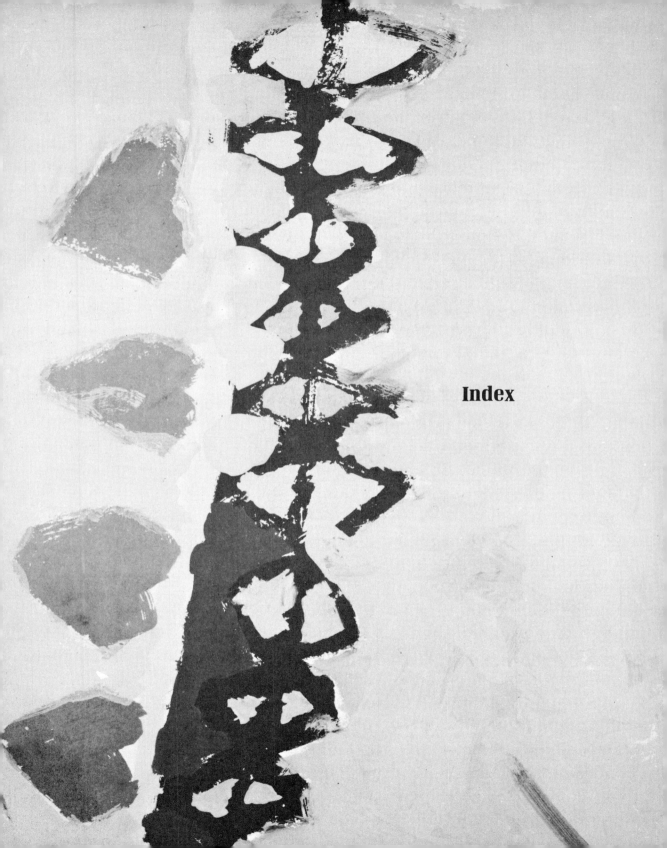

Index

INDEX

(Page numbers in italics indicate illustrations.)